Geopolitics of
the World System

Geopolitics of the World System

SAUL BERNARD COHEN

ROWMAN & LITTLEFIELD PUBLISHERS, INC.
Lanham • Boulder • New York • Oxford

ROWMAN & LITTLEFIELD PUBLISHERS, INC.

Published in the United States of America
by Rowman & Littlefield Publishers, Inc.
A Member of the Rowman & Littlefield Publishing Group
4720 Boston Way, Lanham, Maryland 20706
www.rowmanlittlefield.com

PO Box 317, Oxford OX2 9RU, United Kingdom

British Library Cataloguing in Publication Information Available

Library of Congress Cataloging-in-Publication Data

Cohen, Saul Bernard.
  Geopolitics of the world system / Saul Bernard Cohen.
      p. cm. — (Regional geographies for a new era)
Includes bibliographical references and index.
    ISBN 0-8476-9906-4 (cloth : alk. paper)—ISBN 0-8476-9907-2 (pbk. : alk. paper)
  1. Geopolitics. 2. World politics. 3. Ethnic relations. 4. Security, International. 5. International relations. 6. Low-intensity conflicts (Military science) I. Title. II. Series.
    JC319 .C62 2003
    320.1'2—dc21

                                                                                    2002000615

Printed in the United States of America

∞™ The paper used in this publication meets the minimum requirements of American National Standard for Information Sciences—Permanence of Paper for Printed Library Materials, ANSI/NISO Z39.48-1992.

Contents

Figures

Tables

Abbreviations and Acronyms

ABM	Anti-Ballistic Missile (Treaty)
APEC	Asia-Pacific Economic Cooperation Forum
ASEAN	Association of Southeast Asian Nations
CENTO	Central Treaty Organization
CIA	Central Intelligence Agency
CIS	Commonwealth of Independent States
COMECON	Council for Mutual Economic Assistance
CTBT	Comprehensive Test Ban Treaty
DEW	Distant Early Warning Line
DMZ	Demilitarized Zone (especially Korea)
GDP	gross domestic product
GNP	gross national product
EAC	East Africa Community
ECOWAS	Economic Community of West African States
ENT	Effective National Territory
ERT	Effective Regional Territory
ICBM	intercontinental ballistic missile
ICJ	International Court of Justice
FARC	Revolutionary Armed Forces of Colombia
Frelimo	Mozambique Liberation Front
FSU	Former Soviet Union
GATT	General Agreement on Tarriffs and Trade
Mercosur	Mercado Común del Sur
NAFTA	North American Free Trade Agreement
NATO	North Atlantic Treaty Organization
NMD	National Missile Defense (system)
NORAD	North American Aerospace Defense Command
OAS	Organization of American States
OAU	Organization for African Unity
OPEC	Organization of Petroleum Exporting Countries
RSFSR	Russian Soviet Federal Socialist Republic
SAARC	South Asian Association for Regional Cooperation

SADC	South African Development Community
SDF	(Japanese) Self-Defense Force
SEATO	Southeast Asia Treaty Organization
SSR	Soviet Socialist Republic
UNITA	National Union for Total Independence in Angola
UNTAC	United Nations Transitional Authority in Cambodia
WTO	World Trade Organization

CHAPTER 1

Introduction

One noontime, at the waning of the twentieth century, B-52 strategic and stealth bombers took off from the continental heart of the United States, flew fifty-five hundred miles to deposit their laser-guided military payloads on Serbian targets, and returned to home base. For their pilots, it was a thirty-two-hour work period that enabled them to be home for dinner the next evening. With the help of airborne fuel tankers, this strategic strike force, in combination with tactical fighter-bombers and escorts operating from land bases in Italy and aircraft carriers in the Adriatic, enabled the U.S.-led NATO forces to defeat Serbia without the loss of a single Allied life. For many, that war represented a triumph of technology. The hubris fanned by the liberation of Kosovo nourished the belief that the American superpower could wage war successfully in any part of the world, now that the Soviet empire had collapsed.

If time-distance can be so easily overcome, does this mean the "end of geography" in the strategic or tactical sense? This question was answered unequivocally on September 11, 2001, when terrorists destroyed the New York World Trade Center and a portion of the Pentagon. The strategy of the subsequent campaign against the Osama bin Laden–led al Qaeda terrorist movement and the Taliban regime has been dictated by geography and regional geopolitics. A primary factor is the physical geography of Afghanistan—forbidding mountainous terrain, severe winter climate, a poor land communications infrastructure, and dispersed ethnic populations. Highly sophisticated U.S. air weaponry did not obviate the need for U.S. ground-force combat. This took place first in the unsuccessful hunt for bin Laden in the Tora Bora Mountains. This was followed by a much larger effort by American and Afghan troops in the battle against al Qaeda forces that had dug into the caves of the Shah-i-Kot Mountains. The battle was waged in arduous terrain and under difficult weather conditions.

Geopolitical considerations shaped the coalition sought by the United States to gain access to the landlocked country. Permission had to be secured from a number of countries for airspace overflight, and for the use of air and land bases from countries bordering or near the Afghan border. This required knitting together a coalition that included not only distant and trusted allies, such as Britain and other NATO countries, and friendly nations from other parts of the world, such as Australia, but also the mostly Muslim countries that form a ring around Afghanistan and whose relationships to the United States have been erratic.

Vital elements in the strategic equation involved Pakistan, Uzbekistan, Kyrgyzstan, and Tajikistan: the use of the airspace, air bases, and intelligence capacities of Pakistan, whose Pashtun western provinces adjoined the Pashtun sectors of eastern and southern Afghanistan centering on Kabul and Kandahar; the rolling steppes of southern Uzbekistan, which provided air bases and year-round land access to north-central Afghanistan and the lands to the west and center of the country via Mazar-e-Sharif; Kyrgyzstan's international airport at Manas, which served as a U.S. and allied air force base; and Tajikistan, which afforded direct access to the Northern Alliance–controlled Panjshir Valley, the narrow, tortuous route cutting through the Hindu Kush to within thirty-five miles of the Afghan capital of Kabul, and through which the Russians funneled arms to the Alliance.

The tangled geopolitical web required Washington to include within the coalition states that themselves are sponsors of terrorism, and to make military decisions based on the political interests of some of these states. For example, in the early stages of the campaign, the bombing of Taliban lines north of Kabul was held back in deference to Pakistan's opposition to a post-Taliban government dominated by its enemy, the Northern Alliance. The hope was that an agreement on a postwar coalition government could be quickly reached. The delay had diplomatic as well as military implications, since it was contrary to the policies of India, which favored the Alliance. When this tactic proved unrealistic, and with the imminent onset of Afghanistan's severe winter, carpet bombing of the Taliban lines was initiated, and then followed up by the use of ground forces.

Another dramatic geopolitical turn was the Russian and Chinese support given to the United States in the military campaign. Both of these powers had an interest in suppressing the Afghan terrorist base that backed Muslim extremists in their own countries. Russia was particularly important in providing the use of its own airspace, as well as acquiescing to the positioning of American air and land forces in Uzbekistan and Tajikistan.

The United States has expanded the global War against Terrorism, sending military trainers and advisers to such countries as the Philippines, Yemen, and Georgia and actively planning the overthrow of Saddam Hussein. How long this effort will persist remains to be seen. In any case, the Afghan conflict demonstrates that the interests of other major powers and regional states—allied or competitive—cannot be ignored in forging strategies of war or peace. Even a hyperpower cannot hope to apply a grand strategic master plan to the world system, despite the global reach of communications, economics, and advanced weaponry.

Whereas the United States may see little strategic value in some parts of the world, it must be sensitive to the concerns of other powers. Both Australia and Nigeria are important strategic allies. Yet Washington ignored their vital interests in the conflicts in East Timor and West Africa. The United States sought to appease Indonesia rather than help stop the massacres that took place after the East Timorese voted for independence. This ignored Australia's strategic stake in East Timor because of its proximity to the Australian north and prospective joint development of oil and gas resources within the Timor Sea. While the United States stood back, it was Canberra that pressed for UN intervention and has since assumed the military burden of peacekeeping. Lack of strategic interest was also the basis for the United States ignoring the outbreak of conflict in Liberia and Sierra Leone, with which Nigeria had to contend.

Even though Washington may not be moved to act out of humanitarian considerations perceived to be strategically unimportant, it may have to involve itself in deference to the interests of allied regional states that are important to global geopolitical equilibrium.

The "victories" in the Gulf War, the former Yugoslavia, and Afghanistan promoted the image of the American superpower leading the world into its highest stage of historic development—liberal democracy. This image has been tempting to some scholars, business executives, and policy makers, but it is illusory.[1] Geography still counts. It counts in a strategic and tactical military sense, a political sense, and culturally defined territorial sense, and it counts in terms of the spatial distribution of resources, peoples, and physical systems. Neither 1999 Kosovo nor 1991 Iraq proved that victory can be achieved through high technology alone. Despite the bombing of Kosovo and Serbia, much of the Yugoslav army remained intact and might have proven a formidable foe in a land war. While there is no doubt that the Serbs would ultimately have been defeated, Allied casualties might have been domestically unacceptable. As it was, Russian diplomatic intervention was essential to bringing the Serbs to negotiations. Moreover, attainment of the Allied goal of an autonomous Kosovo loosely linked to Yugoslavia, in which Albanians and Serbs would live together, is highly unlikely. Instead, the seeds of future conflict over a "Greater Albania" conflict may have been planted.

In Iraq, the reluctance of the United States and its allies to push the land war into the heart of the country, leaving the Republican Guard largely intact, assured the survival of Saddam Hussein. "No-fly" zones and economic sanctions have inhibited but not undermined his regime, and the Kurds of the North, as well as the Arab Shiites of the South, are no closer to autonomy. Despite its defeat in the Gulf War, Iraq remains a threat to the Arab Gulf States, a regional destabilizer, and a supporter of global terrorism.

If the geopolitical structure of the twenty-first century is unlikely to emerge under the aegis of a "nonimperialist" American empire, in which order is maintained by the benign, omnipotent hyperpower, what world geopolitical patterns and features may be anticipated? What mechanisms for maintaining global equilibrium can be established as alternatives to the top-down world order that is implicit in the structure of empires? While no single discipline can claim to have the answers to these questions, they can surely be informed by the political-geographical perspective.

The geopolitical perspective is dynamic. It evolves as the international system and its operational environment changes. The dynamic nature of geographical settings accounts, to a considerable extent, for changes in geopolitical patterns and features. These settings change in response to such phenomena as the discovery or depletion of natural resources, the movement of people and capital flows, and long-term alterations in climate. Thus, the shift from rural to urban landscapes, or from manufacturing to service economies, represents geographical change that becomes reflected in changing national ideals and objectives. So does the impact of large-scale immigration. The decline of manufacturing in the United States, its greater reliance on imported goods, the depletion of the nation's petroleum reserves—all have increased the dependency on international trade to the point where "going it alone" as a superpower is not a practical, or even possible, foreign policy. This is a reality that the Bush administration is now confronting in the War against Terrorism, and should give pause to unilateral policies pursued in other spheres.

Geographical dynamism has also influenced changing national and regional outlooks in Maritime Europe as well as South Korea and Taiwan. In the latter case, the massive outsourcing of manufacturing to mainland China's southern and central coasts has pressed Taipei and Seoul, as well as Tokyo and Washington, to rethink their long-term relationships with China. China, in turn, has been forced by changes in the geographical setting of its high-tech "Golden Coast" to open itself to the outside world.

The changes in the world geopolitical map have been more rapid and sweeping during the past century than during the previous two and one-half centuries, when the modern, sovereign national state emerged and the European colonial system was imposed on much of the world. In the twentieth century, the seeds of destruction of the colonial system were planted in the savage conflict of World War I, from which the European powers emerged drained economically and in manpower. The Bolshevik revolution, world economic depression, and the rise of Nazi Germany led to World War II and the complete collapse of the European-imposed world order. The end of that war saw the emergence of the two great superpowers—the United States and the Union of Soviet Socialist Republics (USSR). Unlike their European colonial-imperial predecessors, these Cold War powers dominated their spheres of influence through regional clusters of formally independent allies and vassal states. After half a century, the Soviet Union imploded, laying the groundwork for a new world order, the outlines of which are still being drawn.

The clues to the geopolitical map of the future lie in the patterns of restructuring that have taken shape during the past half century. The bipolarity that characterized the world system in the years that immediately followed World War II gave way to multipolarity as new or revived power centers arose within the geopolitical networks established by the two superpowers. China broke off from its Soviet masters, and Maritime Europe and Japan became economic powers linked to, but also in competition with, the United States. Small satellites also struck independent courses from their former overlords—Yugoslavia and Albania from the USSR and Cuba from the United States. In recent years, South Africa has taken a more assertive role in Sub-Saharan Africa affairs, Brazil has become the "powerhouse" of South America, and India has rapidly moved toward becoming a world power. Especially within the developing world, regional powers have achieved dominance over neighboring states, carving out independent spheres of influence in political and economic affairs. While they possess the capacity to wage wars, they have been loath to do so, and tend to assume the roles of conflict mediators rather than imposing peace upon their neighbors.

Regional geopolitical unity is far more advanced in Maritime Europe than in any other part of the world. Such unity was advocated by Europe's leadership as a prerequisite to the economic recovery that was attained through massive American aid. While loss of colonial empires stimulated the process, what propelled the movement toward unity was the complementary nature of the region's national economies and the benefits to be derived from economies of scale and larger markets. An additional motivation was the recognition that regional political and military institutions would bind West Germany tightly to its neighbors, especially France. This would minimize the threat that a revived Germany might some day plunge Western Europe once again into conflict with the USSR over the issue of German reunification, or that German national resurgence might resurrect dreams of dominance over Western Europe.

The world map was also changed significantly by the proliferation of national states that occurred in the wake of the collapse of colonial empires. These states varied from sovereign entities as large as India and as small as Nauru or Singapore and include highly successful as well as "failed" states. This multiplicity of national nodes and their external links has led to greater system complexity.

Terrorism was a weapon used by many colonial peoples in their drives for independence. It continues to be an important force in the struggles of separatist movements to wrest sovereignty from the national states within which they are located, and is often transferred to the international arena. Terrorism is also a weapon to overthrow existing regimes in order to impose political-ideological or religious systems.

Also contributing to system complexity have been developments at the subnational level, where metropolitan or "megalopolitan" entities emerged with the revolution in highway and air transportation. Such urban agglomerations often compete with state and federal governments, sometimes conducting independent economic activities that have historically been within the province of higher government levels. Prominent among these activities are the promotion of capital investment, overseas markets, and tourism. Examples in the United States are the northeastern coastal megalopolis from southern New Hampshire and southern Maine to northern Virginia and its central and southern California urban complexes.

A related phenomenon is the transnational megalopolis, large conurbations whose interests often compete with those of their national governments. Examples in Maritime Europe include the London, Paris, and Ruhr basins, the urban-industrial triangle from Benelux through the Rhine to Luxembourg and Strasbourg, and the Rhine-North Italy axis.

Another feature of the contemporary world geopolitical map, the "Shatterbelt," was especially prominent during the Cold War. Shatterbelts are regions torn by internal conflicts whose fragmentation is increased by the intervention of external major powers in contention over the region. At a lesser geographical scale are "Compression Zones"—smaller fragmented areas that lie within or between geopolitical regions. Such zones are torn apart by the combination of civil wars and the interventionist actions of neighboring countries. In contrast to Shatterbelts, they are not arenas of Great Power competition. In some cases, these powers may try to bring an end to conflict and to act as peacekeepers.

Over the past half century, a natural order of state levels has evolved within the international system. Competing with major, or first-order, powers are the regional, or second-order, powers. In time, the latter gain enough strength and ambition to try to influence affairs throughout their regions by the application of military and/or economic muscle. A third order of states has also arisen—those with unique ideological or cultural capacities to influence their neighbors, even though they do not possess the military might to enforce these values. Fourth-order states are generally incapable of applying pressure upon their neighbors and those of the fifth order depend upon outside sustenance for survival.

In historic terms, the age of balanced superpower competition was relatively brief—only four and one-half decades. But it was an age of sweeping scientific, technological, economic, and ideological change. Nuclear weapons and space-age capacities, dominated by the United States and the Soviet Union, created a strategic standoff between the two. At first, the equilibrium that was struck was static. This remained so until the Soviet Union leapfrogged the areas surrounding the Continental Eurasian center to penetrate southward into the Middle East and, together with Communist China, eastward into Korea and southward into Southeast Asia. This was later followed by the spread of Soviet influence into Sub-Saharan Africa and Latin America.

The global system became more complex and its structure more flexible, as the new balance struck between the superpowers depended upon a nested system of geopolitical levels whose units were tied to the superpowers as well as to emerging regional powers. This was the system that ended with the collapse of the Soviet Union in 1991 and the end of the Cold War, leaving the United States as the world's sole superpower.

As new geopolitical structures and equilibrial forces begin to emerge, the developmental principles that guided the evolution of the global system during the Cold War retain their validity and provide the basis for anticipating the contours of the geopolitical map of the twenty-first century. Essentially, the principles hold that systems—both human and biological—evolve in stages, from atomization and undifferentiation to differentiation, specialization, and specialization-integration.

Applying these principles to the geopolitical map is complex, for various parts of the world are at different developmental stages. The differences in developmental pace are compounded by different spatial orders, along which geopolitical relations are forged. Broadly speaking, such orders occur at the macro-, meso- and microlevels. The macro-order embraces strategic realms, the meso-order covers tactical regions, and the micro-order includes states and subnational unit areas. As a result of such complexity, change occurs in fits and starts, not in a smooth, orderly fashion.

The capacity of different parts of the system to evolve relates, in great measure, to their distinctive operational environments. Today, three geostrategic realms embrace much, but not all, of the world. The United States is a superpower whose geopolitical arena is the Maritime World of the North Atlantic and North Pacific basins. It both derives strength from its allies within its realm and provides them with strength. For much of the Cold War, and even at times of ideological and military rivalry, the USSR and China were joined together in a Continental Asian geostrategic realm. While they still have common strategic interests in the Northwest Pacific, their paths have diverged. Russia is the core of the continentally rooted realm of the Eurasian Heartland. China, as core of East Asia, has developed a powerful maritime-oriented economic base that, combined with its continental qualities, has enabled it to carve out a separate Continental-Maritime geostrategic realm.

The boundaries of the three geostrategic realms include the areas that the major powers consider to be vital to their national interests. Such interests represent a mix of security, economic, cultural-ethnic-religious, and ideological imperatives. Regional, national, and subnational entities have their own, identified self-interests within the framework of the realm. If these are highly incompatible with those of the realm's major power(s), structural geopolitical changes may result. For example, new Shatterbelts could emerge where competing realms converge. At the same time, where converging realms find mutual self-interest in fostering cooperative relationships, such intermediate regions could become bridges or "Gateways."

Within the geostrategic realms, economic gaps may be closed by surplus energies from core powers that can be directed toward areas of need. Less energy is generally directed to parts of the world that lie outside the realm, especially if they do not adjoin it. The losers in this situation are the Southern Continents of South America and Sub-Saharan Africa. Since the end of the Cold War, these regions have become a "Quarter-Sphere of Geostrategic Marginality." Their teeming populations are mired in poverty and illiteracy, ravaged by disease, and torn by rebellion. In countries torn apart by warring armies and terrorist bands, such as Somalia, the Democratic Republic of Congo, Sierra Leone, and Colombia, governments have lost effective control of large parts of their national territories, and their states scarcely function as organized geopolitical entities.

Following World War II, the Southern Continents emerged from colonial and pseudo-colonial status to become Cold War battlegrounds. With the collapse of the Soviet Union and the Communist movements in most countries on the Southern Continents, the days in which American, European, and Soviet powers waged surrogate wars, propping up satellite regimes or rebellious groups and extending vast amounts of military and economic assistance, are now history.

The major nations of the world now have much less incentive to become deeply involved in directly addressing the poverty, illiteracy, and disease that ravage most of these lands, delegating the amelioration of such problems to international agencies. These agencies, however, lack the massive funding commitments that are needed and that only the major industrialized states can provide.

The Great Powers have also increasingly left the resolution of conflict and peacekeeping within the Quarter-Sphere to regional and local states. While these states may be willing to assume such roles, the success of their efforts depends upon the extent of the military training and equipment, economic assistance, and diplomatic cover that they receive from external powers and international agencies. Without some form of partnership with the major powers of the Maritime realm, these regional policemen are unlikely to stabilize their surround of chronic conflict.

The independent geopolitical region of South Asia also receives a relatively small share of the surplus energies generated from within the three realms. India did secure some military and political support from the Soviet Union during the Cold War, as did Pakistan from the United States during that period and once again as a consequence of its support of the United States in the war in Afghanistan. However, the size of South Asia's population, the magnitude of its economic and social problems, and the historical-cultural uniqueness of its civilizations and peoples set it apart from the contending realms. In particular, the neutralist stance of India gave the region its separate geopolitical identity.

The rapidly evolving globalization of the world's economy and the transformation of communications networks into global-spanning information systems will not erase national boundaries and identities. Globalization does not spell the end of geography and geopolitics, as some have argued.[2] Rather, it makes for a much more complex geopolitical system. Within it, the national state has to deal with far more external and internal pressures and forces, including domestic and international terrorism, than the state has faced over the five centuries since Louis XI (1461–83) destroyed the last vestiges of feudal power and established France as the prototypical modern state.

Globalization does not override geography. Rather, it adjusts to geographical settings and changes them. Its effects are selectively felt within national states and regions, rather than having across-the-board impacts. Capital flows and outsourcing of manufacturing do not touch all parts of the world equally. The movement is largely toward coastal sections of states and regions that possess mass markets, ease of access, and large pools of cheap but trainable labor. Some of these areas have been the homelands of immigrants who have become successful entrepreneurs in the United States, Maritime Europe, and the Asia-Pacific Rim.

The diffusion of modern industry also takes place in response to political considerations. South Korea, Taiwan, and Japan were the objects of U.S. outsourcing when it suited Washington to build up these key portions of the Asia-Pacific Rim to stave off Soviet-Chinese pressures. This, too, was the case for the American initiatives in aiding the reconstruction of Western Europe immediately after World War II. Later, U.S. economic attention shifted to other parts of Asia-Pacifica, such as Indonesia, Thailand, Malaysia, and the Philippines. It then turned toward its southern borderland—to Mexico and Central America.

Maritime Europe first focused its interests on its Maghreb borderland and on Southeast Asia, the former because of geographical proximity and colonial ties, the latter as a continuation of economic links forged during the age of imperialism. Western Europe has now turned its attention to forging economic and political links with Eastern Europe. In recent years, the United States, the European Union, and Japan/Taiwan/South Korea have begun to extend the global economy to China's "Golden Coast" and India's new centers of information technology. However, vast parts of the world remain untouched by economic globalization and are unlikely to be drawn into the world economy for the foreseeable future.

Even in those parts of the developing world that have been strongly affected by globalization, there have been some adverse consequences. Progress is manifested in the creation of large middle classes and pockets of new wealth, despite charges by critics that globalization is another form of capitalist exploitation. However, the gap between the benefiting classes and the low-paid urban and farm workers in these countries has widened, creating new social strains. In addition, the dependence of developing economies on the consumer markets of the world's wealthy countries, as well as on foreign capital and loans, has become dangerously high. When foreign markets shrink due to recession and decreased demand, or to debt overload, there is little to cushion the impact. The economies and finances of Thailand, Indonesia, and Malaysia suffered severe declines in the late 1990s as a result of this vulnerability and have yet to recover. This effect has proliferated with the deep economic recession of 2000–2001.

Entry into the world market economy has had an adverse effect on agriculture in many of the countries that have benefited from globalization, which is linked to freer trade and involves the opening of domestic markets to low-cost farm products from overseas. The output from highly efficient, modernized agricultural sectors, such as those of the United States, Canada, and Australia, can undermine more backward domestic farm economies. The result is growing opposition to free trade agreements by such modernizing countries as Brazil that are reluctant to abandon protective farm tariffs.

While farm protection and preservation of the rural landscape are major concerns in some advanced industrial countries, such as Spain, Italy, France, and Japan, their economies can absorb displaced farm workers. This is not the case within the developing world. There, industrial job creation cannot keep pace with the demand for jobs. Displaced farmers flock to cities that cannot absorb them, or seek relief through emigration, much of which is illegal.

The use of information technology, another aspect of globalization, is also not as far-reaching as some assume. Thanks to the Internet, individuals in the most repressive of states can learn about developments in other parts of the world. But people must have access to the hardware and software, and this is lacking for much of the world's populace. In settings such as China, many along the coastal region are tuned into the global information network and do act as a pressure point against the restrictive aspects of the regime. But this does not apply to the populations of the North and the Interior, who remain rooted to their Communist traditions. Ultimately, the geographically framed gap between the information "haves" and "have-nots" could lead to a political division of China.

Another side of the information revolution is that, while it exposes parts of the developing world to the fruits of economic freedom and consumerism, it also reinforces the realization of the vast gaps in living standards and opportunities between the two worlds. In a country such as Russia, where the introduction of the free market economy has led to such great abuse, including the looting of former state companies by corrupt entrepreneurs, the regime of Vladimir Putin can use information technology to highlight these excesses and tighten its grip on the government. At the same time, the technology makes it harder for the government to hide its own abuses.

Still another example of the differential impact of the forces of globalization has to do with global warming. The "greenhouse effect," which causes rising surface and water temperatures, is an accepted scientific fact, but its impact will vary geographically. Bangladesh could be inundated by rising oceans as ice caps melt. At the same time, the warming might enable agriculture to be extended over more northerly areas and for longer periods in the United States' Great Plains, Canada's Prairie Provinces, and Russia's west and central Siberia. Thus, while globalization is a most important force, and will become increasingly so, its impact will vary with specific national states and regions. In subsequent chapters on the world's geopolitical regions, these variations will be amplified in the discussions on geopolitical patterns and features.

While the United States surely holds considerable responsibility for stabilizing the world system, it cannot be its sole manager. Other geopolitical actors, with their own goals and immediate spheres of interest, have to be enlisted in the efforts. Indeed, in cases in which a stronger power may not be able or willing to apply military force to gain particular objectives, or to use it as a means of halting conflict, international and regional bodies may often be more effective in stabilizing the system. Alan Henrikson has made a cogent case for the increasingly vital role of diplomacy, as distinct from military deterrence, in achieving international equilibrium through the framework of the United Nations and other bodies.[3] If international and regional diplomacy cannot stave off military intervention, it surely has proven a necessary adjunct in separating warring parties and leading them toward peace.

This volume seeks to identify the nature of the world's complex geopolitical structure and the roles and capacities of its various components. It is the hope of this author that a better understanding of the geopolitical forces that shape the international system can lead to shared national strategies that promote the maintenance of global equilibrium.

Notes

1. Thomas Friedman, *The Lexus and the Olive Tree* (New York: Farrar, Straus & Giroux, 1999), 141–63, 297–378; Francis Fukuyama, "The End of History?" *National Interest* 16 (Summer 1989): 3–18.

2. R. O'Brien, *Global Financial Integration: The End of Geography* (New York: Council on Foreign Relations Press, 1992), 1–35, 101–15.

3. Alan K. Henrikson, "Diplomacy for the 21st Century: 'Re-crafting the Old Guild'" (paper presented at the 503d Wilton Park Conference, "Diplomacy: Profession in Peril?"); published in *Current Issues in International Diplomacy and Foreign Policy,* Wilton Park Papers, Vol. 1 (London: H. M. Stationery Office, 1998).

CHAPTER 2

Survey of Geopolitics

The true value of modern geopolitics is as a scholarly analysis of the geographical factors underlying international relations and guiding political interactions. The discipline has had to overcome some controversial roots.

Introduced a century ago as a deterministic field of study and a recipe for statecraft, it was first offered as a set of geographically determined laws governing a state's strategic destinies and evolved as the geographical underpinnings of *realpolitik*. Presented as a science, its scholarly legitimacy was challenged on the grounds that it lacked empirically based principles in its development of doctrines that served the singular needs of particular states. In addition, the focus on *realpolitik* was criticized for the absence of a moral and ethical basis.

Later, in Nazi German hands, *geopolitik* became a distorted pseudoscience, with no scientific bounds. During and since the Cold War, the field has diverged into two competing schools of thought—one nation centered, the other offering universalistic perspectives.

Definitions

Geopolitics is a product of its times, and its definitions have evolved accordingly. Rudolph Kjellén, who coined the term in 1899, described geopolitics as "the theory of the state as a geographical organism or phenomenon in space."[1] For Karl Haushofer, the father of German *geopolitik*, "Geopolitics is the new national science of the state, . . . a doctrine on the spatial determinism of all political processes, based on the broad foundations of geography, especially of political geography.[2] On the eve of World War II, Derwent Whittlesey, the American political geographer, dismissed geopolitics as "a dogma, . . . the faith that the state is inherently entitled to its place in the sun."[3] Richard Hartshorne defined it as "geography utilized for particular purposes that lie beyond the pursuit of knowledge."[4]

In contrast to geographers Whittlesey and Hartshorne, political scientist Edmund Walsh espoused an American geopolitics based upon international justice and that was "a combined study of human geography and applied political science . . . dating back to Aristotle, Montesquieu and Kant."[5]

For Geoffrey Parker, geopolitics is "the study of international relations from a spatial or geographical perspective,"[6] while John Agnew defined the field as "examination of the geographical assumptions, designations and understandings that enter into the making of world politics."[7] Gearold O'Tuathail, an exponent of critical geopolitics, argues that "geopolitics does not have a singular, all-encompassing meaning or identity. . . . [I]t is discourse, a culturally and politically varied way of describing, representing and writing about geography and international politics."[8]

Statesmen and scholars who view geopolitics as a vehicle for integrating geography and international politics may find it useful to define geopolitics, not as a school of thought, but as a mode of analysis, relating diversity in content and scale of geographical settings to exercise of political power, and identifying spatial frameworks through which power flows.

"Geopolitics" is defined in this volume as the analysis of the interaction between, on the one hand, geographical settings and perspectives and, on the other, political processes. The settings are composed of geographical features and patterns and the multilayered regions that they form. The political processes include forces that operate at the international level and those on the domestic scene that influence international behavior. Both geographical settings and political processes are dynamic, and each influences and is influenced by the other. Geopolitics addresses the consequences of this interaction.

The approach that has been taken in this work is regional and developmental. It treats the world's geopolitical structure as an evolving system composed of a hierarchy of levels. National states and their subnational units are framed within geostrategic realms and geopolitical regions.

Because geopolitics straddles two disciplines—geography and politics—its approaches vary according to frameworks of analysis common to each discipline. Since most early theories and concepts of geopolitics grew out of geographical thought, later applications by historians and political scientists often failed because they did not adapt their theories to the dynamic, complex nature of geographical settings.

Stages of Modern Geopolitics

Modern geopolitics has developed through five stages—the race for imperial hegemony; German *geopolitik*; American geopolitics; the Cold War–state-centered versus universalistic geographical; and the post–Cold War period.

STAGE 1: THE RACE FOR IMPERIAL HEGEMONY

Geopolitical thinking can be traced back to Aristotle, Strabo, Bodin, Montesquieu, Kant, and Hegel. Its nineteenth-century precursors include Humboldt, Guyot, Buckle, and Ritter. However, the founders of modern geopolitics were Ratzel, Mackinder, Kjellén, Bowman, and Mahan, whose writings reflected their era of intense nationalism, state expansionism, and overseas empire building. The principles and laws of these leading theoreticians reflected their national perspectives and experiences, as well as the influence of social Darwinism.

Ratzel

Friedrich Ratzel (1844–1904), the German "father" of political geography and a natural scientist, was the first to treat space and location systematically, in his comparative studies of states.[9] He provided successor geopoliticians with a scientific basis for state expansionist doctrines that reflected Germany's nineteenth-century experiences and its ambitions for the future. During the last half of the nineteenth century Germany had emerged as the chief economic and military power on the European continent. Unified under Bismarck's leadership and victorious in its wars with Austria and France, it had enlarged its territory, expanded its heavy industries, and enacted social reform. With the aid of a new, powerful naval fleet, Germany posed a serious threat to Britain and France as it acquired an overseas empire in East and West Africa and the Western Pacific and sought commercial footholds in East Asia.

Ratzel based his system upon principles of evolution and science.[10] He viewed the state as an organism fixed in the soil whose spirit derived from mankind's ties to the land. His geographical "laws" focused on space *(raum)* and location *(lage),* the former dependent upon and contributing to the political character of groups living in the space, the latter providing space with its uniqueness. Frontiers were the "skins" or peripheral organs of states, reflecting growth and decline. When correlated with continental areas organized under a single government, states would generate vast political power. These "organic" theories of state growth fitted Germany's view of its future as a youthful, aggressive, capitalist "giant state."

Mackinder

Halford Mackinder (1861–1947), who established geography as a university discipline in Britain, foresaw the ending of the Victorian era. His concern was safeguarding the British Empire's political, commercial, and industrial primacy at a time when command of the seas no longer appeared to guarantee world supremacy. With the advent of the transcontinental railroad age (the Union Pacific, 1869; Berlin-Baghdad via Anatolia, 1896; and the Trans-Siberian, 1905), Mackinder viewed the rise of Eurasian continental states as the greatest threat to British world hegemony.

For Mackinder, geographical realities lay in the advantages of centrality of place and efficient movement of ideas, goods, and people. In 1904, he theorized that the inner area of Eurasia, characterized by interior or polar drainage and impenetrable by sea power, was the "Pivot Area" of world politics (figure 2.1). He warned that rule of the heart of the world's greatest landmass could become the basis for world domination, owing to the superiority of rail over ships in terms of time and reach. A Eurasian land power (be it Russia, Germany, or even China, and especially an alliance of the first two) that gained control of the Pivot Area would outflank the Maritime world.[11] Eleven years later, the English geographer James Fairgrieve, who introduced the term "Heartland," opined that China was in an excellent position to dominate Eurasia.[12]

In *Democratic Ideals and Realities* (1919), Mackinder, now using the term "Heartland" and taking into account advances in land transportation, population increases, and industrialization, enlarged his map to include Eastern Europe from the Baltic through the Black Sea as Inner Eurasia's strategic annex (figure 2.2).[13] This became the basis for his dictum, "Who rules Eastern Europe commands the Heartland: Who rules the Heartland commands World-Island: Who rules World-Island commands the world." The warning to Western statesmen was clear—the key to world domination lay in the middle tier of German and Slavic states, or Mitteleuropa—a region as accessible to Germans as it was to Russia.

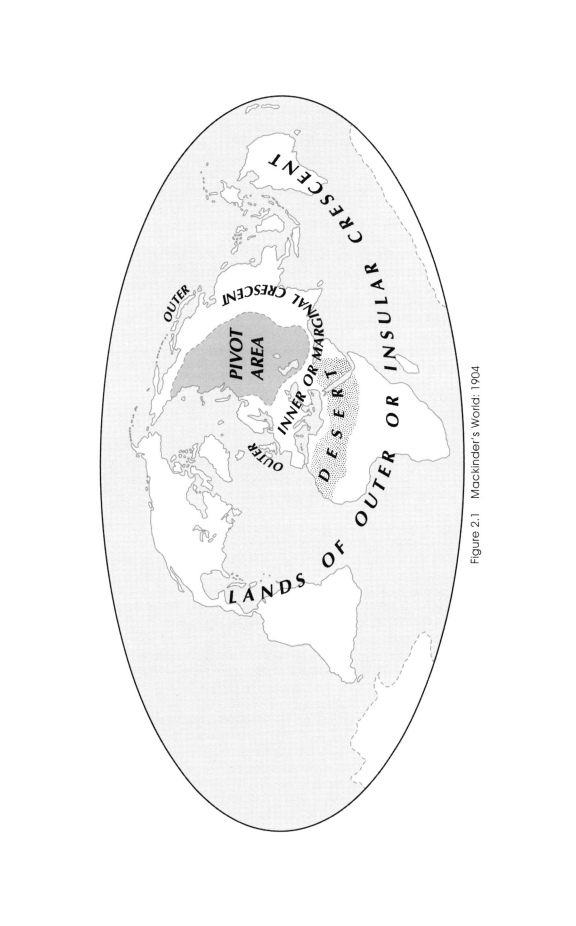

Figure 2.1   Mackinder's World: 1904

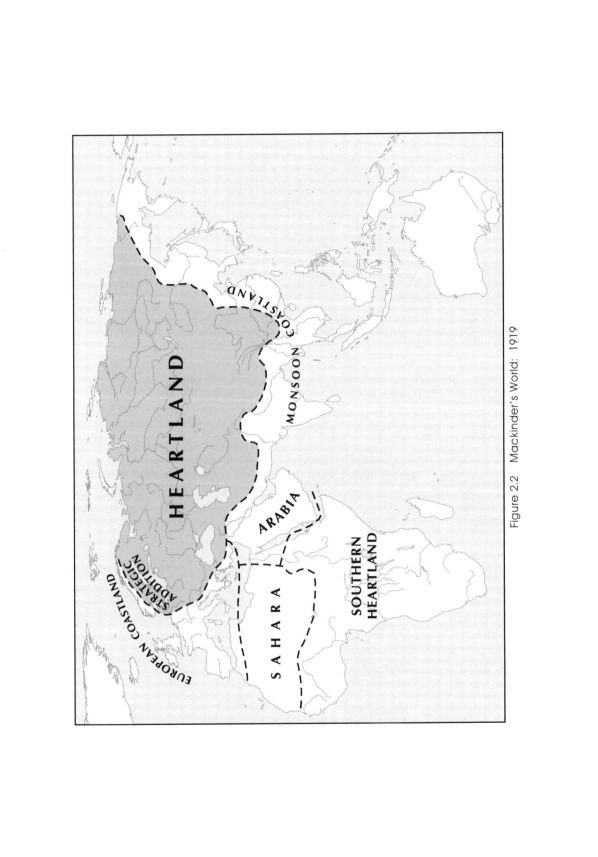

Figure 2.2 Mackinder's World: 1919

Mackinder described the world as a closed system. Nothing could be altered without changing the balance of all, and rule of the world still rested upon force, notwithstanding the juridical assumptions of equality among sovereign states. Mackinder called himself a democratic idealist in advocating equality of opportunity for nations to achieve balanced economic development. He also described himself as a realist who feared that the League of Nations would degenerate into an unbalanced empire, as one or two of the great powers bid for predominance. As a safeguard, he urged smaller powers to federate to increase the number of significant players on the world scene and make it more difficult for hegemony to be attained by potential tyrants. Foreseeing the decline of Britain as the world's leading power, he called for Western Europe and North America to become a single community of nations—a forerunner of the North Atlantic community.

Mackinder remained steadfast in his commitment to the concept of balance. In looking at the shape of the post–World War II order, he foresaw a world geopolitically balanced between a combination of the North Atlantic (Midland Ocean) and Asian Heartland powers. By working together, they could keep future German ambitions in check. The Monsoonal lands of India and China represented an evolving third balancing unit within the world system. He also speculated that the continental masses bordering the South Atlantic might eventually become a unit within the balancing process. The "Mantle of Vacancies," a barrier region extending from the Sahara through the Central Asian deserts that divides the major communities of humankind, might emerge as a fifth component of the system. Mackinder forecast that this barrier region might someday provide solar energy as a substitute for exhaustible resources.

These thoughts were sketched out in a 1943 article entitled "The Round World and the Winning of the Peace."[14] In it, Mackinder discarded his famous 1919 dictum that rule of Heartland meant command of World-Island. He drew no map to accompany his article. Therefore, a map that cartographically expresses what he wrote is presented here (figure 2.3). First, he detached Lenaland (the central Siberian tableland) from the Heartland. Thus, Heartland now consisted largely of the cleared forest and steppe portions of Eurasia. More important, Mackinder's concept of the map of the world had changed, as he introduced the concept of a world balanced by a multiplicity of regions, each with a distinct natural and human resource base.

The yardsticks that Mackinder used in drawing the boundaries of Heartland indicate that the original concept of the Pivot Area of the world had changed from that of an arena of movement (i.e., as a region of mobility for land forces) to one of a "power citadel" based upon people, resources, and interior lines. The three boundaries (figure 2.4) that reflect his changing views of the earth indicate that he was well aware of technological developments, including air power. To place Mackinder's views in historic and contemporary perspectives, Cold War U.S. containment policy was based on his Heartland worlds of 1904 and 1919. Post–Cold War American balance-of-power goals are more in consonance with his 1943 global view.

Whereas Ratzel's theories of the large state were based on concepts of self-sufficiency, closed space, and totalitarian controls, Mackinder was strongly committed to cooperation among states, democratization of the empire into a Commonwealth of Nations, and preservation of small states. He bridged the academy and politics, serving as a Conservative and Unionist member of Parliament (1910–22) and as British high commissioner for South Russia (1919–20). While he was an advocate of open systems, he exhibited ambivalence over trade issues. Initially a Liberal imperialist and proponent of free trade,

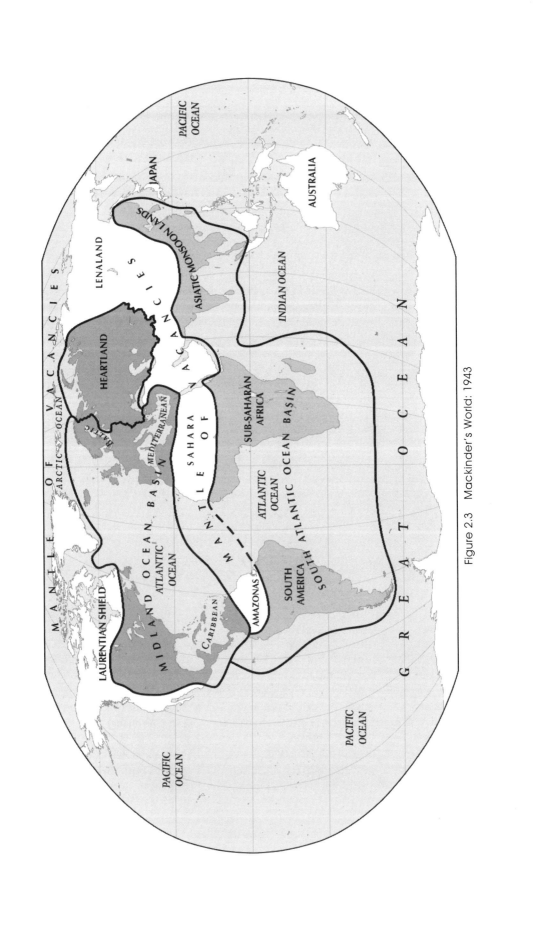

Figure 2.3   Mackinder's World: 1943

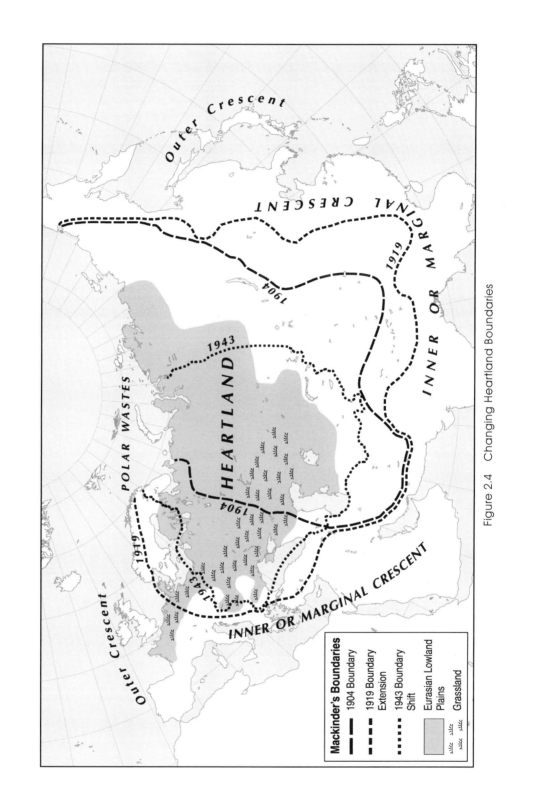

Figure 2.4   Changing Heartland Boundaries

he eventually became committed to a preferential tariff system to protect British imperial unity.[15]

The impact of Mackinder's thinking spanned half a century and his ideas were the cornerstone for generations of strategic policy makers. His view of the world became the basis for Lord Curzon's imperial strategies in South Asia and South Russia, for German *geopolitik* between World War I and II, and for Western containment strategies of the post–World War II era.

Mahan

Admiral Alfred T. Mahan (1849–1914) was a naval historian and second president of the United States Naval War College. His global perspective was also Eurasian centered.[16] For Mahan, the northern land hemisphere, the far-flung parts of which were linked through the passageways offered by the Panama and Suez canals, was the key to world power; within that hemisphere, Eurasia was the most important component. Mahan recognized Russia as the dominant Asian land power, whose location made it unassailable. However, he felt that Russia's landlocked position put it at a disadvantage, because, in his view, sea movement was superior to land movement.

For Mahan, the critical zone of conflict lay between the thirtieth and fortieth parallels in Asia, where Russian land power and British sea power met. He argued that world dominance could be held by an Anglo-American alliance from key bases surrounding Eurasia. Indeed, he predicted that an alliance of the United States, Britain, Germany, and Japan would one day hold common cause against Russia and China.

Mahan developed his geopolitical views as America's frontier history was drawing to a close and the country had begun to look beyond its continental limits to a new role as a world power. He considered the United States to be an outpost of European power and civilization, regarding its Pacific shore and islands to be extensions of the Atlantic-European realm. The United States thus lay within the Western half of a twofold global framework, the Oriental (Asian) being the other half. In many ways, Mahan's view of the world's setting anticipated Mackinder's. Their diametrically opposed strategic conclusions stemmed from different assessments of the comparative effectiveness of land versus sea movement.

Espousing a "blue water strategy," Mahan strongly supported U.S. annexation of the Philippines, Hawaii, Guam, and Puerto Rico; control of the Panama Canal Zone; and tutelage over Cuba. His writings helped bring an end to American isolationism and were highly influential in shaping U.S. foreign policy during the McKinley and Theodore Roosevelt administrations. Roosevelt, in particular, endorsed the Mahan call for a larger navy, as well as his broader geopolitical concepts.[17]

Bowman

Isaiah Bowman (1878–1949), the leading American geographer of his period, was also engaged at policy levels in an attempt to fashion the new world order envisaged by Woodrow Wilson: "The effects of the Great War are so far-reaching that we shall have hence-forth a new world. . . . [T]he new era would date from the years of the First World War, just as Medieval Europe dates from the fall of Rome, or the modern democratic era dates from the Declaration of Independence." Describing the war as the combination of assassination, invasion, and Germanic ambitions, "colored by the desire to control the seats of production and the channels of transportation of all those products," he viewed the relations among states as an evolutionary struggle.[18]

Bowman did not believe that the League of Nations was, in and of itself, the framework for a new world. Rather, he saw different leagues emerging for functional purposes, each designed to advance cooperative plans that would reduce the causes of international trouble. "The world's people are still fundamentally unlike," he wrote, "and the road to success passes through a wilderness of experiment."[19]

No grand theory here, as was Mackinder's, but rather the prescription of an empiricist, of a practitioner grounded on boundaries, resources, national minorities—a world of shifting international parts that was disorganized, unstable, and dangerous and requiring mediating international groups to minimize the dangers. Bowman's idea of a new world was essentially a map of the world as it was, with greater attention to the sovereign interests of certain nationalities and to a need for coordinated international action. His work was, in effect, an explication of what problems would be encountered by Woodrow Wilson's fourteenth point—the call for a general association of nations to guarantee the peace of the world.

Kjellén

Rudolph Kjellén (1864–1922), the political scientist who coined the term "geopolitics" in 1899, was influenced both by his Swedish background and by Germany's growth into a giant state. He viewed the impending breakdown of the Concert of Europe and the drift toward war and chaos as the death knell for a small state like Sweden. Adopting Ratzel's organic state concept, he considered Germany's emergence as a great power inevitable and desirable. The needs of Sweden would be fulfilled within the framework of a new Mitteleuropean bloc from Scandinavia and the Baltic through Eastern Europe and the Balkans, dominated by an ascendant Germany.

A Conservative member of the Swedish parliament, Kjellén viewed geopolitics as the "science of the state," whereby the state's natural environment provided the framework for a power unit's pursuit of "inexorable laws of progress." Geopolitics was initially conceived by Kjellén as one of five major disciplines for understanding the state, the others being termed econo-, demo-, socio-, and crato- (power) politics. As the mainstay of the five, geopolitics came to subsume the others.

The dynamic organic approach led Kjellén to espouse the doctrine that political processes were spatially determined. Moreover, since giant states in Europe could only be created by war, he viewed geopolitics as primarily a science of war.[20]

STAGE 2: GERMAN *GEOPOLITIK*

German *geopolitik* emerged in reaction to Germany's devastating defeat in World War I. Humbled by the Treaty of Versailles, Germany was stripped of its overseas empire and important parts of its national territory. Alsace-Lorraine was returned to France, small border areas were annexed by Belgium, and North Schleswig was returned to Denmark in a plebiscite. Historic Prussia was divided. In West Prussia, Poznan (Posen) went to Poland, as did the land that constituted the Polish Corridor. Danzig became a "free city" and, in the easternmost part of East Prussia, the Memel Territory first came under the League of

Nations, administered by France, and was then annexed by Lithuania. Parts of Upper Silesia went to Poland and Czechoslovakia. The Saar was put under French administration, pending a plebiscite to be held in 1935 to determine its final status, and the Rhineland was occupied by Allied forces. Germany was now but a shadow of the expanding giant state of Ratzel's and Kjellén's imperial era.

In addition, the social cohesion forged by Bismarck's policies was shattered. The socialist Weimar Republic was beleaguered by class warfare and attempts to overthrow it by Communists on the left and racist militant nationalists and aristocratic conservatives on the right. Unemployment was rampant and inflation raged. This was the setting within which Karl Haushofer and his colleagues established the *Zeitschrift für Geopolitik* (1924–39) and the Institute for Geopolitics at the University of Munich. Undoing Versailles by restoring the lost territories and rebuilding Germany as a world power undergirded the pseudoscientific "laws" and principles of *geopolitik* that served Nazi Germany.

Haushofer

Karl Haushofer (1869–1946), the former military commander who became a political geographer, was not an original thinker. The *geopolitik* of the group of German geopoliticians whom he led (Otto Maull, Erich Obst, Ewald Banse, Richard Hennig, Colin Ross, Albrecht Haushofer) was based essentially upon the writings of Kjellén, Ratzel, and Mackinder. Others whose teachings he invoked included Mahan, Fairgrieve, and such geographical determinists as Ellen Churchill Semple, who was Ratzel's leading American disciple.

Much of the organismic Hegelian philosophy of *geopolitik* came from Ratzel, directly or via Kjellén. *Lebensraum* (living space) and autarchy became slogans for doctrines whose consequences were conflict and total war. Three geographical settings permeated the literature of *geopolitik*: Ratzel's large states, Mackinder's World-Island, and panregions. The organic growth of Germany to its west and east was regarded as inevitable. To gain mastery over World-Island, it was necessary to dominate the USSR and destroy British sea power. The geopoliticians posited that German control over Pan-Europe (including Eastern Europe) would force the Soviet Union, regarded as an Asian power, to come to terms.

During most of the 1920s and 1930s, Haushofer espoused continental panregionalism based upon complementarity of resources and peoples: Pan-America, Pan-Eur-Africa, and Pan-Asia, with the United States, Germany, and Japan as respective cores. His position on the USSR was ambiguous. He proposed variously a German-Russian alliance, a Pan-Russia–South Asia grouping, and a Japan-China-Russia bloc. His call for Germany, the USSR, and Japan to form a Eurasian panregion that would dominate World-Island influenced the German-Soviet pact of 1939, but was made moot by Hitler's subsequent invasion of the Soviet Union.

The German School could overlook these contradictions because *geopolitik* made no pretense of objectivity. Its principles were designed to fulfill German national and imperial aims. Doctrines such as *blut und boden* (blood and soil) and *rasse und raum* (race and space) became ideological foundations for the murderous Nazi regime, which plunged the world into history's most devastating war and perpetrated the Jewish holocaust and the murder of millions of Slavic peoples.

While Karl Haushofer was the key figure in *geopolitik*, there were other important contributors. Otto Maull was a cofounder and coeditor of the *Zeitschrift* and subscribed to the theory of the organic state as a collection of spatial cells (regions, cities, etc.) with a life of its own. Erich Obst, the third cofounder of the *Zeitschrift*, sought to establish "objective" standards for *lebensraum*. Richard Hennig developed a doctrine in which land, space, and economics were deemed more important than racial considerations, for which he was bitterly attacked by some of his colleagues. Ewald Banse outlined the strategy and tactics for the coming *blitzkrieg*. Albrecht Haushofer focused on the Atlantic world and on translating geographic data into expansive power politics. An American contributor to the *Zeitschrift* was Colin Ross, an early advocate of Japan's freedom to develop its own "laws of life," independent of German direction. Nevertheless, it was Karl Haushofer who was the architect and mastermind of the *Zeitschrift* and the Institute for Geopolitics—he held the main responsibility for the content and direction taken by German *geopolitik*.

Haushofer's extraordinary influence derived from his close ties to Rudolph Hess, his aide-de-camp in World War I and, subsequently, his student at the University of Munich. Through Hess, he had contact with Hitler from 1923 to 1938. Many of Haushofer's doctrines, especially *lebensraum,* were incorporated into *Mein Kampf* and Haushofer advised Hitler at Munich in 1938.[21] With Hess's flight to England in 1941, the influence of the geopoliticians upon Hitler ended. Indeed, Haushofer was imprisoned briefly at Dachau (ironically, he had a Jewish wife). His son Albrecht, also a geographer with links to aristocrat military circles, was involved in the Generals' Plot to assassinate Hitler in 1944 and was killed by the S.S. Haushofer and his wife committed suicide in 1946.

STAGE 3: GEOPOLITICS IN THE UNITED STATES

Spykman

Most American academic geographers vigorously repudiated German *geopolitik*, resulting in a general reluctance to pursue the study of geopolitics. Nicholas Spykman, a U.S. scholar of international relations who had been born in Amsterdam, was one of the few who did work in the field during this period (1942–44). His "Rimland" theory reflected Mahan's view of the world and was presented as an antidote to the concept of Heartland primacy.[22]

However, Spykman's terminology, his detailed global geographical setting, and the political conclusions that he derived from his views of the world, show that his basic inspiration came from Mackinder, whose strategic conclusions he attempted to refute. Essentially, Spykman sought to arouse the United States against the danger of world domination by Germany.[23] He felt that only a dedicated alliance of Anglo-American sea power and Soviet land power could prevent Germany from seizing control of all the Eurasian shorelines and thereby gaining domination over World-Island.

Spykman considered that the Eurasian coastal lands (including Maritime Europe, the Middle East, India, Southeast Asia, and China) were the keys to world control because of their populations, their rich resources, and their use of interior sea lanes.

In essence, Spykman had the same global view as Mackinder, but he rejected the land-power doctrine to say, "Who controls the Rimland rules Eurasia; who rules Eurasia controls the destinies of the world." To Spykman, the Rimland (Mackinder's "Marginal Crescent") was the key to the struggle for the world. In the past, the fragmentation of the Western European portion of Rimland and the power of the United Kingdom and the United States (parts of what Spykman considered the Offshore Continents and Islands) had made unitary control of the Rimland impossible. (This Offshore region, which included the New World, Sub-Saharan Africa, and Australasia, was equivalent to Mackinder's "Outer Crescent.") Now, however, Spykman feared that a single power, such as Germany, might seize control of the European Rimland and then sweep onto the other portions through various combinations of conquests and alliances, using ship superiority and command of a network of naval and air bases around Eurasia.

Certainly there is still much to be said in favor of sea communication as far as the movement of goods is concerned. Also, aircraft carriers and submarines have given a mobility in the use of aircraft and missiles to ocean basin powers that fixed land bases cannot. The inadequacy of Spykman's doctrine was and remains the fact that no Eurasian Rimland power is capable of organizing all of the Rimland because of the vulnerability of the Rimland to both the Heartland and the Offshore powers. A united Maritime Europe would have to have complete control of the Mediterranean, North Africa, the Middle East, Sub-Saharan Africa, and Australia before it could attempt to exert its strategic dominance upon the remainder of the South and East Asian portions of the Rimland. It could succeed only if the Heartland or the Offshore New World's American power did not intervene. He also held that a Rimland China that swept into control of Offshore or South Asia would be at a disadvantage in seeking to control the Middle East against Heartland-, Western European–, or African-based pressures.

The importance of interior lines of land communication, even between parts of the Rimland, looms greater today than it did in Spykman's considerations. Thus, the Chinese land base was able to sustain North Korea and North Vietnam in spite of the control of the seas and the air by Offshore powers. Communist networks of rails and modern highways (as well as jungle and mountain trails) in South China and North Vietnam were the sinews of politicoeconomic penetration that ultimately defeated the United States in Vietnam, and that have drawn Vietnam, Laos, and Cambodia into China's strategic oversight.

Other Theoreticians

The impact of the air age upon geopolitical thought produced a variety of views. In 1942, George Renner suggested that the air lanes had united the Heartland of Eurasia with a second, somewhat smaller Heartland in Anglo-America, across Arctic ice fields, to form a new, expanded Heartland within the northern hemisphere.[24] A major attribute of this new Heartland was the mutual vulnerability of its Eurasian and its Anglo-American portions across the Arctic. According to Renner, not only would the expanded Heartland be the dominant power center of the world, but it also possessed the advantages of interior air, sea, and land routes across the polar world. Thus the Arctic, as the pivotal world arena of movement, was the key to Heartland and therefore to world control.

Another opinion, that of Alexander de Seversky, has been described by Stephen Jones as "the airman's global view."[25] De Seversky's map of the world, which he presented in 1950, is an azimuthal equidistant projection centered on the North Pole. The western hemisphere lies to the south of the pole, Eurasia and Africa to the north. Here again was an Old World–New World division. North America's area of "air dominance" (its area of reserve for resources and manufacturing) is Latin America; the Soviet Union's area of air dominance is South and Southeast Asia and most of Africa south of the Sahara. De Seversky considered the areas where North American and Soviet air dominance overlapped (this includes Anglo-America, the Eurasian Heartland, Maritime Europe, North Africa, and the Middle East) to be the "Area of Decision." According to this view, air mastery and therefore global control could be gained.[26]

In one sense, this view is an extension of Renner's. In another, however, it led to two different and highly questionable conclusions. The first stems from the distortion of the map projection, which suggests that Africa and South America are so widely separated that they are mutually defensible by their respective senior partners, the Soviet Union and the United States.

Second, de Seversky's view was that air supremacy, and with it control of the northern hemispheric Area of Decision, could be achieved by one power through all-out aerial warfare. While he spoke of only the United States, the USSR, and perhaps, the United Kingdom as having the potentialities of Great Power, in theory any country with the necessary military hardware, recuperative strength, and will could achieve dominance. Thus de Seversky's theories lead to two conclusions: (1) "air isolationism," which suggested a viable division of the world into two, and (2) "a unitary global view," suggesting that, in the event of all-out war, the power that led in military hardware, regardless of its location, could dominate the world. De Seversky's major work, written in 1950, did not anticipate that several powers might achieve the capabilities of mutual destruction.

There are those who held that air power did not add a third dimension to land and sea movement, but simply a complementary dimension to each of these channels. Particularly if all-out nuclear warfare is eliminated, this view of what Jones called the "air-first moderates" held that air power could be decisive only as it lends a comparative advantage to land or sea powers. An influential spokesman for this point of view within the North Atlantic Alliance was the British strategist, air force marshal Sir John Slessor. He was a strong advocate of airborne nuclear weapons as "The Great Deterrent" against total war.[27] Thus ruling out total war, he concluded that the role of air power is to supplement sea- or land-based forces. He held that even an invasion of Western Europe could be countered by a limited type of air attack–land defense to arrest invasion without nuclear war. To Slessor, whose strategic doctrine followed a Rimland-Heartland equilibrium theory, the likely arenas for limited war were the Middle East and Southeast Asia, with air power being the key supplement to sea-supported land actions.

STAGE 4: THE COLD WAR–STATE-CENTERED VS. UNIVERSALISTIC APPROACHES

Onset of the Cold War reawakened Western interest in geopolitics. This came from historians, political scientists, and statesmen, not from geographers, who had distanced themselves from geopolitics because of the taint of German *geopolitik*.

State-Centered Geopolitics

American Cold Warriors embraced geopolitics as a basis for a national policy aimed at confronting the Soviet Union and international communism. Building on early, geographically derived geopolitical theories and holding static interpretations of global and regional spatial patterns, they introduced such political-strategic concepts as containment, domino theory, balance-of-power linkages, and linchpin states into the lexicon of Cold War geopolitics. In this context, Halford Mackinder's Heartland theory played an instrumental role.

George Kennan's 1946 warning of the historical imperative of Soviet expansionism from its Russian Asiatic center was embraced by American anti-Communists as the intellectual basis for containment of the USSR around every point of the Heartland.[28] This was formalized in the Truman doctrine of 1947. Winston Churchill also, in his 1946 speech in Fulton, Missouri, issued a call for containing the expansionist tendencies of the Soviet Union, coining the expression "Iron Curtain."[29]

As a member of the policy planning staff of the U.S. Department of State during the Truman administration, Kennan had promoted the idea of containment. He was the first in a long line of U.S. policy makers to embrace the concept. Other early proponents were Dean Acheson, Paul Nitze, John Foster Dulles, Dwight Eisenhower, Walt Rostow, and Maxwell Taylor. They were later joined by Henry Kissinger, Richard Nixon, Zbigniew Brzezinski, and Alexander Haig, and containment became the keystone of American foreign policy.[30] These versions of the Heartland-Rimland theory remained a tool for containment strategy long after that strategy had proved wanting, as the Soviet Union and China leaped across the Rimland to penetrate parts of the Middle East, Sub-Saharan Africa, the Caribbean and Central America, and Southeast Asia.

Western foreign policy therefore could not confine itself to containment of the Eurasian Continental power along its Heartland borders. Instead, it adopted a strategy of checking the spread of communism throughout the Third World. The idealistic vision that had prompted the United States to support the freedom and democratization of colonial peoples quickly gave way to expedient *realpolitik*—propping up right-wing dictatorships in order to stop the threat of communism wherever that threat was perceived to exist.

Another popular geopolitical doctrine, "domino theory," was first proposed by William Bullit in 1947. He feared that Soviet Communist power would spread via China into Southeast Asia. The concept was adopted by both the Kennedy and Nixon administrations, which rationalized American intervention in Vietnam as a measure to "save" the rest of Southeast Asia.[31]

The domino theory was an important argument for extending Western containment policy well beyond the Southeast Asian and Middle Eastern Shatterbelts into the Horn of Africa and Sub-Saharan Africa, Central America and Cuba, South America, and South Asia. These areas became battlegrounds for the two superpowers, as each supported local surrogates militarily, politically, and economically. The goal was to protect or gain sources of raw materials and markets, while denying military bases to the enemy overseas. The imagery of dominos survives. The threat of the spread of Kosovar Albanian irredentism to Macedonia, Bulgaria, and Greece was one of the factors, along with humanitarian considerations, which precipitated NATO's air war against Yugoslavia in 1998.

A third principle, "linkage," was introduced into geopolitics by Henry Kissinger in 1979.[32] Indeed, Leslie Hepple suggested that Kissinger almost single-handedly reintroduced the term "geopolitics" as synonymous with global balance-of-power politics.[33] Linkage is based upon the theory of a network that connected all parts of the world's trouble spots to the Soviet Union, and that American involvement in any single conflict needed to be viewed for its impact upon overall superpower balance. For Kissinger, display of Western impotence in one part of the world, such as Asia or Africa, would inevitably erode its credibility in other parts of the world, such as the Middle East. Linkage was used to rationalize the Nixon administration's clinging to the war in Vietnam, long after the conflict had clearly been lost. The threat of credibility loss continued to resonate with the West, serving as a driving force in NATO's war against Yugoslavia.

Linkage theory was also applied to détente with the Soviet Union and accommodation with China. To maintain the balance of power, the Nixon administration sought Moscow's agreement on strategic arms limitations and mutual nuclear deterrence and tried to play China off against the USSR. The logical consequence of this policy was acquiescing to the Brezhnev doctrine, which held that military force was justified to keep the socialist countries of Eastern and Central Europe within the Soviet camp.

Zbigniew Brzezinski's geopolitical worldview was based on the struggle between Eurasian land power and sea power. For him, the key to containment and preventing Soviet world dominance lay in U.S. control of "linchpin" states. He defined these by their geographical position, which enabled them to exert economic/military influence, or by their militarily significant geostrategic locations. The designated linchpins were Germany, Poland, Iran or Pakistan-Afghanistan, South Korea, and the Philippines. Their dominance by the United States would effectively contain the Russian "Imperial" power, protecting Europe and Japan and, in the case of South Korea and the Philippines, preventing encirclement of China.[34]

For Brzezinski, the U.S.-Soviet conflict was an endless game, and linchpin control was a necessary part of the U.S. geostrategic game plan. In this approach to geopolitics, there is little consideration of the geopolitical complexity of the global system and of the multiplicity of forces beyond superpower reach that had become active agents in the system. It particularly ignored the innate geopolitical positions and strengths of China and India, and surely underestimated the costs of superpower alliances with weak and unstable regimes.

Universalistic Geopolitics

When geographers reengaged in geopolitics in the 1960s and '70s, they introduced theories based upon universalistic/holistic views of the world and the dynamic nature of geographical space. Three approaches predominated: (1) a polycentric, international power system; (2) a unitary, economically based world system; and (3) an environmental and socially ordered geopolitics.

Because these fresh geographical theories challenged bipolar Cold War geopolitics, they had little appeal to the Cold Warriors and failed to make their way into popular "political" geopolitics, as practiced by statesmen and popularly disseminated through the press. The polycentric or multinodal/multilevel power approach rejected the Heartland theory of world domination, as ironically had Halford Mackinder in his last published work in 1943.

In 1963, this writer proposed a flexible hierarchy (refined in 1973) of geostrategic realms, geopolitical regions, Shatterbelts, national states, and subnational units within a system that evolved through forces of dynamic equilibrium.[35] A decade later, a comparative developmental approach was added that drew on the developmental psychology theories of Heinz Werner and the general systems principles of Ludwig von Bertalanffy.[36] The expanded geopolitical theory posited that the structural components of the global system evolve from stages of atomization and undifferentiation with relatively few parts, to specialized integration with many parts at different geoterritorial scales. Equilibrium is maintained by moving from one stage to another through responses to short-term disturbances.

In England, G. R. Chrone presented a geopolitical system of ten regional groupings that were also hierarchically ordered and had an historical and cultural basis.[37] In Chrone's view, the world power balance was shifting from Europe and the West toward Asia and the Pacific. He predicted that the Pacific Ocean would become the future arena of confrontation for the USSR, the United States, and China.

Two decades later, Peter Taylor, the English geographer, broke away from the "realistic" approach to power-centered geopolitics when he applied a world-systems approach based upon global economics. He drew upon the 1983 work of Immanuel Wallerstein, who argued that the world economy means a single global society, not competing national economies. Integrating the Wallerstein model with George Modelski's cycles of world power, Taylor presented power and politics within the context of a cyclical world economy in which nation states and localities are fitted.[38]

Both Taylor and Wallerstein viewed global conflict in North-South terms (rich nations versus poor nations), rather than in Mackinder's earlier East-West model. Accepting the thesis that capitalist core areas aggrandize themselves at the expense of the peripheral parts of the world, Taylor's radical perspective was offered as a basis for "informing" the political issues of the day.[39]

An environmentally and socially oriented geopolitics was promoted by Yves LaCoste in France with the establishment of the journal *Hérodite* in 1976. In moving toward a "new" *géopolitique,* LaCoste sought to overcome the national chauvinism of the "old" geopolitics by focusing on the land, not on the state. *Hérodite* linked geopolitics to ecology and broader environmental issues, as well as to such matters as world poverty and resource exhaustion.[40] Much of LaCoste's work was inspired by the French human geographer and political anarchist Élisée Reclus, who believed it essential to reshape the world's political structure by abolishing states and establishing a cooperative global system.[41] While this French geopolitics did not produce systematic geopolitical theory, it did put the spotlight on applying geopolitics to significant global problems.

STAGE 5: POST–COLD WAR ERA: COMPETITION OR ACCOMMODATION?

The end of the Cold War era has generated a number of new approaches to geopolitics. For Francis Fukuyama, the passing of Marxism-Leninism and the triumph of Western liberal democracy and "free marketism" portend a universal, homogeneous state. In this idealized worldview, geographical differences, and therefore geopolitics, have little role to play.[42]

For others, the end of the Cold War has heralded a "new world order" and the geopolitics of U.S. global hegemony. President George Bush, addressing Congress in 1990, defined the policy behind the war against Iraq as envisaging a new world order led by the United States and "freer from the threat of terror, stronger in the pursuit of justice, and more secure in the quest for peace, . . . a world in which nations recognize the shared responsibility for freedom and justice."[43]

Still another approach is Robert Kaplan's geopolitics of anarchy. From the perspective of a world divided into the rich North and the poor South, Kaplan concludes that the South, especially Africa, is doomed to anarchy and chaos. His map of the future, dubbed the *Last Map,* is an "ever mutating representation of chaos."[44]

None of these three scenarios has come to pass. In most cases, the overthrow of Communist regimes has not led to stable, free market economies. The restraints upon the unilateral application of U.S. military, economic, and political power are evident from the failures to gain U.S. objectives in Iraq, Somalia, and Haiti, while a geopolitics of chaos gives inadequate attention to the systemic regional and global forces that keep turbulence in check and absorb its positive aspects into the system.

The main thrust of post–Cold War geopolitics, however, continues to follow the two streams of the previous era—the nation-centered/political and the universalistic/geographical. Political geopoliticians advocate projection of Western power into Central and Eastern Europe to weaken Russia's Heartland position at its western edge. They also advance strategies for penetrating the Caucasus and Central Asia and for playing China off against Russia.

Brzezinski's prescription for maintaining U.S. global hegemony is to achieve primacy in three parts of the "Eurasian Chessboard": the West, or Europe; the South, or the Middle East and Central Asia; and the East, or China and Japan.[45] To this end, he advocates pulling Ukraine and the Black Sea into the Western orbit, strong U.S. engagement in Central Asia and the Caucasus (described as "the Eurasian Balkans"), and support of China's aspirations for regional dominance in peninsular Southeast Asia and Pakistan. Despite its expanded influences, China would still be limited to regional power status by the globally framed U.S.-Japan strategic alliance. The objective is to prevent Russia from reasserting strategic control over "near abroad" states or from joining with China and Iran in a Eurasian anti-U.S. coalition. Kissinger's recent oversimplistic foreign policy prescription is for the United States to ensure that no power emerges regionally or globally to unite with others against it.[46]

Advancing a geopolitics of "the West against the rest," Samuel Huntington argues that world primacy can be maintained by dividing and playing off the other civilizations.[47] His thesis is that the fundamental sources of conflict in the world will not be ideological. Instead, the great divisions will be cultural and the fault lines between civilizations will be the battle lines. In dividing the world into Western, Confucian, Japanese, Islamic, Hindu, Slavic-Orthodox, Latin American, and possibly African civilizations, he makes little allowance for internal religious, ethnic, economic, or strategic divisions. He also assumes the permanence of these cultural fault lines, despite the massive demographic changes brought about by migrations and modernization.

Geographical geopolitical theory also continues to reflect the universalistic approaches advanced during the Cold War. Building on the work of Taylor and LaCoste, the "critical" geopolitics represented in the writings of John Agnew and Gearold O'Tuathail applies social scientific critical thinking to ask how power works and might be challenged.[48] Analyses of discourse—of rhetoric, metaphors, symbolism; of feminist approaches to the subject of national security; and of the geographies of social movements, particularly in relation to newly radicalized and participative democracy—are viewed by Joe Painter as central to geopolitical studies.[49]

Conclusion

The reality-based geographical geopolitics that is espoused in this volume is based on polycentrism and builds from the continuous proliferation of the various parts and levels of the world. The current number of two hundred national states could increase to 250–275 within the next quarter of a century. As the pace of devolution quickens, some of these new geoterritorial entities will be highly autonomous "quasi-states." In addition, the network of global cities—centers of capital flows and financial services linked ever more closely by cyberspace, tourism, and immigrant communities—will emerge as a major new geopolitical level, promoting policies sometimes contradictory to national interests. International social movements, such as environmentalism, will also become more influential in shaping national and regional policies, including military ones.

Within this framework, radical geopolitical restructuring is a continuing process. Thus, China has emerged as a separate geostrategic realm. Just as Southeast Asia is no longer a Shatterbelt, so might this be possible for the Middle East, although it is more likely that some part of it will remain a Shatterbelt. Sub-Saharan Africa is in the process of dividing into a number of separate regional units. Western efforts are underway to detach Eastern Europe, the Trans-Caucasus, and Central Asia geostrategically from the Russian Heartland. However, with Russia's revival, these regions could either become new Shatterbelts or, in an era of international accommodation, evolve into Gateways between the West and Russia.

Whatever the course of geopolitical restructuring, we are entering an era of power sharing among a wide variety of regions, states, and other political territorial entities of different sizes and functions. Reality-based geopolitical theory will continue to be a valuable tool for understanding, predicting, and formulating the structure and direction of the world system.

Notes

1. Rudolph Kjellén, *Staten som Lifsform,* 1916. Published in German as *Der Staat also Lebenform* (Leipzig: Hirzel, 1917), 34–35, 203; also cited in Hans Weigert, *Generals and Geographers* (New York: Oxford University Press, 1942), 106–9.

2. Richard Hennig, *Geopolitik: Die Lehre vom Staat als Lebewesen* (Leipzig: Hirzel, 1931), 9; also cited in Andrew Gyorgy, *Geopolitics* (Berkeley: University of California Press, 1944), 183.

3. Derwent Whittlesey, *The Earth and the State* (New York: Holt, 1939), 8.

4. Richard Hartshorne, *The Nature of Geography* (Lancaster, Pa.: Association of American Geographers, 1939), 404.

5. Edmund Walsh, "Geopolitics and International Morals," in *Compass of the World,* ed. H. W. Weigert and V. Stefansson, 12–39 (New York: Macmillan, 1944).

6. Geoffrey Parker, *Geopolitics: Past, Present and Future* (London: Pinter, 1998), 5.

7. John Agnew, *Western Geopolitical Thought in the Twentieth Century* (New York: St. Martin's, 1985), 2.

8. Gearold O'Tuathail, Simon Dalby, and Paul Routledge, *The Geopolitics Reader* (London: Routledge, 1998), 3.

9. Friedrich Ratzel, *Politische Geographie,* 3d ed. (Munich: Oldenbourg, 1923), 4–12.

10. Friedrich Ratzel, "Die Gesetze des Raumlichen Wachstums der Staaten," *Petermanns Mitteilungen* 42 (1896): 97–107. Translated by Ronald Bolin under the title "The Laws of the Spatial Growth of States," in *The Structure of Political Geography,* ed. Roger Kasperson and Julian Minghi, 17–28 (Chicago: Aldine, 1969).

11. Halford Mackinder, "The Geographical Pivot of History," *Geographical Journal* 23, no. 4 (1904), 421–44. Reprinted in Mackinder, *Democratic Ideals and Reality* (London: Constable, 1919; New York: Norton, 1962), 265–78.

12. James Fairgrieve, *Geography and World Power* (London: University of London Press, 1915), 329–46.

13. Mackinder, *Democratic Ideals and Reality,* 104–14, 148–66.

14. Halford Mackinder, "The Round World and the Winning of the Peace," *Foreign Affairs* 21 no. 4 (1943): 595–605. Reprinted in Mackinder, *Democratic Ideals and Reality,* 265–78.

15. Brian Blouet, *Halford Mackinder: A Biography* (College Station: Texas A&M University Press, 1987), 140–45.

16. Alfred T. Mahan, *The Influence of Sea Power upon History: 1660–1783* (Boston: Little, Brown, 1890), 25–89; Mahan, *The Problem of Asia and Its Effect upon International Policy* (Boston: Little, Brown, 1900), 21–26, 63–125.

17. Neil Smith and Jan Nijman, "Alfred Thayer Mahan," in *Dictionary of Geopolitics*, ed., John O'Loughlin, 156–58 (Westport, Conn.: Greenwood, 1994).

18. Isaiah Bowman, *The New World* (Yonkers-on-Hudson, N.Y.: World Book, 1922), 1–2, 8.

19. Bowman, *New World, 11.*

20. Parker, *Geopolitics,* 10–19.

21. Andrew Gyorgy, *Geopolitics,* 180–86; Gearold O'Tuathail, in O'Tuathail et al., *Geopolitics Reader,* 19–24.

22. Nicholas Spykman, *America's Strategy in World Politics* (New York: Harcourt, Brace, 1942), 457–72.

23. Nicholas Spykman, *The Geography of Peace* (New York: Harcourt, Brace, 1944), 38–43, 51–61.

24. George T. Renner, *Human Geography in the Air Age* (New York: Macmillan, 1942), 152–54.

25. Stephen B. Jones, "The Power Inventory and National Strategy," *World Politics* 1, no. 4 (July 1954): 421–52.

26. Alexander de Seversky, *Air Power: Key to Survival* (New York: Simon & Schuster, 1950), 11, map facing 312.

27. John Slessor, *The Great Deterrent* (New York: Praeger, 1957), 264–85.

28. George, Kennan, "The Sources of Soviet Conduct," *Foreign Affairs* 25 (1947): 566–82.

29. Winston Churchill, "Iron Curtain" speech (graduation address given at Westminster College, Fulton, Mo., March 5, 1946). Excerpts in *Internet Modern History Sourcebook* (August 1977), 2 pp.

30. Seyom Brown, "Inherited Geopolitics and Emergent Global Realities," in *America's Global Interests,* ed. Edward K. Hamilton, 166–97 (New York: Norton, 1989), 166–97.

31. Patrick O'Sullivan, "Antidomino," *Political Geography Quarterly* 1 (1982): 57–64.

32. Henry A. Kissinger, *The White House Years* (Boston: Little, Brown, 1979), 127–38.

33. Leslie Hepple, "Geopolitics, Generals and the State in Brazil," *Political Geography Quarterly* 5 (supplement 1986): S79–S90.

34. Zbigniew Brzezinski, *Game Plan* (New York: Atlantic Monthly Press, 1986), 52–65.

35. Saul B. Cohen, *Geography and Politics in a World Divided,* 2d ed.(New York: Oxford University Press, 1973), 59–89.

36. Saul B. Cohen, "A New Map of Geopolitical Equilibrium: A Developmental Approach," *Political Geography Quarterly* 1, no. 3 (1982): 223–42; Heinz Werner, *Comparative Psychology of Mental Development,* rev. ed. (New York: International University Press, 1948), 40–55; Ludwig von Bertalanffy, *General System Theory* (New York: Braziller, 1968), 30–53, 205–21.

37. G. R. Chrone, *Background to Political Geography* (London: Pittman, 1969), 234.

38. Peter J. Taylor, *Political Geography,* 2d ed. (Harlow, England: Longman Scientific and Technical; New York: Wiley, 1989), 2–41; Immanuel Wallerstein, "European Unity and Its Implications for the Interstate System," in *Europe: Dimensions of Peace,* ed. B. Hettne, 27–38 (London: Zed, 1988).Wallerstein, "The World-System after the Cold War," *Journal of Peace Research* 30, no. 1 (1993), 1–6; George Modelski, "The Study of Long Cycles," in *Exploring Long Cycles,* ed. George Modelski, 1–15 (Boulder, Colo.: Rienner, 1987).

39. Taylor, *Political Geography,* 157–69.

40. Yves LaCoste, "Editorial: Les Géographes, l'Action et la Politique, *Hérodite* 33 (1984): 3–32.

41. B. Giblin, "Élisée Reclus, 1830–1905" in *Geographers Bibliographical Studies,* ed. T. W. Freeman, vol. 3, 125–32 (London: Mansell, 1979); Gary Dunbar, *Élisée Reclus, Historian of Nature* (Hamden, Conn.: Archon, 1978), 47–53, 69–97, 112–22.

42. Francis Fukuyama, *The End of History and the Last Man?* (New York: Free Press, 1992), 199–208, 287–99; Fukuyama, *The Great Disruption: Human Nature and the Reconstitution of Social Order* (New York: Free Press, 1999), 10–26, 187–93, 249–82.

43. George H. W. Bush, "Toward a New World Order," 11 September 1990, *Public Papers of the Presidents of the United States, George H. W. Bush, 1990* (Washington, D.C.: Government Printing Office, 1991).

44. Robert D. Kaplan, "The Coming Anarchy," *Atlantic Monthly* 273, no. 2 (1994), 44–46; Kaplan, *The Coming Anarchy: Shattering the Dreams of the Cold War* (New York: Random House, 2000), 37–41, 51–57.

45. Zbigniew Brzezinski, *The Grand Chessboard* (New York: Basic, 1997), 30–56.

46. Henry Kissinger, *Does America Need a Foreign Policy? Towards a Diplomacy for the 21st Century* (New York: Simon & Schuster, 2001).

47. Samuel P. Huntington, "The Clash of Civilizations?" *Foreign Affairs* 72 (1993), 22–49.

48. John Agnew, *Geopolitics: Re-visioning World Politics* (London: Routledge, 1998), 23–30; Gearold O'Tuathail, "Thinking Critically about Geopolitics," in O'Tuathail et al., *The Geopolitics Reader*, 1–11.

49. Joe Painter, *Politics, Geography and "Political Geography"* (London: Arnold, 1995), 151–79.

CHAPTER 3

Geopolitical Structure and Theory

The subjects of this chapter are the geopolitical structures that are formed by the interaction of geographical and political forces and the developmental processes that guide the changes that take place within those structures. Geopolitical structures are composed of geopolitical patterns and features. "Pattern" refers to the shape, size, and physical/human geographical characteristics of the geopolitical units, and the networks that tie them together, and these distinguish geopolitical units from other units. Features are the political-geographical nodes, areas, and boundaries that contribute to the unit's uniqueness and influence its cohesiveness and other measures of its structural effectiveness.

For the most part, geopolitical structures are organized along the following hierarchically ordered spatial levels:

1. the *geostrategic realm*—the most extensive level, or macrolevel;
2. the *geopolitical region*—a subdivision of the realm that represents the middle level, or mesolevel;
3. *national states, quasi-states,* and *territorial subdivisions* within and across states at the lowest level, or microlevel.

Outside of this ordering of structures are regions or clusters of states that are not located within the realm or regional frameworks. These include regions such as *Shatterbelts,* whose internal fragmentation is intensified by pressures of major powers from competing realms; *Compression Zones,* which are torn apart by internal divisions and the interference of neighboring states within the region; and *Gateways,* which serve as bridges between realms, regions, or states.

The maturity of a geopolitical structure is reflected in the extent to which its patterns and features support the unit's political cohesiveness. The developmental approach posits that structures evolve through successive stages—from *atomization/undifferentiation* to *differentiation, specialization,* and, finally, *specialized integration*. Revolutionary or cataclysmic breaks in the process may result in de-development and the beginning of the cycle anew. Another result of such breaks could be rapid movement to a higher stage.

Structure

GEOGRAPHICAL SETTINGS

The earth's two major physical/human geographical settings are the *Maritime* and the *Continental*. These settings provide the arenas for the development of distinctive geopolitical structures. The civilizations, cultures, and political institutions that have evolved within these two settings are fundamentally different in their economies, human cultures and traditions, spirit, and geopolitical outlooks.

Maritime settings are exposed to the open sea, either from coastal reaches or from inland areas with access to the seas. The vast majority of peoples who live there have benefited from climates with moderate temperatures and adequate rainfall, and with ease of contact with other parts of the world, often behind the protective screen of inland physical barriers. Sea trade and immigration have flourished in such settings, contributing to the diversity of their peoples in terms of race, culture, and language. They have also sped up the process of economic specialization. The trading systems that have emerged from this specialization have had open, politically liberalizing effects.

Continental settings are characterized by extreme climates and vast distances from the open seas. Such settings often suffer from lack of intensive interaction with other parts of the world because of the barrier effects of mountains, deserts, and high plateaus, or because of sheer distance. Historically, their economies have been more self-sufficient than maritime ones, while their political systems, more isolated from new influences and ideas, tend to develop as closed and autocratic.

Urbanization and industrialization have come much later to the Continental arena than to the Maritime one. The lag continues in the present, postindustrial age. While Maritime areas have forged ahead by generating and diffusing high-technology innovations, many Continental areas remain heavily rural or are characterized by aging industrial bases that drag down the economies of their urban areas.

Geopolitical structures are shaped by two forces—the centrifugal and the centripetal. At the national level, both are linked to the psychobiological sense of territoriality.[1] The centrifugal force is the drive for political separation that motivates a people to seek territorial separation from those whom they consider outsiders, who might impose different political systems, languages, cultures, or religions upon them. In this context, space with clear boundaries serves as a defining and a defensive mechanism. The centripetal force promotes the drive for political unity that is reinforced by a people's sense of being inextricably linked to a particular territory. Such territoriality is expressed through symbolic as well as physical ties of a people to a particular land.

At one geographical scale, forces of separation may dominate, while forces for unity may prevail at another scale. Thus, centrifugal forces may drive a people to secede from another state in order to protect their unique identity. At the same time, centripetal forces may propel them toward a unity of regional action in such areas as commerce, military defense, or confederation with another state.

While drives for separation and unity are intertwined, they are not always in balance. The imperialist system that kept its form of world balance was destroyed by World War II. Global disequilibrium then followed. Balance was restored when a unifying Europe and a recovering Japan joined in strategic alliance with the United States to counter the Soviet-Chinese drive for Communist world hegemony.

The flow of ideas, migrations, trade, capital, communications, and arms takes place beyond, as well as within, the different structural levels of realm, region, and state. States may move from one level to another. Such change reflects the interplay of political power and ideological, economic, cultural, racial, religious, and national forces, as well as national security concerns and territorial ambitions. The geopolitical restructuring subsequent to the end of the Cold War is testimony to this dynamism. The demise of the former Soviet Union has widened the opportunity for China to emerge as an independent geostrategic realm and enhanced Beijing's role in world affairs. The collapse of the Democratic Republic of Congo (DRC) has provided Nigeria with an opening to expand its role as a regional power, thereby extending its influence from West into Central Africa.

GEOPOLITICAL FEATURES

Despite variations in function and scale, all structures have certain geopolitical features in common:

Historic or Nuclear Cores. This is the area in which a state originates, and out of which the state-idea has developed. The relationship between the physical environment of the core and the political-cultural system that evolves may become embedded and persist as an important element of national or regional identity and ideology.

Capitals or Political Centers. The capital serves as the political and symbolic focus of activities that govern the behavior of people in a politically defined territory. While its functions may be essentially administrative, the built landscape of a national capital— its architectural forms, buildings, monuments, and layout—has considerable symbolic value in mobilizing support for the state. Capitals may be selected for a variety of reasons—for their geographic centrality to the rest of the national space, for the defensive qualities of their sites, or for their frontier locations, either as defensive points or springboards for territorial acquisition.

Ecumenes. These are the areas of greatest density of population and economic activity. Ecumenes have traditionally been mapped by their coincidence with dense transportation networks to reflect economic concentration. In today's postindustrial information age, the boundaries of ecumenes can be expanded to include areas that are linked by modern telecommunications, and therefore ecumenes are less tied to transportation clustering. Because the ecumene is the most advanced portion of the state economically, it is usually its most important political area.

Effective National Territory (ENT) and *Effective Regional Territory (ERT).* These are moderately populated areas with favorable resource bases. As areas of high development potential, they provide outlets for population growth and dispersion and for economic expansion. Their extent is an indication of future strength.

Empty Areas. These are essentially devoid of population, with little prospect for mass human settlement. Depending on their location and extent, they may provide defensive depth and sites for weapons testing. Some are important as sources of minerals.

Boundaries. These mark off political areas. While they are linear, they often occur within broader border zones. Their demarcation may become a source of conflict.

Nonconforming Sectors. These may include minority separatist areas within states and isolated or "rogue" states within regions.

The degree to which geopolitical features are developed and the patterns formed by their interconnections are the bases for determining the stage of maturity of a geopolitical realm or region.

Structural changes produced by these features and patterns may be likened to geological changes that are brought about by the movement of underlying plates and subplates, which eventually regain a new state of balance or equilibrium known as "isostasy." These geopolitical structures are formed by historic civilization-building processes and reconfigured by both short- and long-term geopolitical forces. Geostrategic realms are, in effect, the major structural plates that cover most of the earth's surface. Their movement may result in the addition of some areas to one realm at the expense of another; new realms will be formed when the movements are revolutionary. Shatterbelts, which form zones of contact between realms, may be divided into separate subplates by such movement or totally subsumed within one realm. Regions, or medium-sized plates, may also change their shapes and boundaries as they shift within realms or from one realm to another. Compression zones, or regional subplates, may be formed or disappear with shifting within regional plates.

The most radical shifting of geopolitical plates in recent decades has taken place at the geostrategic level. Following World War II, the world divided into a bipolar and rigidly hierarchical structure. The end of the Cold War signaled a revolution of equal magnitude. With the collapse of the Soviet Union and the crumbling of its empire, the Maritime Realm overrode the Eurasian Continental Realm, detaching substantial portions from the latter's western edge. In addition, the Continental "plate," which had already been weakened by the Sino-Soviet schism, has now broken in two, with East Asia emerging as a separate realm. With the weakening of the Russian core, China has been able to pull away from the Heartland and move partly toward the Maritime Realm through the force of international trade and technology.

Another way of looking at how structures divide and redivide at different levels is to consider the world, not as a pane of glass, but as a diamond. The force of blows shatters glass into fragments of unpredictable sizes and shapes. Diamonds, by contrast, break along existing lines of cleavage, forming new shapes. Geopolitical boundaries follow combinations of physical, cultural, religious, and political cleavages. These boundaries change with shifts in the power balance between political cores, and new boundaries then follow latent cleavages that now come to the surface.

STRUCTURAL LEVELS

The Geostrategic Realm

In the spatial hierarchy of the global structure, the highest level is the geostrategic realm. These realms are parts of the world large enough to possess characteristics and functions that are global influencing and that serve the strategic needs of the major powers, states, and regions they comprise. Their frameworks are shaped by circulation patterns that link people, goods, and ideas and are held together by control of strategically located land and sea passageways.

The overriding factor that distinguishes a realm is the degree to which it is shaped by conditions of "Maritimity" or "Continentality." In today's world, three geostrategic realms have evolved: the Atlantic and Pacific Trade-Dependent Maritime Realm; the Eurasian Continental Russian Heartland; and mixed Continental-Maritime East Asia.

Realms have been a factor of international life from the time that empires first emerged. In modern times, geostrategic realms have been carved out by British Maritime and czarist Russian land-power realms. The United States created a mixed realm consisting of both transcontinental power and maritime sway over the Caribbean and much of the Pacific. Today's Trade-Dependent Maritime Realm, which embraces the Atlantic and Pacific Ocean basins and their interior seas, has been shaped by international exchange. Mercantilism, capitalism, and industrialization gave rise to the maritime-oriented national-state and to economic and political colonialism. Access to the sea facilitated circulation, and moderate coastal climates with habitable interiors offered living conditions that aided economic development. The open systems that ultimately developed within the leading states of this realm have facilitated the struggle for democracy, and movements across the seas have spawned the creation of pluralistic societies.

The bursts in international trade and investment, and in mass migration movements, have defined the Maritime Realm for the past century and a half. From the mid-1890s to World War I, European (and then U.S.) imperialism created a global trading system that was imposed by military force and enhanced by revolutionary advances in transportation and communications. This system was shattered by World War I and the Great Depression of the 1930s.

The global economy was rebuilt under U.S. leadership following World War II. By the 1970s, the share of world goods that entered the arena of international trade had climbed back to its pre-1914 levels. This proportion surged in the 1990s, due in large part to the General Agreement on Tariffs and Trade (GATT) and its successor organization, the World Trade Organization (WTO). It has continued to climb.

The world's leading exporters and importers, the members of the Group of Seven (G-7), are all Maritime Realm nations—the United States, Japan, Germany, France, the United Kingdom, Italy, and Canada. China is rapidly joining these ranks, owing to the economic strength of its maritime south and central coastal regions. The share of world trade enjoyed by the Maritime Realm nations is overwhelming. The four European G-7 members account for over 40 percent of world trade, the United States and Canada 30 percent, and Japan over 10 percent. In contrast, Russia's share is under 2 percent, China's is 5 percent, and India's 1.3 percent. In 1999, the United States was by far the world's single largest trading state, with combined imports and exports of $2.2 trillion.[2] Germany ranked second with $1.1 trillion, Japan third with $765 billion. The intensity of a state's engagement in international trade reflects its maritime and continental setting, as indicated in table 3.1, which shows representative countries. While the 2000 figure for the United States is only 20 percent, this has nearly doubled from 11 percent in 1990 and has only recently been slowed by the world economic recession of 2000–2001.

The Eurasian Continental Realm, which is anchored today by Heartlandic Russia, is inner-oriented and less influenced by outside economic forces or cultural contacts. Until the mid-twentieth century, the major modes of transportation there were land and inland river. The self-sufficient nature of the economy, belated entrance into the industrial age, and lack of sea access to world resources all contributed to politically closed systems and societies. Highly centralized and generally despotic forms of government through the ages became the breeding grounds for the emergence of communism and other forms of authoritarianism in the cores of the realm.

Table 3.1   Percentage of International Trade to GDP by Region
for the Year 2000

Region	Percent
Maritime Realm	
Maritime Europe Region	
Luxembourg	110
Netherlands	106
Belgium	95
Germany	57
United Kingdom	45
France	40
Italy	36
North and Middle America Region	
Canada	66
United States	25
Asia-Pacific Rim Region	
Singapore	150
Taiwan	66
South Korea	44
Japan	25
Eurasian Continental Realm	
Heartlandic Russian Region	14
East Asia Realm	
China Region	9
South Asia Geopolitical Region	
Pakistan	6
India	5

Source: Central Intelligence Agency, *The World Factbook 2001* (Washington,
D.C.: Gov/CIA Publications, 2001).

The Continentality that pervades the Eurasian Realm is both a physical and a psychological condition. Russia/the Soviet Union has historically been hemmed in. Even when technology alters the previous reality (e.g., Soviet conquests in outer space), the earlier mentality persists. The breakup of the Soviet Union and the threat of North Atlantic Treaty Organization (NATO) expansion reinforce the Russian perception of being boxed in by the outside world. While Russia's international trade in 2000 represented 14 percent of its GDP, the statistics mask Russia's self-contained nature. Its GDP of approximately $1.1 trillion is based heavily on Russia's major exports, oil and gas, which reflects the inflated energy prices of those years.

The boundaries of the Heartlandic Russian Realm have changed substantially. To its west, the Eastern European states are no longer tightly within the grip of Moscow, while the boundary between the Heartland and the Maritime Realm has become a zone, rather than a line. The caution with which some NATO states are treating membership applications from the Baltic states, Ukraine, Romania, and Bulgaria reflects a recognition of continuing Russian strategic interests in the eastern Baltic and Black seas.

Elsewhere along the boundaries of the realm, the former Soviet Republics of the Trans-Caucasus and Central Asia are not free of Russia's strategic oversight, although they have gained their independence. The efforts of the West to penetrate these regions in pursuit of oil and gas wealth, as well as the need for military bases in the War against Terrorism in Afghanistan, require Russian cooperation in order to succeed.

China lay within the Continental Eurasian orbit for much of the Cold War, even after the Sino-Soviet schism. However, over the past two decades, a strong maritime economy and orientation has been grafted onto China's politically closed, continental character. The people of the inland-oriented North and Interior, which are essentially rural with urban pockets of heavy industry, are more supportive of autocratic Communist governmental state policies than are the peoples of the south, east and the central coastal regions, which have long been opened to the influences of the outside world. Guangdong/Hong Kong, Fujiang, and Shanghai have been the historic foci of China for trade and cultural exchange with the outside world. The region has also been the source of large-scale emigration, many of whose participants have maintained strong familial and village links with the home country.

Since the lifting of Mao's restrictive policies in the late 1970s by his Communist successors, these regions have once again become the main engines for China's economic growth and entrance into the world of labor-intensive manufacturing of consumer items, high technology, and financial services. This has enabled China to forge ahead of Japan to achieve the world's second largest GDP (although in terms of its modern productive capacity, Japan remains second only to the United States). The coastal regions, collectively known as the "Golden Coast," have reinforced the maritime component of the Chinese setting, allowing Beijing to break the grip of Eurasian Continentality and assume separate geostrategic status.

Despite China's dramatic rise as a trading nation during the 1990s, particularly as an exporter to the United States, it has not become part of the Maritime World, as predicted by Mackinder and Spykman in their times and Richard Nixon in his. The vast majority of Chinese still live off the land and are not employed in manufacturing, trade, and services. Even with China's spurt in commerce, its $429 billion accounts for only 5 percent of the world's merchandise imports and exports, and foreign trade represents only 9 percent of the country's annual GDP of $4.5 trillion (which by many measures is an overestimate).

For the continentally oriented Chinese, the mountains and grasslands, not the sea, hold spiritual, mystical attractions. And it is the common border with Russia that serves as both lure and threat. The Sino-Soviet clash over the present-day boundary had historic roots that go back to Chinese claims on lands annexed by czarist Russia between 1858 and 1881—1.5 million square kilometers in the regions east of Lake Baikal and the Far Eastern provinces. When the rift took place between the two Continental Eurasian Realm powers, beginning with Stalin's death in 1953 and culminating in the breaking of diplomatic relations in 1960, the issue was more than ideology and strategy. It was also China's resentment at being treated as a subordinate power. Reinstitution of diplomatic ties between Moscow and Beijing in 1989 reflected the reality that they had become equals.

Withdrawal of American and Soviet power from Indochina has enabled China to extend the new Continental-Maritime East Asian geostrategic realm southward to include the Indochinese states of Vietnam, Cambodia, and Laos, which constitute a separate geopolitical region within the East Asian Realm. The boundaries of the East Asian Realm are forged by China's reach to other parts of Asia. Tibet and Xinjiang afford contact with South and Central Asia. In the northeast Pacific, where the Maritime, Eurasian, and East Asian realms meet, North Korea is part of East Asia. A reunified Korean Peninsula, however, could become either a Gateway among the three realms or a Compression Zone.

The Geopolitical Region

The second level of geopolitical structure is the geopolitical region. Most regions are sub-divisions of realms, although some may be caught between or independent of them. Regions are connected by geographical contiguity and political, cultural, and military inter-actions, and possibly by the historical migration and intermixture of peoples and shared histories of national emergence.

The regions of the Maritime Realm are North and Middle America, Maritime Europe and the Maghreb, and the Asia-Pacific Rim. The Southern Continents—South America and Sub-Saharan Africa—are dominated by the Maritime Realm and are economically dependent upon it. However, they are of marginal strategic value to the major Maritime powers and are therefore not tightly within their geostrategic orbit. The Eurasian Continental Realm contains two geopolitical regions: (1) the Russian Heartland and (2) the Trans-Caucasus and Central Asia. The East Asian Realm also is divided into two regions: Mainland China and Indochina (the latter consisting of Vietnam, Cambodia, and Laos).

South Asia stands apart from the three realms as an independent geopolitical region that, when linked with the Middle East, forms an "Arc of Instability." The Continental nature of the South Asian subcontinent is strongly reflected in its trade patterns. The ratio of India's international trade of $86 billion to its $1.8 trillion GDP is only 5 percent, while that of Pakistan, with a $280 billion GDP, is only 1 percent higher.

The Middle East Shatterbelt and Eastern Europe, whose future as either a Shatterbelt or as a Gateway geopolitical region remains to be determined, complete the regional geopolitical level (figure 3.1).

Regions range in their stages of development from those that are cohesive to those that are atomized. The prime example of a tightly knit region is Maritime Europe and the Maghreb. Its core, the fifteen-member European Union (EU), has begun to create a "European" culture and identity through regional laws, currency, and regulations. There is considerable speculation as to whether this identity will lead ultimately to a highly centralized body that would override many of the cherished national and political values held by its member-states, or whether the Union will emerge as a loose federation. In contrast, a part of the world such as Sub-Saharan Africa has little, if any, geopolitical cohesion. The end of European colonialism, followed by Cold War–stimulated conflicts and the wars and revolutions that have since raged, have produced a process of de-development and atomization. Efforts during the early years of independence to create subregional federations failed and current ones, such as the Common Market for Eastern and Southern Africa (COMESA), have little prospect of developing into meaningful economic units, let alone geopolitical ones.

Certainly, regional trade and other economic agreements can help foster regional unity. Just as the Common Market ultimately led to the creation of the European Union, so has the North and Middle American Free Trade Agreement strengthened the geopolitical sinews of the North American geopolitical region. But the proposed Free Trade Area of the Americas is unlikely to lead to a unified western hemispheric region because of the wide differences in cultural, political, and social traditions, as well as the distances between the northern and southern continents.

Within South America, the strongest prospects for regional unity rest with Mercosur, the trade bloc formed by Brazil, Uruguay, Paraguay, and Argentina. Under the lead of Brazil, this group could develop sufficient political as well as economic cohesion to emerge as a separate geopolitical region.

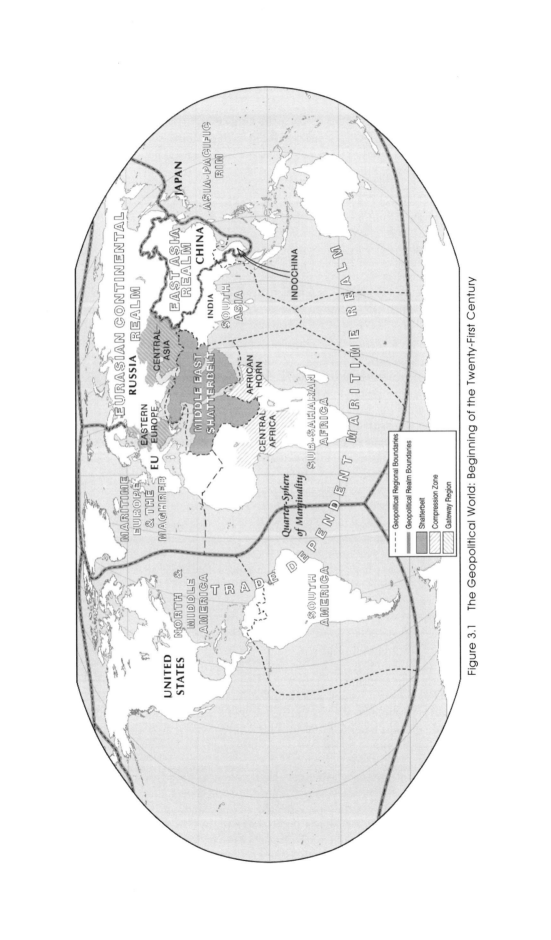

Figure 3.1 The Geopolitical World: Beginning of the Twenty-First Century

Distinctions between realm and region are distinctions between the strategic and the tactical. States operate at both regional and realm levels and sometimes they can maintain ties with two regions and/or two realms. For example, Australia is part of the Asia-Pacific Rim. However, because it belongs also to the Maritime Realm, it is able to benefit from its ties to the two other regions of that realm. Strategically, it serves as a crucial link within the Maritime world's global network. Culturally, politically, and ethnically it retains its historic British roots, as well as its bonds with the United States forged in World War II.

With their continuing development, geopolitical regions have become more important forces within the international system. The larger European states, Japan, and China have gathered sufficient strength and independence of action to focus their attentions on their regional surrounds and to organize them more effectively, as well as to become more assertive on global issues. The emergence of geopolitical regions as power frameworks enhances global stability by strengthening the balance-of-power system. Soviet hegemonic control over the Eurasian Realm was broken when China asserted its strategic independence. The result was that the two former allies began to restrain one another's actions in South and Southeast Asia, East Africa, and Taiwan.

The European Union has been of similar importance in limiting U.S. hegemonic control over the Maritime Realm. In reaction to its loss of global power and its economic and military dependence on the United States, postwar Europe began to build a series of economic and political institutions with an eye to regaining its strength through regional unity.[3] As a renewed center of geopolitical power, Western Europe has been able to reestablish its influence in strategically important areas, such as the Middle East, Sub-Saharan Africa, and Eastern Europe.

The Asia-Pacific Rim has developed its geopolitical unity out of a complementarity of needs among the countries of the region. The role of Japan in the economic development of the region has been pivotal in this process. Of all the world's geopolitical regions, South Asia is the only one that is independent of the three major realms. It is the unit that consciously sought to become a world balancer, with mixed results. India's attempt to project itself as an independent force dedicated to achieving a peaceful, balanced world fell far short of its goal. Rejecting pressures by both the United States and the USSR to join their respective blocs, India adopted a policy of neutrality, and became a leader of the Afro-Asian bloc of nations that sought a "third way" in world affairs.

What undermined India's hopes of becoming a balancer was not only that the superpowers rejected the proffered role. India also found itself in a struggle to exercise its control over the entire continent that had once been British India, but had become politically fragmented when the British Raj left. India has been embroiled in wars with Pakistan over Kashmir and East Bengal, as well as in unsuccessful interventions in Sri Lanka. Despite these setbacks in its efforts to play a balancing role on the world scene, India did partly succeed in the sense that it never fully joined either superpower's camp during the Cold War. However, its dependence upon the Soviet Union for military, economic, and diplomatic support often tilted it toward the latter.

A legitimate question is whether the enhanced role of geopolitical regions may become a factor that will divide, not help to unite, the world system. For example, fears have been expressed that a United Europe, especially with its common currency, growing opposition to immigration from outside the region, farm bloc pressures, and recent commitment to an independent military force, might raise its barriers toward the rest of the world. While there is some basis for such concern, there are powerful offsetting forces.

The special relationships that individual Western European powers have historically enjoyed with such areas as the Maghreb, Sub-Saharan Africa, Central and Eastern Europe, Latin America, and the Middle East mitigate against a "Fortress Europa." So do the historical, cultural, and political-military bonds that link Europe to the North Atlantic world. Indeed, the direction of EU policies is to expand world trade in order to cope with the unemployment that accompanies the downsizing of inefficient industries, as well as to expand its membership into Central and Eastern Europe with the aim of improving the economies and opening the political systems of those countries.

While Europe is hardly typical of the world's geopolitical regions, it should be noted that most of the other regions would be far less capable of attaining higher standards of living and security were they to become more isolated. As regions evolve and become more specialized, their external outreach becomes more, rather than less, of a necessity.

Shatterbelts

While most geopolitical regions have varying degrees of cohesiveness, depending on their stages of maturity, this is not the case for Shatterbelts. Such deeply fragmented regions are global destabilizers.

The concept of the Shatterbelt has long held the attention of geographers, who have also used the terms "Crush Zone" or "Shatter Zone." Alfred Mahan, James Fairgrieve, and Richard Hartshorne contributed pioneering studies of such regions. As early as 1900, Mahan referred to the instability of the zone between the thirty- and forty-degree parallels in Asia as being caught between Britain and Russia.[4] Fifteen years later, Fairgrieve used "Crush Zone" to describe small buffer states between the sea powers and the Eurasian Heartland, from Northern and Eastern Europe to the Balkans, Turkey, Iran, Afghanistan, Siam, and Korea.[5] During World War II, Hartshorne analyzed the "Shatter Zone" of Eastern Europe from the Baltic to the Adriatic, advocating a post–World War II federation for this region.[6]

The operational definition for Shatterbelts used by this author is *strategically oriented regions that are both deeply divided internally and caught up in the competition between Great Powers of the geostrategic realms.* By the end of the 1940s, two such highly fragmented regions had emerged—the Middle East and Southeast Asia. They were not geographically coincident with previous Shatterbelts because the global locus of strategic competition had shifted. The East and Central European Shatterbelt had fallen within the Soviet orbit, as the Maritime and Continental worlds became divided by a sharp boundary in the part of Europe that lay along the Elbe River.

In discussions of the typology of the Shatterbelt, it has been pointed out by Philip Kelly that other parts of the world are also characterized by high degrees of conflict and atomization.[7] It is true that wars, revolts, and coups are chronic in the Caribbean, South America, South Asia, and Africa. The distinguishing feature of the Shatterbelt, however, is that it presents an equal playing field to two or more competing global powers operating from different geostrategic realms.

Not all areas in turmoil are Shatterbelts. Despite the conflicts in South Asia, it is not a Shatterbelt, because India's dominance within the region is not seriously threatened by the United States, Russia, or China, let alone by Pakistan. Similarly, the Caribbean did not become a Shatterbelt, despite Communist regimes in Cuba, Nicaragua, and Grenada and leftist uprisings elsewhere, because the Soviet Union could not threaten U.S. dominance there.

Shatterbelts and their boundaries are fluid. During the 1970s and 1980s, Sub-Saharan Africa became a Shatterbelt as the Soviet Union, Cuba, and China penetrated deeply into the region to compete with European and U.S. influences. Since the collapse of the Soviet Union, war-torn Sub-Saharan Africa is no longer a Shatterbelt. Indeed, it has become strategically marginal to the major Western powers. Southeast Asia, too, has lost its Cold War Shatterbelt status and is now divided between the East Asian and Maritime Realms. Indochina has emerged as a separate geopolitical region within East Asia, while western and southern peninsular Southeast Asia and Indonesia are aligned with the Asia-Pacific Rim.

The Middle East remains a Shatterbelt, its fragmentation reinforced by the strength of a half dozen regional or local states, as well as by the actions of intrusive major powers.

The future may bring additional Shatterbelts onto the world scene. The most likely candidate is the new/old zone from the Baltic through Eastern Europe and the Balkans. A second possibility is the region from the Trans-Caucasus through Central Asia that lies within the Heartlandic Realm, but is so tempting to Western oil interests. The emergence of such Shatterbelts depends upon whether the West tries to overreach by penetrating these regions geostrategically. Should it do so without reference to the security concerns of Russia, Moscow's reaction would quickly convert the two regions into Shatterbelts. Such regions are pivotal in world politics and warrant advance planning strategies rather than ad hoc reactions to crises. Should Afghanistan and Pakistan implode, western Pakistan is likely to be drawn into the Middle East Shatterbelt. Other imploding areas might be Indonesia and northern Andean South America.

Compression Zones

These are fragmented areas that are in turmoil and subject to competition between neighboring states, but not Great Powers. At present, these consist of the Horn of Africa and Central Africa.

NATIONAL STATES

In modern times, the linchpin of the world geopolitical system has been the national state. However, some see the state's demise as a consequence of the rising strength of world and regional governmental bodies, the increased influence of nongovernmental organizations, and the globalization of information and economic forces. Predictions of this demise are hardly novel. Karl Marx held that, with the victory of the workers over the bourgeoisie and the emergence of a classless society, the state would wither away as an instrument of centralized control. More contemporaneously, Peter Drucker says that the new "knowledge society," which transcends national borders, will relegate the state to a mere administrative instrument.[8]

Michael Hardt and Antonio Negri advance the thesis that it is supranational, not national, powers that rule today's global system, and that a new political structure and power ranking is emerging that constitutes a fluid, infinitely expanding, and highly organized system, embracing the entire population of the world. They reason that because power is so widely dispersed, it is possible for anyone to affect the system's course, and that the potential for both revolution and democracy is therefore far greater than it was during the era of nation-states and imperialism.[9]

In reality, globalization is not an independent force, but is the handmaiden of the nation-state system. The global corporations that outsource capital and manufacturing are subject to antitrust laws in their home countries and in many of the countries in which they operate. While the WTO does place restrictions on the application of national quotas, tariffs, and subsidy systems, national restraints continue to affect world trade patterns. Where the national state has agreed to limit its independence of action, this has taken place at the regional, not the global, scale. A prime example is the European Union, whose regional structure is federated, not centralized. The other major regional framework, the North American Free Trade Agreement (NAFTA), is even more subject to national directions and controls. To dismiss the power of the national state is to ignore the political and economic weight, as well as the decision-making capacities, of the major states and regional bodies in the economic, political, military, and cultural arenas.

Theories of globalization present the picture of an emerging world system based upon a seemingly unlimited number of nodes and lines of economic interaction and communication that have the capacity for reshaping global culture and politics. This construct is based, in essence, upon a notion of a structureless world network, devoid of hierarchy, directedness, and spatial differentiation. Globalization may better be described as *anomie,* or the collapse of structures that govern the world system, rather than as the portent of a new, evolving system.

The geopolitical viewpoint of this volume differs markedly from the notion of an emerging world system of globalization. It views the world as organized around core areas that are hierarchically arranged in space and whose functions vary in accordance with the power and reach of these cores. The patterns of interconnection among the nodes are strongly affected by regional settings, as well as by historic and contemporary flows that extend beyond these regions to realms. The major cores of the globalized trading system are the United States, the European Union, Japan, and China, while secondary cores include such countries as South Korea, Taiwan, and Singapore. The economies of these secondary cores first developed as targets for outsourcing, but then expanded to the point where they became independent sources of capital accumulation and have themselves become outsourcers. While neither realms nor regions are self-contained, they nevertheless set the overall geopolitical spatial configurations within which the great majority of political, military, economic, and cultural connections take place.

The role of the national state continues to command vigorous defenders. Peter Taylor argues that the territorial state is vital to the capitalist system, and therefore to the operation of the world economy.[10] Historian Paul Kennedy also holds the view that a nationalist-based, mercantile world order will persist.[11]

However, economics is not the only, or even the major, reason for the national state—the sense of belonging to something socially and territorially is even more important. The state fulfills the cultural and psychological yearnings of particular people. While economic and political interdependence does pose a threat to national cultures, it also provides people with the resources to hold on more tightly to what they most value. For countries that have recently emerged from colonialism or whose economies were dominated by the West, this issue is especially acute. Edward Said cogently observed that, for such countries, there is need for a reconquest of space through a new, decolonized identity.[12] Today, political control of their own territories permits the nations of the former colonial world to be selective in what they accept or reject of Western culture.

There is no question that what transpires within a national state is increasingly influenced by global and regional forces—by international ideological movements, such as environmental and human rights; by global economic institutions and multinational corporations; by the internationalization of politics through foreign monies and other forms of pressure by the world financial markets; and by the media. These forces can also be turned to advantage by the state in advancing its own goals. In the last analysis, the national state remains the glue of the international system, the major mechanism that enables a people to achieve a self-realization inextricably bound with its sense of territoriality. Even the breakup of existing national states, while upsetting the status quo temporarily, is testimony to the power of nationalism, not its decline.

ORDERS OF NATIONAL POWER

The state system consists of five orders or levels. The first consists of major powers—the United States, the collectivity of states embraced by the European Union, Japan, Russia, and China. These all have global reach, serving as the cores of the three geostrategic realms.

The second order of states consists of regional powers whose reach extends over much of their respective geopolitical regions and, in specialized ways, to other parts of the world (see figure 3.2). The third, fourth, and fifth levels are those states whose reach is generally limited to parts of their regions only. In assessing the strategic importance of states, policy makers need to recognize their appropriate levels of power, still keeping in mind that lower-order states are capable of upsetting the system by serving as terrorist bases.

The rank of a nation in this hierarchy can be assessed through a number of socioeconomic, political, and military measures. While power rankings suffer from being somewhat mechanistic, they are commonly used in international assessment. The ranking system used here includes value and political behavior characteristics that reach beyond the traditional emphasis on population, area, economic resources, and military expenditures and technology. Such a ranking method cannot account for idiosyncratic factors, like the length to which the dictator of an impoverished country such as North Korea, or fanatics like the Taliban, will go to influence regional and even global events through threats of war, support of rebellions, and offering a base for terrorism. For the most part, however, "rogue" state leaders must have either access to resources, such as oil, or patrons who will provide them with the needed backing to intervene in affairs outside their borders, for example, Cuba's dependence upon the USSR during the Cold War.

The increased importance of second-order, or regional, states has come at the moment in world history when major powers have begun to distance themselves from regions they no longer consider vital to their own national interests (see figure 3.2). Second-order powerdom is a reflection of the inherent military and economic strength of a state relative to that of its neighbors. It is also a function of its centrality or nodal role in regional transportation, communication, and trade. As important as any of these factors, however, is the ambition and perseverance of the state, not only to impose its influence on others, but to persuade them of their stakes in regional goals and values. Egypt's leadership in the Middle East derives in great measure from its espousal of the pan-Arabism to which the other Arab states also subscribe.

Another criterion for measuring the strength of a regional power is its ability to gain sustenance from one or more major powers without becoming a satellite, or through extraregional

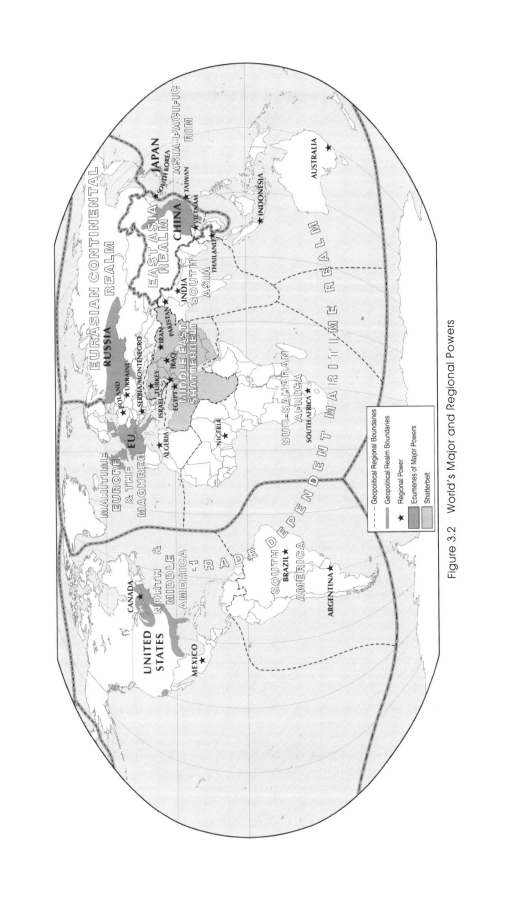

Figure 3.2   World's Major and Regional Powers

Table 3.2   Second-Order Power Rankings

High	Medium	Low
India	Indonesia	Iraq
Brazil	Pakistan	Poland
Canada	Egypt	Serbia/
Turkey	South Korea	Montenegro
Australia	Taiwan	fed.
Iran	Mexico	Algeria
Nigeria	Vietnam	Thailand
Israel		Argentina
South Africa		Ukraine

political-military alliances, trade links, or ideological links. When India took the lead in fostering the concept of Third World neutrality, its inherent power was increased.

Not all regional powers are equal. Table 3.2 is an attempt to rank them in three categories. Members of the European Union are omitted, as the EU is treated collectively as a major power.

Certain regions contain more than one regional power and some states in such regions have developed highly complementary relations with the first-order powers located within the region. This is the case for the U.S. relationship with Canada and Mexico; both of the latter states have gained in strength as a result of their close ties to the North American superpower. Others vie with major powers located in adjoining regions—for example, India with China and Vietnam with China. Still others are heavily influenced by distant first-order states—for example, Israel and Egypt by the United States, Nigeria by the EU. Proximity is important in the capacity of first-order states to influence second-order states militarily and politically psychologically, but it is less of a factor in extending economic influence, because trade more easily spans distance.

Although second-order states may have regional hegemonical aspirations, their goals are constrained by geopolitical realities. With the exception of India and Brazil, second-order powers are unlikely to achieve dominance over an entire geopolitical region. Rather, they can hope to exercise broad regional influence, with hegemony having practical significance only in relation to proximate states.

Third-order states influence regional events in special ways. They may compete with neighboring regional powers on ideological and political grounds or by having a specialized resource base, but they lack the population, military, and general economic capacities of second-order rivals. Examples of third-order states are Saudi Arabia, Ethiopia, Cuba, Angola, Syria, Chile, Colombia, Venezuela, Libya, North Korea, Malaysia, Zimbabwe, Côte d'Ivoire, and Hungary. Fourth-order states such as Sudan, Ecuador, Zambia, Morocco, and Tunisia have impact only on their nearest neighbors. Fifth-order states, such as Nepal, have only marginal external involvement.

Membership in the various orders is fluid. China is now a first-order power. It has gained economic strength through the opening of its system to world market forces, and its military strength has grown through expansion of its air power and its drive to create a "blue ocean" navy. India is moving from second-order status to that of a major power, especially since Pakistan is rapidly losing its stability and cohesiveness due to the clash between its Islamic fundamentalists and its military regimes. While some would downgrade Russia as a major power because of its present economic weakness, its nuclear arsenal, armaments industry, energy resources, and strategic centrality within Eurasia enable it to maintain its first-order status.

Two decades ago, twenty-seven nations could be measured as potential second-order powers. Of these, Saudi Arabia, Morocco, the Democratic Republic of Congo (then Zaire), and Cuba have fallen from the ranking or never attained it. The German Democratic Republic and a greater Yugoslavia have disappeared altogether from the map (as, indeed, has the name "Yugoslavia," for it is now the "federation of Serbia and Montenegro." At the same time, South Korea, Vietnam, and Thailand have now achieved regional power status. Among the most prominent regional states that are extending their influence to neighboring areas are South Africa, Brazil, and Nigeria. However, given Nigeria's domestic instability, it may not be able to sustain such an effort.

Third-order status is also ephemeral. Tunisia, Tanzania, Ghana, and Costa Rica have enjoyed and then lost such ranking with the waning of their ideological influence.

The impacts of major powers and second- and third-order states give regionalism increasingly important geopolitical substance. States that are ideologically at odds with the other states in the region play a special role. They promote turbulence by challenging the norms and injecting unwelcome energy into the system. Examples are pre-1990 revolutionary Cuba, Titoist Yugoslavia, and the market-oriented Côte d'Ivoire of the 1970s.

GATEWAY STATES AND REGIONS

Gateway states play a novel role in linking different parts of the world by facilitating the exchange of peoples, goods, and ideas. There are at present eighteen states that can be classified as Gateways (see table 3.3 and figures 3.3a and 3.3b).

The characteristics of Gateway states vary in detail, but not in the overall context of their strategic economic locations or in the adaptability of their inhabitants to economic

Table 3.3   State Proliferation

Present Region	Present Gateway	Potential Gateway	Postcolonial State	Rejectionist/ Separatist State
North and Middle America	Bahamas Trinidad	Bermuda British Columbia* Quebec* Aruba Curaçao St. Martin No. Mexico* Puerto Rico†	Cayman Islands French Guiana Guadeloupe Martinique	E. Nicaragua
South America				S. Brazil*
Maritime Europe and the Maghreb	Andorra Luxembourg Malta Monaco Finland Tunisia	Gibraltar** Azores Catalonia* Vascongadas*	Canary Islands* Faeroe Islands† Madeira Islands*	Crete* Greenland N. Ireland‡ Scotland Sicily Brittany* Corsica*

Table 3.3   State Proliferation *(continued)*

Present Region	Present Gateway	Potential Gateway	Postcolonial State	Rejectionist/ Separatist State
				Flemishland** Trentino-Alte Adige* Wales* Wallonia Kabylia (Algeria)*
Asia-Pacific Rim	Taiwan Singapore	Guam S.W. Australia*	American Samoa French Polynesia New Caledonia	Ryukyu Islands S. Philippines† Aceh Irian Jaya S. Moluccas
Heartland		Russian Far East*		Chechnya* Tuva Yakutia* Abkhazia**
Caucasus-Central Asia				
China		China "Golden Coast"*		Tibet Xinjiang
Indochina				
South Asia		Pakhtoonistan Tamil Nadu Tamil Eelam†		Baluchistan Kashmir‡ Nagaland Kalistan* N. Myanmar
Middle East	Bahrain Cyprus	Mt. Lebanon*		Arab Palestine S. Iraq Kurdistan Unified Cyprus‡
Central and Eastern Europe	Estonia Latvia Finland Slovenia	Montenegro* Crimea‡		Transnistria* Kosovo*
Sub-Saharan Africa	Djibouti Eritrea	Zanzibar	Mayotte Island Réunion Island	Cabinda Cape Province* Somaliland S. Sudan Shaba S. Nigeria

*Quasi-state (statelet)
**Condominium
†Two stages: quasi-state to independence
‡Two stages: condominium to independence

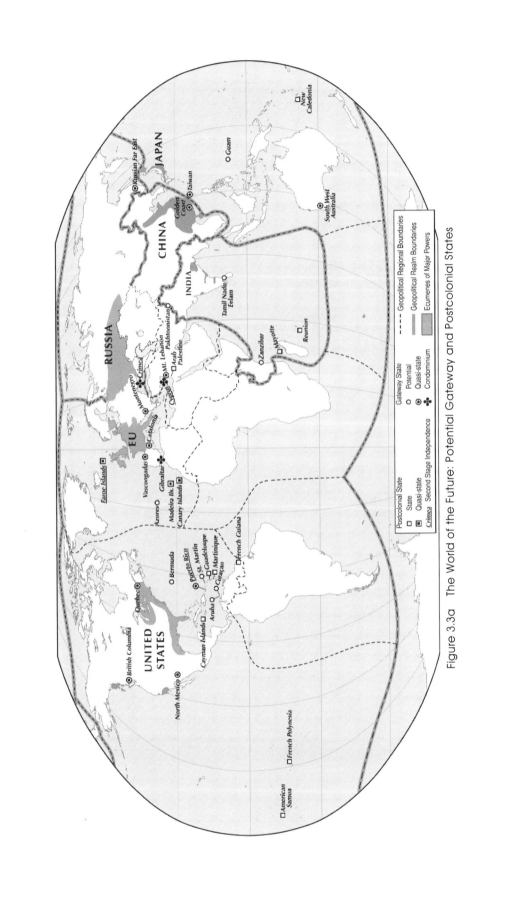

Figure 3.3a The World of the Future: Potential Gateway and Postcolonial States

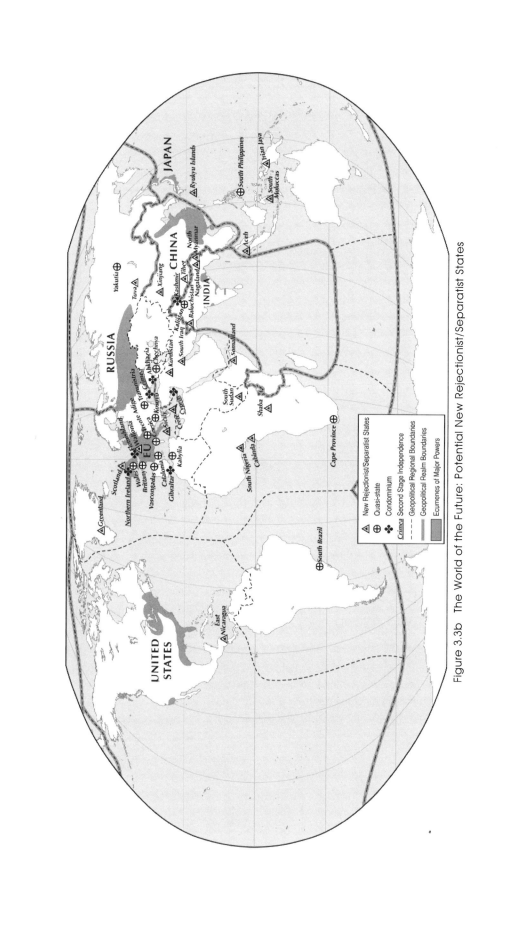

Figure 3.3b The World of the Future: Potential New Rejectionist/Separatist States

opportunities. They are distinct politically and culturally and may often have separate languages or religions, as well as relatively high degrees of education and favorable access to external areas by land or sea.

Small in area and population and frequently lying athwart key access routes, Gateways usually possess highly specialized natural or human resources upon which export economies can be built. Lacking self-sufficiency, they depend upon trade with other countries for many of their raw materials, finished goods, and markets, as well as on specialized manufacturing, tourism, and financial services. Especially when they are sources of out-migration because of their overpopulation, they acquire links to groups overseas that can provide capital flows and technological know-how. The models for such states have existed in such ancient centers as Sheba, Tyre, Nabataea, and Palmyra; in the medieval Hanseatic League and Lombard city-states; in Venice (twelfth to fifteenth centuries); in Manila (seventeenth, eighteenth, and nineteenth centuries); and in Zanzibar (nineteenth century). In the twentieth century, Lebanon was an important Gateway until torn apart by civil strife and war.

Among today's most prominent Gateways are Singapore, Hong Kong, Monaco, Finland, Bahrain, Trinidad, and the Bahamas. The latter, because of its focal location within the Caribbean, its proximity to the United States, its ease of access to Western Europe and South America, and its favorable climate, has become a center for tourism, offshore financial services and banking, international corporate headquarters, as well as, unfortunately, the drug trade.

Hong Kong, although now part of China, continues to play its powerful Gateway role, owing to its special political status. As economic relations between Taiwan and China have greatly expanded and Taipei has become the major source for capital investment on the mainland, Taiwan's role as a Gateway linking the Maritime and East Asian Realms has taken on added significance.

The emergence of Gateways helps to convert former barrier boundaries to borders of accommodation. Estonia is beginning to serve such a role as a link along the geostrategic boundary between the European portion of the Maritime Realm and Heartlandic Russia.

The concept of Gateway regions is a logical extension of the Gateway state concept. Such regions do not yet exist. But Central and Eastern Europe, for example, could develop into a Gateway region between Heartlandic Russia and Maritime Europe, rather than into a Shatterbelt, if it is treated by the major powers as an area of cooperation and not of competition. The countries of such a Gateway, especially the Baltic states, Poland, Hungary, and the Czech Republic, are making their painful transitions to market economies. Their low-cost, fairly skilled labor pools and raw material bases are attracting Western transnational enterprises in areas that range from steel and shipbuilding to telecommunications equipment. These products will be available to the Russian market and the technology used in the modernization of industries can be readily transferred to Russia. Ultimately, an economically recovered Russia would be able to use such a Gateway as a trade bridge to the West and perhaps develop joint enterprises with the West within that region.

Proliferation of National States

The number of national states in the world has trebled in the past half century. In 1945, there were sixty-eight states and the United Nations had fifty-one members, including three memberships allotted to the USSR. In 1991 there were one hundred and sixty-five states, and currently there are two hundred, of which one hundred and ninety belong to the United Nations. The 190th member to be admitted was Switzerland, whose electorate voted to step down from their traditional role of neutrality in international political affairs to join the world body in a March 2002 referendum. East Timor is slated to become the 191st member. This increase in the number of states is likely to continue, as present national sovereignties break apart through either consensus or conflict-driven implosion, with the total possibly reaching 250 to 275 separate national entities within the next quarter century. Paradoxically, the continuing devolution of existing states will also provide long-range opportunities for new kinds of loose confederations, as smaller units feel driven to come together in cooperative frameworks.

State proliferation is the consequence of two forces—the drive of dependent territories for independence and the division of existing sovereign states. Often, although not always, this devolution comes about only after conflict. More than one hundred former colonies and territories have achieved self-determination either as sovereign states or through association with other states. Since the United Nations was founded in 1945, over eighty nations that were once under colonial rule have joined the UN as sovereign states. Of the world's remaining forty dependencies, many have very small populations or provide their administering powers with strategic military bases, so that the latter are reluctant to give up control. Others are so highly dependent economically that they cannot afford the luxury of national independence. Those non–self-governing territories most likely to opt for independence are ones that are sufficiently resource rich, have favorable tourist bases, or are financial havens. As the world becomes a more open system, the advantages that such territories currently enjoy from retaining colonial ties decreases.

POTENTIAL NEW STATES

Table 3.3 and figure 3.3a show the twenty-one colonial areas (including eight gateways) most likely to attain independence soon. Caribbean colonies are more primed than the Pacific dependencies to take advantage of their locations to expand their tourist and financial services economies. The larger number of new states, however, is likely to be those that break away from existing national entities. This category is labeled "Rejectionist-Separatist." Civil and guerrilla wars and active or latent political struggles for independence persist over much of the world. Those that are successful will achieve either full independence or quasi-independence.

Those territories whose prospects for independence are greatest contain peoples who have operated from historic core areas in which they have maintained their cultural, linguistic, religious, or tribal distinctiveness. Many of the prospective states and quasi-states listed in table 3.3 are economically viable because of the strength of their resource bases—for example, Aceh's oil and natural gas; Irian Jaya's copper and gold; Shaba's copper, tin, uranium, diamonds, and fertile grasslands; Xinjiang's oil and gas; South Nigeria's oil and gas; and the grain of Punjab, known as the "granary of India," where the Sikh majority aspires to create a separate county known as "Kalistan."

Some may achieve only qualified forms of sovereignty, thus becoming quasi-states—that is, they may gain qualified political independence. Such states generally lack the military capacities to gain their full objectives. A form of organization for some quasi-states could be the "condominium," whereby two larger powers share oversight for such functions as defense and foreign relations. Political latitude might offer special diplomatic status, including UN membership, as was the case for Belarus and Ukraine when they were within the Soviet Union. Such status might be especially appropriate for Quebec, Vascongadas, Catalonia, Montenegro, Taiwan, China's Golden Coast, and Kashmir. Should the restive Yoruba peoples of southwest Nigeria and the Ibo of the southeast agree to quasi-statehood, rather than try to establish a totally separate state, the two might combine to form South Nigeria and could then join the UN. Twenty-one of the prospective states have been identified as potential Gateways. Some, like China's "Golden Coast," the Russian Far East, and Montenegro, could serve as links to geostrategic regions, as well as to their immediate neighboring states. Were Zanzibar to separate from Tanzania, it could reclaim its historic role as a border Gateway between Sub-Saharan Africa, the Middle East, and South Asia. An independent Puerto Rico could be a bridge between North America and South America. Should they gain their independence, Catalonia (Barcelona), Vascongadas (the Basque Country), and Gibraltar could play useful roles in furthering European integration.

One unfortunate consequence of the proliferation process has been the creation of "failed" nation-states. These are deeply divided, war-torn states, lacking in national cohesiveness, whose governance institutions have collapsed to the point of anarchy or near anarchy. Some divisions are so entrenched and long-standing that they defy international and regional efforts at amelioration.

Models for addressing the "failed state" syndrome include full-scale nation building as proposed for Afghanistan, the NATO peacekeeping effort in Bosnia, and a form of UN trusteeship in East Timor. It remains to be seen how permanent these remedies will be. For the most part, the international community lacks the capacity and geopolitical motivation to mount such operations in most of the world's failed states. It is more likely that massive intervention will continue to be pinpointed for lands that are global geopolitical flash points, and that elsewhere the burden will be left to regional powers to try to mediate conflicts and restore domestic stability.

This need not be the case, however, for states that have yet to emerge. A strategy of early identification of emerging states would permit advance action by international and regional bodies to mount comprehensive infrastructure development programs within prospective states. This could help ward off potential political instability and prepare them to become viable members of the world community when they gain independence. Timely and effective international action could include commitment to technological and capital support for building and maintaining water, sanitation, health, transportation, communications, and education infrastructures. Such comprehensive development efforts would require that, when new states emerge, their fledgling governments demonstrate a "best effort" to share responsibility for these programs, with agreed-upon international monitoring and auditing. This is especially critical for countries with valuable resources that might be siphoned off by ruling cliques.

This continuing struggle for independence has profound implications for U.S. foreign policy making. Concomitant with the objective of eradicating global terrorism, it will be necessary for Washington to promote new approaches that will encourage separatist movements to negotiate their goals peacefully. In many cases, American pressures, sanctions, and rewards by themselves will not be able to dictate peaceful resolutions of irredentist conflicts. Neither is the United Nations equipped to shoulder such a burden. However, a hands-off policy by Washington that simply awaits the implosion of many countries is a recipe for global instability. The challenge is to find new mechanisms for mediating these separatist disputes, based upon a partnership of effort among the United States, other major and regional powers, and regional organizations.

State proliferation is a stage in the evolution of the global system toward specialized integration. States now trying to break away might one day seek confederal ties with their former hosts, especially to fulfill mutual economic self-interest. Table 3.4 suggests possible future confederations.

The creation of fifty to seventy-five additional quasi- or fully independent states over the coming few decades will change the territorial outlines and functions of many major and regional powers. However, these changes are likely to have only limited impact on the power rankings of these states or on world equilibrium.

Among the present regional (second-order) powers, Iraq, Nigeria, and Pakistan could have their territories diminished, reducing them to third-order status. Iraq might be divided into three parts: the Kurdish north, the Shiite south, and the Sunni stronghold centering around Baghdad. Nigeria could split into the Muslim and increasingly fundamentalist Hausa states of the north and the oil-rich south, with its Ibo and Yoruba people. An imploded Pakistan might fragment into four parts: the Pashtun North-West Frontier Province and Tribal Areas as joined with the Pashtun portions of eastern and southeastern Afghanistan to form Pakhtoonistan; northern Kashmir, as part of an independent Kashmir; Baluchistan, a sparsely populated nomadic land in the southwestern part of the country centering around Quetta; and Punjab and Sind, the remaining portions as heir to present-day Pakistan.

Most of the other regional powers should continue to wield substantial influence in spite of possible changes in their territory. For example, the emergence of quasi-states in Canada (Quebec and British Columbia), South Africa (Cape Province), Australia (southwest Australia) and Brazil (the far south) would mean the loss of centralized government

Table 3.4   Potential Confederations

Region	Potential Confederation
North and Middle America	Colombia, Venezuela, "Westindia"
Maritime Europe & Maghreb	Cyprus—North & South
Heartland	"Slavonic Antata" Russia, Belarus, Ukraine, Moldova, Kazakhstan "Greater Turkestan," Uzbekistan, Tajikistan, Kyrgyszstan, Turkmenistan
China	China, Taiwan or Continental China, the Golden Coast, Taiwan
Middle East	Saudi Arabia, Gulf States, Syria, Lebanon, Iraq
Central & Eastern Europe	Baltic States—Estonia, Latvia, Lithuania Former Yugoslav states—Serbia/ Montenegro fed., Croatia, Muslim Bosnia

control over economic, cultural, and local political affairs of significant parts of their territories. However, current exchange patterns would probably remain in force and, in fact, be reinforced by the spur to economic development that results from freedom of economic action by quasi-states and reduction of political tensions.

In the case of Turkey, the emergence of a separate sovereign Kurdistan in its mountainous southeastern portion, joined with Kurdish northern Iraq, would leave intact the Turkish core area of central Anatolia and its rimming coastal lands.

Indonesia shorn of Aceh at the northern tip of Sumatra, of the South Moluccas, and of Iriyan Jaya would continue to exercise its regional influence from its territorial bases of Java and central and south Sumatra. Without having to cope with the rebellions and turmoil of three separatist areas, the Jakarta government would be able to focus on building a more cohesive Indonesian state and forge ahead with economic development. If, however, all of Sumatra were to follow Aceh and break away, Indonesia would be reduced to its overpopulated Javanese core and a few adjoining islands. Without Sumatra's resources of oil, natural gas, and other mineral resources (70 percent of the country's total mineral wealth), Indonesia would be relegated to the status of third-order power.

In Maritime Europe, the proliferation of states may be viewed as an important stage in the developmental process of regional specialization and integration. The territorial impact of this proliferation could affect as many as a dozen European countries. The United Kingdom's influence would be somewhat reduced by the detachment of Scotland, as would Belgium's should Wallonia break away. Spain's central government would lose considerable economic power as well as cultural influence were Vascongadas or Catalonia to become quasi-states, as would the Netherlands with creation of a Flemish quasi-sovereign state.

Such new quasi- and fully sovereign entities would be free of current restraints that might limit their specialized potential and would thus strengthen the EU rather than be an impediment to further integration of its regional structure. France, Germany, and Italy stand to gain political influence within the European Union as a result of reduced power of the diminished states.

India's progress toward becoming a world power is unlikely to be affected by territorial changes. Indeed, its prospects would be enhanced by shedding areas that drain it economically and militarily. Tamil Nadu in the far south, which has been the support base for the Tamil Tiger rebellion in adjoining Sri Lanka, differs from the rest of India racially and linguistically. On the northern periphery, the conflict over Kashmir is costly in lives, resources, and energy. India could benefit from independence of a unified Kashmir, first as a condominium with Pakistan and then as a separate sovereign state.

Emergence of a quasi-independent Sikh state, Kalistan, would resolve another conflict that has bedeviled India. The militant Sikhs, whose religion is a combination of Hinduism and Sufism, have terrorized the Indian states of Punjab (East) and Haryana in their quest for independence. New Delhi can ill afford to lose control over security and foreign affairs of the Sikh homeland, because of its strategic location bordering Punjab (West), which is the heart of Pakistan. However, India would benefit considerably from satisfying the Sikh desire for independence in religious, economic, and local political affairs in order to resolve the bitter conflict that has gone on for decades. An independent Nagaland, the home of Naga tribesmen living in the forested hill country of India's far northeast, would have no impact upon India's economy or security.

Without these separatist states, India could become a more cohesive nation, better able to modernize its economy and human services by reducing its current heavy defense expenditures.

The establishment of Tuva as an independent entity, and of quasi-states in Chechnya, Yakutia and the Russian Far East, would have little impact upon Russia's power position. Indeed, Moscow would be strengthened were it to abandon its long-running conflict in Chechnya. Statehood for the sparsely populated republic of Tuva in south Siberia on the border with Mongolia would have no geopolitical impact whatsoever on Russia. The Turkic-speaking, nomadic Tuvans, who practice Tibetan Buddhism, have long sought the independence that Moscow can well afford to grant at no cost to its national self-interest. Quasi-statehood for Yakutia and the Far Eastern Province would simply formalize and better regulate the conditions of autonomy that already exist within those areas.

In the case of China's rebellious provinces, separation of some would represent a loss and separation of others a gain. Independence of Tibet and Xinjiang would have a negative strategic effect upon China, as well as depriving it of Xinjiang's potentially valuable oil and gas resources. At the same time, resolution of the conflict with Taiwan could be resolved productively by establishing Taiwan as a quasi-state. This would give Taipei unhampered economic and local political control in return for according Beijing jurisdiction over its security and foreign affairs.

The same sort of arrangement could apply if China's "Golden Coast" were to emerge as a quasi-state. This south and central coastal region would be able to build upon its industrial success and accelerate its economic growth. North and Interior China, in turn, would benefit from the increased capital surpluses generated by Golden Coast industries no longer constrained by Beijing's needs and regulations.

Geopolitics and General Systems

Treating the geopolitical world as a general system provides a model for analyzing the relationships between political structures and their geographical environments. These interactions produce the geopolitical forces that shape the geopolitical system, upset it, and then lead it toward new levels of equilibrium. To understand the system's evolution, it is useful to apply a developmental approach derived from theories advanced in sociology, biology, and psychology.

The developmental principle holds that systems evolve in predictably structured ways, that they are open to outside forces, that hierarchy, regulation, and entropy are important characteristics, and that they are self-correcting.

In 1860, Herbert Spencer was among the first to set forth a development hypothesis that drew an analogy between the physical organism and social organization. His evolutionary ideas came from physiology and the proposition that organisms change from homogeneity to heterogeneity. Using the organic growth analogy, Spencer argued that social organizations evolve from indefinite, incoherent homogeneity to relatively definite, coherent heterogeneity. In this hypothesis, state and land meant the combination of social organization and physical organisms.[13]

Combining organismic concepts from Herbert Spencer, the sociologist, with those of Heinz Werner, the psychologist, and Ludwig von Bertalanffy, the psychobiologist, provides the foundations for a spatially structured geopolitical theory.[14] It is a theory that is holistic, is concerned with the order and process of interconnecting parts, and applies at all levels of the political territorial hierarchy, from the subnational to the national to the supranational. Adapting this developmental principle to geopolitical structures, the system progresses through the following. The earliest is *undifferentiated* or atomized. Here, as in feudalism, none of the territorial parts are interconnected and their functions are identical. The next stage is *differentiation*, when parts have distinguishable characteristics but are still isolated. The post-Westphalian states in Europe, or the postcolonial states of the 1950s through the 1970s, all sought to be self-sufficient and to mirror one another. The next stage is *specialization,* which is followed by *specialized integration.* In this last stage, exchange of the complementary outputs of the different territorial parts leads to an integration of the system. The parts of the system are hierarchically ordered, increasing its efficiency, as one level fulfills certain functions but leaves other functions to units belonging to different levels. What helps to bring balance to the system is the drive of less mature parts to rise to higher levels.

Currently, the world geopolitical regions operate at the following stages:

1. specialized integration—Maritime Europe and the Maghreb;
2. specialization—North and Middle America, Asia-Pacific Rim;
3. differentiation—Heartlandic Russia, China, the Middle East, South America, Eastern Europe, South Asia;
4. undifferentiation/atomization—Trans-Caucasus-Central Asia, Indochina, Sub-Saharan Africa.

Geopolitical systems behave like physical systems in that they may exhaust the material and human resources that are the bases of their power unless they are able to recharge their systems with outside energies. In the past, empires did so by exploiting colonies and conquests. In today's world, such energies are best secured through exchange. The Soviet Union collapsed because, in trying to penetrate the far reaches of the globe, it expended its resources and manpower far beyond the benefits it could reap from such penetration. In contrast, a state like Singapore recharges itself through the import of goods and ideas, in exchange for the products and services that it exports. The advantage of most states within the Maritime world is that they can maintain their energy through international exchange. Continental countries, however, especially those that develop closed political systems, have found themselves with less and less energy, not only to influence the world outside, but also to maintain their domestic systems.

Equilibrium, Turbulence, and World Order

The collapse of Soviet communism, the end of the Cold War, and the successful entry of China into the global economy have inspired the hopes that a new order is dawning and fired the debate about the form that such an order will take. The rhetoric is not novel—peace and security, reduction of military weapons, sharing the wealth, justice for national groups. It is the mechanism that is at question. Can there be a truly global system in which the world acts in concert through the United Nations? Is it now feasible to save the world through a *Pax Americana,* or can we count on the world's major power centers—the United States, the European Union, Japan, a reconstituted and loosely federated Russia, and an economically resurgent China—to take collective action to stabilize and enhance the international system?

Military victories in the Gulf War, Bosnia, Kosovo, and Afghanistan have demonstrated the global supremacy of the United States in high-technology military hardware.

However, what has transpired since then has laid bare the difficulties of Washington's efforts to impose a *Pax Americana* on these and other parts of the world, such as the Levant
and Africa.

The events that have plunged so much of the world into chaos during the last decade
demonstrate that world order cannot be imposed by the United States. Washington's need
for an ungainly coalition to conduct its War against Terrorism in Afghanistan is the most
recent example of this reality. The greater promise for a stable world system appears to be
a consensus among the five major power centers and India, with Washington playing the
role of first among equals. In this effort to gain consensus, the UN Security Council, while
it may not have a clear collective interest, nevertheless has proved its importance by serving as a forum that requires agreement among its permanent members and thus has an important role to play in stabilizing the global system.

How we treat the new era's prospects for global stability is very much a matter of con-
ceptualization and perspective. Instead of discussing "world order," we should be speaking
of "global equilibrium," because global stability is a function of equilibrium processes, not
order. Order is static. It speaks to a fixed arrangement, a formal disposition or array by
ranks and clusters that requires strong regulation and implies a sharply defined set of niches
separated by clear-cut boundaries. The niches fit together in an elaborate structure that follows a blueprint designed by some body that operates either hegemonically or consensu-
ally. Essentially, order implies outside regulation.

Equilibrium, by contrast, is dynamic. The term, as applied here, is not being used in
the physical or psychophysical sense that the natural state of an organism is rest or home-
ostasis. Such equilibrium characterizes closed systems but does not fit human organizations
or most natural systems. In these, equilibrium is the quality of dynamic balance between
opposing influences and forces in an open system. Balance is regained after disturbance by
the introduction of new weights and stimuli. Under ideal conditions, such balance is regained through self-correction—through what Adam Smith referred to as the "invisible
hand," or the rational self-interest of peoples.

Of course, because of inertia of the self-interest of governing elites, self-correction may
not always take place. War, terrorism, economic greed, and environmental devastation may
bring people to the breaking point in the absence of reason. So may human interference
with the regenerative powers of the natural environment. When things have gone too far,
there is reaction, correction, and new regulation. Whether equilibrium is maintained
through self-correction or a new level is produced by cataclysmic forces, the balance is accompanied by change, and change by turmoil.

A great deal of turmoil and conflict has taken place in the world since the end of the
Cold War. The collapse of the Soviet Union was not so cataclysmic as to bring on global
conflagration, as hypothesized by such economic determinists as Immanuel Wallerstein
and George Modelski.[15] Communist rule disappeared from the Soviet sphere with a whim-
per, not a "big bang." Even where Communist regimes still prevail, their economies are being liberalized and their systems opened. When these regimes come to an end, the attendant disturbances are likely to be minor tremors.

The difference in the turmoil that plagues the post–Cold War world from that during
the Cold War is not that wars and civil disturbances are less numerous or less lethal, but
that their geographical locations have shifted.[16] Instead of the major conflicts that raged in
the Korean Peninsula, and in the Southeast Asian and Middle Eastern Shatterbelts, the locus of conflict moved to the Balkans and the periphery of the former Soviet Union (FSU).

Only Sub-Saharan Africa has not changed as a region of persistent warfare, while conflict within the Middle East is limited to Israel and the Palestinian territory, Afghanistan, and Sudan. At the same time, as global terrorism has become more sophisticated and more lethal, it has reached into the farthest corners of the earth, affecting major powers and small, weak states alike. It was naive to assume that the end of the Cold War would usher in an era of global peace and harmony. Change and turmoil are intertwined, an unfortunate characteristic of the process of dynamic equilibrium. Because of overlapping spheres of influence and global trade and communications, hierarchy becomes more flexible and national and regional systems become more open. At the same time, the diffusion and decentralization of power makes the system increasingly complex. With the exception of international terrorism, conflict has become more geographically contained. Greater localization and the spread of terrorism offer wider scope for first- and second-order powers to work together cooperatively, using mediation and other approaches to conflict resolution as mechanisms for maintaining dynamic equilibrium.

Notes

1. Robert Ardrey, *The Territorial Imperative* (New York: Atheneum, 1966), 3–41, 108–17.

2. All dollar figures in this work refer to U.S. dollars.

3. Geoffrey Parker, *A Political Geography of Community Europe* (London: Butterworth, 1983), 1–17, 41–61.

4. Alfred T. Mahan, *The Problem of Asia and Its Effect upon International Policy* (Boston: Little, Brown, 1900), 21–26.

5. James Fairgrieve, *Geography and World Power* (London: University of London Press, 1915), 329–30.

6. Richard Hartshorne, "The United States and the 'Shatter Zone' in Europe," in *Compass of the World*, ed. H. Weigert and V. Stefannson (New York: Macmillan, 1944), 203–14.

7. Philip Kelly, "Escalation of Regional Conflict: Testing the Shatterbelt Concept," *Political Geography Quarterly* 5, no. 2 (1986): 161–86.

8. Peter F. Drucker, *The New Realities* (New York: Harper & Row, 1989), 173–86, 255–64.

9. Michael Hardt and Antonio Negri, *Empire* (Cambridge, Mass.: Harvard University Press, 2000).

10. Peter J. Taylor, *Political Geography,* 2d ed. (Harlow, England: Longman Scientific and Technical; New York, Wiley, 1989), 7, 16–41.

11. Paul Kennedy, *Preparing for the Twenty-First Century* (New York: Random House, 1993), 122–34.

12. Edward Said, *Culture and Imperialism* (New York: Vintage Books, 1994), introduction and 3–61.

13. Herbert Spencer, "The Social Organism," reprinted in *The Man versus the State*, ed. Donald Macrae 195–233 (Baltimore: Penguin, 1969).

14. Heinz Werner and Bernard Kaplan, "The Developmental Approach to Cognition," *American Anthropologist* (1956): 866–80; Heinz Elau, "H. D. Lasswell's Developmental Hypothesis," *Western Political Quarterly* 21 (June 1958): 229–42; Saul B. Cohen, "Assymetrical States and Geopolitical Equilibrium," *SAIS Review* 4, no. 2 (summer/fall 1984), 193–212; Ludwig von Bertalanffy, *General System Theory* (New York: Braziller, 1968), 194–213.

15. Immanuel Wallerstein, *The Capitalist World-Economy* (Cambridge: Cambridge University Press, 1979), 6–15, 61–71; George Modelski, *Long Cycles of World Politics* (Seattle: University of Washington Press, 1987), 18–50, 215–48.

16. Dan Smith, *The State of War and Peace Atlas* (London: Penguin, 1997), 16–29, 32–61.

CHAPTER 4

The Cold War and Geopolitical Restructuring

The memory of the Cold War has faded rapidly with the conflicts in Iraq and in Bosnia and Kosovo, and especially with the devastating terrorist attacks on the World Trade Center and the Pentagon, followed by the war in Afghanistan. Nevertheless, it is the geopolitical restructuring that took place as a result of World War II and the Cold War that has shaped the outlines of the current world geopolitical map. The forces behind this restructuring remain important guides to future changes in this map. The Cold War is divisible into three phases: (1) the Maritime Realm's Ring of Containment along the Near-Periphery of the Continental Eurasian Realm; (2) Communist penetration of the Maritime Realm; and (3) Communist retreat from the Maritime Realm and the waning of Soviet power. The geopolitical patterns and features that developed during these phases reflected the changing ideological postures, military capacities, and economic/technological advances among the major Cold War protagonists and other states that had been drawn into the competition.

Phase I: 1945–56

NUCLEAR STALEMATE AND DETERRENCE: DRAWING THE RING OF CONTAINMENT

The first decade of the Cold War was marked by the mutual fears and distrust that prevailed between the American and Soviet superpowers. For Washington, clear evidence of the Soviet threat to world peace was the Berlin blockade (1948), Soviet detonation of an atom bomb (1949), North Korea's invasion of South Korea (1950), the Soviet hydrogen bomb (1953), and the Warsaw Pact (1955). Moscow perceived as major threats to its security the Truman doctrine and Marshall Plan (1947), NATO (1949), American involvement in the Korean War, and the U.S. hydrogen bomb (1952). The various events and perceptions that were formed by the two superpowers during this period resulted in a balance of nuclear terror and nuclear deterrence.

The global geopolitical map of phase I and most of phase II reflected the rigid, hierarchical, bipolar structure imposed on the rest of the world by the United States and

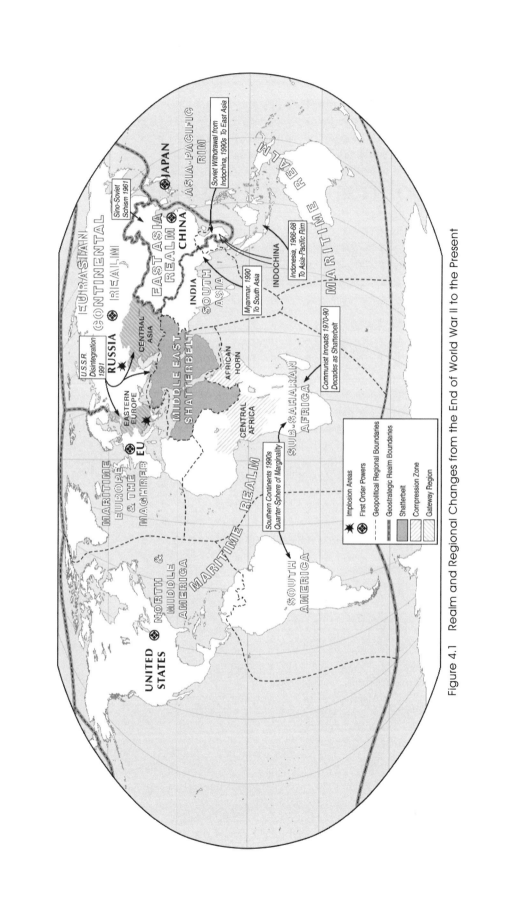

Figure 4.1 Realm and Regional Changes from the End of World War II to the Present

Soviet superpowers (figure 4.1). Most of the world was included within two geostrategic realms—the Eurasian Continental, dominated by the USSR, and the Trade-Dependent Maritime, dominated by the United States. The status of South Asia was that of a geopolitical region independent of the two realms, but subject to continuous pressure from them.

The Eurasian Continental Realm consisted of two geopolitical regions—the Soviet Inner Eurasian Heartland, with its Eastern European strategic attachment, and East Asia. The economic core of the Soviet Heartland had been expanded from its Ukrainian-western Russian base to the Urals when Soviet industry had to be relocated there during World War II. The spread of communism into Central and Eastern Europe immediately after the war provided the USSR with a new, advanced position from which to threaten Western Europe and to seek to undermine the North Atlantic Alliance.

Through its Communist Chinese and North Korean allies, Moscow also posed a major threat to Japan and to the strategic positions of the United States in the Western Pacific. Vulnerability to Soviet power of North and Interior China emphasized China's dependent status. Moreover, Beijing also needed the alliance with Moscow because of its vulnerability to Western naval and air power and the exposure of its coastal reaches to the Nationalists based on Taiwan and U.S. forces based in South Korea.

The Trade-Dependent Maritime Realm included the Atlantic and Pacific basins and their Caribbean and Mediterranean extensions. From its intermediate location between the two oceans, the United States could reinforce its North Atlantic European partners, cast its strategic net over South America, and provide military and economic cover for Japan and other allies along the Pacific Rim.

The regional geopolitical divisions of the Maritime Realm included Anglo-America and the Caribbean, Maritime Europe and the Maghreb, Offshore Asia and Oceania, and South America. Sub-Saharan Africa also lay within the realm, but lacked a distinct geopolitical framework, since it remained divided among the various European colonial powers. The cores of the realm were the manufacturing belt of the northeastern and Midwestern United States and the recovering industrial triangle of northern Europe. They were connected via the sea lanes of the North Atlantic.

The Caribbean was tied to the eastern United States by proximity, capital investment, trade, and U.S. naval bases in Puerto Rico and Guantánamo Bay. South America was under the political and economic shadow of the United States, and the cultural and economic ties between Europe and such countries as Brazil and Argentina reinforced the influence of the Maritime Realm.

The Maghreb was still ruled by France, although independence movements had gathered momentum in Tunisia and Morocco (soon to gain their independence) and rebellion had broken out in Algeria. The presence of large numbers of French settlers, especially in Algeria, plus economic ties helped to keep the Maghreb within France's geopolitical orbit and thus within Maritime Europe's sphere of influence.

In the Pacific, American military power was firmly anchored in South Korea, Japan, Taiwan, the Philippines, Australia, and New Zealand. It was backed by European colonial positions in Malaya, North Borneo, New Guinea, and East Timor. Another important base was Thailand, which had emerged from its World War II occupation (an occupation that it had invited) by Japan. Thailand shook off its historic isolationism and forged a military alliance with the United States. In 1954, Bangkok became the headquarters for the Southeast Asian Treaty Organization (SEATO), which had been established under the leadership of the

United States, Britain, and France immediately after the withdrawal of the latter from Indochina. SEATO also included Australia, New Zealand, Pakistan, Thailand, and the Philippines. The stated purpose of the new alliance was to contain the further spread of communism into Southeast Asia. It ultimately proved helpful to the United States in sanctioning its military presence in Vietnam.

The fundamental weakness of the treaty organization was the fact that only two Southeast Asian states had joined it. Instead, the regional defense role was assumed by Offshore Asia, consisting of South Korea, Taiwan, Japan, the Philippines, peninsular Thailand and Malaya, Australia, and New Zealand. These countries were linked bilaterally to the United States and Britain through economic and military alliances. (In 1977, toward the end of phase II and in the aftermath of the U.S. withdrawal from Vietnam, SEATO was disbanded.)

The countries of Southeast Asia—Indonesia plus the three Indochinese states of Vietnam, Cambodia, and Laos—that were not part of the new Offshore Asian region were soon to become the contested arena between the Eurasian Continental and Maritime Realms and would take the form of a Shatterbelt.

Most of the Middle East had gained independence by the early 1950s, but the region still lay within the orbit of the Maritime Realm. In 1955, under the sponsorship of Great Britain and the United States, Turkey, Iraq, Iran, and Pakistan forged the Baghdad Pact in an effort to create a northern regional screen against the expansion of Soviet influence. This pact was short-lived, collapsing in 1959, when its only Arab member, Iraq, withdrew to pursue a policy of nonalignment. The remaining members were organized within the Central Treaty Organization (CENTO).

Elsewhere within the Middle East, Britain still maintained its rule over the Persian Gulf States, Aden, and the Sudan; its military alliance with Jordan; and its troops in the Suez Canal (although they were in the process of being withdrawn). Saudi Arabia was a firm client state of the United States, and both Israel and Lebanon looked to America as their main supporter. Sub-Saharan Africa, still subject to European colonial rule, was also very much part of the Maritime Realm, and especially important for the realm's strategic minerals and other natural resources.

South Asia, the only independent geopolitical region in the world, stood apart from the two geostrategic realms. Under the leadership of Jawaharlal Nehru, the force of India's commitment to neutrality in the global struggle gave the region unique status. Burma (Myanmar) also took a neutralist course, refusing to join SEATO. Ceylon (Sri Lanka) sought to carve out a role as a leader in the economic development of South and Southeast Asia when it served as host for the Colombo Plan program. However, beset by rebellions, economic crises, and governmental instability, the country had little energy to take on regional initiatives. Nepal, which had for the previous century deliberately isolated itself from foreign influence, continued to pursue nonalignment upon gaining independence. Bhutan, fearing China's claims upon its territory, became even more dependent on India in matters of defense and foreign relations, but remained fairly closed and inaccessible.

Among the states of South Asia, only Pakistan became embroiled in Cold War alliances. This was due, in part, to its geographic split personality as both a Middle Eastern and South Asian state. The seminomadic Pashtuns (Pathans) of Pakistan's North-West Frontier Province, the Tribal Areas and the northern borderlands of Baluchistan, as well as the Baluchi tribesmen, in the southwest, were culturally and linguistically oriented to the

Middle East lands. In contrast, the farmers of Pakistan's Punjab, while Muslims, were culturally and geographically linked to the Indian portion of the Punjab. Similarly, the Muslim Bengali were culturally and linguistically linked to the Hindu Bengali of India. This internal tension eventually erupted in the civil war that brought independence to East Pakistan, which then became firmly tied to India.

During phase I, the USSR and its Communist China ally sought to forge a *cordon sanitaire* around the Sino-Soviet realm by pushing outward from the heart of Continental Eurasia to its surrounding inner seas and passageways to the oceans. With the USSR still reeling from the devastation wrought by the invading armies of Nazi Germany during World War II, Joseph Stalin's goal was to erect a strong defensive screen between the Soviet Union and Western Europe. This was to guard against a recurrence of the *blitzkrieg,* with which the Germans had so recently swept across the Baltic, lain siege to Leningrad (St. Petersburg), penetrated Moscow's suburbs to within twenty miles of the city, reached the Volga at Stalingrad (Volgograd), and seized most of the northern Black Sea coast.[1]

Poland was the key to the Soviet defensive screen. The Allied attempts at Yalta to secure a postwar representative government came to naught, as the controlled elections for the provisional government in 1947 assured a Communist victory.

There were a number of catalysts for the decision of the West to try to block further Soviet expansion by creating a "Ring of Containment" around the Near-Periphery of the Heartland. They included the establishment of the Soviet Zone in Germany in 1945, the outbreak of the civil war in Greece the following year, and the blockade of West Berlin in 1948–49.

The major territorial objective of the Soviet Union during phase I was Eastern and Central Europe—the region that Mackinder had described as the "middle tier of states" between Germany and Russia, populated by Slavs and South Slavs, Bohemians, and Magyars and constituting a strategic addition to the Heartland (figure 4.2).

At the end of World War II, East Prussia was taken from Germany, its northern half, including Memelland, being annexed by the USSR and its southern half being annexed by Poland. The defeat of Germany also enabled the Soviets to retain the Finnish territories that they had seized during the Finno-Russian war of 1940 and the Baltic republics that they had added during that same year. These annexations provided the USSR with a firm grip on the Baltic and gave greater defensive depth to Leningrad. Not only were the Karelian Isthmus and Finnish Karelia acquired, but Finland was forced to lease the Porkkala Peninsula for a Soviet naval base. In the Far North, the Finns lost Pechenga and the Ribachyi Peninsula, adding to the security of Murmansk, which had been so important as the lifeline terminus for supplies from the United States during World War II.

Elsewhere in Europe, the Soviets annexed a wide strip of land from eastern Poland, adding it to Belarus and Ukraine. Prior to Poland's regaining its independence in 1919, these territories had belonged to czarist Russia and the Austro-Hungarian Empire. In addition, eastern Trans-Carpathia was seized from Poland and parts of Bessarabia and Bucovina from Romania, to complete the zone of annexation. With the acquisition of these lands, the USSR gained considerable defensive depth along the invasion routes to Moscow, Stalingrad (Volgograd), Odessa, as well as the Crimea, which had been taken by the invading Nazi armies during the war.

To compensate Poland for its losses in the east, the Soviets added to western Poland thirty-nine thousand square kilometers (twenty-five thousand square miles) of the Third Reich's 1939 territory. The new lands lay east of the Oder and Neisse Rivers and, at their

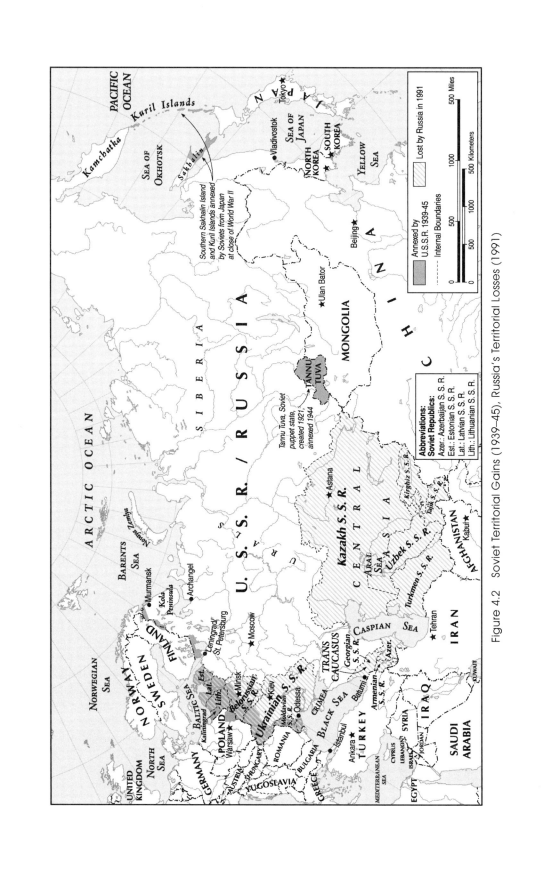

Figure 4.2   Soviet Territorial Gains (1939–45), Russia's Territorial Losses (1991)

northern end, included Gdansk (Danzig) and southern East Prussia. All of these border changes were approved by the West at the 1945 Potsdam Conference.

Soviet security objectives were further satisfied between 1945 and 1948 by Moscow's imposition of Communist regimes upon the belt of Eastern and Central European countries extending from the Gulf of Lübeck and the Elbe River to Thuringia, to the Ore Mountains and the Bohemian Forest, the Middle Danube, the Julian Alps, and the Adriatic. Most of the Black Sea now lay within the Soviet orbit, save its southern Turkish shores. Included were the single-party, vassal Communist states of East Germany, Czechoslovakia, Hungary, Poland, Albania, Yugoslavia, Bulgaria, and Romania. This represented fulfillment of the Soviet strategy of establishing a *cordon sanitaire* along its highly vulnerable western border. Toward the end of phase I, in 1955, the Warsaw Pact formally linked the Eastern European Communist bloc countries militarily with the USSR, as a direct response to remilitarization of West Germany.

Along the southwestern reaches of Soviet power, however, the attempts to draw Greece into the Communist orbit and to pressure Turkey failed. Instead, the North Atlantic Treaty Organization (NATO), which had been created in 1949 in response to the Soviet blockade of Berlin and to defend Western Europe from Soviet expansionism, was enlarged in 1952 to include Greece and Turkey. In addition, Yugoslavia, which had been expelled from the Comintern in 1948, signed a separate military pact with Greece and Turkey in 1954, strengthening the Western containment effort.

During phase I, the Western Ring of Containment was extended eastward to include Iran. In 1946, the Soviet Union withdrew its troops from the northern part of the country, where they had been stationed during World War II, at the time when British and American troops secured the southern part of the country. The Soviet withdrawal came only after intense pressure from the United States and Britain, acting through the United Nations, and with the promise by Iran (which was never fulfilled) to grant Moscow oil concessions. This then enabled the Iranian military to depose Soviet puppet Communist regimes in the Kurdish and Azerbaijani sectors of Iran that had been set up in 1945. In 1952, the anti-U.S. government of Mohammed Mossadegh took power, nationalizing the oil industry and seeking to overthrow the Shah. Two years later, Mossadegh was overthrown, largely by covert activities of the U.S. Central Intelligence Agency (CIA), and the Shah returned to power. The next year (1955), Iran joined with Turkey, Britain, Iraq, and Pakistan in the Baghdad Pact, with the United States as an associate member, strengthening the Ring of Containment along the northern borders of the Middle East.

In South Asia and peninsular Southeast Asia, Indian and Burmese neutrality and Communist revolutionaries in North Vietnam prevented the West from extending Containment to the borders of China. The pervasive influence of Mohandas K. Gandhi's philosophy of nonviolence was not the only source of the Indian policy of neutrality. It related also to New Delhi's ideological differences with the Soviet Union, fears of the Chinese threat to India's territorial integrity, and suspicions that the United States was intent on achieving strategic dominance and imposing American-style capitalism upon the world.

Indian fears of world communism were also fanned by China's annexation of Tibet in 1950, on the basis that the 1914 McMahon line had deprived China of lands that were rightfully its own. Not only was China now perched on India's Himalayan border, but it laid claim to Indian, Nepalese, and Burmese territories, as well as Bhutan in its entirety. In phase II, this dispute would erupt into conflict between India and China. At the same time, New Delhi's distrust of the United States and its former British colonial ruler was fanned by the inclusion of Pakistan within SEATO and the Baghdad Pact. The military support provided by the United States to Pakistan in connection with these pacts was, from the Indian perspective, a direct threat.

Burma maintained its neutrality, refusing to join SEATO and identifying with the other nonaligned Third World states. While recognizing the People's Republic of China diplomatically, it kept its distance, being itself plagued by internal Communist and tribal rebellions. A particular problem for the Burmese was the presence of Nationalist Chinese troops who had fled across the border after their defeat in 1950. The troops remained there for three years, until forced to leave by the United Nations.

In Southeast Asia, the boundary between the Communist and Western worlds remained in flux as the French-Indochina war raged from 1946 to 1954. With the fall of Dienbienphu in 1954, France agreed to an armistice, the terms of which divided Vietnam along the seventeenth north latitude parallel. The North, with its core in the Red River Delta and Hanoi, went to the Communists under the leadership of Ho Chi Minh, while the South, whose core was Cochin China, centering around the Mekong Delta and Saigon, became a French puppet regime led by Bao Dai.

The armistice boundary did not long hold as a line of containment. The very next year the Saigon regime, now led by Ngo Dinh Diem, was recognized by the West as the legal government of all of Vietnam, while North Vietnam began to receive considerable economic as well as military support from the USSR and China. What followed, during much of phase II, was conversion of all of southern peninsular Southeast Asia into a Shatterbelt region, as the Vietnam War engulfed the Great Powers as well as the Vietnamese rivals.

In insular Southeast Asia, the former Dutch East Indies were also part of this Shatterbelt. Indonesia had achieved its independence from the Dutch in 1949, but during the first part of the Cold War it was preoccupied with uniting its diverse peoples in the face of sporadic uprisings and the threat of a highly influential local Communist Party. Moreover, President Sukarno, who had led the fight for Indonesian independence, adopted a socialist and neutralist platform, which fanned Western suspicions.

The northeastern boundary between the Sino-Soviet realm and the United States and its allies was forged by war. Japan's northern limits were drawn after World War II. Then, at Yalta, the Allies agreed to the Soviet annexation of the southern half of the island of Sakhalin and the Kuril Islands, as part of the price for the Soviets having entered the war against Japan. In 1951, the U.S.-Japan security treaty committed Washington to the defense of Japan from external attack.

The victory of the Chinese Communists over the Nationalists in 1949 extended the Eurasian Continental Communist power to the limits of the East Asian mainland and was quickly followed by Beijing's occupation of Tibet in 1950. Offshore, however, the Ring of Containment was sharply drawn during the same year, when the Chinese Communist plans to invade Nationalist-held Taiwan were frustrated by the patrols of the U.S. Seventh Fleet. Thus was the boundary established in the Western Pacific between the two geostrategic realms—down the centers of the Sea of Japan and the East China Sea through the Taiwan Strait. The line was hardened in 1955–56, when the U.S. response to Communist shelling of the Nationalist-held islands of Quemoy (Jinmen) and Matsu (Mazu) was to enter into a mutual security pact with the Nationalists and a promise to defend Taiwan against outside attack.

In the Korean Peninsula, the boundary was stabilized only after a bitter conflict that directly involved American and Chinese forces in the fighting on the ground and in air combat, in which Soviet pilots also joined. While most of the northern boundary divided China from Korea, Soviet concerns over the entry of American troops into the fighting were heightened by the fact that a ten-mile stretch at the eastern end of the boundary that followed the mouth of the Hunchun River served as North Korea's boundary with the USSR, only ninety miles from Vladivostok. After the seesaw battle that raged up and down the peninsula ended, the 1953 armistice line along the thirty-eighth parallel became the basis for the boundary between the two Koreas that persists to this day.

There were unanticipated consequences for the USSR as a result of helping build up the Chinese air force and army. That air force became the third largest in the world and the large Chinese army became battle-hardened. This new strength was instrumental in changing China's view of itself from that of a Soviet satellite to that of a partner. It was an important factor in Mao Zedong's break with Moscow after the death of Joseph Stalin.

The southern end of the Ring of Containment in Offshore Asia included the Philippines, which had received independence in 1947 but continued to house U.S. military, naval, and air bases. These positions overlooked the South China Sea and the shorelands of southern China and Indonesia. The threatened spread of communism to the Philippines was halted in 1954, when indigenous Communist guerrillas (the Hukbalahaps, who operated in Central Luzon) were defeated by the government's forces. However, they regrouped and conducted a campaign of terrorism for the next decade and a half, until crushed by the Philippine military in 1969. They ceased to function the following year.

Rounding off the Heartland's Near-Periphery was the Arctic. There the Cold War balance was maintained through mutual deterrence, as nuclear weapons capable of being delivered by long-range bombers and submarines prowling under the Arctic ice cap became available to both sides. The U.S.-Canadian Distant Early Warning (DEW) line air defense system, begun in 1955, was an important element of the American transpolar security system. Similarly, Soviet meteorological, radio, and scientific posts based on ice floes backed up the country's air, nuclear icebreaker, and submarine defenses.

Expansion of the Communist realm into its Near-Periphery during phase I was greatly facilitated by Moscow's buildup of its nuclear capacity, as well as by the rapid rebuilding of its war-shattered heavy industrial economy. Reconstruction of the economy, including reindustrialization of much of the western Soviet Union, was marked by rapid advances in military technology.

Phase I came to an end in 1956, when Soviet nuclear weapons development led to the establishment of a balance of terror between the two superpowers. Also marking the period's conclusion was the beginning of the Sino-Soviet schism.

Phase II: 1957–79

COMMUNIST DEEP PENETRATION OF THE MARITIME REALM

During this phase, substantial change in the geopolitical map of the world took place, as the Cold War leap-frogged Continental Eurasia's Near-Periphery and spread to the inner and outer reaches of the Maritime world. The bitter rivalry between the superpowers was fanned by a number of events. The 1957 launching of Sputnik, the first artificial satellite, a year before the U.S. launching of Explorer I, was considered a wake-up call to American science and education. In the same year, Moscow announced the development of the first intercontinental ballistic missile (ICBM). In addition, it broke a voluntary moratorium on nuclear testing, which it had signed in 1958, when it resumed testing in 1961. U.S. fears of the Soviet threat were also heightened by the building of the Berlin Wall (1961), the Cuban missile crisis (1962), and the invasion of Czechoslovakia (1968). Soviet fears in turn were intensified by the Bay of Pigs (1961), by U.S. entry into the Vietnam War (1965), and by the American role in the overthrow of Indonesia's President Sukarno (1965).

The penetration of the Maritime world by the Eurasian Continental powers was facilitated by a number of developments. The European colonial era was ending in the Middle East, Southeast Asia, and Sub-Saharan Africa. At the same time, Marxist influence was gathering strength within Third World national liberation movements. The ability of the United States to become directly engaged in additional Cold War conflicts was limited by negative American public opinion stemming from the involvement in the Vietnam War. Development of a massive Soviet arms export industry cemented the dependence upon Moscow of many Third World countries.

The schism between Moscow and Beijing set up a competition between the two for Third World influence. This break began with Mao's ideological opposition to the de-Stalinization policy introduced by Nikita Khrushchev in 1956 and widened with Mao's promotion of the "Great Leap Forward." For Mao and his successors, Khrushchev's disavowal of Stalinism represented abandonment of Marxism. These events led to the withdrawal of Soviet economic aid and technicians from China in 1960. Hostility intensified as China became allied with Albania in 1961 in the wake of the rift between Moscow and Tirana. It increased still further in the late 1960s, when Chinese hard-liners took objection to Leonid Brezhnev's call for peaceful coexistence with the West. Finally, the decade-long border dispute between the two Communist powers erupted into fighting.

A marked ideological shift gave impetus to Moscow's strategic ambitions. The move away from the ideological commitment to support only revolutionary Marxist parties was signaled by the 1956 dissolution of the Cominform. Instead, by joining hands with all who were enemies of imperialism, the USSR could support nationalist movements that were hostile to communism, as well as those that were led by Marxists. The banner was no longer the "*World* Communist Revolution"; it was the "War against Capitalism-Imperialism."

The Soviet Union developed its arms industry to the point of becoming the world's second largest supplier of arms. Whereas in phase I Soviet arms shipments had been limited primarily to the Warsaw Pact countries and China, in phase II, the direction of the flow of weapons shifted to the Third World and to India. While Moscow could not compete with the United States and its allies in trade or in economic assistance to its Third World clients, Soviet military transfers to its clients in the form of sales and grants were generous. Moreover, its improved logistics capabilities enabled it to move large numbers of Cuban troops to Angola and Ethiopia and to ship large quantities of arms and military supplies by sea and air.[2]

Much of what happened in phase II can be traced to the rising influence of Nikita Khrushchev after the deaths of Stalin and Lavrenty Beria. Khrushchev's 1956 speech to the Twentieth All-Union Congress denounced Stalin's dictatorial rule and personality cult and called for decentralized management of the Soviet economy. The address followed up on efforts, initiated in the previous year, to introduce greater flexibility to Soviet foreign policy. This had included a peace treaty with Austria, diplomatic relations with West Germany, and return to Finland of the site of the Porkkala naval base.

Khrushchev also made efforts to place relations with Eastern Europe on more of a partnership basis. The result was establishment of the Council for Mutual Economic Assistance (COMECON) as a broadening of the Warsaw Pact, which had been initiated in response to the remilitarization of West Germany. However, Eastern European hopes that this presaged a loosening of the Soviet grip were quickly dashed when uprisings in Poland by disaffected students and workers were repressed by the Soviets. In Hungary, an anti-Communist revolution that had declared Hungary neutral and withdrew Budapest from the Warsaw Pact was also crushed by Soviet troops.

With Eastern Europe still securely in its hands, the Soviet Union could now challenge the United States and its allies diplomatically and politically, within their own backyard—the Maritime Realm. Soviet aggressiveness was strengthened by advances in military technology, including ICBMs, so that by the 1970s the USSR had achieved nuclear parity with the West.

REGIONS OF PENETRATION

The Soviet strategy of penetrating the Maritime world gathered momentum in the years that followed, as the United States became increasingly bogged down in Vietnam. In addition, starting in 1969–71, the Nixon and Brezhnev administrations pursued a policy of détente in Europe through strategic arms limitation talks (SALT), while the American-supported *ostpolitik* of Germany's Willy Brandt aimed at reducing U.S.-Soviet tensions and achieving mutual force reductions in Europe.

As a general strategy, the Soviet Union sought to establish political and military positions along key Maritime world waterways. Such areas included:

1. the Middle East and the African Horn—the eastern Mediterranean and the Suez Canal, the Red Sea, Bab el-Mandeb, and the Gulf of Aden
2. Southeast and Offshore Asia—the Strait of Malacca and the South China Sea
3. the Caribbean—the Florida Straits and the Yucatan Channel

To carry out such a strategy, a major naval buildup was undertaken.[3] Forming the core of the new Soviet "blue water" navy were missile-carrying nuclear-powered submarines and guided missile cruisers, and intelligence and survey ships. The fleet was backed by long-range naval and giant cargo aircraft. In addition, Soviet shipyards produced one of the largest merchant fleets in the world, including many ships with military mission capabilities. In addition to the Northern, Pacific, Baltic, and Black Sea fleets, the Soviet navy kept permanent forces in the Mediterranean and the Indian Ocean.

The rise of Soviet naval power took place at a time of decline for the U.S. naval program, the fleet having been reduced in number and threatened with obsolescence. Cold War proponents in the United States saw the Soviet buildup as an effort to gain control of the oceans and as a major threat to the security of the seas. However, their call for a strong response to the challenge through the expansion of the U.S. Navy was not answered until the Reagan administration.

Fears of the USSR's threat to Western dominance of the oceans may have been overblown. A more likely explanation for the Soviet naval buildup is that it was done to help defend the footholds that had been secured within the Maritime world, rather than to use naval power as the basis for broader expansion within the realm. A major problem for the Soviet fleets was the undependability of their overseas bases, which were vital to their operations, for they had no independent deep-water capacities. Alexandria, Berbera, Aden, Aseb (Assab), and Massawa were gained and later lost. Cienfuegos was more than offset by the U.S. bases in Guantánamo and Key West; Cam Ranh Bay was neutralized by American air and naval operations in Guam, Okinawa, and the Philippines; and the Conakry base was offset by the U.S. facilities in the Azores and Ascension. Soviet anchorages in the Indian Ocean and the Mediterranean were at the mercy of Western air and sea power.

In the late 1960s and early 1970s, China shifted from a revolutionary policy to a vigorous diplomatic foreign policy, extending aid to selected parts of the underdeveloped world in South America, Africa, and Asia. This new Chinese political assertiveness was facilitated by the self-confidence derived from its development of nuclear bombs and satellites in the 1960s and by the Sino-U.S. détente initiated by President Richard Nixon's dramatic visit to Beijing in 1972.

SHATTERBELTS

During phase II, Soviet penetration of the Maritime Realm resulted in the creation of three Shatterbelts—the Middle East and the African Horn, Sub-Saharan Africa, and Southeast Asia.

The Middle East and the African Horn

The Middle East was the first place in the Maritime Realm where the Soviets penetrated the Western Ring of Containment. There, Syria, Egypt, and South Yemen were Moscow's main targets for extending its influence. Egypt, the largest and most powerful of the Arab states, was the prime objective. As early as 1955, the USSR began to provide aid to Egypt and also to Syria.

Withdrawal of U.S. and British financial support for the proposed Aswan Dam, the centerpiece of Gamal Abdel Nasser's development plans in Egypt, opened the door for the Soviets to provide the funding. Moscow went on to give military support to Cairo after the Egyptian army had been defeated in the Sinai War with Israel. During the next decade and a half, Soviet influence upon Egypt was all-embracing, with vast military, technical, and economic aid. In return, the Soviets acquired access to Egyptian naval bases on the Mediterranean coast, which supported its Mediterranean squadron, a self-contained detachment of the Black Sea fleet.

This penetration of the Arab world's leading nation ended in 1972, when President Anwar al-Sadat made preparations for another war with Israel, against the wishes of the USSR. Sadat ousted Soviet forces and took over their bases. After the defeat of Egypt in this war, the United States moved into the vacuum and, at Camp David, brokered a peace between Egypt and Israel. Egypt then returned to the Maritime orbit through a new alliance with the United States.

Soviet relations with Syria were longer lasting. The Baath Party, which combined socialism and nationalism, had gained power in the mid-1950s. In 1960, its radical wing seized control with Moscow's help. Subsequent economic and military accords provided the Soviets with a strong foothold in Syria, although President Hafez al-Assad, who had seized power and become president in 1971, feared an internal Communist coup and therefore remained wary of Soviet long-range intentions. These fears played a role in Syria's decision to join with Egypt and Libya in the short-lived Federation of Arab Republics (1969–70).

Unlike Egypt, which had swept out Soviet influence in favor of peace with Israel and strong support from the United States, Syria remained at war with the Israelis over possession of the Golan Heights. As a consequence, the USSR continued to maintain considerable influence with Damascus, which still remains heavily dependent on Russian arms.

When Lebanon became embroiled in civil war among Christians, Muslims, and Palestinians in the mid-1970s, Syria seized the opportunity to extend its influence over the country. The Syrian military intervened in 1976 at the invitation of the Christian community to prevent its being overrun by the Lebanese Muslims and Palestinians. Damascus then switched its support to the Muslims and the Palestinians when the Christian-dominated Lebanese army leadership sought to oust the Syrian forces from the country.

Soviet penetration into South Yemen began with the independence of the colony of Aden from Britain in 1967. The new state included the Arab Emirates of south Arabia in the Hadramaut, which lay to the east of Aden. The historic trading center for the southern part of the Arabian Peninsula, Aden had an excellent natural harbor that would well serve Soviet strategic aims in the Red Sea and Indian Ocean.

In 1979, a twenty-year accord between the Soviets and the South Yemen regime provided for Soviet naval bases to be installed. These gave support to the eastern Mediterranean Soviet fleet as it entered or exited the Red Sea at Bab el-Mandeb en route to the Suez Canal. With complementary Soviet bases that had developed earlier, first in Somalia and then on Ethiopia's Eritrean coast, oversight of the southern end of the Red Sea was strengthened.

In Libya in 1969, Muammar al-Qadaffi's overthrow of King Idris and seizure of power led to the closing of the remaining British military bases there, as well as of the U.S. Wheelus Air Base. (Most British troops had been withdrawn three years previously.) This paved the way for the short-lived alliance with Egypt and Syria and for Libya to become a base for international terrorism against Israel and the West.

Qadaffi espoused socialist principles, but was strongly anti-Communist. While he forged military ties with the USSR, which supplied him with vast amounts of advanced military equipment, including missiles, his major interests lay in extending Libya's influence into the Arab world and providing support to Palestinian guerrilla movements. A formal Soviet-Libyan alliance was forged much later, in 1980, when the Libyans came into conflict with Tunisia, and it continued in subsequent years of Libya's conflict with Chad. However, by 1980 the alliance was of little strategic value to the Soviets, inasmuch as Egypt had already made peace with Israel and had become a major client state of the United States.

Relations between the USSR and Iraq took various turns. Initially, in 1955, Iraq severed ties with the Soviet Union over the latter's support of the Kurdish revolt in northern Iraq. Later, in 1972, when Iraq broke its diplomatic links with Britain and Iran, it signed a friendship pact with the Soviets, although its various Baathist regimes continued to be wary of possible Communist coups. Given the strength of the alliance between Washington and the Shah of Iran, Iraq saw its links to the USSR as a valuable countermeasure and purchased substantial amounts of arms from Moscow. The situation changed drastically in 1979, when the virulently anti-American Khomeini regime overthrew the Shah. As Saddam Hussein prepared for war against Iran, the United States considered support of Iraq both desirable and feasible.

During this period of major Soviet inroads into the Arab world, the West maintained its position through strategic alliances with Turkey, the Shah's Iran (until his ouster), Israel, Saudi Arabia, and the Gulf States. It was in early 1979, at the very end of phase II, that the U.S.-Iran alliance was shattered by the overthrow of the Shah and the establishment of the fundamentalist Islamic Republic, led by the Ayatollah Khomeini. Seizure of the American embassy by Iranian militants and the keeping of fifty-two American hostages for 444 days embittered the relations between the two nations for years to come.

From the 1950s onward, oil from the eastern Arabian Peninsula and the Gulf waters, as well as from Iraq and Iran, had become of such global importance that the West had to maintain a strong Middle Eastern presence. In addition, Turkey, the region's largest military power, served as NATO's eastern cornerstone and defensive bastion against the Soviet Black Sea positions.

U.S. support for Israel had begun out of domestic political and humanitarian concerns. However, with American help, Israel had developed a formidable military machine, superior to its combined Arab enemies, and therefore constituted a strong Cold War military counter to Soviet influence among the Arabs. Saudi Arabia and the Gulf States, completely dependent upon Washington for military support and arms to guard against continuing threats from Iraq (and, after 1979, from Iran), provided the West with a firm strategic presence in the Persian/Arab Gulf.

Soviet penetration also extended into the Horn of Africa, where its strategic objective was full command of the southern end of the Red Sea. This involved Moscow in countries bordering the sea along both the Arabian Peninsula and the Horn of Africa. Even though the Suez Canal was now closed, the Horn, a transitional region between the Middle East and Sub-Saharan Africa, was a tempting prize. By linking positions on the coast of the Horn to those held in South Yemen, the Soviet navy would acquire control of both sides of the Gulf of Aden through surveillance installations monitoring the movements of U.S. and allied air and naval power in the Arabian Sea and Indian Ocean.

In the Horn of Africa, the opening for the USSR came in Somalia in 1969, when a military coup brought General Muhammad Siyad Barre to power and established a Marxist-Leninist state that developed strong ties with the Soviet Union. Soviet assistance included considerable arms to build up the Somali forces. In exchange, Moscow was given the right to build naval and missile bases in the north in the port of Berbera (in former British Somaliland), opposite Aden, and in Mogadishu in the south.

Events in Ethiopia soon placed the Soviets in a quandary, forcing them to choose between two allies, Ethiopia and Somalia. In 1974, a Soviet-backed military junta had overthrown Emperor Haile Selassie and installed a marxist regime headed by Haile Maryam Mengistu. Two years later, the Ethiopians formally ended their alliance with the United States and formed one with the USSR. In the long-standing dispute between the Somalis and Ethiopians over the latter's control of the Ogaden Desert, which lay between them, the USSR and Cuba opted for Ethiopia. The Soviets flew in twenty thousand Cuban troops and provided advisers, enabling the Ethiopians to retake the Ogaden in 1978.[4] As the conflict continued, the Somalis turned to Egypt, Saudi Arabia, Iran, and the United States for help.

In 1978, Soviet-Cuban assistance also enabled the Ethiopians to defeat the Eritrean rebels, who had seized most of Eritrea, and clear the way for the Soviets to gain naval and military bases on the Red Sea at Massawa and Aseb.

Sub-Saharan Africa

Sub-Saharan Africa became a second Shatterbelt during this period. With the reopening of the Suez Canal in 1975, the USSR gained direct access to the Red Sea by way of the eastern Mediterranean and the Black Sea. Together with land proximity, this provided the Soviets with a strategic advantage in the Middle East over the more distant Western powers. In most of Sub-Saharan Africa, however, Moscow was at a strategic disadvantage relative to Western Europe. France, Belgium, and Britain were much closer geographically to West and Central Africa and could apply military power there more quickly. In addition, the Europeans had strong economic and cultural ties to those regions. The Soviets, however, had to use lengthy sea routes or overfly the continent to provide military support to Communist movements there.

Only in relatively distant southern Africa did Moscow and its Cuban allies have equal strategic access. There, however, the Soviets had to contend not only with the European powers backed by their transatlantic U.S. partner, but also with white-ruled South Africa, which could directly support the anti-Communist forces in nearby Mozambique and Angola.

An early opportunity for a Soviet foray into Sub-Saharan Africa presented itself within Central Africa, in Congo. Congo attained independence from Belgium in 1960 and its first government was headed by Patrice Lumumba, a Marxist. His Soviet-backed regime was immediately beset by the secession of the mineral-rich Katanga (Shaba), but the USSR's capacity to provide military help was limited. Lumumba was soon overthrown and subsequently murdered and a new national government was established through a combination covert U.S. help, Belgian troops, and white mercenaries. Two years later, Mobutu Sese Seko seized power and the United States became the main supporter of the country (renamed "Zaire"). This ended Soviet hopes of gaining a foothold in Congo—an important source of such strategic minerals as copper, uranium, cobalt, and tin, as well as industrial diamonds, petroleum, and rubber.

The adjoining Republic of the Congo-Brazzaville had received its independence from France at the same time as had Congo. Although a Marxist-Leninist government took power, it steered a neutral course between Moscow and the capitalist world, especially because of its economic dependence upon France. Only at the beginning of phase III of the Cold War did Congo sign a friendship pact with the Soviet Union, a relationship devoid of strategic significance.

In West Africa, Guinea, which had been led to independence from France in 1958 by Ahmed Sekou Toure's radical union movement, cultivated relations with the Soviet Union. In 1961, Toure expelled the Soviet ambassador for seeking undue influence in the country, but relations were restored and Conakry became a base for Soviet military surveillance aircraft and a permanent Soviet naval patrol off the Guinea coast.

Ghana provided no opening for the Soviet Union, although under Kwame Nkrumah (1957–66) it took a strong anticolonial, Pan-African stance, unfriendly to the West. Elsewhere within West Africa, Mali had a flirtation with the USSR in the 1960s and 1970s, when Soviet military advisers provided a small number of tanks and aircraft. While there was a Soviet market for some of its exports, such as hides, groundnuts, and canned fish, the impoverished country still depended mainly upon France for imports and credits, as well as for trade with neighboring African states.

In the latter part of phase II, Benin, which had adopted a Marxist ideology in 1975, sought support from the Communist world. Little was forthcoming, except for a handful of Soviet small naval craft, so the country remained economically tied to Europe. Neither Benin nor Mali offered any strategic advantages for the USSR.

In East Africa, which received its independence from Britain in 1963, only Tanganyika and Zanzibar were realistic targets of opportunity for Communist penetration, as major ethnic divisions, rather than ideology, were the basis for turmoil in Kenya and Uganda. Immediately following independence, Zanzibar was the scene of a leftist revolt, some of whose participants were Cuban trained. However, the island was quickly merged with Tanganyika into Tanzania (1964) and the mainland gradually took control of the island's affairs.

Chinese influence grew in Tanzania, as China provided the aid for building the Tazara (Tan-Zam) railroad from the coast at Dar es Salaam to Zambia in the late 1960s. Nevertheless, the Communist influence was kept within limits, as Julius Nyerere preferred to follow his own brand of socialism, free of Great Power entanglements. Nyerere and his successors continued to steer a course of nonalignment in the Great Power clash. The country did become embroiled in border clashes with Uganda that erupted into full-scale war in 1978–79. It also served as a support base for liberation movements in other parts of Africa.

In the mid-1970s, southern Africa provided the USSR with a new window of opportunity. In Angola, the Communist guerrillas who had led the war of independence from Portugal gained control of the government. In its struggle to keep power against opposition rebel movements, the Marxist regime received large amounts of aid from the Soviet Union and Cuba. In 1976, the opposition National Union for Total Independence of Angola (UNITA) nearly succeeded in capturing Luanda with the help of South African troops and U.S. support. However, Cuban soldiers were flown in by Soviet planes, backed by seaborne supplies, to save the capital and to enable the regime to gain control of the north and much of the rest of the country. With the assistance of Cuba and the USSR, Angola also provided a base for Southwest African guerrillas (the South West Africa People's Organization, SWAPO) in their battle for independence from South Africa.

A Marxist government was also installed in Mozambique when the Mozambique Liberation Front (Frelimo) came to power in 1975. The new regime received aid, equipment, and training support from the USSR and help from Cuban air force personnel. Beira became a base for the Soviet Indian Ocean squadron. The country soon became a haven for the rebels of the Marxist Zimbabwe African National Union, precipitating a brief but devastating invasion from white-dominated Rhodesia.

The Soviet bases on the two coasts of the two southern African allies, Angola and Mozambique, were strategically valuable. From Beira overlooking the Mozambique Channel, the Soviets presented a challenge to the U.S. Fifth Fleet and to its air arm based on the Indian Ocean Island of Diego Garcia, which had been leased from Britain. In addition, Beira provided oversight of the shipping lanes from the eastern Mediterranean and Indian Ocean through the channel to the Cape of Good Hope and of traffic destined for the Atlantic. Angola enabled the Soviet Union to monitor the trans-Cape route from the Atlantic side.

By the end of phase II, the Soviet position in Sub-Saharan Africa had become shaky, despite these widespread efforts to penetrate the region. Its Communist satellites in Ethiopia and Angola remained locked in combat with powerful rebel forces within their countries. Moscow incurred high costs in keeping large numbers of Cuban troops to sustain these regimes, while pumping arms and economic assistance into them. Moreover, in white-dominated South Africa, the Soviets had encountered a regional power with the military capacity and the logistical advantages to help the rebels in both Angola and Mozambique to fight the Marxist governments and their Communist allies to a standstill.

The geopolitical actions of the Soviet Union in Sub-Saharan Africa during phase II had converted the region into a Shatterbelt. Moscow's goals had been twofold—to support Marxist and anticolonial movements of national liberation wherever they took place and to fulfill Soviet geostrategic objectives by securing footholds along the Horn of Africa and other lands and offshore islands bordering the Indian Ocean, thus threatening sea-lanes vital to the Maritime world. The success of these efforts proved to be mixed, however, as so much of Africa continued to depend upon the West for its economic survival and was unwilling to forgo ties with European investors and markets.

Southeast and Offshore Asia

During phase II, the Southeast Asian peninsula and the western portions of Offshore Asia emerged as the third Shatterbelt. Communist control of North Vietnam had been affirmed in the 1954 partition of Vietnam. This partition served as the initial stage of the war that would then engulf all of Indochina and divide the region between the Communist world and the West. The United States failed to contain the spread of Communist power, although it spent over $150 billion in more than a decade of combat.

Despite the rift between the Soviet Union and China, both provided massive military and economic aid to North Vietnam. In 1978, three years after the war's end, China broke with Vietnam over the latter's invasion of Cambodia in support of a Communist faction, led by Hun Sen, that had ousted China-backed Pol Pot and his Khmer Rouge regime. In China's stead, the Soviet Union became Vietnam's chief ally and source of aid, receiving in return a long-term lease for the Cam Ranh Bay naval base overlooking the South China Sea.

Not only had much of the northern half of the Indochinese portion of the Southeast Asian peninsula fallen to the Communists during phase II, but the southern half of the peninsula and Indonesia were also drawn into the East-West conflict.

In Malaysia, a Communist insurrection that lasted through the 1950s ended with the resettlement of nearly five hundred thousand Chinese and the emergence of a strongly Western-supported state that had gained its independence as a member of the Commonwealth of Nations in 1957. Thailand, threatened by its proximity to China and Communist gains in Vietnam, had used SEATO early on for protection. During and following the Vietnam War, it received considerable military and economic aid from the United States. While Communist insurgencies in several parts of the country, especially in the northeast, plagued the Thai regime in the early '70s, they were eventually put down. The Philippines, though wracked by intermittent uprisings, remained resolutely anti-Communist. The Communist-led Hukbalahaps rose up again in the late 1960s and fought intermittently before being finally quashed in 1979. Since that time, the major rebel groups have been the Muslim Moros of Mindanao and the Sulu Archipelago.

During this phase, Indonesia veered from neutralist to pro-Communist to pro-Western stances. The shift toward the West took place in 1966 as a result of an attempted Communist coup, which was repressed by the army, led by General Suharto. Up to three-quarters of a million, many of them ethnic Chinese, were killed in Java and Bali. General Suharto took advantage of the turmoil to strip President Sukarno of his powers and put him under house arrest. He assumed the presidency himself the following year. Suharto then developed close ties with the United States and helped to found the Association of Southeast Asian Nations (ASEAN). This regional bloc of anti-Communist countries included Malaysia, the Philippines, Singapore, and Thailand. (Today, ASEAN also includes Vietnam, Cambodia, Laos, and Brunei.)

OTHER GEOPOLITICAL REGIONS

South Asia

While not of the same strategic imperative to the USSR as the Middle East, Sub-Saharan Africa, and Southeast Asia, South Asia nevertheless became more deeply drawn into the Cold War during this phase. It was China, rather than the Soviet Union, that represented a threat to India. While New Delhi continued its policy of nonalignment, its fears of China were increased as Tibet became more tightly controlled by Beijing, with the settlement there of hundreds of thousands of Chinese.

The ongoing border disputes between India and China erupted into border clashes in Ladakh and Assam in 1959 and a limited war in 1962, whereby China gained some territory in Ladakh. As India's relations with Beijing worsened, its ties with Moscow improved. In 1966, for example, the USSR brokered a troop withdrawal between India and Pakistan that took their forces back to the lines that had been held prior to their war of 1965.

Five years later, Soviet political support and an airlift of military equipment was of assistance to India in its third war with Pakistan, this one over Bangladesh. A new economic assistance plan was subsequently concluded between Moscow and New Delhi. At the same time, India's relations with the United States became increasingly strained over the latter's continuing military and economic support of Pakistan. In spite of all of this, India maintained its posture of neutrality, and ties with the United States gradually improved.

Burma (Myanmar) was not only physically and historically identified with the Indian subcontinent, but it also shared India's commitment to neutrality. In addition to Burma's distrust of Britain, its neutrality had been influenced by its fears of China. Communist rebels and tribal groups, such as the Karens, rose up against the Burmese government shortly after independence and continued their insurgencies over the next two decades with support from Beijing. The military junta that seized power in 1962 increasingly shifted the orientation of the country from its earlier contacts with the nonaligned world to complete isolation.

Latin America

Latin America was another focus for Soviet penetration efforts during phase II. Extending the Cold War to the Caribbean, which lay within the immediate tactical and strategic reach of the United States, represented a daring and costly challenge. Cuba, which overlooks the Straits of Florida and the Gulf of Mexico, provided the USSR with the opportunity to challenge the United States on its own doorstep. When Fidel Castro overthrew Fulgencio Batista in 1959, he nationalized American landholdings and financial and industrial companies, breaking relations with Washington and declaring allegiance with the Eastern bloc. The subsequent failure of the U.S.-sponsored Bay of Pigs invasion in 1961 emboldened Nikita Khrushchev to strengthen the Cuban armed forces significantly and to build Soviet missile bases on the island.

The immediate response of President John Kennedy was to demand that the Soviets dismantle their missiles and to impose a naval blockade, forcing the USSR to back down. In addition, the naval base at Guantánamo remained in U.S. hands, thus allowing the United States control of the Windward Passage and the lanes between the Atlantic and the Caribbean, as well as securing the Panama Canal from the north. While Cuba continued to be a base for Soviet naval and surveillance activities until the disintegration of the Soviet Union, the 1962 missile crisis was a lesson to both superpowers. To avoid similar nuclear confrontations, both adopted strategies of relying upon surrogates in their competition wherever possible. It was Cuba that then took on the mantle of spreading the revolution to other parts of Latin America. However, while Castro became completely dependent upon Soviet arms, economic aid, and fuel, and on the sugar market of the Communist bloc, he was by no means a puppet in the sense that the Eastern European regimes were. Indeed, geographical distance, which was such a considerable liability to the USSR in its efforts to sustain Cuba and spread the revolution within the Western hemisphere, proved to be a political asset to Castro in pursuing some of his domestic and foreign initiatives. This freedom of action was unavailable to Eastern European satellites because of the presence of Soviet forces on their doorsteps or within their territories.

The Bay of Pigs incident stimulated the United States to take an aggressive stance against the Marxist rebellions that began to sweep Latin America. While Cuban influence in Jamaica and Guyana was not negligible, Castro failed to convert the socialist governments there to overt allies. In Venezuela, where two Communist-inspired naval revolts in 1962 and subsequent hit-and-run terrorist actions threatened the Social Democratic government, Washington provided support to suppress the threats.

Elsewhere, the United States had intervened in Guatemala as early as 1954 to topple a Communist-influenced government. Guatemalan bases were then established with U.S. assistance to train anti-Castro guerrillas in the early 1960s. When left-wing terrorism broke out within the country in the mid-1960s and continued in the following years, American support of its military strongly shaped Guatemalan politics.

Only at the very end of phase II, in 1979, did two radical, left-wing governments emerge in the Caribbean that were to become closely allied to Cuba and the Soviet Union during phase III. The Sandinistas gained control of Nicaragua after the lengthy Somoza rule, while a leftist coup supported by Cuban troops seized power in Grenada, to be ousted by U.S. and Caribbean troops four year later.

In South America, Soviet penetration efforts were singularly unsuccessful. In Bolivia, the United States aided the rightist military junta in the struggle against Communist guerrillas led by Castro's chief lieutenant, Ché Guevara, who in 1967 was killed in the fighting. Three years later, a leftist coup resulted in the attempt to develop ties with the Soviet Union, but that government was toppled by a rightist countercoup the following year.

In Chile in 1970, Salvador Allende became the first popularly elected Marxist president in Latin America. He sought close ties with the Communist bloc, only to be overthrown and murdered after three years by the Chilean military, with covert U.S. support. The Marxist revolution spread to Uruguay in 1967 with the establishment of a terrorist group there. Ultimately the campaign of the urban guerrilla movement, the Tupamaros, was put down by a repressive regime installed by the military.

In Argentina, Communist as well as Peronista parties were banned in the 1963 elections by the right-wing regimes that took power. In Brazil, leftist guerrillas were ruthlessly suppressed during the 1960s and early 1970s.

The failure of the Soviet Union to expand its influence in Latin America outside of Cuba (and later Nicaragua) was due, to a considerable extent, to the vigorous countermeasures taken by Washington. Military and police leadership trained by the United States in the Panama Canal Zone's School of the Americas were significant forces in providing security support for the right-wing regimes that dominated most of the countries of the region.

An example of the impact of this training was "Operation Condor," a system developed to share in intelligence and antileftist security actions among Brazil, Argentina, Chile, Paraguay, Uruguay, and Bolivia. The security establishments of these countries and their Washington backers often made little distinction between real and imagined security threats in the effort to stop the spread of Soviet and Cuban-supported Communist movements.

THE ARMS RACE

It was in phase II that the Soviet Union achieved parity with the United States in its military and nuclear buildup. While U.S. arms expenditures had escalated rapidly during the Korean War, they were then scaled back, as President Dwight Eisenhower sought to rein in the "military-industrial complex." By 1961, Soviet military expenditures had nearly caught up with those of the United States. During the 1960s, the two powers kept pace with one another. From 1956 through 1970, for example, Washington's defense outlay totaled $861.7 billion and Moscow's $812.8 billion.[5] The United States forged substantially ahead only during the administration of President Ronald Reagan. U.S. foreign arms sales, mainly to the Middle East, increased exponentially during the 1970s, exceeding those of the USSR.

While the largest portion of Soviet increases in military expenditures was in missiles and air power, and while nuclear parity had been achieved, the buildup of the Soviet fleet also required substantial outlays. The price of this buildup placed a heavy strain on the Soviet economy and society. With a reported gross domestic product that was half that of the United States, and a per capita income that in real terms was probably only one-third that of its rival, the USSR succeeded in matching the United States in military expenditures during phase II. Increasingly plagued by food and consumer goods shortages and lagging in high technology, the Soviet Union was ill-prepared to compete under the further strains that would result from the arms buildup of the Reagan administration.

Phase III: 1980–89

COMMUNIST POWER RETREAT FROM THE MARITIME REALM

In the 1980s the world geopolitical map again underwent major restructuring. Most significantly, China broke away from the Eurasian Continental world to establish a separate East Asian geostrategic realm. Other hallmarks of phase III were the hard-line stance taken against the Soviet Union and other Communist states by the Reagan administration and the rapid decline of Soviet influence in the Middle East, Sub-Saharan Africa, and Latin America.

This phase followed upon the period of détente between the United States and the USSR during the 1970s, which resulted in the Strategic Arms Limitation Talks (SALT I and SALT II)—accords that banned new ICBMs and launchers. The détente ended in early 1980 with the Soviet invasion of Afghanistan and the U.S. boycott of the Moscow Summer Olympic games.

If phase II marked the apogee of Soviet penetration of the Maritime World, phase III was its nadir. The USSR's bloody, and ultimately unsuccessful, war in Afghanistan left it with little surplus energy to devote to its other Cold War pursuits. Considerable pressure was put on Moscow by the decision of the Reagan administration to scrap détente and greatly increase U.S. military expenditures, for it triggered an arms race that the Soviet Union could neither afford nor win.[6] By 1989, the end of phase III, the annual defense expenditures of the United States were $275 billion. The Soviet figure was $190 billion—significantly higher than its average annual expenditures during the previous phase, but inadequate to prevent the arms gap from widening. The United States had extended its lead, particularly in the application of high technology and telecommunications to modern warfare, as it would demonstrate in the Gulf War.

Economically, the situation was worsening in the Soviet Union, as living standards dropped, consumer goods were in short supply, and Soviet agriculture failed to meet the needs of the nation. While the defense budget of the USSR was two-thirds that of the United States, its gross national product had dropped to one-sixth that of the United States. By the end of the decade, it had become evident to Soviet leadership that the costly and uneven arms race could not be sustained, that the country would not have both "guns and butter."

EMERGING MAJOR POWERS

The multipolar nature of the system began to emerge clearly during phase III, as the European Union, Japan, and China became recognized as global power centers. The extraordinary economic growth and prosperity of Maritime Europe and Japan were important factors affecting the Cold War balance during this period. The economic success of Western Europe and the buildup of its military forces within NATO put new pressures on the Soviet position in Eastern Europe. There the unrest over lack of consumer goods, the rise of the Solidarity movement in Poland, and "creeping capitalism," especially in Hungary, were beginning to undermine the foundations of the "command economies" and the stability of the Soviet Union's satellite Communist regimes.

Japan's startling economic and technological success in the 1980s, during which its gross domestic product expanded to become the second largest in the world, enabled it to increase its influence in Southeast Asia, as well as in its own Offshore Asian region. By the end of the decade, Tokyo had forged important economic links with Communist Vietnam, providing investment capital and aid. These links came about as Vietnam redirected its state economy toward privatization and reached out for foreign investment when Moscow was forced to reduce its substantial subsidies. Rebuffed by China, from which it had requested help, Hanoi shifted toward the development of a market economy and turned to Japan. The latter had the financial capacity and the political and economic interest to respond positively, and it did so.

Relations between Moscow and Beijing continued to worsen in the 1980s, not only over Vietnam and Cambodia, but also over the need for the USSR to maintain a large military force along the border with China. The Soviet buildup there had started in 1969, with clashes between the former allies in Manchuria and Xinjiang. Hostility between the two was also fanned by China's opposition to the Soviet invasion of Afghanistan.

During the previous two Cold War phases, China had shared the Eurasian Continental Realm with the Soviet Union, first as its satellite and then as a hostile competitor. While tensions between China and the Soviet Union were high over ideological differences and boundary disputes, their mutual vulnerability along what was then their forty-five-hundred-mile land border had served to keep them geostrategically linked. Moreover, each operated behind closed political and economic systems, reinforcing their common distrust of the Maritime Realm powers.

China's strategic position vis-à-vis the USSR began to change after the mid-'70s, when the United States withdrew from Southeast Asia and Vietnam was reunified under a Communist regime. For China, this was a major geostrategic victory. The perceived Western military threat to its southern provinces was removed and Beijing was free to pursue expansionist aims within the South China Sea region. Deng Xiaoping, Mao's successor, could also now enter into a new political relationship with the United States and other Maritime states that would enable him to introduce badly needed economic reforms into the stagnant socialist state economy. In 1979, diplomatic ties between the United States and China were established and four coastal economic zones were created to attract foreign investment and to spur international trade.

These developments were the necessary preludes to China's vigorous economic growth during the 1980s—a growth that coincided with a period of unprecedented economic expansion throughout the Asia-Pacific Rim. Expansion in that region enabled Japan, Taiwan, Hong Kong, and Singapore to join the United States in providing China with the capital and technology that expanded its manufacturing base and stimulated its export economy.

The foreign policy impact of China's sweeping economic reforms was that it began to seek political accommodation with nations of the Maritime Realm, balancing off its traditional Continental orientation. The strategic consequence was the emergence of East Asia as the world's third geostrategic realm and a new balancer in the global power equation.

THE WANING OF SOVIET INFLUENCE

Southeast Asia

The northern half of peninsular Southeast Asia—Indochina—remained a Shatterbelt, but now the major external interveners were not the Communist powers and the West, but the two opposing Communist states. The Soviet Union was able to maintain some of its past influence in Vietnam, serving as its main political ally and military supplier. Relations between China and Vietnam, on the other hand, worsened because of the dispute between the two over Cambodia. After the Vietnamese invaded the country in 1978 to oust Pol Pot and the Khmer Rouge, their troops remained in Cambodia for the next decade. The Vietnamese also established a military presence in Laos. In addition, Vietnam and China skirmished over territorial claims in the Paracel and Spratly archipelagoes of the South China Sea.

The southern parts of peninsular Southeast Asia, by contrast, became more firmly tied to the Maritime Realm's Asia-Pacific Rim. Singapore, Malaysia, and Thailand benefited from their close economic relations with Japan, as they participated in the region's remarkable economic resurgence. Indonesia, too, made rapid progress as a modernizing industrial power and trading state within Offshore Asia and the broader Maritime world system.

Middle East

Within the Middle East, Soviet influence became substantially diminished during phase III. Moscow's greatest setback came from the entry of Egypt into the Western bloc. Another major Soviet setback in the Middle East was the weakening of its Iraqi ally as a result of the Iran-Iraq war, which lasted from 1981 to 1988. Taking advantage of the turmoil in Iran, the Iraqis launched an invasion to seize the disputed Shatt-al-Arab waterway. Rather than gaining the expected speedy victory, they became mired in a bloody conflict. Ironically, as matters later turned out, Iraq received considerable backing from the United States in this war.

Syria was left as Moscow's main Middle East ally during this period. Damascus was fully dependent upon arms purchases from the Soviet Union to support its military presence in Lebanon and its continuing conflict with Israel. The Syrians were helped by Soviet-maintained economic surveillance stations within the country. However, Syria's economic ties became more balanced. Even though it had formed economic alliances with the USSR and Libya in 1980, and even though the Soviet Union still constituted its largest export market, because of the faltering Soviet economy Damascus forged stronger trade ties with the West, especially the countries of the European Union. During this period, Syria tightened its grip on Lebanon, both militarily and economically, bringing an end to the civil conflict that had continued to rage between the Christians and the Lebanese Muslim and Palestinian communities.

South Yemen was the other remaining Soviet ally within the region during the 1980s. The Marxist regime continued to provide Moscow with the naval base at Aden and sites for communications and electronic intelligence facilities. This enabled the Soviets to retain a strategic presence in the Red and Arabian Seas. A peace treaty was subsequently signed with North Yemen, initiating talks that ultimately led to the unification of the two countries in 1990. When the Marxist state disappeared, the Soviet strategic foothold on the Arabian Red Sea and Gulf of Aden coasts disappeared with it.

Sub-Saharan Africa

In the Horn of Africa, the Marxist regime in Ethiopia, led by Haile Maryam Mengistu, remained in power. However, it was beset by famine and bitter rebellions in Tigre and Eritrea, placing in peril the Soviet African Red Sea bases. Moreover, as economic aid from Moscow and Havana declined during this period, the Ethiopian regime had to look to other sources for economic help.

Elsewhere on the continent, and especially in West Africa, Soviet influence declined rapidly, as Marxist regimes were overthrown in many countries and severely weakened in others. The diminished military and economic support of the Soviet Union and its Cuban ally forced African Marxist regimes to turn to the West economically, thus rebuilding the region's geostrategic ties to the Maritime Realm. Moscow continued to strongly support the Communist regimes in Angola and Mozambique, as well as the Cuban troops who continued to fight side by side with governmental forces against the rebels, who received considerable aid from South Africa.

Toward the end of the decade, however, the Marxist fervor of the Angolan regime weakened, as it began to implement land and industrial privatization programs. In addition, the United States entered the scene directly by providing arms to the UNITA rebels. In Mozambique, as Soviet and Cuban influence faded, the Communist government turned to Zimbabwe for help. The radical leftist regime there responded by sending troops to guard the railway and oil line that extended into Zimbabwe from the port of Beira.

Latin America

During much of the 1980s, Communist attempts to penetrate Latin America had some successes. However, by the end of the decade, these also had largely dissipated. While Cuba remained the Soviet's major power base, in Nicaragua right-wing guerrilla actions and a U.S. trade embargo undermined the economy of the Sandinista government. Economic distress and dissatisfaction with the repressive regime led to the ouster of the regime in the general election held in 1990. In Grenada, the Marxist regime of Maurice Bishop was toppled in a coup, following the invasion and occupation of the island by the United States.

The 1980s were a period of rising strength for leftist rebel movements in Colombia and maoist guerrilla forces in Peru. However, these terrorist groups were internally generated and directed, offering little scope for the Soviet Union and Cuba to extend their influence within the western Andes. Without outside aid, the guerrillas became increasingly dependent on the drug trade to finance their endeavors.

THE WAR IN AFGHANISTAN

Afghanistan was the major focus of Soviet military energies abroad during phase III. While only one of several factors that eventually contributed to collapse of the Soviet empire, the Afghan war had a traumatic effect upon the Soviet military. The conflict began in 1979, when thirty thousand Soviet troops entered Afghanistan to save the Marxist regime that had seized power the previous year and aligned itself with the USSR. Moscow installed Babrak Karmal as prime minister and gradually increased the number of its troops, so that at the height of the conflict as many as one hundred thousand members of the Soviet armed forces were engaged in the fighting. Immense technological power was brought to bear against the outnumbered Mujahedeen, who depended upon arms originating from the United States, Saudi Arabia, and China, and funneled through Pakistan, which also provided the rebels with their main training bases. In the course of the war, over one million Afghans were killed and over five million (one-third of the prewar population) fled the country as refugees. Soviet losses were fifteen thousand killed and thirty-seven thousand wounded.

By the time that Mikhail Gorbachev rose to power in 1985 and instituted his policies of *glasnost* (openness) and *perestroika* (restructuring), it was too late to save the situation. The Soviet Union had exhausted both its capacity and rationale for pursuing the war. Recognizing its futility and burdened by the enormous cost of trying to maintain in power an unpopular Afghan regime, Gorbachev withdrew the Soviet troops in 1988–89, leaving the way clear for the Mujahedeen to sweep into power.

For Moscow, the price of the Afghan war was political as well as economic and military. The unpopularity of the war at home fueled the popular dissatisfaction with the Soviet government's repressiveness and economic failures. The latter had become patently evident with Gorbachev's liberalization policies. Abroad, much of the developing world viewed the Soviet invasion of Afghanistan as an imperialist venture, undermining Moscow's credibility as the patron of anticolonialism.

The Collapse of the Soviet Superpower

While these events were taking place in the Soviet Union, its grip on its Eastern European satellites was weakening. In 1989, democratic movements had gathered stunning momentum. By the end of the year, the Communist governments had been toppled in every one of those countries and the Berlin Wall had fallen, wrenching the European Near-Periphery of the Soviet Heartland from its grasp.

The following year, the Baltic republics demanded independence from the USSR and Moscow signed a pact accepting the reunification of Germany. Thus the Heartland's Eastern European strategic adjunct was lost without a shot being fired, the mighty nuclear arsenal that the USSR had built up having proven valueless. Now the Continental Eurasian Realm has shrunk inland toward the continent's center and geographically it resembles the "Pivot Area" that Halford Mackinder described a century ago.

The dogged determination of the Soviet Union to pursue its strategy of deep penetration of the Maritime Realm proved to be a geostrategic blunder of the greatest magnitude. In extending the Cold War to arenas where the West had an overwhelming military, logistical, and economic advantage, the USSR played to its enemy's strength.

Could the Soviet Union have maintained its superpower status? One alternative strategy for doing so would have been to concentrate on its Near-Periphery and develop the Eurasian Continental Realm into a cohesive unit on a partnership basis. Such a strategy might still have failed, given the sociopolitical rot and the economic weaknesses of the Marxist-Leninist revolutionary state. Indeed, the Brezhnev regime widened the schism through confrontational policies that assumed that Mao could be brought into line by pressure.

The Soviets failed to recognize that Chinese and Soviet communism had emerged from fundamentally different cultures, refusing to respect the ideological legitimacy of Maoism, which focused on its agricultural peasant base and the principle of continuing revolution. Mao's policies of dispersing industry into the interior in the Great Leap Forward of 1958 and the Cultural Revolution of 1966 were clearly resounding failures. But, from the point of view of Moscow, recognition of the principle of separate revolutionary pathways might have cemented a Sino-Soviet partnership and not led the two powers into seeking to play one another off against the United States.

A strategy that sought to craft alliances of equals, between the USSR and Eastern Europe and the USSR and China, would have altered the course of the Cold War. From this perspective, one may conclude that Soviet policies had more to do with losing the Cold War than United States policies had to do with winning it.

Thus geographical factors shape events, but are not deterministic. Within those parameters, it is the policies and decisions of political leaders that determine the geopolitical structures of the globe.

Transition into the Twenty-First Century

THE DECADE OF THE 1990s

The end of the Cold War brought a reordering of the world's geopolitical structures and concomitant changes in expectations and attitudes toward international relations. Three transformations characterized the period.

First, the disintegration of the Soviet Union left only one superpower—the United States. Many expected the United States to impose a *Pax Americana* on the world; the reality was otherwise. Second, although turmoil and conflict continued, it was more limited in scope and geostrategic implications. Third, more open borders allowed globalization and regionalization to flourish, with both positive and negative consequences. Absence of Great

Power control, combined with ease of communications, movement, and capital flows, gave more scope to international terrorism.

These transformations effected change in the world geopolitical structures. With the shrinking of the Eurasian Realm through the implosion of the former Soviet Union and former Yugoslavia, the status of Eastern Europe and Central Asia was significantly altered. In the East Asian Realm, the weakening of Russian pressures enabled China to became more assertive in its relations with the Asia-Pacific Rim and to draw Indochina into its orbit geostrategically. Within the Maritime world, expansion of NATO, as well as the proposed enlargement of the European Union, has affected the existing balance between Maritime Europe and the United States, as well as between the Maritime and Russian Heartlandic Realms.

During this decade, Sub-Saharan Africa and South America became geostrategically marginal to the Maritime powers, even though they were still within the Maritime Realm. The Western powers have stood by passively as Central Africa has broken into a Compression Zone, its internal divisions being reinforced by the intervention of neighboring eastern and southern states.

At the onset of the post–Cold War era, the world's sole hyperpower—the United States—assumed the mantle of global leadership. It quickly met the first international challenge—Iraq's invasion of Kuwait in August 1990. Washington organized and led the coalition of forces that pushed the Iraqis out of Kuwait in January 1991 and, through an unprecedented demonstration of electronic air power, devastated Iraq's major military installations, ports, and cities.

However, in Iraq, Saddam Hussein continued in power behind his Republican Guard, which escaped virtually intact from the massive Allied air bombardment of the Gulf War. In 1992, Saddam ruthlessly crushed the U.S.-encouraged Kurdish rebellion in the north and the Shia uprising in the south.

When the Somali military warlord Muhammad Siyad Barre, was overthrown in 1991, the country fell into chaos and the American response was rapid. Somalia was swept by intertribal warfare and then devastated by the worst drought that Africa had experienced during the century. To protect relief supplies and restore order, Washington dispatched U.S. troops to the stricken country.

These early American initiatives were widely heralded as harbingers of a stable "new world order" guaranteed by a *Pax Americana* imposed by U.S. global economic, military, and informational hegemony. What followed instead was the turbulence that is characteristic of systems undergoing fundamental structural change. The American superpower could neither prevent nor easily put an end to the conflicts that broke out during the 1990s.

In 1994, the U.S. expeditionary force was shocked by an ambush during street fighting in Mogadishu in which eighteen rangers were killed and seventy-five wounded. The troops were quickly withdrawn, as the American public made it clear that it had little stomach for interventions of a humanitarian nature that would cost American lives. The following year, the UN forces also pulled out. Elsewhere, wars in several of the former Soviet republics, especially Georgia, Armenia, and Azerbaijan, were followed by the dismemberment of Yugoslavia, with bloody conflicts in Croatia, Bosnia, and Kosovo.

Where conflict has broken out as the aftermath of the Cold War, its geographic scope has been generally limited. Even in Bosnia, Kosovo, and Rwanda, and in the bloody civil wars in Liberia and Sierra Leone, all of which caused extensive casualties, the conflicts did not spread beyond their own regions. In Afghanistan, the fighting between the Taliban and its tribal opponents did not result in the deaths of hundreds of thousands or the displacement of millions of refugees, as occurred in that country during the Soviet invasion. Nonetheless, the optimism that had given birth to the idea of a new world order quickly gave way to pessimistic scenarios. Zbigniew Brzezinski promoted the view of a world in perpetual turmoil; I. Lukacs predicted that the international system would be ruled by intransigent nationalism; Samuel Huntington saw a future marked by bloody global struggles between great world civilizations and culture; and Robert Kaplan predicted global chaos.[7]

Events of the 1990s suggest that neither the optimists nor the pessimists are correct in their reading of the world geopolitical map. There has, indeed, been considerable turmoil as the result of the profound changes that the international system has undergone; but that turmoil, with the exception of the Gulf War and global terrorism, was confined to areas where it does not threaten global stability.

A balanced perspective of the Cold War's aftermath must also take into account the many peaceful transitions of rule and territorial reconfigurations that have taken place. These include secessions from the FSU by Ukraine, Belarus, the Baltic states, and the former Soviet Central Asian republics; from Yugoslavia by Slovenia and Macedonia; and from Czechoslovakia by Slovakia. The reunification of Germany was accomplished with minor economic or political disruption and the changeover from Communist regimes was relatively smooth in Poland, Romania, Bulgaria, and Mongolia. Elsewhere, South Africa's transformation to a black government was peaceful, as democracy has taken root in that land. As the twenty-first century unfolds, seemingly intractable conflicts appear to be winding down in Angola, Sierra Leone, Sri Lanka, Northern Ireland, and Peru. While they may flare up again, the resolution of these and other conflicts appears to have gained momentum.

Other significant elements of post–Cold War transformation, globalization, and regionalization were present in the 1980s, but could not develop fully until systems became more open and borders could be more easily crossed in those parts of the world that bore the brunt of Cold War competition. Networks of economic and cultural interaction have expanded exponentially since then, bringing prosperity to parts of the developing world. In such areas, international capital flows have facilitated investment and stimulated the outsourcing of manufacturing. The information revolution has broadened the horizons of individuals and made it easier to challenge entrenched authority.

Some of these same factors have their negative aspects. The open system makes it more difficult to contain arms and drug smuggling, and to prevent the spread of international terrorism across more open borders. The transfer of technology has speeded the emergence of India and Pakistan as nuclear powers and enhanced the abilities of North Korea, Iran, and Iraq to develop their own nuclear and biological weapons. Corruption and the ease with which capital can be illegally expatriated have undermined the Russian economy, as well as the economies of many other FSU states. Rapid globalization of culture has deepened the fissures within traditional societies, leading to the spread of Islamic fundamentalism in such countries as Turkey, Egypt, Afghanistan, Pakistan, the states of Central Asia, Nigeria, the Philippines, and Indonesia.

Absent the Cold War competition that stirred up so many wars, conflict mediation has become more widespread. Russia has become involved in helping to mediate regional crises. The Gulf War was contained with Russian collaboration, and Moscow's influence also helped to moderate Serbia's behavior in its fighting with Croatia and, in the latter stages of the war, in Bosnia. It also played an important part in bringing Slobodan Milo-sevic to the negotiation table, and Russia has been supportive of the United States in its conduct of the war in Afghanistan. The United States has played key mediating roles in Northern Ireland and the Middle East, while South Africa has taken the lead in mediating the conflict in Congo. Governments at all levels, as well as the United Nations and regional bodies, are all more fully engaged in the process.

War crimes, violations of human rights, and terrorism, callously ignored during the Cold War, have become important items on the international agenda. This offers the prospect of justice and retribution and holds out the promise of greater respect for human life, dignity, and property.

GLOBAL TERRORISM IN THE NEW MILLENNIUM

September 11, 2001, and its aftermath, the anthrax scare, have severely shaken the Amer-ican public and governments. The loss of an approximately three thousand lives and the devastation wrought upon the country's financial and military nerve centers, as well as the boldness of an attack using terrorist-seized aircraft, had a stunning psychological effect. The Atlantic and Pacific moats, which had lulled the nation into a feeling of security, had been breached. The terrorism that the English, French, Irish, Israeli, and Spanish people had so long endured, not to speak of the atrocities perpetrated upon innocent civilians through-out the developing world, had suddenly become part of the American experience.

Terrorism, both domestic and international, is an age-old phenomenon. Its purposes have ranged from grasping for political power and struggles for national freedom, to the exercise of ideological and religious beliefs, to sheer brigandage. It has been practiced by in-dividuals and small groups, national and transnational movements, empires and states. Practitioners employ surprise and increasingly lethal weapons and techniques to produce widespread panic and fear within the target publics. Kidnappings and ambushes are tradi-tional stratagems, but aircraft and other vehicular hijackings and the use of planes as weapons of direct assault are of recent origin. Even more lethal potentially are biological, chemical, and nuclear weapons of mass destruction.

Despite historic episodes of assassination and other terrorist activities, it was not until the 1980s and 1990s that American citizens and facilities became exposed to large-scale ter-rorist activities. For the most part, they occurred overseas—in Beirut, in West Germany, over Lockerbie, Scotland, in Nairobi and Dar es Salaam, in the Khobar barracks in Saudi Arabia, in the harbor of Aden, Yemen. Bombings and other terrorist attacks took more than one thousand lives in fourteen major incidents, with embassies, aircraft, airports, and ves-sels as major targets. While there was much public surprise and concern within the United States over the attacks, the response from Washington was relatively muted, as it failed to recognize the danger of international terrorism to the stability of the global system.

Nor did scattered incidents at home serve as wake-up calls. The terrorist bombings of Faunces Tavern and the federal courthouse and the 1993 attack on the World Trade Cen-ter, all in New York, as well as a fray outside CIA headquarters in Virginia, cost a limited number of lives and minimal physical dislocation. It took the events of September 11 for Americans to feel the agony of terrorism and to recognize that it was their problem.

Approximately one hundred states have been targeted by terrorist attacks since the end of World War II. Table 4.1 lists countries that have been exposed to major terrorist actions during this period, nearly two-thirds of which have taken place within the last two decades, or remain highly vulnerable to them. Thirty-four of the countries enduring terrorism are Muslim dominated, a reflection of the vulnerability of Muslims themselves to Islamic terrorism.

Under the U.S. Anti-terrorism and Death Penalty Act of 1996, the secretary of state is required to designate foreign terrorist organizations that threaten the country's interests and security. In 2000, twenty-nine such organizations were identified. The largest number of these are Muslim groups, mostly with Arab roots.[8] Al Qaeda, the most lethal of terrorist organizations, is a network whose cells operate in thirty-seven countries (some estimates go as high as sixty countries).

Organized terrorist groups do not operate in a geographical vacuum, but are based in certain countries from which they reach out to others. They derive much of their strength from support obtained from states that sponsor them or offer safe havens. The U.S. State Department's most recent list of such sponsors cites Cuba, North Korea, Iran, Iraq, Libya, Sudan, and Syria. U.S. law requires that sanctions be imposed on these states. For technical reasons, the list has glaring omissions. Afghanistan and the West Bank/Gaza are absent because the Taliban had not been recognized by Washington as a legitimate regime and the Palestinian Authority does not govern a formal state. For political reasons, Pakistan,

Table 4.1   State Targets of Major Terrorist Actions since World War II

Region	Countries
North & Middle America	El Salvador, Guatemala, Nicaragua, United States
South America	Argentina, Bolivia, Chile, Colombia, Ecuador, Peru, Uruguay
Maritime Europe & the Maghreb	Algeria, Austria, France, Germany, Greece, Italy, Morocco, Spain, United Kingdom
Eastern Europe	Albania, Croatia, Cyprus, Kosovo, Macedonia
Heartlandic Russia & Periphery	Armenia, Azerbaijan, Georgia, Kazakhstan, Kyrgyzstan, Russia, Tajikistan, Uzbekistan
Middle East & African Horn	Afghanistan, Bahrain, Djibouti, Egypt, Eritrea, Ethiopia, Iran, Iraq, Israel, Jordan, Kuwait, Lebanon, Palestine (West Bank & Gaza), Saudi Arabia, Sudan, Syria, Tunisia, Turkey, Yemen
South Asia	Bangladesh, Burma, India, Pakistan, Sri Lanka
East Asia	Cambodia, China, Laos, Vietnam
Asia-Pacific Rim	East Timor, Indonesia, Japan, Korea, Malaysia, Philippines, Thailand
Sub-Saharan Africa	Angola, Burundi, Congo, Guinea, Kenya, Liberia, Mozambique, Namibia, Nigeria, Sierra Leone, South Africa, Tanzania, Zimbabwe

Lebanon, Saudi Arabia, and Greece, which either sponsor, finance, or knowingly shelter terrorist groups, are also not listed. Ironically, in forging a coalition to support the War against Terrorism, Washington enlisted such terrorist supporters as Iran, Libya, Pakistan, Saudi Arabia, Sudan, Syria, and Yemen. Beyond the military expedience of seeking support from these states, the position of Washington is that coalition building provides an opportunity to wean some of them away from the support of terrorism. Libya, Yemen, and Sudan have already committed themselves to doing so.

Syria, however, while joining the coalition, refused to end its sponsorship of Damascus-based radical Palestinian terrorist groups or the Iranian-supported Hizbollah, whose headquarters are in Lebanon's Beka Valley. Saudi Arabia also had until recently shown little appetite for cracking down on the various Saudi financial channels that finance terrorism, nor have its rulers any intention of changing a fundamentalist Islamic school system that indoctrinates youngsters from their earliest age with hatred for the United States and other "Western infidels" (including, of course, Israel). Iran condemned the attacks of September 11, but refused to provide U.S. and allied aircraft access to its air space. This despite its bitter opposition to the Sunni Taliban regime.

For a global war on terrorism to succeed, states that support or turn a blind eye to it will have to be pressured to change their behavior or be isolated by the world community. Collective world action is required to address the easy availability of communications, financial instruments, and weaponry to the perpetrators, as well as the economic and political conditions that breed terrorism.

The multilateral approach taken by the United States in its war against the Taliban and bin Laden's al Qaeda has enlisted not only most nations of the Maritime World, but also Russia, China, and Muslim nations. Self-preservation is an imperative for every sovereign state. A state's own vulnerability to terrorism, as well as its desire for economic support and trade with the economically advanced countries of the world, are incentives to act against terrorism.

Since September 11, 2001, some states that sponsor or harbor terrorists have announced a change of direction. With the defeat of the Taliban and the breakup of bin Laden's network, more are likely to follow suit. This is a hopeful sign in the long-term campaign against global terrorism, provided that the United States stays the course in leading the effort, once its objectives in Afghanistan have been realized.

Notes

1. B. Liddell Hart, "The Russo-German Campaign," in *The Red Army*, ed. B. Liddell Hart (New York: Harcourt, Brace, 1956), 100–126.

2. Andrew J. Pierre, *The Global Politics of Arms Sales* (Princeton: Princeton University Press, 1982), 256–62.

3. Paul H. Nitze, Leonard Sullivan Jr., and the Atlantic Council Working Group on Securing the Seas, *Securing the Seas* (Boulder, Colo.: Westview, 1979), 31–118.

4. Daniel A. Korn, *Ethiopia, the United States and the Soviet Union, 1974–1985* (London: Croom Helm, 1986), 23–47.

5. Paul Kennedy, *The Rise and Fall of the Great Powers* (New York: Random House, 1987), 384.

6. Peter Trubowitz, *Defining the National Interest* (Chicago: University of Chicago Press, 1998), 225–34.

7. Zbigniew Brzezinski, *Out of Control: Global Turmoil on the Eve of the Twenty-First Century* (New York: Charles Scribner's Sons, Macmillan, 1993), 181–231; Robert Kaplan, *The Coming Anarchy: Shattering the Dreams of the Cold War* (New York: Random House, 2000), 3–57, 169–85; Samuel P. Huntington, "The Clash of Civilizations," in *The Clash of Civilizations? The Debate* (New York: Council on Foreign Relations, Simon and Schuster, 1996), 12–25; Huntington, *Clash of Civilizations?*, 56–67; John Lukacs, *The End of the Twentieth Century and the End of the Modern Age* (New York: Ticknor and Fields, 1993), 242–91.

8. State Department, *Patterns of Global Terrorism—2000* (Washington, D.C., Counter-terrorism Office, 2001).

CHAPTER 5

North and Middle America

Five major power centers—the United States, the European Union, Japan, Russia, and China—dominate the world geopolitical scene. The capacities, needs, and historic associations of each of these centers shape their respective geostrategic and geographical outlooks and policies. As the cores of these centers change demographically, economically, or politically, so do their strategic policies.

Events of the past half century attest to the dynamic character of core areas. Those of the United States, the European Union, and Japan have expanded geographically and been transformed economically. Russia's core has contracted geographically because of its loss of Ukraine, and it has collapsed economically. China's "Golden Coast" has developed into a global manufacturing and high-tech powerhouse to overshadow its older, antiquated northern heavy-industry core. These changes provide insights into the basis for past and present global power relations and are also harbingers of future geopolitical structures and interactions.

The United States

The five power centers have forged the world's three geostrategic realms, while holding sway over the geopolitical regions within which they are located. The United States, and the North and Middle American geopolitical region within which it is located, will be discussed first. As the world's sole remaining superpower, the United States is uniquely suited to leading the Trade-Dependent Maritime Realm, because of its central location within that realm. Its Atlantic and Pacific geopolitical positions enable it to link the Maritime European and Asia-Pacific Rim geopolitical regions. Moreover, the United States is the only major power possessing both a highly advanced Maritime sector and a fully developed Continental Interior.

GEOPOLITICAL FEATURES

The geopolitical features of the United States include its Historic Core, Current Political Capital(s), Ecumene (area of economic and population concentration), Effective National

Figure 5.1   North and Middle America: Major Geopolitical Features

Territory (ENT), Empty Areas, and Boundaries. The structural patterns laid down by these features provide the basis for analyzing the interrelationships between geography and politics in the United States.

Historic Core

Bostonians are wont to claim Massachusetts as the Historic (Nuclear) Core of the United States, on the basis of Faneuil Hall (the scene of revolutionary meetings), the Boston Massacre, and the Boston Tea Party. Most scholars, however, accord Philadelphia the status of the Historic Core around which the United States was organized. Independence Hall was the scene of the Declaration of Independence in 1776 and the meeting place of the Continental Congress and the Constitutional Convention. Moreover, Philadelphia served as the new nation's first capital.

Whether the honor goes to Massachusetts or Pennsylvania, the birthplace of the revolutionary American state was in the northeastern and middle colonies, not the plantation South. It was among the small merchants and farmers of the colonies that lay along the northeastern coast that the unique American state ideas were formulated—freedom, individual liberty, religious tolerance, and egalitarianism.

Political Capital

With the establishment of the Union, the question of where to locate the new federal capital had to be addressed. There were other candidates to be the capital, but the debate was resolved in favor of what is now Washington, a site that would serve as "neutral ground" between the northern and southern states. The site lay on the fall line of the Potomac River, nearly equally accessible to North and South, and only about fifty-five miles south of the Mason-Dixon line. It was hoped that the new capital would help to bridge the differences between the urbanizing, manufacturing North and the rural, slaveholding South. In the end, however, it was not the geography of the capital that would assure the unity of the nation, but the Civil War.

The federal capital was laid out in 1790, first occupied by Congress a decade later, and became coincident with the District of Columbia in 1878. It is now far from the geographical population center of the country. Moreover, it does not house all of the federal government buildings, which sprawl into nearby Maryland and Virginia, where most federal employees live. Today, the majority of the city's 600,000 inhabitants are black Americans, many of whom are poorly housed, jobless, and impoverished.

For years, the citizens of the district have clamored for political "independence." They have won the right to vote in presidential elections and elect their mayor and city council, but have only a nonvoting delegate in the Congress, which also reviews the council's annual budget. The federal government maintains control over its own buildings, and the district's attempts to gain statehood and voting representation in Congress have failed.

It is ironic that the most prosperous nation in the world has a national capital where the gap between rich and poor is so great. If the capital is to play a new "bridging" role, reflecting the egalitarian ideas of its founding fathers, it is not geographical location that can provide the answer, but socioeconomic and political action.

Ecumenes

At the close of World War II, the U.S. ecumene extended along the Atlantic seaboard from southern New England to Washington, D.C., and westward across New York State and Pennsylvania in two prongs—along the Great Lakes to Detroit and then Chicago, and from Pittsburgh across the southern parts of Ohio, Indiana, and Illinois to St. Louis.

Over the past half century, this ecumene has filled in and expanded, and the California ecumene has emerged. The older ecumene now extends along the northeastern megalopolis from southern Maine and New Hampshire through Virginia and into the North Carolina piedmont. There, two major prongs have developed. One is the research triangle of Raleigh-Durham-Chapel Hill, a major high-tech, pharmaceutical, medical, and scientific center. The other is Charlotte, a leading national financial headquarters city and air transport hub. The southward growth of this ecumene is likely to soon move across the South Carolina and Georgia piedmont to Greater Atlanta.

The economic and population core region has also spread westward from Chicago to the Milwaukee-Madison area of Wisconsin; northward from Buffalo and Detroit to merge with the Canadian ecumene that runs along the northern shores of Lakes Ontario and Erie; and southward from Cincinnati along the lower Ohio Valley to Louisville and then west to St. Louis. Nashville and Memphis are exclaves that may soon be included within the core region. Much of the industrial vitality of the older ecumene has been sapped by the decline of textile and shoe manufacturing in the northeast, as well as by the collapse of heavy industry and the emergence of the "Rust Belt" of western New York and Pennsylvania and the Midwest.

The second ecumene is southern and central California. It extends from San Diego to Los Angeles and Santa Barbara. After a gap along the coast, much of which is taken up by National Forest Service lands and military reservations, the region connects to Silicon Valley (the high-tech hardware and software industry center extending from San Jose to Palo Alto to San Mateo) and then to San Francisco-Oakland. From there, it follows eastern and northeastern prongs into the Central Valley to Sacramento. Phoenix, Arizona, is an exclave of the California region. In addition to being the hub of a rich irrigation agricultural region and a leading center for tourism and recreation, its high-tech and aerospace industries are spillovers from California centers.

An information age view of the dual ecumenes is that their growth and prosperity has in recent years been spurred by two poles—California's Silicon Valley and New York City's "Silicon Alley," the computer graphics and information center of the media age. With the increasing decentralization of high-tech and, in particular, software industries, the core areas are likely to extend their boundaries substantially.

Effective National Territory

The Continental United States does not lack for Effective National Territory (ENT). Approximately two-thirds of the country that is not taken up with its ecumenes is ENT. Within the ENT, Texas and the lower Mississippi Valley, much of the Pacific Northwest, and the eastern Great Plains are capable of absorbing substantial population growth, as their large cities and isolated industrial centers expand into the vast farmland acreage of rural America that is shrinking so rapidly. The ENT also includes the dry western Great Plains, which extend from the one hundredth meridian to the Rockies. They are used for extensive farming and ranching, and are underlain by vast petroleum and natural gas fields.

Empty Areas

Another major feature for the United States is its Empty Areas. Within the "lower forty-eight" states, the Empty Area covers approximately one million square miles from the Rocky Mountains west to the Sierra Nevadas and the Cascades, embracing mountains and deserts to the west of the 105th meridian. It includes the Mojave Desert; the Great Basin of Nevada, which extends into the Salt Lake Desert; and the semiarid to arid Colorado Plateau of Arizona and New Mexico. This Empty Area plays an important role in the defense strategy and economy of the nation. Militarily, the region provides vast spaces for bombing and missile ranges, weapons proving grounds, and nuclear test sites. Yucca Mountain, which is located within the Mojave Desert, ninety miles northwest of Las Vegas, was proposed as a national depository for the nuclear weapons wastes and spent fuels from the 104 U.S. nuclear reactors by the U.S. Department of Energy in February 2002. It remains to be seen whether the plan, which proposes opening the site by 2010, will be implemented in the face of opposition from local and environmental groups, including the governor of Nevada. White Sands Missile Range in south-central New Mexico, which is also a landing site for space shuttles, was the scene of the first atomic explosion in 1945. The spectacular scenery of the region is a major asset for its recreation and tourist industry, and such minerals as copper, coal, lignite, zinc, and nickel, along with petroleum, natural gas, and timber, strengthen the national economy.

The other Empty Area extends over most of Alaska (the total land area of the state is over 650,000 square miles). This Empty Area has considerable strategic and economic value. Alaska provides a military foothold overlooking the Arctic Ocean and hosts defense installations that provide surveillance over the North Pacific. Fort Greely in central Alaska, near Fairbanks, is the command center and testing ground for land-based interceptors designed to shoot down possible North Korean intercontinental ballistic missiles. Kodiak Island in south Alaska is another center for deploying antiballistic missile defenses. In addition, the Arctic North Slope near Prudhoe Bay, an inlet of the Arctic Ocean's Beaufort Sea, has become the most important petroleum producing area in the United States. The eight-hundred-mile oil pipeline from Prudhoe Bay to the port of Valdez on the Gulf of Alaska was completed in 1977. From there, oil is shipped to the continental United States via the Interior Passage, the narrow shipping lane between the coastal and offshore islands that connects Anchorage and the Gulf of Alaska via Prince Rupert Sound to the waters of British Columbia and Seattle.

The environmental hazards involved in using this waterway for shipping oil were dramatized in 1989, when the *Exxon Valdez* tanker ran aground in Prince Rupert Sound, creating the worst oil spill in U.S. history and causing severe damage to the Alaskan ecosystem. Efforts to exploit the natural gas and oil reserves of the Arctic National Wildlife Refuge farther inland have met with vigorous objections from environmentalists. As Prudhoe Bay production declines, the proponents of opening up the refuge to energy exploitation have gathered force.

Most of the state's population is located along the Gulf of Alaska, centering on Anchorage, with an outlying cluster in the south-central region around Fairbanks. Travel within the interior is mainly by air. However, an important strategic and economic land link is the Alaska Highway (or Alcan), the all-weather, graveled road that extends for 1,523 miles from Dawson Creek in British Columbia near the Alberta border to Fairbanks. It was built in the early 1940s as a joint U.S.-Canadian enterprise to supply American military forces in Alaska. Existing highways south of Dawson Creek linked the highway to the U.S.

Pacific Northwest and Midwest, while from Fairbanks the Alaskan road system connected it to Anchorage and the Gulf of Alaska. The Alcan route was critical in World War II in supplying U.S. military bases on the gulf, the Bering Sea, and the Aleutians, from which the Japanese attack on the Aleutian islands of Attu and Kiska were repelled.

The central and western Pacific represents another Empty Area for the United States, one that extends from islands in Polynesia to those in Micronesia. A most important American facility is the Kwajalein Atoll Missile Range—a Micronesian coral atoll in the Marshall Islands where intercontinental missile testing–launching pads and clusters of radars are located. The Marshalls became self-governing in 1979 under U.S. military protection, before being linked to the United States in "free association" seven years later. Bikini and Eniwetok, Marshall Island atolls two hundred and four hundred miles to the west of Kwajalein, were used by Washington as test sites for atomic and hydrogen weapons from 1946 to 1979. The military-strategic significance of Kwajalein was demonstrated once again in July 2001. The atoll served as the base for the testing of the new U.S. antiballistic missile defense system. One of its interceptor missiles succeeded in destroying a dummy nuclear warhead that had been launched from Vandenberg Air Force Base. Vandenberg, located on the Pacific coast, with Los Angeles to the south and the Mojave Desert to the east, may be regarded as the eastern anchor of a gigantic missile range, forty-six hundred miles wide, whose western anchor is Kwajalein.

International Boundaries and External Territories

The international boundaries of the United States with Canada and Mexico are mainly boundaries of attraction, not barriers. Between Canada and the Continental United States, the four-thousand-mile border (excluding Alaska, whose border with Canada extends another fifteen hundred miles) has been a model of peaceful accommodation for over a century and a half, despite its length and complexity. The western half follows an artificial line, the forty-ninth parallel, across mountains and plains. The Red River settlement of 1821 fixed the eastern half of this western boundary. In the Far West, the parallel was extended to Vancouver Island when Britain and the United States settled their dispute over the Oregon Territory.

The eastern part of the U.S.-Canada border is, for the most part, a water boundary that at its western end extends from the Lake of the Woods and the Great Lakes to the upper St. Lawrence. From there, it briefly runs along the forty-fifth parallel to mark the New York–Vermont border, takes a jog along New Hampshire's northern and Maine's northwestern ends, and then follows the St. John and St. Croix Rivers to Passamaquoddy Bay and the Bay of Fundy.

In a unique case of international comity, the boundary that was a fighting front between Britain and the United States in 1812 has evolved into today's unfortified border between the United States and Canada, across which peoples, goods, and ideas flow to the benefit of both countries. Border demarcation has not been uncomplicated, especially in the water areas, and minor adjustments continued to be made by many treaties and conventions until final delimitation in 1925.

The Alaskan boundary between the two nations extends for over fifteen hundred miles. Its northern half follows the 141st meridian from the Arctic Ocean through the Yukon region to British Columbia. The southern half follows the Coast Mountains between southeastern Alaska and British Columbia to the Washington State border. While both nations agreed that the boundary would follow the range's main watershed, its demarcation was complicated, since there is no single crest along which to draw that line.

What is remarkable about this international border of fifty-five hundred miles (including Alaska) is that the remaining disputes are so minor. They center around the precise locations of four maritime borders: the northern end of the Alaska-Canada border in the Beaufort Sea; the Dixon Entrance, between Alaska's southernmost islands and Prince Rupert in British Columbia; the Strait of Juan de Fuca, between Vancouver Island and the northern tip of the state of Washington; and, on the Atlantic side, Machias Seal Island, at the southern end of the Bay of Fundy, on which Canada operates a lighthouse.

The U.S.-Mexican border was established in 1848 by the Treaty of Guadalupe Hidalgo, which ended the Mexican War. This confirmed the U.S. annexation of New Mexico, Utah, and Spanish Upper California. The southernmost strip of this U.S. region was acquired later, via the Gadsden Purchase of 1853. The eastern sector of the 2,075-mile boundary follows the Rio Grande for approximately one thousand miles, from twenty miles north of El Paso to Brownsville at the Gulf of Mexico. The western portion of the border extends from the Rio Grande to the Pacific along artificial lines between New Mexico, Arizona, and California and the Mexican states of Chihuahua, Sonora, and Baja California. While for the most part the boundary traverses semiarid or desert lands, it also cuts across the heavily irrigated farm areas of the Imperial Valley and the lower Colorado River.

The boundary delimitation of the Rio Grande presented problems because the 1848 treaty defined the line as following the center of the normal channel. Since the river was subject to continuous shifting as a result of flooding, there was continuing dispute until 1933, when it was resolved that the deepest continuous channel, the *thalweg,* would become the agreed-upon boundary. Over the decades, the U.S.-Mexico International Boundary Commission has taken responsibility for straightening and stabilizing the river. In addition, the two countries signed a water-sharing pact in 1945, and in 1968 settled their dispute over the location of the border at El Paso.

At the western end, in southern California, where the boundary ran through a heavily populated area, it was completely remarcated between 1891 and 1896. However, wrangling over the use of a canal that had passed through Mexican territory was only resolved when the eighty-mile All-American Canal was built entirely within U.S. territory (1934–40) to tap the waters of the Colorado River.

Off the North American mainland, the United States has two territorial disputes in the Caribbean. Haiti claims U.S.-owned Navassa Island, a tiny islet located between Haiti and Jamaica that once contained guano deposits that have long been mined out and is now used only for its lighthouse. A far more serious dispute is over the U.S. base at Guantánamo Bay. The site covers forty-five square miles at the southeastern end of Cuba. Leased to the United States in 1903, it has become a source of considerable tension between the two countries since Cuba sought its return in 1960 and refused to accept the annual token lease rent.

Another growing source of tension is the island of Vieques, off the eastern coast of Puerto Rico. Its use by the U.S. Navy as a bombing range has sparked considerable local opposition.

The status of the U.S. Trust Territories in the Pacific Ocean has undergone significant change in recent years. In 1986, the Northern Mariana Islands became a commonwealth in political union with the United States. In the same year, the Federated States of Micronesia signed a Compact of Free Association with the United States, as did the Republic of the Marshall Islands. Palau entered into a similar compact in 1994.

Elsewhere in the Pacific, a number of islands remain dependencies (as do the U.S. Virgin Islands in the Caribbean). These include Guam, Midway, and Wake. Guam is by far the most strategically important to Washington. Part of the Marianas chain, Guam is closest to the Philippines and the rest of the Asia-Pacific Rim and possesses major air and naval bases that provide the United States with long-range reach capacity. Wake has both a military and a commercial air base, Midway a military base.

American Samoa remained under U.S. control when the New Zealand Trust Territory of Western Samoa gained its independence in 1990, even though the U.S. eastern portions of the island chain had long ago lost their strategic value. Pago Pago had served the American navy as a fishing and repair base, but was closed in 1951, when administration of the dependency was transferred to the U.S. Department of the Interior. There is now little reason for Washington to retain control of this eastern half of the Samoan chain, whose islanders derive their livelihood from tourism and tuna canning.

THE FOUR STAGES OF U.S. GEOPOLITICAL DEVELOPMENT

The pace of settlement and landscape use in the United States has shaped its geopolitical postures in world and hemispheric affairs. Four successive stages mark the development of the U.S. geopolitical posture: (1) the Maritime, (2) the Continental, (3) the Continental-Maritime, and (4) the Maritime-Continental.

Table 5.1   Four Stages of U.S. Geopolitical Development

| Stages | Inland | | Geopolitical | |
	Time Period	Transport	Power	Orientation
Maritime	Colonial to 1803 (Louisiana Purchase)	River, road, horse	Manual, watermills	Securing Atlantic seaboard
Continental	1803 to 1898 (Spanish-American War)	Rail, river, canal, horse	Coal, watermills	Continental unification and expansion
Continental-Maritime	1898 to World War II outbreak	Rail, highway	Oil, gas, coal, hydroelectric power (penstock turbines), internal combustion engine	Continental development; Caribbean and Pacific expansion
Maritime-Continental	1941 to present	Highway, rail, air	All of above, plus nuclear	U.S. Maritime Ring and global reach

The Maritime Stage

This stage prevailed from colonial times through the Revolutionary War and the Louisiana Purchase of 1803. Expansion of the English colonies from their coastal and piedmont bases involved a series of campaigns against the French and the Indians in the mid-eighteenth century (1745–63). The western limits of colonial settlement were imposed by the Proclamation of 1763, in which the British established a boundary to separate the English settlers from the Indians, with whom the British sought to develop stable relations. Through this edict, Britain tried to put a halt to colonial expansion west of the headwaters of streams flowing into the Atlantic.

The boundary was a watershed line that followed the Appalachians from their southernmost point in northwest Georgia north to the Allegheny Mountains of central Pennsylvania, to northern New York, and then to the Green Mountains of Vermont. This line was substantially breached, both before and after 1763, as settlers pushed out to the Ohio, Tennessee, and Kentucky Rivers.

In the aftermath of the Revolutionary War, the inexorable drive of the settlers in the "western lands" pushed the frontier of settlement to the Mississippi, overrunning the Indian lands that had been set aside by the British. Settlement also penetrated the area north of the Ohio to the Upper Great Lakes, which had been claimed by Britain as an extension of Quebec, but which was ceded to the United States at the end of the Revolutionary War.

Despite the ferment revolving around the westward expansion of the "Old Frontier," the weight of population and economic activities remained along the East Coast and piedmont. Whether acting in concert with Britain or apart from it during the years that led to separation and independence, most Americans had an Atlantic seaboard outlook. Commerce, the main factor in the economy, was based on the export of such agricultural commodities as tobacco, rice, cotton, food grains, cattle, fish, and furs. The imports were manufactured articles from England and sugar, molasses, and rum from the West Indies. For most Americans of this era, therefore, the colonies, and then the fledgling states of the new nation, were part of an exploitable world whose main concern was to secure the Atlantic seaboard.

The Continental Stage

Highlights of the Continental stage were the Louisiana Purchase of 1803, the Lewis and Clark expedition of 1803–1806, and the War of 1812. For nearly a century afterward—until the Spanish-American War—the focus was on conquest of the Continental Interior, to expand the nation's borders from "sea to shining sea." The era was touched off by the purchase from France of a vast area from the Mississippi to the Rocky Mountains and from the Gulf of Mexico to British-controlled North America. The 828,000 square miles thus acquired doubled the land area of the United States and whetted the appetite for more.

Results of the War of 1812 and annexation of Spanish-held West Florida in 1821 sealed U.S. control over its Atlantic and Great Lakes frontiers, as well as over most of the Gulf of Mexico's northern coastlands. Britain's war strategy had included a plan to seize the Mississippi and block the expansion of its former colony into the Continental Interior. The strategy called for troops to seize New Orleans and move upstream to meet forces coming southward from Canada. It failed when Andrew Jackson's sharpshooters repelled the best of the Duke of Wellington's seasoned veterans at the Battle of New Orleans, which ironically took place two weeks after the signing of the Treaty of Ghent and the technical end of the war.

In 1818, the United States and Great Britain came to an agreement over the Continental Interior boundary west of the Great Lakes. The line ran westward from the Lake of the Woods along the forty-ninth parallel to the crest of the Rocky Mountains. As a result of the accord, most of the Red River Valley of the North, south of Winnipeg, became U.S. territory. From the Rockies, the boundary extended along the parallel to the Pacific coast, but excluded Vancouver Island. This line assured U.S. ownership of the middle and lower Columbia River basin.

In the South, the United States gained full control of the northern Gulf Coast when Texas joined the Union in 1845, after American settlers had driven Mexican troops from the territory and declared their independence in 1836. The treaty that followed the U.S.-Mexican War (1846–48) confirmed the Rio Grande as the southern border of Texas. The new boundary ran westward from the Rio Grande at the New Mexico line to the Colorado River, turned to the Colorado's junction with the Gila River, and then followed west to the Pacific just south of San Diego. Thus, all of Upper California was ceded to the United States, while Baja (Lower) California remained within Mexico. Two years later, California entered the Union. Unification of the land from sea to sea had to await the Union victory in the Civil War and the building of the transcontinental railroad system. The earlier system, based on roads, the Erie Canal, and the Ohio-Mississippi-Missouri Rivers, affected only the eastern half of the country and was a slower system of transportation. Construction of the continent-spanning rail line, which had been interrupted by the Civil War, was completed in 1869. On May 10 of that year, the Union Pacific, starting from its Omaha base, met the Central Pacific, which had originated in Sacramento.

Each line had to contend with daunting engineering challenges. Employing Irish laborers, the Union Pacific had to traverse the Laramie and Wasatch ranges after crossing the plains. The Central Pacific, which had brought in Chinese laborers from Canton (Guangzhou), had to climb across the Sierra Nevadas before traversing the deserts of Nevada and Utah. When the two lines met at Promontory Summit, Utah, on the eastern face of the Rockies, development of the interior of the country could progress full scale. Settlements, farming, ranching, mines, commerce, and then industry followed the east-west continental spine, and then the north-south railroads that became linked to it.

In 1893, after nearly a century of efforts by pioneers to settle the Continental Interior, Frederick Jackson Turner called attention to the passing of the American frontier, based upon his evaluation of the 1890 census.[1] Only Utah, Oklahoma, New Mexico, and Arizona remained to be admitted to the Union, and all these states were admitted between 1896 and 1912. Elsewhere on the continent, Alaska, which had been purchased from Russia in 1867, also awaited statehood, but did not receive it until 1959, when Hawaii was also added. The march across the Continental Interior was fueled by the belief of many Americans that it was their "Manifest Destiny" to expand—by force where necessary.

While the Continental outlook dominated this period, there was also a strong belief, held over from the earlier Maritime stage, that American vessels had the right to ply the high seas without interference. This maritime focus led to efforts to strengthen the navy, as well as to develop the merchant marine to carry the increasing products of the American economy in U.S. vessels. After trade wars with Britain had taken a heavy toll, the United States successfully promoted reciprocal trade policies with England, the West Indies, and Canada. But this drive for freedom of the seas and expansion of international trade was secondary to and derived from the overriding quest to unlock the riches of the Continental Interior and achieve self-sufficiency in agriculture, mining, and manufacturing.

In the development of the Interior, the agricultural revolution came first, as settlers moved into the Midwestern prairies and, in the latter part of the century, into the Great Plains beyond. Construction of the Erie Canal in 1825 was a major stimulus for the region's first stage of development. This was soon followed by a railroad-building boom that connected Chicago to the rest of the nation and provided manufacturing with efficient access to raw materials and markets. By the time of the Civil War, manufacturing in the Northeast and Midwest already equaled farm production in those areas in value. The war itself gave a tremendous boost to the intensification of industrialization in these regions, and by the 1880s the United States had emerged as the world's largest producer of steel and farm machinery.

The Continental-Maritime Stage

The next stage, the Continental-Maritime stage, was foretold by the German geographer Friedrich Ratzel. Speculating on the relationship between Continentality and Maritimity, he saw the two elements as complementary. To Ratzel and his American disciple, Ellen Churchill Semple, the conquest of the Interior was made possible by the unifying qualities of the Mississippi drainage system, which had oceanic outlets. The vast North American Continental Interior could be viewed, not in land-oriented isolation, but in a Maritime-connected framework.[2]

This stage began with the Spanish-American War of 1898. Victory in that conflict enabled the United States to project its influence into the Caribbean and the Pacific in pursuit of an expanded version of Manifest Destiny. The era ended with the transitional decades between World Wars I and II.

The Continental-Maritime era was marked both by continuing development of the Interior and outward reach for foreign markets, raw materials, and political influence. Railroad trackage increased from 52,922 miles in 1870 to a peak of 266,381 miles in 1916, to serve both grain exports and new manufacturing centers. (Since World War II, trackage has decreased so precipitously that only 148,000 miles of class I lines now exist.) The railroads enabled agriculture and industry to expand. As a result, farm acreage increased by over one hundred million acres between 1900 and 1920. In addition, Chicago strengthened its position as "Second City" (with New York City the acknowledged "first"), attracting large-scale heavy industry and pioneering American architectural forms that included the skyscraper. Detroit became a leading producer for the military in World War I and St. Louis, already America's fourth largest city by the turn of the century, expanded its position as a center for transportation, commerce, and diversified industry.

This urban growth depended to a considerable extent upon access to a large labor pool, much of which came from new immigrants from Central and Eastern Europe. From 1900 to 1920, 14.5 million immigrants were admitted to the United States, bringing the foreign-born population to 14 percent of the 106 million total. This was a peak percentage never again to be exceeded, as the proportion declined to 4.7 percent in 1970, before rising since then to approximately 10 percent.

Washington's involvement in regional and global politics began with the Spanish-American War and came to full fruition with entry into World War I on the Allied side. However, this involvement did not come at the expense of the focus on the Continental Interior. Instead, it accelerated development of the Interior. World War I stimulated production of corn in the Midwest and wheat in the eastern Great Plains. It also gave considerable impetus to the industrial growth of Chicago and other interior centers.

With the decisive role of the United States in the Allied victory and Woodrow Wilson's rallying cry for the United States to "make the world safe for democracy," it was widely assumed that the global/maritime orientation would displace the domestic focus. This was not to be. While Wilson took the lead in establishing the League of Nations, the U.S. Senate in 1919 refused to approve the Treaty of Versailles, including U.S. membership in the League. This turn inward continued with the strict limitations that were imposed on immigration in 1924 and the Smoot-Hawley Tariff bill in 1930, which raised barriers to world trade. The distancing of Washington from global affairs was reinforced by the Second and Third Neutrality Acts, of 1936 and 1937.

This spirit of isolationism and Continentality continued the focus on the Interior. Flush with the farm prosperity of World War I and the economic boom that followed, the nation converted an additional hundred million acres in the southern Great Plains to cropland in the 1920s. Aided by the large-scale introduction of tractors and other mechanical equipment, this expansion took place in the area from the Texas Panhandle, western Oklahoma, and western Kansas, to eastern New Mexico and eastern Colorado. This raised the total U.S. farm acreage to 990 million in 1930. (It has remained fairly constant since then, amounting to 954 million acres in 1998.)

The postwar era of the 1920s also produced an industrial boom economy for the nation, based upon new techniques of mass factory production of consumer goods—home appliances, automobiles, trucks, and tractors. Most of this new production was centered in the Midwest. As a result, the region, which by 1870 had become the most populous in the United States owing to agricultural settlement, was now able to maintain its lead through the urbanization that accompanied industrialization. By 1920, Illinois, Ohio, Michigan, and Missouri ranked among the most populous states, and Chicago, Detroit, Cleveland, and St. Louis enhanced their positions as major metropolitan centers. Collapse of the U.S. stock market in 1929 triggered the Great Depression, which became worldwide by 1931 and led to overproduction and falling prices in the farm belt. Conditions were further aggravated by the Dust Bowl of 1934 and succeeding years—a product not only of wind and drought, but of soil erosion due to the stripping away of the natural grasslands through cultivation.

During the Depression, the nation had little energy to devote to external affairs. U.S. foreign trade dropped from $6.9 billion in 1930 to $4.3 billion in 1935. (The peak up to this time had been $13.5 billion in 1920, in the aftermath of World War I.) Rampant unemployment reached 25 percent and the displacement of the rural population was especially severe in the Interior. In the southern plains during the 1930s, the record heat, drought, and conversion of grasslands to wheat cultivation that had created the "Dust Bowl" produced a mass exodus. An estimated quarter of the plains populace, mainly tenant farmers known as "Okies" and cotton sharecroppers from the Mississippi Valley (the "Arkies"), pulled up stakes and migrated to California.

Although the emphasis during this stage was Continental, an important Maritime component also developed. Alfred Mahan was a vigorous proponent of the notion that the future of the United States was as a maritime power. In his view, the world was divided into two geopolitical frameworks—the Western or Maritime and the Oriental or Continental.[3] In such a framework, the United States was an outpost of European power and civilization, while its Pacific coastland and the mid-Pacific islands were simply extensions of Atlantic Europe. In keeping with this view, the "Manifest Destiny" of the United States was to expand into the Caribbean and the Pacific, with a canal across Panama serving as the strategic link between the two borders.

During the early twentieth century, Cuba was freed from Spanish rule and, under the Platt Amendment (1901), became a virtual U.S. protectorate. The Platt Amendment also provided for construction of a naval base at Guantánamo Bay. In addition, Spain ceded Puerto Rico to the United States, while in the Pacific they ceded the Philippines, Guam, and Wake Island. At the same time, the United States gained American Samoa through a treaty with Germany and Britain and established a naval base at Pago Pago. This Pacific presence was further expanded by the 1898 annexation of Hawaii, which became a territory two years later. Absorption of Hawaii came after three-quarters of a century of heavy U.S. investment in the sugar industry and the securing of U.S. naval rights to maintain a coaling and repair center at Pearl Harbor in 1887. The facility became a full-scale naval base after 1900.

In 1899 the United States took the initiative in promoting the "Open Door" trade policy in China. This move was designed to help the United States break into the European and Japanese spheres of influence that had been forced on China. For the most part, the success of the policy was limited because it was ignored by the major European powers, which continued to divide China into their own zones of trade, to the exclusion of American commercial activity. U.S. influence in the Caribbean was extended in 1903, when the United States obtained the right to build the proposed Panama Canal and lease the Canal Zone from newly independent Panama, whose successful insurrection against Colombia had been aided by the protective presence of an American warship. The canal was completed in 1914 and was held by the United States until returned to Panamanian control on December 19, 1999.

The United States invaded Haiti in 1915 to protect U.S. investments and properties in a military occupation that lasted until 1934. Another rationale for the invasion was fear that Germany would seize Haiti and threaten the security of the Panama Canal. The American Virgin Islands were purchased from Denmark in 1917.

Cuba, Haiti, and Panama were not the only Caribbean countries to feel the weight of U.S. military intervention. Protection of American corporate interest in bananas, sugar, coffee, cotton, and tobacco in 1912 brought American marines into Honduras, Santo Domingo, and Nicaragua, where they remained for years. Troops were also sent into Mexico in 1914 and 1916.

Hegemony over the islands of the Caribbean and coastal Central America was justified by the Roosevelt corollary to the Monroe Doctrine, whereby President Theodore Roosevelt asserted that instability in a Latin American country might tempt European intervention and therefore justified preemptive military action. The Taft and Wilson administrations used this corollary extensively in intervening militarily and politically within the region, as did subsequent administrations during the 1920s and 1930s. Even after the United States renounced the corollary (the Clark Amendment, 1928) and President Franklin D. Roosevelt introduced the "Good Neighbor Policy," Washington continued to regard the region as its special preserve.

The American presidency itself is a reflection of the pull during this period between the Continental Interior and the Maritime interests of the United States. From the Spanish-American War to the outbreak of World War II, four of the eight presidents had their origins and power bases in the Continental Interior. Their terms for the most part were marked by inward-facing national concerns. The other four presidents were northeast-based and served during interventionist periods.

The Maritime-Continental Stage

This stage began with the outbreak of World War II, as the United States geared up industrially and politically for the global war effort. During the war and into the 1950s and 1960s, the Continental Interior maintained its economic and political parity with the coastal regions of the country. The American manufacturing belt—from Buffalo, Cleveland, and Pittsburgh to Ohio, Indiana, Illinois, and Michigan—which had been the backbone of the defense industry, gained access to the Atlantic when the Saint Lawrence Seaway was opened in 1959. This belt served as the backbone of the U.S. defense industry. By the end of World War II, its steel mills had produced eighty million tons, or 50 percent, of annual world production. With the opening of the seaway, this figure rose to over 130 million tons in 1965, as heavy industry produced motor vehicles, machine tools, rubber, glass, building materials, and a wide variety of appliances, such as washing machines and televisions sets. Most of these came from the factories of the Midwest.

The prosperity of the Interior was augmented by the grains and beef of the prairies and astern plains, which met the needs of both growing domestic consumption and the recovering economies of Maritime Europe and Japan. Adding to the strength of the Interior's economic base were the petroleum and natural gas of Texas and Oklahoma; the coal of Wyoming, Montana, and Utah; and the timber of the Upper Great Lakes.

This growth period seemed to confirm the doctrines that the "Continentalists" of the midcentury had promoted. Historian James Malin, who drew much of his inspiration from the writings of Frederick Jackson Turner, held that the latter's "closed space" theory was based upon the Continental agricultural realm of the nineteenth-century United States, and held little relevance to the urban industrial scene of the twentieth century. Instead, he argued, the Continental Interior held the same wealth of raw materials for industry that it had held for agriculture previously. In Malin's analysis, the open space of the interior would therefore still be the dominant factor in American life.

Malin drew the picture of a central power axis running north to south from Winnipeg to Dallas-Fort Worth, with "power potential distributed along the length of the axis" and the effective center shifting to fit changing requirements. He predicted that industry would migrate deeper into the Interior and that population distribution would accompany the shift.[4] According to this hypothesis, population would move toward the supply of food and toward lightweight metals, petroleum and gas, alloys, plastics, and hydropower, which all lay in the interior. Moreover, north-south mobility would be enhanced by the expansion of major commercial air centers along the central axis.

Giving support to the Midwestern isolationist forces of the interwar period, Malin described the United States as a landmass state that should not extend its commitments across the Pacific, the Atlantic, or south of the Amazon. He felt that the postwar world would hold room for seven or eight major powers—North America, Japan, China, Russia, Germany, Latin Europe, and the British Empire.

An expanded view of the geopolitical significance of the Continental Interior was offered by the geographer George Cressey in 1945.[5] He hypothesized that America had become the real Heartland of the world. Redefining Mackinder's Heartland as a "World Citadel," he argued that North America, not Eurasia, contained this citadel because the core of North America was the one area in the world that possessed all the advantages of interior space, size, and resources, and access to the sea.

Alexander de Seversky, basing his theories on the supremacy of air power in world affairs, felt that the dominance of the United States over the rest of North and South America was balanced by Soviet air superiority over Africa and South Asia.[6] The area of mutual vulnerability for both powers was the North Pole. He argued that superiority in intercontinental bombers and missiles would prevail in an all-out war and that the basis for achieving such superiority lay in the continued development of the U.S. Interior. Indeed, he placed the future center of American power in Kansas.

Theories of the primacy of the Continental Interior were soon to be overtaken by new economic and demographic realities. Starting as early as the 1960s, industry, population, and markets began to grow outside the Interior. Even though the St. Lawrence Seaway had provided the Great Lakes manufacturing area with ocean-going transportation access and attached it geographically to the country's ocean-oriented maritime coastal ring, it could not retain its industrial monopoly. By the beginning of the 1980s, plant closings or consolidations, along with accompanying job losses, foreshadowed the transformation of the Midwest into a "Rust Belt." When new technologies were developed for the steel and motor vehicle industries, most served to spur industrial growth outside the traditional centers of the Great Lakes and the Ohio Valley.

The impact of deindustrialization was particularly devastating for the steel and motor vehicle economy of Michigan, Ohio, Indiana, and Illinois. U.S. raw-steel production dropped from its 1965 peak of 131 million tons to a low of 88 million tons two decades later, due to both the inefficiencies of the older American steel plants and the coastal locations of new industrial centers that used imported steel. With greater efficiencies and the introduction of new technologies, U.S. output rose to 109 million raw tons of steel in 1998, only to drop once more, to 95 million tons, in 2001, when foreign producers in countries like Japan, Russia, South Korea, Brazil, and Ukraine provided approximately one-third of the needs of American industry. The Bush administration introduced tariffs of up to 30 percent in 2002 to arrest the erosion of the domestic steel industry, causing an angry outcry from foreign producers. The possibilities that this action may provoke countermeasures against U.S. exports, as well as the doubt that tariff protection will ultimately save the large, out-of-date, integrated American steel operations, suggest that the decline of the industry has not yet run its course.

Challenged by Japan, which in 1980 took the lead over the United States in world motor vehicle production, the U.S.-based industry surged back in subsequent years so that by the mid-1990s its production represented 25 percent of world total, compared to Japan's 20 percent. The reasons for the resurgence were that Japanese and European manufacturers became market oriented and established production facilities within the continental United States. Most of the new assembly and parts plants that have been built, by both foreign and American-owned producers, have been located in California, the coastal South, and the Mid-South (Tennessee and Kentucky), not in the Continental Interior. As a result of these locational shifts, Detroit's role as the world center for the motor industry has been considerably weakened, despite the fact that U.S. vehicular production more than doubled after 1970, to thirteen million units in 1999. Considerable vehicle assembly and parts manufacturing capacity also has been moved to Canada and Mexico by the U.S. auto industry. This began with the U.S.-Canada Auto Pact of 1965 and accelerated with the establishment of the North American Free Trade Agreement (NAFTA). Imports from Canada and Mexico now account for half of the 4.6 million vehicle imports to the United States.

In addition, the Midwest experienced a drastic decline in defense spending, which had supported much of its industrial base during the Vietnam War. Not only did outlays for national defense decline from 42 percent of the federal budget in 1970 to 15 percent in 1999, but the nature of defense procurement shifted heavily from the tanks and armaments made in Michigan and neighboring states to products made in the Atlantic, Gulf, and Pacific sections of the Maritime Ring—for example, aircraft, electronic weapons systems, and ships. In 1996, for example, awards to states in the Continental Interior and the Great Lakes amounted to approximately $22 billion, or 20 percent of all Department of Defense contracts. California alone received over $18 billion, Texas and Virginia received approximately $9 billion each, and Florida received nearly $6 billion. Michigan's awards, in contrast, amounted to only $1.26 billion. Continental state awards rose to $53 billion in 2001 (18 percent of a total defense budget of $300 billion).

There has also been a marked decline in petroleum production within the United States. Production dropped from 9.6 million barrels per day in 1970, representing over 20 percent of world production at that time, to 6.1 million barrels in 1996, under 10 percent of the world's output. While domestic production rose to 7.8 million barrels in 1999 as a result of OPEC (Organization of Petroleum Exporting Countries) oil price spikes, it fell once more, to 5.8 million barrels in 2001, representing a dependence upon imports for 60 percent of total consumption. The inability of the United States to implement a strong fuel conservation program suggests that this dependence is only likely to increase. Approximately 60 percent of these imports come from Canada, Mexico, and Venezuela, and another 20 percent come from Saudi Arabia and other Gulf States. Much of the remainder is imported from Nigeria and Angola, although Colombia and Ecuador also contribute. This combination of lower production and higher imports has further weakened the economy of the Interior and the Lower Great Lakes, as the petrochemical industry has shifted its location to the nation's ocean ports.

The Interior and the Great Lakes states have lost economic and political influence due to the changing nature of the agricultural sector. Since the output of the Interior states is three and one-half times that of the Midwestern ones that border the lakes, the impact has been greatest upon the former. Postwar farm production and productivity have increased owing to mechanization, application of fertilizers and pesticides, crop hybridization, and farm consolidation. During the same period, the farm population has declined drastically. In 1940, the farm populace represented 23 percent of the total U.S. population; in 1950 it represented 15 percent. By 1970, the figure had dropped to 5 percent, and it is now under 2 percent.

Farm population losses in the grain-growing Continental Interior have been especially heavy since the agriculture there is so highly mechanized and the labor input relatively minimal. With the help of low transportation costs, as a result of access to the St. Lawrence Seaway, and the growth of world market demand for food products, American agriculture has become increasingly export oriented. The United States has become the world leader in farm exports. In 1998, agricultural exports totaled $51 billion, two-thirds of which were in food and feed grains, oil seeds, soybeans, and animal products from the Interior and the Great Lakes/Midwestern states. Still, this represents only 8 percent of all U.S. exports.

In the face of its decline relative to the rest of the economy, the political leverage and influence of the Interior's farm bloc has been substantially reduced. The era of the fiercely independent American farmer, with roots in homesteading, has passed. Today's 1.6 million farmers, especially the very largest corporations, depend heavily on increasingly generous federal subsidies. Farm aid payments are made for keeping land out of agriculture, for drought relief, and for subsidies to large farm corporations to compete in overseas markets. In 2000, such payments amounted to $28 billion, nearly 60 percent of the total value of agricultural exports and 80 percent of the value of exports from the Continental Interior.

Federal agricultural policy has thus become more social policy than farm policy for the small producers, since its major aim appears to be to keep rural farmers afloat and stem farm abandonment. For the rural and small-town sectors of the Continental Interior, such economic dependence is a far cry from the former sturdy independence of rural America. It may be only a matter of time until the combination of congressional impatience and the desire of younger farm generations for a less precarious economic life will further reduce the rural character of the grain-growing Continental Interior. When that takes place, the political power remaining to the farm lobby will rest in the agricultural areas of the Maritime Ring, with the intensive fruit and vegetable-growing sectors of California, Texas, and Florida. These states already have powerful farm lobbies that enable California, in particular, to benefit from highly subsidized irrigation water.

THE MARITIME RING

What has shifted the balance away from Continentality and toward Maritimity in recent decades has been the dramatic growth of population, industry, services, and political power along the nation's coastal reaches. This geographical change has created, in effect, a Maritime Ring that surrounds and dominates the Continental Interior. Specialization has linked the parts of the Ring so that their various economic and political interest groups act in concert across regional lines, rather than dividing along such lines, as in the past. The ring also provides the United States with a central and interconnecting position in relation to the rest of the Trade-Dependent Maritime Realm—a geostrategic realm that includes two-thirds of the earth's water and land surface and one-third of its population.

Contrary to predictions of the Continentalists of days gone by, the use and value of space has been most marked within the highly urbanized and metropolitan Maritime Ring, where most of the population lives, and not within the Continental Interior. This is not to minimize the negative impact of overcrowding within the Ring. The pollution of urban environments is a serious problem, and the density of industrial operations directly contributes to smog and water contamination and has prompted many to relocate to the desert and mountain reaches of the western Interior. But a concerted effort by industry and local and state governments can ameliorate the problems, and federal pressures through the Environmental Protection Agency are beginning to show some positive results.

The Maritime Ring might well be described as the "United States of the Four Seas"—the Atlantic, the Gulf of Mexico, the Pacific, and the Great Lakes (since the 1959 opening of the St. Lawrence Seaway). These coastlands vary in many ways—climate, elevation, landforms, natural vegetation, agriculture, and minerals. But they are similar in very important features—dense population; high degree of urbanization; large number of usable ports and well-integrated land, sea, and air connections; strong concentration of manufacturing and services; tourism; and international trade.

Among the common physical elements are humidity, natural harbors, and the barrier effects of mountains, such as the Appalachians and the western ranges. Average annual rainfall for the Maritime Ring is over thirty inches (save in southwestern Texas and along the southern California coast). In most instances, the rainfall is over forty inches. Such pre-cipitation is adequate for the water needs of both urban centers and productive agricultural hinterlands. The best natural harbors occur along the highland-framed northeast and Pa-cific coasts, and where the coastal plain has been joined to the ocean through submer-gence—from Buzzards Bay to the James River. The South Atlantic, Gulf Coast, and Great Lakes have poorer natural harbors, which have required dredging and, in many cases, up-stream locations. Nonetheless, as we consider the ring in its entirety, we find that no sin-gle maritime state, except perhaps Mississippi, lacks a good deepwater port, be it natural or artificial.

While the mountains have not served as complete barriers between the seas and the In-terior, they have directed the alignment of land transportation lines along specific avenues. The Southeast Atlantic coast has poor overland connections with the Midwest. This has, in turn, given stronger impetus to north-south movement along the Atlantic seaboard. Where the Great Lakes and the Atlantic come closest together—the New York, New England, Penn-sylvania, and Maryland corridors—excellent east-west land links complement the traffic of the St. Lawrence Seaway. Because of the north-south trend of the West's mountain-desert-plateau reaches, land links between the Gulf and the Pacific Northwest coasts have been weak.

Complementary resources and products also help to unify the Maritime Ring. The sorts of materials that are interchanged include petroleum, natural gas, coal, forest prod-ucts, sulfur, cotton, copper, lead, zinc, phosphates, iron, steel, fruit, vegetables, dairy, beef, and poultry.

All of the states within the Maritime Ring have areas that are directly exposed to the open oceans, including those Great Lakes states that have gained access through the sea-way. These thirty maritime states account for well over 80 percent of the nation's mid–2002 population of approximately 281 million, and an even higher share of the country's urban populace. Nine of the ten states that achieved the largest absolute growth in popu-lation over the past two decades are Maritime Ring states, and nine of the ten largest met-ropolitan areas contain Maritime Ring ports. The Ring states account for over 90 percent of both the population and the value added by manufacturing.

Some of the larger cities and population concentrations that are oriented to the Mar-itime Ring are as much as 150 to 250 miles from the sea. Examples are the inner lowland cities of Texas, such as San Antonio and Dallas; the piedmont centers of Charlotte and At-lanta; and the "central place" cities and towns of the farm belt of the Great Lakes states, such as Columbus and Indianapolis. However, most of the Ring's population lives within a two-hour drive of open water in the coastal ocean and Great Lakes counties.

There are 673 counties defined by the U.S. National Oceanographic and Atmospheric Agency as having at least 15 percent of their land in a coastal watershed or interwatershed (interior watershed that leads to the open sea). These counties alone contain over 150 mil-lion people, or approximately 55 percent of the country's total population.

Growth of the Ring has been led in recent decades by the population explosions of California, Texas, and Florida. New York has slipped to third place among the most popu-lous states, with 19 million people, while there are nearly 34 million Californians and 21 million Texans. Florida's population has increased to 16 million. Today the South and Texas, most of whose populations live in the Maritime Ring, is the most populous region, with 35 percent of the nation's total.

Population growth of the Ring has been spearheaded by high-tech industry, as well as by immigration, retirement relocation, financial services, and tourism. Not all of the region has experienced such growth. There have been only moderate to almost no increases in the populations of Great Lakes states such as Michigan, Illinois, and Ohio, and in Pennsylvania and Connecticut. However, one must look to the county level to understand the impact of demographic decline. In their study of U.S. counties from 1990 to 1995, Richard Lonsdale and Clark Archer noted that 635 counties, out of a total of 3,141, lost population.[7] The great majority were within the Continental Interior—in the Great Plains, the Western corn belt, and Appalachia.

The demographic picture within the Interior is not one of across-the-board population stagnation. Nevada, Arizona, Colorado, Utah, and Idaho have experienced population growth. Much of the surge in Nevada and Arizona is a consequence of the spillover of high-tech industry from California, as well as the attractiveness of the environment to retirees. Colorado and Utah have also attracted high-tech industry, in addition to those who relocate to experience life in the "great outdoors." However, by far the greatest population increase has been experienced in the newer parts of the ecumenes—in the southeastern United States, Florida, Texas, and California—the American "Sunbelt."[8]

The growth of the western Interior, along with central city revival, has been cited by some as proof that the digital age has created a "new geography."[9] According to this view, the American landscape is undergoing profound change in scattered, small, uncrowded towns of this part of the Interior because high-technology industry and personnel are free of the older geographical constraints that have focused industry and population within the metropolitan portions of the ecumene. In fact, however, the digital age has done little to alter the geographical population patterns of the nation. Information-age, back-office customer centers in such states as South Dakota and Iowa have not brought major population growth to the Great Plains. And home-based software developers attracted to the uncrowded milieus of the western Interior are far less numerous than the retirees who have moved there.

Neither has the digital age been responsible for gentrifying the landscape of parts of older central cities. Instead, the time-honored banking, financial service, legal, and medical professions provide most of the jobs that draw the gentrifying class into these hubs.

For the most part, the high-tech growth takes place in the suburban metropolitan centers of the ecumenes, in their outliers such as Phoenix, Tucson, and Atlanta, and in independent metropolises such as Seattle-Portland, Salt Lake City-Provo, or Denver. These industries are attracted by the dense road, air, and rail networks; highly developed telecommunications infrastructures; skilled labor pools; the educational and cultural amenities of metropolitan life; and the advantages of industrial agglomeration. So powerful is the role played by the 319 largest U.S. metropolitan regions that their goods and services now account for 85 percent of the national GDP.

There is little likelihood that the digital age will change the overall patterns of the nation's population distribution. Certainly it has energized the national economy and either filled in vacant lands within metropolitan areas or helped to expand metropolitan boundaries. However, this by no means represents a "new geography." It is simply part of the ongoing process of metropolitanization that is tied to those geographical features that initially attracted manufacturing and commerce to favored locations. These centers were linked by transportation and communication networks, allowing them to grow into the continually expanding ecumenes of the country. Now their metropolitan outliers shape and reshape the American landscape.

Diversity of people is a major feature of the two U.S. ecumenes and the nation's ENT. The highly diverse religious, racial, and ethnic character of the ring was marked early on by the immigration from Ireland a century and a half ago and swelled by the immigration from southern and eastern Europe during the period that began in the 1880s and ended in the 1920s. With the loosening of immigration quotas in the 1960s, and especially in the past two decades, the ecumene has been refreshed by the infusion of immigrants from Latin America, Asia, Europe, and Africa. In 1990 the number of new legal immigrants was 1,586,000 and in 1991 it peaked at 1,827,000. While the numbers have since dropped, annual entries still total nearly one million legal immigrants (the figure was 916,000 in 1999) and an estimated 275,000 illegals. Current immigration figures do not include approximately seven million illegals, nearly half of whom are estimated to come from Mexico. All of this has contributed to a new demographic profile in which the non-Hispanic white population of the United States has decreased to 72 percent of the total of 281 million and continues to decrease.

The result of this massive immigration is that one out of every ten Americans is foreign born, a ratio that is beginning to reach toward the peak of the 1920s and early 1930s. In addition to Mexico, which has contributed nearly 30 percent of recent immigrants, the Philippines, China, Cuba, and Vietnam are other leading countries of origin. Throughout the Ring, vast numbers of newcomers now cluster within large and medium-sized cities and are developing new political power bases that are changing local, state, and congressional political maps.[10] Hispanics are now vying for political power with black populations in Los Angeles, Chicago, Newark, and New York. Arab Americans and South Asians are beginning to make an impact upon black-dominated Detroit. In New York City, blacks, Hispanics, and Asians are successfully challenging the old-line white-dominated machines, and Asians are also a growing force in such disparate areas as Seattle, San Francisco, and New Jersey.

This diversity has also brought contrasts in standards of living, educational levels, sociopolitical outlooks, and traditions, changing American society from a melting pot to a society that is challenged and reshaped by cultural pluralism, giving new meaning to democracy. The burden of absorbing less-advantaged immigrants is heavy, requiring massive investments in education, health, and welfare. But the historic results of such processes has been the refreshing and reenergizing of the nation as a whole. In addition, tens of thousands of immigrants to the United States bring with them the scientific and technological skills that enable them to make immediate contributions to national development.

With the rapid growth of racial and ethnic minorities, blacks and Hispanics now make up 12.5 percent each of the total U.S. population, with increasing waves of Asian immigrants bringing the total for Asians to 3.6 percent. Since the vast majority are concentrated within the Maritime Ring, they have added a far richer meaning to the concept of Maritimity than mere trade and climate. For America, Maritimity connotes continuing outreach to peoples and ideas from all parts of the world and feedback by the immigrant communities to the lands of their origin. This gives a unique cast to the role of the Ring as the nation's twenty-first-century frontier.

All along the Maritime Ring, changes that have taken place in the past two decades have reshaped the nature of America's global economic dominance. The location base of the industries that drive the economy is not determined by proximity to the raw materials of the Interior, but by proximity to markets and a highly educated labor force. Within the northeastern megalopolis, financial services, electronics, pharmaceuticals, and chemicals have become the engines of economic growth, spearheading the economic boom that began in March 1991, which by the turn of the century had become the nation's longest period of expansion. The economy took a nosedive in the years 2000 and 2001, however, as manufacturing slumped, the stock market took a sharp downturn, and unemployment rose sharply. Especially hard hit were the high-tech industries, although they remain a vital component of the northeast's economy and the most important engine of the region's future growth and development.

The South, too, participated in the surge. North Carolina, while still a major textile center, has emerged as a center also for high technology, insurance, and banking, and has become an integral part of the ecumene. South Carolina's main industries remain textiles and paper. However, the state has also attracted foreign-owned motor vehicle and tire plants. In addition, while its Savannah River nuclear site at Aiken no longer produces new nuclear materials, the plant still reprocesses nuclear wastes. In Georgia, telecommunications, aircraft assembly, motor vehicles, and finance are among the leading industries. Florida has added defense and space-oriented electronic plants to its tourist and agriculture base, and Cape Canaveral is the principal U.S. launching site for space satellites. In Alabama, manufacturing now exceeds agriculture in importance, with products that range from paper and chemicals to motor vehicles. Louisiana's rich crude oil and natural gas deposits are the basis for its important oil refining and petrochemical industries, but high-tech and auto industries are also located there. Even in Mississippi, long a rural and economically depressed state, manufacturing has overtaken agriculture as the leading economic sector, although the emphasis is upon traditional manufacturing activities such as apparel, furniture, and chemicals.

The most rapidly growing parts of the Maritime Ring have been Texas and the West Coast. In Texas, the aircraft industry that was established in World War II has been surpassed in importance by the high-tech computer and electronics industries in the Dallas-Fort Worth and Austin areas. Houston, the South's largest metropolitan area, is the center for the oil, petrochemical, and heavy industries of East Texas, as well as for finance, electronics, computer technology, and motor vehicle parts. The National Aeronautics and Space Administration's Lyndon B. Johnson Space Center has stimulated a vital aerospace industry. The port of Houston, which extends along the Houston Ship Channel, a fifty-mile dredged waterway to Galveston Bay, is the third busiest in the United States, and the focus for much of the country's Latin American trade.

Building upon its base as the nation's leading agricultural state, a center for the defense industry, and the world center for motion picture and television production, California, with its population of thirty-four million, has emerged as one of the world's industrial powerhouses. Were it an independent country, it would be ranked sixth among nations in GDP. Silicon Valley, stretching from San Jose to San Mateo, is the world's leading producer of semiconductors and software, even though the region was considerably depressed by high-tech industry cutbacks and closings during the recession of 2001–2002. Other key manufacturing activities are motor vehicle and other transportation modes, electronic equipment, machinery, and food processing. Washington, with Greater Seattle as its economic core, is the globe's leading aircraft producer and is a major focus for computer software, including the e-commerce industries, as evidenced by the presence of Microsoft, the world's most highly capitalized company.

California's growth in population and industry has not been an unmixed blessing, for it has created considerable pressures on the landscape. Land and housing costs in southern California and Silicon Valley have escalated and urban sprawl has placed a heavy strain on the transportation systems and other elements of infrastructure. With this growth, demand for electricity has increased rapidly. This demand, coupled with skyrocketing costs, has led to power shortages and created a financial crisis for California's electric companies, as well as the state treasury. While the state came to the aid of the utility companies in the spring of 2001, the long-range problem is far from resolved. California imports much of its power from out-of-state, gas-fired electric plants, which are an insufficient supply. The problem is compounded because drought in the Pacific Northwest has reduced the hydroelectric power surpluses that are usually transmitted to California.

Even in agriculture and mining, the Maritime Ring now substantially outstrips the Continental Interior in value of product. Maritime states contribute 63 percent of the nation's farm output ($130 billion versus $78 billion for the Continental Interior). California, by far the most important farm state in value of both crops and livestock, produces two and half times as much as Iowa, the leading Continental farming state. Agricultural production in Texas, the second-highest-ranking Maritime state, is one and half times that of Nebraska, the second leading Continental state. Reflecting the intensive nature of California's highly irrigated agriculture, the total acreage used there, 18.5 million acres, contrasts with Iowa's 47.5 million acres.

The bulk of the agricultural products grown in the Maritime Ring are consumed domestically, with only 25 percent being exported, the exports consisting mostly of fruit and vegetables, cotton, rice, and tobacco. The majority of U.S. agricultural exports are still the corn, animal feeds, soybeans, wheat, beef, and hides of the Continental Interior and the Great Lakes states. However, this is balanced by national imports of $36 billion of agricultural commodities, or nearly the same amount ($38 billion) exported by the Interior and the Great Lake states.

The intensive movement of goods by sea, along with the region's heavy dependence upon railroads and trucking, is a major feature of the Maritime Ring. Interstate 95, the fifteen-hundred-mile highway from Maine's Canadian border to Miami, Florida, is the primary artery that links the eastern seaboard and the most heavily trafficked route within the federal highway system. Traffic is especially heavy along the stretch from Portland, Maine, to North Carolina. Much of the sea traffic is local and intracoastal. Indeed, of the tonnage handled by the fifty busiest ports in 1997, 58 percent of the total traffic was domestic. On the whole, the goods that are moved by land or water within the Maritime Ring far exceed the movement of products between the Ring and the Continental Interior, reflecting the complementary nature of the trade that takes place within the highly specialized sections of the U.S. seaboards. National political power, as measured by population concentration, is firmly within the Maritime Ring. In the U.S. Electoral College, the Ring states have 401 votes of the 538 total. The closeness of the 2000 presidential election results can be attributed to the fact that, while Albert Gore received nearly 60 percent of those 401 ring state electoral votes, George W. Bush secured 95 percent of those from the Continental Interior.

The politics of the four largest Maritime Ring states, California, Texas, New York, and Florida, are strongly influenced by the role played by international trade of goods, financial services, and tourist services. In addition, these states are the destinations of approximately 60 percent of all legal immigrants and a considerably higher proportion of illegals. Thus their politics is also increasingly influenced by the ties that their immigrants have to their home countries and communities.

Effect on U.S. Foreign Policy and Trade

U.S. foreign policies toward Latin America and, to a lesser extent, Asia have certainly been influenced in recent years by the pressure of immigrant groups from the leading states of the Maritime Ring. In California, for example, where 34 percent of the population is now Hispanic, 12 percent Asian, and 7 percent black, the white proportion of the electorate has fallen to 47 percent in 2000.

The interests of immigrant groups are manifested in pressures upon foreign policies dealing with national immigration and trade toward Mexico, support of Taiwan in its dispute with China, and trade with China, as well as on such domestic issues as bilingual education and health and welfare policies. In New York, similar pressures are generated that contribute to shaping the U.S. outlook toward Puerto Rico and Israel; in Florida such pressures influence policy on Cuba; and in Texas immigrants have an impact on Washington's embrace of NAFTA's *maquiladoras* system. There is growing controversy within the United States over Washington's lax policies toward illegal immigrants, who are both an exploited labor class and, in some cases, involved in the drug trade. U.S. law entitles children of illegals to free public schooling; the amnesty under the 1986 immigration law allowed some, especially farmworkers, to gain green cards. The weight of the Hispanic vote has much to do with the reluctance of Congress and administrators to take a hard line on illegal immigration. This is reinforced by the interests of many U.S. farm and factory employers in exploiting the cheaper labor source.

The strength of Maritimity in the U.S. foreign policies is also directly related to the increasing interdependence of the American and global economies. In 1960, U.S. foreign trade represented only 9 percent of GDP; by 2000, it accounted for 25 percent of the $9.9 trillion GDP, and the percentage continues to rise. This trend line has been especially steep since 1990, with increasing expenditures for petroleum imports, accompanied by widening trade imbalances.

The U.S. foreign trade experience relates to the dramatic rise of world merchandise exports. In 1950, global exports amounted to less than half a trillion dollars. The figure had risen to $2 trillion by 1973 and $3.5 trillion by 1990. The figure nearly doubled by 1998, to $6 trillion, of which the United States accounted for $1.5 trillion. U.S. imports reached $1.2 trillion in 2000, while the exports and services were $1.07 trillion.

Services have become a major factor in international trade, and the United States is particularly well equipped to participate in this sector. U.S. exports of services nearly tripled from 1986 to 1996, when they totaled $220 billion. Service imports, however, only doubled during that period, to $140 billion. U.S. service exports have continued to rise more rapidly than merchandise trade, reaching $296 billion in 2000, compared to $773 billion in merchandise exports. This shift in export emphasis will eventually help to reduce trade imbalance.

All told, 25 percent of U.S. trade is with the Asia-Pacific Rim countries, 22 percent each with Maritime Europe and Canada, 12 percent with Mexico, and 7 percent with the Caribbean and South America. Thus, 85 percent of U.S. trade is within the Maritime Realm. Outside the realm, trade with China represents 5 percent of the total, trade with Russia less than 1 percent.

The Maritime-Continental setting of the United States supports the proposition that America's destiny is now heavily weighted toward the Atlantic and Pacific worlds, as well as balanced between them. Events of the past half century have drawn the United States to the Pacific in definitive ways. The 1959 conferral of statehood on Alaska and Hawaii had significant geopolitical consequences, placing U.S. security interests squarely in the North Pacific. Alaska not only is near Siberia, but is also a short fourteen hundred miles from Hokkaido. Hawaii's nearest neighbors, the Micronesian Islands, are only one thousand miles away. These are short air distances.

Another and more important factor that draws the United States to Asia is the rapid growth of the U.S. Pacific coast states in population, economy, and political power. The increased number of Asian American citizens, especially in California, increases the trans-Pacific pull. External forces are also powerful Pacific magnets. The occupation and reconstruction of Japan, the Korean and Vietnam wars, and the defense of the Taiwan Strait all were early Cold War involvements that left their psychological and political imprints on American public consciousness.

However, the most enduring impact comes from international trade. Japan has emerged as the second most important national economic power in the world, which has had far-reaching consequences for the United States. (Although Japan's GDP has recently been exceeded by that of China, much of the latter's GDP is a measure of subsistence agriculture and it is widely considered to be an inflated figure.) Although the economy of Japan has been in the doldrums since the late 1980s, nine of the world's twenty largest industrial corporations in 1997 were Japanese, as were five of the ten largest banks. As a U.S. merchandise import/export partner, Japan ranks second, just after Canada (Mexico, China, and the EU follow). Japan also has been the source of high-technology innovation that has stimulated American industry. This goes beyond video sets and toys; it includes sophisticated automotive and aircraft components that are so essential to U.S. industry.

President Nixon's opening of China in 1972 signaled a first step in the evolving and sometimes tumultuous relations with that nation, from which neither nation can afford, economically, to step back. Washington's efforts to help China gain entry into the World Trade Organization (WTO) are not based on altruism. China now ranks first as the source of U.S. imports, and second only to Japan in accounting for America's trade deficit. Thus, the volume of Chinese imports makes imperative the opening of the Chinese market to American goods. On the Chinese side, the fact that the United States is its second most important trading partner, after Japan, reflects the importance of the United States to its continued modernization and development.

The United States is the world's greatest trading nation, accounting for one-third of global trade in 2002. When Japan recovers from its lengthy recession of the 1990s, carrying the other Asia-Pacific nations with it, and as China's markets continue to open, there is little doubt that the Pacific will widen its lead over the Atlantic as America's most important trading partner. This factor will cause the further balancing of U.S. interests in both ocean basins.

In summary, the shifting of the American frontier is a continuing process. The frontier of the colonists of the Northeast lost its innovative character as the focus of pioneering moved, first to the trans-Appalachian region and then to the Continental Interior. There, frontiering spawned individualism, Jacksonian democracy, and technological innovation—from the canals and railroads of the nineteenth century to Henry Ford's conveyor belt and assembly-line process that introduced the automotive age. The decline of the frontier quality of the Continental Interior began with the collapse of small Midwestern farms during the Dust Bowl and the virtual abandonment of small prairie and plains farm and cattle towns. This trend was sealed when the adjoining heavy industrial centers of the Great Lakes fell into decline and technological innovation shifted to the coasts, first through the chemical-plastics revolution and then through the computer-technology, information-age, and financial-services revolutions.

This new frontier is augmented by its extension to offshore reaches developed by U.S. initiative, as well as by innovations that are generated offshore that become adopted and adapted to the U.S. scene.

Change is the most striking characteristic of a frontier. Since the Maritime Ring is the most significant generator of change, then surely the new frontier of the United States is the Maritime Ring—the urbanized area within which coping with mounting social, educational, employment, and environmental problems represents the nation's greatest challenge.

Canada

Few nations are as closely linked geopolitically as the United States and Canada. For over a century and a half, they have enjoyed peaceful and open borders, the conflicts between the two over boundaries being now only historic memories.

With the signing of the British North America Act of 1867 (which was absorbed by the Constitution Act of 1982), Canada emerged as the Dominion of Canada, an independent, loosely joined federation, remaining geopolitically oriented to Britain up to World War II. Their economic ties were reinforced by preferential tariffs accorded by London for raw materials and manufactured goods. As a member of the (British) Commonwealth of Nations, Canada followed Britain into World War I and joined the League of Nations at the war's end.

The Canada that emerged after World War II was a substantially more centralized nation, following a process that had begun with Ottawa's initiatives in promoting stronger federal economic policies during the Depression years of the 1930s. Links with Britain loosened as a result of Britain's weakened postwar economic situation and its loss of empire. London's 1973 entry into the European Common Market (now the European Union) further diluted the significance of Commonwealth ties. By the Canada Act of 1982, the British Parliament made Canada fully sovereign, with the right to amend its own constitution. The act replaced the British North America Act of 1867 and made possible the 1982 Constitution Act, which absorbed the British North America Act, as well as subsequent amendments. This only validated the reality of the independent status that Canada had enjoyed since World War I, evident in its membership in the United Nations and NATO. The fully sovereign country already had a strong social welfare commitment and was engaged in coping with Quebec separatism and the issue of native and minority rights, and it needed the new constitutional tools to deal with them, which the act provided.

STRATEGIC AND ECONOMIC TIES WITH THE UNITED STATES

Canada's geopolitical reorientation toward the United States began during World War II, when the two nations developed a close strategic partnership. Ice-free Halifax harbor, the largest in North America, was used as the marshaling and take-off point for American convoys in their crossings of the Atlantic, and Canadian escort vessels shared with the U.S. Navy the task of guarding them. U.S. and Canadian military bases were also established in Labrador and Newfoundland (which voted to join Canada in 1949), as aircraft were ferried across the North Atlantic from Newfoundland and Sydney, Nova Scotia. Canada also provided the vital land link to Alaska during the war, when the Alaska (Alcan) highway was built through its territory.

The Cold War thrust the Canadian Arctic into new strategic prominence. The Distant Early Warning (DEW) Line was constructed as a defense against a transpolar attack and consisted of a series of roughly concentric circles of antiaircraft and antimissile bases in Canada and the northern United States. The North American Aerospace Defense Command (NORAD) became a cornerstone of U.S. strategic policy, as some of its most important bases, both defensive and offensive, were placed on Canadian soil. In addition to the air component, American missile-carrying nuclear submarines prowled the waters below the Arctic ice cap as they maintained their watch over the transpolar rival.

A recent complication of this defense partnership is Washington's proposed defense system against ballistic missiles that, at the outset, would be based in Alaska. One Canadian view is that NORAD should be responsible for the new shield, and that if Ottawa opposes the Alaska system development of the project, Canada should leave NORAD. Many Canadians object to the new defense scheme on the grounds that it would endanger the Anti-Ballistic Missile Treaty with Russia, and also endanger nuclear arms control, triggering a new arms race. These Canadians are sympathetic to Moscow's fears that the system, while proposed as a safeguard against a North Korean missile threat, would also compromise Russian security.

Even more important than common strategic concerns, it is the economic interdependence between Canada and the United States that has sealed their common geopolitical destiny. The postwar demand of the booming U.S. economy for raw materials could not be met by domestic resources. This provided the opportunity for large-scale Canadian exports to the United States of timber, pulp, paper, energy resources, and minerals. In turn, U.S. manufacturers of consumer goods found a ready market in Canada. They also began to invest in Canadian mineral resources and in lower-cost manufacturing plants north of the border. This provoked some political resistance among Canadians in the years that followed. However, the resistance was overcome and the process was accelerated with the subsequent signing of various free trade agreements.

Geopolitical unity has presented Canada with the challenge of maintaining its national cultural distinctiveness and its independence from the United States in foreign policy making, while at the same time it has had to contend with the threat to its national unity by Quebec separatism.

The intertwining of the two economies prompted Prime Minister Pierre Trudeau of the Liberal Party to try to reduce U.S. influence and promote Canadian control of its own industry in the 1970s and early 1980s. A particularly restrictive measure was the requirement that 50 percent of the nation's oil and gas be owned by Canadians. This was revoked when the Conservative Party's Brian Mulroney became prime minister in 1984 and forged close ties with the Reagan administration. These ties led to the U.S.-Canada Free Trade Act of 1987, and ultimately to NAFTA in 1993.

The interdependence of the two nations in trade is now inextricable. Canada ranks first for the United States as the source of imports and a destination for exports. Twenty percent of all imports to the United States come from Canada, and 23 percent of all U.S. exports flow to its northern neighbor, even though the Canadian market offers a population of only thirty-one million. For Canada, the importance of U.S. trade is even greater. Eighty-two percent of all Canadian exports go to the United States and two-thirds of its imports come from there. Because much of the economy in manufacturing, energy, and mining is now controlled by U.S. interests, the economic fate of Canada is increasingly dependent on economic fortunes and market swings in the United States.

Ottawa has endeavored to assert a separate position in certain aspects of international affairs, while at the same time maintaining its close political partnership with the United States. For example, when NORAD was first created, Canada resisted basing nuclear-tipped missiles on its soil, changing its policy only in 1963. Canadians were also widely opposed to the Vietnam War. This was expressed not only in public outcry and in welcoming U.S. citizens who fled to Canada to avoid the draft, but also through recognition of Communist China in 1970.

As an expression of its commitment to world peace, Canada has been in the forefront of promoting international arms control, antinuclear weapons programs, and peacekeeping missions. It was Ottawa that first raised the idea of a UN Emergency Force to replace British and French troops in the wake of the 1956 Suez Canal invasion; Canadian peace-keepers have participated in most such UN actions since then. Moreover, Canada has led the anti–land mine campaign and been an outspoken proponent of international human rights and multilateralism. As a result of these policies, Ottawa has succeeded in shaping a unique and respected role in global affairs, while continuing to enjoy the trust and confidence of its U.S. ally.

Thus, the Canadian culture and sense of nationhood that was forged over two and one half centuries of French and then British rule remains distinct from that of the "Colossus of the South." However, it has also had to make significant adaptations in the light of geopolitical realities.

GEOPOLITICAL FEATURES

Canada has made remarkable progress in little more than half a century as a maturing geopolitical state. Its 1940 population of ten million tripled by the year 2000. Its east-west rail and highway networks, especially the latter, have been considerably extended and improved, while the Prairie provinces, as well as Ontario and Quebec, have benefited substantially from the St. Lawrence Seaway. In addition to the development of these east-west lines of movement, north-south transportation and communication links have become fully developed—a step vital to the integration of the U.S. and Canadian economies that has resulted from the various free trade agreements between them.

Any discussion of Canada's geopolitical features must take into account not only their relationship to the United States, but also the historical development of its French- and English-speaking communities. Profound distinctions characterize the political outlooks of the two Canadian cultures.

Historic Core

It is in the Historic Core that the Canadian state idea emerged. For French Canadians, Old Quebec, the lower part of Quebec City, is their Historic Core. Samuel de Champlain established a French colony there on what is now called the Lower Town, at the foot of a bluff that rises three hundred feet above the St. Lawrence River. By the mid-seventeenth century, Quebec City had emerged as the capital of New France and the center of the fur trade. The city remains the ideological heart of modern-day Quebec separatism.

The location of the Historic Core for English Canada is more ambiguous. For some, it is the Plains of Abraham, which now underlay the upper part (Upper Town) of Quebec

City. It was on this high ground that the English general James Wolfe defeated the French, under the command of General Louis Montcalm, giving birth to English supremacy in Canada. However, a strong argument can be made, as did Derwent Whittlesey, that it was the flight to Canada of American loyalists during and at the end of the Revolutionary War that created the present Canadian state.[11] This would place the birthplace of the Canadian state idea in either the Eastern Townships of south-central Quebec or the upper St. Lawrence and lower Great Lakes.

The townships attracted large numbers of United Empire loyalists, who settled south of the St. Lawrence between Montreal and Quebec. The area extends for about one hundred miles from Granby to Lake Megantic, on a line that is approximately thirty miles north of Vermont, New Hampshire, and the border of Maine. These loyalists and their descendants were tenacious guardians of English culture and gave the area a marked British tinge for over a century.

Another candidate for Historic Core, the limestone lowland of the upper St. Lawrence and the lower Great Lakes, became the seat of Upper Canada. The site of today's Toronto was purchased by the British from Native Americans in 1787 and became the home of many loyalists who had settled in the area after 1783–84.

Still others look to Charlottetown, Prince Edward Island, as the Historic Core of the Canadian Federation and therefore the country's Nuclear Core. In 1864 representatives of the Maritime Provinces (New Brunswick, Nova Scotia, and Prince Edward Island) met at the Charlottetown Conference to seal a union. The conference was also attended by delegates from other provinces and served as the forerunner of the Canadian Federation that was formed three years later.

Political Capital

Ottawa, Canada's federal capital, owes its status to the Constitution Act of 1867, which split Quebec into Lower Canada (present Quebec Province) and Upper Canada (Ontario). The Ottawa River was selected as the boundary divide. The city of Ottawa was founded in 1827 on the south bank of the Ottawa River, fifty miles from its junction with the St. Lawrence, midway between Toronto and Quebec City. It became the capital, first of the United Provinces of Canada (1858) and then of the Dominion of Canada, which was established by the British North America Act of 1867, displacing Quebec City and Montreal, which had briefly served as the capitals of a United Canada after the creation of the Union in 1841.

The selection of Ottawa as federal capital was dictated by the desire for a political center that would be located on "neutral ground," and be able to serve as a link between the two parts of the country. The choice followed an unsuccessful rebellion by the Québecois in 1837. From the onset, however, it did not become the hoped-for bridge, as rebellions in Quebec broke out again in 1870 and 1884. Despite its bilingual status today, Ottawa does not serve as the emotional capital for the Quebec separatists, who remain focused on Quebec City as their future capital.

Ecumenes

Canada's ecumenes are extensions of core portions of the U.S. ecumenes. The main Canadian ecumene runs from the northern shores of Lake Ontario westward along the shores of

Lake Erie, via Hamilton and London, to Windsor. Its major nodes are Toronto-Hamilton and Niagara, which are linked to New York's Buffalo area, and Windsor, which is linked to Detroit and Toledo, Ohio. Much of the ecumene's recent development has been stimulated by the growth of the motor vehicle industry in such southern Ontario centers as Oshawa, Alliston, Cambridge, London, and Windsor, all of which are also hosts to a variety of machinery, chemicals, and electronics manufacturing. Toronto-Hamilton is both the ecumene's industrial powerhouse and its leading financial and services center. Ottawa, an outlier of the ecumene, has become a major focus for Canada's high-tech industry, along with Greater Toronto. The prosperity and economic strength of the heart of the ecumene, from Oshawa through Toronto to Niagara, is such that Canadians refer to it as "the Golden Triangle."

In addition to the major southern Ontario ecumene, Canada has two secondary population and economic core areas—Greater Montreal and Vancouver-Victoria. As the cultural, commercial, financial, and industrial center of French Canada, Montreal's varied industries include steel, electronics, information technology, pharmaceuticals, textiles and apparel, refined petroleum, and transportation equipment. While it has been outstripped by Toronto, it remains Canada's second most important economic center and its leading port. Should the Province of Quebec, with its population of 7.3 million, eventually vote for independence, the connections of Greater Montreal's ecumene with the New York-New England portion of the U.S. ecumene are likely to be expanded.

The Vancouver-Victoria area in southern British Columbia is Canada's third-leading economic center. Vancouver, the chief Canadian Pacific port, has an excellent year-round harbor. A diverse city with a large Asian, especially Chinese, population, its industries include shipbuilding, fish processing, machinery, wood and paper milling, and oil refining. The city has developed as Canada's gateway to China and the Asia-Pacific, thanks to its location at the western terminus for the trans-Canada railroad system and the oil pipeline from Edmonton. Grains, petroleum, and minerals from the Prairie provinces are thus able to tap the growing Asian market. Victoria, the capital of the province, is a major tourist center, as well as the base for a deep-sea fishing fleet and the site of naval installations, grain elevators, and fish processing plants.

Nearly all of the approximately four million population of British Columbia is concentrated along its border with the United States, the remainder of the province being heavily forested, with the Rockies and the Coastal Range extending from the south to the province's northern end. This border location has enabled Vancouver-Victoria to benefit from its economic and commercial ties with Seattle and Portland. Separated from Ontario by twenty-two hundred miles of mountains, grasslands, and the Canadian Shield, and by the Rockies from Alberta four hundred miles to the east, Vancouver-Victoria has developed a distinct political-cultural outlook that reflects both its isolation from the rest of Canada and its proximity to the United States. Should the province respond to separatist stirrings—at this moment a highly unlikely event—it has the potential to become an important Gateway state, bridging the North American and Asian Pacific fringe lands.

Effective National Territory

While Canada is the world's third largest country at 3,851,787 square miles, a large proportion is Empty Area. This leaves a relatively small proportion of the territory to be classified as Effective National Territory, most of which lies within the Prairie provinces and southwestern Ontario west of Lake Superior. The readily developable parts of the Prairie provinces are presently their wheat and general farming areas of southern Manitoba, southern and central Saskatchewan, and southeastern and east-central Alberta.

In addition to the fertile grasslands that have supported large-scale wheat and general farming, the region has a wealth of minerals—especially Alberta's vast oil, natural gas, and coal reserves; Saskatchewan's copper, lead, and zinc; and southwest Manitoba's large oil deposits. The region also has direct access to the sizable timber, precious metals, and minerals resources that lie to their north. The five major urban centers of the provinces—Winnipeg, Edmonton, Calgary, Regina, and Saskatoon—now contain half of the ENT's total population of approximately five million. The continued expansion of these cities and the growth of secondary urban centers can support the expansion of the ENT. Other stretches of ENT include the lands between Lake Ontario and Montreal, with Ottawa as focus, and the lower St. Lawrence between Montreal and Quebec City.

Empty Areas

Canada's Empty Area covers more than three million square miles, or more than 80 percent of the country's total land area. Within this region, the small, scattered populations of Yukon and the Northwest Territories, Nunavut, Labrador, most of British Columbia, the northern and central parts of the Prairie provinces, northern Ontario, and much of Newfoundland are largely indigenous hunters and fishermen, or those engaged in mining.

This Canadian North, which extends across the Canadian Shield to the Arctic, consists largely of bare, windswept rock and treeless tundra. The retreat of the last ice sheet depressed much of the central part of the region's land surface, covering it with lakes and the Great Hudson Bay embayment. The southernmost portion is in thick forests, while the northernmost reaches are covered with ice. For the most part, the North is dry—from under ten inches of rainfall in the Arctic to under twenty inches in the vast areas from the Rockies to Hudson Bay.

While this emptiness cannot sustain population to any extent, it is nevertheless valuable to Canada. The vast space of the North serves as the country's defense shield. Its Arctic ice and waters provide a transpolar route, which in the future could become an important Atlantic-Pacific route for submarine or surface oil tankers and general cargo vessels. Most importantly, the North is a storehouse of minerals, proven and potential, from gold, oil, and natural gas to iron, copper, nickel, and uranium.

Thanks to the oil resources of the northern Alberta sector of the Empty Area, the importance of Canada as a major petroleum supplier to the United States is likely to increase over the next decade. The oil-impregnated sands of the Athabasca region of northeastern Alberta, which center around Fort McMurray, hold vast reserves, perhaps even greater than those of Saudi Arabia. Until now, the cost of recovering the oil has been prohibitively expensive. However, new technologies for separating the oil from the sand deposits have reduced production costs to one-fourth of what they were when the first pilot plant was constructed in 1970.

At the high, OPEC-driven price levels of the year 2000, Athabasca's energy resources have neared a competitive cost level. They were estimated at $9 per barrel, and are expected to be cut to two-thirds of that with newer technologies that are on the horizon. Current projections are that Athabasca will provide one million barrels per day within five years, surpassing the output of Alaska's North Slope. By the end of the decade,

Athabasca's output is expected to reach two million barrels, approximating that of Nigeria. Should this happen, the strategic value of Canada's Empty Area will be considerably enhanced.

In addition, the North's extensive hydropower resources are just beginning to be tapped. The most important of these is the James Bay hydroelectric development in northern Quebec—a colossal project that has been planned in four stages. Phase one, completed in 1985, already supplies more generating power than all of Quebec's coal and nuclear power plants combined. Although the completion of the entire project was scheduled for 2004, objections from environmental groups brought phase two to a halt. Future global energy crises may well lead to its renewal.

Migration

Canada's open border with the United States not only furthers economic exchange, including tourism, but it also facilitates the flow of migrants. In the eighteenth and nineteenth centuries, the movement was of American loyalists and blacks to Canada. For most of the twentieth century, with the exception of U.S. youth seeking to avoid the draft during the Vietnam period, the flow has been from north to south. U.S. immigration law has eased since the signing of the free trade accords, applying to temporary workers as well as permanent migrants. While the years of heaviest out-migration of Canadians, from 1950 to 1970, reflected Canada's immature and still depressed economy, in more recent years, especially the 1990s, Canada has experienced a "brain drain" of professionals.

Other migration factors, both domestic and global, affect the Canadian system. From the mid-1970s to the mid-1990s, the tensions resulting from the Quebec separatist movement prompted over 400,000 English speakers to leave the province for other parts of the country. Toronto in particular was the beneficiary of a substantial inflow of business and professional people, as well as capital.

An even greater force for demographic change has been immigration from abroad. After World War II, Canada became the generous host to hundreds of thousands of Europeans. That welcome mat is still out for immigrants seeking work or refuge, but the pattern of immigration has changed. Over the past decade, the vast majority of immigrants has come from the underdeveloped world, especially South Asia and China. So great has been the impact of immigration that half the population of Toronto, which contains one-fourth of all immigrants in Canada, are foreign born, and over half the city population is nonwhite. Metropolitan Vancouver's population is now one-third Chinese and Offshore Asian. The benefits that Canada's Pacific coast has gained from these immigrants and the capital that many have brought with them have been to expand trade and give the region a strong transpacific orientation.

GEOPOLITICAL FORCES OF ATTRACTION

The following discussion deals with the major elements that shape the intimate geopolitical ties between Canada and the United States. These ties are rooted in the nations' geographical relationships, as well as the depth of the commitment of both people to democratic principles and institutions.

Population Distribution

Canada's population of thirty-one million is distributed in widely separated clusters, confined by the Laurentian Uplands to a narrow zone along the country's lengthy, 3,926-mile southern border with the United States. Much of this population resides within fifty miles of the international boundary. Included in the clusters are the country's leading metropolitan regions—Toronto, 4.8 million people; Montreal, 3.5 million; Vancouver, 1.8 million; and Ottawa, one million. Approximately 85 percent of the population lives within two hundred miles of the border, and very few live more than three hundred miles away.

These population clusters in the Maritime provinces, the middle St. Lawrence, the Ontario Peninsula, and the Pacific coast are linked, not to one another, but to U.S. population concentrations to the south. The distance of these Canadian clusters from each other is reinforced by physical barriers—the bays and gulfs of the Atlantic and the Appalachians; the two prongs of the Laurentian Uplands (the Algonquin Park-Adirondacks district and the upper Great Lakes-Superior highlands); and the Rocky Mountains.

Economic Exchange

As the United States continues to draw down much of its natural resource base, Canada's abundant natural resources have become vital to the U.S. economy. These include freshwater, hydropower, fish, timber and pulp, oil, natural gas, and such minerals as uranium, zinc, potash, asbestos, and nickel. For example, gas from the Canadian Rockies is piped to Chicago and then eastward to the Pennsylvania border, via the big Trans-Canada pipeline. A major exception to this exchange of resources is the grain production of the Prairie provinces, which competes with U.S. commodities for world markets.

Much to the consternation of Canada's western Prairie farmers, the Canadian government has responded to free market agreements by cutting wheat subsidies drastically, from 31 percent of gross receipts in 1991 to 9 percent today. Meanwhile, the U.S. wheat subsidy remains high, at 38 percent. While Canada still produces twenty-one million tons of wheat and controls 20 percent of the world market (two-thirds of the market for durum), the pressures on its Prairie farmers are heavy, and farm population has dwindled. Indeed, what has long been called Canada's "breadbasket" is now more urban than rural. In Manitoba, for example, the 1998 export of grains and seed oils amounted to $677 million, compared with $900 million worth of buses, aircraft parts, furniture, and books. In fact, the single greatest obstacle to manufacturing is the shortage of labor. Ottawa has made the choice—because of its substantial trade balance with the United States, rescuing its western farmers through a reversal of its low-subsidy policy has taken second place to preserving a free market for Canadian goods exported to the United States.

With the implementation, first of the Canada-U.S. Free Trade Agreement in 1989 and then NAFTA in 1994, Canada's manufacturing industries have become heavily geared to the U.S. market and now account for 20 percent of the nation's GDP. Motor vehicles and parts, located mostly in Lower Ontario, are the leading industry. The growth of this industry preceded NAFTA, having begun with the signing of the U.S.-Canada Auto Pact in 1965. However, it was NAFTA that provided the major impetus for the increase in production. Employing half a million workers, the Canadian-based industry's annual output of 2.4 million vehicles, most of which go to the United States, makes Canada the world's seventh-largest motor vehicle producer. Other manufactured products include paper, newsprint, aluminum, chemicals, electronics, machinery, and apparel. This growth of manufacturing is heavily dependent upon U.S. investment, which in 1998 exceeded $100 billion, outranking other U.S. investments abroad, except those that went to Britain. The reverse flow of investment dollars from Canada to the United States, $75 billion, is also substantial, although much of it may originate with Canadian companies whose capital base is in the United States.

As a result of industrial expansion, the nature of the Canadian economy has changed dramatically in the past two decades, with agriculture and resource-based commodities now accounting for only one-third of the foreign trade, compared to 60 percent in 1980. This shift to manufacturing and services has made Canada highly dependent on foreign trade. The value of imports and exports now represents 60 percent of GDP. Since 70 percent of this trade is with the United States (Japan and the United Kingdom account for the rest), it is clear that Canada's economic destiny lies with its southern neighbor.

The complementary and interdependent nature of the economies of the two countries is reinforced by north-south rail, highway, pipeline, airline, water, and telecommunications routes and networks. The exceptions to this directional orientation are the east-west St. Lawrence Seaway and the Trans-Canada gas pipeline. However, even as the seaway has stimulated Canadian global bulk exports, it has also facilitated transborder trade within the Great Lakes region.

THE CHALLENGE OF GEOPOLITICAL PARTNERSHIP

U.S.-Canadian relations appear to be proceeding inexorably in the direction of increasing interdependence. However, given the absence of power symmetry between the two countries, the fear that some Canadians have of sinking from partnership to satellite status is not unwarranted. Environmental issues have become especially contentious. The proposed James Bay Phase II power project to supply energy to New York State raised so much opposition from Canadian (and U.S.) environmentalists and Cree Indians that in 1992 the New York State Power Authority backed away from signing a promised purchase contract. The following year, the government of Quebec decided to shelve the project.

The Northwest Passage, which connects the Pacific to the Atlantic, when finally opened by a U.S. icebreaker/oil tanker in 1969, stimulated U.S. oil company interest in finding a way through the passage to transport petroleum from Alaska's North Slope to the East Coast of the United States. This, in turn, raised the issue of Arctic sovereignty. It was resolved in 1988 with the agreement that U.S. icebreakers could cross the frozen waters of the Arctic Archipelago, but only with case-by-case approval.

Environmental issues yet to be resolved include the opposition in Canada to U.S. proposals to import pure freshwater from Canada's Lake Winnipeg and to U.S. Corps of Engineers flood-control plans to divert flood waters in North Dakota into the Red River. The latter would direct polluted waters into Canada. Another issue is the Alaska-bound cruise ships and commercial vessels operating from the U.S. Pacific coast, which pose environmental threats when they traverse Canada's portion of the Inside Passage—the waterway formed by a deep structural trough that extends along the Canadian coast from Vancouver Island to Prince Rupert and then follows the Alaskan shore to Juneau. The Canadian government cannot allow foreign vessels to continue dumping and spilling.

A recent area of controversy has been the proposed extension of the Trans-Canada natural gas pipeline from Chicago and under Lake Erie through New York State to the southern counties north of New York City. Suburban environmentalists there have argued that the pipeline's construction would have an adverse impact on the landscape.

None of these issues are unsolvable. The export of power and freshwater can be of benefit to Canada if environmental concerns are properly addressed. The use of the Northwest Passage might well lend itself to technological breakthroughs that would permit transit via giant submarine tankers of oil, liquefied gas, and even water, between the Atlantic and Pacific. For the U.S.-Canadian geopolitical partnership to endure, there must be a mutuality of interest. This calls for understanding, sensitivity, and accommodation. Because northern British Columbia and the Yukon Territory do not have direct access to the Pacific, some Canadians have called for the granting of a corridor across Alaskan Panhandle territory. Although this may be passed off as being neither economically nor strategically important to Canada, it is still a sore point in some Canadian circles that the landward boundaries of Canada, which were confirmed in 1903, are denied access to the sea.

Canadian interest in a corridor centers on the Chilkoot and White Passes, which link Whitehorse in the Yukon to the Lynn Canal and the sea via Skagway, Alaska. The granting of a corridor to Canada would not affect the strategic or economic position of the United States, because the major land link, the Alaska Highway, already passes through Canada. A farsighted U.S. policy that respected Canadian political-psychological yearnings in this instance would be a small but significant expression of mutual understanding.

It would behoove Washington to be especially sensitive and attuned to political developments in Canada. This includes respect for the federalism that characterizes the Canadian body politic and that helps to distinguish Canada from the United States. Much of Quebec's drive for separation has had to do with the economic imbalance between French Canada, which accounts for 25 percent of the population, and Ontario, which has a population of 11.4 million, or 36 percent. That imbalance has persisted, as U.S. investment and industry has focused on Lower Ontario. An example is the motor vehicle assembly and parts industry, three-quarters of which is located in Lower Ontario. Washington's encouragement of capital flows and trade expansion with Quebec can yield political as well as economic dividends, for the closing of the economic gap between Ontario and Quebec will help reduce the political tensions between English- and French-speaking Canada. Greater political stability within Canada strengthens the foundations of geopolitical unity between the two countries.

Such capital and trade flows have already begun to help stimulate Montreal's economy. The city has become, in recent years, a major exporting center for the U.S. Northeast, based on its lower labor costs, cheap energy, strong university and R&D centers, and proximity to New York City and Boston, where Montreal's fashion and knit goods, as well as subway cars, find a ready market. Another important basis for exchange is Montreal's growth as a center for finance and high-tech industry. As a result of this recent spurt of activity, Quebec's exports to the United States have risen to one-fourth of the province's GDP; the continued growth of such exchange can play a vital role in closing the gap between French- and English-speaking Canada.

The population of Quebec is almost evenly divided with respect to the independence issue. In a 1995 referendum, 50.6 percent voted against separating from Canada, with 49.4 percent in favor. With such a razor-thin margin, the issue is far from settled. At the end of 1999, the Canadian government tabled a bill seeking to clarify the conditions under which a province might secede. The draft of the proposed legislation has revealed some of the complexities of secession—negotiating Quebec's borders and share of the federal debt and guaranteeing the rights of Indians and linguistic minorities. Quebec separatists would have to grapple with the possible loss of the province's border areas with Ontario and New York, as well as northern parts of the province, where the Indians and Inuit oppose breaking ties with Ottawa. For Washington to be drawn into such political negotiations on any basis save as mediator would be a diplomatic disaster that could jeopardize the geopolitical unity that now prevails.

On a very different political scale, Nunavut, the home to Canada's newest self-governing entity, which was created in 1999, warrants U.S. attention. It was carved out from the eastern portion of what was the Northwest Territories; its boundaries extend along a zigzag line running from the Saskatchewan-Manitoba border to the North Pole, encompassing lands from this boundary east to Hudson Bay. The 17,500 Inuits who inhabit Nunavut have outright title to 20 percent of the territory's 772,260 square miles, including 13,896 square miles of mineral rights. They will also have a share of the petroleum and mineral royalties in all of the territory's federally owned land, and compensation of over one billion Canadian dollars between 1993 and 2007.

In positioning new antiballistic radar systems, as well as maintaining current monitoring systems, the United States needs to be mindful of the rights of the citizens of the new territory, while it negotiates with Ottawa. The new capital of Nunavut is Iqaluit, which has a population of forty-five hundred and is accessible for most of the year only by air or sled. Formerly, Iqaluit was only an outpost for a DEW station. Washington now must take into account the views of the Nunavut government on how the Inuit environment should be used with respect to future joint U.S.-Canadian defense facilities. The confederal nature of the Canadian system may complicate the political dealings between the United States and Canada, but if the common geopolitical destiny of the two countries is to be fulfilled, it is crucial that the decision-making process include all of the relevant constituent parts of the Canadian Confederation.

The strength of the geopolitical relations between Canada and the United States owes much to the geographical settings of the two countries—their complementary resource bases; the openness of their borders, which encourages exchange of ideas, goods, and people; and the merging of ecumenes. However, it is their common outlooks on such fundamental issues as the democratic process, protecting human rights, and international aid, and their mutual respect for those matters on which they differ, that has enabled the two countries to take advantage of the geographical factors that bind them. Above all, the ties between the two are built on a genuine partnership, rather than the dominant-subordinate relationship that so often has been the fate of smaller powers that have lived in the shadow of far larger and stronger neighbors.

Mexico

Geographically and culturally, Mexico belongs to Middle America. Geopolitically, however, its fate has been closely tied to the ambitions and policies of the United States, a condition that made for stormy relations between the two for much of the nineteenth and twentieth centuries. The Mexican War of 1846–48 resulted in the U.S. annexation of 40 percent of Mexico's territory and initiated a century of U.S. intervention in Mexican economic and political affairs.

During the fourth quarter of the nineteenth century and up until the Mexican Revolution of 1910, Mexico was ruled by an oligarch, Porfirio Díaz, whose favorable policies toward large landholders and foreign ownership responded to the interests of American investors in minerals, railroads, and ranching. This policy was extended to petroleum, which was discovered at Tampico along the Gulf of Mexico in 1901. During World War I, the industry grew with the demand for Mexican oil by the Allied forces. U.S. and British capital promoted this growth and the boom continued into the 1918–21 period, when the country became the world's second-highest producer, outranked only by the United States.

During these years, however, the overall political relations between the United States and Mexico deteriorated. The Liberal Party leaders who had come to power in 1910 had begun to squabble among themselves, ushering in a period of political instability and civil war. To protect American interests, the United States intervened militarily in 1914 and 1916, backing the government of Emiliano Carranza, first against counterrevolutionaries and then against Francisco "Pancho" Villa and Emiliano Zapata, revolutionary allies who had fallen out with Carranza.

Tension between the two countries was exacerbated by the strong pro-German sentiment that prevailed in Mexico during World War I, a tension inflamed by the Zimmerman telegram. This message, dated January 19, 1917, was purportedly sent by Germany's foreign minister, Arthur Zimmerman, to the German minister in Mexico City. The message was intercepted and passed on to Washington by a British encryption team; its contents proposed that Mexico be encouraged to form an alliance with Japan and the Central Powers against the United States should the latter enter the war to aid the Allies. In return, Germany would offer to help Mexico regain the territories that it had lost in 1846. Some have held that the Zimmerman telegram was a forgery designed to help justify Woodrow Wilson's decision to enter the war. Whatever the truth, the affair increased the hostility between Washington and Mexico City. This hostility was heightened further that year when Carranza proposed a constitutional change (never enacted) that would have nationalized the country's mineral resources.

Serious controversies over petroleum rights continued from the early 1920s into the 1930s, when the Mexican oil boom offered tempting financial rewards to U.S. companies. Tensions reached new heights when Lázaro Cárdenas became president in 1934 and instituted sweeping reforms centering around land redistribution. He nationalized the railroads and foreign holdings and expropriated the petroleum fields, albeit with compensation.

Relations between the two countries improved in the 1940s, as Mexico entered World War II in 1942 on the Allied side. In return, Mexico received substantial economic aid from the United States, for which Mexican oil had become especially important in supplementing Texas and Oklahoma production. The Inter-American highway, from Nuevo Laredo, Mexico, to Panama City, played an important logistical role during the war. While much of it had been completed before 1941, U.S. funds were appropriated to assist its completion to meet the needs of the war effort. A later example of the growing convergence of the two countries was in the political arena, when Mexico firmly supported Washington's position in the Cuban missile crisis.

The most important factor in increasing the economic interdependence of the two nations is NAFTA, which was signed in 1992 and put into effect on January 1, 1994. That historic accord, coupled with a wave of privatization that had begun in the late 1980s, triggered a rapid growth in the Mexican economy. The growth came to a stunning halt within a year, however, when the Mexican government devalued the peso, setting off the country's worst recession in half a century. The economic collapse was marked by a 52 percent inflation rate, a doubling of unemployment, and a shrinking of economic activity by 6.5 percent.

Responding to the crisis, Washington quickly stepped in to avert disaster. It put together one of the largest financial support packages ever devised—$50 billion—in short- and medium-term loans and guarantees from a combination of U.S. government, International Monetary Fund, and international banking agencies. By 1996, the recovery had begun, and within three years the Mexican economy had more than made up the lost ground.

The rationale offered by Washington for its rapid intervention was not only Mexico's desperate straits, but that its actions sought to protect U. S. interests—exports, jobs, and national security—as well as to stabilize other emerging market economies. This action, reinforced by President Vincente Fox's close U.S. ties, has cemented the relationship between the two countries and presages an era of friendship and cooperation that is in stark contrast to the tensions that marked so much of the nineteenth and twentieth centuries.

GEOPOLITICAL FEATURES

Capital and Historic Core

In the first stages of the postwar period, U.S. attention was focused on the Mexico City national political core and the Gulf of Campeche, which contains the country's major oil- and gas-producing areas and rich reserves. The capital, which is coterminous with the Federal District, is located in the high valley and former lake bed that is the site of Mexico's Historic Core. As the Historic Core, the site dates back to the fourteenth century, when the Aztecs built their capital on the ruins of a pre-Aztec site. When the Spaniards conquered the city in 1521, they expanded the site by filling in the lake with the rubble that covered most of the valley, and by draining the lake, and made the city the political center of the viceroyalty of New Spain.

Mexico City now has a population of 8.5 million, although it has lost close to 600,000 inhabitants to the suburbs in recent years. These suburbs extend outward for as much as one hundred miles in all directions and, together with the capital, have a population approaching twenty million. The crowded metropolis, much of which is in the Valley of Mexico and surrounded by hills and mountains, is plagued by endless traffic jams and serious air pollution. Despite the pressures on land, air, and water, some demographers expect the metropolis to grow into a megalopolis of fifty million by the mid-twenty-first century, and to reach out in a radius of up to 150 miles.

Ecumene

The nation's ecumene—the area containing the highest densities of population and economic activities—has formed around Mexico City. In addition to the Federal District, the ecumene contains the surrounding states of Mexico, Puebla, Morelos, and Tlaxcala and extends out to the Gulf Coast at Vera Cruz. It also contains parts of Michoacán, Hidalgo, and Querétaro.

The total population of the ecumene now exceeds thirty-five million, or one-third of the country's one hundred million inhabitants. The region contains much of Mexico's manufacturing, such as food products, textiles and apparel, motor vehicles, machinery, chemicals, pharmaceuticals, steel, paper, and consumer products. In addition, Mexico City serves as the financial-services and commercial center of the nation.

The center of the coastal extension of the ecumene, the city of Vera Cruz on the Bay of Campeche, is one of the country's two major ports (Tampico is the other) and is a focus for iron and steel, chemicals, and tourism. It is connected by rail and highway to Mexico City. In the northern coastal part of the state, a pipeline from the older oil fields of Tampico and Tuxpam provides refined oil to the capital. The basis for the country's petrochemical industry, however, is the newer oil and natural gas fields south of Vera Cruz City and extending into the adjoining state of Tabasco, where vast offshore reserves were discovered in 1972. These Bay of Campeche oil discoveries triggered the country's second oil boom, which lasted from 1973 to 1982. During that period, oil shipments accounted for three-quarters of the nation's export earnings. Growth then dropped sharply as international prices declined, and Mexico's ability to meet its foreign indebtedness became severely strained. The industry has since recovered and production has stabilized at the earlier peak levels of over three million barrels per day. However, in response to the lessons learned from the sharp fluctuations in oil prices, the government put in place an industrial diversification policy aimed at increasing the export of manufactured goods, metals, and agricultural products, which has succeeded in reducing oil dependence. To a considerable measure, this success now depended upon Mexico's import of foreign capital, as well as upon the access to markets provided by NAFTA. The capital flow has been substantial. Among low- and middle-income countries, Mexico is one of the world's leading importers of private capital, most of which comes from the United States. In addition, access to foreign markets has been broadened by a free trade agreement that was signed with the European Union in 1999, and by agreements with many Latin American countries, such as Chile, Colombia, Venezuela, Uruguay, Bolivia, Costa Rica, and Nicaragua.

Effective National Territory

NAFTA has been instrumental in expanding Mexico's ENT. Most of northern Mexico remains a sparsely inhabited, semiarid to arid grazing region dotted with peasant farms that are heavily dependent upon irrigation. However, its urban clusters and centers of industry have converted what was a backward and largely empty area into part of the country's ENT.

From a geopolitical standpoint, the agreement has drawn the United States and Mexico more closely together, as Mexico's focus on industrial growth has shifted northward to the border zone between the two countries. Thanks to the rapid increase in *maquiladoras*—the assembly plants that import the bulk of their raw materials and parts from the United States and export the finished products on a duty-free basis—this Northern Border Zone has attracted major manufacturing and urbanization.

Few cities and towns located along the boundary lack *maquiladoras* and many, such as Tijuana, Otay Mesa, Mexicali, Nogales, Nuevo Laredo (the country's busiest inland port), and Matamoros, have enjoyed economic booms. This Northern Border Zone also extends southward to cities that have easy access to the border. Monterrey, Mexico's second most important industrial city and its leading iron and steel center, is only seventy-five miles from the border; Chihuahua is 125 miles away; and Hermosillo is 175 miles distant. However, the greatest concentration of activity and employment is in the four border cities—Juárez, Tijuana, Nuevo Laredo, and Matamoros.

The growth of the *maquiladoras* has been so rapid that they account for half of all Mexico's new manufacturing jobs, from textiles, apparel, household appliances, and television sets to high-tech products, chemicals, and metals. In particular, the *maquiladoras* have stimulated the expansion of motor-vehicle assembly and parts plants. Mexico is now the eleventh largest auto-making country in the world, with an annual production of 1.5 million vehicles in plants located in such northern centers as Hermosillo, Chihuahua, Saltillo, Reynosa, and Monterrey, as well as in those in the center of the country, in Puebla and Guanajuato.

The impact of all this activity has been relative prosperity and a higher standard of living for these northern urban centers. Monterrey, for example, where the *maquiladoras* program began, now employs over half a million workers in such industries as glass, cement, steel, chemicals, and furniture, as well as motor vehicles, and has become a center of wealth and capital formation.

This manufacturing growth has created, in effect, a new, industrialized border region between the United States and Mexico. On the Mexican side of the border, the population has increased by nearly 50 percent over the past decade. The growth is concentrated in the dozen Mexican border cities that extend from Tijuana and Mexicali on the Pacific side, to Nogales and Ciudad Juárez in the center, and to Nuevo Laredo, Reynosa, and Matamoros on the Gulf of Mexico. The populations of their twin cities on the U.S. side of the border, from San Diego and Calexico, to Nogales and El Paso, to Laredo, McAllen, and Brownsville, have grown by 20 percent during this period, largely through Hispanic migration—legal and illegal—drawn by U.S. factories and farms in and around these centers. A striking feature of the U.S. side of the border is that it also has shifted rapidly from being an agricultural area to being a mainly industrial area.

Some of the *maquiladoras* are located in the center of the country, in such cities as Aguascalientes, Guadalajara, and Mexico City. They employ only about 40 percent of the number of workers employed in the Northern Border Zone, nearly half of them in clothing and textiles. In contrast, the better-paying, higher-technology industries, such as electronics and motor vehicles, are the dominant ones of the northern zone. A limited number of *maquiladoras* are located in the far south, in Yucatán, where they take advantage of their proximity to the U.S. East Coast by air and sea.

While ownership of the *maquiladoras* is largely a mixture of U.S. and Mexican interests, the ownership share varies with the distance from the border. U.S. companies own over 60 percent of the equity in border centers, with 30 percent owned by Mexican firms and the remainder controlled by foreign interests, mainly Japanese. The U.S. equity drops to under 50 percent in the interior portions of the Northern Border Zone. In the center of the country, Mexican interests own nearly 80 percent. The proportions in the north reflect not only geographic proximity, but also the emphasis of U.S. capital on electronics and motor vehicle industries.[12] The *maquiladoras* program in Central America, as well as in Mexico, is not without its critics. Low wages and substandard workplaces have aroused the opposition of liberal and labor forces within the United States. This has led to sporadic boycotts of firms that contract for or sell goods to U.S. consumers. However, the general response in the producing countries is that the job opportunities afforded by the program to poverty-stricken, jobless native workers outweighs whatever abuses may be taking place.

The *maquiladoras* formally ceased to exist on January 1, 2001, when tariffs on manufactured goods between the United States and Mexico were completely phased out under NAFTA. However, the industrial structural and locational patterns that were set during the

1990s remain firm. In all likelihood, Mexico will continue to emphasize its export industry and the Northern Border Zone will benefit from partnership with the United States. In the near future, the zone may well be converted from ENT to the country's second ecumene.

This is not to imply that the *maquiladoras* have been an unmixed blessing for Mexico's north. The higher wage structure in the zone has contributed to the geographical shift of *maquiladoras* to lower-wage areas within the country's center and south, and to Central America. Whereas 90 percent of these factories were once located along the northern border, the figure is now only 60 percent. The attraction of lower-wage areas, combined with the recent recession in the United States, has caused a loss of an estimated 200,000 factory jobs in the north.

The program had been designed in part to slow legal and illegal immigration from Mexico to the United States, but may have provoked the opposite effect. Urbanized Mexican factory workers who have recently enjoyed higher living standards and now find themselves unemployed feel greater pressures than ever to seek work north of the border. Nevertheless, as the U.S. economy improves, the export base of northern Mexico's industries will be strengthened and the economic and social development of the urban centers of the zone should in all likelihood continue to progress.

While vast disparities of income characterize Mexico, the gap is greatest between the Spanish-Amerindian and white population and the indigenous Amerindian population, who constitute 30 percent of the total population. This disparity is most keenly felt in the ENT's southernmost part, especially in the states of Oaxaca and Chiapas. Poverty has been the driving force in sustaining the Zapatista rebels of Chiapas, drawn from indigenous Indian peasants who have long been exploited by wealthy landholders. Chiapas is a state steeped in ancient Maya traditions and the Zapatista National Liberation Army, which raised the flag of independence in 1994, thrives on this Indian sense of separateness in dialect and social customs.

By 1996, the Mexican army had driven the Zapatistas into jungle hideouts. In the Accord of San Andres, the Mexican government offered limited political autonomy, in response to which the leadership of the Zapatistas adopted a policy of nonviolence. The offer was never put into law by the administration of President Ernesto Zedillo, and discussions broke down. However, since the election of President Vicente Fox Quesada in 2000, peace talks have been renewed and prospects of forging an agreement have greatly improved. Indeed, in a dramatic march to Mexico City in 2001, the Zapatistas declared an end to the war and the conversion of their movement into a political, rather than military, one.

Empty Areas

Mexico has a number of Empty Areas that are either too mountainous or too dry to support populations. The most extensive ones are in the northwest and far south. One of the largest is the arid and desolate Baja California peninsula, which is separated from the rest of the country by the Gulf of California (Mar de Cortés). Stretches of the coast in Sonora, along the eastern side of the gulf, are also desert.

Farther east, the Sierra Madre supports few people, as do its arid interior-facing slopes and the desert basins that lie beyond. In the far south, the Empty Areas include the tropical lowlands of Chiapas that border Guatemala and contain the sites of ruined Maya cities, as well as the interior tropical hardwood forests of southern Campeche state in the Yucatán Peninsula, which adjoin Belize and Guatemala.

Boundaries

Mexico's formal boundaries are not now in dispute. Conflicting claims over the boundary around El Paso were settled in 1964 and 1967, and in 1965 the treaty was signed, committing the United States to maintaining the freshwater content of the Colorado River, whose waters are used for irrigation and household needs in Mexico. These waters are vulnerable to salinity and chemical pollution from the runoff that upstream American farmers return to the river after drawing its waters for irrigation and applying fertilizers and pesticides to the fields.

Policing the 2,075-mile border between the United States and Mexico is not, however, without difficulty, as U.S. immigration officials seek to stanch the flow of illegal Mexican immigrants. For the most part, Mexican authorities cooperate with their northern neighbors, although without the resources or level of commitment of the northern country.

Another boundary of some concern is the border between Chiapas and Guatemala, which has been used as a transshipment zone for drug traffickers and immigrant smugglers. One of the points at issue in the negotiations between the Mexican government and the Zapatistas has been the latter's demand that Mexican troops be withdrawn completely from Chiapas. The government is reluctant to meet this demand fully because of the need to maintain security along the national border.

GEOPOLITICAL FORCES OF ATTRACTION

Trade ties with the United States have deepened with Mexico's industrial diversification. Most of the petroleum and natural gas that is exported goes to the United States (approximately 1.2 million barrels per day). This represents approximately one-fifth of total U.S. imports, which is on a par with U.S. imports from Canada and Venezuela. Over half of the 1.5 million motor vehicles produced go to the United States, one-third are reserved for the domestic market, and the remainder are exported to Latin America. The level of trade has risen dramatically, so that Mexico is topped only by the EU, Canada, and Japan as a leading trading partner. The fact that approximately 85 percent of the country's export trade and 75 percent of its import trade are with the United States creates an overwhelming economic dependence of Mexico on its northern neighbor. While this dependence offers considerable benefits to Mexico in terms of economic growth and prosperity, it carries with it the risk of a sharp economic declines when the United States suffers serious recessions, as was the case in 2001–2002. These trade ties are likely to continue to expand, as European and South American companies, seeking access to a tariff-free U.S. market, locate factories in Mexico. These products then gain duty-free entry into the United States.

Two other important geopolitical forces of attraction between the two countries are immigration and drugs. Mexico is now the country of origin of by far the largest number of immigrants to the United States. By 1998, 28 percent of the U.S. foreign-born had come from Mexico, where approximately 20 percent of the annual immigration originates. If illegal immigrants were counted, the annual figure would be far higher.

So heavy is this flow of immigrants that Hispanics, mainly from Mexico, represented 45 percent of the total population of Los Angeles in 2000 and will soon become a majority, far outnumbering whites, who represented only 31 percent of the population. Many of the immigrants come from Mexico's northern tier of border states. Despite the growth of the economy in this area, the United States remains a magnet not only for unemployed urban *maquiladoras* workers, but also, and even more so, for the northern rural areas, where limited arable land, combined with overpopulation, have produced a large, impoverished populace. Even greater numbers of immigrants to the United States originate from the arid, poverty-stricken farm areas of central Mexico, north of the capital. Population in many parts of such drought-parched agricultural states as Zacatecas, Jalisco, and Guanajuato, has declined precipitously, as illegal migrants from this region have found their way to the United States.

Proximity of the United States and contacts with friends and relatives already living there represent another "pull" factor, as do employment opportunities in agriculture, construction, and services. To complete the loop, the *migro-dollars* that are remitted from the United States stimulate economic activity, especially in the northern section. These remittances, estimated at $6 billion a year, represent 8 percent of Mexico's GDP. They have a powerful political, as well as economic, impact on the country. Indeed, there is a movement within some Mexican political circles to allow migrants who reside in the United States to vote in state and national elections and to draw some of the successful émigrés back into the country to seek public office.

Another interactive force is the flow of drugs across the border from Mexico to the United States. This has increased as Colombian drug cartels have shifted some of their bases to Mexican border cities. To monitor and interdict the flow, U.S. authorities need the cooperation of their Mexican counterparts. While such cooperation has been given only grudgingly in the past, it seems to have been strengthened recently. It is hard to measure the value of such cooperation in monetary terms, but Washington's help in refinancing Mexico's external debt when its economy collapsed in 1995 reflected an acknowledgment that Mexico's importance to the United States had risen with U.S. dependence on Mexico's help in the war against drugs. Recognition of mutual need is a powerful factor in bringing nations together, and the geopolitical ties between the United States and Mexico reflect such need. The political importance of Mexican-U.S. relations was underscored in the summer of 2001, when the U.S. administration began to consider legalizing up to three million Mexicans working illegally within the United States. This is a position that not only has been advocated by Mexico's President Fox, but also has been endorsed by the AFL-CIO. Many of those undocumented immigrants already work on farms, as landscape laborers, and in hotels and factories and have been enrolled in union ranks. Another policy under discussion that would enable temporary work-permit holders to gain permanent residency eventually is an expanded guest-worker program. Although there is considerable opposition to the amnesty proposal from conservative political circles, as well as from U.S. workers who fear job losses or a lowering of wage levels, the political and economic pressures for some kind of amnesty are strong.

The last general amnesty, enacted in 1986, granted legal immigrant status to nearly three million persons who had entered the country illegally prior to 1982 and had remained in continuing residence since then. This status was also extended to those who had worked as farm laborers for over ninety days. The rationale offered at that time was that such a program would reduce the tide of illegal immigrants. This did not prove to be the case. Estimates of the number of illegals now in the United States vary from the official figure of seven million (including over three million Mexicans) to unofficial estimates of up to nine million. A new amnesty program is not likely to stop the flow. Mexico's small farmers continue to be battered by NAFTA free trade policies and plummeting market prices for such crops as corn, rice, coffee, and sugarcane. Thus farm abandonment is not likely to slow down or to cease affecting the annual movement of illegals.

Another rationale for a new program targeted at Mexicans is that it will encourage the Mexican government to be more cooperative with U.S. authorities trying seal the border against future illegal immigration, and that they will also join in a crackdown against drug smuggling. However, the debate over amnesty for Mexicans will no doubt be expanded to the issue of other immigrant groups.

Washington has put these various proposals on hold because of the economic recession of 2001–2002. With the rebounding in the national and global economy, these proposals on the issues of immigrants and immigrant labor are likely to be reintroduced by the administration and gain the approval of the U.S. Congress.

The North American territory that emerged as a unified land under the Spanish and then was separated by U.S. conquests over a century and a half ago has now begun to regain a considerable measure of geopolitical unity through forces that have overcome the barrier effects of the international boundary. These forces are, above all, migration of Mexicans into the U.S. border states as permanent residents and migratory labor and the exchange of goods between the *maquiladoras* zone and the United States. The result is a set of links between Mexico and the United States that are beginning to mirror those between Canada and the United States, and that have made a strong contribution to the forging of a geopolitically unified North America.

In an ironic twist of history, the lands that Mexico lost to the United States in war over a century and a half ago are now being regained in a sociocultural and limited political sense. The rapid increase of the Mexican American and other Hispanic populations owing to immigration and high birthrates could create Hispanic majorities in California, Texas, and New Mexico by the mid-twenty-first century. In addition to the effect on state and congressional politics, voters in these states, along with those in New York and Florida, could affect national politics in a variety of issues, ranging from immigration policies to the level of attention to Mexico and Middle America in economic and foreign policy.

Middle America

Middle America, while geographically distinct, is a subregion that is geopolitically part of North America; both are within the Maritime Realm. The area includes the islands of the Caribbean, Central America, and the northern coastlands of South America, from the Gulf of Darien through Venezuela and the Guyanas. Colombia might also be pulled into the region because of the growing intensity of its relations with the United States.

Approximately a century ago, Ellen Churchill Semple noted the geographical similarities between the New World's Gulf of Mexico-Caribbean basin, which she termed "the American Mediterranean," and the interior sea of the Old World Mediterranean.[13] Nicholas Spykman described the American Mediterranean geopolitically as the area over which the United States held absolute hegemony.[14]

THE FOUR STAGES OF U.S.-MIDDLE AMERICA ASSOCIATION

There is no doubt that the United States has acted as the hegemon of Middle America throughout the twentieth century. Its involvement in Caribbean affairs, however, antedates the era of hegemony, as reflected in the four stages of association that have marked their relationships.

Stage 1: The Era of Defensive Posture

With the emergence of the United States as an independent nation, Americans had a legitimate fear of European states using their Caribbean island bases and Mexico to dominate the Gulf and Mississippi, and thereby confining the United States to the eastern seaboard. In addition, Americans themselves were attracted by the wealth of the Indies—sugar, rum, and slaves—to which the subsistence colonial economy stood in marked contrast.

Stage 2: The Era of Aggressive Intervention

After the issue of slavery had been resolved in the United States by the Civil War, Northern as well as Southern voices were raised in favor of U.S. expansion into the Caribbean and Central America. The interests were commercial, humanitarian, and strategic. By the turn of the century and following the Spanish-American War of 1898, military and economic considerations had become sufficiently pressing to inspire a series of U.S. interventions in Cuba, Haiti, the Dominican Republic, Nicaragua, and Panama. The weight of the strategic considerations increased with the growth of population and industry in the U.S. Gulf states and the opening of the Panama Canal in 1914. The canal permitted California to be more closely tied to the eastern United States and helped Washington to extend its influence across the Pacific. The Good Neighbor Policy of the 1930s represented a less emotional and more sympathetic approach to U.S. relations with Latin America, but without any essential change in its aggressive actions toward the rest of the hemisphere.

Stage 3: The Cold War Fear of Counter-Encirclement

Fidel Castro overthrew the regime of Fulgencio Batista in 1959 and soon declared himself a Marxist-Leninist and allied the country with the Soviet Union. Communist Cuba, in and of itself, represented no military challenge to U.S. security. But the United States indeed would have been threatened had the USSR succeeded in basing nuclear missiles on the island in 1962, as the Soviets attempted to do, following Cuba's crushing of the U.S.-sponsored Bay of Pigs invasion. However, Washington's instantaneous challenge to the Soviet incursion caused Moscow to back off. In so doing, the Soviet Union recognized American strategic primacy within its geopolitical region. U.S. retention of its Guantánamo Bay naval base at the southeastern tip of Cuba helped to assure this primacy. Sometimes referred to as "the Pearl Harbor of the Atlantic," Guantánamo overlooks the Windward Passage, one of the two narrow openings between the Atlantic and the Caribbean. The other opening, the Mona Passage, is controlled by U.S. naval bases in Puerto Rico.

Dismantling of the Soviet missile bases did not restrain the USSR from continuing to pour military and economic aid into Cuba. However, with the exception of Cuban troops who operated in Nicaragua in support of the Sandinistas, direct Cuban military intervention took place outside the western hemisphere—in Angola, Ethiopia, and other countries in Africa and the Middle East.

Castro did seek to export communism to other parts of the Caribbean and South America by supporting revolutionary movements in such countries as Guatemala, El Salvador, Venezuela, Uruguay, and Bolivia. But the support was through arms to guerrilla movements, not through troops. Only in Nicaragua, where the Sandinistas assumed power in 1979, and in Grenada for a limited four-year period did Cuban and Soviet efforts succeed in helping to sustain marxist regimes.

While it was clear to most American and international policy makers that Cuba represented no military threat to the United States, Washington's embargo of Cuba continued, not just through the Cold War era, but into the present. It is an outdated policy that has become increasingly ineffective, as international opinion has overwhelmingly favored the lifting of sanctions, and foreign investors in Cuba have ignored them.

Stage 4: The Era of the "Benevolent Policeman"

Advancing democracy and human rights became the new U.S. Middle American policy in the early 1980s, as Castro's influence had ebbed. In 1982 Washington pressured the Honduran military government to hold free elections, even as the United States continued to support bases in that country to bolster the Contras in their war against Nicaragua's Sandinista government.

In the 1983 "comic opera war," U.S. troops invaded Grenada to "protect" American medical students there and prevent reestablishment of a Marxist regime. The United States promoted democratic elections, rather than permitting the Grenadan army, which had just overthrown the previous revolutionary government and executed Prime Minister Maurice Bishop, to remain in power.

In 1985 Washington withdrew support from the Guatemalan military to permit democratic elections in that country. Four years later, Panama was invaded by twenty-five thousand U.S. troops, who toppled the dictator, Manuel Noriega, and took him to the United States, where he was convicted and jailed for drug trafficking.

The United States continued its "benevolent policeman" policy as the collapse of the Soviet empire in 1989, and the USSR itself in 1991, threw Cuba into an economic tailspin and increased its regional political isolation. With the elimination of the Soviet Union as a factor within Middle America, and with the weakening of Cuba, Washington felt free to abandon right-wing military regimes that it had supported on the basis of their anticommunism. When in 1990 Nicaragua's repressive Sandinista government was ousted in democratic elections, the United States hastened to support the new government. The Sandinistas had called the elections in response to widespread unrest and unpopularity, as the national economy had deteriorated under the pressure of the American trade embargo and the reduction in Soviet economic aid.

Intervention within the region continued, as in 1994 the U.S. military invaded Haiti to restore Jean-Bertrand Aristide to the presidency, from which he had been ousted by a military junta. What followed was an unsuccessful venture in peacekeeping by American troops under the UN banner. The troops were ultimately withdrawn, as bickering among the Haitian political parties led to continuing crises and governmental paralysis.

In Guatemala, Washington welcomed the end of the civil war in 1996. The peace accord signed by the government and the leftist rebels opened the way for constitutional reforms. This later prompted President Bill Clinton to apologize for the considerable military aid that previous U.S. administrations had provided the Guatemalan armed forces and the repressive military regimes.

GEOPOLITICAL FEATURES

The various states and dependent territories of Middle America have, for the most part, immature geopolitical features. There is no historic core or contemporary political capital that has region-wide influence. The only countries that have well-defined ecumenes with substantial industrial features are Cuba, at its western end around Havana; Venezuela, on its northern coast, from Caracas west to Maracaibo; and Puerto Rico, in greater San Juan. Most of the countries of the region also have limited ENTs, the major exception being the grasslands of Venezuela's Orinoco Valley.

Boundaries

Ironically, boundaries, which had given little cause for dispute in modern times, have again become points of contention in Central America. Honduras and Nicaragua clashed over fishing rights in their Pacific waters in the 1980s and are now engaged in a much wider dispute over their sea border in the Caribbean. Under contention is fifty thousand square miles of water and two tiny islets. The Organization of American States (OAS) is attempting to mediate the dispute.

Another boundary quarrel has erupted between Nicaragua and Costa Rica, over the use of the San Juan River, which forms the border between them. Again, the OAS has been asked to intervene.

A third dispute is between Guatemala and Belize, the former British Honduras, which received its independence in 1980.[15] In the negotiations that led up to independence, Guatemala had indicated that it would be satisfied with a more limited area and access to a free port at Belize City. The United Nations affirmed the territorial integrity of Belize and, in 1991, Guatemala dropped most of its claims, except for one regarding a section in the far south. However, in 2000, the dispute over that area broke out again, resulting in some minor skirmishing.

Still another boundary issue has to do with Venezuela's claim to all of Guyana west of the Essequibo River—more than half of Guyana's total land area. The claim surfaces from time to time, although recently it has been quiescent. Venezuela is also in contention with Colombia over the maritime boundary between the two countries in the oil-rich waters of the Gulf of Venezuela. Particularly at issue is control of Los Monjes Islands, which lie off the Goajira Peninsula, at the northeastern tip of Venezuela. The islands were occupied by Venezuela in the 1950s, but the issue of Colombia's oil-drilling rights in the surrounding waters of the gulf is unresolved.

A Middle American boundary that is not in political contention, and yet is probably the most serious of all Central American flash points, is Panama's southern border with Colombia. The 170-mile line cuts across the dense tropical rainforests of the Darien Gap (so named because of the gap in the Pan-American Highway system at Panama's southernmost province of Darién). This boundary is readily crossed by drug traffickers heading north from Colombia and smugglers moving arms southward from such Central American countries as Nicaragua and Panama to Colombian guerrillas.

The Darien Gap has long attracted smuggling, and the unintended consequence of the U.S.-supported Plan Colombia to fight Colombian drug activity is to increase smuggling activities within the province of Darién. While most of the effort under the plan is directed against coca growers and processors in the far south of Colombia (in Putumayo province along the Ecuador border), actions are also directed at another area of production and guerrilla activity, Antioquia, which borders Panama. Narco-guerrillas operating in Antioquia have forced hundreds of refugees to flee across the border into Panama. They use Antioquia's jungles as safe havens, as well as for arms smuggling routes.

For Panama, which has no army, securing the border is difficult. This security situation has increased the burdens on its police, already heavily engaged in trying to crack down on contraband and drugs that flow through Colón, the second-largest free trade zone in the world. Without substantial U.S. financial and other aid to secure the border of Panama, the area is likely to become a tinder-box.

GEOPOLITICAL FORCES OF ATTRACTION AND SEPARATION

Overall, the boundaries and other geopolitical features play relatively minor roles in determining geopolitical destinies in Middle America. The determining elements are those geopolitical forces that shape the subregion's relationships with North America.

Geopolitical Forces of Attraction

The most compelling centripetal, or disruptive, force is location, both strategic and economic-demographic. Strategically, the Caribbean islands may be viewed as the northern and eastern sides of a frame that encloses the interior sea, with the Central American coastlands on the west. The northern side of the island frame is of particular significance to the United States. It consists of two "walls"—the Bahamas, which constitute the outer wall, and the Greater Antilles, which are the inner one. Through this part of the frame, traffic is channeled in three major passageways: the Florida Straits and the Windward and Mona Passages. Atlantic-Gulf shipping of the U.S. Maritime Ring moves via the Florida Straits, while Atlantic-Pacific shipping moves via the Windward Passage and the Panama Canal. Much of the Venezuelan-U.S. traffic uses the Mona Passage, between Puerto Rico and Hispaniola.

The eastern edge of the frame consists of the Lesser Antilles. These smaller and less-populous portions of the Caribbean are mostly European dependencies, although American bases are spotted throughout. Shipping to Europe moves via St. Thomas at the northern end and Trinidad at the southern end of this island string. The U.S. Navy has traditionally guarded the waters of the American Mediterranean from such bases as those at Key West, Florida; Guantánamo Bay, Cuba; Puerto Rico; and Panama. A naval base was established at Chaguaramas, Trinidad, at the onset of World War II, but the lease has recently been abandoned.

Time and technological change have greatly diminished the strategic importance of these bases. Long-range aircraft operating from the U.S. mainland and self-supporting naval battle fleets can easily dominate the Caribbean Sea. The narrowness of the Panama Canal and its locks structure has eliminated its use as a passageway for aircraft carriers and nuclear submarines. Indeed, the canal itself has lost much of its importance to the United States, as it now carries only 12 percent of U.S. waterborne commerce.

In 1979, Washington began to anticipate its eventual withdrawal from the Canal Zone when it signed a treaty with Panama that guaranteed the neutrality of the canal. American support of the right-wing regimes of Omar Torrijos Herrera and Manuel Noriega (until the latter's drug trafficking became an embarrassment) only served to increase popular anti-U.S. sentiment and turn the country toward neutrality. The U.S. Southern Command Headquarters was moved in 1997 from the Canal Zone to an air force station in Miami. By the time the Canal Zone reverted to Panama at the end of 1999, the use of the Howard Air Force Base, located within the zone, had become limited to surveillance efforts seeking to interdict the flow of cocaine and other drugs to the United States. Only a dozen aircraft were permanently stationed there, as it had become a forward-support airfield for fighters, tankers, and surveillance jets that passed through to operate over the skies of Colombia and other Andean countries. To replace this closed U.S. Panama base, alternative sites with only limited military installations and infrastructures are required.

The proximity of much of the Caribbean basin to the U.S. Maritime Ring is an aspect of its locational attraction. The Florida Straits, between the Florida Keys and Cuba, are only ninety miles wide, while the stretch of water between Grand Bahama and West Palm Beach is only sixty-five miles. New York City is seventeen hundred miles from Puerto Rico, fourteen hundred miles from the Dominican Republic, and one thousand miles from the Bahamas—in each case within two to three hours' flying time. New Orleans is six hundred miles from Cuba and one thousand miles from Jamaica, while South Florida is seven hundred and fifty miles from Honduras and twelve hundred miles from the Panama Canal. These distances have made the Caribbean highly accessible to American tourists and businessmen and have facilitated the flow of migrants and visitors from the basin to the mainland United States.

Access cannot be measured solely in miles and time distance, as those who have sought to escape from Cuba will attest, but proximity is a powerful force of attraction. It enables migrants from Middle America to maintain close contacts with families and friends who remain in the homeland. These contacts are the basis for networks that have developed to facilitate additional migration and to direct newcomers to supportive communities on the mainland. They also help to maintain cultural and familial bonds. From cities such as New York, for example, there is an annual exodus of migrants from Puerto Rico, the Dominican Republic, Jamaica, and smaller islands back to their Caribbean homelands for the winter holidays and even longer periods.

Another powerful centripetal force is the complementarity of climate and physiography, as well as of resources. From a strategic point of view, the petroleum that the United States imports from Canada, Mexico, and Venezuela is a compelling factor in the geopolitical linking of North and Middle America. These three countries provide the United States with its nearest and most secure sources of supply.

While other oil-producing regions, such as the Middle East, Nigeria, and Angola, are also important suppliers, they are more volatile politically. The U.S. embargoes on oil from Iran and Iraq are harbingers of what might take place should anti-American stances develop in future regimes in Africa, Saudi Arabia, or other Gulf States. Moreover, the increasing petroleum needs of the Asia-Pacific Rim and China offer closer markets for Middle Eastern and Indonesian exports.

Tourism is a major aspect of the Caribbean basin economy and the mainstay of some of the smaller islands. For visitors from the northern parts of the United States and from Canada, the Caribbean winter's warm climate, clear and warm waters, cooling easterly trade winds, and relatively dry weather are welcome relief from northern winters. In addition, the physical landscapes, which range from low-lying reefs, long sandy beaches, and sheltered coves to volcanic mountains, add to the region's attractiveness to visitors. In Central America, tourism has been stimulated by the wealth of archaeological sites and by ecotourism in the zones of topical forests, with their diversity of plant and animal life.

Complementarity extends also to the agricultural sector. While plantation crops no longer dominate the economy of Middle America, as they once did, sugar remains the economic mainstay of Cuba and is a major component of the economies of Barbados, the

Dominican Republic, and Jamaica. Honduras is still highly dependent upon bananas, Haiti and Guatemala on coffee, and Belize on lumber. These and other plantation crops, such as cacao, henequen, and tobacco, are also widely grown in neighboring countries and find their markets in the United States and Canada.

In 1993 a trade war broke out between Washington and the European Union over the trade preferences accorded by Europe to banana exports from small-scale growers in former and current Caribbean and African dependencies. These included Jamaica, Guyana, Guadeloupe, Martinique, St. Lucia, St. Vincent, and Suriname, as well as such West African countries as Cape Verde, Côte d'Ivoire, and Guinea. The U.S. position has been to promote an open market for Latin America's banana industry, which is dominated by U.S. corporations in Honduras, Guatemala, Costa Rica, Panama, Colombia, and Ecuador. The WTO ruled in favor of the American corporations, whose share of the European market had been cut in half by the EU banana policies. In April 2001 the dispute was finally settled. Terms of the agreement call for a modified system of quotas and tariffs to last until 2006, at which time all quotas will be lifted.

Among the most important Middle American minerals for the United States are bauxite from Jamaica and petroleum from Trinidad and Venezuela. In recent years, ultranationalistic President Hugo Chavez of Venezuela cut oil production to drive up prices, in keeping with OPEC guidelines. As a result, that country, which had been the single largest petroleum exporter to the United States, dropped to number four, behind Canada, Mexico, and Saudi Arabia. This may be only a temporary drop, in light of the vast oil reserves of the Maracaibo basin and the low cost of shipping the product to the United States.

The dependence of the Caribbean basin on farming, tourism, oil, and bauxite provides an inadequate base to meet the employment needs of its growing population. However, with the exception of Puerto Rico and Venezuela, manufacturing has made little headway in most of the region. There has been some outsourcing of apparel production to Costa Rica, Guatemala, Haiti, and Jamaica—the latter is also a substantial producer of alumina—but these activities have done little to change the economic structure of the region.

Thus much of the Caribbean remains mired in poverty, save for areas that specialize in financial services, tourism, or oil exports. Among the pockets of prosperity, the Bahamas have an annual GDP per capita over $20,000; the figures for Barbados and Trinidad are over $10,000 (the former relying on sugar processing and diverse manufactures, the latter on petroleum); and for Venezuela it is over $8,000. For most of the Caribbean and Central America, however, the figures are much lower. Some countries have per capita annual GDPs ranging from $3,500 to $4,500, but the majority are only at the $2,000 range and below. Indeed, for Haiti the figure is only $380, for Honduras $740.[16]

Grinding poverty, poor soils, and lack of land are the "push" factors for migration to the United States. The sixty million population of the Caribbean and Central America accounted for 160,000 immigrants, or 18 percent of all who legally entered the United States in 1996. Of these, the largest number (70 percent) came from five countries—the Dominican Republic, Cuba, Jamaica, Haiti, and El Salvador. Land pressures there are high, with population density exceeding six hundred persons per square mile in the latter three. In Central America, rural overpopulation and limited arable lands are aggravated by birthrates, which in most of the countries range from just under a 2 percent to a 3 percent increase per annum.

Poverty is not the only basis for the magnet effect of the United States. For Cubans and those who have fled other repressive regimes of both the right and left, strong attractions are opportunities for education and political and economic freedom. So is the desire to generate "migro-dollars" to support kinfolk who remain in the home region.

The drug trade and money laundering have also become powerful "pull" factors. While hardly a positive force of attraction, they nevertheless demand a continued U.S. interest and involvement in the region. Interdicting the flow of drugs from the Andean region of South America requires new forward bases for air surveillance. With the closing of the Panama bases, the United States has begun to negotiate with Honduras, where it has had a military base since the 1980s, to lease a field that would support short missions. (For Andes surveillance, an Ecuadorian air force base at the Pacific port city of Manta provides a U.S. air facility that will monitor air and sea activities in southern Colombia.) Two smaller air stations have been secured on the Dutch islands of Aruba and Curaçao to aid in the surveillance of traffic from northern Colombia across the Caribbean. The configuration of land and water explains why Jamaica, Haiti, Cuba, and the Bahamas are the chief stepping-stones for the South American drug trade and why the United States is so intent upon building surveillance mechanisms within or surrounding these islands. Offshore financial service centers have taken advantage of proximity in countries with very permissive tax codes to provide tax havens for investors and centers for laundering money illegally gained. Corporate shells have been established in such centers as the Cayman Islands, Grand Turk, the Bahamas, and Antigua—all close to the United States, but also providing ease of air access to Europe and Brazil.

Geopolitical Forces of Separation

Geopolitical unity between North and Middle America is a logical, but not inevitable, consequence of the geographical, strategic, and economic relations between the two regions. Centripetal forces also characterize these relationships. For the past century, these have been kept in check forcefully by direct or indirect military pressures, in addition to having been submerged by the countervailing forces of attraction that have been cited.

Many of the forces for disruption that were latent are now emerging. The resentment against large U.S. corporations that own vast sugar and banana plantations, as well as mineral interests, is based upon the fact that these raw materials are, for the most part, exported for consumption or processing, bringing little value added to the peoples of Middle America. Genuine complementarity would mean that each possesses its fair share of value added. This would be achieved if more food processing were to take place within the region; if some of the Jamaican bauxite and aluminum that is now shipped to the United States were converted to finished products in Kingston's factories; if Honduran lumber were made into furniture; or if the region's petroleum were made into a wider array of petrochemical and plastic products, and its hides into shoes and sandals. Most of the apparel making that is now being outsourced from the United States focuses on cheap labor and cheap items. There could be far more scope for an industry based on fashion design using local natural dyes and designs. Higher value-added products will be required if wages are to be raised for local workers. This is a policy-planning issue for Middle American governments, U.S. economic development aid, and American manufacturers.

While the era of U.S. support of right-wing dictatorships in Middle America is now over, the question of how to encourage political and economic reform has yet to be adequately addressed. Washington's 1994 military intervention in Haiti went awry because a military presence alone cannot guarantee the transition to democracy. Credible local politicians and a police force free of corruption are necessary to build a full and healthy society. In a country like Haiti, the decade and a half or more that it would have taken to nourish a stable, democratic society proved too long for Washington and the American public. Neither would tolerate keeping forces there indefinitely, as demonstrated by the pullout of U.S. troops in 1999. But Washington must face up to the reality that peacekeeping requires as much energy as waging war. It can and should tolerate a long-range program of aid and investments targeted at building up a middle class, training a governmental bureaucracy, and building a broad educational system.

The bitterness resulting from U.S. support for Middle America's right-wing dictatorships has fostered especially strong movements toward neutrality in world affairs within Venezuela, Panama, and Cuba (now that the former Soviet Union has left the scene). Memories of Washington's support of Venezuela's Marcos Pérez Jiménez, Panama's Torrijos and Noriega, and Cuba's Fulgencio Batista are deeply embedded in the national movements of those countries. Regaining the trust of their peoples is a slow process. The residual effects of these earlier interventions contribute to today's anti-U.S. nationalism within the region, and is a centrifugal force.

U.S. military bases in Cuba and Puerto Rico fuel such anti-Americanism, as they did in Panama. If the Cuban American lobby is so powerful that the U.S. Congress is unable to adopt a rational foreign policy, at least planning for the post-Castro era should take into account the opposition of many Cubans to U.S. retention of its Guantánamo Bay naval base. Nestled within the southern basin of Guantánamo Bay, the forty-five-square-mile naval reserve includes air fields and fortifications, and is a major training center for the U.S. Atlantic fleet. It also became the site of a prison encampment for al Qaeda fighters captured in the war in Afghanistan. The 1903 lease of the land and its 1934 renewal was imposed by the United States. Provisions of the treaty require consent of both governments to revoke it. Since 1960 the Cuban government has rejected these terms and sought return of the land. Just as Washington accepted the inevitability of withdrawal from Panama, so should it prepare to do so at Guantánamo Bay. This would be in the interest of future strong and mutually beneficial relations with Cuba.

Another disruptive military force is the U.S. Navy's continued use of Puerto Rico's island of Vieques, eight miles from the main island's southeast coast. Vieques has become a major issue for Puerto Rican nationalists, environmentalists, and fishermen. The civil disobedience that in April 1999 prevented the navy from using the island as a firing range for the Atlantic fleet war games has become a major political headache for Washington. Bombing, with the use of "dummy bombs," was resumed, as the Clinton administration offered $50 million to the ninety-three hundred inhabitants of the island, an offer suspended by the Bush administration in March 2001. The initial agreement permitting use of the island lasted only until 2002. A storm of opposition to continued use of the range has been generated within both Puerto Rico and areas such as New York, Chicago, and Florida that have large Puerto Rican populations. This resulted in halting live-fire exercises; the Bush administration has promised to leave the island by 2003. The navy plans to compensate for the impending loss of Vieques by increasing its Florida training facilities.

In the 2000 elections for governor of Puerto Rico, the pro-commonwealth party gained 48.5 percent of the vote, the pro-statehood party 45.7 percent, and the independence party only 5.6 percent. With such a razor-thin margin, the statehood forces could prevail in a plebiscite on the future of Puerto Rico and thereby assure that the U.S. military bases will remain in place. If, as seems more likely, the commonwealth forces should prevail, then the future of these bases is more tenuous. In either case, Vieques is a wake-up call to Washington that the United States cannot continue to export to the island undesirable land uses, such as bombing ranges, without the clear support of the Puerto Rican government and people.

At the eastern end of Puerto Rico and across the water from Vieques, the Roosevelt Roads Naval Reservation ship and air installations surround the harbor of Esenda Honda. As one of the U.S. Navy's largest bases and an employer of local inhabitants, the base provides considerable local economic benefits. Nevertheless, local sensitivities do not always take economic gain into account, thus Washington should prepare for the possibility of being asked to vacate Roosevelt Roads.

Before the Vieques-type opposition spreads to Roosevelt Roads, it would be prudent for Washington to settle any outstanding issues that the populace might have about that facility and take steps that will increase the benefits that the island derives from this and all other U.S. military facilities.

With the loss of its Panamanian bases, the near-inevitability of return of Guantánamo to Cuba in a post-Castro era, and the uncertainty that surrounds its Puerto Rican military facilities, the Pentagon needs a long-range strategy for Middle America that is built upon alternative sites.

The surveillance facilities being sought in Honduras, Ecuador, and Peru have only limited functions. For full-scale bases and firing ranges, there may be no alternative, ultimately, but to expand facilities on the U.S. mainland.

Conclusion

The integration of Middle America with North America to form a unified geopolitical region is based upon the dependence of the Caribbean basin lands upon the United States and, to some extent, Canada for investment capital, markets, economic aid, tourism, and emigration outlets. The United States, in turn, needs Venezuelan oil as well as the lesser amounts supplied by Trinidad. Proximity and configuration of its lands and narrow seas combine to make the Caribbean basin strategically vital to the security of the eastern and southern portions of the U.S. Maritime Ring.

Another centripetal force taking on increasing importance within the region has to do with Mexico's leadership in promoting trade with its Central American neighbors. A free trade agreement exists among Mexico, El Salvador, Guatemala, and Honduras, while Mexico has separate agreements with both Costa Rica and Nicaragua. The Mexican government has also proposed a "Puebla-to-Panama" plan to integrate efforts at promoting tourism, trade, education, environmental protection, and disaster relief planning among Mexico's nine southern (and poorest) states and their seven Central American neighbors. The projected linking of electric power, telephone, and gas grids within the region would, if implemented, constitute an important geopolitically integrative force.

While the countries of Middle America are far too small and poor to attain the partnership levels that Canada and Mexico enjoy with the United States, this does not mean that Washington can ignore their political and cultural sensitivities. The Cold War incentive of U.S. support for right-wing dictatorships is over. It has been replaced by emphasis on economic development as well as actions that encourage democratic government and protection of human rights.

There is no guarantee that right- or left-wing regimes will not emerge in the future. However, recent history has demonstrated that heavy-handed military intervention in Middle America does not provide long-range solutions. A more rational policy approach is to expand balanced trade and economic assistance and to use these as leverage when necessary.

Notes

1. Frederick Jackson Turner, "The Significance of the Frontier in American History" (paper delivered at American Historical Association meeting in Chicago, 1893); reprinted in Turner, *The Frontier in American History* (New York: Henry Holt, 1920), 1–38. The superintendent of the Bureau of the Census had concluded that a frontier line could no longer be traced and that discussions of its extent and westward movement would have no place in future census reports. From this, Turner developed his thesis that with the passing of the frontier the first period in American history was over. It was in the period, Turner held, that free western lands served as the safety valve for the discontented population masses of the East and molded the independent spirit of frontierism.

2. Ellen Churchill Semple, *American History and Its Geographic Conditions* (Boston: Houghton Mifflin, 1903), 397–419; Friedrich Ratzel, *Politische Geographie der Vereinigten Staaten* (Leipzig: Oldenburg, 1897), 17.

3. Alfred T. Mahan, *The Problem of Asia and Its Effect upon International Policy* (Boston: Little, Brown, 1900), 24–26, 63–65, 84–86.

4. James Malin, "Space and History: Part 2," *Agricultural History* 18 (July 1944): 65–126.

5. George Cressey, *The Basis of Soviet Strength* (New York: McGraw-Hill, 1945), 245–46.

6. Alexander de Seversky, *Air Power: Key to Survival* (New York: Simon & Schuster, 1950), map facing 312.

7. Richard Lonsdale and J. Clark Archer, "Emptying Areas in the United States, 1990–1995," *Journal of Geography* 96, no. 2 (March/April 1997): 108–22.

8. Fred M. Shelley, J. Clark Archer, Fiona M. Davidson, and Stanley D. Brunn, *Political Geography of the United States* (New York: Guilford, 1996), 235–80.

9. Joel Krotkin, *The New Geography: How the Digital Revolution Is Reshaping the American Landscape* (New York: Random House, 2000), 3–26, 38–51, 130–39.

10. Shelley et al., *Political Geography of the United States*, 308–35.

11. Derwent Whittlesey, *The Earth and the State* (New York: Holt, 1939), 528–29.

12. Ian MacLachlan and Adrian Guillermo Aguilar, "Maquiladora Myths: Locational and Structural Change in Mexico's Export Manufacturing Industry," *Professional Geographer* 50, no. 3 (1998): 315–31.

13. Semple, *American History and Its Geographic Conditions,* 397–419.

14. Nicholas Spykman, *America's Strategy in World Politics* (New York: Harcourt, Brace, 1942), 51–61.

15. "Central America's Border Order," *Economist,* 13 March 2000, 42.

16. Rand McNally, "World Gazetteer: Profiles of Countries and Places," *World Facts and Maps,* 2000 Millennium Edition, 70–224 (Skokie, Ill.: Rand McNally, 2000).

CHAPTER 6

Maritime Europe and the Maghreb

"Maritime Europe" aptly describes the human habitat that lies within the western peninsular and insular reaches of Eurasia, where European civilization evolved. In many ways, Western Europe is the archetypical maritime region. It is characterized not only by a sea-oriented set of physical and economic conditions, but by inhabitants who have developed a distinctive, trade-oriented outlook that stems from their interaction with the sea.

The omnipresent maritime influence is underscored by the fact that most of the region's inhabitants live within 250 miles of open water and that the region is traversed by major rivers and valleys offering ease of access to the coasts. The physical characteristics of the region are highlighted by temperate, moist, marine forest or Mediterranean-type climates and moderately fertile, humid, midlatitude podzolic or terra rossa soils. These, together with timber, waterpower, coal, iron, and chemical resources, fostered intensive agriculture and facilitated Maritime Europe's emergence as the world's leading manufacturing center during the industrial revolution. Toward the end of the twentieth century, the coal reserves were supplemented by North Sea oil and natural gas. The harbors and coves of the deeply evolved, well-stocked fishing waters of the submerged Atlantic coastline, and the more limited fishing grounds off the jagged Mediterranean coast, provided an early basis for a fishing economy, as well as for the development of commerce.

It was within this setting that modern national states arose. Most were organized around Historic Cores nestled within river valleys with access to the seas. The political boundaries that separated them were drawn along such physical barriers as mountains, morainic ridges, marshlands, and open waters. As Western European states developed, they compensated for their relatively limited land bases by trading with far-flung parts of the world and ultimately developing colonial networks. Indeed, the Western European experience demonstrated that a small land area could sometimes be turned to advantage. The land frontiers of the Netherlands needed limited armies, while the nation's fleets had modest manpower requirements. The same holds true for Britain, whose surrounding waters offered considerable protection from outside foes. From their more restricted land bases, both states were able to compete for world power with larger, more populous land powers like France and the German states.

The differences of culture, religion, language, and physical settings that had set European peoples apart from one another during medieval and early modern times intensified with the emergence of the modern national state and the carving out of colonial empires.

What these Western European rivals had in common were not only the material conditions of Maritimity, but also the psychosocial outlooks inherent in the concept of both national state and empire. It was the sea that gave Europeans the opportunity to reach out—to explore and to seek new raw materials, products, and markets in exchange for their manufactured goods. The infinite nature of open-water expanses encouraged a national and regional mindset attuned to opening up new fields of economic activities and pursuing innovations in manufacturing, trade, and services. While from the sixteenth to the twentieth centuries Europe's major powers did, indeed, divide the world into separate colonial sectors, open systems that depended on exchange were developed within those separate spheres of influence that ultimately would become the basis for intraregional exchange and unity.

The European regional trading system goes back to medieval times, and even to the classical Roman era, when traders moved outward with the legions. Thus, a millennium ago, European regional commerce was stimulated by networks of medieval trading centers that linked Anglo-Saxon, Gallic, Germanic, Scandinavian, and Slavic territories. German merchants set up trading houses in London as early as the eleventh century. Two centuries later (1226), the Hanseatic League of north German cities was organized. Over the next four centuries, the league extended its network along the North and Baltic Seas to embrace up to 160 cities and towns, before its collapse in the mid-eighteenth century. A similar alliance among the communes of Lombardy, the Lombard League, had been formed in 1167, but lasted for only a century, torn apart by the wars between the papacy and the German rulers of the Holy Roman Empire.

In early modern times, European focus on commerce took on a global range. British, Dutch, and French trading companies operated within Asia and North America from the seventeenth into the nineteenth centuries, as they vied for control of international trade. In addition, sophisticated banking and finance systems within Europe spurred the region's economic development. An example was the House of Rothschild, which operated branches in Frankfurt, London, Paris, Vienna, and Naples. This network played a major role in financing the operations of various European governments and providing the capital for railroads, mines, and the Suez Canal.

The global economic and political hegemony of Europe ended with two world wars. The first bled it of youthful manpower; the second left the region too devastated to hang on to its global empires. Despite the Allied victory in 1945, Western Europe could not compete with the American and Soviet superpowers. Its condition of geopolitical inferiority was underscored by dependence upon the United States for its military security, as well as its economic recovery.

Three recent forces have enabled the region to overcome its inferior status and take its place as a full partner with the United States within the Trade-Dependent Geostrategic Realm: (1) political and economic unity as expressed by the European Union and other groupings and agencies; (2) the collapse of the Warsaw Pact and dismantling of the Soviet Union, which eliminated the military and political threats that had absorbed so much of Western Europe's political energy; and (3) the vigor with which European corporate and financial sectors have followed the U.S. lead in promoting the global market economy.

Within a brief quarter century, Maritime Europe has emerged as the world's most highly specialized and integrated geopolitical region. The member states of the EU and its neighbors have turned from seeking security exclusively through national economic, political, and military institutions to deriving more and more of this security through common regional agencies and actions.

This concept of security through regional integration derives strength from the broader geostrategic framework within which Europe is embedded—the Maritime Realm, the core of which is the Euro-Atlantic alliance. Indeed, absent such a broader framework, Europe's regional unity goals would probably have been far less ambitious and might never have been attained. It was the North Atlantic Treaty Organization that provided Western Europe with the military shield against Soviet pressures, especially during the early phases of the Cold War, and enabled it to resist powerful internal Communist parties. Moreover, the presence of the United States as the military mainstay of NATO made it possible for Germany and its neighbors to put aside past enmities in favor of a common regional destiny. NATO protected Western Europe from Germany, just as it protected Germany and the rest of the region from the USSR.

It was the economic might of the United States that put Europe on the road to recovery and in the position that it holds today—an economic power, with a population of 375 million, whose combined wealth and financial centers are on a par with those of the United States, despite relative weaknesses in the euro currency. Europe's engineering, electronic, pharmaceutical, and fashion industries both compete for global economic partnership with their American counterparts and work in partnership with them.

While Maritime Europe has clearly emerged as one of the world's major power centers, it nevertheless lacks some of the geopolitical patterns and features that are found in North and Middle America, Heartlandic Russia, and East Asia. First, Maritime Europe's core is not a single, unified national state, but a federation of such states. Its unity derives from a balance between national and regional interests, and there are constant tensions over the striking of such a balance. Second, the region's land base is limited. It lacks such geopolitical features as a lightly populated and extensively exploited Effective Regional Territory (ERT) and a vast Empty Area—features that provide the other regions with defensive depth, room for space-age activities, natural resource reserves, and the potential for population absorption.

Incorporating the Maghreb (western North Africa) and the Sahara into the geopolitical region supplies the desired Empty Area. However, the ERT that links the other regions to their Empty Areas is still missing. The transitional land connection to the Sahara in Morocco, Algeria, and Tunisia consists of a narrow coastal plain backed by the Atlas Mountains. Thus the Maghreb cannot serve as an outlet for European population expansion, as it did during the colonial period. On the contrary, the tide of immigration has been reversed. The overpopulated countries of Morocco and Algeria now provide Europe with much of the large pool of migrant labor that forms an unskilled underclass in urban and rural areas and is a source for growing social tensions.

Thus Maritime Europe holds strategic and economic sway over western North Africa. Now that the Russian sphere of action in Eastern Europe and the eastern Mediterranean has been curtailed, Maritime Europe's reach into these regions is by no means foreclosed. Should Turkey enter the EU and Israel arrive at a peace agreement with the Palestinian Arabs, Syria, and Lebanon, Europe's economic aid and investment will be vital to supporting the peace and promoting eastern Mediterranean development. Under such circumstances, the broadening of Maritime Europe into a Euro-Mediterranean geopolitical region would become a realistic possibility.

The boundaries that set off Maritime Europe and the Maghreb from the rest of the world system are marked by water barriers in three directions—the Atlantic to the west, the Norwegian Sea-Arctic Ocean to the north, and the Mediterranean to the southeast. To the south there are formidable barriers—the Atlas Mountains and the Sahara. The Atlantic water barrier extends from Iceland to the Azores and Canary Islands, excluding Greenland, which is geographically part of North America although it belongs to Europe geopolitically. The northern Norwegian Sea-Arctic Ocean boundary includes the island of Svalbard. The southeastern Mediterranean barrier waters separate Cyprus from the Levant (Israel, Lebanon, Syria, and the Palestinian Authority).

Only in the east does nature play no role in Maritime Europe's geopolitical demarcation. There, beyond the Oder River, the northern European plain broadens into Poland, Belarus, and the Eurasian plain, and Continentality prevails. As a consequence, the geopolitical border between Maritime Europe and the Eurasian Heartland has fluctuated historically across a broad zone of contention within Central and Eastern Europe. It is not nature, but the relative military and economic strengths of competing power cores and the structures of their respective strategic alliances that have fixed the limits of the region.

Soviet power pushed the line westward to the Elbe River in 1945. In the wake of the collapse of the Soviet Union, the boundary now is being shifted eastward by Western European economic might and NATO's military power. The ultimate location of the line will depend to a considerable extent on the force that the West can and wishes to bring to bear, and on the success with which Eastern European countries manage their new market economies. However, the boundary will also be fixed by the counterpressures that Russia can exercise—pressures that will depend on the speed with which Moscow can regain sociopolitical cohesion, modernize its armed forces through sophisticated weaponry and a better-trained professional army, rebuild its failing economy, and uproot the corruption and "crony capitalism" that have become synonymous with the Russian version of the market economy.

Geopolitical Features

The geopolitical features of the Maritime Europe and the Maghreb region include its Historic Cores, Political Capital(s), Ecumene, Effective Regional Territory, Immigration Patterns, Empty Area, and Boundaries.

HISTORIC CORE

Location of a region's Historic Core varies with the regional framework that marks a specific era. The Nuclear Core of Western Europe could be the Plain of Latium, the seat of the Roman Empire. For Eastern Europe and the Mediterranean, the core is Constantinople, capital of the eastern empire. The seat of power of the Carolingian empire was the North Rhine-Westphalian center of Aachen. Paris was the Historic Core for Napoleonic Europe, while Brussels is the nucleus for today's unified Europe. It was Brussels that headquartered the first of the European bodies dedicated to the unity of the region, the European Coal and Steel Community. Subsequently (1958), Brussels became the center for the Economic Union of Belgium, the Netherlands, and Luxembourg, then, in 1967, for the European Economic Community, the forerunner of the European Union.

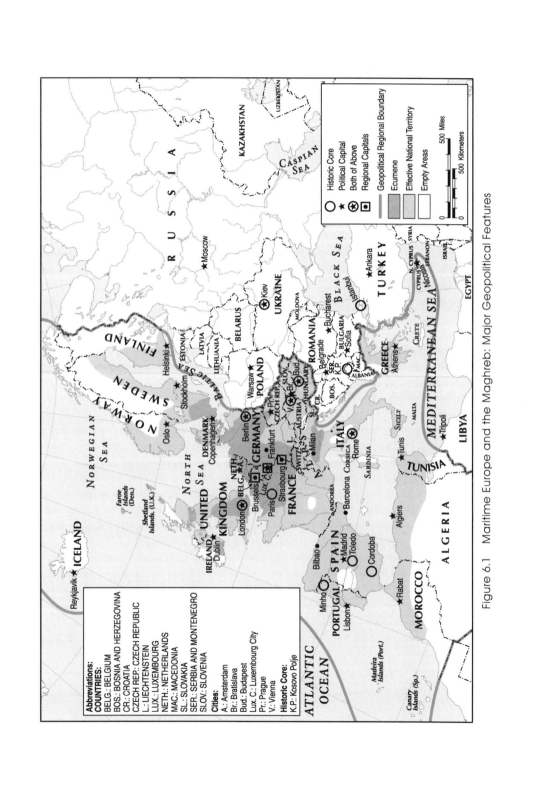

Figure 6.1   Maritime Europe and the Maghreb: Major Geopolitical Features

POLITICAL CAPITAL(S)

Identifying Maritime Europe's political capital is equally complex. The capital of a nation is more easily defined than that of a unified region. The former is the seat of centralizing functions that cast their influence upon the various parts of the state. The capital of a geopolitical region, however, must serve a group of nations with disparate interests, zealous in their own prerogatives. In some situations, including that of Maritime Europe today, such a capital is seen as "neutral ground," possessing a distinctive political-psychological character that can help regional leaders to mobilize public opinion in support of regional aims, and yet not play an overpowering role. At a national level, Ottawa and Canberra fulfill such roles in highly federated states. In other situations, such as that during the Soviet era, Moscow's function and image expressed its regional dominance.

The European solution to the selection of a regional capital eschewed a single, "neutral" site. In the early 1950s, Saarbrücken appealed to many as a possible capital because it was under consideration as an autonomous district within the Western European Union. It fell out of consideration in 1955, when its electorate rejected a Europeanized Saarbrücken, preferring to remain part of West Germany. Geneva, too, was considered as a potential capital, given its location, facilities, history, and tradition as a neutral international center. However, Switzerland remained aloof from the EU and the Western European Union, thereby disqualifying Geneva. The country's strongest concession to formal bonds to a unified Europe are its membership in the European Free Trade Association, along with such other European countries as Norway, Iceland, and the Principality of Liechtenstein.

Rather than one capital being designated for the EU, its political functions were dispersed. Brussels became the seat of the European Commission and the Council of Ministers, Strasbourg of the European Parliament, and Luxembourg City of the European Court of Justice. Of the three centers, Brussels plays the more prominent role because it houses the European Commission, the union's major decision-making body, which is composed of one minister from each member state. The European Parliament in Strasbourg is the popularly elected representative governmental body. However, its legislative powers are largely consultative, save for the fact that it has the final vote on the EU budget. In addition to being the headquarters for the EU Court of Justice, Luxembourg City also houses the European Investment Bank.

The distances between these three "capitals" are short—120 miles separating Brussels from Luxembourg City and 45 miles separating the latter from Strasbourg—thus affording easy communication among the three. Of equal importance is that this "capital corridor" is central to southeastern England, the Paris basin, and the Rhine Valley, and thus lies within the heart of Europe's ecumene.

The appeal of Brussels to be the "first among equals" of the three centers is not only its central location attributes. The city has a cosmopolitan flavor, a moderate climate, and political and economic stability and has long been a center of culture and the arts. It is multilingual and multicultural, with rich traditions in trade and finance. With a history dating back to the sixth century A.D., Brussels can rightly claim that it has been a crossroads of European currents and traditions.

Over and above those cities formally designated as seats of EU functional activities, certain national capitals have strong political or economic influence in determining the destiny of Maritime Europe. London, Paris, and Berlin have played the decisive roles in taking Europe to this stage of regional unity and will clearly continue to influence the future directions of the region. Frankfurt has become the financial capital of the EU, serving as headquarters for its new Central Bank and the twelve-member euro currency zone. Architectural and building plans are underway to enhance the city's foundation and image as the modern European capital.

ECUMENE

The outlines of the Western European ecumene are defined by the region's heaviest concentrations of population and economic activity. The area extends from southeastern Ireland, the English Midlands, and the Thames basin through Paris and northern France, the Low Countries, northern Germany, the Rhine Valley, and the Swiss plain, into northern Italy. Population densities generally exceed three hundred persons per square mile. The ecumene includes such metropolitan centers as London, Paris, Randstad Holland, the Rhine-Ruhr conurbation, and the Hanover-Bremen-Hamburg triangle. From there, a northern prong extends to Copenhagen and Malmö, an eastern prong to Magdeburg-Brannschweig-Berlin, a southern one along the Rhine to include Frankfurt, Mannheim, and Stuttgart, and a southeastern one from Leipzig to Prague. In the Rhine-Ruhr conurbation, Dortmund has become the hub for high-technology firms, which have replaced the declining, older chemical and steel industries. London, Paris, Frankfurt, Geneva, and Milan serve as the driving financial engines.

In the delineation of the ecumene of a nation or a region, small, noncontiguous outliers may also be included. An important outlier is Italy's highly industrialized Po Valley, which extends from Turin through Milan. Southeastern Ireland, a thriving center of high-tech industry, and southern Scotland are recent outlier additions, despite the physical gaps between them and England's portion of the ecumene. The addition of southern Scotland reflects its economic revival, owing to the development of high-tech industry. Moreover, offshore oil and gas pumped from North Sea fields have contributed to the economic boom. Indeed, Scottish nationalists argue that an independent Scotland could become a wealthy country, especially if the deeper offshore fields prove to be as extensive as believed. Whether or not Scotland achieves independence, it is emerging as a northern exclave of Britain's portion of the European ecumene.

The industrial decline of England's Midlands and its northern reaches sets these regions in sharp economic contrast to the high-tech, service-oriented, prosperous southeast, and thus the former are no longer part of the ecumene. The same applies to the "Second England" of the North, where textile and steel mills have closed, the shipbuilding industry has collapsed, and the coal mines no longer operate.

From Bremen-Hamburg, the ecumene extends to the Oresund, where Malmö, Sweden, has been linked to Copenhagen, Denmark, and thence the rest of the continent by a bridge-tunnel system. Copenhagen's airport is a hub for northern European aviation. The dynamic industrial and financial economy of the Oresund is well positioned to reach out to southeastern Norway (Oslo) and southern Finland (Helsinki). Its industrial base includes engineering, motor vehicles and aircraft, pharmaceuticals, shipbuilding, armaments, telecommunication equipment, and a financial sector that has been strengthened by mergers of Nordic banking and insurance firms.

The middle and upper Elbe and Mulde River Valleys of southeastern Germany and the Czech Republic branch southeastward from Hanover to extend the ecumene from

Leipzig to Halle to Dresden to Prague. This area has a heavy concentration of chemicals, machinery, textiles, transportation, optical instruments, electronics, and armament production, besides being a focus for commerce and financial services.

With the growth of the high-tech industry, not only has the European ecumene been revitalized, but also its outer boundaries are being expanded. University centers are playing a key role in attracting venture capital to their cities to support innovations in such fields as software, computer chips, wireless technology, interactive television, and biotechnology. Thus university towns like Cambridge, Leiden, and Louvain have spearheaded developments that have compensated for the decline into rust belts of nearby areas once powered by coal and steel.

In southern Europe, a high-tech industrial arc has developed that extends from the aeronautical factories of Toulouse to the computer chip center of Sophia Antipolis near Nice. This arc is poised to join the Turin-Milan portion of the current ecumene, which is also a focus for software.

North of the Alps, Munich has become a major center for biotechnology and can be expected to pull prosperous southern Germany into the upper Rhine portion of the ecumene, which now extends to Stuttgart.[1] In northern Europe, Stockholm, Uppsala, and the Finnish university town of Tampere are important for telecommunications. However, they are too geographically removed from southern Sweden to join the expanding European ecumene.

EFFECTIVE REGIONAL TERRITORY

Europe's Effective Regional Territory (ERT) includes areas that are more lightly populated than the heavily urbanized ecumene, but are readily "exploitable" due to their locational relationship to the ecumene, favorable soils or minerals, and an adequate transportation and communication net. From one-quarter to one-third of Maritime Europe consists of arable lands that constitute the ERT. These lands are mainly in farming or grazing and support substantial rural populations. For example, the rural populace of Portugal is 64 percent, of Ireland 42 percent, Italy 32 percent, Norway 27 percent, and Spain 23 percent. At the same time, these countries, with the exception of Portugal, have highly modern industrial and postindustrial economies to support this farming sector and to speed its modernization.

Under normal conditions of modern development, one could expect the row-crop and pasture lands of these countries to be converted to more intense economic uses and be rapidly absorbed into the ecumene. However, culture, traditions, and politics tend to maintain the status quo and block an urban expansion that could relieve the ecumene from current "piling up." Exceptions are the Upper Garonne (Toulouse to the Mediterranean) and southern Bavaria (Munich to Augsburg).

European unity has made it possible for poorer countries to support their farm economies because of EU agricultural support policies. The EU annual budget of over $90 billion allocates approximately half to farm subsidies, with French, Italian, and Spanish farmers being the major beneficiaries. Without a change in EU and national farm policies, the ecumene is likely to remain contained spatially, burdened by the weight of population and economic activities, rather than expand into the ERT, as is the normal progression of development. Should there be a change in policy, relatively flexible high-tech, telecommunications, and service industries could readily move into parts of the ERT. Areas with potential for such movement are the Spanish Meseta, Italy's Mezzogiorno, and France's

Aquitaine basin, which covers the area from the Pyrenees through the Lower Garonne (Bordeaux) and then extends northward along the Bay of Biscay to La Rochelle.

IMMIGRATION PATTERNS

Recent immigration has played a key role in the growth of the Maritime European ecumene and expansion of its ERT during the past half century. The region that had for so much of the modern age exported its surplus population has in recent decades become an importer of migrant labor from abroad.

There is, as yet, no common European policy on immigration, leaving it to individual governments. Most of those who have migrated to the EU countries and have remained there are guest laborers, seasonal workers, asylum seekers, or illegals who have been smuggled into Europe through a variety of sea and overland routes. The largest number of migrants settle in the major urban centers of the ecumene or in outlying metropolitan regions. Many, however, come as farm laborers, some on a seasonal basis.

The origins and destinations of these foreigners reflects a combination of geographical proximity, former colonial ties, and acquaintance with the language of the host country. Germany has more foreigners than any other European country—seven million, or 9 percent of its population. From 1960 to 1973, when it terminated the program, the Bonn government heavily recruited guest workers *(gastarbeiters)*, the majority of whom came from Turkey. The Turks, who now number over two million, are joined by the hundreds of thousands of immigrants who have come from Eastern Europe—Poland, Hungary, the Czech Republic, Estonia, Romania, Slovenia—and from North Africa. This flow of immigrants has been augmented by tens of thousands of asylum seekers, especially from the former Yugoslavia and Turkish Kurdistan, but also from the Middle East. The Balkans also serve as a key route for hundreds of thousands of illegals from Asia who seek entry into Europe. While Germany is the most generous of the EU member states toward asylum seekers, there is also widespread racial and religious prejudice within the country toward immigrants on the grounds that their absorption will dilute German culture and nationalism.

In addition to these seven million immigrants, more than three million ethnic Germans have come to Germany since the collapse of the Soviet empire. The majority of these are the *Russland Deutsche*, who are descendants of German settlers who were first invited to the lower Volga region by Russian empress Catherine II in 1763. The others have come from Poland, Romania, the Czech Republic, Slovakia, and the Baltic states.

Over the course of time, the Volga German population grew, until it reached 1.8 million by the end of the nineteenth century. The growth was such that farmland became scarce in the Volga region, so in 1890 a program was launched to settle ethnic Germans in western Siberia. In 1924 the German Volga Autonomous Republic was established in recognition of the unique cultural background of the settlers. However, the republic was dissolved in 1941 and the inhabitants were deported to Siberia and Kazakhstan because of Stalin's fears that they were Nazi collaborators. Few of the ethnic Germans who have migrated from Russia are fluent in German, thus their absorption has been not much easier than that of non-German immigrants. This is true also for many of the ethnic Germans who have come from Poland.

France, with over six million foreigners, is the EU's second most popular destination for immigrants. During the Algerian War of Independence (1954–62), one million French colonists returned to the mother country. Since then, they have been followed by nearly four million Muslims, mostly from Algeria and Morocco, many via the overnight ferry from Algiers to Marseilles. Africans from French West Africa are also numerous. Proximity and fluency in the French language facilitate this migration. Employment is primarily in low-paying service and construction jobs in the large cities of France. Italy attracts illegal migrants from Tunisia and Albania, some of whom then move on to northern Europe.

Spain fills most of its farm labor needs from Morocco. The vast majority of workers are illegals who cross into Spain via the Strait of Gibraltar. Some Moroccans use the Gibraltar route to move on to the urban centers of France or to construction jobs in the Netherlands, whose foreign population is approximately three-quarters of a million, or 4.5 percent of its total population. The Dutch migrant workers come from widely distributed points of origin—from the former colonies of Indonesia and Suriname, the Maghreb, the former Soviet Union, and southeastern Europe. Sweden, too, has a relatively high proportion of foreigners—over half a million, or 6 percent of the populace. Most of them come from eastern and southeastern Europe.

Many refugees came to Britain from Eastern Europe immediately after World War II. The much larger influx, however, is the result of historic ties with former colonies, which accounts for many of Britain's more than two million immigrants. Large numbers of English-speaking South Asians came to Britain to escape the terror of the India-Pakistan War of Partition. They were followed almost immediately by migrants from English-speaking West African and the Caribbean countries. West Indies bus drivers and hospital workers were actively recruited in the 1950s and '60s, before this immigration was closed off in 1971. Now small numbers of seasonal farm laborers are drawn from Eastern Europe.

During the past decade, the demand for outside labor has expanded to include skilled workers. Ireland, with an explosive economy short of labor in the fields of information technology and electronics, has launched a vigorous campaign to attract Irish expatriates from the United States, Canada, and South Africa. In addition, there are job opportunities for hospital and hotel workers.

Most of Maritime Europe's recent migrations have been based on temporary work permits, the granting of asylum, or illegal residence. In many EU countries, the migrants face exploitation, racial bias, and other forms of discrimination. Austria's Jörg Haider and Jean LePen have made political capital by opposing Muslim and black immigrants. Their success has encouraged the rise of right-wing, anti-immigrant parties in Italy and the Netherlands and struck receptive chords among groups in Germany, France, Spain, and Greece.

Ironically, the anti-immigrant bias coincides with a time of declining population growth within the EU. Recent projections of the UN Population Division suggest that the countries of Maritime Europe will need thirty-five million immigrants by 2025, and up to seventy-five million by 2050, simply to maintain the labor force at 1995 levels. The proportion of elderly within the EU is expected to increase from today's 15 percent to 22 percent in 2025. Without continuing immigration, total EU population may drop from today's 375 million, which is 135 percent greater than that of the United States, to less than the total U.S. population.[2] Because of declining birthrates, some European countries, such as Italy and Spain, face a major decline in population within the next two decades.

A major overhaul in immigration policy is required if Europe is to maintain its current living standard, let alone keep pace with the United States. This would involve a systematic approach to instituting a sizable, planned, legal immigration, rather than the unordered response to labor needs. There would also have to be a corresponding change in attitude toward foreigners to replace hostility with an understanding of religious and ethnic pluralism and multiculturalism.

While the record of the United States in its treatment of immigrants is surely not flawless, it has been far more open to them than has Europe. The difference is rooted in the concept of "a nation of immigrants" that is embedded in American myth, law, and reality. The United States today has over thirty million citizens and permanent residents who are foreign born (and from seven to nine million illegals) and another approximately 800,000 legal immigrants enter each year. In general, their contributions are recognized and valued, be these in low-skilled jobs in farms, hotels, restaurants, hospitals, and construction or in the professional and highly skilled technology fields in which one-quarter of all immigrants now work. The EU and its constituent nations could benefit from the U.S. experience, given the reality of having become a region of refugee in-migration and their need of the newcomers for economic health.

EMPTY AREA

Maritime Europe has no vast empty spaces and it is in this connection that the Maghreb is such an important geopolitical adjunct. The Empty Area for the region is the Sahara, the world's largest desert, which has a population of under two million. Vast oil and gas deposits underlie the desert surface in Algeria. In addition, there are extensive deposits of iron ore in Mauritania and western Algeria, as well as phosphates in northern Morocco and Western Sahara—the former Spanish colony that was annexed by Morocco in 1975. A source of conflict in Western Sahara has been the native Polisaro independence movement, which operates out of Algerian bases and is backed by the Algerian government. While a cease-fire agreement a decade ago muted the conflict between the rebels and Morocco, it has recently heated up again.

Until the end of the 1960s, France was able to use the inaccessible and seemingly endless Sahara Desert tracts for nuclear and rocket-launching activities. Colomb-Bechar and Hamiguir in the Western Sahara, as well as Reggane in southern Algeria, were used for missile testing from the late 1940s through the '60s. Reggane alone was the scene of seventeen underground and atmospheric nuclear tests conducted by France. However, because of the tensions between Algeria and France, such tests were moved to the Moruroa and Fangatufa atolls of southern French Polynesia in the Pacific Ocean. Inasmuch as use of the Sahara for space launching sites has also been precluded, France has shifted these activities to Kourou in French Guiana, where the European Space Agency now maintains an active program. This is a far different function than that played by French Guiana up to the end of World War II. For centuries, this overseas department was used by the French as a site for penal colonies, such as Devil's Island, and for sending political exiles.

When Algeria resolves the long-standing Islamic fundamentalist rebellion that, together with Berber unrest, has destabilized the country, and when it is able to offer Europe a reliable staging area for joint space activities, the Sahara is likely to again become an important world arena for civilian as well as military space-launching purposes.

What differentiates the Saharan Empty Area from those of the world's three other major power centers is that the Atlas Mountains are a major barrier to access from southern Europe to the desert region. In contrast, the settled portions of the United States, Russia, and China have direct land connections with their respective Empty Areas. In addition, similar to the case of Russia, which has lost most of its midlatitude desert regions to Kazakhstan and the four other former Soviet Central Asian republics, Europe's access to the Sahara is now highly dependent on stable political relations with the Arab western North African states, especially Algeria.

BOUNDARIES

The Eastern Border Zone

The eastern boundary of Maritime Europe is the region's only undefined boundary from both a physical geographical and a geopolitical standpoint. Most geographical definitions of the European continent describe its eastern border as running along the Ural Mountains and then southward to the Emba River, which flows into the northwestern Caspian Sea. Within this broad geographical framework, the break between Europe's maritime and continental portions follows a broad zone within which the boundary has oscillated.

The boundaries of this zone, one of the oldest geopolitical features in European history, have fluctuated with the relative power and movements of Germanic and Slavonic peoples. There was, indeed, a boundary between these two, set by the Treaty of Verdun, as early as 843 A.D. It ran along the Elbe and Saale Rivers to the Bohemian Forest. For the next five centuries, it was breached by the Germanic peoples, who penetrated into Slavonic territory in a series of forays and invasions.

The deepest early penetration was along the Baltic Sea, where commercial opportunity and large tracts of agricultural lands and forests beckoned. The Hanseatic League created a string of trading centers along the Baltic coastlands in the eleventh century that extended from Lübeck, Copenhagen, and Malmö in the west, through Danzig to Riga, Reval (Tallinn), and Narva in the east.

A more aggressive invasion was that of the Order of the Teutonic Knights, who established control over the whole sweep of the coastal region by the beginning of the fourteenth century. They created large landed estates and strengthened the Germanic hold over these Slavic lands.

In succeeding centuries, the tide turned. The Germans were driven out of the eastern Baltic, which then became a battleground among Poland, Sweden, and Russia. The latter eventually prevailed, gaining control of the region in the eighteenth century. In the western Baltic, however, East Prussia and West Prussia remained German. They joined the Principality of Brandenburg in 1600 and led the eventual unification of the modern German state.

During the first half of the twentieth century, Germany again pressed eastward, invading Russia in World War I and the Soviet Union in World War II. This eastern border zone continued as the meeting point and battleground between Germans and Slavs, but now became part of the broader clash between land and sea power.

In 1915, James Fairgrieve described the belt in Europe between the Eurasian Heartland and the Western European sea powers as a broad "Crush Zone" of buffers, extending on the east from Scandinavia and the Baltic countries through Eastern Europe to the Black Sea, and on the west from the Low Countries and Germany to Switzerland.[3] This was a much broader zone than the one presented by Halford Mackinder in 1943, which extended from the Baltic to the Black Seas and represented the contact area between Eurasian land power and European sea power. Fairgrieve postulated that the boundary line within the zone would shift as technological change and political-economic developments gave one side strategic advantage over the other.[4]

In the struggle between Maritime and Continental Europe that followed World War II, the boundary shifted westward to the Elbe as a result of the extension of Soviet power (see figure 6.1). When the former Third Reich was divided in 1945, West Germany's eastern boundary ran from Lübeck to the lower Elbe and then southward following the Harz Mountains and the Thuringian Forest, before swinging eastward to the Ore Mountains. What became East Germany was stripped of its eastern March Lands (the territories of Prussian expansion), which were transferred to Poland and the Soviet Union. The boundary between East Germany and Poland included Szczecin (Stettin) within Poland and then followed the Oder River to the Neisse River to the Sudeten Mountains and the Czech border. This line was recognized by East Germany in 1950; twenty years later it was recognized by Bonn.

The German lands to the east of this boundary were mostly transferred to Poland, in compensation for the eastern Polish territory that was annexed by the USSR. This territory covered thirty-nine thousand square miles and included western Prussia (Pomerania, Lower Silesia, and Upper Silesia), the independent state of Danzig, and the southern half of East Prussia. Although the German lands that Poland gained had been highly industrialized, they had been devastated by Allied bombing and the ground warfare between Soviet and German troops.

Offsetting this addition, between World Wars I and II, Poland lost to the Soviet Union an even larger area, totaling 68,000 square miles, of what had been eastern Poland. These territorial changes left Poland with a total land area of 121,000 square miles, or a net loss of 20 percent of its prewar area.

In addition to the lands that Germany lost to Poland, the northern half of East Prussia (the Königsberg region) was annexed by the USSR. Renamed Kaliningrad, it was directly affixed to the Russian Federated Republic.

The new post–World War II boundary between Poland and the Soviet Union extended from Kaliningrad and Lithuania south to the Carpathians. This line approximated the proposed Curzon Line, which had been recommended as Poland's border by Lord Curzon at the Versailles Conference following World War I, but had been rejected, first by the new Soviet state and then by the Poles. The Soviets demanded only that the line be redrawn to shift several small areas, five to eight kilometers eastward, to Russia that would have gone to Poland.

The Polish territory that was annexed by the USSR had been part of the Jewish Pale of Settlement—that part of czarist Russia to which Jewish settlement was legally restricted. This included such major Jewish population centers as Vilna, Grodno, Baranowice, Brest, Pinsk, Lviv, and Ternopil. Nearly all of the 1.3 million Jews of the Pale and the rest of Poland's total Jewish population of 3.3 million had perished in the Holocaust, as only a handful survived the concentration camps, fled to the USSR, or remained in hiding during the war.

The Soviet Union also seized Bessarabia from Romania to form the bulk of the Moldavian SSR's territory. The southern part of Bessarabia was added to Ukraine, as was North Bukovina, which lay to the west of Bessarabia. In the Soviet far north, strips of land were taken from Finland for the purpose of adding greater defensive depth to Murmansk, the mining centers of the Kola peninsula, and St. Petersburg. The Baltic countries that had gained their independence in 1919—Lithuania, Latvia, and Estonia—were also reabsorbed as soviet socialist republics.

All told, Soviet land acquisitions in Eastern and Central Europe totaled 265,000 square miles. They contributed substantially to Moscow's ability to keep a firm grip on its Warsaw Pact satellites and to pushing back the eastward reach of Maritime Europe.

In the wake of various territorial changes that took place, nearly ten million ethnic German refugees and expellees moved to West Germany. While most came from the lands east of the Oder-Neisse line in Poland and northern East Prussia, 3.5 million came from the Czech Sudetenland and half a million from Hungary, Yugoslavia, and Romania. Territories that had been Germanized for over twelve hundred years were now back in Slavic hands.

Other Boundaries

There are relatively few internal boundary disputes in Maritime Europe. The most serious are between Greece and Turkey on the eastern edge of the Mediterranean. One is the conflict over Cyprus and the other revolves around competing claims over territorial waters, airspace, and mineral deposits within the Aegean Sea.

The Greek Cypriot area is controlled by the internationally recognized Cypriot government, which holds 59 percent of the island's land area. The Turkish-Cypriot area occupies 37 percent of the island and the two are separated by a UN buffer zone that makes up the remaining 4 percent. Turkey's claims to the continental shelf affect the territorial waters that surround Greece's Aegean islands, like Samothrace, Lesbos, Chios Nikaria, Samos, and Khios. The Turks maintain that these Greek islands, which lie close to the Turkish shores, are entitled to only a six-mile territorial limit beyond their shores, while the Greeks assert that the limit is twelve miles. The dispute affects shipping and airspace rights, and it has been exacerbated by discovery of oil in the Aegean seabed.

The sovereignty of Gibraltar remains contested by Britain and Spain, particularly in the encroachment of Britain into what was established in the eighteenth century (in accordance with the 1713 Treaty of Utrecht) as a neutral zone. Gibraltar's airport is within this zone, around which the British have built a wall and fence.

At the northeastern end of Maritime Europe, Northern Ireland remains a major conflict zone. To be discussed in the section on the Maghreb are the territorial disputes between Spain and Morocco and those among the Arab states of western North Africa.

European Integration

THE MILITARY-STRATEGIC EQUATION

The reunification of Germany, the overthrow of Communist regimes in Central and Eastern Europe, and the collapse of the Soviet Union have made possible the eastward spread of Maritime Europe. The first step was expansion of NATO in 1997 to include Hungary, the Czech Republic, and Poland. NATO is now considering membership applications from Eastern European countries in a line from the Baltic through Poland to Romania and Bulgaria. Hungary's location has particular value to NATO strategically, since it borders six Eastern European and Balkan countries—Ukraine, Romania, the Federation of Serbia and Montenegro, Croatia, Slovakia, and Slovenia—as well as Austria and the Czech Republic in Central Europe.

The basic reasons for the initial enlargement of NATO were twofold. One was to strengthen security and democracy within these countries. The other, as expressed by Zbigniew Brzezinski and some leading German officials, was to reduce the overwhelming power of a reunified Germany by enlarging the alliance, while at the same time reassuring Poland that Germany would become its strategic partner, rather than a threatening neighbor.[5] Some viewed this as merely a first step. Albania, Bulgaria, Estonia, Latvia, Lithuania, Macedonia, Romania, Slovankia, and Slovenia have applied to be considered for full membership at the NATO summit of October 2002. Romania and Bulgaria are the least controversial of the applicants. Croatia, too, is seeking to join this group. The secretary general of NATO, Javier Solana Madriaga, strongly supported this expansion as part of NATO's new strategic concept of protecting Eastern Europe against the possible resurgence of Russia by way of a collective security pact that will have transatlantic links.[6] President George W. Bush has also vigorously advocated NATO's extension eastward to the borders of Russia, arguing that this would erase the "false" geographic divide between Eastern and Western Europe, protect democracy, and represent no threat to Russia. At the same time, Bush speaks of engaging Russia as a security partner, an eventuality that the NATO expansion would surely foreclose.

Such a proposed expansion would be a geopolitical blunder on the part of West. It would be met by bitter opposition from Moscow and rekindle the Cold War in a new form, as Russia would make a vigorous effort to strike up alliances with China, Iran, and possibly Iraq. Admission of the Baltic states into NATO would pose a direct threat to the heart of Russia. Most likely this would lead to the return of short-range nuclear weapons to bases in the Russian enclave of Kaliningrad, which is wedged in between Lithuania and Poland and is the headquarters for the Russian navy's Baltic fleet.

In 2001 Washington accused Moscow of moving tactical nuclear weapons into a storage depot in Kaliningrad, thus violating Russia's stated policy of keeping the Baltic free of nuclear weapons. While Russia vigorously denied such movement, it has also made it clear that it will oppose the expansion of NATO closer to its borders. If this were to happen, Russia would very likely renounce the nuclear-free policy as a way of putting pressure on Lithuania, Latvia, and Estonia. Lithuania lies astride the connections of Russia, through Belarus, to Kaliningrad; Estonia overlooks the approaches to St. Petersburg; and Latvia is on a direct line to Moscow. Should the Baltic states enter into negotiations for admission to NATO, Russia has the further capacity to destabilize them because of their large ethnic Russian populations—approximately 30 percent in Latvia, just under 30 percent in Estonia, and 10 in Lithuania—and to cut off the cheap crude oil that it now supplies to Lithuania's sole oil refinery. The Estonians, in particular, have pressed for rapid admission to NATO, but Germany has indicated its preference to keep all Baltic states out of the alliance.

Entry of Romania and Bulgaria into NATO would add to Moscow's current strategic concerns over its freedom to use the Black Sea. The greatest threat to Russia, however, would be posed by the possible inclusion of Ukraine. At present, a vaguely defined "special partnership" status exists between NATO and Russia. Drawing Ukraine directly into the North Atlantic Alliance would surely upset the current uneasy strategic balance, for it would represent a significant intrusion into the Eurasian Heartland. Moreover, admission of Ukraine would, in all likelihood, influence Moscow to seek to destabilize the Ukrainian government by encouraging the secession of the Russian population in the eastern Ukraine, including heavily industrialized Kharkiv (Kharkov) and the Donets Basin.

The argument that Eastern Europe's admission to NATO would diminish the historic threat of Germany to the region is dubious. Poland's security does not lie with its own armed forces. Even though Poland has been admitted to NATO, its best protection is a strong Germany that remains a cornerstone of the Atlantic Alliance and the proposed new EU Rapid Reaction Force. The security of Poland will also rest heavily on establishing stronger economic ties with Germany, not with the number of missiles and tanks it may possess. These economic links are rapidly being forged—Germany has already become Poland's biggest trading partner, accounting for over one-third of Poland's exports and one-quarter of its imports. Germany has also forgiven half of the debt owed to it by Warsaw. Indeed, it may be argued that the burden of added military expenditures could inhibit Poland's economic growth. Astonishingly, even Ukraine, Georgia, and Azerbaijan are seeking consideration as candidates for NATO membership. Were these applications to be entertained, positive relations between Russia and the West would be seriously undermined. The conflict between Armenia and Azerbaijan would drag NATO into a quagmire. Even George W. Bush, who has become such a staunch supporter of NATO expansion, is unlikely to press for NATO to include Russia's Trans-Caucasus backdoor.

The decision of the EU to build an armed force with the capacity for autonomous action in times of regional crises is a related military-strategic policy issue. The motivation is for Europe to be less dependent upon American-dominated NATO in situations that do not require massive involvement, but might be brought under control by a robust, mobile, sixty-thousand-man force. As conceived, this proposed EU Rapid Reaction Force would absorb the military functions of the dormant ten-nation Western European Union. France in particular views such a defense force as a way for Europe to exercise its separate identity and not have to wait on the action or inaction of the U.S. Congress and administration.

The stimulus for the EU Rapid Reaction Force was the demonstrable inadequacy of Europe's military capacity during the wars in Bosnia and Kosovo. In these conflicts, the European members of NATO found themselves lacking in precision-guided weapons and sophisticated intelligence systems, which inhibited them from having a meaningful role in influencing Washington's political-military policies. In addition, in both campaigns and the peacekeeping actions that have followed, unified command and control of NATO forces has been difficult to achieve. In Kosovo, the peacekeeping forces have been hampered by Washington's restrictions on the disposition of U.S. troops and its desire to keep them out of risky situations. The proponents of an EU Rapid Reaction Force feel that an independent military force will enable the EU to deal rapidly with European crises and eliminate this weakness.

Moscow has backed the concept of a separate EU Rapid Reaction Force for two reasons. First, it views this expression of European military independence as a counterweight to Washington's use of NATO to penetrate Eastern Europe. Second, it has a genuine concern about spot fires in neighboring countries to its west that need speedy attention, lest their destabilization affect Russia negatively.

However, the United States, citing duplication of effort, has been lukewarm in its support of an independent European military command. Another question raised by Washington has to do with the lack of symmetry between the two bodies, with EU members who are not part of NATO (Ireland, Finland, Sweden, and Austria) and the NATO members who are not part of the EU (Iceland, Norway, Turkey, the Czech Republic, Hungary, and Poland).

Turkey's role, especially, presents military and political complexities. The structure of Euro-corps is predicated on its having the use of NATO assets to conduct its operations, both those designed to intervene in wars and those designed to keep the peace. Many of these assets, such as AWAC (Airborne Warning and Control System) radar planes, tanks, helicopters, and military stores, are located in NATO bases in Turkey, where they are geographically close to many European potential trouble spots. Ankara has expressed qualms about the corps, conditioning support on its having a say in the planning of its operations, which may well affect Turkey, especially since its rival, Greece, is a member of the EU.

It could well be that this opposition is a political tactic aimed at using the Euro-corps issue to force a positive decision on Turkey's request for admission to the EU—a request that was snubbed in 1997. Although Ankara is now recognized as a formal candidate, its membership application remains stalled. Consideration has been put off to some indefinite date owing to the insistence of Greece that the Cyprus issue and territorial disputes in the Aegean Sea be resolved before admission of Turkey can be discussed.

THE EUROPEAN INTEGRATION MODEL

The European integration model differs profoundly from other regional integration models. NAFTA, for example, is concerned almost exclusively with economic integration. The former Soviet bloc, while it represented political, military, and economic unity, was built on a top-down model in which the USSR dominated the regional structures that were established. Maritime Europe is unique in that it is based upon a partnership of states, some with highly centralized and others with federal structures that have voluntarily turned over many, varied national functions to the regional body. While the initial foci of a unifying Europe were essentially on eliminating intraregional barriers to trade and movement, and on military security, the region has since evolved into a comprehensive union whose laws and regulations in the economic, social, and political spheres impinge directly on many once fiercely guarded sovereign rights.

Since the formation of a single agricultural market in 1993, the EU has had great influence in shaping a common agricultural policy for its member states, expending nearly half of its total budget on subsidizing agriculture. The consequences of these generous subsidies to full-time farmers, as well as the high tariffs or quotas levied on foods imported from outside the EU, has been to maintain high-cost grain and beef production. This forces European consumers to pay prices much higher than the world market level for these products. Another result is the piling up of stored surpluses, especially dairy products. The policy also tends to keep much of the rural landscape in place, when otherwise it might well have been overrun by forces of urbanization.

It was the restrictions on food imports that brought about the "banana war" with the United States and resulted in the WTO decision against the EU. The resolution of this costly trade dispute, which provoked retaliatory sanctions on European goods exported to the United States, may lead the way to a more flexible and less protectionist EU farm policy.

Achieving European unity is a struggle to find a balance between these national and regional interests, at the same time that Europe is striving for a new equilibrium with the United States within the Atlantic Alliance and the Maritime geostrategic realm. Within the European Union, the struggle focuses particularly on whether the EU should be a highly centralized body, as advocated by Germany, or a looser federation governed essentially by its member states—a position held by France. Britain is ambivalent.

Within the union, there have also been differences over such issues as embargoes on British beef by the continent's member states, British opposition to the euro currency, EU farm policies, the pace of enlarging the union, and the suspicion by some members that France is seeking to undermine NATO in its vision of an independent European military capacity. Nevertheless, the past decade of substantial economic growth and social advances weighs in favor of integration. This is reflected in crossborder corporate mergers; the ascendance of European law over national legislation in such areas as trade, human rights, working conditions, and environmental controls; and the effective loss of sovereign control over monetary policies on the part of the eleven EU members that have joined the euro currency zone. (Britain, Denmark, Sweden, and Greece are not participants in the zone.) To further strengthen economic integration, the introduction of joint customs and tariff policies is scheduled for 2003. Europeans have a long way to go in developing a sense of regional political European identity, but progress is undeniable.

In June 2001, Irish voters rejected in a referendum the Treaty of Nice, which provides for expansion of the EU by twelve members, starting in 2003. Under current union rules, the treaty must be ratified by all of its fifteen members. While the Irish referendum may be overturned in a future vote, use of the veto power by one member has now become a matter of debate within the EU, adding to the pressures for institutional change, which are also addressed in the Treaty of Nice. In addition to their concerns over the economic impact of extension, the Irish also fear having to participate in the proposed EU Rapid Reaction Force, thus undermining the country's traditional neutrality. This is another of the treaty's outstanding issues that will have to be addressed with the EU's proposed constitutional changes.

Even though Maritime Europe is not yet a superpower in the same sense as the United States, goals of achieving political, economic, and military parity are well grounded because of its economic strength and historical-cultural bonds and because its national ecumenes, with their dense communications networks, merge into the highly integrated regional ecumene. The fifteen EU members constitute the world's largest trading bloc and foreign aid donor. Their combined wealth of over $8 trillion in GDP nearly approximates that of the United States and their 375 million population is one-third larger than that of the United States.

Many assume that Wall Street now dominates the global capital market. In fact, the combined EU financial markets are as large, and the euro, despite its failure thus far to maintain parity with the dollar, serves to unify these markets by facilitating capital flow and commerce. Globalization of finance has helped Europe to strengthen its world position and prevented U.S. domination of the international economy. London leads the world in investment banking and fund management, and London and Frankfurt both top New York as the leading exporters of financial services. The wave of international corporate mergers that is so feared by Europeans, who decry the American acquisition of European companies, has been far from one-sided. European corporations have been equally aggressive in taking over U.S. concerns, so that a transatlantic balance exists in the process of corporate agglomeration.

The operating budget of the EU, which has been capped at under $100 billion through 2000, is minuscule compared to Washington's $1.7 trillion and is therefore a far less powerful fiscal instrument for the conduct of foreign policy. Nevertheless, Brussels does use its budget for regional aid to poorer members and, increasingly, for humanitarian assistance to the developing world. The foreign aid component of the budget—more than $6 billion—is already one of the largest in the world. Moreover, the EU has substantial influence upon international financial agencies, as well as on the treasuries of its member states.

In Middle East peace negotiations, for example, the United States has been the chief mediating force between Israel and the Arabs, and is perceived by the contending parties as the sole power that could help bring them to an agreement and then guarantee a peace. Nevertheless, in the event that peace does come to the region some day, it is highly unlikely that Washington will be willing to bear the major share of the financial burden that would go with the implementation of a peace, a cost that has been estimated at $20 billion. The EU and various European nations will be called upon to supply a substantial share of the required funds.

The major factors that contribute to Maritime Europe's march toward political integration are (1) complementary economic and human resources, (2) ease of movement across relatively short distances, and (3) a political commitment to regional unification.

Trade

Maritime Europe has historically been the world center for international trade, and it continues to be so. The exchange of goods and services that so dominates the economy also has shaped its politics and culture. One measure of the importance of foreign trade is that it represents 45 percent of the combined $6 trillion GDP of Western Europe's five largest states—Britain, France, Germany, Italy, and Spain. By contrast, U.S. trade represents over one-quarter of its $9.9 trillion GDP. Seen another way, these five countries, with combined populations of 300 million, generate $2.7 trillion in annual international exchange of goods and services, compared to the $2.2 trillion generated by the 278 million U.S. population.

The revolutionary change that has taken place over the past half century is that so much of this trade is intraregional, now that the movement of peoples, goods, and ideas is unhampered by Western European national boundaries. The five largest states conduct over half their foreign trade within the EU; U.S. trade with its NAFTA neighbors comes to 30 percent.

Trading characteristics are linked directly to the region's prosperity, as well as to its intensive internal links and its ties to the rest of the world.

Europe's larger countries have broader economic bases, but still benefit from specialized roles. Germany's economy is the most varied. With a gross domestic product that ranks fourth among the world's states, it stands out as the world's third-largest manufacturer of motor vehicles, as well as a leading producer of metal, engineering products, and chemicals. France is unique among its European peers in that three-quarters of its electricity is produced by nuclear energy. Chemicals, aircraft, and motor vehicles are major industries, along with wines and fashions.

Italy has retained an important niche in viticulture and the fashion goods industry, while its engineering, steel, and chemical industries are economic mainstays. For Spain, machinery, footwear, chemicals, and food are important exports. In its south, a system of intensive vegetable production for export has developed that uses irrigation and plastic sheeting and draws upon a labor pool from nearby Morocco. This complements the region's traditional sales of olives, fruit, and wines.

Great Britain has offset the decline in its traditional manufactures, such as steel and chemicals, to focus on service-related industries, especially finance and information technology. In combination with France, it also rivals the United States for civilian aircraft manufacturing. Sweden's broad manufacturing base provides exports in forest products, machinery, and transport equipment. Its telecommunications products also command a strong market.

Table 6.1   Maritime Europe Trade and Income

Country	Leading Trading Partner	Trade in Goods & Services (% of GDP)	GDP per Capita ($US in thousands)
European Union			
Austria	Germany, Italy, Switzerland, Japan	64	25
Belgium	Germany, France, Netherlands	134	25
Britain	U.S., Germany, France	45	23
Denmark	Germany, Sweden, Netherlands	70	26
Finland	Germany, Sweden, UK	65	23
France	Germany, Italy, Belgium	40	24
Germany	France, U.S., Italy, UK, Netherlands	57	24
Greece	Germany, Italy, France	27	17
Ireland	UK, Germany, France	146	22
Italy	Germany, France, UK, U.S.	36	22
Luxembourg	Germany, France, Belgium	110	36
Netherlands	Germany, France, Belgium, UK	106	24
Portugal	Germany, France, Spain	42	16
Spain	Germany, France, Italy	38	18
Sweden	Germany, UK, U.S.	89	22

Country	Leading Trading Partner	Trade in Goods & Services (% of GDP)	GDP per Capita ($US in thousands)
European Free Trade Association			
Iceland	UK, Norway, U.S., Germany	64	25
Norway	UK, Sweden, Germany, Netherlands	76	28
Switzerland	Germany, France, U.S.	88	29
Liechtenstein	EU	466	23

Sources: Rand McNally, "World Gazetteer: Profiles of Countries and Places," *World Facts and Maps,* 2000 Millennium Edition, 70–224 (Skokie, Ill.: Rand McNally, 2000); *The World Bank Atlas—1999* (Washington: World Bank, 1999), 56–57; Central Intelligence Agency, *The World Factbook 2001* (Washington, D.C.: Gov/CIA Publications, 2001).

Complementarity of economies enhances specialization among Europe's smaller countries. Thus, Iceland's electronics industry provides equipment for navigation and exploitation of fisheries to much of Europe's and the world's merchant and fishing fleets. Norway was the major producer of heavy water for nuclear reactors until it ceased production in 1989; but its merchant fleet, the third largest in the world, continues to carry 10 percent of global trade, and its fish products are widely exported. This is in addition to its chief exports—oil and natural gas. Greece continues to forge ahead as the world's leading shipping nation, with its fleets accounting for over 20 percent of the world's merchant fleet tonnage.

Luxembourg has overcome its depleted iron ores and its declining steel industry to gain prosperity as a world-class center for banking and finance. The economy of the Netherlands, although varied, has a special niche in hothouse flowers and cheese production, while it derives considerable strength from Europoort, which is the westward extension of the port of Rotterdam, located on the southern bank of the Hook of Holland, where the Rhine-Maas-Waal river system enters the North Sea. Europoort is Western Europe's major oil port and handles container traffic and the bulk movement of raw materials destined for interior Europe. Belgium continues to specialize in iron and steel and in textiles, while maintaining its position as the world's largest diamond-cutting center and specializing in glass production.

While fishing and farming remain mainstays for Ireland, its newly found prosperity is linked to its holding a major share of Europe's PC software and business applications, and to publishing and teleservicing. The products of Finland's telecommunications industry also enjoy a wide global market. Denmark has shifted to electrical and electronic equipment and financial services, with the decline of its agriculture, fishing, and shipbuilding. Microstates such as Liechtenstein and Andorra specialize in tourism and providing tax havens for trade and headquartering of foreign corporations. To these functions Monaco adds gambling as an important activity.

Transportation and Telecommunications

The highly integrated transportation and communications system of Maritime Europe has influenced the process of regional unity, which in turn accelerates the continued development of highways, railroads, rivers and canals, pipelines, and telecommunications networks. These are the sinews that bind Europe together. Among the more recent important links in the system are the auto-rail "Chunnel" under the English Channel and the Oresund Bridge and Tunnel between Denmark and Sweden.

The oil and gas fields of the North Sea are connected by pipelines to refinery centers along the coasts of the British Isles, Norway, Denmark, the Netherlands, and Germany. From there, a pipeline grid extends across Western Europe. A gas pipeline system also extends from North Africa's fields to southern Europe via Sicily and Italy, and to Spain via Gibraltar, while pipelines from Russia reach to the eastern Baltic, Germany, and the head of the Adriatic.

The import of fuels from the North Sea and African fields, as well as the Middle East and other parts of the world, is serviced through port installations all along the European coastline. Also, a dense intraregional grid from northern Scandinavia to the shores of the Mediterranean provides for the efficient sale and exchange of electricity, the net exporters of which are Norway, Sweden, France, Switzerland, Austria, and Spain.

Although road transportation now surpasses railways as the leading carrier of people and goods, the European rail system maintains high standards of efficiency, and high-speed railroads are strong long-distance competitors to aircraft.

Canals carry only 5 percent of the goods of Western Europe, but they continue to play an important role for local traffic, especially in northern Germany and the Low Countries. Intricate systems of canals and rivers connect the Seine to the Loire, the Loire to the Rhone, and the Rhine to the Moselle and the Marne. The Rhine-Moselle-Marne water system is especially useful for exchanging bulk materials such as coal, iron ore, and steel.

The spread of modern telecommunications and information systems is also impressive. The region outranks the United States in the development and use of wireless phone systems, although it lags behind the United States in personal computer and internet technology usage and marketing applications. The heaviest high-technology use centers around Paris, while in much of the rest of France there is cultural resistance to the adoption of home computers. The Netherlands, however, has demonstrated the capacity to develop as a world-class center for software production and e-commerce that is competitive with many U.S. centers.

The Politics of Unification

Initially, the driving forces behind the unification of Maritime Europe were the devastating effects of World War II and the threat of Soviet-exported communism. Economic recovery and military defense took precedence in the creation of European regional bodies. In recent years, however, it has become apparent to most Europeans that the region cannot achieve its fullest geopolitical potential without a unity that is reflected in both law and political outlook.

The key legislative institutions that have emerged in furtherance of European unity are the European Court of Justice in Luxembourg and the European Court of Human Rights in Strasbourg. In recent years, a European body of law has begun to emerge from cases that deal with nuclear waste disposal regulations, emission controls, trade, fishing quotas, working conditions, human rights, and discrimination in the armed forces. The competition between European law and national law is far from resolved, as enforcement of European edicts often encounters resistance from member states. In spite of such resistance, evolution of a supranational body of laws, a sine qua non for regional unity, is progressing steadily.

At the beginning of the year 2000, in an unprecedented display of political pressure, the EU imposed sanctions on Austria over inclusion of the far-right Freedom Party in its coalition government. All of the other fourteen EU members froze relations with Austria and downgraded contacts with its ambassadors to their countries. In a subsequent example of muscle flexing, Brussels put Turkey on formal notice that its imprisonment of the mayors of three largely Kurdish cities in the southeastern part of the country would jeopardize Ankara's application for membership in the EU. While these were early and isolated actions, they represent a growing commitment of the union's members to carving out a European political position based upon widely endorsed, Western ideological beliefs and values.

The two most important issues currently facing the European Union have to do with its governance structure and the management of its expansions. As noted, Germany has been a vigorous proponent of a strong, centralized European federation with a directly elected president and parliament sharing substantial power—in effect, a United States of Europe (as envisaged by Robert Schuman half a century ago). For their part, Britain and the Scandinavian members are opposed to any more dilution of national sovereignty and support only limited European parliamentary and executive powers, as in the current situation. It is premature to predict which view will ultimately prevail—a centralized superstate or a union of nation-states. France, which once espoused a Gaullist vision of a "Europe of Homelands," now also has taken a stand against a strong central governance structure. It favors increased cooperation in defense and economic policies, but opposes a constitution that would create a centralized federation. The French are leaning toward a European Union that is a confederation of nations with a hard core of inner circle members committed to fuller integration (in which the Franco-German alliance would hold the leadership) and an outer circle of members for whom the structure would serve more as a customs union. France is also opposed to reform of Europe's common agricultural policy, while Germany favors reducing farm subsidies. In addition, Paris fears Berlin's domination of the union, and thus opposes the reweighting of votes in the European Council, which would take into account the size of Germany's population—one and a third that of France.[7]

The organizational direction of the EU has profound geopolitical implications. A highly centralized EU expanded to include Eastern Europe to the borders of Russia would put Germany in a central location geographically within the union, in addition to its economic and demographic dominance. It would gain through peaceful politics what it failed to win in two world wars—strategic control of Eastern Europe and a position that could upset the balance between the Maritime Realm and Heartlandic Russia. However, an EU that remains a federation of nation-states would be balanced between England and France, with their Atlantic basin orientations, on the one hand and Germany on the other. Under such circumstances, membership expansion would be less of a threat to Russia and equilibrium would be preserved, not only within Maritime Europe, but also within the Maritime Realm and the world system as a whole. The subject of the future governance structure of the EU will be the focus of deliberation that began in 2002 over the drafting of a constitution for the union. Other questions to be resolved have to do with the extent to which the EU should exercise power over foreign affairs, military policy, and taxation—areas in which it currently has limited authority.

The negotiations over expanding the membership of the EU reflect these varying viewpoints. Those who advocate more stringent economic criteria for admission of new members seek early admission for states whose economies are relatively strong and can be more rapidly integrated within the EU system. These countries include the Czech Republic, Slovenia, Hungary, Poland, and Estonia, some of which could enter as early as 2003. Cyprus also is seeking early admission, although it has not yet been recognized as being in this category. Slovakia, Bulgaria, and Romania are among the countries that are furthest from meeting the EU criteria. Latvia, Malta, and Lithuania form an intermediate group.

Considerations other than economics also come into play. Even when some countries are economically weak, their applications have been promoted by Britain and France on the grounds of their having been strong supporters of the West during the Kosovo war. Applicant countries must also conform to Western requirements in cleaning up their environments. In almost every Central and Eastern European state, air and water pollution and unsafe nuclear reactors compromise health and safety standards. This suggests a long wait for Romania, Bulgaria, Slovakia, and Lithuania.

Those seeking membership must also demonstrate that their political systems are democratic, based on market economies and the legal protection of human rights. Turkey's application has been put off for reasons already cited—its Kurdish policies, the opposition of Greece because of the Cyprus conflict, and military control of substantial parts of Turkey's economy. The Turks are convinced that their being a country of Muslims is the fundamental barrier to their membership. The widespread discrimination that Islamic Turks encounter as guest workers in Germany and the similar hostility met by Muslim immigrants from North Africa are cited as evidence of racial and religious bigotry.

Geopolitically, Europe's failure to make a genuine effort to bring Turkey "into the "club," could have grave consequences. Turkey is a cornerstone of NATO. If rebuffed by Europe, it could refocus its geopolitical attention toward the Middle East and Central Asia, not only to the detriment of the geostrategic interests of the Maritime World, but also at the risk of increasing tensions with Greece and undermining Turkish secularism.

INCOMPATIBILITY OF EASTERN AND WESTERN EUROPE

The EU is trying to reinvent Eastern Europe and pour it into a Western European mold—an unrealistic policy driven less by sociopolitical realities than by the "soft security" argument of needing to wrench the region permanently out of the Russian orbit. Small wonder that the Turks are affronted when Bulgaria and Romania, but not Turkey, are considered appropriate candidate countries.

Prince Klemens von Metternich, the conservative Austrian statesman of the first half of the nineteenth century, sought to balance Central Europe off against a French-Russian alliance. He described Asia as beginning at a street leading out of Vienna called "the Renweg." Translated into modern terms, this suggests that Maritime Europe ends with Central Europe—at Vienna, Prague (Germanized Bohemia, the core of today's Czech Republic), and Budapest (the partially German city of Magyar-populated Hungary). From this line eastward, Continentality is the regional hallmark.

Vienna and Budapest, the two upstream Danubian cities, served as the twin capitals of the Hapsburg's Austro-Hungarian Empire during the latter part of the nineteenth century. Prague, which is linked to Germany by the Vltava River, a tributary of the Elbe, and by a number of valleys to the south that reached to the Danube and Vienna, was the northern terminus of the Central European axis that extended to Vienna and Budapest. By most cultural, economic, and historic measures, the Czech Republic and Hungary should be joined to the EU.

Slovenia, too, once an integral part of the Austrian Empire, has a rich Western heritage. By far the most industrialized, urbanized, and prosperous of the former Yugoslav republics, and strongly linked by trade to Germany and Italy, Slovenia is primed to enter the EU.

From these countries eastward, however, the expanded membership becomes problematic. One of the marks of a Continental orientation is its heavier dependence upon agriculture compared with Maritime trading states. Poland is the largest of the belt of Eastern European countries that border Maritime Europe, with a population of nearly forty million, one-third of which is rural, and one-quarter of its entire workforce still dependent upon farming. While the country has made some progress economically through modest market reforms, its agricultural development lags.

Lithuania, once a major regional power whose rule extended from the Baltic Sea to the Black Sea, was merged with Poland from the sixteenth to the nineteenth centuries, before being annexed by Russia. Russia remains its chief trading partner, particularly for oil imports, and Lithuania's population is 20 percent ethnic Russian. Although industrialized during the Soviet era, Lithuania is still heavily agricultural (27 percent of its population is rural) and remains much poorer than Poland. In southeastern Europe, Romania and Bulgaria are even more dependent upon agriculture—36 percent of the Romanian and 25 percent of the Bulgarian workforce are devoted to agriculture.

The large and inefficient agricultural sectors of these four countries would make their successful absorption within the EU more difficult. Their per capita GDPs range from 40 percent to two-thirds of the average per capita GDP of the Central European candidates. In addition, their industrial plants are antiquated. Their recent political histories of faltering governments, more often than not including ex-Communists in leadership roles, helps to explain their delays in tackling basic market-economy reforms.

A more realistic alternative to the EU's plans to admit this western belt of Eastern European countries might be to create a strong free trade association with these countries that would be similar to the North American Free Trade Agreement. Open markets and capital flow, outsourcing of industry from Western Europe, and ease of movement of people and goods would speed the economic development of Eastern Europe. It would do so without imposing laws and regulations that do not suit the geographical conditions, historical ties, and sociocultural values of this western fringe of Continental Europe.

If such an association were to be seriously considered as an alternative to expansion, the "fast-tracking" of Poland should be put off. So would Estonia's proposed membership, despite its historical-cultural and trade links to Finland and Sweden. (The Estonians are ethnically and linguistically close to the Finns.) Although such ties make Estonia a more feasible EU member, they have to be weighed against the sentiments of the country's large ethnic Russian population, which is opposed to becoming westernized.

State Proliferation

In a geopolitical region, national states are the nodes, and lines of transportation and communications the connectors, that form the regional network. Maritime Europe has the world's densest network of nodes and connectors, enabling it to achieve unmatched levels of specialization and integration. This dense network increases the capacities of the region to maintain a dynamic equilibrium because of the multiplicity of opportunities for feedback and self-correction by its various components. Should a state become destabilized and its connectors to the rest of the region become blocked, the other states have alternative interconnectors to maintain the integrity of the system. Neither civil war in Northern Ireland, nor terrorism in northern Spain, nor the Cyprus conflict has impeded Maritime Europe's drive toward regional unity.

The proliferation of nodes within an integrated system accelerates its development because the nodes can become additional centers of specialization. Thus, the proliferation of states, ministates, and quasi-states in Maritime Europe need not signal fragmentation and anarchy. For example, an independent Slovenia has already carved out its niche as a transit center for goods from Austria and Hungary to southeastern Europe. Should such nodes as Catalonia, the Basque country, and Northern Ireland become independent, could we not expect them to take advantage of their locations, manpower pools, and resources to add to Europe's economic and political power? This would be possible only if they could turn their full attention to national development rather than dissipate so much of their energies in the struggles for political freedom.

State devolution in Europe does not necessarily mean complete sovereignty, but it does mean granting peoples who live in historically held territories the right to self-determination and the freedom to conduct those functions that they consider crucial to their survival as a people. In general, the interests of peoples struggling to gain their freedom from host countries center on being able to decide on matters of language, religion, culture, and economics. They may well be willing to allow the larger state from which they seek to break away to retain functions that relate to foreign policy and military defense. San Marino, which lays claim to being Europe's oldest state, has renounced such rights as establishing a broadcast station and growing tobacco in return for an annual subsidy from Italy. Liechtenstein, one of the world's wealthiest countries and one joined to Switzerland in a customs union, has no army and is represented abroad through Switzerland, but conducts independent taxation and finance policies. Elsewhere, China's recent arrangement with Hong Kong—"two economies, one state"—is another useful model.

One of the consequences of the creation of the European Union has been to spur these national devolutionary trends through the revival of regional cultures and languages. The charter of the forty-one-member Council of Europe encourages indigenous languages in schools, media, and public life, while the EU's Bureau for Lesser-used Languages finances projects that promote minority tongues. Moreover, the reduction or elimination of barriers to trade and the movement of peoples throughout the union reduces the significance of current national boundaries.

Table 6.2 identifies national nodes that could emerge through a variety of new territorial entities within Maritime Europe, including states, quasi-states, confederations, and jointly ruled condominiums.

The Basque country of northern Spain (Vascongadas) extends from the coastal reaches of the Bay of Biscay inland to the Ebra River and into the western Pyrenees. Geographical isolation has helped the five million Basques, who are among Europe's most ancient peoples, to maintain their separate language, traditions, and nationality since the Middle Ages.

Table 6.2   Potential European States and Quasi-States

New National Node	Type
Azores	Gateway state
Basque region (Vascongadas)	Gateway quasi-state
Brittany	Quasi-state
Canary Islands	Quasi-state
Catalonia	Gateway quasi-state
Corsica	Quasi-state
Crete	Quasi-state
Unified Cyprus	Greece-Turkey condominium
Faeroe Islands	Quasi-state (second-stage independence)
Flemishland (Greater Flanders)	Neth.-Belg. condominium/quasi-state
Gibraltar	Gateway state/U.K.-Spain condominium (second-stage independence)
Greenland	State
Madeira Islands	Quasi-state
Northern Ireland	U.K.-Ireland condominium (second-stage independence)
Scotland	State
Trentino-Alto Adige	Quasi-state
Wales	Quasi-state
Wallonia (French-speaking Belgium)	State

During the Spanish civil war, they established an autonomous state that was then crushed by General Francisco Franco. Over the past three decades, the Basque guerrilla movement conducted a fierce battle against Madrid before accepting a cease-fire in 1998. The Basques are divided over their future with Spain. The moderate Basque right-wing and Socialist parties would accept a high degree of autonomy. The more extreme Basque Independence Party uses terrorism to try to achieve full independence.

This wealthy region, whose per capita income exceeds that of Spain as a whole, contains the thriving industrial centers of San Sebastian and the port of Bilbao, a major commercial and financial center with a strong industrial base. Although Bilbao's steel and shipbuilding industries have declined in recent years, its modernized industries include motor vehicles, pharmaceuticals, chemicals, textile machinery, and various consumer goods. Its infrastructure has been modified and its cultural institutions aid in the expansion of tourism. San Sebastian's major seaside resorts have fostered a significant tourist industry, along with its fishing, metallurgy, and machinery. With peace, the Basque region has the economic potential to become an important Gateway linking northern Europe and Iberia.

Catalonia's history of nationhood goes back to its separate political existence from the ninth to the end of the fifteenth centuries. Until the end of the Middle Ages, Barcelona's traders rivaled those of Genoa and Venice for commercial supremacy of the Mediterranean. The region has made consistent attempts to break away from Spain since the seventeenth century. A revolution for independence broke out in 1934, but failed. In the Spanish civil war of 1936–39, Barcelona became the Loyalist Republican capital, before falling to the regime of Francisco Franco, who repressed the Catalán language and culture. In recent years, Catalonia has been bolstered by considerable autonomy from Madrid and the regional Catalán government has made Catalán the official language, making it difficult for the non–Catalán-speaking half of the populace to conduct official business.

Barcelona, the center of Catalonia, is Spain's chief commercial and industrial center, as well as the country's leading port. Its industries include the manufacture of motor vehicles and parts, aircraft, electronics, machinery, and textiles. Catalonia as a whole is the wealthiest of all Spanish regions. With its population of nearly seven million, its well-trained workforce, and its historic Mediterranean leadership traditions, the region is especially well positioned to become a Gateway for the entire western Mediterranean. It could do so while retaining its close economic and security links to Spain, and without undermining Spanish economic and political viability. Gibraltar, another possible Gateway state, might emerge as a condominium between Britain and Spain.

In France, the grounds for Breton autonomy demands are essentially cultural and linguistic. Separate sovereignty has had little backing since Paris loosened its centralized grip by granting budgetary power to Brittany.

Corsica, with its distinct language and culture, has been the traditional scene of separatist movements, banditry, and blood feuds from the Middle Ages, when it was ruled by Genoa, up to its transfer to France in 1768. During the 1970s and '80s, Corsican guerrillas conducted bombing campaigns to advance their independence drives. In recent years, economic development strategies have focused on tourism. At the end of 2001, Corsica was granted limited autonomy, which included the teaching of the Corsican language in schools, but this is unlikely to halt separatist violence. A high degree of autonomy and quasi-statehood would appear to be a practical solution to the Corsica issue.

Crete was the scene of major separatist unrest against the Turks at the turn of the twentieth century, until its incorporation with Greece in 1913. Later, in 1938, Crete independence forces sought freedom from the dictatorship of Greece's Ioannis Metaxas, but the revolt was quashed. During World War II, when Crete fell to the Germans, and then briefly after the war, there was some Communist guerrilla activity on the island, but this did not spur the rise of a strong separatist movement. If the tensions between Greece and Turkey over Cyprus dissipate, and especially if Turkey should enter the EU, Crete's strategic value to Greece will decrease. Under such circumstances, Athens may be inclined to grant the limited powers of a quasi-state to this island home of one of the world's earliest civilizations.

Greek Cyprus has 80 percent of the island's population and nearly 60 percent of its land area. It is internationally recognized, but there will be no peace until a solution is found to the fears of Turkish North Cyprus of being absorbed by the larger, more prosperous Greek sector. Cyprus became independent in 1960 under agreements that forbade either union with Greece (*enosis*) or partition. The 1974 coup by pro-*enosis* forces triggered Turkey's invasion of the northern part of the island to protect its Muslim population. A federation of these two bitterly hostile territories, in isolation of their respective ties to Greece and Turkey, is unlikely. However, a confederation of the southern and northern parts, governed as a condominium by Athens and Ankara, might be acceptable as a near-term solution.

Belgium is an arena that might produce one or two new European national nodes. The political leaders of the Flemish (Dutch-speaking) populace of the prosperous north have expanded their previous demands for Flanders' autonomy within Belgium, to calls for a Greater Flanders, which would include both the Belgian north and the southern part of the Netherlands. Such a "Flemishland" would have a population of twenty-two million and an economy that would rank as the world's tenth largest. Because of its importance to both Belgium and the Netherlands, sovereignty for Flemishland would seem a dim prospect, but some sort of condominial cultural and economic autonomy may be feasible.

In southern Belgium, a separate Wallonia has been the goal of the French-speaking inhabitants. Wallonian nationalism has been strengthened in recent decades by the decline in the south's heavy industrial base and by chronic unemployment. The nationalist political parties are concerned also with protecting the French language and with losing political equality with the faster-growing Flemish parts of Belgium. For their part, many Flemish leaders have expressed little desire to maintain unity with poorer Wallonia. With an independent or quasi-independent Flemishland, a small, separate Walloon state could emerge.

Devolution in Northern Ireland is underway, despite recent stumbling blocks to implementing the accord between Protestants and Catholics that was signed in 1998. The agreement provided for power sharing between the Unionist Protestant majority and Republican Catholic minority. In accordance with its terms, an Assembly, Executive, and Ministerial Council were established. The Assembly was convened on December 2, 1999, however self-rule was surrendered in 2000 because the Irish Republican Army (IRA) was reluctant to disarm. Peace will remain elusive until the IRA, the Catholic Shin Fein Party's military wing, is decommissioned and the Protestant militia groups are dissolved. With peace, Northern Ireland could emerge, first, as a condominium, with such powers as defense and foreign affairs being shared by the United Kingdom and Ireland, and ultimately as a separate state.

There are two different territorially and ethnically separatist forces in northern Italy: Trentino-Alto Adige and Padania. Trentino-Alto Adige was once part of the Austrian Tyrol. Its German-speaking populace (now about half of the total population of the province of Bolzano and Trento) has been backed by Austria in its demands for legislative, administrative, and linguistic autonomy. Rome has already granted the region considerable autonomy, but the issue of return to Austria is not likely to remain quiescent without quasi-statehood in a condominial relationship to Italy and Austria.

"Padania" is an invention of the Northern League, a north Italian, right-wing party established in 1982. Its leaders speak alternately of secession and federalism. The territory generally viewed as Padania takes its name from the Latin name for the Po River and what is sometimes called the Padana Valley. Geographically, this region covers Lombardia, Piemonte, Liguria, the Veneto, and Emilia (half of Emilia-Romagna). There is no historic territorial basis for a Padanian state, nor is it linguistically distinct from the rest of Italy. What drives the secession goals of the Northern League is the desire to separate the richest part of Italy, the north (sometimes they extend their claim to Tuscany and Rome), from the poorer south. While this political movement cannot be lightly dismissed, the prospects for it dismembering Italy are very poor. There are also separatist movements in Sicily and Sardinia. However, since receiving limited autonomy, and because of their economic dependence on Rome, pressures for independence have subsided.

Portugal's Azores and Madeira Islands have already been granted the status of autonomous regions, while the Canary Islands have received greater regional autonomy from Spain—all part of the trend of devolution. Because of their economic dependence on their mother countries, quasi-independence would be most realistic for the Madeiras and the Canaries. The more distant Azores could evolve into a Gateway, given their strategic location one thousand miles west of Portugal, one-third of the way across the Atlantic, and one thousand miles off the northwest African coast. The Azores now accommodate NATO air bases and also have popular resort areas.

The establishment of parliaments in Scotland and Wales is an important milestone in their devolution. Scottish nationalists view this as a step toward independence, especially in the light of Scotland's recent economic upsurge. The growth of the high-tech industry and the prospect of control of offshore oil and gas reserves has heightened the nationalist calls for statehood, despite the greater political autonomy that Scotland now enjoys. Most of Britain's oil fields are located off the Scottish coast, as are 40 percent of the gas fields. In the event that Scotland were to gain its independence, the location of the Anglo-Scottish maritime boundary, which would extend from the River Forth into the North Sea, could become a point of contention. So might the fate of the Orkney and Shetland Islands, which lie off the coast of northeastern Scotland and have their own incipient separatist movements.

The situation differs for Wales. The overriding concerns of Welsh nationalists are education, language, and culture. These can be satisfied by greater autonomy as a quasi-state, particularly since the depressed economy of Wales makes it dependent upon London for long-term revival.

Greenland already enjoys semiautonomous status under the Danish crown, with foreign policy and defense being handled by Copenhagen. Nevertheless, Greenland continues to pursue self-determination for its fifty-six thousand people.[8] In particular, it seeks a stronger voice in the future of the U.S. Thule Air Force Base, which was built during World War II and has been greatly expanded in recent decades. While Denmark has reservations about allowing Thule to be used for the U.S. National Missile Defense system, the Greenlanders appear to favor such an installation and are using the issue as an opportunity to seek Washington's support for gaining a say in the ultimate decision. This ability would represent a form of quasi-statehood. In all likelihood, however, statehood may be the only way to satisfy the self-determination goals of most Greenlanders.

Denmark's Faeroe Islands lie between Iceland and the Shetlands. The Faeroes, which first came under Danish rule in 1380, have had a strong nationalist movement since the nineteenth century. In fact, the islanders declared independence in 1946 after a plebiscite, but then reversed the proclamation, receiving home rule in its place. This rule has enabled the fifty thousand inhabitants to close their fishing waters to EU members, despite their ties to Denmark. The plebesite on independence scheduled for May 2001 was canceled after Copenhagen threatened to cut off its subsidies to the Faroes. What may renew impetus for the new independence drive is the possibility of petroleum finds in the surrounding waters. It is likely that a quasi-statehood formula may satisfy the near-term ambitions of the islanders, especially since traditional fishing remains their economic mainstay and the need for annual subsidies from Denmark remains strong. In the long run, the Faeroes are likely to achieve full statehood, with symbolic ties to the Danish monarchy and close fiscal ties to Denmark.

In summary, territorial devolution of states within Maritime Europe can be expected to take different forms. However, rather than serving to fragment and weaken the region, they are likely to enhance its integration and strengthen it by adding specialized parts that will further bind the region together.

The Maghreb: Maritime Europe's Strategic Annex

The geopolitical relationships between Maritime Europe and North Africa are greatly influenced by the shape and structure of the Mediterranean Sea, its branches, and its surrounding coastlands. The present form of the sea is determined by the mountain ranges that make up three-quarters of its shores. The western Mediterranean basin, which extends from Gibraltar to the narrow waters between Tunisia and Sicily, is completely surrounded by mountains. Within the basin, the islands of Corsica and Sardinia form a north-south wall, to the west of which age-old trans-Mediterranean interactions developed between the Iberian Peninsula and France with Morocco and Algeria. The eastern side of this island wall helps to enclose the Tyrrhenian Sea arm of the Mediterranean, directing traffic between the western side of the Italian peninsula and the northern Tunisian shores.

The eastern Mediterranean basin is rimmed by mountains only on its northern and eastern edges. On its southern shores, from Sinai west to Egypt, Libya, and the Gulf of Tunis, the coast is low and straight, with no natural harbors. The transbasin links between the east coast of Italy and Libya cross the Adriatic and Ionian Seas and branch into the Mediterranean. At the eastern end of the basin, the Aegean Sea also branches into the Mediterranean, connecting Greece and Turkey with Egypt and the Levant.

The western Mediterranean basin has experienced a different history of political development than has the eastern end of the sea. The basin extends from its eastern end at the hundred-mile-wide Strait of Sicily, which lies between Cape Bon in northeastern Tunisia and southwestern Sicily, westward to the Strait of Gibraltar, which is only eight miles in width at its narrowest opening, between the Pillars of Hercules. For the most part, the western Mediterranean is encircled by young fold mountains. There are few breaks across them on the European side, save for the Ebro, Garonne, and Rhone Valleys. In the Maghreb, the limited openings across the parallel Atlas Mountain chains are blocked from the rest of the African continent by the Sahara Desert. A number of islands lie within the sea and serve as stepping-stones to both northern and southern coasts (the Balearics, Corsica, Sardinia, and Sicily). Settled long ago by Europeans, these islands have been outposts for European states in their strategic relationships with the southern shores.

The absence of effective breaks across the surrounding mountains has, until modern times, made the issue of control an internal or "family" matter within the western basin. Thus Carthage, Rome, North Africa, Spain, France, and Italy vied for control of all or parts of the basin, with little outside interference. Because of the limited, and therefore weaker, North African support base, the Moors (as well as the Carthaginians before them) did not penetrate effectively beyond Spain, Sardinia, and parts of Sicily. During the Middle Ages, Spanish-French-Austrian rivalry over Italy diverted the attention of the European powers from the North African coast.

In modern times came two changes: (1) improvements in land communications across Western Europe to the Mediterranean and (2) the Anglo-French alliance, which controlled both the western entrance to the Mediterranean and the trans-Mediterranean sea-lanes. From the second quarter of the nineteenth century to the beginning of the twentieth, France secured strategic control of most of the Maghreb. It first invaded Algeria in 1830, and in 1844 it defeated the sultan of Morocco, who had aided the Algerians in their continuing resistance. Algeria was formally annexed four years later, and French influence in Morocco grew steadily over the second half of the nineteenth century. Tunisia was invaded and became a French protectorate in 1883.

However, Spanish and Italian interests in the Maghreb, as well as interference from Germany and England, prevented the French from achieving total mastery in western North Africa. Paris had to share power with Madrid when, in 1912, Morocco was divided into a French protectorate over 90 percent of the land and a Spanish protectorate over the rest. In Tunisia, the French met with continuing opposition from Italy, which maintained considerable economic influence in Tunisia and a sizable number of its nationals as residents within the country. Ultimately, the geopolitical patterns of colonial association that France forged with this part of the Muslim world proved incompatible with Muslim demands for equality and political self-determination.

Léon Gambetta, the prime minister of France during the occupation of Tunisia, is quoted as having said in 1880 that the configuration of the French coasts and the establishment of French rule in Algeria had made the Mediterranean, and especially the western Mediterranean, France's "scene of action."[9] History has borne him out, but not in the geopolitical form that he had envisaged. After 170 years of colonization and acculturation, France's political influence in the Maghreb, while still strong, is tenuous.

Since the emergence of the Maghreb from colonialism, its relations with Maritime Europe have become ambiguous, despite the reality that France, Italy, Spain, and Germany remain its chief trading partners. The political relationship between France and Algeria still suffers from the legacy of conflict and colonial rule. In addition, with the region's independence, the economic gap that separates western North Africa from Europe has widened, not narrowed, leaving the Maghreb in continued economic dependency. The economy of the Maghreb would be in even greater distress were it not for the safety valve of emigration to Europe by millions of workers, many of them to France.

What gives rise to the hope that a new, trans-Mediterranean political partnership can be forged is that Europe and the Maghreb are now interdependent, and not bound together in the colonial dominant-subordinate mode. The EU needs the Maghreb's oil and gas as well as its labor pool. The Maghreb needs Maritime Europe's capital, technology, finished products, and tourists.

Algeria, the world's second-largest exporter of natural gas, has the fifth largest reserves. Its petroleum reserves rank fourteenth in the world. Currently, most of the oil and gas, which accounts for 25 percent of the country's GDP and nearly all of its exports, is sent to Italy, France, and other EU countries, with 15 percent going to the United States.

Tunisia is also an oil and gas exporter, mainly to the EU. Strategically located within the central Mediterranean and overlooking Libya, it is the Maghreb's gateway to Italy, southeastern Europe, and the eastern Mediterranean. Oil and natural gas pipelines cross Tunisia from eastern and central Algeria to Mediterranean ports and the gas line continues across the sea to Sicily and Italy.

The Maghreb is a focus for European capital investment, not only in energy and other minerals and petrochemicals, but also in its food industries. In addition, the combined population of seventy million for the three countries represents a market with major potential for Europe, as well as a major source for its necessary migrant labor.

Algeria, the regional power within the Maghreb, is the key to balanced relations between that area and Maritime Europe. With a population of over thirty-one million, which is only slightly larger than Morocco's twenty-nine million, Algeria's per capita GDP is one and one-half times that of its western neighbor, because of Algeria's hydrocarbon resources. Also, Algeria's industrial base is somewhat broader than Morocco's due to the former's petrochemical industries. While the armed forces of the two countries are fairly similar in size, Algeria's is the more battle hardened of the two.

Europe's dealings with Algeria, however, are complicated by the latter's political instability. The thirty-year War of Liberation against France, which ended in 1962, left Algeria's economy in ruins and caused half a million military and civilian deaths. In the years that have followed, Algeria has fought border wars with Morocco and has had to cope with political coups and Berber unrest.

The Berbers, who account for one-third of the total population, have struggled for over a decade to gain cultural autonomy, recognition of their language, and a share of political power through democratization of the regime. Their homeland, known as the Kabylia, extends across the mountains and coastal reaches east of Algiers, from their center of Tizi-Ouzou to Skikda. While those living on the coastal plain have become partially Arabized over the centuries, the mountain Berbers have not, having clung to their customs and to the Berber tongue and using French, rather than Arabic, as their second language.

In addition, part of southeast Algeria is claimed by Libya. Since the voiding of 1991 national elections by a military regime, Algeria has also been torn by the terror campaign against the government waged by the outlawed Islamic Salvation Front's fundamentalist guerrilla forces. Charges of vote rigging in the 1998 national elections have been additional barriers to resolving this conflict, in which one hundred thousand lives have been lost.

Berber unrest over failure of the government to officially recognize the Berber language has been quiescent since the riots were repressed in 1980. However, the language issue, coupled with widespread unemployment and governmental oppression, provoked major disturbances in June 2001 within the Berber Kabylia region. The rekindling of a Berber uprising, coupled with the continuing threat of the widening of the Islamic insurgency, continues to keep the country in turmoil. In 2002, as a gesture to the Berbers, the Algerian government agreed to make Tamazight, the Berber language, an official language alongside Arabic. This should reduce Berber unrest, although resentments over discrimination still are widespread and might be satisfied only by quasi-statehood.

Political turmoil has stalled economic reform efforts to change one of the most centrally planned economies in the Arab world and to reduce the overdependence on oil and gas resources. Much of the energy wealth has been dissipated through corruption and bureaucratic inefficiencies, while the bloated governmental workforce (30 percent of all workers) impedes the implementation of change. An added burden is the country's heavy foreign debt, built up by its need for continuing capital investment in its energy sector and its efforts to expand other industries.

Morocco, which gained its independence from France in 1956 and Spain in 1958, did so with minor disturbances, rather than a full-scale rebellion, as was the case for Algeria. In most of the years that have followed, Morocco has enjoyed domestic political stability under the tight rule of an absolute monarchy. The 1963 border conflict with Algeria was resolved by an agreement in 1970. However, the dispute with Mauritania over control of Western Sahara (formerly Spanish Sahara), which Morocco claims and administers, has yet to be adjudicated. After Morocco seized the entire territory and sent 300,000 settlers into the region, Western Sahara guerrillas, backed by Algeria, launched an armed struggle. It lasted throughout the 1980s, ending only when Algeria withdrew its military support. While the decade-long UN-mediated cease-fire still holds, the debate continues over the terms of an independence referendum. The Sahrawis (the "Polisaro"), who oppose the granting of voting rights to the Moroccans who have settled in the Western Sahara, maintain a well-organized government-in-exile in the camps of western Algeria. However, poverty is endemic. The economic plight of the Sahrawis, whose thirst for independence is sharpened by the richness of Western Sahara phosphates currently controlled by Morocco, may drive them to break the truce and drag Algeria into the dispute once again. The conflict in the Sahara, in which 30,000 guerrillas were killed, is far removed from where most of the Moroccan populace lives and has had little effect upon day-to-day life, tourism, or foreign investment. Morocco also disputes Spain's control of the coastal enclaves of Ceuta and Melilla and of three small islands, one in the Mediterranean northeast of Melilla, the others off the coast of Western Sahara.

The main challenge for Morocco today is economic. It is the poorest of the Maghrebian states and has the highest percentage of illiteracy. While the country exports phosphates, some iron ore and copper, and food products, the income derived from these products is only one-tenth of what Algeria receives from its oil and gas revenues. On the positive side, proximity to Europe and the cheap Moroccan labor force have attracted considerable foreign investment in industries and services that are rapidly privatizing, while tourism has been growing steadily. There is also an agreement with the EU for phased tariff-free trade by 2012. With continued political stability, prospects for economic improvement are good.

Tunisia is by far the most economically advanced of the three countries of the Maghreb. Its economy is diverse, with agriculture, mining (phosphates), energy (oil and natural gas), tourism, and manufacturing sectors, and its fiscal affairs are in order. The country had already enjoyed a measure of autonomy before it received its independence in 1956 and, under the leadership of Habib Bourghiba, followed a moderate socialist policy that was generally pro-Western and pro-French. Minor boundary disputes with Algeria were settled in 1970, and a 1980 Libyan invasion of a border mining town was repulsed. (A maritime boundary dispute with Libya remains unresolved.) Despite labor unrest during much of that decade, Tunisia has been generally successful in modernizing its economy, while providing a moderating influence within the Arab world. Its 1998 association agreement with the EU was the first between the union and one of the western Mediterranean Arab states, and since then trade barriers are being gradually removed. With a relatively high economic growth rate and close ties with its European neighbors, Tunisia, already a Gateway to trans-Mediterranean European states, can be the lynchpin in geopolitically connecting the Maghreb to Maritime Europe.

While most Western European leaders have cast their geopolitical gaze eastward, in their plans to expand the EU and NATO they would do well to look southward with equal, if not greater intensity. Europe's southern flank—the Maghreb—is already closely linked through history, trade, proximity, and immigrant labor. As large as is the economic gap between Western Europe and the Maghrebian states, it is no greater than that existing with some of the Eastern European EU candidates.

Creating the geopolitical framework that would extend the Maritime European region across the Mediterranean is a realistic goal. In contrast, deep penetration into the western margins of the Heartland represents a geopolitical overstretch, the strategic costs of which may well exceed the benefits. Regional unity between Maritime Europe and the Maghreb is economically feasible. A hurdle that must be overcome, however, is the racial and religious bias that has for so long distorted the European view of North Africa. Overcoming this bias is both an economic necessity and good geopolitics.

A geopolitically unified Maritime Europe and the Maghreb has many similarities to North and Middle America. The difference is that the Maghreb is much larger and more populous than Middle America and has had a history of hundreds of years of political, economic, and cultural relations with the European lands to its north. Europe enjoys strategic dominance over its southern Arab state neighbors through its overwhelming military power and control over Atlantic and trans-Mediterranean sea-lanes and Mediterranean islands. In addition, the EU has the economic capacity to support Maghrebian economic development.

Many of the elements involved in unifying the western Mediterranean basin are already in place. The challenge is for Maritime Europe to seize the opportunity by developing mechanisms that are not modern versions of the nineteenth- and twentieth-century imperialism that bound the basin together at that time. The requirement today is for institutions based on a mutuality of interests and equality of participation. If, for example, the EU is willing to enlist forces from non-EU member states in the prospective EU Rapid Reaction Force, it might also consider inviting its neighbors from the Maghreb to supply limited numbers of selected troops, an action that would be largely symbolic. A far more important step would be to forge a strong free trade association with Tunisia, Algeria, and Morocco. Such an association could then be incorporated into a broader free trade framework, which could also include the western states of Eastern Europe that are now being considered for EU membership.

Conclusion

As the European Union moves toward higher levels of specialized integration, its geopolitical status as full partner with the United States within the Maritime Realm has led it to take independent initiatives within the global arena. The union has taken a more flexible position on the subject of the sanctions that have been imposed upon Iran and Iraq. It has adopted a different stance from that of Washington on the Arab-Israeli conflict, one which generally exhibits greater sympathy toward the Palestinian Arab position. In North Korea, it has sought to engage Pyongyang diplomatically and economically, with the objective of moderating that regime's nuclear weapons program and helping to alleviate the country's food shortages.

The EU has been vigorous in its opposition to the decision of the Bush administration not to ratify the 1997 Kyoto Protocol. This accord, which has been signed by over one hundred countries, calls for the reduction in the emission of heat-trapping gasses, like carbon dioxide, that contribute to global warming. Since the United States is the source of one-quarter of all "greenhouse gasses," its refusal to support the climate accord would undermine its efficacy. EU leaders have expressed their concern that the American action would scrap the protocol and be a major setback to the urgent need for improving the environment. In addition, the Europeans, especially Germany, have expressed strong reservations about Washington's proposed National Missile Defense shield, on the basis of its flaunting the Anti-Ballistic Missile Treaty, and are strongly opposed to Washington's threats to attack Iraq and overthrow Saddam Hussein.

While the administration of President George W. Bush is drawing back from certain foreign involvements such as the International Criminal Court, the EU is taking a more interventionist approach. Other differences between the EU and the United States that are likely to emerge are differences over operational relationships between NATO and the proposed Euro-Corps and taking a harder versus a softer stance in relations with Russia. Such differences are neither unexpected nor unhealthy. In a genuine partnership they are likely to be resolved through a balanced approach to the issues in question.

Within Maritime Europe, the reunification of Germany and NATO's expansion into Central Europe and Poland have changed Germany's geographical position from that of border state to one of centrality. The geopolitical consequences of this centrality have a profound bearing on the strategic balance between Paris and Berlin, the states with the two largest economies. If the EU does expand eastward, Germany's position will be enhanced because of its central location within Europe, as well as its historic ties to the countries to its east and their increasing dependence on the Federal Republic for trade and economic aid. France's fear of being overshadowed may slow down this eastward expansion and increase the pressure for a looser, rather than a more centralized, regional governing body.

It is likely that Britain will become more fully engaged in EU affairs, which would maintain the balance among the union's leading members, rather than shift it toward German dominance. At the same time, the strength of the historic alliance between the United States and Britain will serve to preserve the partnership of interest between the United States and the EU within the Maritime Realm.

Notes

1. William Drozdiak, "Old World Reinvents Itself as Model for New Economy," *International Herald Tribune,* 19 February, 2001, 1, 11.

2. Barbara Crosette, "Europe Stares at a Future Built by Immigrants," *New York Times Week in Review,* 2 January 2000, 1, 4.

3. James Fairgrieve, *Geography and World Power* (London: University of London Press, 1962), 329–30.

4. Halford Mackinder, "The Round World and the Winning of the Peace," *Foreign Affairs* 21, no. 4 (1943): 268–73.

5. Jane Perlez, "Blunt Reason for Enlarging NATO: Curbs on Germany," *New York Times,* 7 December 1997, A17.

6. Javier Solana Madriaga, "Growing the Alliance," *Economist,* 13 March 1999, 23–28.

7. "France and Germany—Scenes from a Marriage," *Economist,* 24 March 2001, 27–30.

8. "Denmark and Greenland: Ultima Motives," *Economist,* 17 February 2001, 55.

9. Léon Gambetta, as quoted in Norman Harris, *Intervention and Colonization in Africa* (Boston: Houghton Mifflin, 1914), 238.

CHAPTER 7

Russia and the Heartlandic Periphery

When Halford Mackinder delivered his paper "The Geographical Pivot of History" to the Royal Geographical Society in 1904, the czarist Russian empire was in full control of the core of Eurasia—the pivot region, or Heartland, of the world, which he had deemed impenetrable to maritime powers.[1] The Russians had begun their transcontinental expansion eastward to the Pacific with the crossing of the Urals in 1581. During the subsequent centuries, they pushed settlement across the southern parts of Siberia. The Far Eastern Territory was annexed from China in 1860, when construction began on what was to become the chief Russian port on the Pacific, Vladivostok. Control over all of Siberia was assured in 1905 with the construction of the 5,575-mile Trans-Siberian Railroad from Moscow to Vladivostok. The expansion southward was completed in the late nineteenth century, when the Russians swept over the remainder of the Trans-Caucasus not yet under their control and also seized Central Asia.

Mackinder's 1919 volume, *Democratic Ideals and Realities,* was written after the Bolshevik revolution had toppled the czar and proclaimed the Soviet state.[2] In it, he voiced the fear that communism might sweep across Eastern and Central Europe and engulf the seven independent states of the "Middle Tier" between Germany and Russia, which extended from the Adriatic and Black Seas to the Baltic. Not only was the new Soviet state in control of the Eurasian Heartland but, Mackinder warned, it was now in a position to rule Eastern Europe, the strategic annex of the Heartland. He hypothesized that, in an alternate scenario, Germany might succeed in winning control over a divided Eastern Europe and thus command the Heartland. In either case, control of World-Island and command of the world would follow.

In "The Round World and the Winning of the Peace," written in 1943 at the height of World War II, Mackinder restated the proposition that the Eurasian Heartland was the "greatest natural fortress in the world."[3] This version of the Heartland omitted Lenaland, the region extending from the Yenisey River eastward to the Pacific. Control of this new Heartland of four and a quarter million square miles and 170 million people would, in Mackinder's opinion, provide the Soviet Union with a strategically invulnerable defensive position in its conflict with Nazi Germany. Repudiating his 1919 dictum, Mackinder asserted that rule of the Heartland no longer guaranteed control of World-Island. Instead, the strength of the Heartland was now offset by the inherent power of a unified North Atlantic basin. He predicted that this global balance-of-power system was destined to be strengthened as the Monsoonal Asian lands of India and China developed into new geostrategic power centers.

In the wake of its victory in World War II, the USSR gained complete command over its Eastern and Central European "strategic annex." This was accomplished through the direct absorption of the wide swath of territory from southeastern Finland, the Baltic states, and East Prussia to eastern Poland, eastern Czechoslovakia, and northern Romania, as well as by the installation of Communist satellite regimes in the remainder of the region. At the height of the Cold War in the 1960s and '70s, the Heartland further extended its power by leapfrogging the Ring of Containment that the West had established along the perimeter of Continental Eurasia, penetrating the Maritime Realm in Southeast Asia, the Middle East, Sub-Saharan Africa, and the Caribbean.

The Soviet drive for global command was relatively short-lived. In overreaching its strategic and economic capacities and maintaining a tyrannical and corrupt Communist regime, Moscow hastened the collapse of the Soviet empire and the loss of a considerable part of the Heartland. Far from being the strongest land power in the world, Russia today is strategically weak, exposed to NATO's eastward expansionist policies, the inroads of Maritime and fundamentalist Islamic influences into the Trans-Caucasus and Central Asia, and pressures from China along its North Pacific territories.

As the West looks to the future, however, it should not take for granted that Russia's post–Cold War collapse, with its political instability, endemic corruption, impoverishment, plummeting health standards, declining population, and weakened armed forces, is a permanent condition. The country has great inherent strengths. Rich in natural resources, it is the world's largest producer and exporter of natural gas, with 60 percent of world gas reserves and 10 percent of its oil reserves. In addition, Russia has a vast nuclear arsenal, a substantial scientific and engineering population, spatial depth, and a strategically central position within Eurasia. Should reforms sweep away crony capitalism and build a healthy market economy, Russia's recovery is likely to be accompanied by a revived nationalism, probably linked to the Russian Orthodox Church.

Loss of the non-Russian former Soviet republics has left the new Russia with a population of 145 million that is, for the most part, ethnically Russian and increasingly responsive to the lure of nationalistic slogans and initiatives. (The major minorities are the Muslim peoples in the North Caucasus and in Tatarstan in the Middle Volga.) Nationalism is a force that can be harnessed in positive ways by a strong central government that reasserts control over the distant regions, which in recent years have exploited the Kremlin's weakness in order to pursue relatively independent economic and foreign policies.

Large numbers of geographically concentrated ethnic Russian populations are located in the regions close to Russia's borders in such former Soviet republics as Estonia, Latvia, Ukraine, Moldova, and Kazakhstan. The presence of these Russians is likely to prove a major obstacle to Western efforts to wean these newly independent states away from the Russian strategic grasp. A sound Maritime Realm policy would be to recognize Russia's strategic interests in Eastern Europe and seek a partnership with Moscow that aims at building up Eastern Europe as a Gateway, rather than risk it becoming a Shatterbelt.

In the Caucasus and Central Asia, international oil interests and some American Cold Warriors are strong advocates for involvement of the West in a replay of the "Great Game."[4] The Great Game was conducted by Britain a century ago, when it sought to displace Russian influence in Central Asia, as well as to penetrate the Black Sea and the Caucasus. An initial step in the new Great Game took place in 1996, when the United States provided modest military aid to Georgia and Azerbaijan when these states joined with Ukraine and Moldova to form a mutual-support group. Uzbekistan was added to the group three years later. Under the acronym GUUAM (from the first initial of each member's name), the organization set the goals of negotiating reduction of Russian troops within or along their borders and promoting the construction of pipelines that would reduce their dependence upon Russia for the supply or transit of oil and gas. The dispatch of American military personnel to Georgia in 2002 to train Georgian troops in antiterrorist tactics is a recent example of U.S. efforts to penetrate the region.

The Great Game strategy has as little likelihood of long-term success today as it had when Britain sought to undermine Russia's strategic interests during the earlier period. Russia has an overwhelming geopolitical advantage in a contest with the West for strategic influence over the Black Sea, the Caucasus, the Caspian Sea, and interior Central Asian areas. It is an advantage similar to that which the United States enjoys in the Caribbean, Maritime Europe in the Maghreb, and China in Indochina. Penetration of geopolitically subordinate regions by distant external powers usually turns out to be short-lived and counterproductive.

The Changing National Territory

Present-day Russia, like all territorial states, including the Soviet Union and the czarist empire before it, is the expression of the interaction of a people with the landscape it occupies. The political marking off of the state produces a national landscape—the arena for its economic, cultural, and political activities. When the political territory changes, national characteristics and objectives change.

A national landscape becomes altered in two ways: vertically, through new internal forms, and horizontally, through the addition of external areas or the loss of existing territory. Vertical changes occur as new sets of environmental conditions emerge or new uses are made of the existing environment. Examples of changed environmental conditions are the Dutch conquest of the sea, climatic desiccation in the African Sahel, and the shrinking of the Aral Sea due to the diversion for irrigation of the waters that feed it. New uses of the existing environment include urbanization, the introduction of new crops, the discovery of new mineral resources, and changing systems of land tenure.

Horizontal change may not immediately affect the existing grain of the national landscape, but it does ultimately. Since West Germany has reabsorbed East Germany, the East has begun to change from an older and inefficient heavy manufacturing base in steel and chemicals to a more high-tech, service-oriented economy. After Singapore seceded from Malaysia, it soon became a leading Asian economic power—a global financial center and a leading producer of chemicals, electronics, and refined petroleum products.

Within half a century, Russia has experienced radical horizontal change, first through the direct addition of territory to the Soviet state and domination of the vast belt of surrounding satellite territory, and now through the stripping of much of its former national territory as well as the loss of direct control over its Eastern European strategic annex. The challenge for Russia, if it is to pull out of its current quagmire, is to "grow" vertically—through modernization of industry, agriculture, and services; application of high technology; and judicious use of its natural resources.

The horizontal expansion of the Russian empire began in the late sixteenth century, as it proceeded to swallow up dozens of non-Slavic peoples. A century later, the czars embarked also on vertical expansion through modernization. From then on, the two types of change occurred in tandem.

The year after Peter the Great captured Ingerman (the region drained by the Neva River and the eastern shores of the Gulf of Finland) from Sweden in 1702, he began to build St. Petersburg. In 1712, he moved the capital from Moscow to the new city. For Peter, St. Petersburg was to be more than a "window looking on Europe." It was to be used to spearhead Russia's changeover into a modern industrial state. The port that was built became Russia's leading port on the White Sea, supplanting Archangel (Arkhangelsk), which had to be kept open by icebreakers during much of the year. Peter's modernization plans included the building of a navy, and St. Petersburg's outer port on Kotlin Island provided the site for the Kronshtadt Naval Base.

Other goals of modernization included industrialization, the subordination of the Russian Orthodox Church to the Crown, and an efficient centralized state administration. Diverse manufacturing enterprises, such as shipbuilding, engineering, and textiles, were rapidly introduced into the city, so that by the mid-eighteenth century, the new capital had overtaken Moscow as Russia's leading industrial center. Spacious classical buildings and ornamental parks and gardens were designed by French and Italian architects to help make St. Petersburg a world-class cultural center. In a remarkably brief period, the fruits of vertical change had exceeded those of the horizontal expansion.

Peter the Great viewed St. Petersburg as the national engine of change and the instrument of Russia's securing what it needed from Europe to help fulfill its modernization plans. He by no means saw Russia's future as European, however. His goal was for Russia to take what it could from the West and, when it could compete on equal terms, to turn its back on Europe and devote its energies to expanding the czarist empire eastward and southward.

In contrast to the new capital, the country's political center and primary city at the turn of the eighteenth century, Moscow, represented Russia's inward-oriented and landlocked spiritual, as well as geographical, forms and traditions. The city, which had developed from its mid-twelfth-century village origins to become the seat of the Vladimir-Muscovite princes in 1271, lay in a basin at the junction of the Upper Volga plain and the central Russian uplands. It was thus strategically located to enable the rulers of Muscovy to gain dominance over the surrounding Russian lands.

Moscow's built form, as well as the social and military organization of the Muscovite state, reflected an amalgam of influences—Byzantine, Tatar, and Slavic. The dukes of Moscow had to share their power with the Russian Orthodox Church, whose seat had been moved to Moscow in the mid-fourteenth century. Moreover, during the centuries of their struggle with the Tatars, Russian noble families had intermarried with them and adopted many Tatar customs and traditions. Moscow's early public buildings and churches, including the Kremlin, the city's walled center and citadel, were started in the fourteenth century and represented an attempt to create a uniquely Russian architectural version from the amalgam of these influences. The wooden building materials, as well as the bricks of later construction periods, were drawn from locally available sources; the cupolas and towers so characteristic of the city provide a Russian Byzantine form that is derivative, but nevertheless *sui generis*.

By the time of Peter's accession to the throne, Moscow had experienced large-scale growth. The market for its products, however, was essentially restricted to the territory embraced by the landlocked Muscovite state, thus limiting continued growth. This commercial consideration weighed heavily in Peter's decision to build St. Petersburg and to try to extend the economic reach of the state beyond its existing territorial bounds.

TERRITORIAL EXPANSION OF CZARIST RUSSIA

The historical development of the Russian state, from the onset of modern times to the present, has been characterized by alternating periods of territorial expansion and contraction. Blocked by the powerful Mongol-Tatar empires in the south, which by the twelfth century had overrun the lands north of the Black and Caspian Seas, and by the Grand Duchy of Lithuania, which had incorporated most of Ukraine and White Russia, the Dukes of Moscow expanded their control over territories to their north and eastward to the Volga.

In 1552 Ivan broke the Tatar military power that had confined his predecessors to the territories of Muscovy and Novgorod, sacking Kazan, which had become the capital of the Tatar khanate of Kazan, one of the four independent khanates to emerge from the 1480 breakup of the Mongol empire of the "Golden Horde," which was also known as the Kipchax Khanate. Kazan, five hundred kilometers east of Moscow, was the gateway through and around the southern Urals into the central Urals. The central Urals were crossed in 1581 by Yermak Timofeyev and his band of Cossacks, who then took the city of Sibir (near the present city of Tobelsk), capital of the Tatar khanate of Sibir.

By the end of the reign of Ivan IV, Czar of All Russia (1584), the Russian-controlled territory, shaped as an inverted triangle, extended in the north from the Kola Peninsula, the island of Novya Zemlya, and the frozen waters of the White, Barents, and Kara Seas. Archangel, at the mouth of the Dvina on the White Sea, was founded during the last year of Ivan's reign. Despite being icebound for much of the year, it became Russia's principal port, until displaced by St. Petersburg over a century later. The port regained importance after a rail line to Moscow was completed in 1898. However, from the time that Murmansk, on the Barents Sea, was developed as an ice-free port during World War I, Archangel has had to share its role as a port for the north. Murmansk became the major supply base for Allied convoys to the USSR in World War II. It is now a major naval base and home port for the nuclear submarine fleet, as well as a leading freight port and fishing center.

The conquest of the Tatar khanate of Sibir was completed in 1598, after which time the road to all of West Siberia was open. During the seventeenth century, West Siberia was annexed to Russia and the Cossacks moved eastward, building fortresses and trading in furs. The advance of the Cossacks across Siberia was rapid. In short order, they reached the Sea of Okhotsk, an arm of the north Pacific, establishing the fishing and trading settlement of Okhotsk in 1649, although they soon had to abandon the territory, later to be known as the Russian Far East, in the face of Chinese military pressure. The Russians did not return to the Siberian Pacific coastlands for nearly two hundred years, when they occupied all of the territory north of the Amur and east of the Ussuri River (1856–60) and built a military post at Vladivostok (1860). The Siberian fur trade had become a major source of wealth for Russia. When it declined in the early eighteenth century, it was replaced by silver, copper, and lead mining, much of which was carried out by convict labor. In contrast, gold mining, which became Siberia's leading source of wealth in the nineteenth century, was carried out mostly by free laborers.

European Russia's penetration of the lands along its Baltic and Black Sea coasts began more than a century after its push into Siberia. The leading power in the Baltic was Sweden, and it took a coalition of Russia, Denmark, Poland, Saxony, Hanover, and Prussia to wage a twenty-one year conflict (the Northern War of 1700 to 1721) to defeat the forces of Sweden's Charles XII. Early in that war, Peter captured Ingermanland (1702); eight years later, he took Swedish Livonia (present-day Estonia and parts of Latvia). The Peace Treaty of Nystad (1721) confirmed the annexation of these territories, as well as of most of Karelia, but did not give Finland to Russia. Russia conquered and annexed Finland during the Napoleonic Wars a century later (1809). Finland remained under Russian control until the chaotic conditions of the Bolshevik revolution enabled the Finns to break away and regain their independence.

While the foothold on the Baltic permitted Peter to realize many of his ambitions, Russia still lacked a year-round, open-water port, because the Gulf of Finland was icebound three to four months during the year. The Black Sea offered Peter warm-water ports, but the path from there was blocked by the Ottomans.

As early as 1696, Peter conquered the area around the Sea of Azov, the northern arm of the Black Sea, into which the Don River system flowed, although the Ottomans regained it in 1711. Russian control of the western (Derbent and Baku) and southern shores of the Caspian Sea, seized in a war with Persia (1722–23), was also short-lived. While Russia eventually regained the Azov region in 1735, it was not until Catherine the Great's two major wars with the Ottomans that the northern Black Sea coast was conquered and annexed in its entirety. The Crimean peninsula was gained in 1783, bringing the khanate of Crimea to an end, and Odessa fell in 1791.

During the first half of the nineteenth century (1806–55), Russia's hold on the Black Sea was extended by its conquest in the Caucasus of Greater Georgia on the eastern shores of the sea. Batum (Batumi), Erevan (Yerevan), Tiflis (Tbilisi), and Baku were now part of the empire. In addition, annexation of much of Bessarabia (1812) provided Odessa with greater defensive depth. In the latter half of the century (1868–84), Russia also succeeded in gaining all of the southeastern shore of the Caspian Sea from Persia, as well as the southern part of (Russian) Central Asia (1864–78). The Bukhara and Khiva khanates, while overrun during this period, remained nominally independent under Russian protection. (The northern half, Kazakhstan, had already been seized from Tatar khanates in wars that had lasted for over a century, from 1730 to 1840.)

Russian control of the Central Asia region was additionally strengthened toward the end of the nineteenth century with the construction of the Trans-Caspian Railroad, which extended from Krasnovodsk on the Caspian Sea eastward through Ashkabad, Bukhara, and Samarkand into Turkestan and then northward to Tashkent in southernmost Kazakhstan. Branches of the system connected to the fertile Fergana Valley and its ancient oasis cities that lay astride the silk route between China and the Mediterranean. This line would much later be connected to the Trans-Siberian Railroad by the Turk-Sib Railroad (completed in 1931), which ran from Tashkent to Novosibirsk.

The prize that eluded Russia during these two centuries of conquest and expansion was control of the Bosporus and the Dardanelles—the exits of the Black Sea to the Mediterranean. The Western powers rose to the defense of the Ottomans during the Crimean War (1853–56), putting an end to czarist dreams of breaking the strategic noose that enclosed Russia's warm-water ports.

Nineteenth-Century Expansion into the Far Eastern Territory

The pace of expansion to the east during this period was guided essentially by economic opportunities, the availability of labor, and access. When the Cossacks first conquered

Siberia during the seventeenth century, they moved by horse and riverboat, traversing the level portages that linked the east-west Siberian river systems. Native Siberian peoples in the north were few and offered little opposition, as they were incorporated into the fur trade. Agricultural developments were limited and spotty, oriented to the needs of the trading centers, military outposts, and mining communities. In the nineteenth century (1861), emancipated Russian serfs were given free land. This stimulated settlement of the wooded and the black earth soils in the steppes of the southern part of West Siberia, which were suitable for both row crops and dairying.

From there came the moves across Central Siberia in the mid-nineteenth century, to the region later known as the Far Eastern Territory. The Russians took advantage of the weakness of the Chinese empire to gain control of all of the territory north of the Amur and east of the Ussuri, extending from Yakutia and the Lena River eastward to the entire northeast Asian coast.

For the most part, Russian efforts in the Far East were oriented to the Pacific coastlands. The interior section of the region, Yakutia (modern Sakha), extended from the Central Siberian Uplands in the west to the Verkoyansk Range in the east. It covered an area of 1.2 million square miles, or half of the total Far Eastern Territory. Yakutia is one of the coldest inhabited parts of the earth, much of it lying within the Arctic Circle. In the early period of Russian colonization, the small group of settlers were confined to the upper (southern) part of the Lena River Valley, where Yakutsk had been established as a fort in 1632. Until the twentieth century, Yakutia remained essentially a region of herding, hunting, lumbering, and gold mining. Today the major source of income is diamond mining. The one million people who now live in a handful of cities and towns are supported by tin, natural gas, oil, coal, and phosphate deposits, along with wood products, paper, and food processing.

The major settlements of the Russian Pacific Far East were oriented to the lower courses of the major rivers and to the Sea of Okhotsk, the Sea of Japan, and the Bering Sea. Their growth into important centers had to await completion of the Trans-Siberian Railroad (1891–1905). Vladivostok, the eastern terminus for both the railroad and the Northern Sea Route, and whose port is kept open in winter by icebreakers, became the chief base of the navy on the Pacific and a center for the fishing and whaling fleet. Vladivostok assumed its importance as a naval base after the Russians lost Port Arthur (the present Chinese port of Lushun) as a result of their defeat in the Russo-Japanese War (1904–05).

The Russians had developed Port Arthur in 1898 as a lynchpin of the Chinese-Russian strategic alliance against Japan. Situated at the southern tip of the Liaodung Peninsula in southern Manchuria and overlooking the Yellow Sea, the base was designed to protect the peninsula from the threat of Japanese seizure. For the Russians, as well as the Japanese, Manchuria was a major prize. Its vast grasslands provided the potential for large-scale agricultural settlement and it was rich in mineral resources, especially coal, iron, and timber. Moreover, it was the strategic gateway to North China.

With their victory in the war, the Japanese took control of Port Arthur and southern Manchuria, limiting Russian influence to the northern half of the province and causing them to shift their naval operations to Vladivostok. Russia had first begun its penetration of northern Manchuria in the early nineteenth century and continued to retain influence there until World War I.

As early as the seventeenth century, Russians had also explored the island of Sakhalin across the Tatar Strait from their Far Eastern mainland and just to the north of Japan's northern island of Hokkaido. In the following two centuries, Russian and Japanese settlers jointly colonized the island. For a brief period, Russia gained full control, but after its defeat by Japan in 1905 it was forced to limit its sovereignty to that half of the island that lay north of fifty degrees north latitude. After World War II, the USSR regained sovereignty over the entirety of Sakhalin, and the Japanese renounced their claim to it. The current value of Sakhalin to the Russians is enhanced by its oil and offshore gas deposits and by oil pipelines that run from the island under the Tatar Strait to the Russian mainland.

Another strategic objective of both the Russians and the Japanese was the Kuril Island chain, which extends for 775 miles from the tip of Kamchatka to the north of Hokkaido and encloses the Sea of Okhotsk and Sakhalin. Both countries laid claim to the islands in the eighteenth century. Japan held them from 1875 to the end of World War II, when Soviet forces occupied the islands. Possession of the chain remains a point of diplomatic contention, as Japan demands return of the four southernmost and largest islands. Because of the dispute, no peace treaty was signed between the USSR and Japan following World War II. The Kurils are important for their deepwater, ice-free harbors and the space that they offer for air and naval bases to overlook the North Pacific. In addition, their surrounding waters contain rich fisheries.

Farther north, in the Far Eastern Territory on the Kamchatka Peninsula, is Petropavlovsk, founded by Vitus Jonassen Bering in 1741. Earlier, the Danish explorer had been employed by Peter the Great to explore the eastern part of the Northwest Passage—the water route sought by the Russians along their northern Arctic coast to connect the Atlantic and the Pacific. Bering had then discovered Kamchatka when he sailed through the strait that now bears his name in an effort to reach Alaska. The center for a fishing fleet during its early period, Petropavlovsk is now an important Russian naval base and the location of shipyards. It is also the center for the modern-day trawling and factory fishing fleet.

Another early settlement, Khabarovsk, at the junction of the lower Amur and Ussuri Rivers, was founded as a trading post. Khabarovsk experienced considerable growth and prosperity with the coming of the railroad in 1905 and is now a major industrial center and port, with air connections to Alaska and Japan.

Westward Expansion

While the czarist empire was able to expand steadily to the north, south, and east over a period of four centuries, its territorial expansion along its western perimeter was blocked by several power centers, first Lithuania and Poland, then later the German and Hapsburg empires. Kievan Russia, the cradle of Russian nationalism, was captured by the Mongols of the Golden Horde in the thirteenth century. A century later, rule of Ukraine passed to Lithuania-Poland, although the Crimea remained in Tatar hands. For much of its early modern history, Ukraine was under Polish rule.

Growing interest in Ukraine—the "Land of the Little Russians"—brought Russia into conflict with Poland. The Russo-Polish War of 1667 ended with the partition of Ukraine, Russia obtaining left-bank Ukraine east of the Dnieper River, including Kiev, and Poland retaining the right bank. A century later, the left and right banks were united, as Catherine the Great annexed western Ukraine following the Partitions of Poland (1772, 1793, 1795). In the twentieth century, eastern Ukraine proved to be of major value to the Russians. They moved large numbers of ethnic Russians into the Donets Basin (Donbas) and Kharkov (Kharkiv) areas, which bordered the Russian centers of Rostov, Belograd, and Kursk. The vast coking coal deposits of the Donabas and the rich iron ores of Krivoy Rog

(Krivyy Rih) became the bases for the emergence of Donbas and Kharkov as two of the most heavily industrialized steel and metallurgical centers of the world.

Belorussia ("White Russia," now Belarus) posed an equally formidable challenge to czarist expansionism. It, too, had been conquered by the dukes of Lithuania and remained under the rule of Lithuania and Poland during the sixteenth- to eighteenth-century wars between Russia and Poland. As with Ukraine, Belorussia finally passed to the czarist empire with the partitions of Poland. After World War I, in 1921, Poland retook western Belorussia, while the eastern, larger part was retained by the USSR. In 1939, the Soviet army moved into the western region and incorporated it into Belorussia, which retains the territory to this day.

Lithuania, which had been one of medieval Europe's largest and most powerful states, gradually came under Polish rule. It joined in a union with Poland in 1569 as a defensive measure against the pressures of Ivan IV and became Polonized. With the partitions of Poland, Lithuania was annexed to Russia. When Russia collapsed after World War I, Lithuania regained its independence, but lost its Vilna region to Poland. In 1923 Lithuania seized the Memel territory (Klaipeda), which had formerly been part of East Prussia. Vilna was passed back to Lithuania as part of the Soviet-German partition of Poland in 1939, while Memel was returned to Germany. Lithuania was occupied by the USSR the following year and forced to become a constituent Soviet Republic. After being occupied by Germany during the war with the Soviet Union, Lithuania was regained by the USSR in 1944 and remained a Soviet Republic until its independence in 1990.

While Peter the Great had seized eastern Latvia (Livonia) from Sweden, the western part of the country, south of the Western Dvina River and known as Courland, with its Baltic ports of Liepaja and Ventspils, did not pass into Russian hands until the third partition of Poland in 1795. Latvia had for centuries been dominated by German merchants who had settled there with the Hanseatic League. Its landowning aristocracy, the "Baltic Barons," was also of German origin. The collapse of Russia and Germany made Latvian independence possible in 1918. The country was conquered by the Soviets in 1940 and absorbed into the USSR, but its Lettish population strongly supported the German troops who occupied Latvia during the war.

At the onset of World War I, the czarist empire was at its territorial peak, extending for 5,700 miles from the Baltic to the Pacific and covering a total land area of 8,647,660 square miles (including Bukhara and Khiva). Its population of 145 million was heavily concentrated in European Russia. Despite relatively large-scale movement of settlers into Siberia between 1891 and 1911, the overall population of that region was only eight million, nearly all of whom were Russian. All told, approximately three-quarters of the population of the empire was Slavic, with Turkic as the second-largest ethnic grouping.

By all accounts, Russia had fallen far short of achieving the modernization to which Peter the Great aspired. Its economy was still largely agricultural and underdeveloped. Industry, dependent upon foreign capital, was concentrated in only a few places—St. Petersburg, the leading manufacturing and financial center; Moscow, a major textile and metallurgical center; Baku, the focus of Russia's oil industry; and the Donbas/Kharkov iron and steel region. The rail network was woefully inadequate, with a density of mileage that was only one-tenth that of the United Kingdom, France, or Germany.

The czarist regime was despotic and corrupt, with an ineffective, centralized civilian and military bureaucracy that was ill prepared to lead the nation into World War I. While Russia now extended beyond the bounds of Mackinder's "Pivot Area," it was hardly in a position to be a strategic threat to the Maritime reaches of Eurasia that surrounded it. Such a threat would come only after the Bolshevik revolution, the victory of Soviet forces in World War II, and the spread of communism into East and Central Europe and East Asia.

TERRITORIAL CHANGES IN THE SOVIET ERA

During the period following the Bolshevik revolution and its aftermath, the territory that had been embraced by the Russian empire shrank by 405,740 square miles. The "White" (anti-Bolshevik) republics of Georgia, Armenia, and Azerbaijan in the Caucasus did not long survive, and were regained by the Soviet Union. Those territories that were lost to the Soviet Union included Finland, Estonia, Latvia, Lithuania, the Polish provinces that had been held by Russia, Bessarabia (to Romania), and Kars and Ardahan in the far south (which were restored to Turkey). Thus in 1938 the area of the USSR amounted to 8,340,479 square miles, or approximately 300,000 square miles less than Russia in the czarist period.

The Soviet state expanded once more, first as a result of the seizure of lands in 1939–40 in accordance with the pact with Nazi Germany and later with the territorial spoils that were confirmed by Soviet victory in World War II. Most of the annexations were in Eastern Europe, although as previously noted southern Sakhalin and the four southern Kuril Islands were taken from Japan. In addition, in 1984, nominally independent Tannu Tuva, bordering Mongolia, was formally absorbed.

Table 7.1   Post–World War II Soviet Land Annexations

Area	Former Colony	Soviet Republic
Pechenga District	Finland	Murmansk Oblast (RSFSR)
Karelia (Salla)	Finland	Karelian ASSR (RSFSR)
Vyborg District	Finland	Leningrad Oblast
Northern East Prussia and Memelland	Germany	Kaliningrad Oblast (RSFSR) and Klaipeda Oblast (Lithuanian SSR)
Estonia	Independent	Estonian Union Republic
Latvia	Independent	Latvian Union Republic
Lithuania	Independent	Lithuanian Union Republic
Eastern Estonia and Latvia	Estonia and Latvia	Pskov Oblast (RSFSR)
Eastern Poland (Western Belorussia)	Poland	Four oblasts in Belorussian SSR and Vinla Oblast in Lithuanian SSR
Transcarpathia (Ruthenia)	Czechoslovakia	Transcarpathian Oblast (Ukrainian SSR)
Central Bessarabia	Romania	Moldavian SSR
Southern Bessarabia	Romania	Izmail Oblast (Ukrainian SSR)
Tannu Tuva	Independent	Tuva ASSR (RSFSR)
Southern Sakhalin	Japan	Sakhalin Oblast (RSFSR)
Kuril Islands	Japan	Sakhalin Oblast (RSFSR)

Note: SSR – Soviet Socialist Republic; ASSR – Autonomous Soviet Socialist Republic; RSFSR – Russian Soviet Federal Socialist Republic

The basis for Soviet territorial expansion was threefold: strategic, economic, and nationalistic. Historic claims were important only as they related to these factors, as they played an unimportant role within the Soviet propaganda mechanism.

The strategic objective was defensively motivated: to assure command of interior and marginal seas and land gateways. It also served an offensive function in increasing the vulnerability of neighboring states to Soviet pressure.

Economic objectives played a major role in providing the Russian ecumene with improved port facilities in the Baltic for foreign trade. Nationality goals related not only to pan-Slavic ambitions, but also to the unity of minority peoples living within the Soviet nationality-based administrative framework. Not only were Russian-inhabited parts of Latvia annexed and combined with the Russian Soviet Federal Socialist Republic (RSFSR) and Ruthenian portions of Poland merged with Ukraine, but also much of the Karelian-inhabited portion of east-central Finland was added to Soviet Karelia.

There were two overriding elements in these territorial annexations—the need for strategic depth in some of the most important cities of the USSR (which had proved vulnerable during the German invasion) and fear of any future invasion from Germany. The principal international ports of the USSR in 1939 were Odessa, Leningrad (St. Petersburg), Murmansk, Archangel, and Vladivostok. Of these ports, all save Archangel were frontier cities. Odessa and Leningrad were twenty and twelve miles respectively from the pre–World War II Romanian border. Murmansk was fifty miles from Finnish territory, while Vladivostok was thirty-five miles from Japanese Manchuria. Sovetskaya Gavan (Soviet Harbor), developed during World War II on the Gulf of Tartary as a deepwater naval base and commercial port for the Amur Valley, was only seventy miles from Japanese-held southern Sakhalin. With the territorial changes that occurred during and immediately after World War II, Odessa was now fifty, Leningrad ninety, and Murmansk eighty miles from the borders of the Soviet Union, while Vladivostok was shielded by both southern Sakhalin and the North Korean satellite state.

For Moscow, these additional few miles had psychological as well as strategic significance. Leningrad had been besieged for more than two years by the invading Nazi armies and Odessa had temporarily fallen to the onslaught of combined German and Romanian forces. Murmansk was bombarded by the Germans, who had seized the nearby Norwegian city of Kirkenes in 1940, and the chief Russian supply line was in constant danger of being cut. Moreover, the Soviets well remembered the occupation of Murmansk by Allied troops from 1918 to 1920, during the Russian civil war. They had historic recall also of the vulnerability of Vladivostok, which had been occupied during the revolution by Japanese and other Allied troops, who remained until 1922.

Soviet territorial annexations in the west were designed to provide a buffer against future attack by a revived Germany or by an alliance of hostile Western powers. For example, Hitler's first plans for Operation Barbarossa, the invasion of the Soviet Union during World War II, were to strike the Soviet Union simultaneously through several corridors: (1) northern Finland against Murmansk and Archangel; (2) the Baltic Sea, via southern Finland and the Baltic states toward Leningrad; (3) Belorussia, from along the Warsaw-Bialystok-Minsk land corridor north of the Pripet Marshes and thence northward to Leningrad; (4) southern Poland and the Donets Basin (Donbas); and (5) through Romania to Odessa and the Black Sea.

The post–World War II annexation of the Pechenga district in northern Finland, including the western Rybachyi Peninsula, provided defensive depth for the ice-free port of Murmansk. It also helped to secure the nearby Kola Peninsula's apatite resources, which were the basis for Russia's phosphate industry. South of Pechenga lies Russian Pasvik, which had been annexed by Finland in 1920 to provide access to Pechenga. This corridor and its nickel resources were now in Soviet hands and, as a consequence of this annexation, the Soviets gained a common border with Norway. The latter's taconite ore mining town of Kirkenes lay exposed and the population of northern Norway became subject to strong Communist propaganda pressures.

Despite all these territorial additions in the North, the entrances to the Barents Sea were still not in Soviet hands. The Svalbard Island group was still owned by Norway, which rejected Soviet claims to this coal-mining Arctic archipelago.

The most important boundary change that occurred was the annexation of the Baltic republics. Soviet geographer Nicholas Baransky offered this apt summary: "Owing to its geographical position, the Soviet Baltic region is of prime importance for the external connections of the U.S.S.R. . . . [It is] a natural harbor which serves the Central U.S.S.R."[5] Although not entirely ice free, Riga, the largest city and a major rail terminus, presented the Soviet Union with its best Baltic port. Klaipeda (Memel) and Ventspils (Windau) offered newly developed oil ports and Tallinn offered a natural gas terminus. Kaliningrad (Königsberg) was an important ice-free addition to the eastern Baltic ports.

The Kaliningrad Oblast, cleared of Germans and populated by Russians, became part of the RSFSR, although separated from it by the Lithuanian and Belorussian republics. Kaliningrad provided direct access to the Polish and East German satellites' ports of Gdansk, Szczecin, and Rostock. Slight internal territorial changes also strengthened the Russian position in the Baltic vis-à-vis both satellite states and non-Russian Soviet republics. A portion of Estonia lying along the right bank of the River Narva was detached, to be added directly to the Leningrad Oblast. Finally, Russian-inhabited rural districts of Estonia (Petseri) and Latvia (Abrene and Kacanava), all east of the Gulf of Riga, were detached and added to the Pskov Oblast within the RSFSR. Pskov, at the southern end of Lake Peipus, was important as the land gateway to Leningrad.

Also, following the principle of drawing boundaries based on nationalities, a Lithuanian-inhabited strip of Belorussia was added to the Lithuanian Soviet Socialist Republic (SSR), which had reincorporated Vilna from Poland. With Vilna and Pskov both in Soviet territory, the Vilna corridor, which follows the high Baltic end-moraine (the ridge that marked the edge of glaciation) northeastward to Leningrad, was more secure. Soviet actions in the Baltic, in a broad sense, can be described as defensively oriented, owing to the exposure of the Russian core to the European lands to the west.

The westward shift of the boundary in Belorussia brought the Pripet marshes completely within the Soviet fold. This boundary was restored to the Curzon Line of 1919, as the Soviets reclaimed territory lost to Poland after their 1920 war. Return to the Curzon Line completed Russian control over the Vilna Gap, thus blocking the high-ground route to Leningrad and Moscow. In addition, the Curzon Line gave the USSR possession of the most direct route to Moscow, high ground from Brest to Minsk that skirts the northern edge of the Pripet marshes. Moreover, western Belorussia was claimed on the basis of nationality, White Russians being in the majority over Poles.

Western Ukraine lands taken from Poland included Lviv and Drogobych. The former was a rail hub on the upper Bug River whose industries served the agricultural areas to the east. The latter was a district on the northern slopes of the Carpathians that was once Poland's major petroleum-producing region. Its strategic and economic implications lay in its being denied to Poland, as well as in its availability to Kiev. In the case of western

Ukraine, unity of the Ukrainian people was an important basis for the claim, although another reason for Soviet interest was the fact that the Soviet border was now but 130 miles from Krakow and just another 50 miles from industrialized Upper Silesia. With the absorption of Transcarpathia, the Russians accomplished much more than the union of Ruthenians with their kindred Ukrainians. This land annexation gave the Soviet Union complete control of the eastern Carpathian Mountains and a base on their southern slopes from which to overlook the Tisa River and all of the Hungarian plain. Czechoslovakia and Hungary now shared common borders with the USSR and Budapest lay exposed to a Soviet border only 150 miles away. Belgrade and Vienna were also affected by this new Danubian position of the USSR.

The border changes in northern Bukovina and Bessarabia were justified as absorptions of predominantly Ukrainian peoples, but they also served broader Soviet strategic and economic interests. They gave to the Soviets the lands between the Dniester and the Prut, as well as the northernmost mouth of the Danube. The Ploesti oil fields and Bucharest were about 125 miles from the Soviet border—another example of the vulnerability into which a satellite state had been pushed.

Boundary adjustments in Siberia were less important to Moscow strategically than were those in Europe. In the Pacific Territories, annexation of Sakhalin and the Kurils (which enclosed the Sea of Okhotsk) pointed a double dagger toward northern Japan. However, these acquisitions did not substantially affect the security of Russia's Sea of Japan coast and Vladivostok, because the Sovietization of North Korea provided for greater protection.

In south-central Siberia, annexation of nominally independent Tannu Tuva in 1944 may have been viewed as a precedent for eventual Soviet annexation (which never took place) of the Mongolian People's Republic. A lightly populated and underdeveloped land, the Tuva Autonomous Soviet Socialist Republic (ASSR) is at the headwaters of the Yenisey and overlooks Irkutsk and the Trans-Siberian Railroad from the eastern end of the Western Sayan Mountains.

At the onset of the Cold War, the USSR unsuccessfully revived claims to Ardahan, Kars, and Artvin on the borders of the Middle East in Turkey. These were areas that Russia had once seized from the Ottoman Empire and that the Soviets now wished to add to Georgia and Armenia. Moscow also failed to gain the demilitarization of the Turkish straits. The waterway that connected the Black and Mediterranean Seas had been briefly internationalized and demilitarized in the early 1920s, but had been refortified by Turkey in 1936.

Soviet territorial pressures were also mounted against Iran. In 1945 Soviet troops that had been garrisoned in the northern part of the country during World War II supported the establishment of a separatist Communist republic in the oil-rich Iranian Azerbaijan province. Soviet troops also backed a Kurdish separatist republic in the lands to the west and south of Lake Urmia, overlooking Iraq's northern oil fields. The rebellions were quashed the following year and the USSR had to remove its troops owing to UN Security Council pressures.

Offsetting these failed territorial efforts, however, were later Soviet successes in forging a ring of bases in the Mediterranean and Indian Oceans. From the 1960s to the 1980s, the USSR established naval facilities at Marsah Matruh, Alexandria, and Port Said in Egypt and at Latakia in Syria. South of Suez, along the Red Sea, installations were built at Ras Benas in Egypt, Port Sudan in the Sudan, and Hodeida in Yemen. In addition, the Soviet bases at Aden (overlooking the Gulf of Aden) and on the island of Socotra provided a strong presence in the waters east of Suez leading to the Indian Ocean.

Since the Suez Canal had been blocked by Egypt as a result of its loss of Sinai to Israel in the 1967 war, leaving the canal out of use until 1975, Moscow's efforts to create a Soviet-controlled Black Sea-Mediterranean-Suez-Indian Ocean route to the Far East came to naught. The peace settlement between Egypt and Israel that was negotiated in 1978 and formally ratified in 1979 ended all Soviet hopes of using Suez as a strategic weapon in the Cold War.

TERRITORIAL CONTRACTION IN POST-SOVIET RUSSIA

The USSR that emerged after World War II had acquired 265,000 additional square miles. This increased its size to 8,600,660 square miles—only 50,000 square miles less than the territories held by the czarist empire at its zenith. When the Soviet Union collapsed forty-five years later, the territorial dissolution stripped the Russian core of fifteen of the FSU's constituent republics. The land that remained to the new Russian Federation was reduced by nearly two million square miles, to 6,592,735. Its 1991 population was reduced to 154 million, as compared with the FSU's 293 million. Since then, Russia's population has dropped to 145 million as a consequence of lower birth rates, higher death rates, and out-migration. The collapse of the health-care system, as well as a number of economic and social factors, is responsible for the continuing population shrinkage. Unless the trend is dramatically reversed, the country could be left with only 135 million people by the end of the present decade and its economic recovery could be hampered by severe labor shortages.

In contrast to the highly multiethnic character of the USSR, where ethnic Russians were only 53 percent of the total population, Russians now constitute 82 percent of the populace of the Russian Federation. This is not to suggest that Russia is no longer ethnically and religiously diverse. Within its twenty-one republics and other political subdivisions, it has over sixty different recognized groups, including large numbers of Ukrainians, Tatars, Yakuts, Ossetians, Buryats, Chechens, Ingush, Bashkiris, Chuvash, Komi, Mari, Jews, Germans, and Armenians. However, forging a new state based on the present multinational profile is far less challenging than the task faced by the Soviet Union, which tried to forge a cohesive state out of 108 distinct nationalities.

Implosion of the Soviet State

Implosion of the Soviet Union came after eight decades in which the regime was held together by internal terror and fear of external enemies, as well as by the dream of a classless and more just society. The state had been established on the principles of Marxism and the rights of all ethnic groups within the USSR. (There were twenty-two nationalities, each with over one million in population.) However, all were forced into linguistic and cultural assimilation, as tolerance for ethnic equality remained an empty promise. During World War II, millions of minority peoples, including Crimean Tatars, Chechens, Ingush, Volga Germans, and Kalmyks, were deported to Central Asia and Siberia. Economically, the failure of the command economy to provide a better life for the mass of people stood in sharp contrast to the prosperity of the Western world. The Communist system was riddled with inefficiencies and heavy outlays on defense, which sapped the system even further. It was only a matter of time before the implosion took place, as occurred formally in September 1991.

The dissolution was consensual. Eleven of the newly independent states agreed to the establishment of the Commonwealth of Independent States (CIS) on the basis of an expected benefit from a common framework within which disputes could be mediated and trade promoted. Only Georgia and the Baltic states did not join. In fact, however, the CIS remained a hollow organization, as only Russia and Belarus have retained substantive ties.

The conflicts that followed the devolution of the FSU were confined mainly to internal strife within the newly independent states. The exception was the bitter war between Armenia and Azerbaijan over the Armenian Christian enclave of Nagorno-Karabakh in southeastern Azerbaijan, which had held the status of an autonomous region. The fighting between the Armenians and the Azeri had begun even before the breakup of the FSU, but peaked after the Armenian population declared the region to be an independent state. Armenian troops entered the conflict and drove out most of the Azeri populace from the enclave and the lands that connect it to Armenia proper. Moscow originally sided with Azerbaijan, but then tilted toward Armenia. It now operates air and missile bases in Armenian territory, while Russian troops help guard Armenia's Turkish border. Turkey, meanwhile, has increased its military and economic influence in Azerbaijan and, in 1993, placed Armenia under a trade blockade. This has had little economic effect.

In Georgia, civil war broke out almost immediately after the dissolution of the FSU. In addition, a separatist revolt erupted in Georgia's Muslim Abkhazia, which adjoins Russia's Black Sea coast and its North Caucasus reaches, and seeks to make Abkhazia an associated state within Russia. Russian troops aided the separatists and eventually Moscow settled the conflict, leaving Abkhazia as an autonomous republic within Georgia, but under virtual Russian control.

Russian intervention imposed a similar solution in South Ossetia. There the Farsi-speaking Ossetians revolted against Georgia in 1992, with the goal of joining North Ossetia, which lies along the northern slopes of the main Caucasus range in Russia. Russian troops intervened on behalf of the Ossetians and the outcome was a South Ossetian autonomous republic in Georgia that remains under Russian protection. Moscow extracted a price for helping to stabilize the Shevardnadze regime in Tbilisi. Georgia joined the CIS, permitted the Russian navy to use the base at Batumi, and sanctioned the presence of Russian troops in its sovereign territory.

A war of secession broke out also in eastern Moldova, along the eastern bank of the Dniester, adjoining Ukraine. There, toward the end of 1991, the region's majority Russians and Ukrainians declared their independence, establishing the self-styled pseudostate of the Trans-Dniester Republic, whose leadership seeks unity of the "republic" with Russia.[6]

Elsewhere, the dissolution of the FSU created considerable tension between Russia and Ukraine over Ukraine's independence, and also over the sovereignty of the Crimea. A great deal of the Russian sense of nationhood is derived from Russia's historic and symbolic identification with Kievan Rus (located in the modern Ukraine), the medieval Slavic state that many Russians regard as the historic core of Russia. Many consider the Kievan state to be the common heritage of modern Russians, Ukrainians, and Belorussians. One of the consequences of the tension between Russia and Ukraine over Kiev was that Ukraine did not join the CIS. In the Crimea, now part of Ukraine but with a majority Russian population, Russian separatists called upon Moscow to retain the region. Their grounds were that the port city of Sevastopol, the home of the former Soviet Black Sea fleet, was indispensable to Russian security.

Both of these issues were peacefully resolved eventually, although the debate was sharp. In 1997 Russia accepted Ukraine's existing national borders and recognized its sovereignty over the Crimea and Sevastopol. In exchange, Ukraine accorded Russia the right to base its Black Sea fleet in Sevastopol.[7]

With the exception of Tajikistan, the former Soviet Central Asian republics were not torn by the kind of conflict experienced by the newly independent Caucasus states. However, in Tajikistan, the poorest of all former Soviet republics, a civil war broke out in 1992 between the Moscow-backed regime led by former Communists and the Islamic United Tajik opposition. Despite a shaky peace that was signed in 1997, the Dushanbe regime has since had to call upon Russian troops to sustain it against attacks from the fundamentalist eastern highlanders.

Russia itself has not been immune from internal conflict. In the North Caucasus, Muslim Chechen rebels inflicted a humiliating defeat upon the Russian army in their 1994–96 war, at the end of which the rebels announced the creation of an Islamic fundamentalist state. This state was short-lived—its economy collapsed, its territory served as a haven for terrorism, and its central government proved incapable of exercising control over the territory. The war resumed two years later.

From a Russian strategic viewpoint, revolts by Russian North Caucasus territories lying between the Caspian and Black Seas represent a threat to the lines of communication that traverse them, particularly railways and pipelines. Moreover, the fact that the region is located along an international border provides separatist groups with the option of linking up physically with Azerbaijan and Georgia.

Unlike in Chechnya, the separatist movement in the interior of the country, in Tatarstan, represents only a minor threat to Russia. Located within the center of European Russia, along the Volga and Kama Rivers, the oil-rich Tatar Republic is landlocked, with no access to external support bases. Thus, when in 1991 the leaders of the former Tatar ASSR declared the independent state of Tatarstan (Tataria), the act was strategically irrelevant. Also, the fact that ethnic Russians are as numerous there as Tatars ruled out any serious threat of conflict. While Tataria was not signatory to the 1992 treaty that established the Russian Federation, it subsequently made its own treaty with Moscow.

Geopolitical Features

Dismemberment of the Soviet Union has had a substantial impact upon the geopolitical features of the "New Russia," particularly with respect to the contraction of its former ecumene, the loss of some of its mineral-rich Effective National Territory and Empty Area, and its changed territorial boundaries. Nevertheless, Russia remains a formidable state, the largest political landmass in the world, extending for five thousand miles from west to east across eleven time zones and for fifteen hundred miles from its Arctic North to the Black Sea, the Caucasus, and the mountains of southern Siberia. No other national state possesses Russia's spatial depth.

This factor is reinforced by the massive nuclear arsenal that is to be modernized at the same time that it is reduced in accordance with U.S.-Russian nuclear arms agreements. An analysis of Russia's geopolitical features leads to the conclusion that its inherent strength will enable it to recover from its current condition of political and social instability and economic disarray. Even if it has lost its superpower status, it is likely to reemerge before too long as one of the world's major geostrategic powers.

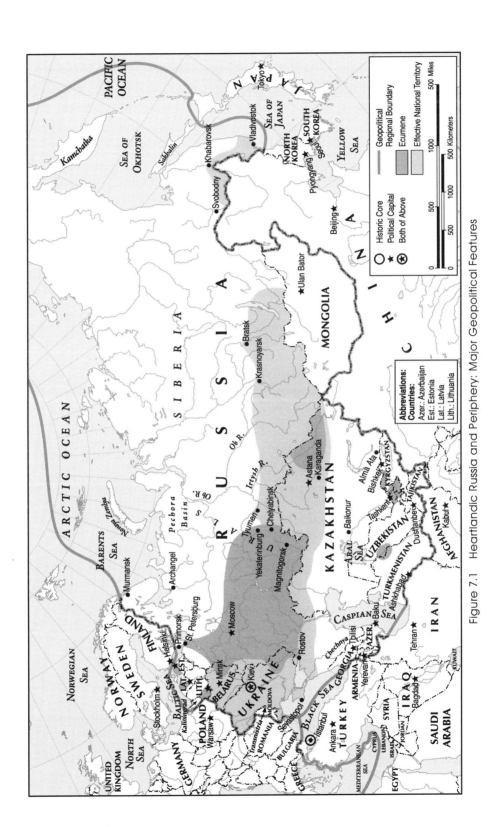

Figure 7.1　Heartlandic Russia and Periphery: Major Geopolitical Features

HISTORIC CORE

Russia's Historic Core—the area in which the Russian state originated—is generally considered to be the medieval principality of Kievan Rus, although Novgorod also may lay claim to this status. The origins of Russia may be traced to the arrival of the Varangians, the Scandinavian traders and warriors led by Rurik, who founded his dynasty in Novgorod in 862 A.D. Located in northwestern Russia, Novgorod was situated on the Volkhov River, on the major trade route that led from the Baltic to the headwaters of the Volga, then south and southeast to the Black and Caspian Seas. Novgorod's location eventually enabled it to become one of the four chief centers of the Hanseatic League, along with London, Bruges, and Bergen.

Rurik's successor, Oleg, transferred the capital to Kiev, the center of the Kievan Rus state, in 879. However, Novgorod continued to be the main center for foreign trade and ultimately (from the early twelfth to the fifteenth centuries) was capital of all of northern Russia to the Urals.

Vladimir defeated his brother, Oleg, in 880 to become grand duke of Kiev. He then conquered distant Slavic tribes and waged successful wars with Lithuanians, Bulgars, and Byzantines to expand his kingdom. For Russians, the defining moment of their nationhood took place in 988–89, when Vladimir converted to Christianity and made the Greek Orthodox Church the religion of his people, linking secular rule and the church.

Kiev was chosen to become the new seat of the Varangian dynasty because its location along the Dnieper River was better sited for the Scandinavian-Black Sea-Constantinople trade. As the capital of Kievan Rus, Kiev became a leading European commercial and cultural center. Surrounded by the fertile crop- and grasslands of southern Russia, the city had a more prosperous agricultural area than Novgorod, which was located within the cool, marshy, and thin-soiled glaciated section of northern Russia.

The name "Russ" initially described the Varangians, who then applied it to the Eastern Slavs who had settled around Kiev and gave their name to the new state—Kievan Rus. Kiev became known to the Russians as the "mother of cities," even after political power shifted to Moscow. Kiev remained the capital until 1169, during which time Eastern Orthodox Christianity consolidated its position among the Slavs and Byzantine culture predominated. It was during this period that the Russian Orthodox Church became an essential part of Russian nationalism and Church Slavonic became the liturgical and literary language of the Russians.

Because the Kievan state was, in effect, a frontier state, exposed to the nomadic attacks of the Mongols who swept out of the Eurasian steppe lands, it finally succumbed to the invading Mongol armies (1237–40), who established their control over southern and eastern Russia.

POLITICAL CAPITALS

With the breakup of the Kievan Rus state, Russian power shifted northward. The most powerful of the political units to emerge under the Tatar yoke was the principality of Vladimir-Suzdal, which centered around Moscow. Moscow's nodal location in a basin at the juncture of the Volga plain and the central Russian uplands had been advantageous for its development as a medieval trade center and the seat of the Duchy of Vladimir (part of the Kievan dynasty). The city had ease of access in all directions, the surrounding Valday hills, Smolensk ridge, and central uplands serving as the basis for a great watershed system. Moscow was a strategic crossroads for medieval trade routes—the Moskva River runs southeast into the Oka, and thence to the Volga River as it flows southward into the Caspian Sea. An arm of the Moskva also flows north into the Upper Volga, which is connected by river systems that flow into the Baltic and White Seas. The Oka River also connects to the Don River immediately to Moscow's south and to the Dnieper to the west; both drain into the Black Sea. Later, canals would effectively link these river systems. The centrality of the city was again reinforced by its radial railway network and by more recent air, electric power, and pipeline links.

In addition to access, Moscow's site had natural defensive advantages. It was protected on the east by the Klyazma-Oka marshy plain, on the north by the marshy plain of the Upper Volga, and on the west and northwest by the Smolensk-Moscow ridge. Farther to the northwest lay the Valday hills. Even though the city was sacked by the Mongols in 1238, it recovered to become the core of the Grand Duchy of Muscovy and the seat of the Russian Orthodox Church. By 1328, it had emerged as the main political and economic center of the duchy and in 1380 it became the capital of a unified Russian state. By the mid-sixteenth century, the Muscovite rulers took the lead in throwing off the Tatar yoke and began the state's southern and eastern expansion.

Moscow grew as the main manufacturing center of the state and served as the capital of Russia until, in 1712, Peter the Great built the new capital of St. Petersburg on the Baltic Sea to spearhead Russian commercial expansion. For the next two centuries, Moscow remained the religious core and second most important economic center. It resumed its role of political capital in 1918. That shift was both symbolic of Bolshevik rejection of the czarist cultural and economic turn to the West over the previous two centuries and the strategic expression of the Soviet desire for greater defensive depth. St. Petersburg was exposed geographically to invading forces from the west and the north, whereas Moscow had the advantage of being removed from the borders.

The alternating of the base of political power between Moscow and St. Petersburg represented antithetical points of view. Moscow reflected the inward-turning of medieval and early-modern-age Russia and the Soviet state. St. Petersburg represented czarist efforts to open the state to external technological innovations, cultural influences, and financial capital. It was from St. Petersburg (Petrograd from 1914 to 1924, Leningrad in 1924, and now St. Petersburg once more) that the city's industrial workers, soldiers, and sailors spearheaded the Russian revolutions of February and October 1917.

ECUMENE

The ecumene of Russia, defined by its highest density of population and economic activities, is shaped like a triangle that lies on its side pointing eastward. Its wide base on the west extends from St. Petersburg to Smolensk (facing Belarus), then to Briansk and Kursk, which adjoin the northeastern Ukraine, and continues southward to Rostov-on-Don at the eastern edge of the Donets Basin, which was once a major part of the Soviet ecumene but now lies mostly within Ukraine. From the western base line, the core area extends eastward, embracing Moscow and south-central Russia and then narrowing as it extends to Nizhny Novgorod (Gorki), Kazan, and Perm on its northern edge and Samara (Kuibyshev, on the great bend of the Middle Volga) and Ufa on its southern border. Crossing the Urals, the ecumene includes the West Siberian centers of Magnitogorsk, Yekaterinburg (Sverdlovsk), and Chelyabinsk. These cities form a triangular wedge from which the core area then extends eastward to Tyumen, a major center for the oil, natural gas, and chemical industries, and southward to Kurgan, which manufactures agricultural and chemical machinery. Both of these cities are on tributaries of the Ob-Irtysh River, which is the current boundary of the ecumene.

In much of the European portion of the ecumene, the population density ranges between 200 and 330 persons per square mile. From the Urals through West Siberia, peak densities are from 120 to 150 per square mile, while densities on the northern and southern edges of the ecumene range from 60 to 120 per square mile.

Major coal deposits are located in the eastern Donbas and north of Perm, while lignite deposits are in the areas surrounding the Moscow basin. The deposits of petroleum and natural gas in the region that extends from Saratov in the middle Volga northeastward along the Kama River basin to Perm, in the western Ural foothills, were so extensive that this area was called the "Second Baku." From 1950 to 1975, it was the Soviet Union's largest oil producing and refining center. Since then, it has been overtaken by energy-rich West Siberia. Now described as the "Third Baku," the Tyumen oblast, extending the length of the Ob-Irtysh basin, holds vast natural gas reserves—the largest in the world—and its petroleum deposits have made Russia into the world's second-leading oil exporter and third largest producer with 9 percent of total output. The oil exports go mainly to Western Europe. Russia now provides Western Europe with only one-fifth of its gas imports, much of which flows through the pipelines that cross through Ukraine. This figure will double with lines under construction, through Belarus, Poland, and Slovakia. Substantial new oil reserves that will enhance Russia's energy-producing capacities have been found in the Pechora basin north of the Arctic Circle to the immediate west of northern Siberia.

Rich iron ore deposits in western Russia south of Kursk, and scattered mining centers for molybdenum, copper, lead, zinc, and bauxite, are also located within the ecumene. This rich mineral base served as the foundation for the development of Russia's heavy industry—in the eastern Donbas, Moscow, Kursk, and Urals regions.

While the Urals had first developed metallurgical and ironworks in the early eighteenth century, its great industrial spurt occurred during World War II. Then, in the face of invading Nazi armies, much of Soviet industry was transferred from European Russia to the secure reaches of such Ural centers as Sverdlovsk (Yekaterinburg), Chelyabinsk, and Magnitogorsk.

Yekaterinburg today is not only the capital of the Sverdlovsk Oblast, with its population of five million, but it is also the center for a regional grouping of Urals provinces whose populations total twenty-three million. The city was closed to foreigners until 1992 because of its secret nuclear-weapons-assembly and uranium-enrichment plants. It has now begun to attract foreign investment and serves as Russia's third busiest diplomatic center.

Chelyabinsk's initial industrialization steps took place with the building of the Trans-Siberian Railroad; its steel and tractor industries were developed in the 1930s. It too was a closed city, serving as a center for the design of nuclear weapons and uranium processing. It now suffers from radioactive contamination due to nuclear waste disposal and nuclear accidents. During the Soviet era, there were ten such closed nuclear cities, with populations totaling seven million. Redirecting their large pool of scientific and technical personnel to civilian projects is an enormous challenge to Moscow, but also a major element in its strategy of economic recovery.

Mayak, the largest nuclear complex in the world, is located just north of Chelyabinsk on the Techa River, a headwater of the Irtysh-Ob River system, which drains the West Siberia Empty Area. The Mayak complex lies within the city of Ozyorsky (formerly the secret city of Chelyabinsk-65). Mayak currently reprocesses fuels from nuclear submarines, icebreakers, and breeder reactors and was the scene of reprocessing accidents in 1949, 1957, and 1967. In 1996, Moscow began construction of a fissile material storage facility there that is slated to become the world's largest depository of nuclear waste from power plants and serve customers from throughout Europe and Asia. Completion is scheduled for 2002. While Washington first supported the project, it now has voiced reservations because the plans include reprocessing and resale of some of the spent fuel, rather than merely storing the waste. The fear is that some of the reprocessed fuels could be diverted to nuclear weapons programs.

The other key Urals center is Magnitogorsk. Once the largest steel producer in the FSU, it produces only half of the raw steel that it did before the collapse of the Soviet state. Its ills are representative of those of Russia's rust belt generally—a bloated labor force, antiquated equipment, air pollution, and dependence on a single industry. With the opening of the country's markets to cheaper foreign steel imports, Russia's steel production has dropped from eighty million tons per annum to under fifty million. Built in 1929 as a factory town around the Magnitogorsk Metal Works, Magnitogorsk must now find a way to reinvent itself economically.

The current inability of the Moscow government to exercise strong controls over important parts of its ecumene, such as the Urals, is a major challenge. Some of Russia's farflung regions have been bolstering their positions at the expense of the Russian center, but these are economically unimportant. The Urals, however, are too wealthy and too important to the Russian state to be allowed to move off in independent economic and political directions—a tendency that has been fostered by the governor of the Sverdlovsk province in the Urals.

Urbanization and industrialization are now the economic mainstays of the ecumene, whose population is 76 percent urban. However, agriculture, the initial support basis of the ecumene, remains a prominent feature of the landscape. In the northern European sections of the ecumene, mixed farming emphasizes potatoes, rice and other grains, sugar beets, livestock, and flax. In addition, a belt of "suburban farming" around the big cities produces vegetables, dairy products, and pork. The fertile chernozem (black earth) soils at the southerly edge of the European ecumene are major producers of wheat, rye, sugar beets, and sunflowers. The introduction of grains at this edge took place in the 1930s. Over the intervening decades, production has suffered from soil and wind erosion, as well as periodic drought.

With the political upheavals of 1991 and the breakup of the USSR, the future of growth of the ecumene lies in its expansion into what remains of Russia's Effective National Territory.

EFFECTIVE NATIONAL TERRITORY

Just as the dismemberment of the Soviet Union has truncated the Russian ecumene, so has it deprived Russia of vast portions of its former ENT—in eastern Ukraine, the Trans-Caucasus, and northern Kazakhstan. Despite the loss of these territories, Russia's ENT is still large. It includes substantial lands in the North Caucasus and in lands eastward through the Lower Volga and Lower Ural basins, into the southern fringes of West and Central Siberia. Present population densities in the ENT range from twenty-five to sixty persons per square mile; the ENT can support heavier densities through modern urban, industrial, and agricultural development.

Much of this region fell under Nikita Khrushchev's Virgin Lands program, initiated in the 1950s. The aim of the program was to promote large-scale, mechanized grain farming in the belt of long-fallow, chestnut-colored and brown soils that underlay the steppe lands extending from the northern Caucasus through northern Kazakhstan and into West Siberia. Approximately 90 percent of the lands in this development scheme were in Kazakhstan. The plan drew substantial numbers of Russian colonists into the region, as well as engaging the large ethnic German population that was expelled to Kazakhstan during World War II. (Many of the latter have been repatriated to Germany since Kazakhstan's independence.)

In addition to wheat and other grains, livestock farming for dairy and meat products was developed in the northern portions of the steppe, while cattle ranching for beef was the focus in the southern fringe. Irrigated rice, cotton, and fruit were introduced into the Lower Volga, from Stalingrad to the Caspian Sea, and in the North Caucasus.

The Virgin Lands program introduced reforms, such as turning over farm equipment from centralized machine tractor stations to the collective farms and reducing taxation on the private plots of collective farmers. However, low and variable rainfall and susceptibility to drought limited the region's agricultural potential. Much of the newly plowed soil was swept away by dust storms, many of the shelter belts planted under the plan were in areas too dry to sustain tree growth, and soil erosion was widespread. A gamble because it focused on a climatically marginal region, the program failed to meet expectations.

The larger part of the present ENT lies in the strip of land that extends for eight hundred miles from Omsk in the southern part of the West Siberian Lowland to Tomsk, as well as to Krasnoyark in Central Siberia. The Trans-Siberian Railroad serves as the spine for this region. Hemmed in on the north by the cold, marshy sector of the West Siberian Lowland and on the south by the boundary of Kazakhstan and the Altay and Western Sayan mountains, the strip varies from 100 to 250 miles in width. Omsk, at the western end of the ENT, at the confluence of the Om and upper Irtysh Rivers, is Siberia's second-largest city and the center of its most advanced agroindustrial region.

Farther east, the main urban centers of the ENT include Tomsk on the Upper Ob and the belt of heavy industrial cities in the coal-rich Kuznetsk Basin (Kuzbas) that cluster around Novosibirsk, Siberia's largest city and its leading industrial and scientific center. Tomsk, a center for heavy machinery and chemicals, is especially at risk from its nuclear past. Its adjoining city, Seversk, was established to produce materials for the Soviet nuclear weapons program. This nuclear complex—perhaps the largest on earth—contains antiquated nuclear reactors that produce plutonium and have been prone to accidents. In addition, the complex currently contains one of the largest nuclear waste sites. These industrial centers are surrounded by the farmlands of the Baraba steppe.

Still farther to the east, the region terminates at Krasnoyarsk, the capital for the Central Siberian Territory, located along the Yenisey River, which flows twelve hundred miles north to the Arctic. Like Tomsk, Krasnoyarsk was a closed nuclear city with facilities for plutonium production and uranium-enrichment processing. Both cities are struggling to transform themselves into modern commercial and industrial centers.

An outlier of the main ENT lies five hundred to six hundred miles deeper into Siberia. It extends from Bratsk, at the northern head of the Bratsk Reservoir, to a cluster of industrial centers that lie between the reservoir's southern end and the westernmost tip of Lake Baikal. This outlier is hemmed in by the cold, barren Siberian Plateau to its north and the Eastern Sayan Mountains to the south. Bratsk is a single-industry city, a major aluminum producer. In contrast, cities such as Cheremkhovo, Angarsk, and Irkutsk, which are at the southern end of the reservoir and form a land bridge with Lake Baikal, have a diverse industrial base, ranging from machinery, aluminum, chemicals, and textiles to food products.

A second ENT outlier fifteen hundred miles farther east is located within the Russian Far East in the grassland areas north of the middle Amur and east of the lower Ussuri River. This outlier is an interrupted rather than a continuous strip. The westernmost point is Blagoveschensk, capital of the Amur region and across the border from the Chinese city of Heihe, an agricultural and gold mining center. Blagoveschensk's economy is based on local lignite deposits and food-processing plants. Khabarovsk, on the Amur near its junction with the Ussuri, is a major industrial city and transport hub, with oil refineries, shipyards, lumber processing plants, and engineering works.

The outlier ends at Vladivostok, where the Ussuri empties into the Sea of Japan. Vladivostok is the chief Russian port and naval base on the Pacific. Kept open by icebreakers in the winter, it is the capital of the Maritime Territory. As terminus of the Trans-Siberian Railroad and the Northern Sea Route, Vladivostok has developed a diverse industrial base, with shipyards, chemical and engineering factories, fish canneries, and food processing factories. The city also serves as the Russian Far Eastern Territory's major cultural and education center.

On the east side of the bay, opposite Vladivostok, lies the town of Bolshoi Kamen, a closed city that is home to a naval shipyard that specializes in scrapping nuclear submarines, and where the Russian navy has been dumping radioactive waste. The building of waste-treatment plants with Japanese financing and the assistance of U.S. contractors has been progressing slowly. Japan's stake in cleaning up contamination in the Sea of Japan reflects the strategically sensitive role of Russia's Far Eastern Territory, vis-à-vis not only Japan, but also North and South Korea.

Vostchony, a container port on the Sea of Japan sixty miles east of Vladivostok, has modernized its facility with the help of foreign investment. It has begun to attract increasing business from Japan, China, and South Korea. Containers shipped from these countries are loaded directly onto the Trans-Siberian Railroad and moved westward over a six-thousand-mile route to western Russia, Eastern Europe, and Finland.

Areas of modest development are the lower Amur, with its manufacturing center of Komsomolsk-na-Amure, the naval base of Sovetskaya Gavan on the coast southeast of Komsomolsk, and Sakhalin Island across the Tatar Strait from the mouth of the Amur. However, Sakhalin's coal and oil deposits are of growing importance. Promise of larger-scale economic and settlement activities is offered by oil and gas drilling on the northeastern end of the island, as well as offshore in the Sea of Okhotsk.

The development of Russia's Siberian ENT, first by farmers, herdsmen, and the military, then by mining and forestry, and in recent times by urbanization and industrialization, has been a centrally organized process. It remains to be seen what effect Russia's turn to a market economy and individual initiative will have on the development of the region. Central government support continues to be important during the transition from military industry and nuclear research and production activities. Moreover, reestablishment of Moscow's political and fiscal oversight of its outlying regions is a prerequisite to the political stability that capital investors require. Therefore it appears that the future of ENT expansion will depend on a blend of governmental and private initiatives, rather than on the free market forces that have been dominant in the development of similar regions in the West.

The likelihood is that Russia's ecumene will continue to expand into the western and southern portions of the ENT. However, unlike the U.S. West Coast, the Central Siberian and Far Eastern ENT outliers are unlikely to produce separate, secondary ecumenes, because they are too constrained by the rigorous climate, poor soils, and vast distances from the heart of Russia. Growth of these eastern areas in Siberia and along the Pacific is likely to be relatively slow. If economic conditions continue to lag there, the possibility will increase that a disaffected Far Eastern Territory might seek greater autonomy or quasi-independence.

EMPTY AREA

Siberia occupies most of the Empty Area of Russia. It is a region of over four million square miles—from Arctic ice fields, tundra, and taiga forests to high and mid-latitude mountains and plateaus, to the vast marshy West Siberia Lowland. Russia's additional former empty spaces of temperate and subtropical steppes and deserts now belong to the independent Central Asian republics.

The Empty Area is essentially uninhabitable, since it is mostly covered by permafrost and exposed to frigid winters. Therefore, nearly all of Siberia's thirty-two million residents (22 percent of Russia's total population) live within its ecumene or ENT.

In the north, the region's few inhabitants are indigenous Finno-Ugric and other peoples who subsist on hunting, fishing, and reindeer herding. The south is populated by Turkic-speaking and Mongol peoples who raise cattle. Scattered Slavic settlements engage in mining and forestry, while a handful of urban communities serve as processing centers for Siberia's resources.

The rich natural resources of the Empty Area, including oil and natural gas, nonferrous precious metals, and timber, have been a major support base for the economic development of the ecumene and ENT of Russia. East Siberia remains a storehouse of gold, silver, diamonds, mica, and bauxite. Its giant hydroelectric power stations along the Yenisey and the Angara Rivers, as well as hydropower plants elsewhere, are important components of the national electricity grid.

The Empty Area's vast West Siberian Lowland oil and gas fields, which have been exploited since 1965, enabled the FSU to become the world's largest natural gas producer. They remain Russia's top source of foreign currency. These fields lie within the Middle Ob basin and are served by Surgut, Neftejungansk, and Nizhnevartovsk, which were constructed in the 1960s and house tens of thousands of energy industry workers. The oil and gas pipelines that radiate from the "Third Baku" serve the West Siberian ENT and its Central Siberian outlier, as well as the Urals and European sections of the ecumene.

In addition to these rich gas and oil deposits, Siberia's Empty Area contains a few cities scattered across Central and East Siberia. Norilsk, Russia's northernmost major city and the second largest located above the Arctic Circle, is linked to the mouth of the Yenisey by the port of Dudinka. Norilsk's local minerals—nickel, copper, cobalt, platinum, and coal—as well as power from nearby hydroelectric plants, support diverse metal smelters. Yakutsk, with access to nearby coal and gas deposits, is a major port on the Lena River and has food, textile, and leather goods industries, sawmills, and a shipyard, as well as being the region's cultural and scientific studies center. Magadan, on the Sea of Okhotsk, is the center for the gold mining region of the upper Kolyma River, manufactures mining machinery, and hosts fish canneries and shipyards.

Siberia has historically served the czars and the communists not only as a storehouse of minerals to support Russia's settled regions, but also as the home to penal colonies and concentration camps. In the air age, its vast, empty space was put to a new use—to serve the FSU's defensive/offensive strategic purposes. During the Cold War, a network of missile and early-warning radar sites were constructed along the Arctic coast, facing the U.S.-Canadian NORAD system. In addition, nuclear-missile-bearing Soviet submarines maintained a constant vigil beneath the Arctic ice cap and waters, facing off against their American submarine opponents in a continuous game of "nuclear tag."

The hilly island archipelago of Novaya Zemlya, five hundred miles east of Murmansk and approximately six degrees north of the Arctic Circle, has been the scene of nuclear testing since 1995. Over one hundred nuclear blasts have been conducted on its snowy and icy wastelands. While the last large explosion took place in 1990, the Russians have continued to use the island for underground experiments that test the reliability of their nuclear arsenal.

With the advent of the space age, the FSU found a new strategic use for its Empty Area. The region has provided launching pads for space vehicles for both military and commercial operations. The locus of the Soviet/Russian space activity has been, and continues to be, in Kazakhstan. The Baikonur Cosmodrome was developed north of Tyura-Tam, one hundred miles east of the Aral Sea. Starting with Sputnik in 1957, most of the Soviet Union's and Russia's space and ballistic missiles have been launched from the Cosmodrome's three major sites. In addition, the major targeted site for space landings has been nearby at the city of Aral, just to the northeast of the Aral Sea. Vozrozhdneniya Island, which is located within the sea, was the site of the world's largest anthrax burial ground and the Soviet's major open-air biological testing station. Uzbekistan has had to reach out to international agencies for help in cleaning up the sites.

Plesetsk, in northern Russia, 125 miles south of Archangel, has served as a site for a few high-inclination launches, but the Russians have continued to focus their space activities at Baikonur, leasing an area of six thousand square miles from Kazakhstan at an annual rental of $115 million and maintaining ownership of the facilities. Recently they also developed a new launch site at Svobodny in the South Amur Oblast of the Russian Far East, one hundred miles north of the Amur River. In addition, Orsk, in Russia's southern Urals, and Dzhezkazgan, at the western edge of the Kazakh Uplands, are used as supplements to the Aral landing site. It is clear that Russia regards this part of Kazakhstan as a vital part of its Empty Area and is not prepared to give up its use.

With the end of the Cold War, Siberia's globally central Empty Area has assumed new and valuable commercial importance. Long-range jet-plane flight routes are being developed across the Arctic and Siberia to connect the major cities of North America directly to such points as Beijing, Bangkok, Shanghai, Hong Kong, and Cairo. Considerable savings in fuel and labor are provided by shortening flight times by up to five hours. Russia and Canada can expect to derive substantial fees from airspace overflight charges. As one dividend of the end of the Cold War, the military air control networks that were developed by both the United States and the Soviet Union across the Arctic space can now be turned to supplementary commercial applications as well.

BOUNDARIES

Russia's Cold War land-border disputes with China have been part of much broader conflicting territorial claims. The conflict goes back to the nineteenth century, when China was forced to cede 580,000 square miles of territory to czarist Russia. These lands lay in the Tajik and Kyrgyz sectors of the Pamirs; in a large part of southern and eastern Kazakhstan; and in the Soviet Far East, north of the Amur and east of the Ussuri River. The latter territory contains such centers as Vladivostok, Khabarovsk, and Petropavlovsk in the Kamchatka Peninsula. In essence, the claim was against lands in Turkestan, Siberia, and parts of Mongolia that had been colonized by Russians and were the core of what Mackinder described as the Heartland. These lands, which were originally populated by Central or East Asian peoples with no historic racial or linguistic connections to Slavs or Han Chinese, nevertheless became the basis for historic claims between Russia and China.

After the Sino-Soviet split, Beijing reasserted its claims to the section of the Pamir that adjoined western Xinjiang and an area in southeastern Kazakhstan that is drained by the Ili and Irtysh Rivers, whose headwaters are in northern Xinjiang. Beijing's most strident claims were focused on sections of the border with the Soviet Far East, along the Amur and Ussuri Rivers, involving twelve hundred square miles of territory. It was there that serious military clashes erupted between the two powers in 1969.[8] The Chinese held that the main channel of the Amur ran northeast to Khabarovsk, while the Russians claimed that the channel ran southeast to the Ussuri. The fighting centered around Damansky (Chenpao) Island, a small, uninhabited island in the Ussuri River just south of the Amur River, near Khabarovsk. Both sides sustained heavy casualties, after which inconclusive negotiations took place.

While this border region became heavily militarized in the 1970s, further fighting has not taken place. An agreement was finally reached in 1997 that left in dispute only two small sections of the current 2,300-mile boundary between the two countries and that reduces the border's militarization.[9]

In accordance with the 1945 Yalta accord, the USSR occupied the entire Kuril Island chain in the Pacific, which had long been in dispute between Russia and Japan, and had been occupied by Japan since 1875. The Kurils overlook Russia's Kamchatka Peninsula—Russia's closest point to the Aleutian Islands and the Bering Sea. However, Japan has continued to demand return of the four southernmost islands, immediately to the north of Hokkaido, which it regards as its Northern Territories. These are the islands of Etorofu, Kunashiri, and Shikotan and the Habomai group. The dispute over these islands has marred the diplomatic relations between the two countries for the past half century and has hindered Japanese investment in Russia. A recent Russo-Japanese agreement to seek a settlement of the southern Kuril dispute and to sign a peace accord is testimony to Moscow's current desire to move toward overall stability in the North Pacific. Accommodation with Japan would be a useful step, although genuine stability will have to await peace in the Korean Peninsula.

Another dispute is over the maritime boundary of the Svalbard Archipelago, whose main island is Spitzbergen. The archipelago belongs to Norway and, in accordance with the

1920 Treaty of Paris, is to remain demilitarized. Briefly invaded by the Germans in 1942, the islands were recaptured by Norway, which has since rejected the requests of Moscow that it be allowed to share in their defense. The economic value of Svalbard lies in its minerals, especially coal. The Russian coal-mining concessions represent 60 percent of the island's coal exports and the Russian miners account for a similar percentage of the small population of three thousand.

Since the collapse of the Soviet Union, a number of other issues have remained unresolved along Russia's 12,375-mile border.[10] The boundaries within the shared waters of the Caspian Sea have yet to be delineated among Azerbaijan, Iran, Kazakhstan, Turkmenistan, and Russia. In the Baltic, Russia's most sensitive boundary issue is with Estonia. The latter claims 770 square miles in the areas of Narva, just west of St. Petersburg, and Petseri, which lies to the west of Pskov. While the two parties came to an agreement in 1996, at this writing it has yet to be ratified. The same holds true for a 1997 border agreement with Lithuania that reaffirms Lithuania's title to the Klaipeda (Memel) area. Latvia lays claim to a section of the border that was transferred from the Latvian to the Russian Republic in 1944—the Abrene Pytalovo district on the Ukroya River, sixty-five miles southwest of Pskov. While both sides came to an agreement here in 1997, it too remains to be ratified. None of the Baltic border issues represent strategic threats to Russia today. However, should the Baltic states join NATO, the disputes could become inflamed.

The Heartlandic Periphery

The Eurasian Periphery of Heartlandic Russia has undergone revolutionary geopolitical change since the dissolution of the Warsaw Pact and the breakup of the USSR. Once allies of the Soviet Union, and bases from which the USSR could control the Eurasian Rimland, the former Communist satellites within the Periphery have now become a base that can be turned against Russia. In addition, Russia considers the fourteen constituent republics that broke away as its "Near Abroad," because of their defensive and economic value, and because approximately 18 percent of the total ethnic Russian population lives within their borders.

Western policy makers may dismiss as groundless, and even paranoid, Moscow's concerns about NATO's expansion, but memories are indelibly etched of the German invasion during World War II, in which an estimated twenty million Soviets died and many of the nation's cities and industries were devastated.

When Russians look to their western Periphery for defensive depth, they recall the wartime vulnerability of the line from Leningrad (St. Petersburg) to Moscow to Tula to Stalingrad (Volgograd) to the northeastern shore of the Black Sea at Novorossiisk. This line held only because the defensive depth to the west provided the time for the broken Russian armies to regroup.

Russian historic memories of outside invasions reach back well before World War II. In 1812, Napoleon's Grande Armée seized Moscow and burned much of the city, before being forced to retreat after one month. During the Crimean War of 1854–56, Anglo-French forces allied with Turkey penetrated the Black Sea and laid siege to Russia's naval base of Sevastopol. In two years of fighting, the invaders won half of the city and the stalemate bled both sides dry. At the war's end, neither side had accomplished its goals, but all participants were severely weakened. From 1918 to 1920, Archangel, Russia's main White

Sea port and the terminus of the Northern Sea route, and Murmansk were occupied by Allied forces and the Russian White Army in their unsuccessful campaign to overthrow the Bolsheviks. Also during the civil war, Polish troops seized Ukraine in the course of their dispute with the Bolsheviks over the Russo-Polish frontier, while Vladivostok was occupied by Allied forces, including the Japanese, until 1922.

Russia's current security concerns are also focused southward. Western political and commercial encroachment in the Trans-Caucasus states of Georgia and Azerbaijan have raised suspicions in Moscow. This also applies to Central Asia, where international oil interests have focused investments in the energy resources of the region. These include plans to build oil pipelines that would circumvent existing lines that run through Russia and are regarded as part of a Western strategy to draw the region out of Moscow's strategic sway. U.S. military bases in Central Asia that were developed to support the war in Afghanistan against the Taliban and al Qaeda, along with U.S. military training missions in Georgia, have added to Russia's disquiet.

Only Mongolia, in the heart of Eurasia, seems safely within Russia's orbit, although China could seek to play a stronger role there. Another of Moscow's worries is the vulnerability to Chinese pressures on Russia's Far Eastern Territory. However, recent tensions there have been reduced, as both countries have become alarmed over U.S. nuclear strategic arms policies.

All of these concerns color Russia's current behavior toward its Heartlandic Periphery. Resurgent Russian nationalism, reinforced by the renewed strength of the Russian Orthodox Church and by the interests of the military-industrial establishment in regaining past prestige and power, affects policies toward the Periphery. These concerns are also linked to the presence of twenty-five million Russians living in the Periphery, mostly in areas that border Russia and contain the seeds of a drive for a "Greater Russia." Finally, one cannot discount the importance to Russia of Kazakhstan's Empty Area, or of the Caspian Sea's oil reserves, which Moscow so recently commanded in totality and over which it now seeks to exercise some measure of control.

GEOPOLITICAL FEATURES OF THE HEARTLANDIC PERIPHERY

The vulnerability of much of the Heartlandic Periphery to Moscow's pressures is especially great among the states that adjoin Russia to its west and south. This vulnerability stems from their geopolitical features, especially their political capitals, ecumenes, and boundaries.

Capitals

The proximity of the capitals of most of Russia's nearest neighbors leaves those cities strategically exposed. The following distances to the closest Russian territory illustrate this point: Tallinn (in Estonia), 120 miles (and 200 miles from St. Petersburg); Riga (Latvia), 130 miles; Vilna (Lithuania), 200 miles; Kiev (Ukraine), 170 miles; Tbilisi (Georgia), 70 miles; Yerevan (Armenia), 100 miles; Baku (Azerbaijan), 120 miles; and Ulan Bator (Mongolia), 150 miles. Astana (Akmola), which replaced Almaty as the capital of Kazakhstan in 1997, is located within the Kazakh ecumene in the north-central steppe lands, 200 miles from the Russian border. Known as Tselinograd when it was the administrative center for the Soviet Virgin Lands agricultural program, it grew rapidly in the 1950s and '60s, attracting a mainly Russian population. It is now being developed as a Special Economic Zone to generate foreign capital and spur industrial growth, as well as to attract more ethnic Kazakhs to the city.

Ecumenes

The ecumenes of these states are equally close to Russian territory and, in some cases, actually merge with those of Russia. Estonia's economic and population core area follows the Baltic coast from Tallinn to Narva, where it joins the Russian core west of St. Petersburg. The Latvian ecumene, which centers around Riga, is only 150 miles from the St. Petersburg core, while the Belarus ecumene, running from Minsk to Vitebsk and Mogilev, merges with Russia's core at Smolensk. Lithuania's economic core region, stretching from Kaunas (Kovno) to Vilna, is only 100 miles from the western edge of the Belarus ecumene. Ukraine's economic and population core extends from the lower Dnieper (at Dnipropetrovsk) northeastward to Kharkiv at the Russian border and eastward to Donetsk and its associated industrial centers of the Donets Basin, where it merges with the Russian part of the basin at Rostov.

In the Caucasus, Georgia's major economic core area extends northward along the Black Sea at Batumi and northeastward to the Kutaisi area, approximately 200 to 300 miles from the southern edges of Russia's ecumene along the Sea of Azov and Rostov. Armenia's industrial centers of Yerevan and Kumayri are 250 to 300 miles from the Russian ecumene, while Azerbaijan's core is farther away—550 miles.

Kazakhstan's ecumene extends from Karaganda and Temirtau northeastward to the Russian border at Pavlodar, where it is approximately 250 miles from both the Omsk and the Novosibirsk industrialized clusters of West Siberia's ENT. Mongolia's very limited ecumene extends north from Ulan Bator to the Russian border, where it is less than 150 miles from the Lake Baikal industrial centers of south-central Siberia.

BOUNDARIES

As discussed, Russia now has no active boundary disputes with its neighbors, although the lines with each of the Baltic states await final ratification and there remains the issue of the Svalbard Archipelago maritime boundary. However, territory and boundary conflicts among the Periphery neighbors have been serious obstacles to economic and political development in some of them. Armenia and Azerbaijan went to war over the largely Armenian-populated autonomous region of Nagorno-Karabakh, which lies within Azerbaijan. The fighting led to great losses of life and property and to massive displacement of people. Similarly, Serbia's conflicts over Bosnia and Kosovo have substantially weakened Belgrade. In both cases, Russia is in a position to help mediate the conflicts, and may therefore be able to strengthen its influence in these parts of its Periphery.

Russia has played a dual role relative to the separatist revolts that have broken out in Transnistria in Moldova and in the Abkhazia and South Ossetia regions of Georgia. While it provided military support to the separatists, it has at the same time played a moderating and stabilizing role, helping to limit the fighting by placing peacekeepers in Abkhazia and keeping Transnistrian separatism at a de facto level.

Ukraine has a dispute with Romania over the continental shelf of the Black Sea, under which significant oil and gas deposits may exist. This, however, has little relevance for

Russia, which has a far greater stake in the Caspian Sea boundaries that have yet to be de-termined among all the coriparians—Azerbaijan, Iran, Kazakhstan, Turkmenistan, and Russia.

In Tajikistan, the former Communist and now Nationalist government faced an Is-lamic fundamentalist revolt from 1992 to 1997. Moscow came to the aid of Tajikistan, sending troops to the Tajik border with Afghanistan to try to block assistance to the rebels from fellow Tajiks in Afghanistan. Turkmenistan also has turned to Russia for help in guarding its borders with Iran and Afghanistan, while Moscow has had to keep a watchful eye over Uzbekistan's land disputes with Kazakhstan, Turkmenistan, and Tajikistan.

It is clear that boundary and territorial disputes among the neighbors of Russia's Cen-tral Asian Periphery have served to strengthen the influence of Russia there. This and the nearness of the political centers and economic core areas of the Central Asian states rein-force Moscow's strategic weight within the region.

Eastern Europe

THE BALTIC STATES

During World War I, Halford Mackinder argued that stability in Europe depended upon a Middle Tier of independent states between Russia and Germany.[11] After the war, Isaiah Bow-man advocated the establishment of such a tier, to be led by an expanded Poland and Roma-nia, as a *cordon sanitaire* between the historically antagonistic Russian and German powers.[12]

What has transpired since these writings has been quite different. First, the "Middle Tier" was conquered by Germany during World War II, but afterward the states became satellites of the Soviet Union. Now the West is expanding into the region. Should the EU and NATO in combination absorb this belt of Middle Tier states, the imbalance between the West and Russia will become profound and the situation in Eurasia unstable. As previ-ously discussed, decoupling the military and economic links between Western and Eastern Europe would represent a more viable geopolitical solution. While NATO membership for the Central European states of Hungary and the Czech Republic represents no threat to long-term stability, the participation of Poland does—particularly since it has agreed to de-ploy nuclear weapons on its territory should NATO so request.

The application of the Baltic states for NATO membership has profoundly disturbed Moscow. Not only do these countries hold the key to the approaches to St. Petersburg, but also their ports handle a significant share of Russia's foreign trade. Moreover, Lithuania, along with Poland, surrounds Russia's naval base of Baltisk in the Kaliningrad Oblast—home port for Russia's Baltic fleet and for its Eleventh Army. Kaliningrad (the former Prussian city of Königsberg), with a population of one million people, has become a cen-ter for smuggling and corruption. Under different circumstances, it could develop along positive economic lines into an important gateway to Poland and Lithuania. To compen-sate for its lack of a direct connection to Kaliningrad, and as an alternative to the present routes through Lithuania, Moscow has pressed for a secure highway corridor to the exclave via Belarus and Poland. This proposal is supported by Belarus, but thus far has not been accepted by Poland.

Russia has already taken steps to enhance its security interests in the Baltic by con-structing a large oil export terminal at Primorsk, one hundred miles northwest of St. Petersburg, at the eastern end of the Gulf of Finland. The facility is connected to a newly completed pipeline that is the first section of the Baltic Pipeline Project. This project will expand the present pipeline system to open up large-scale exploitation of the Pechora oil and gas reserves of Russia's Arctic Far North, and to better serve the fields of West Siberia and some of Kazakhstan.

A substantial share of Russian oil exports now moves through Baltic Sea terminals in Latvia and Estonia. The largest of these terminals, Ventspils in Latvia, alone takes 15 percent of Russia's petroleum shipments. The Primorsk terminal will facilitate the expansion of the country's overall production and, in an emergency, bypass the Baltic state transit ways. In addition, Russia has expanded St. Petersburg to become its largest port, with the goal of reducing Russia's dependence on dry cargo ports in Estonia and Latvia.

Added to these strategic concerns are Moscow's interests in the rights of Russians who live in the Baltic states. While Russians constitute less then 9 percent of Lithuania's populace, they are much more important factors in Estonia, where they are nearly 30 percent, and in Latvia, where they are now 30 percent of the total (having dropped from 40 percent during the Soviet era).

One of the most reckless and politically motivated policies to come out of Washington in recent years has been the 1998 pledge President Clinton made when he signed a charter of partnership with the Baltic presidents to support the aspirations of the three Baltic countries to join NATO. The argument was that the security of Europe depends upon Baltic security. Fortunately, NATO's European leadership has been more cautious about admission of the Baltic states. While the clock cannot be turned back on NATO's absorption of Poland, requests for membership of the Baltic states would best be turned down by the Alliance. For the Russians, the Finnish model of military neutrality, even as it is a member of the EU, represents a direction for the Baltic states that would meet the security needs of Moscow.

Estonia is the most economically advanced of the Baltic countries and a heavy user of information technology. Along with Slovenia, it is a top candidate for the admission to the EU and could be a useful bridge between the EU and Russia.

BELARUS AND UKRAINE

Belarus and Ukraine are equally sensitive strategic areas for Russia. Historically, Belarus has been a crossroads for invading armies heading for Moscow along the Smolensk-Moscow plateau. Also known as "White Russians," the Slavic Belorussians never developed a distinct culture, language, or identity apart from the Russians. During the Soviet era, the Belorussian Republic was developed as an industrial hub for the manufacture of armaments, machinery, motor vehicles, chemicals, textiles, and electrical equipment. However, it remained a relatively poor area, saddled with inefficient, Soviet-era state collective farms and state-owned industries.

The Russians regard Belarus as the key buffer against NATO, now that Poland, which adjoins Belarus on its west, has joined the Western alliance. The Communist president of Belarus, Alexander Lukashenko, has pressed for a full reunion with Russia. While a reunification agreement was signed in 1997, this does not provide for the full merger desired by the autocratic Belorussian president. Nevertheless, Minsk is meeting the security aims of Moscow by reintegrating its air defense, intelligence, and arms production, which includes mobile Scud missile launchers. In addition, the Belarus economy is totally dependent upon Russia for its oil and gas supplies, most of which it receives as a gift.

Ukraine is of equal strategic importance to Russia, both because it is the land gateway to southwestern Russia and because the Crimea overlooks Russia's now limited Black Sea coast. Thus far, Ukrainian governments have refrained from requesting admission to NATO and there has been little inclination on the part of European states to utilize the NATO-Ukraine Partnership for Peace Charter as a basis for advancing military cooperation.

However, any form of military alliance between the West and Ukraine would precipitate Russian countermeasures. Not only is 23 percent of Ukraine's fifty million population Russian, but those 11.5 million Russians are concentrated in two strategic parts of the country—east of the Dnieper and in the Crimea—and Russian separatist sentiment in both of these areas is widespread. Moreover, the majority of religious Ukrainians belong to the Russian Orthodox Church and pay allegiance to the patriarchate in Moscow.

The Russified Dnieper region extends from Kharkiv, Ukraine's second-largest city and a major industrial center, through the provinces of Lugansk and Donetsk—the heart of the Donbas, with its heavy industry and coal. Ukrainians are a bare majority in this region and the highly urbanized Russians dominate many of the urban centers. A Russian-inspired separatist movement could dismember the country. Even Kiev has a 20 percent Russian population that, in times of conflict, could threaten government stability.

The substantial Russian population of the Crimea (estimated at two-thirds of the total) posed a problem for Ukraine in the mid-1990s because of the Crimea's separatist sentiments during the negotiations over the future of Sevastopol and the surrounding region. The Crimea had been a Tatar autonomous republic until the republic was dissolved in 1945. The Tatars were forcibly resettled in Soviet Asia at that time, because they had been charged with collaborating with the German occupiers during the war. Initially, the region was annexed to the Russian SFSR. In 1954 it was transferred to the Ukrainian SSR, but pro-Moscow feelings remained strong.

Crimean separation was tied up with the negotiations over the disposition of the Soviet fleet. The resolution of this issue was that 80 percent of the ships, as well as 50 percent of the facilities of the naval base at Sevastopol, would remain in Russian hands, with the rest going to the new Ukrainian navy. Sevastopol thus continues to serve the Russian Black Sea fleet, which shares the base with Ukraine's naval vessels. In an attempt to mollify the separatists, who include not only the Russians, but a residual Tatar minority, Ukraine established the Autonomous Republic of Crimea within its governance structure in 1993. Nevertheless, the Crimea would clearly be vulnerable to a Russian-inspired separatist revolt should Ukraine join NATO.

Another manifestation of Ukraine's vulnerability to Russian pressures was Russia's involvement in the establishment of the breakaway Trans-Dniester Republic in Moldova's Transnistria region, which is wedged in between Moldova and southwestern Ukraine. Half of the Transnistria's population consists of Russians and Ukrainians. When armed clashes broke out between the secessionist elements and the Moldovan forces, the Russian Fourteenth Army, which has been stationed in the region since World War II, intervened on behalf of the secessionists. Moldova's dependence upon Russia is heightened by its heavy indebtedness to Moscow for the natural gas supplied to it.

A second separatist force, the Turkish Gagz ethnic group in the far southeast of Moldova, also declared independence at this time, with the support of the Transnistrians. This area overlooks the lower Prut, a few miles from where it joins the mouth of the

Danube and in between Romania and Ukraine. The status of the Gaganz "Republic" remains in question.

Further compounding the danger to Ukraine inherent in the possible dismemberment of Moldova, and indeed threatening Moldova's very survival as an independent entity, is the claim that Romania has on the larger part of Bessarabia, located between the Prut and Dniester Rivers. Bessarabia is the gateway from Russia to the Danube Valley. Historically, its control has shifted back and forth between Russia and modern Romania. Romania absorbed the region in 1918, but was forced to cede it back to Russia in 1940. Moscow then merged the larger part of the region into the Moldavian SSR.

Bessarabia's northern and southern sections, which were predominantly Ukrainian speaking, were incorporated into Ukraine. Romania has forsaken its claim to the territory now held by Ukraine. However, it maintains its claim on the Bessarabian part of Moldova, which constitutes most of the country.

Moldova and Romania maintain close ties. At the end of World War I, Bessarabia declared itself an independent Moldovan republic and then voted for a union with Romania that was internationally recognized at the Paris Peace Treaty (1920). Ethnically and linguistically, Moldovans are akin to the Romanians; support for reunification with Bucharest remained widespread within Moldova until its recent independence, when the subject of reunification was dropped. For Moscow, Romanian control of Moldova would undermine the position of the Russian-speaking people of Transnistria, as well as giving a Western-leaning Romania direct access to the open plains of western Ukraine—another unwelcome prospect.

Russia's current major leverage against Ukraine is the former's commitment to protecting all Russians living in the CIS. The CIS is the community of former Soviet republics, except for the Baltic states. It was established in 1991 as a successor to the Soviet Union to coordinate trade policies and mediate disputes. Over the past decade, it has become essentially a "paper" organization, but is frequently used by Moscow as a diplomatic cover to pressure its neighbors. As a measure of the declining economic importance of the CIS, intra-CIS trade fell from 21 percent of its members' GDP in 1992 to 7 percent in 1997.[13]

Although rich in natural resources and the recipient of considerable foreign aid since it broke away from the Soviet Union, Ukraine remains impoverished. The Kiev regime has failed to restructure the country's economy or to modernize its inefficient industrial plants. Moreover, the government is riddled with corruption, politically divided, and heavily in debt (especially to Russia, for unpaid natural gas purchases from the corporation Gazprom). A substantial proportion of the electorate, frustrated that independence has brought with it economic decline rather than prosperity, supports reunification with Russia. However, it is highly unlikely that Ukraine would give up its sovereignty. Moreover, western Ukraine (centering around Lviv), which was known as "Galicia" and was ruled by Poland between the two world wars, has never been Russified. It might well try to break away should Ukraine move too close to Russia. The western Ukrainians, many of whom are Catholic, would prefer to move Ukraine closer to Poland and the EU, and to have greater autonomy. The Catholic population numbers one million Roman Catholics and five million Eastern Catholics or Uniates. The latter subscribe to Eastern Orthodox rituals, but pay allegiance to the Pope. The Uniate Church was established in 1596, in response to the pressures upon the Orthodox bishops by Polish Catholic rulers who had assumed control of Ukraine from Lithuania in 1569.

Russia remains the leading trade partner of Ukraine and supplies it with most of its energy via natural gas and oil pipelines. Moreover, Ukraine's agricultural strength can benefit from a recovering Russian market. During the Soviet era, the farms and black earth soils of Ukraine's steppes produced one-quarter of all Soviet agricultural production, while the West offers little in the way of an alternative market for Ukraine's meat, milk, grain, and vegetable exports. In addition, should Kiev succeed in privatizing its economy and attracting Western capital for certain industrial niche products, it can serve as an important gateway to Russia. It would be well for both the West and the government in Kiev to recognize that Ukraine's best prospects lie in its becoming a bridge between Russia and the West, not a spearhead of NATO.

THE IMPLOSION OF YUGOSLAVIA AND THE BALKANS

Geographically, the Balkan Peninsula includes Albania, most of the former Yugoslavia, Bulgaria, southeastern Romania, northern Greece, and European Turkey. Historically and politically, these six countries have been referred to as "the Balkan states." Geopolitically, Greece and Turkey are now part of Maritime Europe, while Romania and Bulgaria are geostrategically vital to Russia. A major concern for Moscow has been the efforts of Bulgaria and Romania to join NATO. Membership of these two countries, along with Turkey, in NATO would provide the West with control of much of the Black Sea littoral. Should Ukraine also join the Alliance, Russia would then be squeezed into a very small section of the northeastern coast. Naval exercises that NATO has held within the Black Sea, with the inclusion of U.S. forces, has further heightened Russia's sense of vulnerability and increased its fears of Western containment.

However, neither Russia nor the Maritime powers now have substantial strategic interests in the states of former Yugoslavia—Croatia, Bosnia, Macedonia, Slovenia, and Serbia/Montenegro—or Albania. It is for this reason that this war-torn area has not become a Shatterbelt. The West and Moscow are not competing to stop the conflict or to impose a peace upon peoples who are bitterly divided religiously, ethnically, and culturally.

Dissolution of the Yugoslav federal empire involved far greater conflict than was experienced in the breakup of the Soviet state. The first stages of the breakup were relatively peaceful. Slovenia, the most economically advanced of Yugoslavia's federal republics, was allowed to leave after only limited fighting, while Macedonia declared its independence under the cover of a small UN force. However, Slobodan Milosevic's dreams of a "Greater Serbia" included large parts of Croatia plus Bosnia, Montenegro, and the autonomous regions of Vojvodina and Kosovo that lay within Serbia. The wars in Croatia and Bosnia raged for four years. They ended in 1995, with the U.S.-brokered Dayton agreement for Bosnia and the Croatian recapture of all Serb-held parts of Croatia. Serbs were then expelled from all parts of Croatia except Eastern Slavonia, where a UN peacekeeping force was installed.

The unrestrained fighting, mass killings, and ethnic cleansings carried out by Serbs, Bosnian Muslims, and Croats in Bosnia and Croatia were followed four years later by similar Serb actions in Kosovo. This was brought to an end by massive NATO air warfare against the Serbs. The peace accords in both Bosnia and Kosovo are maintained through the large-scale intervention of NATO troops, supplemented by Russian forces and UN police units.

The outcome of NATO's military campaign in Bosnia, far from assuring a multiethnic independent republic, has reinforced the division of the country into two largely autonomous units—a Serb republic (Rupublika Srpska) and a federation of Muslims and

Croats in which the Muslims dominate in an uneasy alliance. The Croats, who are concentrated in southwestern Bosnia, adjoining the Dalmatian coast, seek to break this alliance and rejoin Croatia. In 2001, the National Executive of the Bosnian Croats voted for self-rule as a step toward independence.

The situation in Bosnia brings into question the West's policy of trying to preserve a unified state composed of people who support different sovereignties. In the long run, regional stability will be better served if the Serb part of Bosnia joins Serbia and the Croatian section in western Bosnia is allowed to join Croatia, leaving a smaller, but cohesive Muslim Bosnia. The results of the Kosovo intervention have been even less successful. The Serb military remained intact, despite relentless NATO bombing. Since the end of the conflict, hundreds of thousands of Albanians who fled or were expelled during the war have returned and the Albanians have driven out most of the Serbs. The one hundred thousand Serbs who remain continue to receive support from Belgrade, but their future is uncertain. Ultimately, the fiction of an autonomous Kosovo still tied to Yugoslavia is likely to be set aside, with most of Kosovo joining Albania. The Serb sector in the northern part of Kosovo centers around Mitrovice in the Ibar River Valley, an area with rich copper and zinc deposits. Mitrovice might be annexed to Serbia, should Belgrade also be guaranteed control of key national and religious shrines located in other parts of the region.

Kosovo has special mythic importance to Serbia as the historic core of Serbian nationalism. Slavs initially settled there in the seventh century and fully colonized it by the end of the eighth, before converting to Eastern Christianity in the next century. The region was seized by the Turks, who defeated the Serbs in the battle of Kosovo Polje (the Kosovo Plain) in 1389. The battlefield site has since become a shrine and pilgrimage site for Serbian nationalism and the Serbian Orthodox Church.

Under the Ottomans, in the fifteenth and sixteenth centuries, the vast majority of Kosovo's population that was ethnic Albanian was converted to Islam. Thus, the Orthodox Serbs found themselves in a minority when Kosovo was regained from Turkish rule by Serbia and Montenegro during the Balkan War (1913) and formally incorporated into Yugoslavia after World War I (which was initially named the Kingdom of Serbs, Croats, and Slovenes). Serbs have remained as a minority, ranging from a high of 38 percent, owing to a government resettlement policy in the 1920s, to a low of less than 20 percent of the population at the time of the Kosovo War.

What complicates the prospects for a compromise based on a partition of Kosovo between Serbia and Albania is the geographical distribution of Serbs and Albanians. While Mitrovice at the northern end of the fifty-mile-long Polje Plain is ethnically Serb and adjoins Serbia, the Kosovo Polje battlefield and associated tombs and monasteries are located five miles southwest of Pristina, the regional capital that is now ethnically Albanian. Moreover, Pec, a city of revered churches and shrines on the western edge of Kosovo, is also surrounded by ethnic Albanians, as is Prizren, a town in the far south that has numerous ancient monasteries and churches. Without ironclad guarantees of Serb control and access to these sites, there is little likelihood of Serbia's acceptance of a partition.

Kosovo has unlocked a new set of boundary disputes that are linked to ethnic Albanian populations in southern Serbia and Macedonia. Kosovar guerrilla activity has spread to those areas, despite the efforts of the NATO peacekeeping force to contain them. While Yugoslavia and Macedonia have recently resolved their border dispute and demarcated the line, the Albanian guerrillas now threaten to destabilize the situation in their drive to create a Greater Albania.

Approximately 30 percent of the two million Macedonians are ethnic Albanians, including many refugees from the Kosovo conflict who were granted entry. Many of these ethnic Albanians have long held grievances against the country's Slavic majority in the areas of job and language discrimination, but the political parties that represent the Albanians in the Macedonian parliament and government are opposed to the Kosovar-led insurgency. The bulk of the Albanian population lives in three districts along the western border with Albania and adjoining Kosovo and Serbia in the north. Tetovo, the country's second-largest city and the center for Macedonia's Albanians, lies within ten miles of the Kosovo border in the northwestern part of the country. Skopje, Macedonia's capital, is located only ten to twenty miles from the territorial crescent formed by this Albanian population and is therefore highly vulnerable to guerrilla activities.

Macedonia had just emerged from the isolation cast upon it by Bulgaria, Serbia, and Greece (Athens had even challenged its right to call itself by that name), and had developed positive relations with these neighbors, when the Kosovar guerrillas violated its territory. For NATO, this was both a political and military setback. The Alliance had armed and trained the Kosovars during the war with Serbia and had looked the other way when the Kosovars drove tens of thousands of Serbs out of the province. Now it found itself turning to Serbia to make common cause in containing the Albanians, who also sought control of the ethnic-Albanian-inhabited Presevo Valley in southern Serbia, adjoining Kosovo. NATO has permitted the Serbs to send troops into a part of the three-mile buffer zone bordering Macedonia that it had previously established within Serbia to separate Serb from Kosovar forces; Belgrade, rather than the Albanian Kosovars, has become NATO's hope for stabilizing the situation.

Serbia's most pressing problem currently is its relationship with Montenegro. While still formally a republic within a part of the Yugoslav Federation with Serbia, Montenegro's leadership has expressed the desire to be independent of Belgrade. While the Montenegrans claim to be a separate ethnic nationality, they are mostly Serbs and belong to the Orthodox faith. Russia has had an historic alliance with Montenegro and may be expected to seek a mediating role in the current tensions between the two former Yugoslav republics. However loose the ties among its parts, a unified Serbia/Montenegro provides Moscow with an opening to the Adriatic. Moreover, hemmed in by the Catholic Croats to the north and the Muslim Albanians to their south, the 650,000 Montenegrans (compared to Serbia's 9.6 million population) have no other natural allies than the Serbs and the Russians. The Serbs would be landlocked should Montenegro break away. A solution to the issue came with the decision of the two republics to form a loose federation named the federation of Serbia and Montenegro. This took place on March 14, 2002, when Yugoslavia was officially declared "dead." The federation will control foreign and defense policy, while there will be considerable economic and political autonomy.

In the face of all the turmoil in this portion of the Balkans, Russia continues to be the primary backer of Serbia, supplying it with oil and other commodities. NATO continues to strive for that most elusive of goals—peace and stability. For neither is this imploded area strategically vital.

The Trans-Caucasus and Central Asia

What links the Trans-Caucasus and Central Asia regions is the Caspian Sea. The export of much of the petroleum and natural gas resources of the Central Asian countries of Kazakhstan and Turkmenistan requires pipelines that traverse parts of the Trans-Caucasus.

THE TRANS-CAUCASUS

The extensive Russian military involvement in the affairs of Georgia, Armenia, and Azerbaijan during the 1990s reflects the depth of its strategic interests in the Trans-Caucasus. Russia's relations with Georgia, the only mainly Christian country within the largely Muslim world of the Caucasus, have been especially tense because of Moscow's support of the separatist movement in Abkhazia, as well as its ambiguous role in the South Ossetian rebellion.

Abkhazia, the Muslim region within northwestern Georgia, extends from the Black Sea to the south of Russia's Sochi resort area, north to Russia's Karakchevo-Cherkess Republic. The main Abkhazian city, the port of Sukhumi, a resort as well as a manufacturing center, is also the southern terminus of the 120-mile Sukhumi Military Road, which crosses the Greater Caucasus through the Klukhori Pass into Russia. The road provides Russia with an important land link to the Black Sea and, until recently, Moscow kept a military base at Gudauta, north of Sukhumi, as well as three other bases in Georgia.

The rebellion in Abkhazia broke out in 1992 and was supported, according the Georgian charges, by the Russians. There, at the onset of the fighting, Muslim separatists expelled 260,000 Christian ethnic Georgians, creating a major refugee problem for the Tbilisi government. Russian and Georgian peacekeepers stabilized the situation by 1994, but in 1999 the pressures for separation mounted and Abkhazia held a referendum on independence, which passed by a large majority. Its political status remains ambiguous today. It continues to operate with quasi-independence, and sentiment for reunion with Russia remains strong, while an Abkhazi government-in-exile sits in Tbilisi.

In South Ossetia, the rebellion against Georgia broke out in 1992, two years after Tbilisi had taken away the autonomous status that the region, together with North Ossetia, had enjoyed as part of the Mountain Autonomous Republic during the Soviet era. Russian and North Ossetian troops intervened to quell the rioting, and autonomy was restored. In 1995 sporadic fighting erupted once more, as the Christian South Ossetians demanded either independence or to be linked to the Muslim Russian republic of North Ossetia. Again the Russians quieted the unrest, this time stationing troops in the region to guarantee its autonomy. South Ossetia has less strategic importance to the Russians than Abkhazia, although the 170-mile Ossetian Military Road that traverses Ossetia, connecting Alagir in North Ossetia to Georgia's Kutaisi and the Batumi coastal region, is one of the two main routes across the North Caucasus.

Russia's desire to maintain a substantial military presence in Georgia also relates to security concerns within its own North Caucasus territory. The most serious of the rebellions there is in Chechnya, which has a seventy-five-mile border with Georgia. Underscoring the importance of Chechnya to Russia is that a major oil pipeline and railroad from Baku in Azerbaijan to Novorossiisk on the Black Sea runs through Chechnya. (The new pipeline from the northeast Caspian shores to Novorossiisk bypasses Chechnya.) Moscow has wished to seal the Chechen-Georgia border by keeping troops in the Pankisi Gorge, a narrow valley that leads to the Shatili Pass across the crest of the mountains and marks the boundary between the two countries. The gorge, long a transit route for drugs and for arms smuggling from Afghanistan to the Chechen Muslim rebels, has also been an escape hatch for the rebels and, according to Moscow, the site for their training camps. However, Georgia has refused to allow the Russians to station their troops in the gorge, but has been helpless to prevent the heavy bombings of the valley. It is not only the presence of Russian bases in Georgia and the proximity of Russian troops to its borders that limits the ability of

Georgia to ignore pressures from Moscow. The Tbilisi government is also dependent on and in considerable debt to Russia for the natural gas that is the basis for the country's supply of electricity and heating. Moscow has not hesitated to slow down or even temporarily cut off supplies during the winter, as political leverage.

Impoverished, riddled by corruption and lawlessness, devastated by the wars of insurrection, and overwhelmed by the collapse of its farm economy, Georgia is caught between the pressures of Russia and the West. In 1998 Moscow removed its troops from Georgia's Black Sea coast and half of Georgia's land border with Turkey. The following year, it agreed to close its base in Abkhazia and an air base near Tbilisi. Nevertheless, tensions persist as President Eduard Shevardnadze of Georgia has insisted repeatedly that Georgia's future is with the West, and has expressed his intentions of making application for NATO membership.

Washington is making considerable efforts to expand its influence within Georgia. Its direct foreign aid contribution now represents one-third of the Georgian budget; also, it has been highly supportive of the arrangement that President Shevardnadze has made with Western oil interests to build a major new pipeline to carry Caspian Sea oil from Baku across Georgian territory to the Black Sea. From there the oil would have to move by tanker through the Black Sea and out to the Mediterranean. Turkey has been opposed to this line, fearing increased shipping traffic through the already crowded straits and possible oil spills. It adds to Moscow's concerns that the Georgian government has invited U.S. military forces to train Georgian troops with the objective of clearing the Pankisi Gorge of Chechen and other guerrilla and terrorist bands.

If the West were to be so reckless as to extend NATO to include Georgia, as well as to respond favorably to the applications of Romania and Bulgaria, it would be following a path of serious geopolitical folly. Trying to make a Western lake of the Black Sea would turn the entire region into a Shatterbelt, the consequences of which would be a spate of local wars, as well as resumption of the Cold War.

Another problem for the Russians has been the 1999 Chechen rebel penetration into the neighboring Russian republic of Dagestan, which lies on the shores of the Caspian, north of Azerbaijan. This incursion, as well as penetration of southern Russia, brought on the second Chechen war. Large-scale Russian air attacks upon Chechnya continued in the fall of 1999, in response to terrorist bombings within Russian cities. Since then, the government of Vladimir Putin in Moscow has reoccupied most of Chechnya, although the conflict continues with guerrilla hit-and-run tactics.

The Caspian Sea oil and natural gas pipelines that extend through Chechnya to Russia's Black Sea coast or northward into Russia first traverse Dagestan. Control of Dagestan, which is Russia's only land contact with Azerbaijan, also strengthens Moscow's military leverage over the oil-rich Azeris. Dagestan militants, who favor an independent Islamic state, are but a minority. The majority of Dagestanis, who are moderate followers of Sufi Islam, have expressed no desire to leave the Russian federation or forgo Russian economic subsidies. Another reason for the strategic importance of Dagestan to Moscow is that it adjoins northeastern Georgia, placing Russian forces within 70 miles of Tbilisi.

The two other Trans-Caucasus states, Armenia and Azerbaijan, have been joined in conflict over Nagorno-Karabakh since 1988, blocking the building of pipelines across the Trans-Caucasus to the Black Sea or the Bay of Iskenderun. At that time, Nagorno-Karabakh was an autonomous Soviet region located within Azerbaijan. Its population of 200,000 was more than three-quarters Armenian. When the two countries became independent, Armenian nationalists demanded that the region be included within Armenia. By

1992 Armenian troops, with military support from Russia, had captured the mountainous enclave, as well as a corridor of Azerbaijani territory connecting it to Armenia. In the years of fighting, up to 800,000 Azeris and 400,000 Armenians have been displaced, while 35,000 have died in the conflict. A cease-fire was negotiated in 1994, but three years later Nagorno-Karabakh declared independence; Armenia, while renouncing its claim to the breakaway territory, continues to occupy it militarily.

Economically, Azerbaijan is of far greater importance to the outside world than is Armenia, although the latter has a considerably higher income, owing to its machinery equipment manufacturing, gold, jewelry, and hydroelectric power, as well as investments and remittances from prosperous Armenian communities living abroad. Azerbaijan's significance is its oil production and refining center at Baku on the Apsheron Peninsula. The peninsula and its offshore waters once constituted one of the world's richest oil regions, the main petroleum-producing center of the Soviet Union until World War II. The reserves have declined, but Baku remains important as the primary pipeline terminal for oil coming west from the Central Asian oil-producing countries, as well as for its large refineries.

Azerbaijan has without success sought military and diplomatic aid from the United States in its conflict with Russian-backed Armenia and has offered both the United States and Turkey military bases on Azeri soil. Recently, however, Washington and Moscow have joined in seeking a negotiated peace. The outcome could be establishment of a self-governing, quasi-state in Nagorno-Karabakh and in the adjoining Lachin region, which links Nagorno-Karabakh geographically to Armenia. In exchange, Azerbaijan could receive a security corridor to its Nakichevan enclave in southwest Armenia. Also, Russia and Azerbaijan have signed a ten-year agreement permitting Moscow to continue to operate a Soviet-built missile-tracking station within Azerbaijan that provides coverage of the airspace over South Asia and the Gulf region.

It is Moscow, not Washington, that holds the key to this peace, for the United States is ill equipped to challenge Russia within its Trans-Caucasus backyard. The question looming in the background is whether the West will engage Russia as a full partner in the proposed pipeline developments of the region and acknowledge Russia's interests in protecting the pipelines that now extend from the Caspian Sea through its territories.

THE CENTRAL ASIAN "NEAR-ABROAD" COUNTRIES

The five independent Central Asian states that broke off from the FSU—Kazakhstan, Kyrgyzstan, Tajikistan, Turkmenistan, and Uzbekistan—occupy a vast land area of 1,542,000 square miles, with a combined population of fifty-six million. Landlocked and surrounded by Russia on the north, Iran and Afghanistan on the south, and China on the east, this region of steppe, desert, and mountain is lightly populated and impoverished. It would be of little geopolitical interest to the West were it not for the relatively recent discovery of vast new energy reserves in and around the eastern shores of the Caspian Sea in Kazakhstan and Turkmenistan. As a result of this potential, the Clinton administration embraced the entire Caspian Sea region as a key strategic and commercial objective, thereby asserting a geopolitical interest in the region that has traditionally been Russia's backyard.

Pressured by international oil interests, Washington has taken the position that securing a reliable pipeline system that bypasses Russian territory in bringing the energy exports to market requires aggressive U.S. political and economic support of Central Asian states, as well as Azerbaijan and Georgia. Indeed, playing upon the historic role of Central Asia as the locus of the Silk Road, based on the trading of silk and gold between the West and China, American oil interests have pressed the Congress for an Energy Silk Road Strategy Act, which would encourage U.S. governmental intervention in the affairs of the region.

The geopolitics of oil and pipelines is complex. Russia's involvement in Caspian Sea oil already includes its control of two pipeline routes. One, which taps the Mangyshlak and Tenghiz oil fields, runs from Atrau in Kazakhstan northward into Russia to the Baltic Sea. A second line extends westward from Makhachkala in Dagestan on the western shore of the Caspian Sea, through Russia (via Chechnya) to the port of Novorossiisk on the Black Sea. In 2001, this line was supplemented by a much larger, new, nine-hundred-mile pipeline constructed by Russia, Kazakhstan, and international oil companies. It bypasses Chechnya and moves oil more cheaply than the older lines, from the Mangyshlak and Tenghiz fields to Novorossiisk. It is also expected to carry the initial output of the huge Kashagan oil field, which was discovered under the Caspian Sea in Kazakh waters and is due to open in 2005.

Kashagan's reserves have been estimated variously at from 1 billion to nearly 7 billion tons. They could be the biggest petroleum find of the past two decades. These deposits heightened the American interest in the region and prompted Washington to give strong backing to a proposed 1,080-mile pipeline under the Caspian Sea to Baku and thence across Azerbaijan, Georgia, and Turkey to the port of Ceyhan on the northeastern shore of the Mediterranean.

Feeders to the line could serve potentially rich oil and natural gas fields in Turkmenistan's Caspian waters, which have also attracted international oil and gas interests. While such a line would bypass the Bosporus shipping route, and therefore be more ecologically sound, it would be far more expensive to build and to operate than the new Russian line. Moreover, the Ceyhan line would run through southeastern Turkey and therefore be vulnerable to being cut by Kurdish rebels, through whose homeland the route would travel. Another line that has been proposed by some international oil companies would run from the Caspian through Iran to its Kharg Island oil terminus on the Persian Gulf. In addition to being more expensive, this route is anathema to Washington because of its tense relations with Iran.

In a recent exercise of its pipeline politics power, Russia has begun the last stage of construction of a natural gas pipeline to Turkey. This pipeline would extend under the Black Sea at a seven-thousand-foot floor depth, from the Novorossiisk area in Russia to the Turkish Black Sea port of Samsun. The overland section from Samsun to Ankara has already been constructed. The pipeline will increase Turkey's dependence upon Russia for natural gas from 60 percent of what they currently use to 90 percent. Fields in Russia and Kazakhstan, and probably Turkmenistan in the future, will be the sources of supply for the line. The project gives further emphasis to the geographical advantages of Russia in the competition to control oil and gas routes from the Caspian Sea and Central Asia.

A more prudent and less provocative U.S. policy would be to support a mixed set of pipeline routes, starting with the one that was recently constructed across Russia and perhaps eventually including an agreement to supplement this one with the Iranian route. Such lines would not be needed for a few years, during which time events in Iran might produce a more favorable climate for restoration of U.S.-Iranian relations. Whatever the direction and timing of the routes, the inclusion of Moscow as a co-owner/shareholder of the emerging pipeline network would reduce tensions between Russia and the United States, while assuring Russia of increased benefits in transit fees from those lines that now cross its territory or may be built in the future.

The aim of Washington in all of this pipeline geopolitics is clear—to end Russian domination of the Caspian. The consequences of such a policy would be to ignite another Great Game in Central Asia and help to drive Russia and Iran into each other's arms.[14] Through much of the nineteenth century, the British had maneuvered to prevent Russian control of the region. They failed in their efforts to establish alliances with the emirs of the Silk Road kingdoms and (in the First Afghan War, in 1839) lost in their attempt to gain control of Afghanistan, the rugged approach land to the deserts and steppes of Central Asia. Their military expeditions into Tibet in 1905, southeast of the ancient routes to China, had no lasting effect either. The race for empire ended in the late nineteenth century with Russia controlling Central Asia to the borders of Persia, Afghanistan, the Tien Shan and Altai Mountains, and to Mongolia.

A new Great Game, this time headed by the United States, has even less chance of long-term Western success than the one played by Britain, which had the Indian subcontinent available as its base. Russia has two major advantages. The first is its strategic location abutting the Caspian Sea and Kazakhstan, by far the largest and most powerful of the Central Asian states and the one with the richest oil reserves. The second is the substantial Russian population located in Kazakhstan and Kyrgyzstan. Slavic organizations in these two countries, playing upon suspicions of China and popular fears of vulnerability to Islamic fundamentalism, have called for a referendum on joining the Belarus-Russian union. Thus far, these calls have not been acted on, but they cannot be lightly dismissed. The leaders of these two regimes and those of the other Central Asian states are fully aware of their continuing dependence upon the military support of Moscow to maintain the stability of the region.

Over ten million people in Central Asia, or 18 percent of the region, are Russian. Well over half, or six million, live in northern Kazakhstan, where they represent 38 percent of the population (Ukrainians and Germans are another 10 percent). The north, which is the center for the country's manufacturing and its major farming area, also houses Russia's space industries and its nuclear testing sites. The Kazakhs are a minority in much of their own country, but they hold the key to its stability, and thus to the prospects for fully exploiting the land and offshore oil deposits.

Eastern Kazakhstan, centering on Ust-Kamenogorsk (Oskemen) on the upper Irtysh near the Russian border, is predominantly Russian. Support there is particularly strong for Kazakhstan joining the proposed Belarus-Russia union. Much of that population is Cossack in origin, their settlement dating back to the late seventeenth century. (Cossacks have also lived in southern Kazakhstan since the early nineteenth century.) Indeed, the northern part of eastern Kazakhstan was part of Siberia until 1936. While separation is currently not a serious issue, an effort to wean the country away from Russia could result in its dismemberment, for the Russians have made it clear that defense of ethnic Russians has a high priority.

Boundaries are another point of possible contention, should the Great Game be injected into Kazakh politics. The boundary of northern Kazakhstan, long regarded as an old colonial settlement area by the Russians and a focus for settlement during the Virgin Lands program, is still not fixed. This is true also for the dividing lines within the territorial waters of the northern Caspian Sea, which are underlain by rich energy deposits.

Dividing the seabed of the northern Caspian has not yet become a matter of serious regional dispute. Iran has proposed a joint area in the middle of the sea to be shared by the five riparians beyond their coastal zones. Kazakhstan, Azerbaijan, and Turkmenistan have at times argued for using median points to divide the sea into national sectors, while Russia,

Kazakhstan, and Azerbaijan have also proposed relating jurisdiction over the waters to length of coast.[15] Russia could use this issue as leverage in arresting Western attempts to wean Kazakhstan away from the Russian sphere of influence.

Russia's second most important area of concern in Central Asia is Kyrgyzstan. As is the case with Kazakhstan, Russia is Kyrgyzstan's chief trading partner. Large numbers of Russians and Ukrainians settled there during World War II, and they now represent half of the population of Bishkek (Frunze), by far the largest urban and industrial center of the country. All told, one million of Kyrgyzstan's people, or 22 percent of the population of 4.5 million, are Russian. Their status is of considerable concern to Moscow, as well as a strategic asset. Because of its location, bounded by Kazakhstan to the north, Uzbekistan to the south, Tajikistan to the west, and China to the southeast, Kyrgyzstan could prove of importance to future Russian-Chinese relations. Both Kyrgyzstan and Kazakhstan border China's Muslim Xinjiang Uighur Autonomous Region. The Russian military presence along the borders of the Central Asian countries might be helpful to China should Xinjiang's separatist movement become a serious threat to Beijing, for China and Russia have a common interest in containing the spread of Islamic fundamentalism within Central Asia.

Russia is far better positioned than the West to take a hand militarily in stabilizing Central Asia. The countries of that region are beset with disputes over land and water boundaries and by the threatened spread of Islamic fundamentalism emanating from Afghanistan and Iran. Russian troops have been stationed in all five countries. Since helping to quell the civil war in Tajikistan between the government and a fundamentalist Islamic opposition group, Moscow has stationed troops along the Afghan frontier, across which the Islamic militants received arms from the Taliban. They also patrolled Turkmenistan's border to protect against incursions from Iran and Afghanistan. Moscow's military support of Turkmenistan has been accompanied by agreements on joint exploration of the rich natural gas and offshore Caspian oil fields that the country possesses. Kyrgyzstan, too, needed Russian help to combat Islamic guerrillas sponsored by Afghanistan, and Russia has been sympathetic to the Uzbek government's repression of Islamic fundamentalism in the wake of 1999 terrorist bombings. A further reflection of Russia's military importance to the region is the agreement signed by Moscow in May 2001 with Kazakhstan, Kyrgyzstan, and Tajikistan to form a joint Rapid Reaction Force to combat Islamic insurgencies. The force is to be based in Bishkek, the capital of Kyrgyzstan.

Uzbekistan, for its part, claims border lands in the mountainous section of southern Kazakhstan, thus in the year 2000 Uzbekistan's border guards seized some stretches of land. The strength of the Uzbek army makes Kazakhstan particularly dependent on the Russian arms provided to it as part of its annual lease payments for the Baikonur space-rocket site. In addition to Uzbekistan's claim in southern Kazakhstan, Uzbekistan has claims on the Tajik section of the Fergana Valley, while Turkmenistan and Uzbekistan are at odds over Karakalpakia, the region of western Uzbekistan on the Aral Sea at the delta of the Amu Darya. A month after Uzbekistan's seizure of land in southern Kazakhstan, Turkmenistan and Uzbekistan joined with Russia and China, along with Kyrgyzstan and Kazakhstan, to form the Shanghai Cooperation Council. The purpose of the council is to resolve border disputes and to fight Islamic militancy.

Turkey has sought to extend its influence into Uzbekistan by offering arms and military training to combat the latter's extremist Muslim rebels, but so far the offer has not been accepted. Rigid governmental policies have discouraged foreign investors, who were attracted initially by the country's irrigated cotton production and its substantial natural gas deposits. The uranium that once supplied most of the FSU's needs no longer has the strategic significance that it had during the Cold War.

Mongolia

East of Central Asia lies the Mongolian Republic, covering a vast area of 604,000 square miles, bordered by Russia on the north and China on the south. Mongolia was under Chinese influence during the eighteenth and nineteenth centuries and came under Soviet sway after World War I, as the People's Republic of Mongolia. The sparse population of 2.5 million, which had long followed a nomadic way of life, changed to urban pursuits and settled agriculture under the influence of communism. Sixty percent of the populace is now urbanized and a number of industrial centers have been developed. Nevertheless, the economy remains dependent on the export of livestock, minerals, wool, and cashmere.

The landlocked status of Mongolia reinforces its continued dependence upon Russia for trade, although China has become its second most important commercial partner. The Altai Mountains and the Gobi Desert separate Mongolia from China's Inner Mongolia region, while Ulan Bator (Ulaanbaatar), the capital and main industrial city, and most of the other major cities of the country are located 150 to 200 miles from the Russian border, with relatively easy access to Russia across high, grassy steppes and low mountains. The strategic vulnerability of this part of Mongolia suggests that the Russian influence of the past century will persist well into the twenty-first century and that Russia's Inner Asian reaches will remain secure from outside penetration.

Halford Mackinder's inspiration for the Heartland theory was the role that the center of what he called "Euro-Asia" had played between the fifth and sixteenth centuries as the source of the waves of nomads sweeping out of its steppes to conquer so much of the continent's ocean-facing margins. Of these groups, the Mongols made the deepest and most lasting impact upon the Eurasian margins, using the horse as the military tank of that era. Superior horsemanship, together with centrality of location and short interior lines enabled them to move outward in any direction, employing the elements of speed and surprise. This gave them a major geostrategic advantage over the relatively immobile European and East Asian farmers and forest dwellers.

Between the first quarter of the thirteenth to the mid-nineteenth centuries, Genghis Khan, Kublai Khan, Tamerlane, and Babur swept out of the Mongolian Plateau to seize such areas as North and South China, Persia, the Black Sea coast, southern Russia, Baghdad, Aleppo, Turkey, Afghanistan, and India. In another example of the mobility of the horse, Yermak, the leader of the Russian Cossacks, crossed the same grassy gateway between the southern Urals and the Caspian Sea in 1582 to penetrate Siberia. Even though the Mongol threat dissipated in the west by the end of the fifteenth century, a branch of the Mongols, the Mogul (Mughal) empire, established itself in India in 1526 and lasted until 1857, when the British formally took over.

Mackinder viewed the Trans-Siberian Railroad, which was completed the year after he wrote his article "Geographical Pivot of History," as the successor to the horsemen and camel men of the Mongol empire and the riders of the steppes who followed them. He saw the rail as the key to Russian control of the Pivot Area of Eurasia.

Events of the past century have proven that, while Mongolia remains geographically in the center of Eurasia, the center of the Heartland lies to the west—in West Siberia.

World power is now determined more by where natural and human resources are concentrated than by centrality and mobile lines of transportation. Mongolia is now but a small and strategically marginal country. It has been bypassed by time and technology and is dependent upon Heartlandic Russia for its viability.

Conclusion

Events of the past century have demonstrated that the centrality of the Heartland within the Eurasian continent does not mean command of the Old World or control of the continent in its entirety, and certainly not control of the globe. However, Heartlandic Russia's location does enable it to use its centrality to exercise strategic dominance over its Periphery. The bases for such dominance are proximity, short interior lines of transportation and communication, historical/cultural ties, control over militarily and economically important land passageways, and the spread of ethnic Russians and other Slavic peoples into parts of the Periphery. These factors provide Moscow with a strategic advantage over outside powers in influencing the course of events in Eastern and southeastern Europe, the Trans-Caucasus, Central Asia, and Mongolia.

This centrality is also a factor in enabling Russia to play a continuing role within the Northern Highland Zone of the Middle East. This geographical advantage has permitted Russia to continue to sell arms to Iran, in spite of Washington's efforts to block such sales. At the same time, South Asia is well outside the strategic reach of Heartlandic Russia. Moreover, East Siberia, which lies east of Lake Baikal and the Lena River, and especially the Far Eastern Territory are vulnerable to the pressures of China, the Asia-Pacific Rim, and the United States (from its Alaska base). In the unlikely event that Beijing and Washington were to develop a strategic alliance directed against Moscow, East Siberia might become a Compression Zone because of its remoteness from the Heartland.

The prevailing physical and geopolitical character of Heartlandic Russia is Continentality. The vast Eurasian expanses, wealth of mineral resources, and broad agricultural and forestry base have historically focused the energies of the Heartland's rulers on development of the Interior, and not on foreign exchange. In modern times, this Continentality was reflected in the czarist and Soviet drives for national self-sufficiency, usually behind closed political-economic systems.

There have been brief periods during which Russia has opened itself to the outside world. Peter the Great did so as he sought to modernize the country by importing Western ideas, technology, and workmen. With national and international communism as its defining ideology, the Stalinist Soviet Union closed its own system to the outside world, as it developed heavy industry, agriculture, and a sophisticated scientific-technological military base.

When Moscow did reach outward beyond the Eurasian Rimland during the Cold War, it was to support Communist revolutions in the Third World for the strategic advantages that Moscow could gain in its competition with the United States. This outreach was a one-way street—it exported arms, economic aid, and political guidance, but did not open the Soviet system to external influences. The reforms instituted by Mikhail Gorbachev represented a major break in the Soviet closed system policy, but came too late to forestall the collapse of the Soviet empire and the dismantling of the USSR.

During the initial phases of the post-Soviet era, the new Russian leadership based its hopes for economic recovery on a free market system tied to global forces. That recovery has not taken place. Instead there has been a de-development of manufacturing and a collapse of agriculture, as state industries and farms have been looted and sold off, as debt has been recklessly incurred, and as cheaper and better foreign goods have entered Russia. Widespread poverty, not prosperity, has been the fruit of Russia's efforts to increase capital investment inflow and trade with its main European partners—Germany, the United Kingdom, and Italy—and with the United States.

Promotion of Western capitalist ideals of minimizing government interference in the market process has a hollow ring to a people who have seen the rise of a class of corrupt Russian oligarchs who practice an extreme form of crony capitalism. For many Russians, the Americanization of the world economy and culture is seen as a challenge to Russian culture and is likely to fuel nationalism and militarism, rather than weaken their impact.

With the exception of international capital investment for the oil and gas industry, most of the investment inflows now are directed toward goods and services for the Russian consumer, not toward building export industries, as was the case for Western investment in the trade-oriented Asia-Pacific Rim countries. Moreover, much of the capital generated by privatization of industry and by energy exports has been sent abroad, rather than being reinvested in the domestic economy.

Russia's current economic weakness masks its inherent strengths—its relative ethnic homogeneity, its high degree of urbanization (76 percent) and literacy (98 percent), and its large pool of well-trained scientific and technological personnel. These are complemented by the wealth of energy and other mineral resources, abundant forestry and animal products, a strong agricultural base, and the country's advantageous global strategic location. An added source of strength is that the burden on Russia's resources has been greatly reduced because it no longer needs to support its former satellites economically and militarily and the cost of maintaining its huge nuclear arsenal, offensive navy, and massive land force is being greatly reduced.

Reinventing its economy may prove less of a challenge to Russia than restructuring its political system and restoring the national cohesiveness now so sorely lacking. The centralized political control during the Communist era was maintained by terror and repression, as well as World War II–inspired patriotism and Cold War fears of the outside world. By contrast, centrifugal forces, at times verging on anarchy, brought central government almost to a state of paralysis, particularly in the last few years of the presidency of Boris Yeltsin. Many of Russia's eighty-nine regions had become essentially private fiefdoms that were badly and corruptly governed and that ignored directions from Moscow. These forces were especially strong in oil-rich Bashkortostan and Tatarstan in the European Russian far east, Sverdlovsk in the Urals, the state of Sakha in Yakutia in the Far East, and Primorsky on the Pacific.

The election to the presidency of Vladimir Putin has signaled the restoration of strong central government. Crony capitalism has been partly, but not fully, attacked, and governors responsive to Moscow have been put in place. Nevertheless, developing a cohesive governmental system requires more. It will have to take into account the devolutionary forces that are sweeping across Russia. The Putin government will therefore have to find a balance between regional desires and needs on the one hand and national requirements on the other.

In the North Caucasus, adherence to the Russian Federation by Chechnya, the Ingush Republic, Dagestan, and North Ossetia will depend upon introducing a structure of genuine autonomy that satisfies the Islamic religion, culture, mores, and economic needs of these minority lands. In the Far Eastern Territory and Yakutia—so far removed from Moscow and the ecumene—the central government must reinvest much of the regional wealth for local development, rather than exploit these resources largely for the benefit of the ecumene.

One cannot dismiss the possibility that these regions might eventually break away from the Russian state. If Moscow persists in seeking a military solution in Chechnya without a concomitant political formula that guarantees Chechen quasi-independence, it risks continuing a lengthy guerrilla war that may eventually prove unacceptable to the Russian people.

In the Far Eastern Territory, the temptation of separatist elements to take an independent economic course is tempered by the strategic vulnerability of the region to China and Japan. This should not lull Moscow into indifference toward separatism.

Without speedy improvement in the Russian economy, there may well be a return to the historic pattern of national behavior that was based upon the bedrock of continental self-containment. Even if there should be a rapid economic turnaround, with open markets and trade, elements of the authoritarian and social welfare tradition of the Soviet state are likely to be built into the evolving Russian political system.

Moscow's concerns over separatist movements within its new borders are likely to limit the degree of democracy permitted by the government. Russian democracy cannot be expected to mirror that of the United States or Maritime Europe. Western outcry over human rights violations in Chechnya are legitimate, but have to be balanced with the recognition that Russia will act to preserve its territorial integrity. It will counter Chechen guerrilla attacks in the same fashion that Spain deals with Basque terrorism and other countries have fought civil wars to overcome separatism.

Russia has also begun to take important foreign policy initiatives. It has conducted discussions with the EU aimed at strengthening its ties with the union, including cooperation with the West European Rapid Defense Force. It has joined the EU in trying to mediate the Korean conflict and urging North Korea to abandon its missile program. Moscow has made a particular effort to strengthen its ties with Berlin, to which it owes half of its $40 billion foreign debt. It is likely that Germany will respond by devising a debt relief formula that could be followed by the other major debt holders.

In the year 2000 Russia approved the START II Treaty as well as the Comprehensive Test Ban Treaty (CTBT). While the United States had approved START II in 1996, the U.S. Senate, along with other holdouts such as China, Pakistan, India, North Korea, and Egypt, has rejected ratification of the CTBT. Moscow sought deeper future reduction of nuclear warheads for START III than was first envisaged by the United States. However, in May 2002, both parties agreed to deep reductions of between 1,700 and 2,200 missles, representing a cut of approximately two-thirds of the current arsenals. Washington has also reserved the right to store some of the missles.

Reviving a Cold War atmosphere is in the interest of neither the United States nor Russia. While pressures and blandishments from the United States may ultimately succeed in gaining the grudging approval of Russia to amend the 1972 Anti-Ballistic Missile (ABM) Treaty, the costs might well outweigh the benefits. Given its massive nuclear arsenal, Russia has little to fear from the NMD, the first phase of which is to include new radar and missile interceptor systems at Shemya Islands in the westernmost part of the Aleutian chain, 550 miles east of Russia's Kamchatka Peninsula. Russia clearly stands to gain from a strategy that might restrain a possible nuclear strike by an unstable North Korea. However,

Moscow has legitimate misgivings that scrapping the ABM Treaty could force it into an unwanted renewal of the arms race.

Russia is sensitive also to China's objections to NMD, based on the latter's limited nuclear arsenal. Moscow does not want to put in jeopardy its recent progress toward developing a strategic alliance with Beijing by giving in to U.S. pressures on this issue. If Russia were to accept the U.S. position, this might reignite major competition between the Chinese and the Russians in North Korea, Vietnam, and South Asia. U.S. policy makers should consider whether the price of trying to contain the "rogue" North Korean regime is worth the possibility that the North Pacific, as well as Indochina and South Asia, could become destabilized by a new round of Sino-Russian geostrategic competition. A sounder policy for restraining the North Koreans would involve Russia, China, South Korea, and Japan as major players in the quest for security in the North Pacific.

September 2001 and its aftermath introduced a new era in U.S.-Russian relations. Moscow responded positively when Washington requested support in the War against Terrorism in Afghanistan. It consented to the use of air and land bases in Uzbekistan, Tajikistan, and Kyrgyzstan, and permitted the overflight of its own territory by U.S. aircraft. An even more positive development has been the signing of the NATO-Russian Partnership Accord on May 28, 2002—an event that has been heralded as signifying the formal end of the Cold War. Russia will be a partner in discussions and actions over such issues as military cooperation and nonproliferation; NATO retains control over key military decisions.

Russia has made clear its desire to become part of the Western community of nations, resurrecting the drive for westernization launched by Peter the Great three centuries ago. As a measure of its commitment to the economic and military health of the West, President Putin has undertaken to ensure the energy security of the West by pledging to make Russian oil available in time of war or disturbances in the Middle East and other export regions. Moscow and Washington have also come to an agreement on the opening of Russia's energy and other mineral resources to Western technology and investment.

At this writing, it is unclear how Russia can relate in a meaningful economic way to the EU structure or how quickly Russia can adjust its economic policies and regulations to warrant admission to the World Trade Organization. However, if there were any lingering questions as to whether the Cold War was really over, these have been dispelled by post–September 11 events. A genuine partnership between the United States and Russia appears to be developing, which augurs well for the future stability of the world.

Notes

1. Halford Mackinder, "The Geographical Pivot of History," *Geographical Journal* 23, no. 4 (1904): 421–44.

2. Halford Mackinder, *Democratic Ideals and Realities* (London: Constable, 1919), 148–66.

3. Halford Mackinder, "The Round World and the Winning of the Peace," *Foreign Affairs* 21, no. 4 (1943): 595–605.

4. Zbigniew Brzezinski, *The Grand Chessboard* (New York: Basic, 1997), 123–50.

5. N. M. Baransky, *Economic Geography of the U.S.S.R.*, trans. S. Belsky (Moscow: Foreign Languages, 1956), 318.

6. Vladimir Kolossov and John O'Loughlin, "Pseudo-States as the Harbingers of a New Geopolitics: The Example of the Trans-Dniester Moldovan Republic," *Geopolitics* 3, no. 1 (Summer 1998): 151–76.

7. Taras Kuzio, "Borders, Symbolism and Nation-State Building," *Geopolitics and International Boundaries* 2, no. 2 (Autumn 1997): 36–56.

8. Alan J. Day, ed., *Border and Territorial Disputes* (Harlow, England: Longman, 1982), 264–66.

9. Central Intelligence Agency, *The World Factbook 2000* (Washington, D.C.: Gov/CIA Publications, 2000), 2, 11.

10. Central Intelligence Agency, *The World Factbook 2000*, 11.

11. Mackinder, *Democratic Ideals and Realities,* 158–81.

12. Isaiah Bowman, *The New World* (Yonkers-on-Hudson, N.Y.: World Book, 1922), 5–11, 278–94, 328–56.

13. "Russia's World," *Economist,* 9 May 1998, 21.

14. Karl E. Meyer and Shareen Blair Brysac, *Tournament of Shadows: The Great Game and Race for Empire in Central Asia* (Washington: Corneial and Michael Bessie/Counterpoint, 1999), 283–309, 554–73.

15. Elaine Sciolino, "It's a Sea! It's a Lake! No. It's a Pool of Oil," *New York Times,* 21 June 1998, 16.

CHAPTER 8

The East Asia Geostrategic Realm

The defeat of the United States in the Vietnam War and the collapse of the Soviet Union have freed China to enlarge its power base within East Asia, as well as to play an expanded role along the Asia-Pacific Rim and in South and Central Asia. Within a brief period, Beijing has become an acknowledged global power and forged a third geostrategic realm that competes with the Eurasian Continental and Maritime worlds.

The East Asian realm that is dominated by China embraces North Korea and a separate Indochinese geopolitical region that includes Vietnam, Laos, and Cambodia. North Korea, while dominated by China, is part of the Korean Peninsula—a small Shatterbelt that is caught between the Maritime, East Asian, and Heartlandic Realms.

The strengthened position of China within the Yellow, East, and South China Seas presents a serious challenge to the U.S. western Pacific strategy of the past half century. That strategy has been to create a geopolitical region within the Asia-Pacific Rim (Asia-Pacifica) as part of the Maritime Realm and to build up South Korea and Taiwan, to both contain China and protect Japan. The boundaries of Asia-Pacifica are in flux. South and North Korea are moving cautiously toward rapprochement, which could in the long run lead to unification and to geopolitical neutralization of the Korean Peninsula. In addition, Taiwan's place within the region is by no means assured, as the Beijing and Taipei regimes both continue to accept a "One China" policy, despite profound differences over the structure and timing of reunification.

China

The emergence of China as the center of a new geostrategic region results not only from the weakening of U.S. and Russian influence in the western and North Pacific. It relates even more to changes that have taken place within China itself. For much of the past half century, China was oriented to the Eurasian Continental Realm—first as a geopolitical region subordinate to the Soviet Heartland and then as its hostile competitor. The country's Continentality was expressed by its closed, heavily rural system and Mao Zedong's efforts to shift the locus of economic power, which was in the North and the Interior regions.

With the end of Maoism and the Vietnam War, China has reopened its economic system, enabling forces of Maritimity to emerge from the strangling grip of Continentality.

Farming in the northern and interior rural areas is subject to frequent droughts, while growing urban centers, including Beijing, suffer from chronic water shortages that are aggravated by industrial pollution that makes much of the urban water supply unpotable. This has unleashed the entrepreneurial talents of the peoples of the south and central coasts—from Guangdong (with centers at Guangzhou and Shenzhen), Hong Kong, and Fujian to Zhejiang, Shanghai, and now Jiangsu, north of Shanghai. The Chinese of this region have taken advantage of foreign investment and trade opportunities to make Maritime China a world economic powerhouse. This coastal region, sometimes called the "Golden Coast of China," is home to most of China's rapidly growing middle class and has the country's highest per capita income and largest share of foreign-funded companies. The focus of these companies is foreign trade.

Continental China has undergone considerable upheaval. The state-owned, large-scale industrial structure in the North and Northeast has shrunk, and the system of agricultural communes has been disbanded, causing massive displacement of farmers, who have migrated to the cities, where they form a huge underclass. While China's center of economic gravity has now shifted to its Maritime-facing "Golden Coast," the great majority of the nation's population and landmass remains in the North and the Interior—from Manchuria and North China, where most of the old heavy industry is located, to the country's outer provinces of Inner Mongolia and Xinjiang in the far west and Tibet in the southwest. The heavily rural middle and upper parts of the Yellow and Yangtze River basins, as well as southwest China, are parts of this region, which remains caught in the grip of Continentality.

The Continental-Maritime split personality of China distinguishes East Asia from its competing realms. The Maritime Realm, with its seaman's point of view, is the open-system sector whose outlook is based upon exchange—of peoples, goods, and ideas. Heartlandic Russia, with its landsman's perspective, is inward facing and has traditionally pursued a closed system based upon internal resources. China encompasses both of these contrasting world orientations, retaining its repressive, top-down Communist governance apparatus, while encouraging a market-oriented economy. The competition is played out within two different geographical arenas—in the North and the Interior and in the "Golden Coast"— with varying political, economic, and cultural outlooks. How to reconcile the geopolitical contradictions that grow out of these two outlooks represents China's greatest internal geopolitical challenge. Its outcome will determine whether China will remain united or its destiny is to be divided into two separate states.

CONTINENTALITY VS. MARITIMITY

For most of China's four millennia of recorded history, its geopolitical orientation has been Continental. It was this landsman's China that shaped the closed culture, religion, dominant language (Mandarin), and imperial bureaucratic system of the nation. This is the culture that nurtured China's high degree of ethnocentrism and its deep-rooted sense of racial superiority. It was a culture that looked down upon foreigners as barbarians and sought to wall itself off from the outside world, psychologically as well as physically. The vastness of the Chinese landmass supported the development of the concept of Continental self-sufficiency and isolation.

It was the North that nurtured the regimes that organized China, starting with the Yin dynasty (1523 B.C. to 1027 B.C.), the first historic dynasty located in modern-day Henan, north of the Huang He (Hwang Ho, or Yellow) River. The North spawned dynasties established by such nomadic invaders as the Huns, Mongols, and Manchus, as well as the Chinese Sung and Ming empires. Much of China's history is represented in the clash between nomadic forces sweeping into China from the north and west and the native Chinese dynasties that emerged out of the middle valley of the Huang He to counter and ultimately overthrow the Central Asian invaders.

Various Chinese rulers from the Qin, who first built the Great Wall of China in the third century B.C., to the Ming (1368–1644 A.D.), who restored the wall in its present form, sought to protect China from the nomads. The wall extended across the Inner Mongolian plain from the Qilian Shan (mountains) north of the Huang He headwaters for fifteen hundred miles, until it reached the Yellow Sea. It embraced Hebei (Hopei) Province, where it was designed to protect Beijing and Tianjin (Tientsin).

While China's geopolitical orientation and development has historically been Continental, Maritimity has also placed its stamp upon the nation's personality and focus. The locus of the early Maritime orientation was the southeastern and central coast, extending from Guangzhou (Canton) on the Pearl River Delta northward for six hundred miles to the Ningba flats of the Yangtze Plain, just south of Shanghai. The rocky and highly irregular shoreline, with many offshore islands, was backed by mountains that provided protective defense screens, but offered little space for population to spread. Early on the innumerable harbors of the coast became the bases for fishing and exchange of farm products. In modern times this coast became the locus of the great commercial ports and manufacturing centers developed by Western powers that opened South China, and its central coastal extension, to the outside world. Hong Kong, on the estuary of the Pearl River, and Shanghai, connected to the Yangtze estuary by the Huanpu River, were the keystones of this development.

Han people, coming from the North, first populated the southern coastal region fifteen hundred years ago, when they displaced the indigenous Thai and Tibetan hill tribes. They crowded into the narrow coastal zones and pushed inland up the narrow river valleys that had cut into the mountains. In these plains and interior valleys, the humid, subtropical climate was favorable for the intensive cultivation on small plots of double-cropped rice, tea, tobacco, mulberry trees for silk, and poppies for opium.

It was this Maritime China of the South that produced the fishermen, sailors, traders, and farmers who created the Chinese exchange economy and, in modern times, the great trading cities of Guangzhou and Hong Kong, one of the world's busiest seaports. This was also the overcrowded China from which millions of emigrants—the overseas Chinese—went forth to Southeast Asia and North America. Initially, most the emigrants came from Guangzhou (in Guangdong Province); in recent decades, Fujian has been the major source of out-migration. The south and central coasts are where the Cantonese, Fukienese, and Wu (Shanghai) tongues developed, as separate from the Mandarin of the North. The latter, historically the language of the ruling classes, is the official national language of the country and is spoken in most of China, but not in the Southeast.

Guangzhou's port was known to ancient Europe through Arab and Hindu merchants and had extensive political and economic connections with Southeast and Offshore Asia for centuries. Nevertheless, it was only in the nineteenth century that China fully entered the global Maritime arena. Prior to that time, there had been an initial contact with European trade and political influence when Portugal established the settlement of Macao (Macau) in 1557 on the western side of the Pearl River estuary. However, the antiforeigner policies of the Ming and Qing (Manchu) dynasties kept China relatively closed to modern Maritime influences.

Great Britain opened China to the Maritime world when it waged the First Opium War (1839–42) because of its dissatisfaction with the limited trade agreements that it had been granted by the Qing emperor. Over the next century, foreign trade zones and footholds were established along the coast. Guangzhou became the first of the treaty ports in 1842. Treaty ports were opened to foreign trade by bilateral treaties between China and foreign governments, and they provided areas available for settlement as well as mercantile activities. Because of the shallowness of its harbor, the British obtained the concession of the twenty-nine-square-mile rocky island of Hong Kong, ninety miles to Guangzhou's southeast, on the eastern side of the Pearl River estuary. A small area on the mainland, Kowloon, was added in 1860. In 1898 the Crown Colony of Hong Kong secured a ninety-eight-year lease on the New Territories, 366 square miles of adjoining mainland next to the city of Kowloon, and developed it as a twin city to Hong Kong. The Hong Kong harbor at Victoria is one of the finest natural harbors in the world; thus the Crown Colony quickly became the gateway to South China, as well as the country's leading link with the Maritime world.

While the origins of Shanghai go back to the eleventh century, and while it became a walled city in the sixteenth century, it remained unimportant until it was opened to foreign trade with its establishment as a treaty port the year after Guangzhou. In 1843, Britain received a commercial concession. This was followed by a concession to the United States in 1862, and the two concessions were merged into the International Settlement in 1863, which put the greater part of Shanghai under extraterritorial control. The French maintained a separate concession within the city, which they had first gained in 1849, and substantial numbers of foreigners, including Japanese, Russian, British, and Americans, took up residence there. Subsequently, the international settlements were added in several other Chinese cities. In the Shanghai and other international settlements, foreigners received deeds to the land within the bounds of the settlement, and were permitted to organize themselves into municipal councils governed by their own administrative, judicial, and legislative institutions.[1]

Shanghai was the world's fastest-growing city from the mid-nineteenth to the mid-twentieth centuries and rivaled Hong Kong as a great world port, despite its location five miles from the open ocean on a tidal creek and tributary of the Yangtze. The port extends for fifteen miles along the creek, which is called the Huangpu. Initially built on the opium trade—it became notorious as a city of sin, gambling, and corruption—but it soon developed into the country's leading industrial center.

Approximately seventy treaty ports were ultimately opened along the China coast, mostly along the south and center, but extending as far north as the Liaodong Peninsula on the Bay of Korea in Manchuria. These were ports opened to a foreign trade by treaties, within which large areas were available for foreign trade and settlement. In addition, another twenty-two were designated as open ports, which were opened voluntarily by the Chinese government, although land leases to foreigners were limited in duration. Among the major ports of the South were Shantou (Swatow) at the northern end of Guangdong Province; Amoy (Xiamien), a major port for immigrants to Southeast Asia; and Fuzhou (Foochow), on the central Fujian coast. By 1850 Fuzhou rose to become China's chief port by virtue of its being the world's largest tea export center. Ningbo (Ningpo), just south of Shanghai in Central China's Zhejiang Province, which had been an early port of entry for Japanese missions to the Chinese court and a sixteenth-century Portuguese trading settlement, also expanded its commercial activities.

The treaty ports of the North extended to the Yellow Sea and its northern arms, the Gulf of Bo Hai and the Bay of Korea. Tianjin, thirty miles upstream on the Hai River and connected to the Huang He by the Grand Canal, was developed by British and French concessions as the major port of the region. Despite its relatively poor harbor, Tianjin became a major international port because it served as the gateway to the North China Plain and the rail terminus for Manchuria. On the southern shore of the Bo Hai, at the eastern end of the Shandong (Shantung) Peninsula, Britain held a concession at the territory of Weihaiwei. In northeastern Shandong, Germany controlled a major treaty port on the southern coast of the peninsula at Qingdao (Tsingtao) on the Yellow Sea, losing it, along with the surrounding German territory of Jiaozhou, to Japan at the outbreak of World War I.

Dalian (Dairen), the chief commercial port for Manchuria, was at the northern end of the Yellow Sea, at the tip of the Liaodong Peninsula, between the Bay of Korea and the Gulf of Bo Hai. The city, combined with Port Arthur (Lushun), was administered by the Russians as a naval base and southern terminus of the South Manchurian Railway, until its acquisition by Japan as a result of the Russo-Japanese War of 1904–05. In a repetition of history, Dalian was reoccupied by Russian troops at the end of World War II, and it remained a Russian leasehold for a decade, under both the Chinese Nationalists (Guomindang) and the Chinese Communists.

Some inland centers were also designated as treaty ports. The most notable was Nanjing (Nanking), the largest interior river port of China, located on the Yangtze and connected to Shanghai by the Grand Canal. Much farther inland, along the central Yangtze River, was Hankou (Hankow), which is now part of the urban conurbation of Wuhan. Although six hundred miles from the sea, the port was capable of handling ocean-going vessels. Foreign penetration of the Yangtze Valley reached as far inland as the Japanese settlement at Chongqing (Chunking), which became a treaty port in 1891, and in Manchuria at Haerbin (Harbin) on the middle Sungari River. There the Russians obtained a concession in 1896.

The burst of economic development in all of these foreign-controlled treaty ports, concessions, settlements, and territories brought industrialization to China and opened the country to outside capital investment and trade. But this Maritime orientation was imposed on China. Nineteen different countries obtained unilateral rights and privileges that were deeply resented by the Chinese. Foreign armed forces and warships were stationed, not only along the coasts, but within inland waters as well. In addition, the imperialist powers mounted intrusions deep into the Chinese Periphery—Britain in Tibet, Russia in Xinjiang (Sinkiang) and Outer Mongolia, and Japan in Manchuria.[2]

The Manchu regime of the nineteenth and early twentieth centuries was too corrupt and impotent to loosen the foreign grip on China. When it was overthrown in 1911 and a republic was established under the leadership of Sun Yat-sen, the Chinese government sought to revise or abolish the treaty system, but failed. The Chinese had invested great hopes in the Paris Peace Conference of 1919, but these were dashed when the Great Powers failed to reject Japan's claims in Shandong. This led to the increased strength of the anti-imperialist movement in China, evident when a violent student protest was put down by the Beijing dictatorship, which was backed by warlords who had wrested power from Sun.

Conflict continued in the years that followed. While Sun Yat-sen had sought inspiration from Western ideals, his failure to gain support from the West led him to turn to Russia for help in his struggle against the regime in Beijing. The tangled web of events during this period was marked by the military victories of Chiang Kai-shek and the return of the Guomindang to power in 1925; the long civil war resulting from the break between the Guomindang and the Chinese Communist Party; the Japanese invasion of Manchuria

(Manchukuo) and establishment of a puppet regime there; and the Japanese attack in 1937, leading to its lengthy occupation of North China, the Yangtze Valley, and the coastal areas.

The Nationalists had moved the capital from Beijing to Nanjing (the "Southern Capital") on the lower Yangtze River, a reflection of their outward orientation. However, a decade later they were forced to flee from the Japanese and move deep into the Interior to Chongqing along the upper Yangtze, in the southwestern province of Sichuan (Szechwan). This fertile area is known as fertile Red Basin for its reddish sandstone-derived soils, which have made it the "rice bowl" of China. There the Nationalists were supplied by the Allies through the Burma Road, which extended from Lashio through Yunnan Province to Chongqing. Several years previously, the Interior had provided similar sanctuary to the Communists, who in 1935 had retreated from the Nationalists in their "Long March" to Shaanxi (Shensi) in the Northwest. They made their headquarters in Yanan (Yenan) at the northern end of the province, which served as their capital until they took power in 1949.

At the height of World War II, the United States and the other Western powers signed treaties with China abolishing the foreign concessions and privileges that had been unilaterally imposed over the previous century. With the defeat of Japan, Germany, and Italy, the Chinese assumed that the era of imperialistic penetration was finally over. To their surprise, Chinese officials learned that the Yalta agreement on the Far East, signed by Roosevelt, Churchill, and Stalin, forced China to grant Moscow territorial and political concessions.

Moscow acquired joint rights to a new railway system, under Soviet control, that would combine the Chinese Eastern and South Manchurian Railways, linking Inner Mongolia and the Soviet Far East to Harbin and Dalian. The USSR was also to enjoy a free lease over the commercial port of Dalian and restoration of the Russian naval base at Port Arthur (Lushun). In addition, China would have to recognize the independence of Outer Mongolia.

These vestiges of nineteenth- and early twentieth-century imperial penetration remained until 1955, when Soviet troops were withdrawn and China regained control of the port, base, and railroad. Moreover, although in the early days under Communist rule China was highly dependent on its Soviet ally and patron, the suspicions of Soviet imperialistic intentions had been fanned by these postwar concessions and would play a role in Beijing's hostility to Moscow, which would lead soon to the Sino-Soviet break.

The Maoist Era (1949–76)

By the end of World War II, the Communists controlled much of interior North and Central China. They quickly took control of Manchuria (the Northeast), turned over to them by the Russian armies that had occupied the region after the defeat of Japan. The ensuing conflict between the Beijing-based Communists and the Nationalists in Nanjing ended in 1949 with the defeat of Chiang Kai-shek's armies and their flight to Taiwan, where they established their seat of government in Taipei.

With the Communist takeover, China's orientation once more shifted inward. For the next three decades the strategy of the system was Continentality, first as subordinate to Moscow and then as an independent geopolitical power in competition with the Soviets. China's goal was self-containment. Its foreign trade with the other Continental power, the USSR, under the Sino-Soviet Treaty of Friendship, Alliance, and Mutual Assistance continued until the open split between them in 1960.

For Mao Zedong, Maritimity and the opening to the West had degraded and corrupted China. In particular, he had come to despise the social impacts of Western influence as represented by the hedonism and corruption of the wealthy classes of Shanghai and the great gap between those who had been enriched by foreign-supported manufacturing and trade and the millions of the city's poor. Mao was determined to turn away from the world beyond the sea and become self-reliant in food and the products of China's natural resources.

For the most part, China's exports at that time were food, textiles, and minerals, while its imports were heavy industrial products. Trade with Japan and the West, the country's leading trading partners in the 1930s, now became negligible as the focus shifted to the Soviet Union and some of its satellites.

During the Vietnam War, China provided the North Vietnamese with substantial supplies and military equipment. As its foreign policy aim became the spread of maoist revolutionary philosophy to South America, Africa, and Asia, Beijing extended economic aid to countries that it sought to influence. However, the main emphasis of the Chinese regime was economic development of its own country. In former Manchuria, where the chief coal and iron resources of the country are to be found, the heavy industry base was rapidly expanded with the help of Soviet technicians.

Between 1957 and 1960 Mao Zedong organized the "Great Leap Forward" which sought to focus the nation's attention on the rural areas of the Interior. The Communist regime forced millions of people out of the cities into huge farming communes in the countryside. It also promoted the establishment of thousands of small factories that used "backyard" furnaces that produced metals aimed at attaining the revolution's goal of local self-sufficiency. The purpose of locating manufacturing in the Interior was to reduce the country's dependence on the heavy industries of the Northeast, which was strategically exposed to the Soviet Union. Most of the metals turned out to be useless.

The social upheaval caused by the communization of agriculture, as well as three successive years of drought, resulted in dramatic crop reductions and widespread famine. Millions of Chinese starved to death during this period. The Great Leap Forward, an outgrowth of Mao's ideological opposition to the de-Stalinization policy introduced in 1956 by Nikita Khrushchev, became a major factor in China's break with the USSR. The hostility between Beijing and Moscow led to the withdrawal of Soviet economic aid and technicians from the country in 1960. The enmity intensified the following year, when China allied itself with Albania in the wake of the rift between the USSR and the Communist regime in Tirana. The rift increased further in the 1960s, when China's hard-liners objected to Leonid Brezhnev's call for peaceful coexistence with the West. At that point, a simmering border dispute between the two Communist powers erupted into fighting.

The Cultural Revolution of 1966–76 was another great national trauma. Mao swept aside the five-year planning process to focus on the production of staple, high-yield crops at the expense of agricultural diversity. In addition, he initiated a massive, antiurban program aimed at building scattered factories throughout the rural parts of the country. The goal was not only to disperse industrial enterprises, but also to arrest manufacturing growth in the big cities. Industrial production dropped rapidly during this period. The Cultural Revolution also involved mass mobilization of youth, encouraging them to join the Red Guard, which persecuted technical experts, teachers, and intellectuals and enforced Mao's cult of personality. Universities were closed and thousands were purged. Only Mao's death in 1976 put an end to the excesses of the Cultural Revolution and returned the country to political stability and rational economic development.

Reemergence of Maritimity: Post Maoism (1976–)

Under Mao's successors, Deng Xiaopeng and Zhou Enlai, China's farms were decollectivized, industry was modernized, and diplomatic relations were developed with the West. The year that diplomatic relations were established with the United States—1979—was also the year that four coastal cities were declared special economic zones, to attract trade, foreign investment, and technology. Fourteen more cities were added to this group in 1984 and eventually Shanghai was added in 1990. Such steps reflected the abandonment of the Soviet-style, centrally planned economy and the move to a market-oriented economic system, although still within the rigid framework of Communist Party control.

The 1980s and '90s have been years of major progress for China. GDP has quadrupled to over $4 trillion by Chinese estimates in the past twenty years, millions of surplus farmworkers have moved to the city, and foreign trade has expanded, reaching $325 billion in 1998. In the words of a Chinese Young Pioneer (one of the urban youth sent to the farming areas): "Chairman Mao founded China, Deng Xiaopeng made us rich, and now Jiang Zemin is leading us into the future."[3]

Maritimity involves far more than economics, however. The seafarer's outlook is one of exploration—the search for new places, new ideas, and new contacts. It represents the opening of a system. Land conflict and threats had long been the main concern of China, so that its military defense was continentally oriented. The new focus on Maritimity has called for a radical rethinking of the role that its navy is to play in the years ahead.

Until recently, China's naval strategy was geared to its near coasts. With a small "brown-water" fleet, whose capacity was limited to coastal operations, China was helpless to interfere with the operations of the U.S. and Russian "blue-water" fleets, which were capable of staying in the middle of the ocean for extended periods. Communist China could not prevent the U.S. Seventh Fleet from blocking its planned invasion of Taiwan in 1950 or its threatened invasion of Taiwan in the tense period that followed the intensive shelling of the Nationalist-held islands of Quemoy (Jinmen) and Matsu (mazu) just off the coast of Fujian. The Vietnam War brought the naval power of the U.S. Third and Seventh Fleets to the South China Sea, where it was applied with impunity against the North Vietnamese and their Chinese allies.

The Chinese naval weakness was further underscored when a Soviet blue-water fleet began to operate in the South China Sea after the withdrawal of American forces from the Indochinese arena. The mounting tensions between China and Vietnam that culminated in the brief border war of 1979 made a stronger alliance with the Soviet Union crucial for Hanoi. As part of the new military agreements between the two, Vietnam turned over the Cam Ranh Bay naval and air bases to the Soviet navy under a lease that extends to 2004. Cam Ranh had been expanded in 1965 as a deepwater port by the United States, which built its main naval base there. When the Soviets took it over in the early 1980s, they made it the largest Soviet naval base outside the USSR. The fleet that they stationed there housed an aircraft carrier and over one hundred submarines, as well as other warships and land-based bombers. An added threat to China was the Soviet development of electronic facilities to monitor Chinese communications in the South China Sea, especially around Hainan.

China's recent history of naval inferiority, in combination with the collapse of the Soviet Union and the end of the land threat to its northern borders, has inspired Beijing to focus on building up its naval forces and expanding its maritime reach. In 1992 Beijing promulgated its Laws of Territorial Waters and Contiguous Zones, which claimed jurisdiction over a two-hundred-mile-wide area beyond its coasts. Under these laws, the Chinese claim sovereignty over the waters of the Taiwan Strait in their entirety, and therefore could evict the foreign naval vessels and fishermen that use these waters. Those nations that do recognize a two-hundred-mile exclusionary zone do so only with respect to fishing and underwater mining rights, not air or sea transportation, civilian or military.

In addition, the Chinese claim the Senkaku (Diaoku) Islands, one hundred miles northeast of Taiwan in Japan's southeastern Ryukyu chain, as well as the Paracel and Spratly Island groups in the South China Sea. Inclusion of the waters surrounding these islands under Chinese jurisdiction would extend Chinese control to the eastern borders of the East China Sea and the southern borders of the South China Sea, near the coasts of southern Vietnam, northern Borneo, and the southern Philippines. In the unlikely event that the Spratlys are recognized as Chinese, the reach of these laws would extend one thousand miles beyond the Chinese mainland.

As long as China's navy remained a small, obsolete, coastal force, there was little that it could do to enforce its new territorial waters laws. Transformation of the navy began in 1994, with the purchase of state-of-the-art destroyers, submarines, and missiles from Russia and the establishment of a training program for Chinese naval personnel. Two years before, China had made an unsuccessful attempt to purchase old aircraft carriers from Russia and Ukraine. This new strategic relationship was one of the first products of the entente that had been reached in 1994 between the two former foes. Since then, China has moved forward with efforts aimed at both purchasing vessels and electronic equipment from abroad and developing its own production capacity in these areas.

In 1999, navy Chief Vice-Admiral Shi Yunsheng announced a ten-year modernization program, to include battleships, submarines, aircraft carriers, destroyers, frigates, and missiles.[4] The formal announcement stated the navy's mission, which emphasized near-coast defense, rather than blue-water capabilities. However, the very reference to aircraft carriers, and subsequent indications of plans to form a fourth Chinese fleet for the Indian and near-Pacific Oceans, suggest that the distinction between regional defense and more broadly projected naval power may be a matter of semantics.[5]

While China now has northern, eastern, and southern fleets to serve its security needs in its adjoining seas, a fleet such as envisaged by Admiral Shi would have considerable striking power, reaching to the Sea of Japan, the Philippine Sea, and the Malacca Strait. This would threaten much of Japan's oil and natural gas imports, as well as Singapore, and the energy exports of Malaysia and Indonesia. There are also persistent Chinese attempts to secure naval rights at the port of Sittwe (formerly Akyab), on Myanmar's Andaman Sea.[6]

In the face of U.S. naval pressure, and without aircraft carriers, China's ambition to play a powerful strategic naval role is still limited, even in its regional waters. This applies to its threats against Taiwan, let alone in the southernmost parts of the South China Sea and the Bay of Bengal, where the Indian navy is the dominant presence. Nevertheless, the buildup of Chinese air, naval, and missile power along the Strait of Taiwan has been of sufficient magnitude to be regarded as a serious threat to Taiwan, whose government has pressed Washington to sell it state-of-the art destroyers and antimissile systems. Beijing's objections to such sales have been vigorous.

China is clearly intent on reinventing itself as a naval power. There is little doubt that, sooner or later, this power will be in a position to neutralize or at least pose a serious threat to the American naval presence in the Taiwan Strait and off the Korean Peninsula. Such an eventuality would have an important impact upon such issues as Korean unification and China-Taiwan relations.

China's continuing maritime development seems assured, given its diplomatic successes in achieving trade agreements with the United States and the European Union and its membership in the World Trade Organization. However, this does not mean that Continentality is about to disappear as a geopolitical motif. China's international trade represented only 7.5 percent of its $4.5 billion GDP in 2000, while the country's economic growth continues to be generated domestically to a large extent, rather than by exports.[7] No matter how quickly trade increases as a result of the reduction of trade barriers, the dividends from the trading policy are likely to remain confined to the south and central coasts and the Beijing area.

At best, only about 20 percent of China's 1.3 trillion people are likely to be significantly affected by the forces of Maritimity. Nearly 70 percent of China is rural, with about half of the people living as farmers in the North, the Northeast, and the Interior. Millions from these areas seek to escape rural poverty and estimates are that 80 to 130 million have moved from rural parts to the large urban centers of the coastal provinces.[8] In all likelihood, the rural population of the three regions will continue to be caught in the grip of Continentality—closed to the economic and cultural forces of the outside world and far more accepting of Communist political controls than fellow citizens who live in the prospering coastlands. It is this rural populace, whose farm incomes are one-third that of farmers located within the ecumene, that is the mainstay of the regime as it seeks to direct the hybrid socialist-capitalist system that is evolving.

Most of the urban migrants suffer from conditions reminiscent of the lives of the poor in the Shanghai of the 1920s and '30s. As they fail to become successfully absorbed in urban life, they too may become a major force for the reimposition of a centralized command economy.

In the decades ahead, the forces of Continentality and Maritimity will compete for dominance. Whether the current regime can successfully resolve the economic, cultural, and political contradictions between them remains the key to China's future geopolitical stability and its very existence as an integrated state.

THE LOCATIONAL PERSPECTIVE

It is not only the geographic setting of a nation but also how it perceives that setting that influences the conduct of foreign policy. Locational "facts" are transmitted by leadership to the public and become embodied in national folklore and myths that drive future generations of leaders to shape foreign policies that conform to that perspective.

Millennia of historic and cultural postures of national egocentrism have led to China's present locational perspective—the perspective of China as the "Middle Kingdom," the center of the world.[9] This perspective evolved from a local to a regional to a global geographical scale. The local sense of space goes back to the period when China was a loose collection of small states that had expanded from the northern part of the country to the Yangtze, and then to the South (1500 to 200 B.C.). Their Middle Kingdom was differentiated from those around them by agriculture—the essence of the civilized world. What lay beyond the limits of this sown world was of no consequence because it was peopled by uncivilized nomads—"the Barbarians."

The regional sense of space developed when the Han Empire united China through a strongly centralized government in 200 B.C. During the following two millennia, China met other worlds through intermittent foreign trade, the import of Buddhism from India, and nomadic rulers who overthrew their dynasties.

In the early part of this period, the Chinese reached into surrounding areas by conquering and colonizing Korea and the Tonkin Delta (618 to 907 A.D.). They treated these areas as non-Chinese tributary kingdoms, offering protection in return, but not absorbing them as provinces within the Chinese space. The exception was Taiwan, which had a small aboriginal populace before it was seized from the Dutch in 1622 A.D. and settled by Han peoples. (In 1895 the island was acquired by Japan, which called it "Formosa.")

Toward the end of this period, from the eighteenth to the twentieth centuries, the encounter with Europe confronted the Chinese with the challenge of modernity. All contacts, with the exception of the introduction of Buddhism, did little to transform Chinese culture and civilization. A society that had invented the civil service, the wheelbarrow, the compass, and gunpowder had little to learn from "foreigners."

The territorial encroachments and introduction of alien cultures by Europeans, Russians, and Japanese from the mid-nineteenth to the mid-twentieth centuries shook, but did not alter, the Chinese view of themselves as being at the center of the world. The goal became to dislodge the foreigners and restore territorial integrity and regional hegemony. The strength of antiforeigner feeling was evidenced in the Boxer uprising (1898–1900), when the secret society of Boxers, supported by the dowager empress, rebelled against foreign influences, including Christianity, railroad building, and the system of extraterritoriality whereby foreign powers exercised their own economic, diplomatic, judicial, and policing functions over wide areas within China, including the stationing of military forces and warships. The conflict swept over much of North China, although the governors of the southern provinces refused to back it. The rebels occupied Beijing for two months, until the rebellion was finally put down by British, French, Russian, American, and Japanese troops. The failed uprising left foreign spheres of influence entrenched more strongly than ever within the Chinese landscape.

The Chinese Communist revolution introduced the global perspective of a China that continued to be differentiated from the rest of the world, but held a central place within it by being the leader of the revolutionary Third World. Norton Ginsburg presented a Chinese model of the world that was formed by four concentric zones. The fourth or outer zone distinguished the underdeveloped rural world from both the capitalist and socialist urban realms.[10] This global view helped the Chinese to reject satellite status vis-à-vis the USSR, while providing a defensive strategy against the West. After the Sino-Soviet schism, Lin Pao advanced the concept that China could exploit its position of centrality within the Third World to counterencircle both the West and the Soviet Union from rural bases in Asia, Africa, and Latin America, and thus break the ring of containment that had been drawn around it.[11]

In the light of the sweeping changes that have occurred within the global geopolitical system during the past decade, centrality within the underdeveloped world has little relevance for China's current foreign policy. The period of Communist revolution within Sub-Saharan Africa, Latin America, and Southeast Asia is over and the pursuit of influence within economically and strategically unimportant parts of the world has little appeal to Beijing. For China today, the perspective of centrality is evolving within a new geopolitical order in which China, as the core of the world's third geostrategic realm, holds a position that is centrally located between the Heartlandic and Maritime Realms—independent of them, but interconnected to them in matters of China's choice. The geopolitical regions of greatest strategic concern to Beijing are those bordering Russia and the Asia-Pacific Rim.

Controlling a geostrategic realm that lies between the Continental and Maritime worlds, the Chinese can expand their classical perspective of centrality to pursue policies that pit the other realms against one another. In military-strategic terms, China can forge an alliance with Russia without fear of being dominated. Recent examples include Sino-Russian support of Iran and Serbia, expanding Russian oil sales to China, and cooperation with Russia in space technology to develop a Chinese-manned spacecraft. In addition, with the upgrading of its armed forces, China has turned to Russia to purchase jet fighters, naval vessels, and other equipment. At the same time, tensions with the Maritime Realm have increased over Taiwan, the possible development of a National Missile Defense by Japan, and China's securing of the air over its two-hundred-mile exclusive economic maritime zone—the cause of the "spy plane" incident with the United States in April 2001. Economically, China has launched an all-out effort to expand its reach to the Maritime world. This began with its economic liberalization during the last two decades and the normalizing of trade relations with the United States. China's admission to the World Trade Organization in November 2001 means the reduction of tariffs and other barriers to trade, foreign investment, and the establishment of foreign company operations. The trade-off for opening Beijing's markets, including to cheap farm products from U.S. agrobusiness, is the anticipated expansion of markets in the West and Offshore Asia. This has already meant breaking out from economic isolation and decreased self-sufficiency. Should this trend be extended, it would bring even greater changes to the economic landscape of China. The consequences of further concentration of manufacturing and services along the coast also means greater strategic vulnerability. This has made the buildup of offensive and defensive coastal air, missile, and sea power a strategic imperative.

While there are considerable risks to pursuing such an opening, the Chinese Communist leadership expresses confidence in its ability to pursue economic reform without losing political control. It remains to be seen whether China's second economic revolution will destroy or save the current regime. However, it should be recalled that the party survived the massive economic failure of the Great Leap Forward and the social chaos of the Cultural Revolution. It has kept a tight political grip on the country, despite the 1989 massacre of democratic reformers at Tiananmen Square and the more recent turmoil surrounding its vigorous crackdown on the Falun Gong. A pacifist, spiritually based movement, reportedly with millions of followers, the Falun Gong was banned as a "counterrevolutionary cult" in 1999 but continues its activities. So far, the party has weathered these signs of resistance, as well as the poverty of the rural population and the tens of millions of migrants to the city who remain untouched by the prosperity generated by the export economy.

GEOPOLITICAL FEATURES

Nineteenth- and twentieth-century foreign imperialism, the Communist revolution, and the recent opening to the outside world have contributed substantially to the shaping of the geopolitical features that have characterized China's historic development as an organized state. What follows is a discussion of these features and their evolution, meaning, and trends.

Historic Core

The geopolitical roots of the first historic dynasty of China, the Yin (Shang), which ruled from 1523 B.C. to 1027 B.C., were in what is now Henan Province, which is traversed by

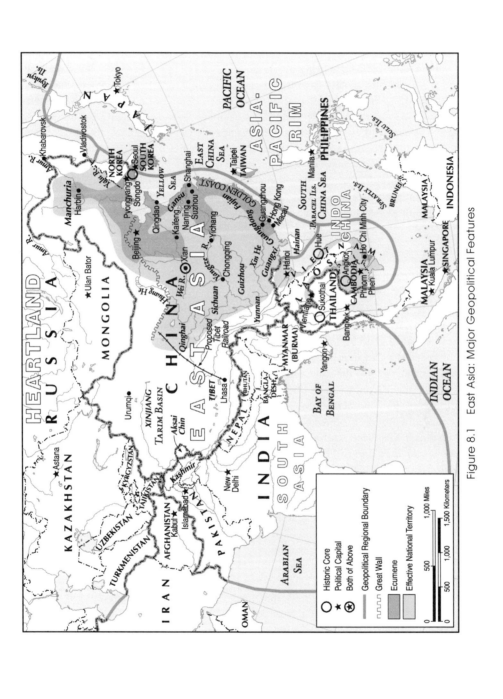

Figure 8.1 East Asia: Major Geopolitical Features

the Yellow River (Huang He) on the North China Plain. One of the capitals of the Yin, a site near Anyang at the northern edge of the province, could be described as the Historic Core of the country—the cradle of the Chinese nation. However, the dynasty of this era was based only upon control of a small city-state that exercised dominance of neighboring city-states of the plains.

A more solid claimant to being the cradle of modern China may be the Wei River Valley. The Qin, the first dynasty to unify China (221–206 B.C.), gave its name to the country. It extended the limits of China north to the province of Gansu bordering Inner Mongolia, west to Guizhou and the border of the Yunnan Plateau, and south to the Gulf of Tonkin. The seat of the Qin was Xian (Xianyang), the most splendid Chinese city of its time, which was located in North China's current Shaanxi province on the Wei River. Whichever site one determines to be the cradle of the Chinese state, it is clear that the locus is Interior North China near the Huang He and on its tributaries. The Continental perspective and inward-turning of Chinese civilization may, in great measure, be attributed to the sense of nationhood that evolved from this region.

Capitals

While China has had a number of different capitals, for most of its history they have been located in the North, reflecting the country's Continental orientation and concerns. The wide Wei River Valley provided capitals for several early dynasties subsequent to the Qin. They were attracted to the valley by its well-watered, fertile, alluvial soils, which supported the cultivation of grain and fruit. The capital of the Zhou (1027–256 B.C.), the dynasty that preceded the Qin, was at Changan, one of several sites adjoining the modern city of Xian. Changan was also the seat of the Han dynasty (202 B.C.–220 A.D.), which followed the Qin and made Confucianism the basis for the bureaucratic state. The city was also the political center for Tang dynasty (618–906 A.D.), which introduced the system of civil service exams and brought Confucian culture to a highly developed form. These various capitals sited near Xian were on the major east-west grassy gateway route from the steppes of Mongolia and Turkestan (Xinjiang) to the North China Plain, approximately one hundred miles upstream on the Wei from its junction with the Huang He.

Kaifeng, which lay farther to the east on the Huang He, served as the capital of the Five Dynasties and then the Northern Sung Dynasty (906 to 1127 A.D.). This location commanded the heart of the Yangtze Plain. When the Sung were overthrown and their court fled southward, they established their capital at Hangzhou (Hangchow) on the East China Sea, near the mouth of the Yangtze—the first capital to be located outside the Northern Interior. The purpose of this move was to remove the seat of government from the Mongol incursions from inner Asia.

Beijing (Chinese for "northern capital") had once been the capital of the Tsin dynasty (265–420 A.D.) and served as the seat of power for warlords, until its capture in 1215 by the Mongol Genghis Khan. The eastward migration of capitals within North China came to an end with this Mongol seizure of power. Kublai Khan (1260–90 A.D.) constructed Cambuluc, the nucleus of today's Beijing. The Mongol capital was transferred in 1267 from Karakoram in central Mongolia to the Beijing site, which was renamed Khanbaliq. The site lay at the northern edge of the North China Plain and was the gateway to both Mongolia and northeast China. From their new capital, the Mongols gained control over one-third of the then known world—the largest land empire in history to date.

The Ming dynasty, which overthrew the Mongols in 1368 and unified all of China, had its power base and capital in Nanjing near the Yangtze Delta, but moved it to Beijing in 1421. The Ming centerpiece, the Forbidden City, remains the largest palace complex in the world. When the Manchus swept into China from the north to establish their dynasty in the seventeenth century, they retained Beijing as their capital.

The city had unique strategic advantages that made it an ideal forward-based capital. Fifty miles to its northwest lay the northern end of Nankou Pass, the chief gateway from Mongolia, which provided a secure route for communication lines from Central Asia. Less than two hundred miles to the east, the Great Wall ended at the sea, and this point served the Manchus as their secure gateway to Manchuria. Another advantage was the absence of physical barriers between Beijing and the rest of North China and the Yangtze Delta region of Central China, where Nanjing, the historic "Southern Capital," is located. After the mid-nineteenth century, Shanghai became connected to North China by a combination of the Grand Canal and river ways. This water route ran northward, crossing the Huang He, and then on to Tianjin, and from there it continued to Beijing or to the sea. Shanghai was also connected to the west via the Yangtze.

The periods during which the capital shifted to the coastal reaches of Central China reflect the pull of Maritimity, but they were brief. Nanjing had served as the capital of China from the third to the sixth centuries, as well as being the seat of the Ming from 1368 to 1421. When Sun Yat-sen's revolutionary forces took power in 1912, the city served as Sun's first capital. During the next decade and a half of turmoil, Guangzhou, Beijing, and Hankou also alternated as the country's political centers.

In 1928, Chiang Kai-shek reestablished Nanjing as China's capital, moving it a decade later, after the Japanese conquest, to Chongqing. In 1949 the Republic of China fell to the Communists, who returned the capital to Beijing, where it has remained. So once again, the political center is in the North, while economic modernization and expansion takes place in the coastal provinces of South and Central China. The blending of the Continental and Maritime outlooks as reflected in these dual power centers presents China with both pitfalls and opportunities.

Ecumene

The ecumene of China currently stretches from the coastal sectors of the South a few miles from the Vietnam border, through Guangdong, Hong Kong, and Fujian to Shanghai and the lower Yangtze Valley and the Great Yangtze Delta on the central coast. From there, it extends in two directions—westward, upstream to the middle Yangtze basin, and northward, through the North China Plain into southern Manchuria. The total area of this vast Chinese economic and population core region is 580,000 square miles, an area with a population of over 700 million.

The westward spread of the ecumene extends beyond the middle Yangtze basin's Wuhan urban conurbation and rich, lake-studded agricultural areas until it is blocked by the gorges of the Yangtze. These begin just beyond Yichang, which is the head of navigation of the river, one thousand miles from the sea. It is along this stretch of the river, extending for nearly 120 miles, that construction of the Three Gorges (Yangtze) dams and reservoir system has been going on for nearly a decade. This is a mammoth hydroelectric power, navigation, irrigation, and industrial and agricultural land-use project. When the dam is completed, a 244-square-mile lake will be created that will displace over one million people and inundate countless historic sites.

Environmentalists have been highly critical of the project, arguing that, in addition to the destruction and displacement, China has little need for the capacity that will be added to the country's electricity supply. The counterargument is that the new hydro power will enable the government to retire many coal-burning plants. China now depends on fossil fuels, mostly domestic coal, for 80 percent of its energy. Use of domestic oil is also on the rise, and in the year 2000 China had to import petroleum for the first time. As a result of its dependence on fossil fuels, it has become one of the most highly polluted countries in the world, and air pollution in the big cities is a major health hazard. With the completion of the Three Gorges project some time after the end of the next decade, China's ecumene is likely to extend into the Red River basin of Sichuan Province, now a part of the Effective National Territory.

Another project that has drawn criticism form environmentalists is located far from the ecumene, in the province of Yunnan in southwest China. There, on the Upper Mekong River, a large hydroelectric power scheme is underway, the first of eight dams having been completed at the end of 2001. The electricity generated by these dams is scheduled to serve Yunnan's development needs. However, the project threatens Cambodia's fisheries and will reduce the flow of silt to Laos.

North of the Yangtze, the ecumene includes the rest of the lower Yangtze Plains province of Jiangsu and those parts of the province of Anhui that are traversed by the Huai River as it winds its way to the delta. Still farther to the north, the population and economic core grades into the North China Plain, embracing the lower Huang He Valley and Delta provinces of Henan and Shandong. It then continues northward through the Huang He Plain and Hebei Province to Beijing, Tianjin, and the Gulf of Bo Hai. From there, it reaches into Liaoning Province of southern Manchuria, focusing on the Shenyang-Fushun-Anshan industrial conurbation.

Sixty percent of China's 1.3 billion people live in the ecumene, on a land base that is only about 15 percent of the country's total land area of 3,690,000 square miles. In many places, the densities substantially exceed the average of thirteen hundred per square mile of the economic and population core, not only in its urban portions, but within the highly fertile coastal and interior plains and villages, where thousands of rural villages have attracted the majority of China's farm families. This rural population still accounts for the majority of the ecumene's population.

As China has moved toward a market economy, income distribution within the economic core, as well as between it and other parts of the country, has become increasingly uneven within the past two decades. Per capita income is highest in Guangdong and Zhejiang Provinces and, especially, in such urban centers as Shanghai, Beijing, and Tianjin. In Hong King and Macau, the respective average per capita incomes of $23,000 and $18,000 rival those of the most advanced nations.

Economic disparities within the ecumene are considerable, not only between its rural and urban areas, but also within and among its urban centers. Many of the estimated one hundred million farmers displaced by the disbanding of the agricultural collectives have moved to the cities from the rural sectors of the ecumene, such as Anhui, Henan, Guangdong, and Shandong. Classified as temporary workers who lack permanent residence certificates, they are legally banned from most employment save garbage collection, the building trades, sidewalk vending, household work, or unskilled factory jobs. Living in sprawling shantytowns or illegally built rented rooms, they suffer from poverty and discrimination, have no health care, and lack access to education for their children. Yet they cannot or will not return to the countryside, where jobs are unavailable. This group represents a permanent, floating population that will continue to grow with rural overpopulation, agricultural modernization, and China's increasing openness to foreign food imports, as the government seeks to open the economy to more foreign trade.

Just as the temporary workers represent a potential source of urban unrest and political instability, so do the workers in those parts of the ecumene and areas outside of it in the Interior, the North, and the Northeast that have become rust belts or are likely to be otherwise affected by the shrinking of state enterprises. Unemployment is widespread in southern Manchuria, the northeastern end of the ecumene, where so many of China's heavy industries were located to take advantage of the rich coal, iron-ore, and petroleum deposits of the province. The industries include massive iron and steel works; aluminum and paper plants; machinery, tractor, locomotive, and aircraft factories; and chemical and petroleum complexes. With these industries now antiquated and inefficient, as much as one-fifth of their labor force has been cut back, as the state-run enterprises have modernized. The same fate awaits other large, national industries both within and outside of the ecumene, such as the state-owned motor vehicles plants of North China and Sichuan or the big steel and aluminum plants of Shandong.

Beijing, the nation's second-largest city, with a population of over seven million, also has massive industrial complexes that manufacture steel, chemicals, plastics, machinery, and electronic equipment, many of which have become outdated. Their cutback began as early as the 1970s and '80s because of concerns over pollution.

In the Interior and those parts of North China that are not part of the ecumene, the state still controls 60 to 80 percent of industrial output, much of it built along the Soviet Communist model. This sector will now have to compete with more efficient industries within the ecumene that have been established or modernized by foreign-financed and Chinese entrepreneurial initiatives. These new industries are the basis for China's "Golden Coast"—the locus of the export-driven economy where per capita incomes are five to ten times higher than in the Interior.

In provinces such as Guangdong and Fujian, where foreign investments are heaviest, the import of modern industrialization has been most striking. China's version of Silicon Valley, located around Shenzhen, produces a wide array of telecommunications, medical technology, engineering, electronics, and computer hardware and software. In nearby villages and towns, hundreds of small factories produce consumer goods that include toys, lighting fixtures, footwear, apparel, and textiles. This part of the coastal South began to benefit from the shift of Hong Kong's factories and the diffusion of its technological know-how to Guangdong, even before the Crown Colony reverted to China in 1997. The process has since accelerated, so that much of what is today labeled as "made in Hong Kong" is actually produced outside its borders. The prosperity of Hong Kong, now that it is no longer an important manufacturing center, is based primarily upon its role as the country's premier business and financial center and its container cargo port. The city's financial and commercial power is a major element in the continued industrial growth of the South, while its port, the largest of its kind in the world, now handles nearly half of all China's exports.

Hong Kong is likely to lose some of its transfer trade to Chinese ports that will benefit from direct importing upon the entry of China into the WTO. If Taiwan also joins the WTO, Hong Kong's loss will be even greater because Taiwan currently does not trade directly with China, but transships through Hong Kong. However, the overwhelming financial and commercial weight of Hong Kong, along with its advanced technology, will in all likelihood enable it to retain its role as the leading force in the continuing economic growth of China's South.

Northward along the coast, development of manufacturing in Fujian Province, whose coast is 100 to 150 miles from Taiwan, is in great measure owed to Taiwanese capital investment and trade. Most of Taiwan's twenty-two million inhabitants are descendants of Chinese who immigrated from the southern and central coastlands in the eighteenth and nineteenth centuries and speak the Fujianese or Hakka dialects that are common to Fujian, Guangdong, and Jiangsu. The vast majority of the island's population is concentrated along Taiwan's broad west coastal plain, which faces China and is backed by the heavily forested hills and mountains of the central and eastern parts of the island.

This dense concentration of agricultural and manufacturing activities, as well as its crowded urban centers (Taiwan is over 70 percent urban), constitute Taiwan's ecumene, which functionally is rapidly becoming part of the Chinese mainland ecumene. When and if China and Taiwan enter into some kind of reunification agreement, the two ecumenes will also be fully merged.

Still farther northward, along the coast in Zhejiang Province, the city of Wenzhou has developed as a major center for Chinese private enterprise, producing a variety of items from buttons to electronics. The prosperity of Shanghai, China's largest city and industrial center, with a population of twelve million, depends more and more on its light industry, such as electronics, computer software, and publishing, and on foreign-developed factories such as the Volkswagen and General Motors auto plants. In addition, the city retains its traditional base of large steel, textile, shipbuilding, machinery, and chemical production and oil refining, with a major seaport, including deepwater container facilities, and serving as the country's largest financial and commercial center. A new, world-class "Silicon Valley," focusing on information hardware, is developing along a sixty-mile corridor extending westward from Shanghai to Suzhou. It is powered by capital investment and large-scale manufacturing outsourcing from Taiwan, as well as by the engineering and management talents of émigrés who have returned on a temporary or full-time basis.

The economic strength of China's "Golden Coast" has been the basis for the country's 8 percent average annual increase in GDP during the 1980s and '90s. However, this very prosperity contains the seeds of political instability because of the widening gaps between various groups—between the employed and the unemployed; in terms of wage disparity, between high-tech employees and those in the traditional consumer industries; and, in terms of living and working conditions, between temporary migrants from the rural areas and the city dwellers with permanent jobs and housing.

As previously noted, environmental pollution is another major problem created by the intensification of economic activities within the Chinese ecumene. Air and water pollution is widespread. Industrial and consumer electricity consumption is now met essentially by soft-coal generating plants, which have increased the amount of acid rain that affects the ecumene's farms, water supply, and urban populace. The rapid increase in motor vehicles as a result of economic prosperity and the construction of seventy-five hundred miles of modern highway has also contributed substantially to rising pollution levels, especially in the big cities.

China is currently the world's seventh-largest oil producer—160 million tons in 1999. However, increased oil consumption needs have changed China from being self-sufficient in this regard to becoming increasingly dependent upon imports. In the year 2000, crude petroleum imports exceeded sixty million tons, and they are projected to rise to one hundred million tons within a decade, largely from the Middle East and Russia. This may result in China becoming more involved in the oil politics of the Middle East.

Oil adds another strategic dimension to Beijing's concerns over the separatist movement in the far western frontier province of Xinjiang, led by the Muslim Turkic Uighurs, who form the province's majority. Critical to China's economy are the vast oil fields of Karamay, near the borders of Kazakhstan, Russia, and Mongolia, and the new oil and natural gas reserves discovered in southwestern Xinjiang's Tarim Basin Desert. The need for oil also partly accounts for China's claims to the Spratlys and Paracels.

Effective National Territory

The areas embraced by China's ENT include the Interior provinces that extend from Guanxi and Hainan in the southeast to Guizhou and eastern Yunnan in the southwest. The ENT then stretches northward to the Sichuan (Red) basin in eastern Sichuan Province to Shaanxi's Wei River Valley and to the fertile but dry loesslands of the northern part of Sichuan Province, where it is bracketed by eastern Gansu to the west and Shanxi to the east. Its northern reaches include a narrow fringe of southwestern Inner Mongolia south of the Great Wall (Ningxia Province). The fringe extends eastward along the dry, grassy tablelands that border the wall until it broadens into the grasslands of central and northern Manchuria.

While these regions form a semicircle around the ecumene, their development has for the most part been hampered by topographic barriers, long distances, and poor communication lines with the core. This stands in marked contrast to the ENTs of Russia and the United States, which directly adjoin their ecumenes without intervening physical barriers or lengthy distances. As a consequence, the population and economic cores of these two major powers have been able to expand into the easily developable parts of their countries and thus more easily serve as safety valves for natural growth or as areas of absorption for new immigrant populations.

By contrast, the area that constitutes China's ENT is already heavily settled. Approximately 1.2 million square miles contain a population of 450 million and have an overall density of 430 persons per square mile. Much of the region suitable for farming has long become overpopulated because arable land with available water is so limited. The carrying capacity of the grasslands for pastoralism is also overtaxed and the urban centers are burdened with inefficient industries.

The ENT has little capacity to absorb many of the fifty million Chinese who are added each year through the average annual growth at a rate of 1.3 percent. Therefore, it is the overcrowded ecumene that will have to continue to bear the major burden of supporting China's population growth. Past efforts to industrialize the ENT have had mixed results, despite its abundance of energy resources and metallic and nonmetallic minerals, especially in Yunnan and Sichuan. In the 1960s and '70s Mao moved much of China's heavy and military industry from the strategically vulnerable coast and the Northeast, deep into the Interior. Fear of nuclear attack from either the United States or the Soviet Union motivated the Communist government to establish a "Third Line" region of defense in the canyons and caves of Sichuan, Guizhou, Yunnan, and Gansu. This Third Line was so named to differentiate the region from the "First Line" defense region along the coast and the "Second Line" of the middle Yangtze basin.

During the Cultural Revolution, when Mao sought to eliminate the educated classes and moved many small factories into the countryside, the move to the Interior took on a revolutionary ideological rationale. During the 1960s and '70s nearly half of the available national investment was spent on relocating hundreds of key industries into these remote provinces. Nuclear weapons and ammunition plants, military research laboratories, steel mills, and truck assembly plants were moved over new highways and railroads, while power plants were constructed to provide industry with the necessary power. History proved the Third Line a colossal waste of manpower and money.

In the past two decades, many of these remote plants have been closed or moved to the valley areas around such Interior centers as Chongqing and Chengdu in Sichuan, Guiyang in Guizhou, and Kunming in Yunnan. For the most part, these are the large, state-run factories that produce steel, machinery, chemicals, textiles, aluminum, and motor vehicles. Plagued by antiquated equipment, bureaucratic management, lengthy distance to market, and lack of foreign investment to modernize, most have continued to survive only through state subsidies. Some new industries, such as electronics and telecommunications equipment, motorcycles, and television equipment, have been able to thrive, but their employment base is not wide enough to absorb workers from factory closures or shrinkage in the older, basic industries. As a result, the provinces of the Interior remain among the poorest in China. While Beijing has initiated a "go west" campaign to attract young Chinese to the ENT and the country's Empty Area beyond, there is little evidence that such a campaign is likely to attract enough settlers to address the overpopulation problem.[12]

Empty Area

The Empty Area of China is vast—nearly two million square miles covering 80 percent of the entire country and with a population of forty million. The provinces included within the area are Tibet (Xizang), Xinjiang, Qinghai, western Sichuan, western Gansu, northern Shaanxi, and most of Inner Mongolia. The overall population density of the Empty Area, twenty persons per square mile, masks its uneven distribution. For the most part, the densities are two persons per square mile or less. However, a considerable proportion of the population is concentrated in urban oasis centers, especially on the rim of the desert of Xinjiang's Tarim Basin, in the western half of the province and on the steppes and semidesert lands of the Dzungaria (Junggar) Basin in the northern part of the province.

The relative geographical location of China's Empty Area is quite different from those of the United States and Russia. The Empty Area of the continental United States is bordered on the east by the country's ENT and on the west by the Pacific coast ecumene. Only to its south and along the Rockies to its north does it adjoin the foreign countries of Mexico and Canada. The separate Empty Area of Alaska borders Canada and Russia. Russia's Empty Area is also quite isolated from these neighboring countries. With the exception of the lands that adjoin the Bering Strait across from Alaska, the region lies to the north and northeast of Russia's ecumene and ENT, extending to the Arctic.

In contrast, the Chinese Empty Area adjoins eleven different countries, which provides the heavily populated core regions of the country with a deep, protective, strategic spatial screen against a hostile military land invasion. It also offers Beijing advanced forward bases from which to threaten its neighbors.

This strategic advantage, however, is offset by two factors. Much of the Empty Area is populated by minority, non-Han people—Tibetans, Tibeto-Burmans, Turkics, and Mongols. Some of these minorities have long sought to break away from the rule of Beijing. In addition, China faces the strategic liability of having its main population centers far removed from the outer edges of its Empty Area, while the centers of South Asia, Central Asia, and Russia are closer to this Chinese region.

The geopolitical consequence of these factors is that political separation sentiment finds support from contact with adjoining countries. Tibet was made a nominally national autonomous region under the control of the Dalai Lama, according to a 1951 agreement. Today it is in reality ruled by a Chinese Communist Commission. Land reforms and the sharp curtailing of the powers of the monasteries led to full-scale revolt in 1959. The Tibetans were ruthlessly suppressed and the Dalai Lama fled to India. It is estimated that a million Tibetans were killed and thousands of monasteries were burned during the years that followed. Establishing his government-in-exile at Dharamsala at the base of the Himalayas in northern India, the Tibetan leader still commands the allegiance of most of the 2.5 million Tibetans, as he continues to try to mobilize worldwide support to regain Tibet's freedom.

In Xinjiang, the Turkic-speaking Uighur tribesmen have waged a half-century struggle for independence. This started in 1950, after the Chinese had crushed the sovereign state of East Turkestan, which the Muslim Uighurs had managed to establish in 1944 during the wartime chaos that engulfed China. The creation of the independent Muslim states of Central Asia following the breakup of the Soviet Union has given new hope to the eight million Uighurs whose hold on their national homeland has been threatened by the mass migration of Chinese into Xinjiang. In addition, rising Islamic fundamentalism among these Muslim tribesmen has been fanned by the growing influence of the fundamentalists of neighboring Pakistan and Afghanistan (which has a twenty-mile border with Xinjiang) and by the strength of the fundamentalist rebels who have been seeking to overthrow the government of adjoining Tajikistan. However, the major force behind Uighur separatism is the nationalism that grows out of language, culture, history, and ties to the land, as well as the desire to control the province's newly found oil reserves.

To link the Empty Area more closely to China, Beijing has promoted the settlement of considerable numbers of ethnic Chinese colonists in eastern Tibet. It has also sponsored the move of Chinese to Xinjiang on a very large scale, so that the six million Han people of the province now represent over one-third of the population and threaten to overtake in numbers the seven to eight million Uighur tribesmen and the other minorities, such as Kazakhs, Mongols, Hui, and Kirghizi. Many of these new settlers have been organized in paramilitary fashion within a string of agricultural colonies along the border.

Transportation lines are being constructed or improved to link the Empty Area to eastern China. They include the rebuilding of the Beijing to Lhasa highway and the decision to construct a 680-mile railroad from Golmud in Qinghai Province to Lhasa, Tibet. From Golmud, the line will connect to the existing railway in Xining, and from there it will connect to the main Chinese rail system. Most of the line will be more than thirteen thousand feet above sea level and it must cross a pass in Tibet that is over sixteen thousand feet in elevation, which will make it the highest railroad in the world. Economic justification for the project is that it will permit the development of Tibet's oil and gold resources as well as greatly increase the export of meat to the rest of China. However, Tibetans fear that its goal is essentially to bind the autonomous region more tightly to the rule of Beijing.

In southern Xinjiang, where Chinese presence has been slight, a highway has been built across the Talakman desert to spur the development of oil fields. A one-thousand-mile railroad was completed along the northern edge of the desert to connect the provincial capital of Urumqi with the western oasis town of Kashi (Kashgar), a bastion of Uighur culture near the border with Kyrgyzstan and Tajikistan. Also, a natural gas pipeline from the Tarim Basin to Shanghai is being planned. These developments serve the dual purpose of exploiting the Empty Area's riches and stimulating the settlement of Han peoples to offset the separatist drives of restive minorities.

Despite all of these efforts, the drives for independence in both provinces remain active. In the long run, an acceptable solution in both Tibet and Xinjiang might be some sort of full independence and guarantees of noninterference in the political and economic affairs of these countries, but with the treaty arrangements that provide for Beijing to maintain defense forces there.

The Empty Area is of importance to China in other ways. The Dzungaria Basin of northern Xinjiang contains coal, iron, tin, gold, silver, and uranium, as well as the vast oil fields already noted. These have been the basis for the industrialization of the region. In Urumqi, Xinjiang's main manufacturing and service center, the developments have included steelworks, oil refineries, machinery, chemicals, and motor vehicle plants. Another industrial center, Yumen in northwestern Gansu, is China's oldest and still one of its leading oil centers, based on rich oil deposits to its northwest. The area's minerals also support light, nonferrous metal smelting works. In addition, as previously mentioned, extensive deposits of oil and natural gas lie beneath the Tarim Basin Desert of Xinjiang.

Still another strategic value of the Empty Area lies in the sites that it provides for space launchings and nuclear testing. Jiaquan, in northern Gansu east of Yumen, and Xichang, in southwest Sichuan south of Kanding, are China's main space satellite launch centers. Secret sites until the 1990s, they have since been opened to foreign tourists. Another launch site is near Taiyuan in northern Shanxi. The country's nuclear test sites are also located deep within the Interior—in central Xinjiang within the Tarim desert, near the town of Yuli in eastern Tibet, and in Inner Mongolia.

China has signed the Nuclear Non-Proliferation Pact and the Comprehensive Test Ban Treaty (CTBT). Moreover, as one of the five major nuclear powers, it has joined with the others in agreeing to the eventual elimination of all nuclear weapons. However, Beijing signed the CTBT only grudgingly and it continues to seek an amendment that will permit nuclear testing for peaceful purposes. In the light of this policy objective, the nuclear test sites of the Empty Area may well not have outlived their usefulness. Certainly the importance of the space launch sites for commercial satellites will continue to grow as the demand for telecommunications increases.

Boundaries

The concerns of China over its international boundaries have brought it into conflict with India and the FSU over land borders and with several countries over the Spratly and Paracel Islands in the South China Sea.

Disputes over the forty-five-hundred-mile Sino-Soviet border led to conflict between China and the Soviet Union in 1969. Serious fighting broke out over control of Damansky Island in the Ussuri River north of Vladivostok, while conflict also erupted over the border between Xinjiang and the USSR in Kazakhstan.

Since the Soviet divestiture of Kazakhstan and Kyrgyzstan, the Sino-Russian boundary has been reduced to twenty-three hundred miles in length. With the improvement in recent years of relations between Russia and China, tension over this boundary has eased and there have been substantial troop reductions all along the border. All that remains in dispute is ownership of two small sections of the boundary. The border between China's Xinjiang Province and Tajikistan also remains to be settled, but is not a cause for tension.

The most serious of the boundary controversies is with India.[13] This has led to two wars and, until 1999, the closing of border trade between the two countries. At this time the two nations also agreed to partial demilitarization of their borders. The first conflict broke out in 1959 over the Longju incident, when the Chinese seized control of a small garrison in India's North-East Frontier Agency (Arunachal Pradesh) at the southeastern edge of the Tibetan Plateau, which they continue to occupy.

The second and more major war erupted in 1962, not only over this eastern Himalayan border, but over the western end as well. There the Chinese territorial claim embraced the Ladakh region of northernmost India, in Jammu and Kashmir state, and northeasternmost Pakistan. Ladakh is sometimes referred to as "Little Tibet" or the "India Tibet" and is ethnically and geographically allied with Tibet. Its population is predominantly Lamaist Buddhist. The region was a dependency of Tibet until annexed by Britain and attached to Kashmir in the nineteenth century. It was divided between India and Pakistan during the partition of India. There had been some skirmishing over the region in 1959, and the 1962 full-scale war broke out over a strategic highway that the Chinese had built across the barren and uninhabited Aksai Chin high plain in northern Ladakh to connect western Tibet with Xinjiang. For China, this was a war over regional security. For India, Chinese control of the territory meant the strategic exposure of the northern Indian plain to Chinese forces via passes cutting through and around the Karakoram range. The area is also the transit way for China to the Pakistani-held sector of Kashmir and northern Pakistan.

China's victory in the 1962 war has left its troops in control of 5,985 square miles, or over 40 percent of Ladakh. To complicate the situation, a Sino-Pakistani protocol of 1987 recognized the boundary as terminating at the Karakoram Pass, thus accepting Chinese sovereignty over three thousand square miles of the disputed area. In addition, Chinese troops continue to occupy the area west of Aksai Chin and two small pockets on the southwest Tibet border that were at issue in the 1959 conflict.

During the 1962 war, China also launched an offensive that overran India's North-East Frontier Agency (Arunachal Pradesh). After a cease-fire, it withdrew its troops to a line of control that approximated the border between India and Tibet, known as the McMahon Line, that had been established by Britain in 1914. However, Beijing continues to maintain its claim to the region. Chinese and Indian troops clashed once again in Arunachal in 1986–87. A decade later, the two countries agreed to a no-fly zone and partial demilitarization over the line of control, but this did not prevent subsequent Chinese incursions in Arunachal and in the southwestern Tibet area bordering India's Uttar Pradesh.

Still another focus of contention in the Himalayan region has to do with Sikkim. India absorbed the mountain kingdom in 1975, but Beijing continues to insist upon the independence of this Buddhist land, which was ruled by Tibet for two centuries and in the nineteenth century came under nominal Chinese suzerainty.

Two other boundaries are in dispute between China and its land neighbors. One is a twenty-mile section of the North Korean border in the Paektu-san (mountain) area. Another revolves around sections of the land border with Vietnam, where the line is indefinite. There, clashes over disputed areas broke out as early as 1974, and in 1979 culminated in China's invasion across the seven-hundred-mile frontier. This was a counterinvasion to that mounted by Vietnam against the Cambodian Khmer Rouge regime of Pol Pot, which resulted in his ouster in favor of a Vietnamese-supported government.[14]

China has also been involved in a number of maritime boundary conflicts. The dispute between China and Vietnam in the Gulf of Tonkin stemmed from Vietnamese fears that China intends to control the "East" (South China) Sea, and thus the Indochinese peninsula, as a springboard to the rest of Southeast Asia. The issue was resolved by two agreements—one an accord over the Vietnam-China land boundary in 1999 and the second an agreement in 2000 to the demarcation of territorial waters and fishing rights in Beipu Bay.

Elsewhere, China's territorial claims to South China Sea waters off the shoals of Sarawak and Indonesia's Natuna Islands have increased the tensions in that region. Both of these areas are rich in natural gas and Beijing has announced its rights to award exploration concessions there. The Natuna offshore gas field, one of the largest in the world, is a particularly tempting prize. The island lies 130 miles off the northern tip of the Indonesian province of Kalimantan, but the field extends northeast of Natuna, within waters that lie in part within two hundred miles of the Spratlys, which are claimed by Beijing. China also claims the Senkaku Islands, off the coast of southwestern Japan. Thus far China has not supported these claims with a naval presence, but this could change as its navy acquires a greater long-range capacity.

The most important, by far, of China's maritime conflicts is with several countries over possession of two island groupings far off its mainland coast in the South China Seas. This issue will be discussed in the chapter that deals with the Asia-Pacific Rim.

The above-mentioned boundary issues, as well as the overriding goals of China to reestablish control over Taiwan, must be kept in mind as Washington pursues its hopes for a strategic alliance with China. Beijing is quite capable of separating its economic policies from its geostrategic aims, and the assumption that the latter will be abandoned as the price for expanded international trade is probably wishful thinking.

The East Asia Rim Periphery

The waters that border mainland China are partially enclosed to their east by a peninsular-insular rim. This rim is formed by the Korean Peninsula, Taiwan, the Philippines, and the Indochinese peninsula. Since South Korea and the Philippines are clearly parts of the Asia-Pacific Rim geopolitical region, and thus under the military shield of the United States, the focus of China's strategic aims are, at least for the present, North Korea; the Indochinese peninsular states of Vietnam, Laos, and Cambodia; and Taiwan.

For much of the past half century, the Soviet Union acted in either partnership or as a competitor with China in support of North Korea and the Indochinese countries in their wars against the United States and France. While Russia's influence has waned, it is by no means negligible. In North Korea it has assumed the role of mediator, rather than intervener, as it has become active in promoting negotiations over the unification of the two Koreas. In Vietnam, it is seeking to reinforce its former strategic partnership by selling advanced weapons to Hanoi. In spite of Moscow's activism, China clearly has a much stronger geopolitical hand in the relations with North Korea and Indochina than was the case before the collapse of the Soviet Union. The new reality is that the two geostrategic realms that now clash directly in this contact zone are the Maritime and East Asian, not the Heartlandic.

In both North Korea and Indochina, China must exercise its strategic superiority judiciously in dealing with these battle-hardened nations that jealously guard their independence of action. To draw them firmly into the East Asian orbit, Beijing will have to develop partnerships based on fulfilling mutual strategic needs, rather than seeking to create a dominant-subordinate relationship.

TAIWAN

The situation with Taiwan presents China with both dangers and opportunities. Currently, China lacks the sea power to reunify the mainland and the island militarily. Both the Beijing and Taipei regimes are in agreement that Taiwan is politically indivisible from the mainland, and its increasing capital investments in China are an important element in the development of the Golden Coast. However, Taiwan is economically and geopolitically a member of the Asia-Pacific Rim region and the Maritime world as a whole. Only if a geopolitical structure is developed that would enable the island to serve as a bridge, or Gateway, between the two realms will China be likely to fulfill its strategic and historic territorial ambitions.

What might be acceptable to the disputing parties is a "Hong Kong Plus" model, which would provide Taiwan with greater freedom than the "two economies-one state" system that characterizes Hong Kong's current status within the framework of Chinese sovereignty. Taiwan can hardly be satisfied with less than complete economic, cultural, and political freedom, including retaining its own elected legislature, whereas China's 1997 agreement with Hong Kong guarantees the retention of the latter's present economic system for only half a century. A confederated political framework that would permit Taiwan to retain special trading ties with closely related neighbors, such as in the Asia-Pacific Economic Cooperation Forum (APEC), or to join the Association of Southeast Asian Nations (ASEAN), might satisfy Taipei.

From China's standpoint, maintaining and increasing the flow of investment capital from Taiwan is essential. Nearly half of all the foreign investments in China are in the electronics area, and Taiwanese computer companies account for over half of these investments. Using the formula that permitted Ukraine and Belarus to hold membership in the United Nations, it might be possible for China to agree to the restoration of a seat for Taiwan within the UN General Assembly, from which it was expelled in 1971. China would have little to lose, owing to its own role as a permanent member of the Security Council, which would guarantee Beijing's dominance within the United Nations of a China Federation, were it to be created.

A small, but possibly significant step toward an eventual political agreement is the accord signed by Taipei and Beijing to permit limited exchanges between the heavily fortified Taiwanese Islands of Jinmen (Quemoy) and Mazu (Matsu) and the province of Fujian. Passengers and goods now may cross the narrow Taiwan Strait, rather than travel via third countries, as Taipei long required. There is also discussion of developing a commercial port on Jinmen as another step in expanding the direct trade, transport, and postal exchanges that Beijing has long desired, not merely with the tiny offshore islands, but between the mainland and Taiwan.

NORTH KOREA

North Korea, the last of the Stalinist states and heir to the tradition of the "Hermit Kingdom" of seventeenth- to nineteenth-century Korea, lies within the geostrategic orbit of China. This dependence is relatively recent, stemming from the collapse of the Soviet Union and the disappearance of Moscow's military and economic aid. Previously, Pyongyang was able to call upon both the Soviet Union and China for strategic support, playing its patrons off against one another and thereby maintaining a degree of independence.

Russia has continued to provide North Korea with international diplomatic backing in support of the coexistence of two Korean states, although it has recently begun to serve as a mediator in South Korea's efforts to draw North Korea into greater engagement. Moscow is using its influence to counter the U.S.-inspired image of North Korea as what used to be described as a "rogue state," against which Washington is proposing to develop its new National Missile Defense system. In this case, China has joined Russia in opposition to the proposal. However, Moscow cannot offer Pyongyang the military support that Beijing can provide in times of crisis.

That North Korea has little alternative but to seek the strategic patronage of Beijing is evidenced in the international negotiations that have taken place sporadically during the past decade. These have been over nuclear weapons policy issues, tensions in the Demilitarized Zone (DMZ) between North Korea and South Korea at the thirty-eighth parallel, terrorist attacks, and on-and-off unification talks between the Koreas. Negotiations have increasingly evolved into a four-party structure, including South Korea and the United States on one side and North Korea and China on the other.

When Korea emerged from World War II, it was the North that had the bulk of the peninsula's industry and its mineral resources. In this part of the country were 90 percent of Korea's minerals (coal, iron, copper, lead, uranium, manganese), its hydroelectric power resources, and its forest products. The industrial base included steel and chemicals, and the North was by far wealthier than the South. Although devastated during the Korean War, North Korea was able to recover quickly with massive Soviet and Chinese aid. The state-owned industrial base was rebuilt and expanded by the addition of armament and aircraft as well as machinery and petrochemicals plants, and by the modernization of the steel, chemical, and textile industries.

The Achilles' heel of the North is agriculture. Little farmland was available because of the rocky and mountainous terrain, poor soils, and a short growing season. The peninsula in its entirety is only 20 percent arable land because of the terrain, but there is even less land proportionally available in the North, where the mountainous landscape gives way to the broad flood plains formed by the Taidong, Chongchon, and Yalu Rivers, which face Korea Bay at northeast China. Farms were collectivized and mechanized, while irrigation facilities were expanded in pursuit of agricultural self-sufficiency, but the climate is too cold for paddy rice, the staple of the South, and grain supplies have been erratic owing to the vicissitudes of climate.

Since the postwar recovery period, North Korea has become the poor neighbor of the South. Its economy has been weighed down by the cost of seeking food and industrial self-sufficiency and by extraordinarily heavy military expenditures, including its nuclear and ballistic missiles program and a million-man army. As North Korea has struggled with the inefficiencies of its Soviet-style, state-run economic system, the previously poorer South Korea has surpassed it economically.

With the collapse of the Soviet Union and the attendant loss of heavy Soviet aid, North Korea has been ill equipped to cope with the series of natural disasters that have come upon it in recent years—floods and droughts that have brought famine and disease and taken hundreds of thousands of lives. Grain production has dropped by 40 percent. Plagued by food, fertilizer, and fuel shortages, the country must depend upon foreign aid from Japan, China, South Korea, the United States, and international agencies in order to cope with the crises.

Thanks to massive U.S. aid after the Korean War, South Korea rebuilt its economy, changing from an impoverished, heavily populated, agricultural country into a prosperous, highly industrialized one. Agriculture was surpassed in importance by manufacturing as early as the 1960s, and today farm output represents only 6 percent of GDP, while industry accounts for 43 percent and services 51 percent. The South Korean economy is fully integrated within the global economy. It exports such products as electronics, electrical equipment, steel, machinery, autos, ships, and textiles, and its total foreign trade in goods represents 35 percent of GDP. The 47 million South Koreans, 83 percent of whom are urban, enjoy a standard of living with a per capita GDP of nearly $14,000, in stark contrast to the standards of the 21 million North Koreans (62 percent of whom are urban), whose per capita GDP is less than $1,000.

North Korea is still the world's most centrally planned industrial economy. State-owned industries provide 60 percent of the GDP, and collectivized agriculture 25 percent, while the service sector is minuscule—only 15 percent of GDP. International trade represents only 11 percent of GDP, reflecting the isolated nature of the economy and the burden of military expenditures. This burden is overwhelming, accounting for approximately 30 percent of GDP, in contrast with South Korea's 3 percent. Recently, China has been encouraging the North Korean leadership to initiate economic reforms by moving in part toward a market economy, thus emulating the reforms that Beijing has undertaken in recent years.

In addition to this grim economic picture, North Korea has been cast as a pariah nation by the United States and much of the rest of the world over its nuclear threat and sponsorship of international terrorism. This makes it even more dependent on the patronage of Communist China, which has evolved as the main power broker on the North Pacific mainland. There have been some recent tensions between Beijing and Pyongyang over the expansion of the latter's economic ties with South Korea—a position contradicted by the fact that China itself is now the second-largest importer of South Korean goods and a recipient of substantial capital investment from that country. The explanation for this position lies in the opposition of Beijing to Korean unification.

The dependence of Communist Korea upon China has its roots in the Korean War. At that time 300,000 Chinese "volunteers" joined the North Korean troops that had been driven back to the Yalu River to push the American-led UN forces back below the thirty-eighth parallel. The line had been arbitrarily established at the end of World War II as a temporary means of separating the northern, Soviet-occupied zone of the country from the southern, U.S.-occupied zone. The thirty-eighth parallel became a formal boundary in 1948, when the two separate regimes—the northern Democratic People's Republic of Korea and the southern Republic of Korea—were established, and the Soviet and American troops were withdrawn. The sudden invasion by the North Korean army in 1950 breached the boundary and pushed back the South Koreans, and the American troops who had been rushed to their aid, to the small pocket around Pusan at the southeastern tip of the peninsula.

The subsequent U.S. counterattack, initiated by the landing at Inchon on the west-central coast near Seoul, drove the North Koreans back to the Yalu River border with China. This brought China directly into the war, as they pushed the UN forces back. Ultimately up to one million Chinese troops became engaged, and their casualties were estimated at up to a half million. The bitter fighting ended with the armistice in 1953 and the establishment of the DMZ, which ran from the Han Estuary northeast across the thirty-eighth parallel. The boundary does not follow the parallel precisely, but cuts across it diagonally. In actuality, North Korea has 850 square miles south of the parallel along the west coast, including Kaesong, a commercial and industrial center, which from the tenth century to the end of the fourteenth century had served as the capital for Korean dynasties. As the gateway for rail and road traffic to the Korean south from Manchuria and North Korea, Kaesong was a major battleground during the war. South Korea holds 2,350 square miles north of the parallel in the center and along the east coast. This area includes the fishing port of Sokcho, on the Sea of Japan and backed by the Taibak Mountains.

For China, the exact location of the boundary between North and South was not the issue. Of crucial importance to Beijing was the preservation of the boundary zone as buffer and, indeed, all of North Korea as a security screen for Manchuria. In this sense, China perceived the Yalu River as its final line of defense, not its first line. General Douglas MacArthur had taken as saber rattling the Chinese warnings against his pushing north of the thirty-eighth parallel. He underestimated Beijing's resolve. Under the urging of Stalin, and with his military support, the Chinese attacked and overwhelmed the much smaller UN force that had reached the Yalu.

China had a genuine fear of an attack by the United States in support of a Guomindang effort to return to the mainland. Moreover, the Chinese entered the war because Stalin's request that they do so included the promise of air cover; the training of pilots for the MIGs that were given to them, which would enable the Chinese to participate with the Russians in the air war; and the massive supply of military equipment. Despite their heavy casualties, the Chinese armed forces emerged from the war with far more effectiveness and power than they possessed before the war, while the Chinese air force became the third largest in the world.

For the same security reasons that prompted its military response half a century ago, Beijing continues to prop up the Pyongyang regime economically and politically. China is North Korea's main trading partner and the two countries share the enormous quantity of hydroelectric power supplied by waters impounded by the Supung Dam on the Yalu River, one of the largest dams in Asia. In fact, China has electric power facilities on the North Korean side of the Yalu.

After the war, China helped North Korea on the manpower front. The flight of several million people to the South had caused serious worker shortages. These were partly offset by Chinese colonists from Manchuria, as well as repatriated Koreans from Manchuria and Japan. On this score, however, there has been an ironic turnabout since the mid-1990s. Seeking to escape the famine that has raged in the North since 1995, tens of thousands of North Korean refugees have crossed the border to China seeking food and jobs. Approximately 100,000 to 300,000 of these migrants, who have fled mostly to the border provinces, are to be found seeking shelter among China's ethnic Koreans, who constitute up to 40 percent of the population of some of the districts of northeast China. Some are sent onward by underground networks into Mongolia and then by circuitous routes into Thailand and, eventually, South Korea. The majority, however, are trapped in these border provinces, where they live and work under most difficult conditions and in constant fear of being sent back by Chinese authorities. Initially Beijing turned a blind eye toward their presence. Now, however, considerable numbers are being returned, both because of Beijing's concern that the area will be overrun by the refugees and out of deference to the North Korean regime's policy of trying to prevent such flight. When caught by the police, the refugees are handed over to border guards to face possible punishment in North Korea for having left the country illegally.

The agreement of June 14, 2000, between Presidents Kim Jong Il of North Korea and Kim Dae Jung of South Korea was heralded as a historic breakthrough. The two leaders agreed to seek reconciliation and unification, the establishment of peace, furtherance of family visitations, cultural exchange, and restoration of railroad and road links between the two countries. This accord has profound implications for both China and the United States, as well as for the Koreans. The North Koreans are adamant in seeking the withdrawal of U.S. troops from South Korea, while China's interests require guarantees that a merged Korea not be drawn into the Maritime Realm strategic alliance. Moreover, the North Korean leadership is hardly prepared to jeopardize Communist control of its country, while the South Koreans will in no way take any steps that would undermine their economic system and weaken their ties with Japan, the broader Asia-Pacific region, and the Maritime Realm.

The signing of this accord had an immediate effect upon U.S. relations with North Korea. Washington eased trade sanctions and softened the rhetoric it had long used to describe North Korea. "Rogue state" was dropped from the lexicon of the U.S. State Department in favor of "state of concern." (This new terminology applies as well to Cuba, Iran, Iraq, Libya, Sudan, and Syria.) The easing of the sanctions reflects an important policy change, moving toward greater emphasis on negotiating differences, rather than on punishment. However, when in February 2002 President George W. Bush lumped North Korea together with Iraq and Iran as the "axis of evil" for their alleged support of terrorism, this rhetoric threatened to undermine South Korea's policy of seeking accommodation with North Korea. Seoul immediately distanced itself from the Bush statement and continued to pursue its "Sunshine Policy," which seeks open doors to the north. Washington, too, has toned down its rhetoric, preferring to focus on "evil-doers," the chief one being Iraq.

Moscow has seized upon the changing relations between North and South Korea to assume a mediating role between them. The negotiations that have followed between the two Koreas have enabled Moscow to expand its influence with both countries. The South Koreans have sided with Moscow in seeking a diplomatic approach to the resolution of the North Korean missile threat, rather than supporting the American National Missile Defense project. In addition, in an effort to draw Seoul and Pyongyang more closely together, the Russians have proposed linking the Pacific coast railroad systems of the two Koreas to the Trans-Siberian Railroad terminal at Vladivostok. This overland rail system would cut to twelve days the time required for goods from Korea's ports to reach Russia and Europe, as compared with the current twenty-four-day sea route. China is also interested in the North and South Korean link, which would provide it with access to South Korea via the existing rail line between Pyongyang and Manchuria. Another desire of Russia is to develop a pipeline network from its border through North Korea to the South, to open the Korean market to its new East Siberian natural gas fields. The North Koreans have requested that Moscow sell them military weapons, especially naval equipment. Both Koreas seem to be open to improved relations with Russia.

When and if Korea does unite, the United States, China, and Russia will have to find a formula that neutralizes the country militarily and encourages it to serve as a bridge between the three geostrategic realms. At present, reunification is a hope, not a reality. However, reduction of tensions and peace along the world's most heavily militarized border seems close at hand, given the June 2000 agreement.

Perhaps the current atmosphere can breathe life into a long-discussed proposal by peace seekers, who have sought to persuade the two Koreas to convert the 150-mile-long, 2.5-mile-wide DMZ into a nature reserve. The zone is currently ringed by hundreds of thousands of troops and studded with military installations. Environmentalists have emphasized its ecological uniqueness. Because of disuse by humans, it has evolved over the years into a nature sanctuary. Such use could serve as a basis for ecotourism that could benefit both states and help to reinforce the current efforts to bring stability and greater openness to the relations between North and South. Converting the Korean Peninsula to a Gateway region that would link all three realms is an important goal in the quest for global geopolitical equilibrium.

INDOCHINA

Vietnam

The geopolitical relations between China and Vietnam have followed a highly tortuous course. The depth of China's involvement in the Vietnam War was evidence of the strategic importance it gives to the Indochinese peninsula. South China's coastal provinces are directly exposed to the threat of hostile forces in the Gulf of Tonkin and coastal Vietnam. Moreover, Yunnan, in southwest China, is open to land invasion from forces moving up North Vietnam's Red River Valley or up the Mekong from Saigon (Ho Chi Minh City) through Laos and Cambodia. Having American troops on China's doorstep was a strategic nightmare to the Chinese leadership, which explains China's vigorous support of North Vietnam during the Vietnam War.

Following the withdrawal of France from Vietnam in 1954 and the division of the country into North and South along the seventeenth parallel, both China and the Soviet Union provided the Ho Chi Minh regime with enormous amounts of economic and military aid. Even after the Sino-Soviet split, the two Communist powers continued to finance the development of industry and agriculture. Focus of industrial development was in the Red River Delta, coastal areas of the Gulf of Tonkin, and the port city of Haiphong, which brought the ecumene of the country to the doorstep of South China.

As the Viet Minh launched their guerrilla warfare against South Vietnam, the Chinese supplied them with the bulk of their military equipment. The flow increased when the United States entered the war directly in 1964 and the North became exposed to systematic bombing from U.S. land bases in the South and aircraft carriers in the Gulf of Tonkin. Much of the Chinese equipment was moved southward by the Viet Minh along the Ho Chi Minh trail—a network of jungle-covered mountain tracks that extended along the eastern border of Laos to South Vietnam and Cambodia.

The United States effectively withdrew from the war in 1973, two years before its official termination. While North Korea's alliance with both China and the Soviet Union had held during the war there, the first break between China and the now united Socialist Republic of Vietnam came quickly, precipitated by China's seizure of the Paracels in 1974, which they continue to administer to the present day. The schism widened in the late 1970s and early 1980s. Vietnamese forces invaded Cambodia in 1978 and drove Pol Pot's Khmer Rouge from power after the excesses of that regime had caused the deaths of three million people and emptied out the cities. Pol Pot, who had seized control of the government in 1975, had exiled most Cambodians to the countryside in an action reminiscent of Mao's Cultural Revolution of 1966–76, which had similarly devastated China.

The presence of Vietnamese troops in Cambodia triggered a brief Chinese invasion of Vietnam's border provinces in 1979, during which China captured several border towns.

Minor clashes had broken out between China and Vietnam as early as 1974 along their 750-mile disputed border, which had never been clearly delineated. Despite protracted negotiations between them, there had been no resolution of the dispute.

The primary factors that led to the war were the installation of a Vietnamese-sponsored government in Cambodia, which displaced the Chinese-supported regime, and the discriminatory treatment by the Vietnamese of their ethnic Chinese. This discrimination was highlighted by Hanoi's clampdown on the large body of Chinese traders whose activities as private businessmen raised the ire of the Communist government. During this period, over a quarter of a million ethnic Chinese fled Vietnam. Most of those living in the Vietnamese provinces that bordered China made their way by land to the People's Republic of China or to Hong Kong. Those who fled to China from the South went by boat. The Chinese troops withdrew from Vietnam after two months, having suffered heavy casualties. The two countries then entered upon years of negotiations over their land-border dispute, which was not formally concluded until an agreement signed in December 1999. The rift with China gave great urgency to Hanoi for seeking the patronage of Russia as a counterbalancing force. In 1978, just before the Chinese invasion, Vietnam had joined the Soviet-led Council for Mutual Economic Assistance (COMECON) and concluded a treaty of friendship with the Soviet Union. Now, with Beijing ending its economic aid program, Soviet assistance became crucial. From the signing of the friendship treaty to the time of the Soviet collapse a decade later, the Soviet Union was the major supporter of Vietnam, supplying arms, economic aid, and fuel. In return, Moscow received the rights to operate and expand the Cam Ranh Bay naval and air bases, which had been abandoned by the United States, thus strengthening its strategic position in both the South China Sea and the Indian Ocean. Adding to the Chinese-Vietnamese friction in the 1980s, China foiled Vietnamese incursion into the Paracels.

In the 1990s, tensions between China and Vietnam lessened as a result of a series of economic and political agreements between the two. Since normalization of relations in 1991, China has become a major importer of Vietnamese products and a major source for capital investment. The countries share similar approaches to their market reforms, following "open door" economic policies while clinging to their Communist governing structures. Vietnam's withdrawal of its troops from Cambodia in 1988 and its recognition of China's rule over Taiwan eased tensions and paved the way for a joint declaration of friendship between the two countries. The agreement commited the two countries to resolving their land and maritime border disputes and to opening the land border fully, save for a military intelligence station that monitors shipping in the South China Sea. This helped to ease China's security concerns and led to the final border accords.

Vietnam's strategic vulnerability to Chinese pressure partly relates to the location of its northern ecumene. As previously noted, the center of North Vietnamese industry and agriculture is the Tonkin Delta, especially around Hanoi and Haiphong, whose development was fostered by both China and the USSR from the 1960s to the 1980s. This region merges geographically into the southern end of the Chinese ecumene's densely populated industrial and agricultural centers in the province of Guangxi Zhuangzu, such as the coastal cities of Beihai and Hepu and the inland cities of Nanning and Wuzhou. Nanning has played a singular role in Chinese-Vietnamese relations as the gateway for Chinese supplies to North Vietnam during the war.

China lacks the surplus capital and is too absorbed with its own development needs to provide Vietnam with the level of economic aid and investment that is required to pull the latter out of its current economic distress. Vietnam remains one of the world's poorer countries, with a per capita income less than half that of China's, and with eighty million people economic gains are quickly absorbed by population growth. This condition exists despite considerable capital investments over the past decade from Singapore, Taiwan, Hong Kong, and Japan, as well as the change in relations with the United States, which included lifting of the trade embargo in 1994, reestablishment of diplomatic ties, and the recent normalization of relations.

With its aging industry being privatized slowly, and with a labor force that is still two-thirds agricultural, Vietnam has not generated the revenues needed for structural economic reform, forcing the country to assume a heavy foreign debt. It was in recognition of its need to look to the Asia-Pacific Rim and the rest of the Maritime world for economic links that, in 1995, Vietnam joined the ASEAN. However, with foreign trade representing only 15 percent of its GDP, Vietnam has a long way to go before it can reach a par with its trade-oriented, more prosperous Asia-Pacific Rim neighbors. Despite the commitment of the Communist regime to a free market economy, foreign investors remain discouraged by governmental red tape and corruption. Evidence of this is the fact that investments, which spurted with the lifting of the U.S. trade embargo, have since declined from a 1996 peak to a level that approximates that of 1991.

The efforts of Hanoi to close the growing economic gap between the northern and southern halves of the country have thus far failed. Those foreign investments that do flow into Vietnam are attracted to the freewheeling capitalist atmosphere of Ho Chi Minh City (formerly Saigon), not to the centrally planned industrial zones of the North. Thus the country that was officially reunified in 1975 remains far from unified economically. The South is the source of two-thirds of Vietnam's wealth, sends 90 percent of its tax revenues to Hanoi, and is the recipient of most of the cash remittances from families abroad. This economic gap is hardly a recipe for healthy political relations between the two parts of the country.

With the Hanoi regime's uncertainty over its ability to retain its centralized powers, and despite its still bitter memories of the Vietnam War, in which three million Vietnamese lost their lives, it will continue to seek whatever help it can get from the Maritime world. At the same time, it accepts the realities of China's growing strategic power in East Asia. From the standpoint of Beijing, eliminating the vestiges of territorial conflicts with Vietnam is the most direct way of rebuilding a strategic alliance.

Vietnam is far from being a satellite of China, however, having struggled against Chinese domination for two thousand years. Both sides appear to have concluded that they can deal with one another as partners better than as opponents. A recent sign of China's recognition of its need to treat Vietnam as a partner within the East Asian Realm was its settlement of the land and coastal water boundary disputes that had marred relations between the two countries for so many years.

Additional steps that could be taken, such as agreeing to a condominium over the Paracels and joint sponsorship of claims and energy concessions in the Spratlys, would reassure Hanoi of Beijing's intentions as it seeks to develop a strategic partnership with its neighbor to the south. For its part, Hanoi might open its doors to the return of ethnic Chinese who fled, not only to redress an old wrong, but to benefit from the economic dividends that come from strengthened familial ties with overseas Chinese and mainlanders.

Russia's relationships with Vietnam are in flux. From 1978 until the end of the 1980s Moscow was the major foreign influence in the country, as the Soviets expanded their Cam Ranh Bay naval base and provided Hanoi with substantial military and economic assistance.

One of the finest deepwater shelters in Southeast Asia, Cam Ranh served as the Soviet Union's major military beachhead within the region and as its largest naval and staging area outside the USSR. The warships and aircraft based there, as well as electronic listening facilities, facilitated surveillance over both the South China Sea and the Indian Ocean.

As the Soviet empire began to crumble at the end of the 1980s, Moscow withdrew from most of Cam Ranh Bay, leaving only a few auxiliary vessels and a small military force there to maintain the intelligence station and using the port for occasional merchant ship repairs.[15] At the same time, it drastically lowered its economic support of Vietnam—a factor that influenced Hanoi's decision to seek repair of its relations with China.

Vladimir Putin's visit to Hanoi early in 2001 signaled Russia's interest in reengaging Vietnam. The two countries signed a "strategic partnership" accord that awarded Moscow exploration rights in a thirty-eight-square-mile tract of Vietnam's oil-rich continental shelf. In addition, it provided for Russia's sale to Hanoi of advanced arms, especially naval weapons, and promised help in constructing Vietnam's first nuclear power plant. The Russians also agreed to forgive nearly all of the $11 billion debt owed to them. The two parties used the signing of the agreement as an occasion to voice their common objection to the proposed U.S. National Missile Defense (NMD) system.

Part of Moscow's objective in the new "strategic partnership" is to renew the lease on Cam Ranh Bay beyond its 2004 expiration date, in the hope that some day the base may become a spearhead for Russia's strategic return to the region. At the same time, the Vietnamese government feels that it cannot afford to let the large, well-situated harbor and its adjoining airport lie idle, and it has signaled its intention not to renew the lease. It has indicated a desire to put them to economic use by remodeling the facility for cruise ships and merchant vessels. To further complicate the situation, both China and the United States have evinced an interest in gaining access to the base.

The Russian actions in Vietnam are in keeping with an "Orient Policy" enunciated by former Prime Minister Yevgeny Primakov, who advocated regaining political influence in North Korea, Vietnam, and India through military assistance programs.[16] Vietnam may see its purchase of arms from Russia as an expression of the former's intent to maintain a measure of strategic independence from China. However, there is little likelihood that the agreements between Moscow and Hanoi can alter the fundamental reality that Indochina now lies within the geostrategic orbit of East Asia.

Washington's efforts to forge a new partnership with Vietnam were highlighted by the visit of President Clinton in December 2000. While the focus of the visit and of U.S. policy initiatives is trade and free markets, the American initiative may also have had the objectives of offsetting Chinese pressures on Vietnam and containing China's southward expansion. These objectives are unrealistic. Whatever directions the relations between Beijing and Hanoi may take, the United States has neither the capacity nor the will to try to affect the strategic relationships between these Asian powers. To suggest to the Vietnamese leadership that the United States might help them to break off China's strategic embrace might encourage them to challenge China, only to discover that there is no American safety net.

Laos and Cambodia

As poor a nation as Vietnam is, it is clearly the dominant state among the nations of Indochina. The economy of Cambodia (Kampuchea) is deeply depressed—the country's per capita income is one-third that of Vietnam—and based almost entirely on agriculture. A trade agreement between the United States and Cambodia in 1996 has led to the rapid expansion of the country's garment industry, with more than three-quarters of a billion dollars of exports being shipped to the United States. The low U.S. tariff on Cambodian goods has attracted dozens of investors from Taiwan, Singapore, Hong Kong, and China, as garments have become the country's biggest export earner. Nevertheless, the number of these newly employed factory workers (under 200,000) does little to reduce Cambodia's rural poverty, inasmuch as 80 percent of the entire population lives as farmers or farm laborers.

Cambodia's domestic politics remain unstable, despite the efforts of the United Nations to bring stability to the country. From 1991 to 1993 Cambodia was virtually a UN protectorate, under the UN Transitional Authority in Cambodia (UNTAC), as twenty thousand peacekeeping troops sought to pacify the country. UNTAC withdrew after elections were held, but the Khmer Rouge continued their activities until the movement split in 1996. Pol Pot was captured the following year and he died in captivity. A coup in 1998 brought the Communist Party, led by Hun Sen, to power.

In the midst of such instability, the country's military vulnerability to Vietnam remains a powerful element in the political relations between the two countries. Unlike in Laos, which is separated from Vietnam by heavily forested mountains, Cambodia's border with its larger neighbor is completely open. Most of its eleven million people, concentrated in the lower Mekong, are geographically connected with the river's delta area and Ho Chi Minh City.

Laos is lightly settled, with a population of a little over five million and one-third the population density of Cambodia's. Its per capita income is double that of Cambodia, but two-thirds that of Vietnam. Laos, too, has suffered from its landlocked position and from years of warfare. Ruled by the Communist Pathet Lao, which came to power with the help of the Vietnamese, its economy remains underdeveloped, with Vietnam as its largest trading partner. Mountains cover most of the country. The rapids of the Mekong River, along which half of the Laotian population lives, impede movement along this, the nation's main communications artery, while land and air connections are limited.

The result of this isolation is that most Laotians are subsistence farmers, with rice as the main crop. Exports are mainly tin, timber, and coffee, as well as electric power, most of which now goes to Thailand. The planned Nam Theun River dam in Central Laos, which will flood one-fourth of the Nakay Plateau, will cause displacement of four thousand villagers and considerable ecological damage. It will enable the Laotians to export surplus electricity to Vietnam, as well as to Thailand.

Viangchan (Vientiane), the capital and largest city of Laos, is located on the Mekong River on the border with northeastern Thailand and is a center for trade with that country. However, there is at present little possibility that Communist Laos will move out of the geopolitical orbit of Vietnam. In addition to the strategic advantage that Vietnam holds over Laos, the contrast between the democratic political system of Thailand and that of Communist Laos makes it even more unlikely that Laos would move away from Vietnam and toward Thailand.

Conclusion

A clear geopolitical hierarchy in the East Asian Realm has evolved over many years of turbulence. Indochina is dominated by Vietnam, the second-order power of its geopolitical region. The region, in turn, is under the strategic sway of China, the primary geopolitical force of the East Asian Realm. While China has major differences with Vietnam, especially over territorial waters that hold gas and oil reserves, it is unlikely to plunge into conflict with its battle-hardened neighbor. On the contrary, the two nations have strengthened their ties since resuming diplomatic relations in 1991 and, in 1999, they resolved all outstanding disputes along their common 740-mile land border. However, Vietnam, as well as Laos and Cambodia, are scarcely in position to challenge their northern neighbor's strategic pressures, and China's claims to South China Sea waters are likely to persist and eventually prevail.

Is China a world power or is it merely a regional power whose strategic weight has been inflated by some Western leaders and scholars? The general consensus is that China is indisputably a world power. Indeed, many feel that it has become the foremost rival of the United States, given its economic and technological growth. Others question its capacity to achieve world status, describing it as a second-rank, middle power and pointing to the obsolescence of its navy and air force. They suggest that the inflation of Chinese military capacities is irresponsible and politically dangerous and could lead to an unwarranted revival of the Cold War or, conversely, overindulgence of Beijing.[17]

From a geostrategic point of view, China's unique regional reach to so many important parts of the world gives it the potential to become a strong global power. To dismiss this possibility because it currently lacks the sophisticated weaponry of the United States is to ignore Beijing's direct geographical impact upon so much of the world. China has land boundaries with fourteen countries and sea borders with three others—South Korea, Japan, and the Philippines—as well as with Taiwan. Altogether, the seventeen neighbors have a combined population of nearly two billion. Adding China's own populace brings the total to well over three billion, or slightly more than half of the people of the world, who are affected by the actions of Beijing.

In geospatial terms, the East Asian geostrategic realm that is led by China impinges upon the Heartlandic geostrategic realm, the Maritime Realm's Asia-Pacific Rim, the South Asian geopolitical region, and the Central Asian arena. This is a position of centrality that, in some ways, competes with the centrality of Russia. The latter has eleven landward neighbors and four with which it shares intermediate water or frozen waste spaces (Iran, Japan, the United States, and Canada). Heartlandic Russia lies between the Maritime Realm to its west, north, and east (where it faces Maritime Europe, North America, and Offshore Asia, respectively), East Asia to its southeast, and Central Asia to its south. The United States centrality is more limited. It holds an intermediate position within the Maritime Realm between Maritime Europe and the Asia-Pacific Rim, while overlooking Middle America to its south. Surely a Chinese paradigm based on global centrality has as much of a spatial claim as those of its two major competitors.

Notwithstanding its economic weakness, when measured in terms of low per capita income and low industrial productivity per worker, its limited nuclear arsenal, and its deficiencies in military technology, China is now in a position to exercise military and political pressure on the greater part of Eurasia. Its past sales of ballistic technology to Pakistan and Iran reflect its strategic interests in the Asian lands to its southwest, as such sales to North Korea reflect Chinese interests to the northeast. In addition, China's claims to Taiwan and its location on the East and South China Seas make China a nearest neighbor and strategic threat to the Asia-Pacific Rim. China's inability to compete militarily with the United States in Africa, Latin America, and Europe does not diminish its world-power status.

At present, China depends increasingly upon imports of military equipment and the purchase of avionics technology from Russia and other countries to modernize its armed forces. Within the next quarter-century, however, China is likely to acquire independent military armament capacities. In the interim, its power is felt by many of its neighbors, which are in geographical settings that are more removed from the security umbrella of the U.S. superpower.

The end of the Cold War has seen efforts by both Moscow and Washington to strike up strategic alliances with China. Indeed, both President Boris Yeltsin and President Bill Clinton agreed with President Jiang Zemin to develop separate "strategic partnerships." In this burst of enthusiasm for partnerships, Prime Minister Yevgeny Primakov of Russia went so far as to advocate a Russian-Chinese-Indian strategic triangle (as distinct from the previously mentioned Orient Policy, which would have linked North Korea, Vietnam, and India to Russia). The goal of such a triangular relationship would be to maintain Russia's Cold War alliance with India while rebuilding its strategic ties with China. The prospects for such a triangular partnership, however, are dim now that the Cold War is over. The United States and India have been drawn closer in recent years. The need for Washington to aid Pakistan militarily and economically will lose its strategic rationale when the war in Afghanistan has ended. At that time, given India's growing strength in South Asia and the Indian Ocean, the United States is likely to seek a strategic alliance with India.

Although China and India normalized their relationships in 1993 and opened cross-border trade six years later, the outstanding territorial disputes between them persist. In addition, an expanding Chinese influence in Myanmar adds to India's suspicions. Beijing has assisted the Burmese junta in developing its naval ports on the Andaman coast at the eastern edge of the Bay of Bengal. It has also been reported to have been allowed to establish an electronic listening post on Burma's Coco Island, just north of India's Andaman Islands. The Indian navy has reacted by strengthening its Andaman Island naval base. A Chinese threat to New Delhi's dominance of the Indian Ocean is bound to add further strain to the Sino-Indian relationship.

Until the issues of the status of Taiwan and the possible reunification of Korea are settled, a strategic partnership between the United States and China represents essentially a public relations slogan designed by Washington to justify its desire for increased trade links with Beijing, now its largest source of imports. Indeed, it would be more accurate for American leadership to speak of economic, not strategic, partnership.

Japan, the anchor of U.S. geostrategic policy in the Western Pacific, has yet to sort out its long-range strategic relations with China, a major trading partner. Tokyo values its own security arrangement with the United States. However, one of its concerns is that U.S. sales of sophisticated weapons systems to Taiwan could raise the level of Chinese antagonism toward Japan, which provides the major bases for U.S. forces in the Pacific.

Japan's strategic relationship with China also may be affected by events that unfold within the Korean Peninsula. Should the status quo change and the two Koreas become unified, Korea might shift toward neutrality and the American military screen in South Korea would be eliminated. Given these uncertainties, Washington would do well to recall that no strategic partnership between China and the United States would offer America geopolitical security in the western Pacific unless it were to safeguard the strategic interests of Japan.

The boundary between the East Asian Realm and the Maritime Realm's Asia-Pacific Rim region has become a source of renewed tensions with the rise of China as an economic and military power. The buildup of Chinese forces along the Strait of Taiwan was followed by the U.S. "spy-plane" incident of April 2001 and the detention of the crew of the American plane. Irrespective of the specific circumstances that led to the collision of the Chinese jet fighter with the U.S. aircraft, and its subsequent landing in Hainan, the incident reflects China's much broader strategic objective of gaining control over the air and waters of its two-hundred-mile economic exclusion zone.

Washington cannot accept any limitation on its use of international waters to oversee Chinese military activities and communications. Without this surveillance, the U.S. shield over Taiwan would be greatly weakened, as would the defenses of South Korea and Japan. In addition, such limitation could be used as a precedent to foreclose the airspace and waters around the Paracel Islands, two hundred miles off the coast of Hainan, to Vietnam and Taiwan, which also lay claim to them.

The spy-plane incident put the spotlight on two realities in the relationship between China and the United States. The first is the strategic vulnerability to American air and sea power of the coastal regions containing China's most important economic centers. The second is the economic interdependence of the two countries, which acted as a restraint on the behavior of both during the crisis. China cannot afford to have U.S. sanctions imposed on trade and capital investment. The stake held by U.S. corporations in Chinese manufacturing operations is too large, and the thirst of U.S. consumers for low-cost imports too great, for the United States to impose trade sanctions—a weapon of last resort.

Mutual economic vulnerability may be as powerful a balancing force as mutual strategic vulnerability. The strategic equilibrium that has developed between Washington and Moscow stems from mutual nuclear deterrence; the balance between Washington and Beijing has grown from their increasing economic interdependence.

A more likely scenario than a U.S.-China strategic partnership is the renewal of the former strategic alliance between Heartlandic Russia and China. Moscow's interest is in containing U.S. expansion into the Baltic countries and Ukraine via NATO and warding off Western geopolitical penetration of Central Asia through control of energy resources and pipelines. China's interest is in curbing the extension of U.S. power into the Southeast Asian mainland. Both China and Russia share the common goal of keeping a unified Korean Peninsula from becoming absorbed within the Asia-Pacific Rim and thus the Maritime Realm, thereby weakening their North Pacific positions. Together, therefore, the two neighboring Continental Asian powers have a stake in putting their decades of feuding behind them and seeking jointly to counterbalance the American superpower.

The fruits of the new strategic partnership are already evident. China's substantial purchase of Russian fighter jets, submarines, and other weapons has been accompanied by a border agreement. Nearly all of the twenty-three-hundred-mile boundary between the two countries, which was the site of conflicts in the 1960s, has been demarcated. Expanding trade, especially in oil, and the 1997 agreement between the two countries to settle all border disputes is recognition of this mutual interest. It reflects the perception in both regimes that they are in danger of being penetrated from various directions because of their vulnerability to American-led strategic pressures. For Russians, the threat is Western military and economic intrusion into its periphery. For China, the Maritime military threat is exacerbated by the economic muscle of its Asia-Pacific Rim neighbors and the growing dependence of its own industrial base upon Western capital and trade.

The proposed U.S. NMD shield has served to emphasize the common strategic interests of Moscow and Beijing. Russia is strongly opposed to such a system, although the thousands of Russian missiles are a deterrent against any American nuclear attack. China is even more opposed to NMD because it fears the deployment of the sensors, missiles, and yet-to-be-developed weapons designed to destroy a small number of incoming missiles. The Chinese arsenal has only a small number of land-based missiles, and these could be overwhelmed by the thousands of U.S. warheads. Placing the shield in the Aleutian Islands, as proposed, has been rationalized as a means of protecting the continental United States against a North Korean nuclear missile. However, the Chinese suspect that it would also be used to protect Taiwan.

A likely consequence of this proposed U.S. strategy to contain North Korea would be to push China to expand its own nuclear capacity. This would be a far more destabilizing element than the threatened North Korean arms development. China and Russia are better positioned to restrain North Korea than would be the American NMD. They could guarantee North Korean security and, together with South Korea, help it to redevelop its agricultural and industrial base. There is no guarantee that this would alter North Korea's behavior, but since it would take several years to put the NMD in place, there would be time to test North Korea's intentions.

A similar rationale of behavior modification through economic development was offered by the Clinton administration when the U.S. Congress passed the China trade bill in 2000—that not only is trade good for both countries, but that it would soften China's behavior regarding human rights and cause it to act with greater restraint vis-à-vis unification with Taiwan. Time will tell.

Any look into China's geopolitical future should take into account the possibility that its entry into the global market, and attendant economic and social influences and strains, might undermine Chinese communism. What could follow? Highly unlikely would be a smooth transition to a cohesive, market-oriented, liberal democratic state. This did not take place in the wake of the collapse of the Soviet Union. It is even less likely to happen in China, where the contradictory outlooks of the closed, heavily rural, and decaying industrial Continental North and Interior and the more open Maritime south and central coasts would no longer be reconciled by a strong, central government.

While it is not likely that the country would succumb to the warlordism of the past, some sections of China might well strike out for their independence. This course would be particularly likely for Xinjiang, where Uighur separatism has never been eliminated, and also for Tibet. Taiwan might renounce the "One China" concept and reinforce its current position as an integral part of the Asia-Pacific Rim and the community of world nations. However, the more likely scenario is that Taiwan would become a gateway quasi-state linked to China through a "Hong Kong plus" formula. The massive outsourcing of Taiwanese manufacturing to the "Golden Coast" during the 1990s, accompanied by large-scale capital flows and the technical advice of skilled Taiwanese engineers, has led to the rapid merging of the high-tech economies of the two countries. Since political institutions tend to adjust to economic realities, a political compromise will probably be struck by the two parties. Such a compromise is likely to fall short of Taiwan's total formal independence, but would enable the island to fulfill its potential as a powerful Gateway linking China to the Asia-Pacific Rim and the Maritime Realm as a whole. A "Hong Kong plus" formula is also more feasible than independence for the "Golden Coast," because of its vulnerability to Beijing's overwhelming military force and the absence of geographical barriers to shield the coastal regions from the North.

In this circumstance, a loose federation would probably be necessary to hold Inner Mongolia and central and northern Manchuria within the remainder of China. The gap between the rest of the Continental North and the South would undermine the chances for cohesion for decades. Within such a scenario, revolution and counterrevolution might continue to keep the country in turmoil.

The direction Beijing takes depends on whether it can move successfully toward change in an evolutionary fashion. Economic improvements that continue to benefit only the Maritime portions of China may well result in internal stresses that lead to political fragmentation. Foreign efforts to effect rapid political reform by using economic leverage could also lead to unforeseen consequences, and even chaos, if they come without alleviating the plight of the rural masses of the country.

Notes

1. William L. Tung, *China and the Foreign Powers* (Dobbs Ferry, N.Y.: Oceana, 1970), 69–89.

2. Tung, *China and the Foreign Powers*, 69–89.

3. Erik Ekholm, "After Fifty Years, China Youth Remain Mao's Pioneers," *New York Times,* 26 September, 1999, A12.

4. Oliver Chou, "Navy Boss Outlines Force of the Future," *South China Morning Post,* 22 April 1999.

5. Anthony Davis, "Blue Water Ambitions," *Asia Week* 26, no. 11 (24 March 2000): 1.

6. "Myanmar's Where the Indian and Chinese Navies Meet," *Stratfor Commentary*, 27 January 2000.

7. Central Intelligence Agency, *The World Factbook 2000* (Washington, D.C.: Gov/CIA Publications, 2000), 6.

8. "China Survey," *Economist,* 8 April 2000, 13.

9. C. P. Fitzgerald, The Chinese View of Their Place in the World (London: Oxford University Press, 1964), 68–72; Andrew L. March, *The Idea of China* (New York: Praeger, 1974), 7–22; Benjamin I. Schwartz, "The Maoist Image of World Order," in *Image and Reality in World Politics,* ed. John C. Farrell and Asa P. Smith (New York: Columbia University Press, 1968), 92–102; Derwent Whittlesey, "The Horizon of Geography," *Annals of the Association of American Geographer,* 35, no. 1 (March 1945): 1–36.

10. Norton Ginsburg, "On the Chinese Perception of World Order," in *China's Policies in Asia and America's Alternatives*, ed. Tang Tsou (Chicago: University of Chicago Press, 1968), 73–96.

11. Lin Pao, Excerpts from "Peking Declaration Urging 'People's War' to Destroy U.S.," *New York Times,* 4 September 1965, 2.

12. "Go West Young Han," *Economist,* 23 December 2000, 45–46.

13. Alan J. Day, ed. *Border and Territorial Disputes* (Harlow, England: Longmans, 1982), 252–57.

14. Day, *Border and Territorial Disputes,* 276–80.

15. Nayan Chanda, "Cam Ranh Bay Manoeuvres," *FEER,* 28 December 2000, 4 January 2000.

16. Gerald Segal, "Does China Matter?" *Foreign Affairs* 78, no. 5 (June 1999): 24–36.

17. Patrick E. Tyler, "The China Threat, Some Experts Insist, Is Overrated," *International Herald Tribune,* 16 February 1999, 2.

CHAPTER 9

The Asia-Pacific Rim

The Asia-Pacific Rim, or Asia-Pacifica, is the third major geopolitical power center of the Maritime Realm. This region extends from South Korea, Japan, and Taiwan (at least for the present) through the Philippines, Singapore, Malaysia, Thailand, Indonesia, East Timor, and Papua New Guinea to Australia and New Zealand. Thus it embraces the string of island states of Offshore Asia that border the China Seas and reach into the southwest Pacific and the peninsular lands that adjoin this string on both its northern and southwestern ends. The countries of the Indochinese peninsula—Vietnam, Laos, and Cambodia—plus North Korea are excluded from the region on the grounds that they lie within China's geostrategic orbit.

The overriding geopolitical characteristic of Asia-Pacifica is its Maritimity. Its island and peninsular states are well positioned to engage in international trade because of the comparative advantages of sea transportation over movement of goods by land. The strategic downside of this dependence upon trade is that sea lanes are vulnerable to interdiction, especially since so much of the traffic that moves within the region and to and from other parts of the world must pass through a substantial number of straits and narrow seas. The rim depends heavily upon U.S. naval and air power to secure these shipping lanes.

Another aspect of this Maritimity is the region's climatic patterns. They grade southward from the humid, moderate climates of the continental, temperate and subtropical zones of the northern parts, to the tropical, rainy areas straddling the equator. The zones then reverse to Australia's humid subtropical east and southwest coasts and New Zealand's humid temperate clime. Only Australia's interior is desert and semi-arid. The initial stimulus for the early dense settlement of much of the region was the favorable conditions for agriculture within its temperate and tropical zones. Modern colonial economic development was based on significant trade in plantation and forest products.

In preliterate and ancient times, the region's narrow and shallow seas facilitated the diffusion of races, languages, religion, crops, cultures, and technologies from mainland Asia. Colonizing European powers were able to use their naval superiority to secure the territories that they ruled and to control access to them. Today's independent states continue to use the seas to their advantage through control of coastal waters and airspace. In effect, the waters on the one hand have become isolating screens behind which diverse national cultures have been able to strengthen themselves, while on the other they connect the various countries by trade.

A most striking example of the advantage of naval and air power over land power has been the case of Taiwan. Taiwan occupies the island of Jinmen (Quemoy), which is only four miles from China's coastal port of Xiamen (Amoy). Nevertheless, China has been unwilling to risk deployment of its massive military manpower across this water to seize that island from Taiwan. Likewise, it has not been able to invade Mazu (Matsu), which lies immediately off the coast from Fuzhou (Foochow), let alone to sweep across the ninety-mile-wide Taiwan Strait to "liberate" Taiwan.

Beijing was able to exploit its manpower advantages to help the North Koreans fight the U.S. superpower and its allies to a standstill in the Korean War and to use its land connections to Vietnam to contribute substantially to the U.S. defeat in the Vietnam War. However, it could not cope with American naval and air superiority within the waters of its own geographical backyard when it tried to seize the Chinese Nationalist-held islands. The recent buildup of Chinese air, naval, and missile forces along the Taiwan Strait, and the efforts of Taipei to counter this by purchasing state-of-the-art destroyers and antimissile radar from the United States, represent a new phase in the naval conflict.

Evolution of the Region

The Asia-Pacific Rim geopolitical region has emerged during the past half century, having overcome the effects of the Japanese occupation, the devastation of World War II bombing, and postwar Communist rebellions supported by the USSR and China. Asia-Pacifica lacks the politically integrative structures, and concomitant economic and social institutions, that have forged Maritime European unity. However, the region has attained a high degree of integration through its intraregional economic ties and security framework backed by U.S. military power. Its geopolitical unity has been achieved through a community of interests and partnerships. While Japan is clearly the dominant core of the rim, the political and geographic framework that has evolved is a far cry from the "Co-Prosperity Sphere" that Tokyo imposed upon conquered nations during the 1930s and 1940s. At that time, political unity was enforced by arms and the greatest part of the region was the East Asian mainland.

The seeds of modern Pan-Asianism were planted after the Meiji restoration of 1868. Japanese imperialists at that time promoted the spiritual bond of Asian brotherhood as their rationale for leading a unified Asia that would be morally and culturally superior to the materialistic world of the West. Panregionalism envisaged a three- or fourfold division of the world, based upon great or panregions arranged along a north-south axis and organized around a dominant northern core. Karl Haushofer, the father of German *geopolitik*, knew Japan well. He had served as Germany's military observer in Japan from 1908 to 1910 and wrote his Ph.D. thesis on the geographic foundations of Japanese power. He saw Japan as the core of the Pan–East Asia region, with its industrial and military center drawing food and raw materials from the resources of the periphery in exchange for finished goods.

The region that he anticipated included not only Japan, Southeast Asia, and Australia, but also China and East Siberia. While Haushofer viewed Japan as the leader, he also believed that China, and possibly Russia, had to be embraced as its partners. The influence of Haushofer and his school of *geopolitik* on Japanese military and industrial leaders was profound, and many of the basic ideas of German geopolitics were incorporated within

Japanese politics. Thus, Tokyo's concept of a "Greater Asia Co-Prosperity Sphere" was the outcome of Japanese studies of the German "Great Space Economy."[1]

The Japanese failed, however, to heed Haushofer's warning not to be drawn into war with China, but rather to seek a partnership with it. Tokyo's taste for territorial spoils had been whetted by its seizure of Formosa (Taiwan) and the Pescadores Islands from China after the Sino-Japanese War of 1894–95. Following Japan's victory in the Russo-Japanese War (1904–05), during which China allied itself with Russia, Japan created a protectorate in Korea, which it formally annexed five years later. It also gained economic control over southern Manchuria in 1905, built the southern Manchurian Railroad, and developed the economy of the region. However, Chinese warlords continued to exercise military control over the province, a situation ultimately unacceptable to the Japanese militants. They invaded the province in 1931, occupied it, and established the puppet state of Manchukuo the following year. Through this action, the Japanese eliminated Russian influence from northern Manchuria, building up the province as a base for initiating the second Sino-Japanese War in 1937, during which they overran northern and east coastal China during the next three years.

After the fall of France in 1940, the Japanese moved southward to conquer Vietnam, where they allowed Vichy France to maintain a puppet administration until 1945. This was the next step in the creation of the Greater East Asia Co-Prosperity Sphere. Following the Japanese attacks upon Pearl Harbor and Singapore, which marked Tokyo's entry into World War II, their troops quickly overran Southeast Asia, from Burma, the Malay Peninsula, and Singapore to the Philippines, Indonesia, and the islands of the western Pacific.

Thailand was spared an invasion because it was already a satellite of Japan. The military regime that seized power in Bangkok in 1938 turned to Japan for support in advancing Thai territorial claims in Cambodia, Laos, northern Malaya, and the Shan states of northeastern Burma.

The Thai alliance was strategically important to Tokyo, for it permitted the stationing of Japanese military forces at bases on the eastern and southern Thai coasts. These bases became launching sites for the invasions of the Malay Peninsula and the Dutch East Indies that began on December 8, 1941, when the Thai government permitted Japanese forces to enter their country. The oil resources of the Indies were especially crucial to the Japanese, whose U.S. supply had been cut off by Washington's embargo. That embargo, as well as the neutrality treaty signed with the Soviet Union, were major factors behind the attacks upon Pearl Harbor and Singapore, which initiated the war in the Pacific.

By the 1930s Australia had become an important trading partner of Japan—a valuable source of wool, wheat, and pig iron in return for finished goods. While Australia had long been included in Tokyo's Pan-Asian plans, the Japanese failed to invade Australia during World War II. They did manage to bomb and shell Darwin in the far north on the Timor Sea, the industrialized port city of Newcastle northeast of Sydney, and Port Jackson (Sydney Harbor). However, their plans to invade the island continent were dashed by the 1942 battle of the Coral Sea, in which U.S. naval and air power defeated the Japanese fleet, stopping its southward advance.

The Japanese envisioned the Co-Prosperity Sphere fashioned by their conquests as an East Asian mercantile system, within which their *zaibatsu*, the great trading enterprises, were to play pivotal roles. Japan's World War II defeat, and its devastation from U.S. bombing and the atom bombs that were dropped on Hiroshima and Nagasaki, put a conclusive end to the Japanese dream of creating such a sphere. Replacing this framework was the geopolitical region that first emerged as Offshore Asia. With the end of the Vietnam War, Southeast Asia's Shatterbelt status came to an end. The Indochinese peninsula now clearly lay within the Eurasian Continental framework, while the peninsular and insular parts of Southeast Asia (Thailand, Malaysia, Singapore, and Indonesia) just as clearly belonged to what now could be called the Asia-Pacific Rim region.

LINKING AUSTRALIA TO ASIA-PACIFICA

When the Japanese threat to Australian security became overwhelming, Australia's strategic fate (and that of New Zealand) became inextricably linked to the island-peninsular region to its north. Until then, Australians had accepted the traditional British view of Australia as the "end of the line," as belonging to the peripheral portion of South Asia. In such a view, Australia was located on the "farther" side of Asia and part of "Further India" or the "Farther East."

The threatened invasion of their country in World War II and the United Kingdom's divestiture of its South Asian empire gave Australians a new perspective on their place in the world. Offshore Asia and peninsular Southeast Asia had become meaningful neighbors.

The shift in Australia's geopolitical orientation brought about a change in its attitude toward immigration. Immediately after World War II, large numbers of Eastern Europeans were admitted, but Canberra continued to practice an Asian exclusion policy that was discordant with the new geopolitical realities. This policy was officially discarded in 1973. By 1998 about 40 percent of all immigrants to Australia had been born in Asia, as the total number of Asians exceeded 1.3 million, or 7 percent of the population.

The new orientation was further reflected in international trade. Whereas before the 1950s half of Australia's imports and exports went to Britain, and much of the remainder went to other European countries and the United States, the main flow shifted to the rest of the Asia-Pacific Rim. A major factor in the redirection was the elimination of the imperial trade system, which accorded tariff preferences to the territories of the British Empire, and then to the members of the Commonwealth, such as Australia. The elimination of this system was a condition for the admission of Britain to the European Community in 1973—the same year that Australia opened its gates to Asian immigrants.[2] Today the major share of Australia's international trade—over half of its imports and three-quarters of its exports—is with other Asia-Pacific members. This is a powerful illustration of the importance of its regional links.

Politically, Australia's ties with the United Kingdom were not formally severed until 1986, when Britain passed the Australia Act, which terminated the power of the United Kingdom's Parliament to legislate for Australia. However, Canberra's loss of its British security umbrella occurred much earlier. In 1951 the Australia, New Zealand, United States (ANZUS) Treaty was concluded as a substitute for the vanishing British military presence. This pact committed Australia and New Zealand to serving as forward bases to support U.S. strategic interests in the Pacific and Indian Oceans, with the focus on securing Japan's sea lanes.[3]

Three years later, Australia became increasingly involved in military ties with the countries to its north. Together with three of its Pacific Rim neighbors—Thailand, the Philippines, and New Zealand—Canberra joined the United States, Britain, France, and Pakistan in the Southeast Asia Treaty Organization (SEATO). The purpose of SEATO was to oppose the advance of communism in Vietnam and other parts of Southeast Asia, especially Indonesia and Malaysia. The organization became redundant, as the Communist threat weakened in Indonesia with the 1966 massacre of hundreds of thousands of alleged Communists (many of whom were ethnic Chinese) and the ousting of pro-Chinese President Sukarno the following year. In addition, Communist rebellions were put down in the Philippines in the late 1960s and early 1970s. South Vietnam fell to the North Vietnamese in 1976 and SEATO was formally disbanded the following year.

The creation of another regional organization, the Association of Southeast Asian Nations (ASEAN), in 1967 did not directly involve Australia. However, the regional economic growth that ASEAN fostered provided considerable market opportunities for Australia. Another political mechanism that helped to bind Australia to its near north was UNTAC, which was established in 1991. This peacekeeping and civilian administration body included not only the five permanent members of the UN Security Council, but also Japan, Australia, Indonesia, and Thailand, in recognition of the important role that could be played by these regional states in helping to stabilize the Cambodian situation. When order was restored in the country and free elections were held in 1993, the Cambodians who had fled to Thailand as a result of Khmer Rouge actions began to return.

A REGION OF TRADING STATES

A quarter century ago the region that now embraces the Asia-Pacific Rim included only Offshore Asia. South Korea, Japan, Taiwan, the Philippines, Australia, and New Zealand were already closely linked by trade, by their military treaties with the United States, and by their common experiences in war. Southeast Asia, however, was a Shatterbelt, within which external powers—the United States, the Soviet Union, and China—exploited intraregional differences to further both Cold War and "hot" war aims.

Thailand, Malaysia, Singapore, and Indonesia began to see that their strategic interests lay within the Maritime Realm. Similarly, the Offshore Asian nations and their Western supporters came to the conclusion that these Southeast Asian nations were vital to Maritime geostrategic security, because they could assure control of the links between the Indian and Pacific Ocean. Moreover, by the mid-1970s one-third of the trade of Japan and Taiwan, and 15 percent of Australia's international trade, was already with Southeast Asia, and the potential for its increase was considerable.

Since then, the geopolitical status of Southeast Asia has fundamentally changed. Most of the Southeast Asian Shatterbelt has merged with Offshore Asia, as Russian influence has all but disappeared and China's strategic concerns have focused on relations with the former Indochinese countries. Australia and Japan have emerged as the northern and southern strategic cornerstones of the new Asia-Pacific Rim region. This flies in the face of geopolitical analyses offered by some scholars who discount Japan's regional power role within the western Pacific and hold that the fate of Southeast Asia and Australia rests exclusively with a U.S.-China accord.[4] This view underestimates the economic and political weight of Japan within the Rim. Asia-Pacifica is an integral part of the Maritime Realm. In a matter of but a few decades, the Rim has carved out a regional identity, the future of which rests to a considerable extent on the strength and prospects of its member states, rather than on outside powers.

As suggested at the beginning of this chapter, trade among the member states of Asia-Pacifica, and between them and other parts of the world, especially the United States, gives the region a distinct maritime stamp. Trade orientation can be expressed in various ways. Table 9.1 presents this orientation in terms of ratio of trade to national GDP, manufactured goods as a percent of total exports, foreign direct investments as a percentage of GDP, and trading partners. Unlike in other parts of the former colonial world or other Third World countries, which are also dependent upon trade, a high proportion of the Asia-Pacific Rim's exports are in manufactured goods and therefore possess a high value-added dimension. Since so much of this trade is intraregional, it serves as a very strong regional centripetal force.

The Chinese populations of several of the countries of the region have played a very important role in the region's industrial and commercial development and in its intrare-

Table 9.1   The Asia-Pacific Rim: A Region of Trading States

Country	Trade in Goods & Services (% of GDP)	Main Trading Partners	Manufactures as % of Merchandise Exports	Foreign Direct Investments (% of GDP)
Singapore	150	Japan, U.S., Malaysia	84	9.0
Malaysia	82	Japan, U.S., Singapore	76	5.2
South Korea	44	Japan, U.S., China, Germany	92	0.6
New Zealand	43	Australia, Japan, U.S.	29	9.0
Australia	33	Japan, U.S., U.K., N.Z.	29	2.3
Thailand	31	Japan, U.S., Singapore	71	2.4
Japan	25	U.S., China, So. Korea	95	0.1
Philippines	24	U.S., Japan, Singapore	45	1.5
Indonesia	16	Japan, U.S., Singapore, Germany	42	2.2
	Trade in Goods (% of GDP)			
Brunei	64	Japan, Thailand, Singapore, So. Korea	NA	NA
Taiwan	64	Japan, U.S., Singapore, EU	NA	NA
Papua New Guinea	32	Japan, Australia, U.S., Singapore	NA	NA

Sources: World Bank Atlas, 1999, 56-57; Central Intelligence Agency, *The World Factbook 2001* (Washington, D.C.: Gov/CIA Publications, 2001).

gional trade. Singapore has a large majority of Chinese (78 percent) and Malaysia a substantial number (30 percent). Elsewhere, the proportions drop to 14 percent in Thailand, 3 to 4 percent in Indonesia, and 2 percent in the Philippines. However, they provide a significant share of the wealth and market capitalization of their host countries. The large transnational conglomerates that are controlled by Chinese entrepreneurs are linked by informal networks that facilitate trade and capital investments among them.

Another characteristic of the region is its high proportion of urban population and the fact that so many of its member states have high- or medium-income levels. This is illustrated in table 9.2.

Tables 9.1 and 9.2 tell the extraordinary story of the economic progress of the region over the past half century from an underdeveloped, essentially colonial and shattered set of countries to the thriving economies of today. Maritime Europe also made a remarkable recovery during this period, but it was able to build on an advanced human and natural resource base. In addition, it called on unprecedented financial, technological, and political support from the United States, not only in restoring its economy but also in establishing innovative, regional political and economic institutions that have taken it to unprecedented levels of prosperity.

What is remarkable about Asia-Pacifica is that its recent development has not followed traditional colonial and neocolonial lines of economic complementarity, whereby the underdeveloped portions of the region provided the low value-added raw materials in exchange for the developed sector's high value-added finished goods. The tropical monsoonal areas do, indeed, possess such raw materials as rubber, timber, rice, sugar, palm oil, copra, petroleum, iron, chrome, and manganese. And Japan and Australia do have advanced manufacturing bases, which draw on these resources to a considerable extent. But early on, the Japanese organized a complementary manufacturing strategy that built upon the market potential as well as the large, cheap labor supply, of the rest of the region, to diffuse man-

Table 9.2   Asia-Pacific Rim Population and Income

Country	Pop. (millions)	Urban Pop. (%)	Pop. per sq. mile	GDP ($billion)	GDP per capita ($thousand)
Australia	19	85	63	446	23.2
Brunei*	0.34	70	150	6	17.6
Indonesia*	228	36	303	654	2.9
Japan	127	78	868	3,150	24.9
Malaysia*	22	54	173	224	10.3
New Zealand	3.9	86	38	68	17.7
Papua New Guinea*	5.0	16	28	12	2.5
Philippines*	83	55	713	310	3.8
Singapore*	4.3	100	17,480	85	26.5
South Korea	48	83	1,260	764	16.1
Taiwan	22	71	1,610	386	17.4
Thailand*	62	20	312	413	6.7

Note: East Timor is excluded from the table because of its marginal status as an independent state.

* Members of ASEAN (other ASEAN states are Cambodia, Laos, and Vietnam, which belong to the East Asia Realm.)

Sources: Rand McNally, "World Gazetteer: Profiles of Countries and Places," World Facts and Maps, 2000 Millennium Edition, 70–224 (Skokie, Ill.: Rand McNally, 2000); Central Intelligence Agency, The World Factbook 2001 (Washington, D.C.: Gov/CIA Publications, 2001).

ufacturing abroad. Japanese multinational auto companies established factories that built components in various countries, such as engines in Thailand and batteries in Indonesia. Computer companies outsourced electrical components to Singapore and assembled fax machines and microcomputers in Malaysia. The South Korean steel, semiconductor, and automotive industries gained their start by depending upon Japan for technology and parts. Together with Japan, they created shipping cartels that built three-quarters of the world's ships during this period. Today, Japan ranks second only to Greece in its ownership of merchant fleets, while South Korea is the eighth leading owner.

Japan was not alone in pursuing this complementary manufacturing strategy within the region. U.S. and European companies did so also. Dutch and British oil interests built refineries in Singapore based on petroleum from nearby Indonesia, while Singapore's shipbuilding industry purchased steel from South Korea. In South Korea, much of the textile, apparel, shoe, and later the electronics industries were developed by the outsourcing of production from the United States and Japan. The same was the case for Taiwan and, to a lesser extent, Thailand. Indonesia exports nearly half of the world's hardwood, but also engages in wood processing and a variety of outsourced computer products.

The Philippines, with a large, technologically literate labor pool, has become one of the fastest-growing importers of high-tech parts from the United States, as well as one of the fastest-growing exporters of high-tech goods to the United States. Philippine specialties include the assembly of computer hardware and the development of software. The progression has been from the subcontracting of parts and finished products by American and Japanese multinational firms to the creation of Internet ventures and global customer-support services.

The Japanese and Australian economies remain the strongest in the region and Japan continues to run trade surpluses with its neighbors. However, although it exports machinery, motor vehicles, and consumer electronics, and imports most of its raw materials, Japan also imports manufactured goods. Australia, with the most balanced of the region's economies, is an exporter of wheat, wool, coal and ores, machinery, and transportation equipment, but it also imports these last two items, as well as telecommunications products and computers. Japan is particularly interested in expanding its trade with Australia, New Zealand, South Korea, and Singapore through free trade agreements with these countries.

This adds up to a region of increasingly balanced exchange, powered by the great financial centers of Tokyo and Singapore. The regional trend is for the most advanced countries to shift more and more of their manufacturing abroad and concentrate on the service aspects of their economies, such as Tokyo's focus on telecommunications, software development, and financial services. Singapore reexports half of what the country imports.

Political Stability and Instability

A geopolitical region is more than an economic or strategic unit. Its character is also defined by the political conditions that prevail among its constituent parts. In this regard, the Asia-Pacific Rim is divided between politically stable states and states plagued by instability.

POLITICALLY STABLE COUNTRIES

Japan and Australia, the regional anchors, are highly stable politically, as is New Zealand. Malaysia has prospered within an atmosphere of political calm, as its ruling coalition, dominated by Malays with the support of Chinese and Indian parties, has provided a framework for ethnic harmony. This is despite long-standing tensions between the Malay Muslim (60 percent of the population), Chinese (30 percent), and South Asian (10 percent) communities. Singapore has enjoyed political stability since its split from the Federation of Malaysia in 1965. It has flourished economically within an authoritarian political environment, becoming a world leader in high-technology manufacturing.

South Korea and Taiwan

South Korea and Taiwan have also benefited from internal political stability, even as their relations with their Communist neighbors have kept both countries in states of continuing international tension. Seoul responded to its financial crisis of 1997–98 by electing a reform government that has not only guided economic recovery, but has also succeeded in reducing frictions with North Korea.

Taiwan, one of the great economic successes of modern times, has matured politically. Its new generation of native Taiwanese leaders has thrown off the lengthy rule of the authoritarian Guomindang (Nationalist Party) of the mainlanders to establish a democracy. The current government, led by the Independence Party, is taking a cautious approach to its relations with China, not forcing the issue of independence. Patient negotiations could ultimately find a confederated formula that might satisfy mainland China's claim to sovereignty over the island nation, without Taiwan sacrificing most of its current freedom of action.

The Philippines and Thailand

The Philippines and Thailand are still beset by the political uncertainties of countries that have thrown off dictatorships and military rule. However, they have gained in political stability in two ways: they have weathered the transition to democracy under popularly elected (if not always corruption-free) governments and they have substantially quashed the insurgency movements that have menaced their countries. While the Philippines is still plagued by the small Abu Sayyaf terrorist band, this does not threaten the government's durability.

The Philippines have enjoyed political stability under three popularly elected governments, even though Joseph Estrada, who won the presidency in 1998, was driven from office by popular protest in the wake of a bribery scandal and impeachment proceedings. He was replaced by the vice president, in accordance with Filipino law.

A developing country by most standards, the economic growth of the Philippines, especially in the high-tech area, can be attributed to the political stability that has followed the overthrow in 1986 of the corrupt dictatorship of Ferdinand Marcos. A further factor was the removal of U.S. military bases in the early 1990s, which defused tensions between Manila and Washington and paved the way for a new and healthier era of cooperation between the two countries. The former U.S. Clark Air Force Base and Subic Bay Naval Base, to the west and north of Manila, respectively, have since been transformed into special economic zones, with seaport, international air, and manufacturing facilities. These zones complement the industrial and financial centers of Manila and areas to the south of the capital, where the country's high-tech electronics industry is rapidly growing.

Internal unrest continues to plague the country. However, the scale of violence is far lower than in the past, and on-and-off peace negotiations reflect the substantial weakening of guerrilla groups. The Communist (Huk) insurgency that dragged on for decades on Luzon suffered heavy casualties in the 1980s and has been virtually eliminated as the government waged a vigorous counterinsurgency campaign after 1992.

The Muslim rebellion in Mindanao may be entering a final phase. That conflict erupted in 1971. It had been precipitated in great measure by large-scale resettlement projects initiated by the Philippine government after World War II that brought tens of thousands of Christians from Luzon to Mindanao. By the early 1980s the island had become 80 percent Christian and the threatened Moro (Muslim) minority increased its separatist demands and the scope of the conflict. In response to a raging insurgency in 1990, Manila established an autonomous region for Muslim Mindanao that included the adjoining Sulu Archipelago, where islands of Basilan and Jolo have served as centers for the separatist movement. This was followed six years later by a peace with the main Moro group. Terrorist attacks and kidnappings by the small breakaway Abu Sayyaf faction continued to cause turmoil. Prompted by fears that al Qaeda members might move a base to the southern Philippines, and by the seizure of two American hostages, Washington accepted the government of the Philippines' request to send U.S. military forces to work with Filipino soldiers to destroy the terrorist band. While this operation may well succeed, by no means are the separatist goals of the Moros of the Sulu Archipelago, once home to the Sulu Sultanate, likely to be quenched. While quasi-statehood may bring a temporary respite to the conflict, in the long run the southern Philippines are likely to win independence.

In Thailand, too, there has been progress toward achieving political stability. The only Southeast Asian country to have escaped colonialism, Thailand emerged from its World War II alliance with Japan to become strongly allied with the United States during the Vietnam War. Until 1988 the internal political climate was highly unstable, as a succession of military rulers quashed efforts to maintain civilian government. In that year, the first prime minister not imposed by the army was popularly elected. The new system survived a bloody military revolt four years later. The country has since been governed by a series of multiparty coalitions in an unwieldy, but nevertheless democratic, system. Various attempts have been made to introduce economic reforms and to clean up widespread political corruption. The former have met with greater success than the latter.

An added factor in the country's march toward political stability has been the stamping out of a long-running "Free Thai" Communist rebellion based in the North that had derived support from bases in China and Vietnam. An Islamic separatist movement in southern Thailand, adjoining Malaysia, where Malaysian Communists had established bases for operations in that country, has also been largely suppressed.

With the closing of U.S. bases in Thailand after the Vietnam War, Bangkok has been able to improve its relations with both China and Vietnam, while remaining allied with the West. The changed relationships have been helpful in Bangkok's successful campaign against the Thai Communists. With peace along the Cambodian border, Thailand has recently begun to invest in tourism and gambling in Cambodia. Angkor Wat's temples have stimulated Thai investment in hotels close to that world-class archaeological site, while gambling resorts have been developed in towns directly across Cambodia's western boundary with Thailand, as well as on Cambodian islands in the Gulf of Thailand.

THE AREAS OF POLITICAL INSTABILITY

The glaring exceptions to the general trend toward political stability within the Asia-Pacific Rim are Indonesia, East Timor, and the small Pacific Island countries of Fiji and the Solomons.

Fiji

Fiji, the most populous of the South Pacific islands, with a population of 800,000, has been torn by ethnic tensions and army coups since its independence in 1970. Many of the inhabitants of the island had migrated there over the previous century as plantation workers from India. These migrants became a majority, until the unrest of the postindependence period prompted many of them to emigrate, leaving the native Fijians as the majority. The exodus was especially heavy after the adoption of the 1990 constitution, which favored native Fijian control of the government. The main struggle is carried on by the traditional Fijian tribal chiefs, who refuse to yield to the authority of elected governments when led by Indo-Fijians, and who resent the long-term land leases held by the Indian sugarcane farmers. Following one of the military coups that took place in 1987, Fiji was suspended from and then quit the British Commonwealth. The overthrow of a government in 2000 that had been led by Indo-Fijians who had been elected the previous year has been followed by continuing turmoil. This has exacerbated the country's economic difficulties stemming from a severe drop in the world price of sugarcane, Fiji's main export.

The Solomon Islands

The situation in the Solomon Islands has been equally turbulent. Since the islands gained their independence in 1978, militias representing immigrants from different island communities have fought with each other, keeping the country in chronic turmoil. Guadalcanal, the largest and most important of the islands in the archipelago, contains the town of Honiara, the capital. The country's economy, based essentially on the export of timber, is depressed.

The population of the islands, numbering 430,000, is mainly Melanesian, but is divided into over eighty different language and cultural groups. Conflicts over landownership and bias against immigrants from neighboring islands led to the overthrow of the government of the Solomons by immigrants to Guadalcanal from Malaita. The counteraction of Guadalcanal's ruling Istabu ethnic group forced twenty thousand Malaitans out of their homes. Australia then brokered a peace deal between the warring groups, but it has been totally ignored; continued strife led to the withdrawal of the peace monitors in March 2002. In both Fiji and the Solomons, the political chasm between traditional leadership and those seeking governmental reform shows little sign of narrowing.

Indonesia

Indonesia is widely recognized as an "Arc of Instability."[5] The Suharto regime (1966–98) clamped down on many of the separatist groups that had threatened to tear the archipelago state apart in the 1950s and '60s. However, Indonesian politics has been tranquil neither during that period nor since. The so-called "stability" during the Suharto era was based upon ruthless repression, corruption, and the self-enrichment of a small military and political elite.

The difficulty of forging a unified state out of the Dutch East Indies was manifest from the time that Indonesia proclaimed itself independent, shortly after the Japanese surrender in 1945. The highly centralized government in Java had to impose its sovereign control on a region extending for over three thousand miles, from the Indian Ocean into the western Pacific. The island republic includes over 13,600 islands (three thousand of which are inhabited), the most important culturally and economically being Java, Sumatra, and Bali. Moreover, it must fashion a nation out of over three hundred diverse ethnic groups and 350 indigenous languages. The national slogan may be "One Country, One People, One Language," but the reality is such overwhelming diversity that national unity remains highly elusive.

The core of the country consists of the very densely populated and developed islands of Java and Madura, whose linguistic stock is Deutero-Malay. They are ringed by the great arc of islands to their west, north, and east that are commonly referred to as the "Outer Islands."

Separatism is encouraged by the combination of the sheer size of the country (752,410 square miles), the poor transportation and communications, and the resentment against the Javanese, who constitute over half of Indonesia's 220 million people. The Ambonese Christians of the Moluccas (Malaku) Islands, once called the "Spice Islands," established the short-lived South Molucca Republic at the southwestern end of the archipelago. The republic was annexed by Indonesia in 1950, but remained in open rebellion until 1956.

In 1958 rebellions also broke out in Sumatra, Sulawesi (the Celebes), and Kalimantan (Borneo), where Islamic parties had strong bases and were in opposition to the secular state program of President Sukarno's Nationalist Party. The Sumatra rebellion was the most serious, fanned by general dislike of the Javanese and the fact that most of the country's exports came from Sumatra's petroleum and natural gas (Indonesia is the world's largest exporter of liquefied natural gas), palm oil, rubber, and tropical hardwoods, while most of the national expenditures went to Java. Although the rebellion ended three years later with reassertion of full authority by the government, the resentment has continued.

Aceh, the northernmost province of Sumatra, which had been a Muslim sultanate since the sixteenth century, has also been the scene of unrest and rebellion. The Dutch gained control in the nineteenth and twentieth centuries, but the Acehnese waged guerrilla war for decades. This devoutly Islamic province set up an independent Muslim state in 1848 that remained formally independent from the Dutch until 1903, and maintained a quasi-independent status until the Acehnese rebels were crushed at the end of the Sumatra war in 1961. The province was then designated a special territory with autonomy in religion, culture, and education, but it has remained a powder keg for Jakarta.

Sukarno, the country's first president and a leader of the independence movement against the Dutch, had created a "guided democracy" in 1956, as he skillfully balanced the competing interests of the army and the rapidly growing Communist Party. As convener of the Bandung Conference the previous year, he had gained a position of leadership within the Asian-African world with his anticolonial rhetoric and his call for Third World economic cooperation and independence from Western influences.

In the late 1950s Sukarno began to lean toward the powerful Indonesian Communist Party and toward China. He launched undeclared war against Malaysia in 1962 in opposition to the creation of the independent Malaysian Federation, which he considered a British imperialist subterfuge. Indonesian military raids were mounted against Malaysia's North Borneo territory from Kalimantan, the southern two-thirds of the island of Borneo and part of Indonesia. In addition, Jakarta withdrew from the United Nations in 1965, a gesture of opposition to Malaysia's having been granted a seat on the Security Council.

Indonesia's course of direction changed abruptly during that year, when an attempted Communist coup against the military was repulsed by the army, led by the pro-Western General Suharto. In this operation, half a million Chinese and Indonesians were killed and 200,000 were imprisoned on political grounds. Suharto, in effect, replaced Sukarno in that year, and two years later he became president, ushering in what many Western statesmen considered an era of stability.

In fact, while the highly centralized Jakarta regime kept the lid on most of the separatist movements during this period, it could not eliminate them. Although crushed in 1961, the Acehnese declared their independence once again in 1976 and established a government-in-exile as they continued their conflict. The South Moluccans, who had created a government-in-exile in 1966, persisted in their resistance.

Western (Dutch) New Guinea, which had been seized by Indonesian troops in 1962 and formally annexed in 1969, remained a source of unrest. The Free Papua movement rebels, who declared an independent state in 1961, have waged guerrilla warfare from their jungle refuges for four decades. The settlement of over sixty thousand Javanese families as part of Jakarta's voluntary resettlement program (known as "transmigration") further aggravated the situation in the province (first called West Irian and now Irian Jaya). The clashes were particularly intense in 1977 and 1984.

East Timor was also a focus of major unrest during the Suharto era. The Indonesians seized the former Portuguese colony in 1975, touching off a war with the Timorese that devastated much of the country. Washington gave unwavering support to General Suharto for this annexation, ignoring the fact that he used American arms in the invasion and subsequent slaughter of 200,000 East Timorese. The U.S. rationale was Indonesia's strategic importance in terms of its location, size, resources, and market potential. Nevertheless, the Timorese persisted in their drive for independence.

Although it had also originally supported Indonesia's annexation, by the 1990s Australia had changed its position owing to popular outrage over the abuses perpetrated by the Indonesians on the East Timorese. This outrage was coupled with the growing geopolitical importance of East Timor to Australia, based on the proximity of the territory—less than three hundred miles away—the oil and gas potential of the Timor Sea, and fear of a flood of Timorese refugees.

Suharto was ousted in 1998 and the president to follow him, B. J. Habibie, agreed in 1999 to a referendum in which the Timorese voted overwhelmingly for independence. This touched off an even worse bloodbath by progovernment militia and some Indonesian troops that ended with the intervention of Australian armed forces, but only after much of the territory had been destroyed and fifty thousand Timorese had been killed.

The events that centered around East Timor reflected contrasting strategic priorities for the United States and Australia. Unlike Australia, the United States did not have a primary geopolitical interest in East Timor. Its concern was the oil of Indonesia located far to the west, in Sumatra. As a result, Washington procrastinated while Australia took the lead in the intervention.

East Timor became independent in May 2002, making the transition from UN tutelage, as it rebuilds its devastated country and develops the frameworks of statehood. While most of the 800,000 Timorese are impoverished and depend largely on agriculture, their hopes for a brighter economic future rest on the proven oil and gas reserves that underlie the Timor Sea. This area, called the Timor Gap, lies midway between Australia and East Timor. Australia initially claimed half of the reserves based upon a boundary agreement it had made with Indonesia in 1972. The Timor Gap is less than four hundred miles wide, therefore drawing a boundary based upon an international standard of two hundred miles would result in overlapping claims. Australia recently agreed to accept the consequences of a median line boundary, placing 90 percent of the Timor Gap under East Timor's sovereignty. The fields will still be treated as a single, shared entity, without for the moment formally fixing the new boundary along this median line.[6]

The "stability" of the Suharto era was based on repression. Little wonder that, with the end of the military regime, many of the rebellions that had been repressed or brutally contained again rose to the surface. The strongest separatist movements remain in the northernmost and easternmost sections of the archipelago, far removed from Jakarta.

Aceh constitutes the most serious military challenge to Jakarta's rule and is the most important of the separatist provinces. Adjoining the northwestern entrance to the Strait of Malacca, the world's busiest shipping lane, it lies eleven hundred miles northwest of Jakarta. The population is five million (out of Sumatra's total of approximately forty million) in an area of twenty-one thousand square miles. Aceh accounts for half of Indonesia's oil and natural gas production and also produces coffee, pepper, rice, tobacco, rubber, and timber.

The Acehnese rebel movement is well supported financially and powerfully motivated by the history of the region as an independent principality. The Indonesian government and the military oppose Aceh's claims for independence, not only for economic reasons and on the grounds of the province's being an integral part of the national territory, but also for its strategic location along the Strait of Malacca. Fighting has recently disrupted production from onshore and offshore gas fields around Arun, where a liquefaction plant is located that ships its products to Japan and South Korea—a matter of concern, not only to the international companies operating in the area, but also to Indonesia and its international customers.

Indonesian insistence on holding onto the territory ignores the centuries of Acehnese history as an independent Muslim sultanate. Its economic importance to Jakarta, albeit substantial, needs to be considered within the broader economic context. Aceh's oil and gas exports contribute over $2.5 billion in revenues to the government, which is only 5 percent of Indonesia's total exports of $50 billion, and only 0.5 percent of the national GDP of nearly $1 trillion. The financial benefits that the province brings to the Jakarta government must be weighed against the costs of continuing conflict and the subjecting of Aceh to martial law.

In 1989 the Indonesian government initiated a campaign (which lasted for nine years) to crush the rebellion. This did not put an end to the separatist goals of the devout Acehnese Muslims and since 1998 the fighting has spread. The push for independence has accelerated since East Timor's successful referendum and subsequent freedom.

In July 2001 Indonesia's parliament passed a bill granting broad autonomy to Aceh. In addition to allowing the province to impose Muslim Sharia law, the bill called for granting it 70 percent of the royalties collected from its oil and natural gas fields. These favorable terms may encourage fundamentalist forces elsewhere in the country.

The focus for separatism in the remote South Moluccas (the islands of Ambon, Buru, and Seram) is Ambon, the provincial capital and largest town, which is fourteen hundred miles from Jakarta. The basis for the separatist drive is historic and religious, for half of the one million population of the South Moluccas (an area of 10,500 square miles) is Christian. Five hundred years ago, the Spice Islands were important because they were the only source of nutmeg and cloves; Dutch traders in these items brought Christianity to the islands. Today the islands are unimportant agriculturally and economically in general. The Christian-based separatist movement is not propelled by concerns of economic discrimination, but by fear of being swamped by Muslim immigrants who have settled on the island as part of the "transmigration" program. If a small, Christian-dominated state or quasi-state were to be established in these islands, which lie just to the west of Irian Jaya, it would have little negative strategic or economic consequence for Indonesia. Christian communities in Halmahera in the North Moluccas, where communal strife is widespread, might then choose to relocate to a new South Moluccan Republic.

Irian Jaya is the locus of the third major separatist conflict. This western half of the island of New Guinea has a population of under two million in a land area of 163,000 square miles. Most of the Irianese (also known as Papuans) are indigenous Melanesian tribesmen who live on subsistence farming in the jungle areas and have little in common with the Javanese.

These native Papuan rebels have continued a struggle for independence that first broke out four decades ago and has lasted into the post-Suharto era. Their resentment over loss of lands to timber interests that have overexploited the province's tropical hardwoods is intensified by their failure to derive any benefits from the large-scale copper, gold, and silver mining operations that are conducted by foreign corporations under lease from Jakarta, or from the island's oil deposits. One of the corporations operating in Irian Jaya is the single largest in Indonesia.

Recent offers of special autonomy by the Indonesian government have been spurned by the Free Papua Congress, which has declared independence for the country. The Papuans are armed with only bows and arrows, in contrast to the rebels in wealthy Aceh province, who are well equipped with modern weapons with which to conduct full-scale operations against the Indonesian army. Nevertheless, the Papuans have attacked and killed non-Papuan migrant settlers in the towns of Merauke and Fafak and have stepped up guerrilla warfare within the entire province. In response, Indonesia has poured troops into Irian Jaya's capital of Jayapura and cracked down heavily on the native population, committing widespread human rights abuses.

The West Papuans might well seek a federation with Papua New Guinea, the independent state that covers the eastern half of the island. With more than twice the population of Irian Jaya, Papua New Guinea is part of the British Commonwealth and has a relatively strong agricultural base, with important oil, mineral, and forestry resources. Under Australian rule for most of the twentieth century, until it gained independence in 1975, its major trading partner remains Australia. Its capital, Port Moresby, is located on the Coral Sea, three hundred miles from northeastern Australia and within the Australian security umbrella. While Papua New Guinea itself has had to deal with a separatist movement on its island of Bougainville, it might be receptive to a federation with Irian Jaya, which is also much closer to Australia than it is to most of Indonesia.

These three areas—Aceh, Irian Jaya, and the South Moluccas—are the main, but not the only, trouble spots in Indonesia. There is major unrest in Kalimantan, the southern 70 percent of the island of Borneo. (North Borneo contains the Malaysian states of Sabah and Sarawak and the independent, oil-rich Sultanate of Brunei.) Although sparsely populated by indigenous native tribes, Kalimantan is wealthy in oil, gold, natural gas, and valuable tropical hardwoods. A government transmigration program that brought tens of thousands of Madurese farmers to the island has provoked violence by the Dayaks in West Kalimantan against the Madurese, forcing many to flee back to their island of origin. The unrest has stimulated calls for independence, especially in East Kalimantan, where the oil resources are located. In addition, in the Indonesian waters, especially those north of Borneo leading to the South China Sea and the Pacific, piracy is rampant. Over 50 percent of the world incidence of piracy occurs in these waters or those of the Strait of Malacca.

Separatist movements also exist in Christian North Sulawesi (the northern Celebes) and in the Muslim-populated Ujung Pandang (Makasar), the capital and largest city of South Sulawesi. The latter, at the juncture of the Makasar Strait and the Flores Sea, was a historic center for the spice trade and is now a major distribution and transshipment point for goods from Europe and Asia. It had a long history as an independent sultanate, until it was conquered by the Dutch in the mid-seventeenth century.

Potentially the most serious breakaway threat besides those in Aceh, Irian Jaya, and the South Moluccas lies in the province of Riau in west-central Sumatra, opposite Singapore at the southeastern end of the Strait of Malacca. Riau's vast oil and gas reserves rival those of Aceh. These include the huge gas fields that lie under the territorial waters surrounding the province's Natuna Islands, in the shallow waters of the South China Sea. The islands are closer to the Malay Peninsula and eastern Malaysia (on the Island of Borneo) than to Riau's mainland, and proposals have been made to tap the West Natuna gas field by pipelines to Singapore and possibly the southern tip of the Malay Peninsula. Bintan Island in the Riau Archipelago has extensive bauxite and tin mines.

Riau is three hundred miles from Aceh and separated from it by the province of Sumatra Utara. The two rebellious territories have little in common except their mutual grievances at having their wealth siphoned off by Jakarta. It is unlikely that they would unify or federate. The great threat to Indonesia of Riau's separatist movement is that its success could trigger breakaway sentiments within the rest of Sumatra and lead to a repeat of the island's rebellion of 1958–61.

The Indonesian military has been adamant about retaining all of these rebellious regions. The argument used in the East Timor case—that freedom for the former Portuguese province would be the start of national disintegration—is much more compelling when applied to former Dutch territories, and particularly Aceh because of its economic importance. There is a less persuasive case to be made for holding on to remote Irian Jaya, which is over two thousand miles from Jakarta and populated by Melanesians. That region has been exploited by Indonesian military leaders for self-enrichment through control of coffee plantations and the awarding of mining concessions, but its economic importance to the country as a whole is minor.

Indonesia is a state waiting to implode. If it can confine this implosion to Aceh, the South Moluccas, and Irian Jaya, its prospects are favorable for surviving as a strong and influential power. However, should all of the island of Sumatra, with its wealth of natural resources, break away, those prospects would be considerably diminished.

Java is overpopulated, with a density of more than two thousand persons per square mile—one of the highest in the world. While agricultural productivity on the island has increased in recent years, and while most of Indonesia's industry is located within the island's centers of Jakarta, Surabaya, and Sandung, Java would be hard-pressed without access to part of Sumatra. Java's land area is one-tenth that of Sumatra, while the population is three times as large (Sumatra has a population of approximately forty million). Sumatra has been an outlet for modest transmigration from its crowded neighboring island, in addition to its value for its natural resources. The wealth of its oil, gas, minerals, timber, and crops produces the major share of Indonesia's GDP. Without Sumatra, Indonesia would be impoverished.

Transmigration cannot solve the problems of overcrowded Java, Madura, and Bali. During the Suharto-initiated program, six million settlers were transferred, mainly to the Outer Islands, but this did not compensate for the natural increase in population of the overcrowded islands. However, settlement in Sumatra has not stirred the ethnic passions that have torn the rest of the Outer Islands.

While loss of the three main separatist provinces, especially Aceh, would have substantial negative economic impact, the benefits of keeping these eight million people within the republic are outweighed by the military costs of fighting the rebellions and the diversion of political attention from some of the country's major economic problems. The challenge to Jakarta is to reorganize its political structure to satisfy the needs of the other Outer Islands. With approximately 60 percent of the population of the country, Java need not fear losing its leadership within a reconstituted state, provided that it changes its current hegemonic rule to one based upon partnership with federated units. Such a policy would be especially reassuring to Bali, with its unique Hindu/Buddhist culture and rituals that are akin to the ancient Javanese Hindu culture, and would make this small island of three million people a major attraction for international tourism.

An Indonesia at peace, and without its three breakaway territories, could become a genuine keystone of Asia-Pacifica and a fitting partner of Japan and Australia in the continued development of the region. It would remain the most populous Muslim country in the world and the fourth most populous national state. An Indonesia in continuing strife, with unwilling and unassimilable parts, will fall far short of realizing its national potential and will be a drag on prospects for regional unity.

Democracy alone is no guarantee of Indonesian stability. Although the Indonesian Parliament was democratically elected after the ouster of General Suharto in 1998, the country has suffered from considerable political instability. Within a three-year period (1998–2001), it had three presidents—B. J. Habibie, Abdurrahman Wahid, and Megawati Sukarnoputri. The latter replaced Wahid in July 2001, when he was ousted for incompetence by the People's Consultative Assembly, which consists of the Parliament plus military, regional, and special interest groups. President Sukarnoputri, a daughter of Indonesia's founding father, Sukarno, may have to depend heavily on the military for support in stabilizing the country, because of the fractious nature of Indonesian politics. A unity based upon the reemergence of powerful military influence is less likely to seek a compromise that will address the separatist issues.

Geopolitical Features

HISTORIC CORE

The Asia-Pacific Rim has no regional historic core, inasmuch as there was no single defining political event to initiate the process of regional geopolitical cohesion. National historic cores include Kyoto, Songdo, Sukothai, and Borobudur.

POLITICAL CAPITALS

The Asia-Pacific Rim has no single, formal political capital. Bangkok served as the capital of the now-defunct military alliance, SEATO. ASEAN, the current economic, social, and cultural alliance, is headquartered in Jakarta, while the seat of the Asia-Pacific Economic Cooperation Forum (APEC) is Singapore. However, neither ASEAN nor APEC is coterminus with the boundaries of Asia-Pacifica.

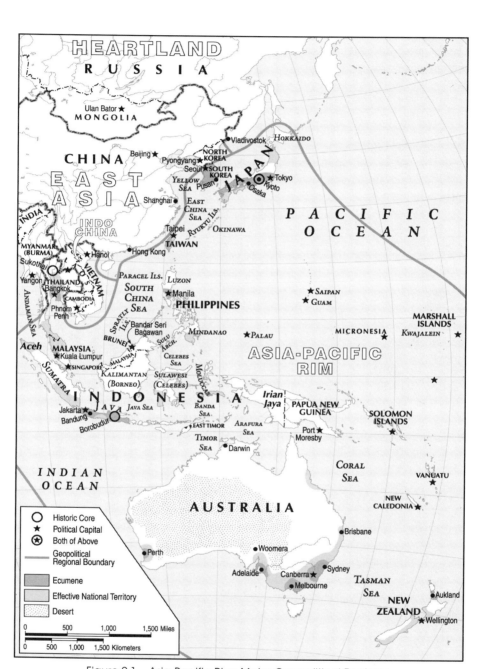

Figure 9.1   Asia-Pacific Rim: Major Geopolitical Features

The political capitals with the greatest political-economic impact upon Asia-Pacifica are Tokyo and Singapore. Tokyo represents the region's leading economic, political, and military power (although constitutionally the military can be applied only for self-defense). Singapore, Asia-Pacifica's leading international trading center, lies at the convergence of some of the world's major sea lanes between Europe and East Asia. It is a major center for international finance, vying with Tokyo in this respect, and is regional headquarters for many world-class, multinational corporations.

ECUMENE

The map of the Asia-Pacific Rim displays a geopolitical region of mostly island states, separated by narrow waters and broader seas, and nearby mainland peninsular countries. For most purposes, an ecumene is defined as a contiguous area of densest populations, transportation and communications networks, and clustering of economic activities. Contiguity can include narrow seas, as well as land, and in a water-oriented region, where seas are connectors rather than barriers, a chain of national ecumenes that link up with one another form a regional ecumene.

The most important of such ecumenes in Asia-Pacifica extends along the east coast of Japan's island of Honshu, from metropolitan Tokyo-Yokohama southward through Nagoya, Osaka, and Kobe, to Hiroshima and Shimonoseki at the southern tip of the island. From there, it is connected by a railroad tunnel and bridge southward across the very narrow Shimonoseki Strait to Kitakyushu, along the northwestern coast of Kyushu, to Fukuoko and Nagasaki, as well as into the north-central part of the island to Kurume and along its northeastern coast.

This water-connected national ecumene is the economic powerhouse of the Asia-Pacific Rim. It contains approximately 100 million, or 80 percent, of Japan's 127 million people and the vast majority of Japan's electronics, metallurgical, motor vehicle, ship, chemical, and textile production. Together with commerce, finance, and services, this concentration of population and economic activity has made the modern economy of Japan second only to that of the United States. Population densities within the ecumene range from ten thousand per square mile in the Kanto Plain (Tokyo-Yokohama) to three thousand per square mile in Nagoya.

The Honshu ecumene also extends westward across the 100-mile-wide Korean Strait into South Korea. This South Korean extension forms the other part of the regional ecumene. It is a major independent global economic force, formed in great measure by Japanese investment and supplemented by U.S. aid. The Japanese outsourcing of manufactures and export of capital investment and technology that followed the Korean War provided the spurt for what has become a varied and cutting-edge economy.

Most of South Korea's manufacturing takes place within its ecumene, which contains thirty million people, representing 60 percent of the nation's total of forty-eight million. Population densities of the ecumene average three thousand persons per square mile and continue to increase because so much of the eastern half of the peninsula is mountainous and unsuitable for the spread of population.

The Korean and Japanese ecumenes are linked at Pusan, Korea's second-largest city (population four million) and its largest port, which handles most of the country's foreign trade and serves as the gateway to Japan. The economic core area then runs inland through Taigu, the third-largest city, and on to Taijon on the west coast. It then follows the coast northward to Seoul, the capital and the most important urban and industrial center of the country, with a population of 10.3 million, over 20 percent of South Korea's total. The city, which is located on the broad plain of the Han, the largest river in the country, is backed by a rim of mountains. Historically, it served as a junction for routes connecting the entire peninsula, extending northward to Pyongyang, northeastward across the mountains to Wonsan (both now in North Korea), and southeastward across the peninsula to Pusan. As large as it is, Seoul has not been able to absorb all of the population that its industrial base supports, and a megalopolis has grown up within an approximately thirty-mile radius. Another ten million people now live in these outer centers, including the industrial port of Inchon, and the city of Suwon. Each of these two cities has a population of 2.5 million, and both are connected by subway to the capital.[7]

The Seoul megalopolis now both dominates the country and mirrors its remarkable industrial growth. Its motor vehicle, shipping, steel, chemical, machinery, and textile industries have pushed into the outer periphery of the region. Electronics, including semiconductors, computer and telecommunications equipment, and financial, insurance, and information services are more concentrated within the central city.

The South Korean ecumene extends to the northern suburbs of Seoul, only twenty miles from the DMZ, which marks the border between the two Koreas. While Seoul is now a frontier city, it does not stretch the imagination to envisage its eventual reemergence as the center of the peninsula—if not of a united Korea, then at least as a link between two Koreas that are open to economic and social interchange. The current distance between the northern edge of the South Korean ecumene and the North Korean economic core area, centering around Pyongyang-Nampo, is only sixty miles. This gap would be quickly filled by the spillover of Seoul's industries, should political conditions permit.

With political unity, one could expect the Korean ecumene eventually to expand northward from Pyongyang along the Yellow Sea to the Yalu River and link up with the industrial complexes of southern Manchuria. At such time, the vision could well be realized of Seoul as the hub of northeast Asia, linking Japan, Korea, and northeast China. A unified ecumene would then extend from Honshu and northern Kyushu across the Korean Strait and then along the full length of Korea's west coast. From there it would connect northwestward to Manchuria's Liaodong Peninsula and then into the industrial heart of Liaoning Province from Shenyang to Bohai Bay (Gulf of Chili) at the northern end of the Yellow Sea. Russia's South Maritime Territory, centering around Vladivostok and the Upper Ussuri Valley, could become an important outlier.

The Asia-Pacific Rim also includes several significant but scattered secondary ecumenes: Southwestern Malaysia-Singapore; the northwest coast of Java; the southeast coast of Australia, with one cluster extending from Newcastle through Sydney and Wollongong to Canberra and the other extending from Melbourne to Geelong; and western Taiwan.

Taiwan is the most important of these secondary core areas, extending from the northern tip of the island at Taipei along the length of the western coast through Taoyuan, Taichung, and Tainan, to the southernmost end at Gaoxiong. While Formosa, as the Japanese called Taiwan, had undergone modest modernization under the Japanese occupation (1905 until the end of World War II), it was still largely agricultural when the Chinese Nationalists gained control of the island in 1949, after being driven from the mainland. Most of the population during that period lived, as it still does, on the semitropical, broad, fertile west coast plain, since the central and eastern parts of the island are heavily forested hills and high mountains.

Over the next half century, massive U.S. aid spurred industrial development, mainly in light industry, producing consumer and food products. The development shifted to heavy industry at the start, and then to high-technology and services. Chemicals, steel, motor vehicles, pharmaceuticals, electronics, electrical goods, telecommunications, and transport equipment now are spread throughout the Taiwanese ecumene.

An example of Taiwan's economic strength is Hsinchu Science Park, located outside Taipei. Known as Silicon Valley East, this center is the core of the world's third-largest high-tech industry concentration and accounts for one-third of Taiwan's manufacturing exports and a large share of the world's computer production.[8]

An outstanding characteristic of Taiwan's industry is that small and medium-sized companies predominate. These companies are flexibly structured and have shown an aptitude for developing innovative technologies and organizational systems. When China's reforms in the 1990s provided an opening for Taiwanese investment, Taiwan was prepared. Within the past decade, thousands of businesses were set up in China, as well as in Southeast Asia. In a massive shift, many of Taiwan's labor-intensive manufacturing enterprises have been relocated to the Chinese ecumene in Hong Kong and the provinces of Guangdong and Fujian, just one hundred miles across the Taiwan Strait from Taiwan's ecumene. Recently, a considerable amount of Taiwan's high-tech computer hardware and software production has been outsourced to jointly owned Chinese coastal industries; up to one-third of all Chinese exports are now estimated to be made by Taiwanese-owned manufacturing firms.[9] The United States and Japan have long been the leading trade partners of Taiwan, although recently China has become Taipei's second most important export market.

There are profound geopolitical consequences of what is becoming, in effect, a merged Taiwan-China ecumene. As Taiwan's economic success becomes increasingly bound up with that of Maritime China, its role as a Gateway to the mainland increases. Despite serious political differences between the two countries, the reality of a merged economy may lead to a peaceful unification more quickly than many currently anticipate. This is despite occasional aggressive actions by mainland China toward Taiwan, and native Taiwanese leadership's continuing affirmation of the goal of independence.

EFFECTIVE REGIONAL TERRITORY

Lack of regional land contiguity mitigates against the delineation of a coherent Effective Regional Territory. National immigration laws also work against the possibility of settlement on a regional basis of less densely populated areas possessing favorable climatic and terrain features.

Only Australia has vast amounts of Effective National Territory (ENT). These developable lands form an arc that borders the ecumene from Brisbane west to Adelaide and the Murray River Valley. In addition, they include areas that lie in Perth's interior in southwest Australia. The ranching and commercial farming areas of the semitropical northeast (the coastal sectors of Queensland), where pockets of urbanization already exist, also belong to the ENT. Despite the elimination of the Asian Exclusion Laws, the numbers of legally admitted immigrants from within and outside the region still remain limited to eighty thousand per annum and do little to relieve the population pressures of Asia-Pacifica.

The extent and proportion of ENT in other countries within the region are much more restricted. Japan's ENT includes much of western and southern Hokkaido and Shikoku, as well as parts of northern Honshu. In the Philippines, there is development potential in Mindanao, some parts of Leyte, and the smaller islands that all lie to the south of Luzon. So is there potential in portions of tropical peninsular southern Thailand and areas within its semiarid savannah northeast. The lowland and upland jungles of much of Malaysia are unfavorable for human settlement, although the northwest around George Town and the northeast coast do offer some room for expansion.

Indonesia's ENT includes southern Sumatra and that island's west-central and northeast coast. In addition, there are expansion prospects in some of the Outer Islands east of Java, such as Lombok, western Sumbawa in the Lesser Sundas, southern Flores, and southern Sulawesi.

Most of New Zealand's population is concentrated in the urban centers of the North Island, as is the bulk of its agricultural production. The plains on the eastern side of the South Island, the larger of the country's two main islands, represent New Zealand's ENT.

Singapore has no ENT, being completely filled by its ecumene. Likewise, there is very little ENT in South Korea or Taiwan, because most of the land outside their ecumenes is mountainous.

What blocks the development of some of these ENTs is political unrest, as well as lack of development capital. This is reflected especially in Indonesia. Past efforts to resettle Javanese, Balinese, and Madurese in developable parts of Irian Jaya, the South Moluccas, and Kalimantan have contributed to political unrest and turmoil, which in turn inhibits such development.

EMPTY AREA

Many of the countries of the Asia-Pacific Rim have Empty Areas in their mountainous and jungle sectors. Very sparsely inhabited, the jungles serve as bases or places of refuge for guerrilla groups, support indigenous cultures and tribal ways of life, or provide a basis for large-scale timber operations and the destruction of the ecological balance. But only one part of the Rim has a vast empty area—Australia.

Most of the interior of Australia, especially the western and central portions, is desert that covers about one-third of the continental landmass of nearly three million square miles. This Interior is a flat, dry, and uninhabited plateau with no permanent rivers or lakes. The country's population of nineteen million hugs the eastern and southwestern coasts, while the rainy tropical northern coasts are also virtually uninhabited.

The deserts of the Interior include the Great Sandy, Gibson, Great Victoria, Tanami, and Simpson. In the east-central portion of Australia's deserts, the monotony of the landscape is broken by the Macdonnell Ranges (which overlook the town of Alice Springs) and the Musgrave Ranges. North of the latter is the sandstone monolith of Ayers Rock (Uluru), which rises boldly above the plain and is, like Alice Springs, a tourist attraction.

The empty Interior does hold some mineral wealth—gold, copper, molybdenum, oil, and natural gas—and in the Kimberley Plateau in northwest Australia is the world's largest diamond mine. However, the Interior's greatest strategic value is in the realm of space rocketry and stellar observation. Woomera, on the fringe of the desert in South Australia near the usually dry saltwater Lake Torrens, is the site of the major missile testing range used by Australia and its allies. This testing range extends deep into Western Australia and was once the biggest land rocket range in the world. It was from here that Australia's only space satellite was launched in 1967 and here that the British multiple reentry nuclear warhead testing program was conducted in the early 1970s. The town of Woomera now has a population of fifteen hundred, or one-quarter of its size during the height of rocketry activities.

In addition to the range, the Interior provides tracking stations in Western Australia and Queensland. Geraldton, two hundred miles north of Perth on the desert's coastal edge, is part of a network of ground stations that monitor North Korea and Pakistan and are operated by the United States, Britain, Canada, Australia, and New Zealand. The clear, dark skies and excellent viewing conditions have also attracted important observatories to east-central New South Wales, at Siding Spring and Trunkey Creek, in the semiarid grasslands that lie to the east of the desert.

The Pine Gap Joint Defense Space facility in a remote part of central Australia is an electronic spying base operated jointly by Australia and the United States. Its large antennae, which pick up signals from U.S. space satellites, have the potential of playing a key role in an early warning system for the proposed American NMD system. This possibility has become a source of controversy within Australia. The Labor Party has announced its opposition to the use of Pine Gap for such a purpose, for fear of the impact of such use on the relations between Canberra and both China and some of the Asia-Pacific states.

BOUNDARIES

Most of the important boundary disputes involving Asia-Pacifica are not intraregional, but involve issues with nations that border the region. These are strategic boundaries because of their substantial impact upon the relation of Asia-Pacifica with its neighboring geostrategic realms. The boundary controversies among Asia-Pacific state members have only tactical or local impacts.

The dispute between Japan and Russia over four islands held by Russia—Etorofu and Kunashiri, the southernmost of the Kuril Islands chain, and Habomai and Shikotan—involves the definition of the boundary between the Heartlandic Russian and Maritime Realms, as well as the border between the two countries. In the light of Japan's expanding trade and economic assistance to Russia since 1997, there may be a possibility of ending what has been a bitter dispute since the end of World War II. However, unless some compromise on these islands can be reached, a peace treaty between Russia and Japan will remain elusive.

The North-South Korea and China-Taiwan conflicts over unification of their territories are disputes not about the drawing of boundary lines, but about territorial sovereignty. As such, these relate to the boundary between the East Asia and Maritime geostrategic realms. There is also controversy over the line of demarcation between North and South Korea. The North Koreans assert their title to five small islands in the Yellow Sea off Panmunjon that are occupied by South Korea. They also claim a two-hundred-mile economic zone in the waters of the Sea of Japan off their east coast, and this has precipitated armed clashes over the rights of South Korean and Japanese fishing boats.

Both China and Taiwan have sought to exercise sovereignty over Japan's Senkaku (Diaoku) Island group in the Ryukyu (Nansei) archipelago south of Okinawa—the Senkaku Islands are five uninhabited coral islands that lie only one hundred miles off the east coast of Taiwan. The geopolitical impacts of these disputes are minor because of the relative insignificance of the areas that are involved.

The major disputes over the strategic boundary between East Asia and Asia-Pacific Rim countries revolve around the Spratly and Paracel Island groupings. The Spratlys are located at the southern end of the South China Sea, midway between Vietnam, Malaysia, and the Philippines and 650 miles southeast of Hainan. They were held in the 1930s by France and during World War II by Japan, which built a submarine base on Spratly (Storm) Island, the largest in the chain. In 1946, the Chinese Nationalists declared sovereignty over the islands and left a garrison on one of them.

Called the Nansha Islands by the Chinese and the Kalayaan Islands by the Philippines, this archipelago consists of nearly two hundred islands, scattered coral reefs, and sandbars that lie astride the sea passage between Singapore and Japan and guard the southern entrance to the South China Sea.

Both historic and strategic arguments were the basis for the initial claims to the Spratlys by China, the Philippines, Taiwan, Vietnam, Malaysia, and Brunei. These claims took on greater urgency when in 1976 oil was discovered at Reed Bank, midway between the Spratly group and the Philippine island of Palawan. Oil production began there in 1979 by a consortium to which the Philippine government granted the concession. Since then, natural gas reserves have been discovered that are potentially richer than even the petroleum deposits.

The overlapping claims by the various parties have led to a series of naval and troop clashes in the Spratlys between China and the Philippines, the Philippines and Vietnam, and China and Vietnam. The clashes between China and Vietnam were one of several factors in the deterioration of their relations after the unification of Vietnam.[10] Incidents occurred as early as 1974, but the most serious clashes took place in 1988, when the Chinese navy sank several Vietnamese naval vessels.

The dispute between China and the Philippines has been sparked by facilities constructed by the Chinese on Mischief Reef, which lies west of Palawan and falls within the two-hundred-mile exclusive economic maritime zone of the Philippines. The Chinese claim them to be fishing shelters, but Manila insists that they are military installations. In addition, Brunei established an exclusive fishing zone around Louisa Reef in the southern Spratly Islands, but does not formally claim the island. Despite the attempts of ASEAN to develop a regional code of conduct to prevent the use of force, China refuses to recognize the dispute as a multilateral one. It is unlikely that Beijing will yield on the Spratlys because of their oil and gas potential and China's growing dependence upon imported energy supplies.

In the northern part of the South China Sea, the Paracel (Xisha) Islands are also in dispute. These 130 barren coral islands and reefs lie 175 miles southeast of China's Hainan Island and 230 miles off the Vietnam coast. Chinese armed forces seized the Paracels from the Vietnamese in 1974, following Saigon's announced intention of conducting oil surveys there. The Chinese continue to administer them in the face of Vietnamese claims to the chain. Although the waters of the island are now used by fishermen, their economic significance is in the oil reserves that underlie them. While the boundary controversy is essentially between the two East Asian mainland powers, Taiwan still formally claims them on the basis of being the legitimate government of China, adding a strategic dimension to the dispute. As with the Spratlys, the oil potential of the Paracels is likely to block a speedy resolution of the dispute, though both countries have agreed to negotiate their differences. The Chinese claim is reinforced by the fact that the Paracels are close, not only to Hainan, but also to Hong Kong and Guangzhou, which are only 450 miles away.

The outstanding intraregional boundary disputes are relatively minor. One has to do with conflicting claims between Japan and South Korea over the uninhabited Tok Do islets (Liancourt Rocks), which lie between the coasts of southwestern Honshu and east-central

Korea. Another dispute is over two small coral islands off the coast of Sabah that have been developed as resorts by Malaysia, but are claimed by Indonesia. Both sides have agreed to submit this dispute to international arbitration. Malaysia and Singapore also have conflicting claims to two small islands.

A far more important territorial issue between Malaysia and Indonesia was resolved in 1974. Then, thanks to the reduction in tension between the two countries that occurred after Indonesia joined ASEAN (Malaysia, Thailand, and the Philippines had been its founding members), Jakarta recognized the incorporation of Sabah (northern Borneo) into the federation of Malaysia. The Philippines renounced its claim to the former British protectorate three years later as its contribution to ASEAN unity, although it has not formally revoked its rights.[11]

With the resolution of the East Timor conflict, the three remaining major territorial disputes within Indonesia—Aceh, Irian Jaya, and the South Moluccas—remain as significant issues. In these cases, it is not the demarcation of the boundaries that are in dispute. If these areas were to win their independence, their current provincial boundaries would become the national boundaries, although there might be some difficulties in drawing a separation line between the South and North Moluccas.

On the landward western side of the Asia-Pacific Rim, alignment of Thailand's border with Burma is in dispute and has occasioned sporadic conflict. Tensions between the two countries have recently increased, as Bangkok has tried to seal its borders against the flow of illicit drugs from eastern Myanmar's processing factories. Parts of Thailand's borders with Laos and Cambodia are also indefinite, but this has occasioned only minor friction. Thailand and Vietnam came to an agreement over their border in 1997.

Conclusion

The Asia-Pacific Rim is a less geopolitically mature region than the others within the American and Maritime European Realms. Before it can achieve parity with those regions as an integrated geopolitical force, it needs to establish a stronger regional political, economic, and military framework and to reduce its dependence on the U.S. military-strategic umbrella.

The frameworks that presently bind the region are either too narrowly or too broadly drawn. ASEAN excludes South Korea, Japan, Taiwan, Australia, and New Zealand—the most economically advanced portions of the region. Under such circumstances, the poorer Southeast Asian states are dependent upon ad hoc aid from their more affluent neighbors. What they lack is a structural form of subsidiarity developed within a regional body, such as the EU, whose policies they could help to shape.

ASEAN's ten-member group (Myanmar, Thailand, the three Indochina states, Malaysia, Singapore, the Philippines, Indonesia, and Brunei) has developed an ASEAN Free Trade Area, and negotiations are underway to link it with the Australia-New Zealand free trade area. However, Japan, South Korea, and Taiwan have evinced little interest in joining. An economic framework that does not include these three advanced economies will have little impact upon ASEAN's tariff reduction policies designed to stimulate trade and facilitate economic specialization among the poorer states of Southeast Asia. To accomplish this, an Asia-Pacific Rim economic framework is needed whereby the region's stronger states can take the lead in reducing regional economic inequalities. Models include NAFTA and the single market, such as was represented by the European Economic Community, which preceded the

EU. Another drawback of ASEAN is that it includes Vietnam, Cambodia, and Laos, which lie within the East Asia geostrategic orbit and have very different strategic interests from their Asia-Pacific Rim neighbors. It also includes Myanmar, which is caught between East and South Asia.

APEC is far too broad a framework to meet the direct economic needs of Asia-Pacifica. Established under the leadership of the United States in 1989, APEC was founded to liberalize trans-Pacific trade. In addition to the ASEAN states, Japan, South Korea, Australia, and New Zealand, the organization's members include countries with very divergent strategic interests—China, Russia, the United States, Canada, Mexico, Peru, and Chile. While APEC can serve the important purpose of binding the Asia-Pacific Rim to the entire Pacific world, including the Western hemispheric portions and the north Eurasian Pacific, it is an inadequate forum for addressing such regional issues as intraregional migration, short-term labor exchanges, smuggling of drugs and other goods, and narrowing the economic gap. Nor can ASEAN tackle these issues unless it is expanded to include the geopolitical region in its entirety.

Still another economic organization under development is an East Asia Economic group that has become known as "ASEAN + 3"—the ASEAN states plus Japan, South Korea, and China. This expression of economic regionalism has focused initially on financial issues, such as currency swaps and monitoring of capital movement. The trade emphasis is not toward a free trade area, but rather toward bilateral preferential arrangements led by Japan and South Korea. Such an East Asian economic bloc has the potential to compete with the EU and NAFTA in size and economic strength. However, it cannot take on the integrated geopolitical characteristics of the latter two regions, because of fundamental geostrategic and ideological differences between the East Asian mainland and the Asia-Pacific Rim.

Regional geopolitical unity is the outgrowth of political, social, and military/strategic bonds, as well as economic linkages. Such bonds are still in an incipient stage within the Asia-Pacific Rim. Instead, bilateral agreements, especially those between the region's member states and the United States, characterize the region. This is especially the case for military affairs, in which the American military shield protects South Korea, Japan, Taiwan, Thailand, Australia, and New Zealand. A common regional strategic framework would strengthen the geopolitical unity of Asia-Pacifica. A major step in building such a framework would be the creation of an Asia-Pacific rapid-response regional defense force by those six states. Such a force could play a vital role in heading off local conflicts or minimizing the impact of wars that erupt.

The regional approach to peacemaking and peacekeeping would be politically more effective than the efforts of individual countries or of international agencies. Moreover, a regional military command would help to build a spirit of confidence and cooperation between countries that have long harbored suspicions about one another over boundary issues or support of separatist groups. Such a regional defense arm would not diminish the need for the American strategic air and naval forces that help to secure the Asia-Pacific Rim from Chinese and Russian geostrategic pressures. It could, however, substantially reduce the number of U.S. armed forces now stationed in South Korea (thirty-seven thousand) and Japan (forty-five thousand), which represent nearly 80 percent of all American troops that are "forward-deployed" in Asia and the Pacific.

Asia-Pacific security cooperation will depend heavily upon Japan's agreement to assume a major regional defense role, and upon the willingness of its neighbors to accept such a role. The present Japanese constitution, which renounces war but does not rule out self-defense, was adopted in part to reassure those countries that had suffered under Japanese militarism. Just as Germany has become militarily integrated with its former Western European enemies, so may Japan's neighbors come to see that the twenty-first century requires a regional security architecture that parallels regional economic ties.

The major debate that is now taking place in Japan over the future of its armed forces has to do with a proposed constitutional change that would enable Japan to exercise military power in an unhampered way—a change favored by Washington. This reflects the struggle between resurgent Japanese nationalism and those who remain committed to pacifism. Part of the nationalist argument is that greater military might, combined with Japan's status as the world's second-largest economic power, would strengthen Japan's case to become the sixth permanent member of the UN Security Council. For China, new strategic concerns are raised by the possibility that a militarily powerful Japan, freed from restraints, might be tempted to take an interventionist position in conflicts within the Asia-Pacific Rim. The same might hold true for Russia, which could conceivably move Moscow and Beijing more closely together.

A broadened security role for Japan requires more than a constitutional change. Japan currently has no long-range bombers, missiles, or carriers, since its defense strategy is confined to the home islands. Instead, it relies on the United States to keep its sea lanes open or to deal with territorial disputes that might destabilize the region.

A more assertive Japanese Self-Defense Forces (SDF) role in regional affairs would enable the United States to reduce substantially the number of its troops stationed in Okinawa. This small, agricultural, tourist-oriented island in the southern part of the Ryukyu (Nansei) chain south of the main Japanese islands is strategically important because it lies midway between Taiwan and South Korea. When Okinawa was returned to Japan in 1972, the United States retained 20 percent of the densely populated southern part of Okinawa, for military facilities. These include two large air bases, a helicopter base, and the infrastructure that supports a full U.S. Marine division. Opposition to this U.S. presence has added fuel to the deeply-rooted Okinawan independence drive.

The Pentagon has attempted to mollify the Okinawans by consolidating some of its facilities. Indeed, long-term consideration has been given to shifting the marine base to the relatively empty northern part of the island, or even to northern Australia. For the present, however, the controversy remains, to the acute discomfort of both Washington and Tokyo.

Should the Japanese SDF assume many of the security functions now being carried out by U.S. armed forces stationed in Japan, the Japanese government would have to weigh the costs and benefits of placing such a heavy defense burden on such a small island as Okinawa, which covers only 1 percent of the nation's total land area. Shifting the responsibility to Tokyo for finding an equitable, long-range solution to the problems of siting military facilities within the Japanese archipelago would defuse an increasingly ugly domestic and international situation, as well as involve Tokyo more heavily in the defense of the region. As a short-term solution, the U.S. Marines could well be redeployed from Okinawa to ships operating from fleet bases in the Pacific (e.g., Guam or Japanese larger island harbors) in a strategy known as maritime prepositioning.[12] The air base problems are more intractable.

Major issues that threaten Asia-Pacific security include North Korea, Taiwan, the Spratlys, and separatism in Indonesia. After half a century of shouldering the security burdens of the region, Washington inevitably will wish to reduce its defense responsibilities. Under such circumstances, the need for an Asia-Pacific regional defense force will become even more urgent. This urgency will be reinforced by China's pursuit of its goals of modernizing its armed forces and creating a blue-water navy. Japan's security, as well as that of its regional neighbors, is heavily influenced by China's strategic policies in the South and East China Seas, as well as the Sea of Japan.

Another force that can further regional integration is a planned approach to immigration. Japan and Australia can benefit from large-scale immigration. Japanese demographic projections suggest a major decline in its current population of 127 million, based upon a rapidly declining birthrate and an aging populace. This is an unexpected reversal for a nation that, during the first half of the twentieth century, sought to create a Pacific empire that would be able to absorb colonists from the overcrowded Japanese islands. However, it is not surprising in the light of Japan's shift from an essentially rural nation to a highly urbanized one based on industry and services. A United Nations study has suggested that 600,000 immigrants per year will be needed to maintain the present workforce.[13] The population of the country is aging more rapidly than that of any other country in the world, making immigration a pressing need.

To develop an open and coherent immigration policy will require a fundamental change in Japanese attitude. Historically, the country is more hostile to immigration than any other industrialized nation. The largest immigrant group, approximately one million Koreans, stemmed from those who were brought to Japan as laborers or military conscripts between Japan's annexation of Korea in 1910 and the end of World War II in 1945. Their descendants have never been fully accepted into Japanese society. Neither have the tens of thousands of Chinese who have entered illegally in recent years to take on menial jobs, or the handful of Southeast Asian refugees who have been given entry by Tokyo. As difficult as it will be for Japan to open its society to outsiders, the alternative of economic decline is even less acceptable. Both economic necessity and the fostering of regional ties with its Asia-Pacific neighbors are likely to force the Japanese to face up to the challenge.

While Australia has become open to immigration during the past half century—first from Eastern Europe and then from Asia—the numbers of legal immigrants remain low. Recently, illegal immigrants, many seeking refuge from war-torn Middle Eastern and southeastern European counties, have entered Australia via Southeast Asia; while their numbers are small, the government has begun to crack down on asylum seekers.

As the Australian economy matures, shifting from farming, extractive industries, and manufacturing to high-tech and information-age industries and services, the current labor pool that can be drawn from its nineteen million population will need to be augmented. The Philippines, Malaysia, Thailand, Indonesia, Taiwan and India are likely sources for future immigration. Working against this long-term manpower need is a growing fear among white Australians of being swamped by Asians. This has given rise to racist and anti-immigrant sentiment and precipitated a national debate on immigration policy.

Japan is the major economic and political core of the Asia-Pacific Rim. The fortunes of its neighbors are tied to its fortunes. When Tokyo experienced the breathtaking economic and technological development that propelled it into becoming the world's second-largest economy in the 1970s and '80s, its Asian neighbors benefited from Japanese capital and outsourcing. The demand-side stagnation that engulfed the Japanese economy in the 1990s brought on financial crises and economic slumps among its neighbors also.

Japan's mounting trade deficit (over $25 billion per annum) has caused strains with China and moved nationalists to call for a more restrictive trade policy. The strongest protectionist voices come from the Japanese farm lobby, which fears being inundated by cheaper Chinese vegetables, which in recent years have won nearly half the Japanese market. However, most of the trade deficit comes from the import of consumer products made by Japanese manufacturing plants that have been established in China. This makes it un-likely that Tokyo will reverse its trade policies. However, such rising economic tensions could spill over into the political area.

Despite its current economic problems, and the inability of increased government in-vestments to turn the tide, Japan remains by far the richest and most-advanced state in Asia-Pacifica and, indeed, in all of East and South Asia. Japan's leadership role is solidly based. It has been, and will doubtless continue to be, a generous provider of development aid to its poorer Pacific Rim neighbors. Indeed, at the end of the twentieth century, Japan led all of the world's nations as a donor of overseas development aid, with an annual total of $15 billion, ranking it ahead of the United States and Germany. It is also likely to main-tain its role as a primary generator of capital investment, outsourcing of manufacturing, and trade.

There has been a weakening of the "old boy" business network, the grip of the giant conglomerates, and governmental restrictions. This should help Japanese industry to de-centralize, with a great increase in smaller, more nimble enterprises that can adapt more quickly to the needs for innovation in this information age. The Asia-Pacific Rim's popu-lation of 600 million is a significant market for Japan's creative economic energies, as is the nearby East Asia Realm, with its 1.4 billion populace. The history of Japan's economic suc-cesses suggests that it will be able to retain its economic leadership within the region.

The geopolitical relations between Japan and the United States have been dominated by the latter since the end of World War II. This is not only because of the American role in rebuilding the devastated Japanese landscape and economy and Tokyo's Cold War fears of the former Soviet Union and China. It has also been influenced by the nature of the post-war economy that became so heavily dependent upon Japanese exports to the United States.

Since the mid-1990s, Japan has been forced to lessen its overwhelming dependence upon trade with the United States, not only because of the impact of the American reces-sion on its import of Japanese manufactured goods, but also because Japan is in the throes of a fundamental economic restructuring. Confronted by high wages and labor shortages, Japanese manufacturers are shifting their production operations to other Asia-Pacific Rim countries and to China. Earnings from overseas investments in 2002 exceeded merchandise export earnings, and manufacturing's share of Japan's GDP has dropped to 20 percent. Con-tinuation of this trend, with increasing focus on design and marketing of high-technology, high-quality products and financial services, mirrors U.S. economic structural trends, where manufacturing now accounts for only 15 percent of the GDP. The main difference between the two economies is that the United States will continue to have a powerful agricultural sec-tor, while Japan depends upon food imports.

As Japan's economy becomes more similar to that of the United States, it becomes more competitive in the search for manufacturing outsourcing and financial investment opportunities. Geopolitically economic competition might encourage Tokyo to adopt a more independent course in international affairs, especially with issues that concern the Korean peninsula, China, Indonesia, and the Middle East—the latter being Japan's major oil supplier.

While China has become Japan's second largest trading partner, Tokyo remains firmly linked geopolitically to the Maritime Realm. Together with its Asia-Pacific Rim neigh-bors, it continues to look to the American military shield as the guarantor of its national and regional independence and to the Maritime World for the largest share of its market opportunities.

A more independent international political and economic course for Japan will not weaken the Maritime Realm geopolitically. Rather, in tandem with Maritime Europe's increasingly independent posture, this will lead to a more balanced, multipolar geostrategic realm within which Washington's propensity to take political and military initiatives without consulting its allies is likely to be curbed.

Geopolitical regions are dynamic. Their nature and orientation may change as their geographic and economic landscapes are altered, or as the political/ideological, religious, and social forces that shape these landscapes undergo change. Through time, peripheral parts of a region may become detached and added to an adjoining region. At present, the center of the Korean Peninsula and the Strait of Taiwan form boundaries of tension between the Asia-Pacific Rim and the East Asia Realm. This could change. Taiwan and China have accepted the principle of "One China," although they differ in their interpretations of its meaning. Future negotiations may find an accommodation whereby Taipei accepts Beijing's political sovereignty, while China permits Taiwan to pursue an independent economic and domestic political path, but as a demilitarized entity.

The opening of relations between North and South Korea, along with the "Sunshine Policy" being pursued by the South, are not aimed at reunification in the near future. Each country belongs to a different geostrategic realm and the economic and ideological gap between them is too great. However, a formal peace between the North and the South is a realistic prospect. With peace would come open borders, the exchange of people, and the flow of capital and technology from the South in exchange for low-cost goods from the North.

Should the above scenarios come to pass, the boundary between Asia-Pacifica and East Asia would become a boundary of accommodation and South Korea and Taiwan would serve as Gateways between the two worlds. Under such circumstances, the reduction of the U.S. strategic presence would inevitably follow and Japan's leadership role as economic, political, and military core of the Asia-Pacific Rim would be enhanced within a regional framework of cooperative action.

Notes

1. Hans Weigert, *Generals and Geographers* (New York: Oxford University Press, 1942), 167–91.

2. Bruce Ryan, "Australia's Place in the World," in *The Australian Experience,* ed. R. L. Heathcote (Melbourne: Longman's, 1988), 305–17.

3. Robert O'Neill, "Australia and the Indian Ocean," in *The Southern Ocean and the Security of the Free World*, ed. Patrick Wall (London: Stacey, 1977), 177–89.

4. Zbigniew Brzezinski, *The Grand Chessboard* (New York: Basic, (1977), 151–93.

5. Thomas Friedman, "The Mean Season," *New York Times,* 9 September 1999, A23.

6. Seth Mydans, "East Timor's Dream of Oil," *New York Times,* 20 October 2000, A13.

7. Wook-ik Yu, "Seoul: The City of Vitality," *I.G.U. Bulletin* 50, no. 1 (2000): 5–19.

8. "Survey Taiwan," *Economist,* 7 November 1998, 14.

9. "Survey Taiwan," 14.

10. Alan J. Day, ed. *Border and Territorial Disputes* (Longman, 1982), 327.

11. Day, *Border and Territorial Disputes,* 330–31.

12. Paul Bracken, *Fire in the East* (New York: HarperCollins, 1999), 164–68.

13. Howard W. French, "Still Wary of Outsiders, Japan Expects Immigration Boom," *New York Times,* 14 March 2000, A1, A14.

CHAPTER 10

The Arc of Geostrategic Instability, Part I: South Asia

The Eurasian Heartland, the Maritime, and the East Asian geostrategic realms converge around a broad, tricontinental zone that embraces the lands rimming the northern Indian Ocean, the Persian/Arab Gulf, and the eastern Mediterranean/Red Sea. This zone contains two geopolitical regions—South Asia, which is separate from and independent of the three geostrategic realms, and the Middle East Shatterbelt, whose fragmentation is caused, in considerable measure, by the intrusive actions of the major powers that are located within the realms that surround it.

The two regions are geographically connected by Pakistan, a state whose territory has been historically linked to South Asia and which has been in conflict with India since its independence. Pakistan has become increasingly involved in Middle Eastern affairs through its ties to Afghanistan.

While South Asia is a region of three major religions—Hinduism, Buddhism, and Islam—India's regional dominance makes Hinduism the main religious force. The Middle East is Islamic, with the exceptions of Israel, Lebanon's Mount Lebanon section, and South Sudan. The major religious differences in the region stem from the Sunni-Shia schism and the clash between secularism and religion, especially Islamic fundamentalism.

This tricontinental zone forms an "Arc of Geostrategic Instability," within which nearly every country has been caught up in conflicts with its neighbors or torn by civil wars. The end of the Cold War has done little to defuse tensions within the Arc. Acquisition of nuclear weapons capacity by Pakistan to match that of India, as well as the progress made by Iran and, putatively, Iraq to join the nuclear club, makes for a most dangerous situation. Israel, too, has nuclear capabilities. Moreover, the rise of militant Islam has fueled civil strife and increased the threat of terrorism within much of the Arc, as well as outside its bounds.

Under the British Raj, most of South Asia was a unified geopolitical region. Only Nepal and part of Bhutan lay outside the boundaries of British India. Since the end of British rule and the emergence of the subcontinent's independent states, a divided South Asia has known little but conflict. The 1947–48 War of Partition between India and Pakistan resulted in over one million people killed and fourteen million refugees—8.6 million of which were Muslims and 5.3 million of which were Hindus. From the time that Myanmar (then Burma) gained its independence in 1948, it has been torn by civil war; since 1962 it has been led by unstable and repressive military juntas. For nearly two decades, Sri

Lanka (formerly Ceylon), which also became independent in 1948, has been in the grip of a bloody separatist rebellion by Tamils against the ruling majority Buddhist Sinhalese. The Tamils live in the north and east of the country and are Hindu. The independent state of Bangladesh was created when East Bengal, which was then East Pakistan, split off from West Pakistan in the war of 1971–72, in which 500,000 were killed.

Thus, the unity which the Mughal (Mogul) and British empires imposed on South Asia has been shattered by the political divisions and religious and sectarian strife of the past half century. While neither of those empires fully encompassed all parts of the region, their rules embraced most of its territories and brought administrative order. The Muslim Mughal empire reached its greatest territorial expanse by the end of the seventeenth century, when it extended east to Orissa on the Bay of Bengal and south through nearly all of the Deccan. Only the island of Ceylon, the northern Himalayas, and Burma lay outside its bounds.

As Mughal rule crumbled in the eighteenth and nineteenth centuries, British power began to extend over the subcontinent. The British Raj, too, never succeeded in fully encompassing all of South Asia. Not only had it failed to conquer Nepal and much of Bhutan, but while Burma proper had become a British colony, the rebellious Shan states of eastern Burma had only protectorate status, their local chiefs exercising political controls. At that time, the Government of India Act established the All-India Federation, and a framework of unity was put firmly into place. In accordance with this act, the native states were given freedom in domestic policies in exchange for British control of foreign affairs, defense, and communications.[1]

While South Asia is not, and never was, a completely unified geopolitical region, it is a distinct geographical region, possessing many cultural and human similarities and separated from the rest of Asia. The Indian subcontinent stands aloof from its neighbors, behind a barrier of rimming deserts, mountains, and monsoonal forests. Its best connections to the outside are via the Indian Ocean.

Within South Asia, the population is most heavily concentrated along the Brahmaputra, Ganges, and Indus River valleys in the north and along the east and west coasts. It thereby forms an almost continuous population ring around the Deccan—the highly dissected southern half of the Indian subcontinent whose center is semiarid. While population densities in the rural Deccan are high—over six hundred persons per square mile—they do not begin to compare with the densities of the great northern interior valleys that form the Hindustan Plain, nor with the densities of the east and west coastal plains, which contain most of the big cities, industries, and transportation networks. There the mixed rural and urban populations range from twelve hundred to over five thousand persons per square mile. The populations of the Hindustan Plain cross national boundaries in both the Punjab and Bengal to intertwine further the geopolitical fates of Pakistan and Bangladesh with that of India.

South Asia's geopolitical distinctiveness is influenced by its dependence upon agriculture and its inward economic orientation, as well as its geographical isolation caused by its rimming mountains. Two-thirds of the workforce of the region is dependent upon agriculture (table 10.1). Much of this agriculture is traditional farming, although significant strides in modernization have been made in parts of India, Pakistan, and Sri Lanka. For the most part, the region feeds itself, the exception being Bangladesh, one of the world's poorest countries. Bangladesh's agricultural production is subject to the vicissitudes of disastrous floods, droughts, and monsoonal storms, making it dependent on food aid imports.

Table 10.1   South Asia Population and Trade

Country	Population in Millions	Population Density (per sq. mile)	% of Workforce in Agriculture	Main Trading Partners
India	1,000	800	67	U.S., Germany, Japan
Pakistan	145	425	50	U.S., Japan, China, Germany
Bangladesh	131	2,355	75	India, U.S., China, Germany
Myanmar	42	160	67	Japan, China, India, Thailand
Sri Lanka	19	775	75	Japan, U.S., India, U.K.
Nepal	25	440	89	India, U.S., Singapore, Germany
Bhutan	2	110	94	India
Maldives*	0.3	2,550	NA	Sri Lanka, Singapore, India, U.K.

*2.5 percent of the Maldivian labor force engages in fishing and, minimally, in agriculture because of the infertility of its coral soils.
Sources: Rand McNally "World Gazetteer: Profiles of Countries and Places," *World Facts and Maps*, 2000 Millennium Edition, 70–224 (Skokie, Ill.: Rand McNally, 2000); "Nations of the World," *World Almanac and Book of Facts 2000*, 768–877 (Mahwah, N.J.: Primedia Reference, 1999); Central Intelligence Agency, *The World Factbook 2001* (Washington, D.C.: Gov/CIA Publications, 2001).

Exchange with other nations is of secondary concern to most of South Asia, whose trade in goods and services, as a percentage of GDP, averages a little over 5 percent. Two exceptions are Sri Lanka, whose exports of textiles, clothing, tea, gems, and rubber and imports of machinery, transportation equipment, petroleum, and sugar represent over 20 percent of its GDP, and the Maldives, whose economy is based on tourism, shipping, and fishing.

Because of its large pool of scientists and skilled technology workers, India has considerable potential for expanding its high-tech industry. Software exports, mostly to the United States, have been growing rapidly, as have exports of pharmaceuticals. However, the software industry still represents only 3 percent of the country's total GDP of $1.8 trillion. The GDP that educated, highly trained Indian emigrés generate in Silicon Valley probably exceeds India's total high-tech GDP.

The concept of South Asia as an independent geopolitical region separated from surrounding geostrategic realms and their regional subdivisions was first advanced by this writer in 1963.[2] It diverged from the worldview of Halford Mackinder, who had considered India, the Southeast Asian peninsula, and China to be a unified Monsoonal coastland. In his 1919 volume, he depicted this region as one of the six "natural" regions of the world.[3] In continued support of this thesis, he argued in 1943 that "a thousand million people of ancient oriental civilization inhabit the lands of India and China. They must grow to prosperity. . . . Then they will balance the other thousand million who live between the Missouri and the Yenisei."[4] The latter reference is to the Heartland and North Atlantic units working in cooperation with one another.

What this worldview failed to appreciate was that the geopolitical destinies of India and China could not be shared because of their unique geographical and cultural-historical settings. In Mackinder's time, as today, the two had different demographic and resource bases and different sets of strategic concerns. China was an essentially homogeneous nation caught between the Eurasian Heartland and Asia-Pacifica, with much of its space belonging to the Continental Interior. In contrast, India's populace was highly diverse racially, ethnically, linguistically, and religiously. Its Indian Ocean strategic orientation was reflected in the historic reach of its sailors and merchants to Southeast Asia's islands and to the eastern and southern coasts of Africa—the two major regions where the Indian diaspora first took root. In addition, the ecumenes of the two great civilizations were too far removed from one another geographically to develop significant interaction or to enable one power to dominate the other militarily.

Although the historic buffer zone of Tibet and the Himalayas that lies between East and South Asia has been breached by China in recent decades, India's dominant position within its region remains unchallenged. In general, the towering Himalayan mountain ranges continue to bar the route to northern India. They wall off Tibet from the lands to the south and, while the northern part of Azad Kashmir, which Pakistan ceded to China, now connects China's Xinjiang to Pakistan, it is too remote an outpost to serve the Chinese as a serious military threat to northern India.

During the course of the Cold War, the USSR was able to gain some influence in India, while at various times China and the United States became important military backers of Pakistan. However, these inroads did not fundamentally alter the geopolitical status of South Asia. It remained a separate and inwardly oriented geopolitical region, most of which took a neutralist posture in the struggle between the Western and Communist realms. Pakistan's ties to the West and China did not alter its fundamental geostrategic orientation, which remained South Asian. Its major concern was its struggle with India over Kashmir, but it also felt threatened by the Soviet inroads into Afghanistan. South Asia was spared from becoming another Cold War Shatterbelt by the combination of physical vastness, a population that has now reached 1.35 billion, an inward economic and cultural orientation, a common political history, and India's dominant role. However, while it stands apart from adjoining geostrategic realms and maintains independent geopolitical regional status, the unity that the Indian subcontinent once enjoyed eludes it today. Until South Asia can overcome its internal divisions, its independence is likely to remain an isolating force, and its role on the global scene will continue to be limited.

Regional Geopolitical Orientation

INDIA AND PAKISTAN

India gained its independence in 1947. It adopted a policy of nonalignment or neutralism in the Cold War, based in part on what Jawaharlal Nehru described as its geographical position: "India is big and India is happily situated. . . . [A]n invasion or attack on India . . . will give [other countries] no profit."[5] The main preoccupation of India's leadership was its disputes with Pakistan over Kashmir, water rights, and East Pakistan.

India did have a broader view that extended beyond the region. This was reflected in its leadership role within the "Third Force"—the grouping of Asian and African states initially assembled in 1955 at Bandung, Indonesia, where Nehru expressed his opposition to military alliances and called for a moratorium on nuclear testing. However, he had doubts as to whether the Asian-African conference could ever develop into a cohesive group.[6] In this, he was being realistic. India was so preoccupied with its conflict with Muslim Pakistan and binding together the Union of India that it had little surplus energy, beyond moral exhortations, to look beyond the subcontinent. The partition of British India has left 120 million Muslims within India. They represent 12 percent of India's population, including heavy concentrations in Mumbai and Bangalore. Intercommunal strife between the Hindus and the Muslims, who constitute the fourth-largest concentration of Muslims in one country, remains a serious threat to India's unity, particularly since Hindu militants have gained political influence with the rise of the Bharatiya Janata Party, which now heads the national coalition government.

The response of Washington to India's neutralism was to draw Pakistan into a military alliance, first in 1955 through the short-lived Central Treaty Organization (CENTO), which also included Turkey, Iraq, and Iran, and later through bilateral arrangements. Also in 1955 Pakistan joined the now-defunct SEATO, which together with its involvement with CENTO reflected both westward and eastward strategic pulls.

Hindsight teaches us that the Cold War policy of tolerating no neutrals pursued by U.S. Secretary of State John Foster Dulles was a major blunder. For Dulles, the nonalignment of India was "immoral," regardless of whether India was the world's largest democracy. He therefore turned to the alliance with Pakistan, which was to be plagued by corrupt and often dictatorial military rule and chronic political instability throughout the Cold War and beyond.

India's hopes for nonalignment were severely shaken by the intrusion into the region of both the United States and China. With its mortal enemy, Pakistan, in alliance with the United States and its relations with China deteriorating because of border disputes, New Delhi had to open itself to Soviet military, economic, and political support to gain Moscow's backing for its position on Kashmir.

In the 1959 Lonju incident, China occupied a garrison post in India's North-East Frontier Agency (which in 1987 was renamed Arunachal Pradesh state). Khrushchev sought unsuccessfully to mediate the dispute, as he tried to balance Soviet-Indian ties with the ideological and strategic Sino-Soviet bonds. However, just before the 1962 war broke out between India and China, the Soviets agreed to build and deliver jets for India. Moreover, rather than backing Beijing, Moscow remained neutral when the war broke out. All of this contributed to the eventual Sino-Soviet schism, for it fanned Mao's fears that the USSR was seeking to outflank China through an alliance with India. As noted in the previous chapter's discussion of China's borders, Beijing has remained in control of over 40 percent of Aksai Chin—that cold, high desert plain in the northeasternmost part of Jammu and Kashmir that is bordered by Xinjiang on its northeast and Tibet on its southeast. The Chinese also invaded India's North-East Frontier Agency, which lies north of Assam, but withdrew at the end of the war.

Beijing's speedy reaction to the Soviet-Indian ties was to settle outstanding differences with Pakistan over their common border in northern Kashmir in 1963. At that time, Pakistan ceded to China 2,050 square miles of the northern Azad Kashmir territory also claimed by India. Beijing, in turn, became Pakistan's major arms supplier. The two countries agreed to build the Karakoram Peace Highway—a 750-mile, all-weather road over the Karakoram Range from Rawalpindi, Pakistan, to Kashi (Kashgar) in Xinjiang that crossed the mountains at the 15,420-foot Khunjerab Pass. (It was completed only in 1978.) The road is the sole paved section of the historic silk route from the Mediterranean to China.

By 1971, when the Bangladesh rebellion broke out in East Pakistan (which is separated from the western half of Pakistan by eleven hundred miles), China openly supported Pakistan, while Moscow backed India. Washington supported neither its Pakistani ally nor India, whose troops quickly triumphed over those of Pakistan. In the months of civil war that had preceded India's intervention, an estimated one million native Bengalis had been killed in East Pakistan and several million had fled into exile in India.

Beijing subsequently supplied Islamabad with nuclear technology. At the same time, while the United States was decrying the spread of nuclear weapons in South Asia, it was building up Pakistan militarily to support the Afghan rebels in their war against the Soviet Union.

The second war between India and Pakistan over Kashmir took place in 1965 and caused the United States and Britain to impose an embargo on the sale of arms to both countries. This further strengthened the bonds that India and Pakistan had, respectively, with the USSR and China. The embargo was lifted in 1975, but in the meantime India had turned to Moscow for new and major infusions of weapons, as part of a 1973 aid agreement that Prime Minister Indira Gandhi had forged with Moscow. New Delhi abandoned its antinuclear policy the following year, when it exploded an underground nuclear test device in the Thar Desert.

When the Soviet Union invaded Afghanistan in 1979 to prop up its Marxist governmental ally in Kabul against Islamic fundamentalist rebels, Washington called upon Islamabad to help foil the Russian move. Pakistan became the main arms conduit from the United States to the rebels and provided the Afghan Mujahedeen and volunteers from other Islamic countries with major training and supply bases. Also, since this period, it has sheltered well over two million Afghan refugees. Saudi Arabia, which was also enlisted in the effort in Afghanistan, provided considerable financial support to the rebels. The magnitude of U.S. military and economic aid to Pakistan during the 1980s—$600 million per annum—made Pakistan the third largest recipient of U.S. aid, after Israel and Egypt. Adding to India's fears over the resurrected U.S.-Pakistan alliance was the continuing thaw in the relations between Washington and Beijing. For India, this raised the specter of encirclement and provided additional justification for its drawing closer to the Soviet Union.

The sudden pullout of Soviet troops from Afghanistan in 1989, and U.S. suspension the following year of all military and economic aid to Pakistan because of its nuclear weapons program, appeared to set the scene for a radical restructuring of alliances in South Asia. India had become far more attractive to Washington as a potential ally on several grounds: (1) its significance as a potential market (India's economy has grown by approximately 6 percent per annum in the past decade), (2) its pool of technological brain-power, (3) its role as a leader of developing countries in bridging the differences between the Third World and the World Trade Organization, and (4) its importance as the world's largest democracy.

The convergence of U.S. and Indian interests also related to the deterioration of ties between Washington and Islamabad, until the exigencies of the U.S. war in Afghanistan restored these relations. The collapse of the Soviet Union had undercut the strategic rationale for the U.S.-Pakistani military alliance of the 1980s. Tensions then increased between the two countries because of Pakistan's role in supporting the Taliban and Osama bin Laden's terrorist base in Afghanistan. The unintended consequences of the American effort to support the Afghan Mujahedeen against the Soviet forces and their Afghan allies had been the rise to power of the fundamentalist Sunni Taliban. There are strong bonds based on Pashtun lineage, between the Taliban and the twenty million Pashtuns who live within Pakistan's western borderlands, from Peshawar to Quetta. Pakistan now harbors many Islamic fundamentalist guerrillas who have been redirected from the Afghan war to support Muslim militants in the Indian-held part of Kashmir, and Pakistan also has become a refuge for al Qaeda forces who have escaped the rout of the Taliban. A major obstacle to full-scale rapprochement between the United States and India is Russia's continuing role as the main supplier of arms to New Delhi, although the sale of American arms is being negotiated. While the government of India has a long-term objective of creating a self-sufficient armaments industry, until this is achieved, it will remain dependent upon such imports. The rebuilding of military and economic ties between Washington and Islamabad in the War against Terrorism may prove a temporary setback to U.S.-India relations.

In its relations with the United States, India is also disturbed by the intensity of American efforts to strengthen economic and political ties with China. China's retention of part of Indian-claimed Aksai Chin, and its role as a major supplier of arms to Pakistan, adds to New Delhi's suspicions that the United States is unlikely to take a balanced approach in its relations with the two Asian states.

Despite India's suspicions of U.S. intentions, the likelihood is that the United States will seek closer relations with India in the years to come. This is in recognition of India's strategic importance as the potentially dominant power over the Indian Ocean region.

SRI LANKA

In Sri Lanka, civil war broke out in full force in 1986 between the Sinhalese government and the independence-seeking Tamil Eelam "Liberation Tigers." It continued to rage until the cease-fire of 2002. India's involvement had begun three years earlier, when Indira Gandhi ordered the covert arming and training of the Tamil rebels. The Tamils, who live mainly in the northern and eastern parts of the island and represent 25 percent of the country's population, are mainly Hindu, while the Sinhalese, who are three-quarters of the populace, are Buddhist. New Delhi's motives were to court the political support of its own fifty million Tamils in the Indian southern state of Tamil Nadu by allowing the Sri Lankan Tamil militants to set up bases on Indian soil.

However, growing concern that the creation of an independent Tamil state in northeastern Sri Lanka might encourage separatism among the Tamils of Tamil Nadu caused the Indian government of Rajiv Gandhi to do a policy about-face in 1987. An added complication for India was that Tamil Nadu adjoins Kerala—long a bastion of Communist Party strength and plagued by a separatist movement. Accepting the Sri Lankan government's request for assistance in securing a peace with the separatists, New Delhi sent more than seventy-five thousand troops to help quell the rebellion and broker a peace. The effort failed and India pulled out its forces in 1990 at the request of Sri Lanka. Nevertheless, the ties between Sri Lanka and India have continued to be strong, especially since the Sinhalese-dominated government in Colombo has sentenced to death the Tamil Tiger leader held responsible for the revenge assassination of Rajiv Gandhi in 1991, when he was already out of office. New Delhi can be expected to continue its support of the Sri Lankan government, while cautiously promoting the cause of peace. Meanwhile, the conflict, which has taken over sixty thousand lives and caused the displacement of one million Tamils, has yet to be resolved despite the current cease-fire.

MYANMAR (BURMA)

The political relations of Myanmar with India and the rest of South Asia have become more tenuous since the Burmese gained their independence in 1948. During much of the nineteenth century, most of the country was controlled by British India. While Burma was given a new constitution in 1935, separating it from the rest of British India, the Japanese invasion during World War II gave Burma little opportunity to exercise its newly won freedom.

Since its postwar independence, the country has been torn geopolitically by pressures from both India and China. Indian strategic interests lie in Myanmar's location overlooking the Bay of Bengal, and in the oil and gas reserves of Lower Burma. Another strategic consideration for New Delhi is that its provinces of Assam, Nagaland, and Arunachal Pradesh adjoin the northwestern part of Upper Burma, which is exposed to the Chinese military threat. Were Myanmar allied with India, it could be a helpful buffer.

Beijing's interests in Upper Burma stem from the geographical proximity of the region to Yunnan Province and Tibet. If Myanmar were drawn into Beijing's orbit, it would also enable China to exercise greater leverage upon Laos and northern Thailand, which adjoin Myanmar along its northeastern and eastern border.

Shortly after the Union of Burma was established, its government sought to loosen ties it had developed with India during the British Raj. To offset India's pressures, the Yangon (Rangoon) government cautiously reached out to the new Communist regime in Beijing, looking for help in ousting the Chinese Nationalists who had been driven across the border into Burma, where they had quickly organized the drug trade. The Nationalist troops did leave Burma in 1953, although in response to the orders of the United Nations, not because of actions by Beijing.

Myanmar-China-India Relations

Trying to maintain a balancing act between India and China, the Socialist government of U Nu adopted an approach that fit a broader ideological position of nonalignment and orientation to the Third World—a policy that paralleled that of Nehru's India. In keeping with this spirit of nonalignment, and to further relations with China, Yangon refused to join SEATO.

In 1960 China and Burma signed a Treaty of Friendship and Non-aggression in which China relinquished claims upon Burma for territories in the far north (Kachin state) and the northeast (Nam Wan and the Wa states). In return, Beijing received five small villages in these border areas.[7] With these provisos, Beijing accepted on a de facto (but not a de jure) basis the Sino-Burmese section of the McMahon Line, which had been drawn in 1900 by a joint Anglo-Chinese boundary commission.

In 1962, beset by insurgencies in the north, east, and southeast, Burma plunged into chaos and a military junta seized power. The pro-Chinese "White Flag" majority Communist Party of Burma (the minority "Red Flag" Communists had split off and operated in the south) gained control of much of the northeast, along the border with China. Elsewhere in the north, Shans and Kachins captured considerable territory. The Chinese provided the insurgents with arms and even sent Red Guard volunteers to the "White Flag" Communists. Despite the fact that at one point the various rebel groups had seized control of nearly one-third of the country, they failed to overthrow the government, and China's efforts to penetrate Burma came to naught.

With the disintegration of the Communist Party in the 1980s, and after making peace agreements with other rebel movements, Burma (renamed Myanmar in 1989) appreciably improved its relationship with China. Beijing became the main supplier of arms to the Yangon government, while trade links were established that opened Burma's market to a flood of Chinese consumer goods. In addition, China has permitted its territory to become the conduit by which heroin is transported from the "Golden Triangle" to Hong Kong and thence to the United States, Australia, Southeast Asia, and Europe. Since much of the heroin is controlled by Myanmar's military junta, China's cooperation in shipping the drug to Western markets was eagerly sought by Myanmar.[8]

The relations between India and Myanmar have been strained since the military junta overthrew the U Nu government in 1962. This despite the fact that India is the single largest market for Myanmar's exports. One of the major issues between the two countries has been the aid provided by Yangon to the Naga rebels, who have fought for nearly half a century for Nagaland's independence from India.

Nagaland is a small state in northeastern India, wedged in between Bangladesh and Myanmar. When the Naga army was driven out of India in the mid-1970s, it took refuge in the Burmese Naga hill lands and used the transborder sanctuaries as bases from which to mount raids against Indian forces. For many years, the Indian government was unsuccessful in its attempts to enlist Yangon's support against the Naga rebels. However, in 1999 India and Myanmar signed an agreement to promote joint action against the Nagas (the Burmese Naga tribesmen had risen up against the Yangon regime) and against the drug traders operating along their mutual border.

A major cause of friction between the two countries has been India's firm support of the prodemocracy forces in Myanmar in the face of their persecution by the ruling junta. Thousands of Burmese dissidents were given refuge in India when they fled Yangon's repression of antigovernment riots that followed the junta's invalidation of the 1990 democratic elections. The arrest of the leaders of the victorious democratic party led by Aung San Suu Kyi evoked strong criticism from New Delhi, while Beijing backed the crackdown against the dissidents.

Recent negotiations over the export of hydroelectric power from India to Myanmar, as well as the accord on military cooperation against the Nagas and the reestablishment of transborder trade, are portents of warming relations between the two countries. However, the development of strong ties between them hinges upon the restoration of democracy in Myanmar.

At the onset of the twenty-first century, slight openings began to appear in the hitherto tightly closed Burmese political system. A number of opposition leaders who had been imprisoned were released and Mrs. Suu Kyi, the symbol of the Burmese peoples' yearnings for democracy, has been released after a lengthy house arrest. In addition, the generals, who control the country not only politically, but also economically, have begun to allow private investors to buy into the industrial and farm businesses that the government has expropriated and mismanaged over the years. This is seen as a desperate attempt to save an economy that is in grave difficulties, with rampant inflation and collapsing government services. The country that was once one of the world's largest rice producers and exporters is now only a minor factor in the world market.

Economic sanctions by the EU over the human rights abuses of the junta (known as the State Law and Order Restoration Council, SLORC) have also had an effect and the efforts to reestablish a democratic system appear to be gathering momentum. When the country does emerge from its current repressive isolation, it is likely to become geopolitically oriented toward India, while its economic development needs will, for the most part, depend upon Japanese and European grants and investments.

THE MALDIVES REPUBLIC AND DIEGO GARCIA

The Maldives Republic, within the Indian Ocean extension of South Asia, has a tiny population (approximately 300,000) that depends upon tourism, fishing, coconut products, shipping, and apparel. It enjoyed strategic importance until Britain withdrew from the naval base in the southernmost island of Gan in 1976, replacing it with facilities on the island of Diego Garcia, which lies eight hundred miles to the south of the Maldives. That island is part of the Chagos Archipelago, a series of tiny coral atolls that were part of Mauritius until they were detached from that former British colony in 1965, at the height of the Vietnam War. The central location of Diego Garcia within the Indian Ocean, twelve hundred miles northeast of Mauritius, made it an ideal site for a strategic "floating" base that would be secured from attack by its distance and isolation. Britain later leased the base to the United States, which developed it as a base for long-range strategic bombers and for refueling naval vessels. The island proved its worth as part of the Maritime Realm's global security network, not only during the Vietnam and Gulf Wars, but also in the War against Terrorism in Afghanistan.

A complicating political factor is that now-independent Mauritius continues to claim the Chagos chain, while Diego Garcia's native islanders, who were moved to Mauritius when the American base was built, have lodged legal proceedings to be allowed to return to Diego Garcia or go to other parts of the Chagos chain.

Geopolitical Features

HISTORIC CORE

An area that might be considered South Asia's historic political core is Rajputana, the center of the historic region within the northwestern part of the Indian subcontinent that is coextensive with the modern Indian state of Rajasthan. It was there that the ancient Hindu warrior caste came to power in the seventh century and held sway for nearly a millennium, until the several Rajput princely territories were conquered by the Mughals in the late sixteenth century. Tribal divisiveness during that Hindu era prevented the establishment of a single, great political capital. Today, Rajasthan remains the bastion of conservative Hinduism, as the region plays a major role in the shift of India's politics toward right-wing religious nationalism.

Delhi's historic function as the site for the capitals of both the Mughal and British empires gives it a more clear-cut claim to being South Asia's historic core. For both empires, it was the nerve center that unified most of the subcontinent during the periods in which they held power. As the crossroads of routes leading to all parts of India, the Delhi area had been strategically important to early Hindu and Rajput dynasties. The site of the present city is the head of the two great sections of the Hindustan Plain (the valleys of the Ganges

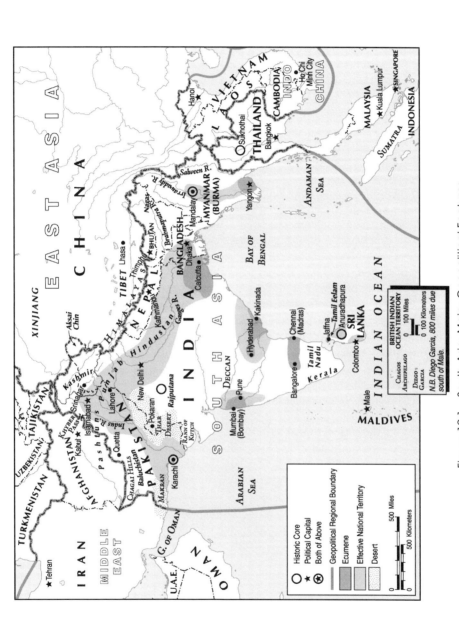

Figure 10.1   South Asia: Major Geopolitical Features

and upper Indus), on the Jumna River, a major tributary of the Ganges. Delhi dates back to the twelfth century, when it became the capital of Turko-Afghan rulers. In the seventeenth century, the Mughals built the city of Old Delhi (1658) to serve their empire, moving the capital from nearby Agra, which they had founded a century before (1556) as the seat of the Mughal court. These Muslim overlords merged the various parts of their empire with an effective administrative system that laid the groundwork for the idea of Indian nationhood. When the British Raj embraced the subcontinent in its entirety, Old Delhi served as the capital until it was replaced by Calcutta.

CAPITALS

The modern political capital of India is New Delhi, but Calcutta played a unifying role as the earlier capital of British India. The rise of Calcutta is related to the centralization of the activities of the British East India Company. During the seventeenth and eighteenth centuries, the company established three settlements or "presidencies," in Bombay (Mumbai), Madras (Chennai), and Calcutta. The latter is located on the Hoogly River at the delta formed by the confluence of the Ganges and the Brahmaputra on the Bay of Bengal. It was from Calcutta, which Robert Clive had made the main center of British commercial power and rule, that Britain was able to establish dominance over the Bengal region and oust its French East India Company rivals.

Calcutta's port and its role as the center, or entrepôt, for jute production and milling, textiles, and tea exports were the bases for the city's preeminence. Boats could move from Delhi, at the head of navigation of the Jumna River, downstream to Calcutta, thus traversing the entire Gangetic Plain. The formal shift of British India's capital from Old Delhi to Calcutta did not take place until 1833, but the political center of gravity had shifted there decades before. By the time Britain moved the capital back to Old Delhi in 1912 to strengthen its position in the Hindustan Plain against the Russian threat from Central Asia, Calcutta had already become South Asia's largest city and port.

New Delhi, the current capital of India, was inaugurated in 1931, the Delhi Cantonment serving as interim capital while New Delhi was under construction. Designed as a resplendent city whose architecture would express the grandeur and power of British India, the capital was expanded over the years from administrative center to the home of commercial and modern industrial functions.

Two hundred miles to the north of New Delhi, at an elevation of over seven thousand feet on the Himalayan ridge, was Shimla (Simla)—the hot-weather seat of government, to which the British annually migrated. When the British shifted their capital back to Delhi, they did not anticipate that the western part of the great Hindustan Plain would some day break away to form the separate country of Pakistan, and thus deprive New Delhi of its strategic continental bridging position.

During the period of British control of South Asia, India's political impact upon the region's outer parts was limited. Ceylon (Sri Lanka) had acquired separate political status as a crown colony when the British displaced the Dutch in 1798. Four years later, the ancient city of Colombo, which had been modernized as a port by the Dutch, became the capital of the colony.

Burma, too, was removed from British India's administration during much of the time that it was under British rule. The Burmese kingdom was not fully conquered by Britain until 1887 and, unlike India, enjoyed no self-government until 1923. Until this time, all Burmese capitals had been sited in the "Dry Zone" of the Middle Irrawaddy Valley in central Burma, a scrub-covered region where agriculture is essentially restricted to dry farming, with emphasis on millet, pulses, and beans, and minimal land and is available for irrigation. There, Mandalay, which had been the capital of the Burmese kingdom from 1860 to 1885, reflected the historic geographical focus of Burmese culture and civilization that was distinctly non-Indian. Britain finally recognized the cultural difference in 1937 and separated Burma from British India.

In 1923 Rangoon (Yangon) had been selected as capital, replacing Mandalay, because of its location on the Bay of Bengal in the south-central part of the country. It was built up as the country's chief port and relied for its labor force upon the large Indian population that had earlier settled in the lower Irrawaddy Valley, and served as a labor pool for the surrounding plantation areas.

The capital of Nepal, Kathmandu, is only fifty miles from the border of the Indian Hindustan Plain and therefore is especially vulnerable to pressure from New Delhi. However, Indian influence never fully penetrated the country politically, despite the fact that Nepalese royalty, whose sovereignty had been recognized in 1923, is Hindu. During the Cold War, Nepal's monarchs sought to distance themselves from Indian control by balancing their relationships with China, the Soviet Union, the United States, and India and maintaining a nonaligned policy. Nevertheless, and especially since the end of the Cold War, India remains the most influential foreign power in Nepal, because of their geographical proximity, their cultural affinity, and the substantial economic aid that India renders to Nepal. In recent years, Nepal has been plagued by Maoist rebel attackers seeking to overthrow the constitutional monarchy and establish a one-point republic.

The inaccessible Himalayan Buddhist kingdom of Bhutan was more heavily penetrated than was Nepal by British India, which took control of Bhutan's foreign affairs. When India gained its independence, London turned over this function to New Delhi. India continues to oversee Bhutan's diplomatic affairs, despite the kingdom's nominal independence and its membership in the United Nations. Even though Bhutan is remote and landlocked, its capital of Thimphu, which lies along a tributary of the Brahmaputra River, is accessible to Indian military forces from the province of Assam. When China seized Tibet, which borders Bhutan from the north, India closed the Bhutan border and built military roads into the kingdom. China's claim that Bhutan is part of Greater Tibet has reinforced India's commitment to asserting its dominance in Bhutan's military affairs.

Buddhist Sikkim, another Himalayan land, which lies wedged between Nepal and Bhutan, became an Indian protectorate in 1950. Its capital and only town, Gangtok, was relegated to the status of a state capital when, in 1975, the kingdom was formally annexed to India. At that time, New Delhi deposed Sikkim's traditional chogyal leader and converted the country into India's twenty-second state.

Pakistan's current capital, Islamabad, lies in the western Punjab within the Himalayan foothills, only forty miles west of the border with Indian-held Kashmir. It is also only ninety miles east of the Khyber Pass and the Afghan border, and thus very much a "frontier" capital. Located on the main highway and railway route from Afghanistan and Pakistan's North West Frontier Province, Islamabad was completed as a planned city adjoining Rawalpindi, the chief urban center of the northern Punjab. Rawalpindi had served as the country's interim capital from 1959, when the capital was moved there from Karachi, to 1970.

Siting Islamabad in the northern Punjab was not only a statement designed to emphasize the strategic importance of the region to Pakistan vis-à-vis its Kashmir and Afghanistan interests. It was also a move to reinforce Pakistan's commitment to securing its North-West Frontier Province and the Tribal Areas against the separatist ambitions of its Pathan (Pashtun) tribesmen. With its capital now located in the Punjab, which contains half of the country's total population as well as the army headquarters in Rawalpindi, the country's political-military center of gravity lies firmly in the northwest.

ECUMENE

Not only does South Asia lack the semblance of a regional ecumene, but India itself has no unified population or economic core area. Instead, it possesses three widely separated ecumenes: West Bengal-Bihar, focusing on Calcutta at the northern end of the Bay of Bengal; Mumbai (Bombay) on the Arabian Sea, with an extension inland across the Western Ghats onto the western edge of the Deccan in the Mumbai-Pune (Poona) district; and a zone that extends from the south central Deccan at Bangalore on the Arabian Sea eastward across the Deccan to the coast at Chennai (Madras) on the Bay of Bengal. As a historical note, these areas include the same locales that were the seats of the East India Company presidencies. While Delhi, the center of the northwestern part of the Hindustan Plain, is densely populated, it is an essentially agricultural region lacking the depth of industrial activity that a modern-day ecumene requires.

Calcutta, now India's second-largest city, with a metropolitan population of over ten million, is also its second-largest port and is served by a major network of rail, highway, river, and ocean transport facilities. Its dense population concentration ranges between fifteen hundred and two thousand persons per square mile. The major industries are the older, traditional light and heavy ones—textiles, food processing, shoes, paper, steel, chemicals, aluminum, transportation equipment, and shipbuilding. The region is the focus for traffic from eastern India and Nepal. Calcutta itself, teeming with refugees from Bangladesh, has become overwhelmingly crowded.

Mumbai, the only deepwater harbor on the west coast, is India's largest city, with a population of over twelve million, and also the country's leading port. In addition to its industries, it owes much of its preeminence to being the center of India's finance and banking, as well as of its film and other media production industries. Pune is the country's center for chemicals, oil refining, motor vehicle and machinery manufactures, textiles, fish products, pharmaceuticals, and electronics.

The Bangalore-Chennai ecumene is a mixture of old and new industrial India. Chennai, the capital of the state of Tamil Nadu, is a focus for chemicals, machinery, textiles, motor vehicles, and tanneries. Its harbor on the Bay of Bengal is the node for transportation links that radiate outward across peninsular India. Bangalore, the inland hub for this southern part of India, has become the core of the country's high-tech industry and is known as the "Silicon Valley of India" and its "Science Capital." As the newest and fastest-growing sector of an Indian ecumene, it plays a prominent role in India's plans for becoming a world software power. Its computer, electronics, telecommunications, and aircraft industries are likely to spill out and fill the corridor that now connects the Bangalore district to Chennai on the coast.

The seeds of a fourth ecumene are to be found in Hyderabad, which is situated in the central Deccan in Andhra Pradesh. The city has become India's newest software center, benefiting from the presence of several scientific and technological institutions, and is beginning to compete with Bangalore for the "Silicon Valley" title. Hyderabad is three hundred miles from the heavily populated east coastal centers of Andhra Pradesh, which are surrounded by intensively cultivated areas of rice, sugar, cotton, and palm-oil production. One can envisage the development, over the next few decades, of a corridor of modern industry cutting eastward to the coast through this agricultural zone that will serve as the basis for a new ecumene.

It is only in the Ganges Delta that a major Indian ecumene merges with that of a heavily populated neighboring country. The international boundary between India and Bangladesh divides Hindu West Bengal, which is economically dominated by Calcutta, from Muslim East Bengal. Dhaka, the Bangladeshi capital, with a population of nearly ten million, has its country's greatest concentration of industry—textiles, apparel, jute products, and handicrafts. Moreover, it is the heart of a densely populated and fertile agricultural region that is the world's largest producer of jute. However, it is an area subject to severe flooding from monsoonal rains, cyclones, and tidal waves, and land connections from Calcutta are poor and unreliable. Bangladesh is overwhelmingly poor and overpopulated, its 2,250-persons-per-square-mile population density being the highest in the world except for some small island states, and it is also lacking in mineral resources. Although the distance between Dhaka and Calcutta is only 150 miles, there is little prospect that the limited ecumene of Bangladesh will ever benefit from and merge with that of Calcutta.

The economy of Sri Lanka is based essentially upon the export of plantation crops. The country's small and underdeveloped ecumene, which centers around Colombo in the southeastern part of the island, has made progress in expanding the manufacture of textiles, clothing, rubber, and food products. However, it remains a minor economic core in comparison with those of India.

Elsewhere in the region, neither Nepal nor Bhutan possesses population and economic core areas of any magnitude. The growth of Myanmar's limited ecumene, which focuses on Yangon, has been stunted by the military government's closing of the country's economy to outside contacts.

India's ecumenes completely dominate those of its neighbors. The prospects for the development of a regionwide ecumene are negligible. While India is an important trading partner for Bangladesh, Sri Lanka, Nepal, Bhutan, and Myanmar, these heavily agricultural countries are only marginal markets for New Delhi. With the exception of Bangladesh, they are self-sufficient in food, but because of their widespread poverty they can import few finished goods and services.

Thus, India's main economic links lie outside South Asia. Its leading trading partners are the United States, Germany, and Japan. Moreover, the Indian market itself, rather than international trade, is the main catalyst for the growth of its ecumenes. The country's middle class, estimated at two hundred million people, is potentially one of the world's largest consumer markets and accounts for a disproportionate share of the nation's $2.2 trillion GDP. Even though India now has the world's fourth-largest GDP, its per capita income of $2,000 is approximately half that of China, while its ratio of trade to GDP is only 5 percent.

The modernized sector of the Indian economy is the engine of growth that offers the greatest long-range hope for pulling the impoverished rural portions of the country and the urban poor out of their present miseries. But, for the foreseeable future, the middle class will remain a relatively self-contained segment of relative prosperity, with all too little impact upon the impoverished classes. India therefore remains vulnerable to social upheavals, as the poor flock to the great cities, where only a small proportion of them succeed in securing employment, housing, and adequate health services.

EFFECTIVE REGIONAL/NATIONAL TERRITORY

South Asia's countries possess few lands that are now only moderately settled and that therefore could attract substantial new population growth. (See table 10.1 for population densities.) Most of Pakistan is mountain or desert, with most of the population crowded onto the Indus Plain. Bangladesh, one of the world's most densely populated nations, is one great floodplain with no room for expansion. Mountainous Nepal and Bhutan have limited narrow valleys that hold nearly all of their populations.

Sri Lanka's landscape is characterized by a central mass of mountains surrounded by wide coastal plains that are very densely populated in the wet western and southern portions of the island. The "Dry Zone" of the northeast has for decades been heralded by Colombo governments as a resettlement area that could absorb the overpopulated reaches of the country. In historic times, this region was heavily populated through the use of "tanks," or basins that could store water for irrigation. However, diseases and wars caused it to become deserted over the centuries and it is now largely covered with swamps and dense jungles.

Converting the Dry Zone, where populations are under fifty persons per square mile, to Effective National Territory has been a slow process. Malarial swamps have been cleared and irrigation schemes have been initiated, including the diversion of waters from the Mahweli dam in the moist central highlands. However, settlement efforts have lagged behind the country's population growth for political reasons that have hampered the development of infrastructure. The zone is largely in the poor, Tamil-inhabited regions and the Tamils oppose the large-scale movement of Sinhalese farmers from the overcrowded "wet zones," where population densities range from 600 to 3,000 persons per square mile.

Extreme nationalists among the Sinhalese majority are opposed to regional autonomy for the Tamils, which the Sri Lanka government has proposed in order to end the rebellion. As the reason for their opposition, the nationalists cite the need for continuing central governmental controls of the Dry Zone. So the dilemma remains. Without peace, most of the goals for restoring the Dry Zone and providing Effective National Territory for Sri Lanka's burgeoning population, currently at twenty million, are likely to remain unrealized. But the price of peace may be Tamil political control of immigration into the zone, which could block Sinhalese resettlement prospects.

Myanmar, with its central core of forests and mountains running from the northern borders to the delta of the Irrawaddy, has little expansion room. The dry belt is the central Irrawaddy Valley, which is already densely populated. It contains such former capitals as Mandalay and two cities that lie immediately to the south of Mandalay, Amarapura and Ava. For reasons of politics and terrain, the northern and western hills and the eastern Shan plateau also hold little promise of absorbing large numbers of additional people. Instead, the crowding is likely to continue within the Irrawaddy Valley and Delta, the Arakan coast facing the Bay of Bengal, and the Tenasserim coastal region that fronts the Andaman Sea.

India, too, has little available land for agricultural expansion. Whatever areas might be described as Effective National Territory are the already densely populated farm regions, where the replacement of agriculture by urban industrial activities is serving to expand existing ecumenes. These areas include the western portion of Bihar in the lower Gangetic Plain, the Western Ghats to the east of Mumbai, and the Hyderabad-Chennai corridor.

EMPTY AREAS

South Asia possesses four main Empty Areas: (1) the Thar (Great Indian) Desert of western India, which extends into Pakistan's southeastern Sind Province; (2) the Rann of Cutch, which is the vast salt waste and swamp that lies mostly in India's Gujarat state south of the Thar desert, but extends into southern Sind; (3) the Khara and Makran deserts of Pakistan's southwestern Baluchistan; and (4) the Himalayas.

The value of the Thar Desert to India is essentially strategic. It was at Pokaran, in the east-central Thar, that India exploded its first nuclear device in 1974 and conducted its underground nuclear tests in 1998. The Chagai Hills, along the northern rim of the Khara Desert in Baluchistan, straddle the Afghan border and provide Islamabad with its nuclear testing sites, including those where the 1998 tests took place.

The Rann of Cutch, originally an arm of the Arabian Sea, is now a vast salt waste and swamp depression. The dispute over its boundary was one of the causes of the 1965 India-Pakistan war. In a 1968 international arbitration, India was awarded more than 95 percent of the Rann's eighty-four hundred square miles. The area's sole economic resource is salt, which can be extracted only in the dry season. As pointed out by Govind Singh, it was hardly worth fighting for, but both sides saw this as an issue of historic territorial rights and were willing to go to war over what each regarded as its territorial integrity.[9]

The Himalayas, Asia's great mountain system, extend for fifteen hundred miles from northern Pakistan across northern India, Tibet, and Nepal to eastern India, Bhutan, and Nepal. A series of parallel ranges, the towering southern (Great) Himalayas, are snow-covered year-round. Little of the region is inhabited, save the southern foothills. Its main geopolitical function is as a frontier barrier between India and China. The Himalayas also serve as the source of the largest rivers of the Indian subcontinent, on which Pakistan, India, and Bangladesh are so dependent. The Karakoram, the major pass across the Karakoram Mountains, enables traffic to skirt the western end of the Himalayas. The Diphu pass, at the eastern end of the Himalayan range, serves as the main crossing point there. Both passes have been important objectives in the competing Indian and Chinese territorial claims. Control of the Karakoram pass by China affords Pakistan direct access to Xinjiang Province. India's control of the Diphu Pass blocks China's access to Assam.

BOUNDARIES

The major conflict over boundaries between South Asia and an adjoining geopolitical realm is the one between China and India over the territories at the western and eastern edges of the Himalayas, as previously discussed. Elsewhere, along the region's outer rim, there is a minor dispute that has caused sporadic conflict between Myanmar and Thailand over alignment of the border.

The most serious and widespread border disputes, however, are intraregional. The territorial dispute between India and Pakistan over the status of Kashmir has not only triggered three wars, but it also has brought the two nations into the dangerous nuclear confrontation that threatens to destabilize the entire region. "Liberation" of Indian-held Jammu and Kashmir—India's only heavily Muslim state—has been the consistent objective of Pakistani military and civilian rulers. At the time of the partition of India, Kashmir was ruled by a Hindu prince who, despite the region's mainly Muslim population, placed Kashmir under India. A Muslim revolt ousted the prince, but he was reinstalled by Indian troops who were flown to Kashmir to repulse the Pakistani-supported rebels.

The present cease-fire line divides the region in two—the lightly populated, half Muslim and half Buddhist northern and western portion in Pakistan known as Azad Kashmir, and the southern and more populous region, the Indian state of Jammu and Kashmir. The latter contains the heavily Muslim-populated Vale of Kashmir, including Srinagar, capital of the state. The Vale of Kashmir is the most populous part of the region and its economic heart. Jammu, in the south, is two-thirds Hindu.

The emotional and ideological pull of Kashmir on both Indians and Pakistanis has been the major stumbling block to mediation of the dispute. However, over the years the strategic issue has intensified. The part of Aksai Chin that China occupies is in eastern Ladakh, one of Kashmir's subregions, and forms an important link between Tibet and Xinjiang. In addition, the Pakistani-Chinese boundary agreement of 1962, whereby China was granted 2,050 square miles of northern Azad Kashmir that had been in dispute between India and China, provided for highway links between Pakistan and Xinjiang (the Karakoram Highway and an earlier one built through the Mintaka pass in 1968).[10] The Pakistani shift of this territory to China was a strategic gain for Pakistan as well as for China, while it was viewed by India as a strategic setback.

The economic cost of the Kashmir conflict has been enormous. For example, the Kargil campaign caused a 28 percent increase in India's 1999 military budget, or in other words accounted for over one-fifth of total federal expenditures. Pakistan's military expenditures are proportionally the same, although the 4.4 percent of GDP that this represents is substantially higher than India's 2.7 percent.[11]

The waters of the Indus River basin are also an issue in the Kashmir conflict. The Indus, Jhelum, and Chenab Rivers flow through the state of Jammu and Kashmir before entering Pakistan. They are crucial to agriculture in Pakistan's Punjab and Sind. The 1960 Indus Water Basin Treaty did not provide for integrated water development, but rather for each country to develop and manage its own water resources. Construction of upstream dams for power and irrigation by India remains a point of contention for its potential impact on downstream Pakistani users.

Another river boundary controversy between the two countries revolves around Sir Creek—the stream that separates India and Pakistan at the southwestern edge of the Rann of Cutch. India claims that the boundary is midchannel of the creek where it enters the Arabian Sea, just below the mouths of the Indus; Pakistan claims the right bank, thus the stream exit in its entirety. The precise location of the boundary here is important in fixing its maritime extension. What is at stake for Pakistan is that its claim would permit the seaward extension of its exclusive economic zone to include another 250 square miles of water whose seabed holds promise of oil and gas reserves.

Two minor disputes, one between India and Bangladesh and one between India and Nepal, are worthy of mention because of the broader principles that are involved. The first dispute is over a small island that was formed in 1979 after a cyclone and tidal wave in the Bay of Bengal. The island lies in the estuary of the Hariabhanga River, the main channel of which forms the boundary between India and Bangladesh. The bank of the river on the

Indian side is three miles west of the island, while the Bangladeshi bank is five miles to the island's east.[12] The island—"New Moore" to India and "South Talpatty" to Bangladesh—has no intrinsic value. The dispute relates to control of the maritime zone of the continental shelf that extends out from the island. The shelf possesses rich oil and gas reserves—an extension of the delta's resources. While there have been no military incidents since the navies of the two countries skirmished in 1981, the definition of the maritime zone remains an important issue to both countries.

India and Nepal were in dispute over control of thirty square miles at the source of the Mahakali (Sarda) River along the border between the two countries, where India constructed the Sarda dam on the river, despite Nepal's objections. In 1996 the two countries came to an agreement on sharing the dam's water and hydroelectric supplies and established the Mahakali River Commission to adjudicate future disputes. The principle of the agreement was that the India-built dam did not prejudice Nepal's sovereign rights. The agreement permitted both parties to cooperate while continuing to disagree on the boundary location.

China considers its forty-three-mile border with Afghanistan to be a strategic problem, although it is not in dispute. This boundary is at the eastern end of Afghanistan's Wakhan salient, which cuts between the Pamirs in Tajikistan and the Hindu Kush in Pakistan and adjoins China's Xinjiang Province. The Taliban and al Qaeda were able to smuggle arms via the Wakhan to the province's Muslim Uighur rebels and to bring them to Afghanistan's terrorist training bases. This is one of the factors in China's cooperation with the United States in the War against Terrorism.

Conclusion

South Asia is a distinct geopolitical region, separated from surrounding realms and regions by nature, culture, social difference, politics, and to a considerable extent, religion. It can be neither dominated by Great Powers nor absorbed into adjoining geopolitical frameworks, although Pakistan and Myanmar, on the region's western and eastern margins respectively, have strong links with bordering geopolitical regions.

As a geopolitical region, South Asia lacks internal unity because of its deep divisions—religious, racial, ethnic, linguistic, and social. The depth of these divisions is such that significant regional frameworks of cooperation have yet to evolve. The Colombo Plan for Cooperative Regional Development, aimed at strengthening the economies of various members through economic and technical assistance, was signed in 1951. It then embraced Southeast and South Asia as well as the United Kingdom. The United States, which joined later, has become the largest donor among its twenty-six members. The plan, which provides for educational, health, and technical aid as well as food supplies, overall has had a marginal impact on the economy of South Asia.

Equally ineffective in attaining the stated goals has been the South Asian Association for Regional Cooperation (SAARC). Established in 1985 with a membership that included all of the region's states (save Pakistan, which joined later), SAARC's goals include cooperation in such areas as easing poverty, environment, education, controlling drug trafficking, and trade liberalization. It has created the South Asia Preferential Trade Association to stimulate regional trade and development and founded a regional development fund, which has almost no money available for stimulating the economies of the region's least-developed countries. SAARC's main achievement lies within the realm of publishing studies, but it falls far short of being an instrument for furthering regional unity.

The divisiveness of South Asia has been a major factor in its development lag over the past half century. Looming above the other regional conflicts is that between India and Pakistan over Kashmir. The dispute has led the two countries into an expensive arms race and a dangerous nuclear weapons competition. In addition to the full-scale wars waged between the two countries, Muslim guerrillas supported by Pakistan have mounted actions within India's Jammu and Kashmir state that have caused twenty-five thousand deaths in the past decade. Fighting broke out between India and Pakistan over Islamabad's support of these guerrillas, although this conflict did not erupt into a full-scale war between the two countries.

Prospects for resolution of the conflict through outside mediation have shown little evidence of improvement since the end of the Cold War. The web of foreign power entanglement continues to complicate the dispute. Russian arms sales to India and Chinese military support of Pakistan sustain the disputing parties. The situation has been further complicated by renewal of U.S. economic and military aid to Islamabad. Its military rulers, led by President Pervez Musharraf, joined the coalition against the Taliban in the face of enormous opposition by Pakistan's Islamic fundamentalists, who are especially strong in the Pashtun areas of the country, where many al Qaeda and Taliban guerrillas are in hiding.

While the United States has made efforts to improve relations with India, its recent rapprochement with Pakistan, and its even-handed efforts to halt the nuclear arms race between India and Pakistan, remain obstacles to the development of strong ties between Washington and New Delhi. U.S. policy makers rarely take into account that India's goal of becoming a nuclear power derives from its fears of China even more than its enmity with Pakistan. If mutual deterrence is both a practical and morally defensible strategy for U.S. relations with Russia and China, then Indians ask why nuclear deterrence between India and China is not equally defensible.

A U.S. policy that would acknowledge the legitimacy of India's goal to become a nuclear power would clear the air for improved ties between the two countries. It might also pave the way for a major effort by the United States and other Maritime world nations to spur India's economic development. Such a policy need not attempt to wean India away from its ties with Russia and seek to embrace it geostrategically within the Maritime Realm—a prospect that is neither politically realistic nor geopolitically necessary. However, it could lead to a new role of balanced engagement in world affairs for India in place of its failed nonalignment policies. This would be based on convergent relationships with both the United States and Russia. A stronger India would not only counterbalance the weight of China in Asia and further strengthen the foundations of global geopolitical equilibrium, but it would secure India's dominance within South Asia.

High technology represents India's most promising avenue for economic development. The large Indian middle class generates a pool of well-trained scientific and technological personnel who use English to communicate with each other. This manpower pool has already made a global impact through the Indian émigrés, who play so important a role in the U.S. and other Western high-technology worlds. These émigrés have been helpful in stimulating India's rapidly growing software and pharmaceutical industries, as more and more outsourcing of software activities and services has been directed toward India. In 1999 Indian software exports totaled $5 billion, or over 7 percent of all exports, and they are increasing exponentially. Some projections are for a tenfold growth within a decade.

The high-technology industry alone cannot directly solve the country's massive unemployment problem. It can, however, generate billions of dollars in exports that can then be plowed back into the nation's physical and social infrastructure—roads, water, electricity, communications, wiring, education, and health. Its application to older manufacturing industries can also bring about dramatic productivity increases there and help to modernize India's agriculture.

All of this would expand the domestic and foreign market for Indian goods and services, which would in turn further stimulate the flow of outside capital investment. Manufacturing and information services that are outsourced to India could eventually raise India to the level of China as one of the great trading nations of the world. However, India has a long way to go before it can close the current gap with China as a focus for outsourcing. One measure of this gap is that India's current foreign trade is only one-fourth that of China and its exports to the United States only one-eighth the level of Chinese exports.

Changes in South Asia's external boundary contours depend upon the geopolitical directions that Pakistan and Myanmar may take. Pakistan, together with Afghanistan, may become a Shatterbelt, internally divided and caught in the vise between Iran, India, China, and Russia. As Pakistan has strengthened its ties with Afghanistan, and Islamic fundamentalism has gathered momentum within Pakistan, Islamabad's Middle Eastern orientation has become stronger.

One possibility is that a postwar Pashtun-controlled Afghan government, hostile to Pakistan, might revive historic claims within Afghanistan for the unification of all Pashtun peoples, who had been divided by the boundary known as the "Durand Line" when British India was separated from Afghanistan in 1893. This boundary was delineated by a survey party headed by Sir Mortimer Durand. The agreement accepting this line put an end to the tension that existed between Britain and Afghanistan since the conflict of 1878 to 1880. Alternatively, should Afghanistan break apart, its Pashtuns might mount a drive for reestablishment of an independent state that includes western Pakistan in an area that has been called Pakhtoonistan. The cause of an independent Pakhtoonistan was pursued by Kabul at the time of the creation of Pakistan and clouded relations between the two countries from the 1950s to the 1970s.[13]

Also, Afghanistan supported guerrilla activities in Pakistan's central and southern Baluchistan Province during this earlier period, on the grounds of the tribal links between its inhabitants and those of Baluchistan. Absorption of the province would provide landlocked Afghanistan with an outlet to the Arabian Sea. This Baluchi guerrilla separatist movement has been quiescent since the rapprochement between Afghanistan and Pakistan that took place at the time of the Soviet-Afghan War.

Pakistan might well become dismembered through the loss of its North-West Frontier the Tribal Areas, and Baluchistan Provinces, and through changes in the status of Kashmir. What would remain of Pakistan would be a much more cohesive state extending across the Indus Plain to include the provinces of (West) Punjab and Sind. Such a state would include more than 80 percent of the country's current population and its two ecumenes, and would be a far more stable entity than present-day Pakistan.

Elsewhere within the region, additional proliferation of states may take place, in the wake of new strife and conflict. This proliferation could take two forms—statehood or quasi-statehood. For example, one option for resolving the Kashmir dispute would be for Kashmir to become a quasi-independent state through the joining of Azad Kashmir, which Pakistan now controls, with Indian-held Jammu and Kashmir in a condominium administered by India and Pakistan. Ultimately, the condominium might evolve into an independent state. "Nagaland," in India's state of Arunachal Pradesh, is probably too small and weak to win its rebellion. However, New Delhi could satisfy the mostly Christian Nagas by offering a Bhutan-like sovereignty whereby India would retain responsibility for diplomatic relations and have assured military access to the country, while the Nagas would preserve their traditional culture, tribal modes of governance, and religion.

Ending the war in Sri Lanka is still doubtful despite the cease-fire. The Buddhist Sinhalese leadership has taken a hard line against consideration of a governmental structure that would offer the Hindu Tamils quasi-statehood. A war-weary Sri Lankan government might eventually offer quasi-statehood to the Tamil Eelam. In the long run, however, this would not satisfy the Tamil Tigers, who would exploit such autonomy to seek full independence. The outcome might result in not just a Tamil state on the northern and eastern coasts of the island, but also perhaps a Greater Tamil state straddling the Palk Strait that would combine the Indian state of Tamil Nadu with Sri Lankan Tamil Eelam.

Since the partition of the Indian Subcontinent, militant Sikhs in India's Punjab state have sought an autonomous Sikh state, which they would call "Kalistan." The Punjab was the historic center for Sikh kingdoms and Amritsar is their sacred city. It was the seizure of the Golden Temple in that city by militant Sikhs and the subsequent storming of the temple by the Indian army troops that led to the assassination of Prime Minister Indira Gandhi by her Sikh bodyguards in 1984. The violence that shook the Punjab in the 1980s has abated somewhat, but the Sikhs, who constitute 60 percent of the total population of India's Punjab, continue to have separatist aspirations.

The importance to India of this province, the eastern half of the historic Punjab, is too great for New Delhi to grant it full independence. It is a vital part of the Hindustan Plain, its economy having national significance as the country's granary, and it serves as a frontier province vis-à-vis Pakistan's western half of the Punjab region. Still, quasi-statehood is a possible solution.

Myanmar's current leanings toward China are not likely to survive the fall of the Yangon military regime and restoration of democracy to the country. The government of India has allied itself strongly with the Burmese freedom cause, while China supports the junta. However, governmental collapse in Myanmar could provide an opening for the separatist forces in the country to revive their independence drives. The Shan people in eastern Myanmar, who live in the hills and valleys that adjoin China, Laos, and Thailand, retain a strong drive for freedom. They derive considerable strength from the opium and heroin trade of the Golden Triangle.

The number of possible new South Asian states or pseudostates is limited by the strengths of the central governments involved, particularly that of India. However, proliferation of states has not run its course in this subcontinent of 1.35 billion people—22 percent of the world's population living in only 4 percent of the world's states. It cannot be predicted whether separatism can be guided into constructive frameworks of negotiation or violence will continue to prevail. Nevertheless, in assessing the geopolitical near future of South Asia, it is fairly safe to predict that some devolution can be anticipated.

Should India remain unified in the face of the various devolutionary currents that may sweep across the region, and resolve the Kashmir conflict, its regional dominance will be reinforced. With its large and efficient army and nuclear capacity, its high-tech industrial leadership, and a population that is likely to overtake that of China in size, it could become the core of a new Indian Ocean geostrategic realm.

Such a realm would embrace eastern coastal Africa, especially Tanzania (with its islands of Zanzibar and Pemba) and Kenya. It would also include Myanmar, which borders the eastern Bay of Bengal and the Andaman Sea. In addition, the realm would include the Indian Ocean island states of the Maldives, the Seychelles, the Comoros, Madagascar, and Mauritius, as well as the French dependencies of Réunion, Mayotte, and Iles Glorieuses, and the British Indian Ocean territory of the Chagos Archipelago that contains Diego Garcia.

Traders and settlers from India have long influenced the lands around the Indian Ocean. Two millennia ago, Hindu civilization spread to Sumatra and much of Java and Bali, as well as to the Malay Peninsula, and Indian traders were active in Zanzibar. Over the centuries, small but influential Indian populations have settled along the fringes of the ocean, including South Africa, where they have engaged in commerce and, in some instances, plantation agriculture. These communities could play an important role in reconstructing the trading networks that linked the basin a millennium ago, and thereby reinforce the geostrategic influence of the prospective realm upon neighboring realms.

Notes

1. Percival Spear, *Modern India* (Ann Arbor: University of Michigan Press, 1961), 386–406.

2. Saul B. Cohen, *Geography and Politics in a World Divided* (New York: Random House, 1963), 280–84.

3. Halford Mackinder, *Democratic Ideals and Reality* (London: Constable, 1919), map facing 77, 83–104.

4. Halford Mackinder, "The Round World and the Winning of the Peace," *Foreign Affairs* 21, no. 4 (1943): 278.

5. Michael Brecher, *The New States of Asia* (New York: Oxford University Press, 1966), 205.

6. Brecher, *New States of Asia*, 210.

7. Bertil Lintner, *Cross-Border Trade in the Golden Triangle* (Durham, England: Boundaries Research Press-University of Durham, 1991), 13–22.

8. Lintner, *Cross-Border Trade*, 1, 25–26.

9. Govand Singh, *A Political Geography of India* (Allahabad, India: Central Book Deposit, 1969), 134–37.

10. Alan J. Day, *Border and Territorial Disputes* (Harlow, England: Longman, 1982), 255–57.

11. Central Intelligence Agency, *The World Factbook 2000* (Washington, D.C.: Gov/CIA Publications, 2000), 9, 10.

12. Day, *Border and Territorial Disputes*, 251.

13. Day, *Border and Territorial Disputes*, 236–50.

CHAPTER 11

The Arc of Geostrategic Instability, Part II: The Middle East Shatterbelt

The western portion of the Arc of Geostrategic Instability—the Middle East Shatterbelt—is even more fragmented and unstable than South Asia because the strength of Great Power penetration has exacerbated the already deep internal rifts.

Sunni and Shia Muslims; Christians and Jews; Arabs, Turks, and Persians; Azeris, Kurds, and Druze; Alawites and Maronites; Nilotic blacks and Sudanese Arabs; Bedouins and farmers; religious fundamentalists and secularists—all are part of the human landscape of the Middle East. Rather than forming a coherent mosaic, however, the parts overlap and rub against one another, fitting poorly into the national frameworks that are the region's political overlay. The ethnic, religious, and racial strife engendered by these differences is further intensified by disputes over the scarce commodities of water and arable land, and by conflicting claims over oil and natural gas resources.

The location of the Middle East at the junction of the Old World's three continents has long given global strategic importance to its water and land transit ways. These transit ways, as well as the vast petroleum reserves of the region, are the magnets that now draw outside powers to the region. In their efforts to gain competitive advantages, outside powers build upon and reinforce the internal divisions. The result of such intense geopolitical fragmentation is to turn the region into a Shatterbelt.

This was not always the case in the Middle East. Indeed, it has experienced lengthy periods of unification imposed by imperial powers, interspersed with periods of political fragmentation. The fall of Constantinople to the Ottoman Turks in 1453 signaled the rise of the Ottoman Empire and an era of regional unity that would last for four centuries. Weakened by military defeats at the hands of European powers and Russia, and sapped by the "capitulations" system, which awarded commercial rights to the Europeans, the empire began to decline in the mid-nineteenth century. By the end of World War I, it had formally dissolved. In its stead came the European imperial rule that segmented the Middle East into spheres of influence.

Modern Colonial Penetration

Throughout the nineteenth and twentieth centuries, Western European powers and Russia jockeyed for bases and influence within the region. Even before the collapse of the Ottoman

Empire, Britain, the most powerful colonial force, had a number of strategic goals, the most important of which was securing the sea lanes to India. The acquisition of bases in Suez, at the southern entrance of the Red Sea, and along the Persian/Arab Gulf provided control over this route. The opening of the Suez Canal in 1869 enabled Britain to expand its trade with South and East Asia, making it the dominant commercial power in the world.

Cyprus provided Britain with the forward base for the occupation of Egypt in 1882, and for command of the canal. Defeat of the Mahdists, who had wrested control of the Sudan from Egypt, by Ango-Egyptian forces enabled the British to establish the Anglo-Egyptian Sudan condominium in 1879. This gave Britain oversight of the western shores of the Red Sea to complement the base on the other side at Aden, which commanded the Strait of Bab el-Mandeb, the exit to the Indian Ocean. Rule over Sudan also assured control of the waters of the upper Nile, thus strengthening Britain's hold on Egypt.

Another British goal was to eliminate piracy in the Arabian Sea and the Indian Ocean, and to halt the slave trade from East Africa that moved along these waters.[1] British protectorates were established over Bahrain (1867), the Trucial States (1892), and Kuwait (1899), which became bases from which to pursue this struggle.

Afghanistan was the land gateway to India, and fear of Russian and Persian penetration of Afghan territory led the British to take preemptive steps. They became embroiled in a series of wars with the Afghans, who were forced to cede the Khyber Pass and other border areas in the east to British India. Later the situation was stabilized when the Afghans signed formal border agreements with Russia and Persia, as well as with Britain.

Other European powers also actively engaged within the region. France sent troops to Christian Mount Lebanon to put a halt to the massacres by the Druze of the area's Catholic population. This became the foothold within the Levant from which Paris ultimately gained control over all of Lebanon and Syria. The French also seized Djibouti on the African shore of the Gulf of Aden, where they developed the port into a commercial and strategic rival to British Aden.

Italy seized Eritrea, along the southwestern shores of the Red Sea. The Eritrean ports of Asab and Massawa commanded the access to landlocked Ethiopia, which was to become the main focus for Italy's imperial ambitions in northeastern Africa.

Russian penetration of the region during the nineteenth century was confined to securing territories around the Caspian Sea. This brought the czars into conflict with both the Ottoman Empire and Persia. The lands on the eastern shores of the Caspian were taken from Persia, while on the western shore the Ottomans ceded northern Azerbaijan to Russia.

At the dawn of the twentieth century, Britain, out of fear of German and Russian designs on the region, felt obliged to strengthen its position in the Persian Gulf through control of overland routes leading there. Turkey and Germany had signed an accord in 1896 to extend the German-owned Anatolian Railway from Konya in southeastern Anatolia to Baghdad and Basra, and then to the open waters. Russia also put forward claims for concessions in the Gulf. For London, such moves represented a threat to vital communication lines needed for the defense of India.[2] British and French opposition held up the line to Baghdad until construction was resumed in 1911 and completed by the end of World War I.

However, none of the above considerations were to become as important to Britain's Persian Gulf strategy as its twentieth-century efforts to exploit and safeguard the oil resources of the region. William D'Arcy had been granted a concession by Persia to drill for oil in 1901. By 1908, the oil fields of Khuzestan, Persia's Arab-populated southwestern province, were revealed to be among the richest in the world.

Meanwhile, Russia sought to penetrate Persia from its Caspian Sea bases. In 1907, it carved out a sphere of influence in northern Persia that extended in the west from Tabriz (nominally under Ottoman control) through Tehran to Mashad in the east, and that reached south to Esfahan. This coincided with the establishment of a British zone of influence covering the southwestern part of the country, extending from the Persian Gulf port of Bandar Abbas northeastward to the borders of British India and Afghanistan and backed by British bases along the western coast of the Gulf.

The Anglo-Iranian oil company then commissioned the building of a refinery at Abadan, whose production was to prove of great importance to the Allied war effort during World War I. It was the defense of the oil fields and facilities that prompted the British to attack the Turks in Iraq, seizing Baghdad in 1917 and then moving on to Mosul. (Abadan was to be expanded into the world's largest oil refinery in the 1970s.)

Britain reinforced its grip on the Gulf by becoming the protector of Ibn Saud, ruler of the Nejd in the center of Arabia, against the Turks. This close relationship between Britain and Saudi Arabia was later affirmed in a 1924 treaty that recognized Britain's special status in Kuwait, Bahrain, Qatar, and the Oman coast. The accord was, in part, a quid pro quo for Britain's acceptance of Ibn Saud's conquest of the Hejaz, which had been ruled by Husayn ibn Ali, Sherif of Makka and head of the Hashemite family—a branch of the tribe to which Mohammed the Prophet had belonged. This paved the way for a unified state from the Red Sea to the Gulf. Even though driven out of Arabia, the Hashemite dynasty retained a prominent role within the region, as in 1921 the British had put one of Husayn's sons, Faisal, on the throne of Iraq and installed another, Abdullah, as head of Trans-Jordan.

From the end of World War I through World War II, much of the region was divided among European colonial powers into fairly coherent subunits—the British in Palestine, Trans-Jordan, Iraq, Southern Yemen (the Aden Protectorate), Egypt, and Sudan; the French in Lebanon and Syria; and the Italians in Libya (which they had conquered in 1912).

Modern Turkey, now limited territorially to Anatolia and Turkish Thrace in Europe, took the path of isolation and initiated a drive toward Westernization, secularization, and self-sufficiency under the leadership of Kemal Atatürk. Saudi Arabia, Yemen, and Iran also remained independent of colonial rule. While Britain remained the major Western supporter of the Saudi Wahhabite dynasty during the 1920s and 1930s, the United States entered the Saudi Arabian scene in 1936 with the discovery of oil by an American oil company, which eventually became the Arab American Oil Company. Commercial production began two years later at Al-Dammam on the Al-Ahsa coastal plain, although it was not until 1951 that a gusher was brought in at nearby Al-Hofuf that, three years later, would prove to be part of the Ghafar structure—the world's largest oil field. The new Pahlavi dynasty in Persia, meanwhile, managed to free itself of the British and Soviet spheres of influence that had been established in the north and south of the country.

While the Middle East had become a highly divided region from the end of World War I to the mid-twentieth century, it also had enjoyed a degree of geopolitical stability. The European powers had struck a balance of power within the territories under their control and had limited the spread of Soviet influence. It was during the Cold War that the deep divisions and instability that have come to be associated with the Middle East converted the region into today's Shatterbelt.

The end of the Mandate system and of colonial rule in general following World War II produced a multiplicity of national states within the region—stretching from Turkey,

Cyprus, and Afghanistan in the north, south through Israel and a politically divided Arab Levant and Mesopotamia, and into Africa, from Libya and Egypt down through Sudan. The conflicts within and among the twenty-four diverse sovereign states of the region were inflamed and expanded by Cold War competition. This struggle, between the Maritime Realm democracies and the Eurasian Heartland Soviet Union, for influence and control of strategically important spaces and for access to oil and gas reserves tore the Middle East asunder. Alliances forged by the outside powers with states and opposition groups removed all semblance of the geopolitical unity that had been achieved within the region in previous eras.

Great Power Rivalry: Cold War Period

The Cold War competition within the Middle East between the West and the Soviet Union was initiated by Soviet efforts to detach northern Iran from the rest of the country in 1945–46. At that time, Moscow supported breakaway Communist republics in the Iranian portions of Azerbaijan and Kurdistan. The seeds of this intervention had been planted in the early years of World War II, when Soviet troops had occupied Iranian Azerbaijan to establish a supply line for Allied military aid being transshipped to the USSR via the Persian Gulf.

Toward the end of the war, Moscow asked for a concession to explore the northern region for oil, but was put off by Tehran. A major worry for the Soviets was that their Baku oil fields were aging.

The Soviets also resurrected historic Russian ambitions for a corridor to the Persian/Arab Gulf, their appetite now whetted by the region's oil deposits that extended along the flanks of the Zagros and from there along the coast to Qatar and the Arab emirates. When the USSR agreed to withdraw from Iran, it did so with the promise that oil concessions would be granted, subject to parliamentary approval. However, the Iranian Parliament resoundingly rejected the proposal the following year, further worsening the relations between the two countries.

Moscow then sought to penetrate Iran through support of the Iranian Tudeh (Communist) Party and the Iranian National Front, headed by Mohammed Mossadegh. Mossadegh came to power in 1951, when the Front gained enough seats within the parliament to pass an oil nationalization act. He was opposed both to foreign oil interests and to the Shah's rule. The Shah then fled, but was returned to power in 1953 when Mossadegh was forced from office (with covert help from the CIA). A firm military alliance with the United States then emerged, foreclosing Iran to penetration by Moscow.

Another Soviet attempt to inject itself into the region failed when Ankara refused to revise the Montreux Convention and give the USSR joint control of the Turkish straits— the entranceway to the Black Sea. Turkey countered the Soviet threat by turning strongly to the West and becoming a full member of NATO in 1952.

In the meantime, the position of the West within the Middle East was undergoing rapid change. In the Levant (Lebanon, Palestine, and Syria), France gave up its mandate over Lebanon in 1945 and over Syria the following year. Britain, which had split off Trans-Jordan from Palestine in 1922, granted the kingdom its independence in 1946, although Britain maintained its influence there by continuing to subsidize and train the Jordanian armed forces. A year later, London gave up its mandate over Palestine, whereupon the first Arab-Israeli war erupted. Israel won its War of Independence in 1948. In the following years, a military and economic alliance developed between Israel and the United States, which helped the former to develop a powerful military machine and a strong modern economy. Washington gained an important strategic asset with the region, but at the cost of bitter and enduring Arab opposition. British military influence in Iraq, where it had relinquished its mandate in 1934, weakened in 1948 as the Iraqi parliament refused London's request for modifications in the treaty of alliance between the two countries. Libya, which had been placed under joint Anglo-French military government after the Allied victory over German and Italian forces in North Africa in 1943, became independent in 1951. Libya subsequently signed military treaties with Britain and the United States, permitting the establishment of military bases on its soil, including the large American Wheelus air base. Sudan gained its independence from Britain in 1956.

With the passing of the European colonial era, the United States moved onto the Middle Eastern scene, replacing Britain and France as the primary Western external power. Because war-torn Europe was in economic shambles, it was left to Washington to apply its military and financial leverage to defend the interests of the Maritime Realm within the region. This it did by placing large NATO bases in Turkey and providing it with massive economic aid, developing strong military and economic ties with Saudi Arabia, forging close relations with Israel, and giving powerful support to the monarchy in Iran.

In response to the West's policy of containment along the Middle East's Northern Tier, which included formation of the Baghdad Pact in 1955, Moscow developed a strategy of alliances that leapfrogged the ring that had been drawn along its borders. The situation in Egypt offered the Soviet Union its first major opportunity to gain a strong foothold within the heart of the Middle East. When British troops completed their evacuation of the Suez Canal Zone in 1956, Colonel Gamal Abdel Nasser nationalized the Suez Canal and broke relations with London.

Three months after the canal had been nationalized, Britain and France moved to regain control of the waterway, in tandem with Israeli land forces. Israel's motives were to block Palestinian guerrilla attacks from Egyptian-controlled Gaza and Sinai and to regain access to the canal, which had been denied to it by Cairo since 1950. An additional goal was to break the Arab blockade of the Straits of Tiran at the southern end of the Gulf of Aqaba, Israel's only alternative access to oil supplies from Iran and trade with the Far East. The campaign to seize the canal was foiled by UN intervention, led by the United States and the Soviet Union. The war ended with an armistice whose terms included the withdrawal of the attacking forces.

In the wake of these events, Moscow emerged as Egypt's major patron, providing it with the funds for the Aswan Dam, supplying it with massive military and economic aid, and establishing military and air bases within the country. The Egyptians pursued economic development in the Soviet style, nationalizing their industries. This relationship lasted until Anwar Sadat suddenly expelled the Soviet military personnel from Egypt as a prelude to the attack upon Israel by Cairo and Damascus that opened the October 1973 war—a conflict that the USSR had been reluctant to support.

The close ties between Egypt, the leader of the Arab world, and the Soviet Union had facilitated the rapid spread of Soviet influence within the region. When Cairo signed a military accord with Moscow in 1956, Damascus followed suit. These alliances were designed to counter the Baghdad Pact. Led by the Baath Party, which combined socialism and nationalism, Syria formed a union with Egypt in 1958 called the United Arab Republic. Yemen soon joined the union, which was renamed the United Arab States. The merger lasted only three years, until a military coup against the Baathists led to the withdrawal of Damascus from the union. In 1966 the radical wing of the Baathists regained power with support from the Soviet Union, which then equipped the Syrian army with modern weapons.

The Arab strategy of dual attacks upon Israel from both the north and south was the cornerstone of the 1967 and 1973 wars. Despite the purchase of substantial arms from the USSR and modernization of their armed forces by the Soviets during this period, the Syrians and Egyptians together proved no more of a match for Israel than had Egypt in 1956.

During the Cold War, many of the carefully constructed efforts by the West to maintain its position in the Middle East were undermined by changes of regimes and shifting alliances. Iraq, the link between Turkey and Iran, joined the Baghdad Pact in 1955, but withdrew in 1959 after a coup that overthrew its monarchy. It then turned toward Moscow. In subsequent years, the Iraqi Baath Party came to power. With its nationalist and socialist ideology, the Baathists were, for quite some time, wary of Moscow. However, in 1972 they signed a fifteen-year friendship treaty with the Soviet Union, legalized the Iraqi Communist Party, and thus expanded the sphere of Soviet influence.

South Yemen, which had received its independence from Britain in 1967, formed the Democratic People's Republic of Yemen, the only official Marxist state in the region. As Soviet influence expanded, Aden, the historic British naval base, became available to Moscow's naval forces, which continued to operate from this base until South Yemen merged with North Yemen in 1990.

Afghanistan sought to play a neutral role in the Cold War until the 1970s, receiving aid from both the United States and the Soviet Union. After the king was deposed in 1973, however, a Marxist government emerged and oriented the country toward Moscow. Guerrilla opposition to the Kabul regime ultimately led to Soviet intervention and the decade-long Afghanistan War (1979–89), which not only devastated the country, but also sapped Moscow's military forces to the point that they had to withdraw.

The Soviet position within the region during much of the Cold War also benefited from the wave of nationalist revolutions that swept Libya, Sudan, and Iran. In Libya, Muammar al-Qadaffi ousted King Idris in 1969. He forced Britain and the United States to evacuate their military bases in Libya, thus strengthening Moscow, and allowed the Soviets access to naval shore bases.

Colonel Muhammed al-Nimeiry seized power in Sudan during the same year, banned all political parties, and nationalized much of the country's industry and the banks. Nimeiry forged strong ties with Cairo, which had broken with the West, and later instituted strict Islamic law, further isolating the country from its former Western supporters. Successor Sudanese regimes reinforced this isolation, as Khartoum strengthened ties with Libya and supported Iraq in the Gulf War.

The Iranian revolution of 1979, which was led by the Ayatollah Ruhollah Khomeini, toppled the Shah, one of the closest allies of the West. Khomeini exploited the widespread resentment against the Shah's autocratic regime, which had become repressive and corrupt. This was the most severe blow to U.S. interests in the Middle East. While the fundamentalist Iranian regime was far removed ideologically from Moscow, its virulent anti-Americanism served the strategic interests of the USSR by breaking the Ring of Containment in the northeastern part of the region. Tensions between Washington and Tehran rose to a fever pitch in late 1979, when militants seized the U.S. embassy and held Americans there hostage for 444 days.

In sum, Moscow's various Middle East alliances made possible the deployment of powerful naval forces in the eastern Mediterranean, the Gulf of Aden, and the Indian Ocean. At different periods, the Soviet navy had access to bases in Libya, Egypt, Syria, Aden, and across the Red Sea and Gulf of Aden waters, in Ethiopia's Eritrean province and Somalia. In addition, it maintained several permanent anchorages in the Mediterranean and the Indian Oceans.

The extensive Soviet penetration of the region required major strategic realignments on the part of the Maritime Realm powers. The most important anchors in this strategy were Turkey, Saudi Arabia, Israel, and after 1976, Egypt. These countries provided stable bases from which the United States and Maritime Europe could respond to the upheavals that brought Soviet military power into much of the Arab world, Iran, and Afghanistan. In addition, on the margins of the Middle East, the competition between the superpowers extended into the Horn of Africa.

Israel played a pivotal role in two dramatic episodes that affected Great Power strategic relationships in the region during the Cold War. During the 1967 Arab-Israeli war, Israel invaded the Sinai, seizing control of the entire peninsula and reaching the east bank of the Suez Canal. During the course of the fighting, the canal was blocked by sunken ships and became the boundary between the two countries. The Egyptians refused to clear the wreckage, so that the waterway remained closed to all shipping. For the USSR, this closure represented a strategic gain in that it forced vessels that normally used the canal to link Europe and the North Atlantic with the Persian Gulf, Indian Ocean, and Asia-Pacifica to take the longer and more costly route around the Cape of Good Hope. The canal remained closed until 1975, when it was cleared with the help of the U.S. Navy, after Egypt and Israel had signed an agreement for military disengagement and withdrawal of Israeli troops from Sinai.

The second episode had to do with the consequences of the October 1973 war. Israel emerged victorious after warding off surprise attacks by Egypt and Syria on its southern and northern fronts. Given the debacle of that war, President Anwar Sadat concluded that Egypt had no prospect of defeating Israel militarily. Moreover, the alliance with Moscow that had provided so much military and economic aid had ended when Sadat ousted Soviet personnel before the outbreak of the war. A 1976 U.S. agreement to provide Egypt with aid in developing nuclear technology for peaceful purposes, as well as the prospect of peace with Israel, pointed to a reorientation of Cairo's foreign policy back toward the West.

The Camp David accord of 1978, brokered by U.S. President James Earl Carter, was followed by a formal peace between Egypt and Israel the next year. President Sadat was then free to pursue a full military and economic alliance with the United States. When he was assassinated in 1981, his successor, President Hosni Mubarak, greatly expanded these ties. The relationship was strengthened by Cairo's participation as a full-fledged member of the Allied coalition during the Gulf War against Iraq. As a result of its return to the Western camp, Egypt has been rewarded by being made the second highest recipient of annual U.S. aid.

The Geographical Setting

A unique geographical characteristic of the Middle East is that its landmass is almost completely surrounded and interpenetrated by major water bodies. It is rimmed by five seas—the Caspian, Black, eastern Mediterranean, Red Sea/Gulf of Aden, and Arabian/Persian

Gulf. These water bodies not only define the Middle East, they are also strategically important to external powers that have historically sought to gain full control over them.

The region is divisible into three east-west trending structural zones—the Northern Highland, Intermediate, and Southern Desert. Each of the zones has distinct physical and resource characteristics that have influenced its economic, cultural, and political development.

THE NORTHERN HIGHLAND ZONE

The Northern Highland Zone consists of high, folded, earthquake-prone mountains that are part of the Alpine-Himalayan system and rim high interior plateaus. A good deal of this mountainous area is subject to widespread tectonic activity, thus earthquakes are a major hazard. Most of Turkey and Iran, and all of Afghanistan, lie within the zone, as does Iraq's northeastern highlands, which are home to the country's Kurdish populace. The parts of Turkey that lie outside the Northern Highland Zone are its narrow Aegean and Mediterranean coastal fringes and its southeastern Mesopotamian plains, the latter being part of the Intermediate Zone.

The Highland region is vast, extending over nearly 1.5 million square miles, and has a population of 150 million—sixty-five million each in Turkey and Iran and over twenty million in Afghanistan. While Turks and Persians form the preponderance of the populations of their nations, each country has large ethnic minorities that have long sought independence within their remote highland territorial bases. The ancient homeland of Kurdistan extends in an arc from the plateaus and mountains of southeastern Anatolia where ten million Kurds live, through northeastern Iraq and northwestern Iran where Kurds number five million in each area. The homeland has smaller outliers in northeast Syria and parts of Armenia. Kurdish independence aspirations date back to the nineteenth century. In 1946, a revolt whose goal was a Soviet-supported Kurdish Communist state, was crushed by Tehran. In Turkey the Kurds have been in rebellion for decades, using terrorism as an instrument of war. At the end of the Gulf War, the Iraqi Kurds, encouraged by the United States launched a rebellion that was ruthlessly quashed by Saddam Hussein. Washington stood by as three hundred thousand Kurds were killed.

The other large minority within the zone is the ten million Azeris of northwestern Iran. Their rebellion, also in 1946, led to a short-lived Communist state, supported by the USSR, but it was quickly put down by the Iranian military.

Afghanistan is divided into towering mountainous highland, inland valley, and desert regions. Within each, various ethnic groups have developed separate linguistic and cultural characteristics. The Pashtuns (Pathans), the largest regional ethnic group, constituting 40 percent of the population, live in the east, along the Pakistan border and in the south; the Tajiks, making up 25 percent of the total, live in the west and northeast; the Shiite Hazaras, about 20 percent, are in the central mountains; and a smaller Uzbek minority is in the north. While most Afghans are Sunni Muslim, the ethnic divisions have long been a basis for civil strife, compounded by the civil war between the Communists and the Mujahedeen during the 1980s. The extreme Sunni fundamentalist Taliban, who are mostly Pashtuns, imposed their rule upon most of the country in the civil war of 1996, after defeating the Mujahedeen forces. The Mujahedeen were composed largely of other ethnic groups and had taken control of the government following the Soviet defeat.

Afghanistan's ethnic and tribal divisions are reinforced by nature, as the core areas for these different groups have developed within river valleys that are separated by mountains and deserts. The Kabul River valley is the focus for the Pashtun core around the city of

Kabul—the gateway to the Khyber Pass and South Asia. The focus for the Pashtuns of Qandahar in the southeastern part of the country is the middle portion of the Helmand River, which originates in the Hindu Kush and flows southwest to Iran. They are separated from the nomadic Baluchis of Rejistan's semiarid and desert lands to their southwest.

The Tajiks of western Afghanistan are concentrated around Herat, a large oasis within the Hari Rud Valley. The north, where the Amu Darya River forms the border with Uzbekistan and part of Turkmenistan, is the homeland of the Uzbeks, who are centered around Mazar-e-Sharif, which is located on the Balkh River, a tributary of the Amu Darya. The Tajiks of the northeast also are concentrated along the Amu Darya plain. The Hazarahs have maintained their separate Shiite religion from their mountain bastions within the center of the country.

The political organization of the country is deeply rooted in a system based on fiercely independent tribal chiefs and warlords. This system is strongly reinforced not only by nature, but also by the poor transportation and communications that inhibit the interconnections among the country's different parts. The nation-building that is envisaged for the post-Taliban era by the United States and its allies will have to adopt strategies that incorporate this cultural-physical mosaic that has endured for so many centuries.

After coming to power, the Taliban provided sanctuary and training bases for networks of Islamic extremists, the most prominent of which was Osama bin Laden's al Qaeda group. These groups are dedicated to exporting terror to many parts of the world in order to further their fundamentalist aims. Afghan-trained guerrillas, including veterans of the Afghan war, have targeted Chechnya, Xinjiang, Uzbekistan, and Kashmir, as well as the Middle East, North Africa, and most dramatically, the United States. To compound the problems of Afghanistan, the country has suffered from a lengthy period of drought and famine that has caused millions of its rural poor to leave their villages in an effort to avoid war and starvation. As many as five million Afghans have fled across the border into Pakistan or Iran, where they are gathered in refugee camps, or have flocked to Afghanistan's larger cities, which lack the means to sustain them. The flow of refugees was renewed when the United States began its heavy bombing campaign in October 2001. Both Pakistan and Iran sought to close their borders, but were only partially successful.

Tensions between Shiite Iran and the Sunni Taliban were long strained over religious differences, exacerbated in 1998 by the murder of Iranian consular officials in Mazar-e-Sharif, the major center of northern Afghanistan. This nearly led to war between the two countries.

While the population of the Northern Highland Zone is engaged mainly in farming, grazing, and handicrafts, the country's nonferrous and ferrous minerals have been important to the industrialization of Turkey and Iran. In the first half of the twentieth century, coal and iron ore became the basis for heavy industry, especially steel, enabling Kemal Atatürk, the founding father of modern Turkey, to pursue the policy of self-sufficiency under state ownership, without dependence upon foreign capital and influence. The economy broadened as oil was discovered in southern Turkey (part of the Intermediate Zone) and came to support a petrochemical and chemical fertilizer industry.

Turkey's situation changed after World War II, when it abandoned its policy of neutrality and moved toward democracy and alignment with the West. Massive aid from the United States began to flow into the country with the Marshall Plan Recovery Program and state capitalism was relaxed in favor of private enterprise. These conditions attracted foreign investment that, combined with continued large-scale American aid, considerably expanded industrialization and moved Turkey into an international exchange economy.

A more recent stimulus for growth in both industry and agriculture has been the Guney-dogu Anadolu Project in southeast Anatolia—the giant Atatürk Dam and Reservoir, supplemented by a string of smaller dams and hydroelectric plants that draw on the waters of the upper Euphrates and upper Tigris Rivers. The project has been bitterly opposed by Syria and Iraq, the downstream riparians of these rivers, and plagued by the conflict between Ankara and the Kurdish separatists of the region. Nevertheless, it has begun to bring industrial and agricultural prosperity to the southern and southeastern parts of the country. In the past, most of Turkey's farm areas were located in the wetter, western part of the plateau, with grazing taking place in the semiarid interior. Today, irrigated cotton, fruit, vegetables, and tobacco have been rapidly expanded into the areas affected by the project, as has manufacturing.

Iran also possesses a variety of minerals, such as iron, coal, copper, chromium, and zinc, and has developed the manufacturing of steel, carpets, textiles, chemicals, and food products. However, it has not felt the pressure to industrialize as keenly as has Turkey, because of its wealth of oil and natural gas resources. The country remains dependent upon petroleum for over 90 percent of its exports, and its economy is therefore subject to the wild swings of the world oil market prices.

During the first three decades of the Cold War, Turkey and Iran served as the Middle Eastern mainstays of the West. With their Turkish and Aryan/Persian populations and long histories of conflict with the Russians to the north and Arabs to the south, they were logical allies for Washington, especially since so much of the Arab world had been convulsed by upheavals in the 1950s and 1960s and some Arab countries had aligned themselves with the Soviet Union.

In the past two decades, the orientation of the zone has changed drastically. After the takeover of the American embassy in Tehran in 1979 and the ensuing hostage crisis, Washington became so obsessively anti-Iranian, matching Iran's virulent anti-Americanism, that it had no compunctions about supporting the ruthless dictatorship of Saddam Hussein in Iraq's war against Ayatollah Khomeini's Iran. The arms supplied to Iraq would later be turned against Kuwait and the West—a prospect that should have been anticipated by Pentagon planners in view of Iraq's long-standing disputes with Kuwait.

While Iran dropped out of the Western strategic fold in 1979, Turkey has remained a cornerstone of the Western alliance. U.S. air and missile bases in that country played a significant role in the Gulf War, and they support the aircraft that impose the no-fly zones over Iraq today. In addition, these bases have played an important role in the War against Terrorism. However, the once highly secularized Turkish society is feeling the influence of a growing Islamic movement that is making considerable inroads within the Sunni Muslim populace. Moreover, the fate of Ankara's application for EU membership may affect its overall relationship with the West. Now that it no longer needs the NATO shield for protection from Moscow, Turkey's attention is focused on prospects for economic improvement through economic integration with Maritime Europe. Should it be spurned by the EU because of its human rights abuses, Kurdish problem, and differing economic policies, Turkey might turn to a more neutral geopolitical orientation.

THE INTERMEDIATE ZONE

This zone stands apart from the Highland Zone to its north and the Desert Zone to its south. The Levant (Israel, Lebanon, Syria, and the Palestinian Authority) and

Mesopotamia (the ancient "Fertile Crescent"), which includes the northern and western shores of the Persian/Arab Gulf, are a physical unit. Structurally, all of this area, save the eastern Mediterranean coast, is part of the Arabian tectonic plate. (The Northern Highlands have been formed from the Turkish and Iranian plates.) Most of the Intermediate Zone is exposed to the influence of the eastern Mediterranean Sea or the Persian/Arab Gulf. Low coastal mountains and adjoining plateaus along the more moist western half of the zone in Lebanon, Syria, and Israel provide ease of land access to the drier eastern half of the zone in Jordan, Iraq, Kuwait, eastern Saudi Arabia, Bahrain, Qatar, and the United Arab Emirates (UAE).

The gentle geological downward warp of Mesopotamia, from northeastern Syria to the head of the Persian Gulf, as well as the western and northeastern shores of that body of water, are overlain by tertiary- and quaternary-age sedimentary layers. Their porous limestones and sandstones have trapped oil in their slight structural foldings to create storage places for the world's richest petroleum reserves. While the bulk of these deposits lie in the semicircle that runs on and off the Gulf shore from Khuzestan in southwestern Iran through southern Iraq, Kuwait, Saudi Arabia, Qatar, the UAE, and Oman, substantial oil is also produced in the fields of northern Mesopotamia—in northern Iraq, northeastern Syria, and the southern edge of southeastern Turkey.

The Persian Gulf-Mesopotamian countries possess two-thirds of the world's petroleum reserves and a considerable quantity of its natural gas deposits. Half of the latter are located within Saudi Arabia and much of the rest of these Middle Eastern gas reserves are in Iraq and Iran. Not only does Saudi Arabia have the world's largest onshore oil field (Ghawar), but it also possesses the largest offshore field (Safaniya). The Burgan field in Kuwait ranks second only to Ghawar.

As important as Middle Eastern oil fields are today, accounting for over one-third of the world's production, their future role may be even greater, if new finds elsewhere fail to keep up with rising demand worldwide or if stringent conservation methods are not adopted by the United States. In fact, one estimate is that, by the year 2040, only the Middle East will be a petroleum exporting region.[3]

The states of the Levant are well situated to serve as Gateways to Iraq and the northern Gulf. This applies not only to their potential for transferring goods and serving as communication links from the eastern Mediterranean. It also refers to the agricultural and consumer products and services that they can generate to be exchanged with Mesopotamia and the Gulf.

As wealthy as this Intermediate Zone is in oil, it is poor in water resources. Water scarcity has been a traditional source of tribal disputes and armed conflicts in the Middle East, as well as a stimulus for technological innovations in water reuse and desalinization. Recycling sewerage waters for agricultural purposes is practiced in Israel, while desalinization plants to convert seawater to freshwater have been constructed along the Gulf coast. A manifestation of the need for and value of freshwater is the water transfer agreement between Turkey and Israel whereby Turkey would ship surplus waters by tanker from the Manavgat River in southeastern Anatolia near Antalya to Ashkelon on the southern coast of Israel, from where it would be sent by pipeline to the country's national water system. The accord is for a ten-year period, at a cost that is comparable to that of desalinized water. Deliveries represent 5 percent of Israel's annual needs—a significant amount—and they are possibly a forerunner of expanded water imports.

There are limitations to how widely Lebanon can increase its production of fruit and vegetables, because of the restricted amount of available flat lands. However, additional irrigated waters in the semiarid Beqa'a Valley could raise this output. The specialized agricultural crops of Israel and Gaza cannot be greatly expanded under its current irrigation water restrictions. With peace and the implementation of a rational water-sharing scheme for the Jordan-Yarmuk River and Lebanon's Litani River, production from these countries could become an important source of exports to Saudi Arabia and neighboring Gulf States.

The greatest potential for agricultural growth within the region is in Syria. Thirty percent of Syrian land is arable, but this land requires irrigation for its optimal development. Measures to expand irrigation works have been taken for the past three decades in the following areas: (1) the northern part of the Ghab (an extension of the Beqa'a) that parallels the coast within the Mediterranean climate belt, and through which the Orontes River flows before emptying into the Mediterranean at the southwest corner of Turkey; (2) the northern steppe zone, from Homs to Halab (Aleppo), where the dry farming of these grasslands for grain is now marginal because of variable rainfall; and (3) the arid lands of the northeast.

For agriculture to become fully developed in the North, a radical change is required in the political relations of the three Euphrates riparian states: Turkey, Syria, and Iraq. Damascus and Baghdad came close to war in 1974 as a result of their dispute over Syria's building of the Tabaka Dam on the Euphrates to form Lake Assad. In addition, Turkey's control of the river's headwaters leaves Damascus vulnerable to Ankara's major long-range plans for exploiting the headwaters. Politics further complicates possibilities for water sharing. Syria backed Iran in its war with Iraq, and then supported the Allies in the Gulf War. Both Syria and Iraq have also provided safe haven for Kurdish Workers' Party guerrillas in their struggle for independence from Ankara.

In the far southwest of Syria, the Yarmuk River, whose main headwaters rise in Syrian territory, forms the border between Syria and Jordan. It also serves as the boundary between Israel and Jordan south of the Sea of Galilee, before entering the Jordan Rift Valley. Most of the waters of the Yarmuk between Syria and Jordan are used for irrigation. Jordan has built a dam across the river and diverted some of the flow to the East Ghor Canal. Before Syria can exploit more of the Yarmuk waters, it would have to invest substantially in irrigation works. By the same token, Damascus would have to expend considerable sums of money were Syria to develop an agreement with Lebanon to enable it to exploit waters of the Litani River that flow through the Lebanese part of Al Bika and then into the Mediterranean at Tyre. Syria's attempt to divert the headwaters of the Jordan River by constructing a diversionary canal was foiled by Israeli military actions between 1964 and 1967. This was a major factor in Israel's initiation of the June 1967 war against Egypt and Syria.

Therefore, both politics and capital are involved in Syria's agricultural expansion. Syria will be unable to realize its fullest agricultural potential without agreements with Turkey and Iraq, and without a resolution of the conflict with Israel. The capacity of Damascus to invest some of its petroleum proceeds (the country's most important source of income) in agriculture is constrained by the emphasis on expanding its civilian industrial base, its heavy investments in the development of a domestic military industry, and its purchase of armaments from abroad.

Economic development within the Intermediate Zone is frustrated not only by inter-Arab and inter-Islamic disputes, but also by the Arab-Israeli conflict. The peace between Jordan and Israel helped to expand tourism in both countries, while Jordan has benefited from water transfers when it has experienced shortages. An end to the Arab-Israeli conflict might stimulate exchanges that would be of mutual benefit to Saudi Arabia, the Gulf countries, and Israel.

For the present, however, there is little prospect that such peaceful economic relations will soon be realized. Instead, the Intermediate Zone remains conflict ridden and highly unstable. Particularly intractable are the conflicts between Iraq and the West and between Israel and the Palestinians. These affect the region in its entirety and contribute heavily to its Shatterbelt status.

THE SOUTHERN DESERT ZONE

Structurally, this zone extends across the African plate from Libya through Egypt and Sudan, and then eastward along the Arabian plate that underlies the Arabian Peninsula. It is an essentially desert region, with under ten inches of annual rainfall. The population of the zone is concentrated along the Nile, in parts of the Red Sea and southeastern Mediterranean coasts, and in interior desert oases. In northeast Africa, exceptions to the area's desert character include the northern coastal tip of Cyrenaica in northeastern Libya, which has a Mediterranean-type climate and vegetation in an area backed by a narrow, semiarid belt, and Libya's coastal northwestern Tripolitania, which borders Tunisia and is also characterized by semiaridity.

For the most part, however, Egypt and Libya are northern and eastern extensions of the Sahara, as is northern Sudan. In Sudan, the twelve degrees north latitude line, which runs to the south of Khartoum, is the boundary between the desert of the north and the semiarid savannah region of the center that grades into the south. There, the landscape changes into the permanent and seasonally flooded swamplands of the Sudd, a semitropical region with higher rainfall rates that is subject to flooding from the Nile headwaters and covered with thick, aquatic vegetation.

From the very onset of Sudan's independence in 1955, the rebels have been able to sustain their war against Arab Muslim northern regimes from within the inaccessible reaches of South Sudan—a region populated by negroid Sudanic, Nilotic, and Nubian animists and Christians. The intensity of the conflict has sharpened as Islamic law has been reinforced by Khartoum. In the adjoining Sub-Saharan Compression Zone of the Horn of Africa, deserts also cover Eritrea, most of Somalia, and southeastern Ethiopia, which shares the Ogaden with Somalia.

Most of Saudi Arabia is situated within the Southern Desert Zone. However, the country belongs to both the Southern Desert and Intermediate Zones because its important oil resources lie along its northeastern Gulf coast in the Intermediate Zone, while its major population concentrations, as well as Makka (Mecca) and Medina, are located on or close to the coast in the Southern Desert Zone.

The portion of Saudi Arabia that lies in the Desert Zone is a plateau of ancient crystalline rocks, parts of which are desert and parts of which are semiarid. Nafud, to the north of the sparse grasslands of the Nejd, is desert. So is Rub al Khali in the southeastern corner of the country—one of the world's largest sand deserts and an uninhabited area known as the "Empty Quarter."

The climatic and vegetational exceptions to this desert pattern are the southwest coast of Saudi Arabia—the province of Asir—and northern Yemen, where lofty coastal mountains rise up from the Red Sea to intercept summer monsoon winds. These well-watered areas support dense human settlement and traditional production of coffee, grains, and fruit.

Farther north from Asir, along the Red Sea coast, lies the Hejaz, which consists of a narrow coast backed by highlands with steep slopes dissected by narrow valleys that have been shaped by water and wind. The region's leading city, Jidda (population 2.6 million), is the country's historic seaport and trading center. Jidda is the main port for imports and for pilgrims to nearby Makka and Medina, and the country's commercial and business center. Makka, Islam's holiest city, has a population of over one million and is the destination for two million Muslims who make the annual Haj. However, it also represents a flash point for Muslim fundamentalists, both Saudi and foreign, who have clashed with Saudi troops. Medina, with approximately three-quarters of a million people, is Islam's second-holiest city. An ancient oasis, it lies inland from the Red Sea and is generally visited by those who make the pilgrimage to Makka.

While the Hejaz contained the older Saudi ecumene because of its farming oases, livestock grazing lands, and access for Muslim pilgrims via the Red Sea, in recent decades it has been eclipsed in political and economic importance by the new ecumene that extends from Riyadh to the Gulf centers. This is not to minimize the continued rapid growth of Jidda, Makka, and the planned city of Yanbu (the terminal for the pipelines from the Gulf and a focus for the petrochemical and other industries).

The geographical shift of power from the Hejaz to the Interior and the Gulf coast is not without its liabilities. One-third of the Eastern Province's population of 1.5 million are Shia, whose discontent with Riyadh's Wahhabi Sunni regime has been fanned since the Iranian revolution. Moreover, the majority of the country's five million foreign workers are located in the Gulf area. Since they outnumber the Saudi labor force by two to one and are nearly one-quarter of the country's total population of twenty-one million, they are potentially a highly destabilizing force.

Saudi Arabia's split geopolitical personality could become the basis for political divisiveness in times of domestic stress. Thus far the Saudi government has maintained the military and political power that it needs to strengthen the unity of the kingdom through petroleum wealth, repression, U.S. military support, and an alliance with the country's fundamentalist religious leadership.

In the African sector of the Southern Desert Zone, major petroleum and natural gas deposits lie at Egypt's portion of the northern end of the Red Sea trough, where the African and Arabian plates meet. There the sedimentary strata that overlie the ancient rock base of most of the zone yield petroleum within the fields of the Gulf of Suez waters and natural gas deposits that extend along the coast from the Nile Delta westward.

One of the dividends to Israel of its peace with Egypt is that it is able to purchase energy from Egypt. An agreement has been signed to construct a joint Egyptian-Israeli underwater pipeline to carry natural gas from the Egyptian gas fields to Israel, where the gas will replace imported oil as the main fuel for Israel's power plants. Negotiations are also underway that would extend the line underwater to Turkey, thus further strengthening Cairo's eastern Mediterranean ties.

Petroleum and petroleum products have become Egypt's single-largest export, but agriculture remains an economic mainstay, with over half the population being rural. The country's fairly broad economic base includes tourism, chemicals, textiles, cement, steel, and foodstuffs. However, Egypt's population of over sixty-five million is crowded onto 4 percent of the land—not enough to support the vast farm labor force. Therefore Cairo is heavily dependent for its financial stability on foreign aid, mainly from the United States, on Suez Canal revenues, and on cash remittances from Egyptians working abroad. This state of dependency results in Egypt's need for close relations with the Maritime world, as well as for firm alliances with Saudi Arabia and the Gulf States.

Geopolitical Features

The geopolitical immaturity of the Middle East Shatterbelt is reflected in the absence of significant regional geopolitical features. The region lacks either a Historic or a current Political Core to serve as a unifying force, and its national Ecumenes and Effective National Territories are, in most cases, so physically distant from one another that they inhibit even subregional unity. Those features that do have a regional impact are Boundaries and Empty Areas, and they have served as barriers to interaction, rather than as facilitators.

HISTORIC CORE

The Middle East lacks a single, unifying historic regional core. This is because the capitals of the empires that had ruled the region in various eras—from Nineveh, Memphis, Babylon, and Persepolis to Alexandria, Antioch, Constantinople, and Baghdad—do not serve as rallying points today for the concept of a unified Middle East.

REGIONAL POLITICAL CAPITALS

A modern, Middle Eastern regional political capital is an equally remote concept. There is no regional organization whose seat might be viewed as the forerunner of a political core. In fact, there are only two frameworks that make a pretense of serving the goal of regional unity. One is the geographically limited Gulf Co-operation Council, which includes Saudi Arabia, Kuwait, Bahrain, Qatar, the United Arab Emirates, and Oman. Headquartered in Riyadh, the council promotes cooperation in economics, agriculture, industry, education, and culture; sponsors free trade in the exchange of agricultural, industrial, and mineral products; and has established an investment corporation. One of its functions is the settlement of disputes, but while it has been effective in this area among its own members, it has not been successful in avoiding war in disputes with outsiders.

The League of Arab States (the Arab League), which was formed in 1945, now includes not only the Arab states of the Middle East, but also those of northwest Africa, as well as Somalia and Sudan. The non–Arab Middle Eastern states of Turkey, Iran, and Israel are excluded. Cairo is the league's headquarters, but inter-Arab conflicts have thus far prevented it from being accepted as a regional capital. (When Egypt's membership was suspended from 1979 to 1989, the seat was moved to Tunis.) Moreover, the stated functions of the league—promotion of economic, social, political, and military cooperation and the mediation of disputes—have rarely been implemented.

Efforts to unify even parts of the region have generally ended poorly. The merger between Egypt and Syria, with the later addition of Yemen, fell apart. So did attempts to form a Federation of Arab Republics by Egypt, Syria, and Libya and a unified state between Libya and Egypt. The federation never became operational. Still another short-lived effort

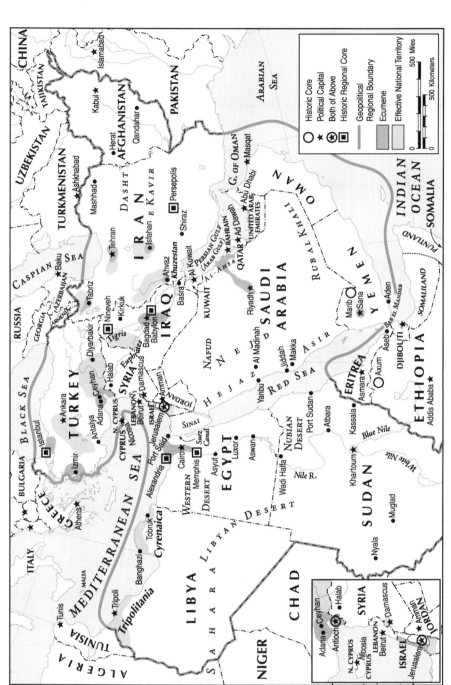

Figure 11.1 Middle East Shatterbelt: Major Geopolitical Features

at unified political action was the Arab Cooperation Council, which was formed by Egypt, Iraq, Jordan, and Yemen in 1989, but broke up the following year when Iraq invaded Kuwait. The merged states of North and South Yemen have been torn by civil war since they joined together in 1990. The sole example of a successful merger is the United Arab Emirates, which was established in 1971–72.

ECUMENES

Geography and politics have conspired to separate the national ecumenes of the Middle East from one another. The areas of densest population concentration and economic activity are generally removed from one another by mountains, plateaus, or deserts. There are three exceptions, where ecumenes cut across national boundaries.

The largest of these transnational convergence areas is located at the head of the Persian/Arab Gulf. It extends along the coast from Kuwait to Basra, Iraq's second-largest city, on the Shatt al Arab; to the Iranian centers of Abadan, on an island in the delta of the Shatt al Arab; and to Khorramshahr, at the confluence of the Karun River and the Shatt. Rather than serving as a unifying force, this convergence has been the focus of two wars—one between Iraq and Iran, the other between Iraq and Kuwait. The economies of these adjoining core areas are based upon the oil fields of Kuwait, southern Iraq, and southwestern Iran. However, their pipelines, ports, refineries, petrochemical industries, and cities have no connections with one another because of the deep hostilities among the three countries.

Another transnational convergence cluster rims the Bay of Iskenderun (Alexandretta). There, where the Orontes River flows into the sea, Syria and Turkey meet. Latakia, Syria's leading port, and Halab, the country's second-largest city and leading manufacturing center, adjoin the Turkish province of Hatay (Alexandretta), whose possession was long disputed by Syria. Antakya (Antioch) and Iskenderun are the major urban centers of Hatay; from here, the population concentration continues westward along the coast to the large Turkish manufacturing center of Adana, capital of Adana Province.

Under different political circumstances, this region might have developed as a unified ecumene. It is served by a nexus of ports, highways, and railroads that radiate outward to Turkey, Syria, and Iraq. However, the hostility between Turkey and Syria has limited the region's development. Instead of here, Turkey's economic and population core areas center around Ankara in the interior of the country, Izmir along the Aegean coast, and the area from Istanbul to Izmit along the Bosporus and the Sea of Marmara. Syria's ecumene is focused around Damascus, with an outlier at Homs (Hims) to its north.

The third transnational ecumene, linking Saudi Arabia to Bahrain, straddles the Intermediate and Southern Desert Zones. It extends for 240 miles from Riyadh in the desert interior to the Saudi shore of the Persian/Arab Gulf centers of Al-Dammam and Al-Jubail, and from there across narrow waters to include the archipelago of Bahrain.

Riyadh, the capital and fastest-growing urban center of Saudi Arabia, has approximately 20 percent of the country's total population of 23 million. It is expected to double from its current populace of four million, to eight million, in a little over a decade. As the nation's political, cultural, financial, and transportation center, the capital played a special geopolitical role in the creation of Saudi Arabia. It is the center of the Nejd, the peninsula's ancient heartland, which never fell to the Ottomans but remained under the control of its desert tribes. From their Riyadh oasis base, the Saudi rulers have drawn upon the desert's culture, its strict Wahhabite religious system, and its social traditions to adapt Bedouin life, first to the sedentary oasis world, and now to the modern urban era. Fanning out from the Nejd, the Saudis developed highway, rail, and air links to the Gulf and the wealth generated by its coastal and offshore oil resources.

The Gulf region, which is the coastal portion of this third ecumene, contains the major industrial center of Al-Dammam and its associated towns, with a population of over two million. Dammam was developed as a deepwater port and the eastern terminal of the railway from Riyadh. Adjoining it is the oil center of Dhahran, which is also an international air hub and the site of a large U.S. air base. Jubail, to the north, is the largest of Saudi Arabia's two planned industrial cities and a major petrochemical center. Backing these coastal urban concentrations is the Al-Ahsa coastal plain (the Eastern Province), which includes some of the country's most fertile agricultural oases and is its chief oil-producing center.

The Saudi ecumene also extends directly across a narrow stretch of water to Bahrain, one of the most important banking and financial centers of the Middle East. While Bahrain's oil reserves are modest, the refineries that were built there after the discovery of oil in 1931 have become important for processing Saudi crude. Britain also developed a major naval base and refueling station at the Bahraini port of Manamah, which played an important strategic role during the Cold War, the Gulf War, and most recently, the War against Terrorism in Afghanistan.

Elsewhere, national ecumenes are geographically removed from those of their neighbors. Iraq's ecumene centers around its capital and largest city, Baghdad, which holds nearly 20 percent of the country's total population of 22 million and most of Iraq's manufacturing industries. From there, it extends southward for approximately one hundred miles, through the densely populated agricultural Mesopotamian plain and the cities of Karbala and An-Najaf. In Iran, no single ecumene dominates the country. Tehran, in the north, with 10 percent of the country's population of 65 million and half its industrial output, is the major economic and population core area. Other important clusters center around Tabriz, the capital of Iranian Azerbaijan in the northwest; oil-rich Khuzestan in the southwest; and the manufacturing city of Esfahan in the center. The spread of the Tehran ecumene is limited by the Elburz Mountains to its north and the semiarid to arid lands to its south and west, so that it does not connect to the country's other industrial and population clusters. Other important national ecumenes are those of Egypt and Israel. The Egyptian economic and population core area extends southward from the Nile Delta, upstream through Cairo to El Faiyum, a distance of approximately 150 miles. It also extends for one hundred miles along the delta's coast from Port Said, at the entrance to the Suez Canal, to Alexandria.

Alexandria, Egypt's great ancient metropolis, now has over 3.5 million people and is the country's leading port; a major industrial center for petroleum products, textiles, food, and consumer goods; and home to a naval base. However, it is dwarfed in importance by Cairo, the largest city, with a population of seven million and a total metropolitan populace of over fifteen million. As the capital of the country's highly centralized political system, it is its chief financial and industrial center and the major focus for tourism, one of Egypt's most important economic resources.

The Israeli ecumene extends along two-thirds of its coastal plain, for approximately eighty miles, from the port of Ashdod in the south, through the metropolitan Tel Aviv region, to Greater Haifa. Its width, only between six and fifteen miles, is constricted by the Green Line, the pre-1967 division between Israel and the Jordanian-held West Bank. The population density of the Israeli ecumene is over two thousand per square mile, its 3.5 million people accounting for 60 percent of the nation's total population of over six million. The overall population density of seven hundred per square mile is an unusually high figure for a total country and is exceeded only by the Netherlands and Belgium among comparably advanced states.

The ecumene contains most of Israel's manufacturing and services, including cut diamonds, military industry, pharmaceuticals, finance, tourism, and high technology. The latter is the fastest-growing part of the economy, with emphasis on computers, software, telecommunications, biotechnology, medical technology, and avionics. Research and development centers that belong to the world's leading computer hardware and software companies help to drive the high-technology industry, which accounts for 60 percent of the country's total exports and is the largest sector of the Israeli economy.

The rest of the national ecumenes of the Middle East are small and underdeveloped. The larger among them are the landlocked core areas of Greater Khartoum in Sudan and Sana, Yemen's capital and largest city, which is located in the center of the country's high plateau.

EFFECTIVE REGIONAL/NATIONAL TERRITORY

Just as there is no unified regional ecumene within the Middle East, so is it lacking in an Effective Regional Territory. For the most part, the Effective National Territories, of the individual countries are both limited and separated from one another by desert conditions. The only point where ENTs meet is in the grasslands of Upper Mesopotamia, where Syria and Iraq converge. In ancient times, this was the main contact zone of the Fertile Crescent. The depth of the political rift between the two states has barred the cooperative ventures that might unify these two ENTs.

EMPTY AREAS

For the most part, the Empty Areas of the region are the deserts across which national boundaries run, and which serve as barriers. Vast, barren reaches separate Egypt from Libya, Israel, and Jordan; Saudi Arabia from Jordan; Syria, Iraq, the Gulf States, and Yemen from one another; and Iran from Afghanistan. Only Iran, Turkey, Syria, and Iraq are not blocked from one another by Empty Areas. However, the mountains and hills of Kurdistan do inhibit ease of communication in the Kurdish region that extends from eastern Turkey and northeastern Syria through northern Iraq and into northwestern Iran.

BOUNDARIES

Boundaries are important geopolitical features within the Middle East and disputes over their locations, as well as over territorial sovereignty, have been major forces in creating and maintaining the Shatterbelt character of the region.

Table 11.1 is a summary of the region's current boundary disputes and disputed areas. Table 11.2 lists recent dispute resolutions and table 11.3 lists the major irredentist areas.[4] The most prominent of these various disputes have been the ones over the Shatt al Arab, Kuwait, and the occupied West Bank and Gaza.

Table 11.1   Current Middle East Boundary Disputes

Countries	Disputed Boundaries	Disputed Areas
Iraq-Iran	Shatt al Arab	
Saudi Arabia-Kuwait		Qaresh and Umm al Madarim Islands
Iran-UAE		Lesser & Greater Tunb Island, Abu Musa Island
Israel-Palestinian Authority	Future boundary of Palestinian state	West Bank, Gaza
Israel-Syria	Golan boundary along the Sea of Galilee's northeast coast	
Cyprus	Land boundary	Division into Greek & Turkish sectors
Turkey-Greece		Sea, air, & territorial claims in Aegean Sea, width of Turkish continental shelf
Libya-Tunisia	Maritime boundary	
Libya-Algeria		Libya claims part of southeast Algeria
Libya-Niger	Land boundary	Libya claims part of northern Niger
Egypt-Sudan	Red Sea coast boundary	Halaib Triangle occupied by Sudan
Caspian Sea	Indeterminate water boundary	Azerbaijan, Iran, Kazakhstan, Russia, Turkmenistan
Latent Disputes		
Iran-Bahrain		Iran claim to Bahrain
Iraq-Iran		Iran claim to Khuzestan
Lebanon-Syria		Syrian de facto occupation cause of recent discontent

Iraq and Iran: The Shatt al Arab Dispute

The eight-year war between Iraq and Iran, which cost over a million lives, was fought over control of the Shatt al Arab, the tidal waterway formed by the confluence of the Tigris and Euphrates Rivers and flowing into the Persian/Arab Gulf. The river supplies freshwater to southern Iraq. After decades of dispute over the boundary, the two countries signed an agreement in 1975 establishing the line as following the *thalweg*—the deepest channel of the river—thus assuring Iran access to Abadan at the head of the estuary.[5] In exchange, Tehran agreed to end its support of the Iraqi Kurdish rebellion.

With the Islamic revolution in Iran in early 1979, relations between the two countries deteriorated. Saddam Hussein, who had seized power in Iraq that same year, abrogated the treaty and proclaimed Iraqi sovereignty over both banks of the Shatt. His assumption was that, since Iran was then in turmoil, it would offer little resistance. This was not the case, and an eight-year war ensued. Iraq invaded Iran through oil-rich Khuzestan, the southwesternmost province of Iran, capturing Khorramshah on the east bank and surrounding

Table 11.2   Recent Middle East Dispute Territorial Resolutions

Countries	Disputed Boundaries	Disputed Areas
Iraq-Kuwait	Land boundary	Warba & Bubiyan Islands; Iraq renounced claim in favor of Kuwait, 1994
Israel-Lebanon	Land boundary demarcated, 2000 (save one very small segment)	South Lebanese Zone, Israel withdrew
Yemen-Oman	Land boundary resolved, 1992	Delimitation of desert area that lies between them
Yemen-Saudi Arabia	Land boundary delimited, 2000	All of Najran & most of Rub al Khali are within Saudi Arabia
Yemen-Eritrea		Hanish al Kabir Island awarded to Yemen; rest of Hanish Islands divided between the two, 1998
Libya-Chad		Aouzou Strip returned to Chad, 1994
Bahrain-Qatar	Maritime boundary resolved, 2001	Larger Hawar Island awarded to Bahrain, smaller island to Qatar

Table 11.3   Middle East Irredentism

Country	Irredentist Movements and Areas
Turkey	Kurds, southeastern Turkey
Iraq	Kurds, northern Iraq; Arabs, southwestern Iran (Khuzestan)
Iran	Azeris, Iranian Azerbaijan
Israel	Palestinian Arabs, Occupied West Bank & Gaza
Sudan	Christian and animist Africans, south Sudan
Afghanistan/ Pakistan	Pashtuns, Pakhtoonistan

the Abadan refinery. While Baghdad asserted its historic right to Khuzestan, it promised that it would support an independent state should its irredentist Arab inhabitants so wish. However, within two years, the Iraqis were driven from the east bank, bringing the war to a stalemate. With its conclusion in 1988, the status quo ante was restored, thus the *thalweg* remains the boundary today. Although the dispute has not been fully resolved, the Algiers accord of September 30, 2000, signed by Baghdad and Tehran, reinstituted the 1975 agreement.

Iraq Invasion of Kuwait

The invasion of Kuwait by Iraq in 1990 was essentially over a long-standing border dispute, although contributing factors were Kuwait's refusal to forgive a $30 billion debt incurred by Baghdad during its war with Iran and Kuwait's exceeding OPEC export quotas. The roots of the controversy lay in Britain's post–World War I territorial policies. In the early 1920s London created Kuwait by carving out a portion of Iraq's desert on the Gulf coast. When oil was discovered in Kuwait in 1936, the Iraqis revived their claim that the kingdom was part of their southern province of Basra.

The British-drawn boundary, which had been validated by the United Nations after World War II, included the large island of Bubiyan and the smaller Warba to its north. These islands commanded the approach to the new Iraqi port of Umm Qasr, which had been built in 1961 as an alternative to Basra. Baghdad became more assertive in its claims to the islands after it initiated the war with Iran.[6]

In addition, the Iraqis held that the Kuwaitis had extended their part of the Rumaila oil fields into Iraqi territory during the Iraq-Iran war and that they were stealing oil through slant drilling into the Iraqi portion of the field. The resulting invasion of Kuwait and its devastation, as well as the ensuing the Gulf War, is well known. However, even in defeat Iraq continued to cling to its claims and, at one point in 1994, moved Republican Guards toward the Kuwait border. As pressures mounted, Iraq reconsidered its stance, and shortly afterward agreed to recognize Kuwait's independence and its borders.

The victory over Iraq by the American-led coalition of twenty-five nations (including the Soviet Union) was followed by a series of economic sanctions and inspection requirements to assure that Iraq is not secretly engaged in the research and manufacturing of nuclear and biological weapons. For the most part, the Iraqis evaded the inspection efforts and, toward the end of the decade, Saddam Hussein ousted the UN inspectors. A low-level conflict still simmers, as U.S. and British planes counter Iraqi attempts to impede their coverage of the "no-fly" zones in the north and the south. Moreover, the boycott has weakened and some countries have moved to restore diplomatic relations with Baghdad.

Arab-Israeli Conflict

After five wars, the Arab-Israeli conflict shifted in emphasis a decade ago from the Arab challenge to Israel's right to exist to Arab demand for an independent Palestinian Arab state within part of the Holy Land. Although Arab extremists still refused to recognize the Zionist state, and Jewish extremists clung to the concept of an undivided Land of Israel, at the Madrid Conference of 1991 both sides moved toward territorial compromise as a basis for resolving the conflict.

This was followed by the Oslo I (1993) and Oslo II (1995) agreements between Israel and the Palestine Liberation Organization, which were endorsed by the two Arab states—Egypt and Jordan—that were formally at peace with Israel. Oslo called for the Palestinian Authority to gain military and/or civilian control of up to 42 percent of the total area held by Israel in the West Bank and 60 percent of Gaza, including all of the larger cities and towns, in a step-by-step process that would lead to an eventual peace. However, Oslo promised only autonomy—statehood was to come with a permanent peace and after most of the Palestinian areas had been returned to an elected Palestinian government. During this interim period, the two parties agreed to take joint security actions to prevent violence by extremists on either side.

The lagging pace of the Oslo process influenced Prime Minister Ehud Barak of Israel to drop the step-by-step strategy and seek a speedy, comprehensive peace. President Clinton then assumed a proactive role in the negotiations between the Israelis and the Palestinians, following up the Camp David Summit of July 2000 with continued participation. Far-reaching terms offered by Barak at the subsequent Wye Plantation Summit and subsequent negotiations at Taba were rejected by Palestinian chairman Yasser Arafat.

The peace process was derailed with the total breakdown of the negotiations in February 2001, followed by the outbreak of the Al-Aqsa Intifada and the election as Israel's prime minister of Ariel Sharon, leader of the populist-nationalist Likud Party. Sharon has repeatedly expressed his opposition to withdrawing from the 145 Jewish settlements with a population of 210,000 that are such an obstacle to negotiating a peace. He heads an ungainly coalition of Likud and other hard-line, right-wing, and religious parties along with left-leaning Labor and centrist parties. Israel's intensive military response to the Intifada has caused the rapid deterioration of the Palestinian Arab economy and its governing structure.

When both sides eventually agree to return to the bargaining table, they will be faced with a different situation than prevailed before the failed peace negotiations. For the first time, an Israeli government (the one headed by Labor's Ehud Barak) had put forth a concrete formula for the conflict's resolution: recognition of a Palestinian state; return to that state of nearly all of the West Bank and Gaza, with its 3.1 million population, and the turnover of a small amount of Israeli territory in partial compensation for lands beyond the "Green Line" retained by Israel; sharing of sovereignty with the Palestinians in Jerusalem ("Al Quds" in Arabic) and establishment of a Palestinian capital in that part of the city; and Israeli security arrangements in the Jordan Valley, perhaps through lease arrangements.

While calling for the annexation of lands adjoining Israel's Green Line (the pre-1967 border) containing up to 150,000 Israeli settlers, the Barak government indicated a readiness to relocate the other 60,000 settlers now living in small, scattered West Bank settlements. Also, while it rejected the Palestinian insistence of the "Right-of-Return" of Arab refugees who had fled or been driven from their homes during the 1947–48 war, it offered to participate in an international effort to provide financial compensation to the refugees and their families. Finally, it agreed to search for a formula that would guarantee Arab control over the top of the Temple Mount (Haram esh-Sherif) and direct access to the Mount.

Even though the Palestinians rejected the Camp David proposal, maps were presented there that detailed Israel's "red line" for the boundaries of territorial compromise. The Palestinian Arabs are likely to insist that this be the starting point in future negotiations. Prime Minister Sharon has ruled this out as a starting point.

Because of the need to include Arab states within the coalition in the War against Terrorism, the Bush administration has had to abandon its earlier hands-off policy and put pressure on both sides, not only to agree to a cease-fire, but to resume negotiations that would lead to peace. EU nations, and particularly Britain, have also taken active roles in pressing for a solution, while Egypt, Jordan, and Saudi Arabia have proposed full peace between Israel and all Arab states, in exchange for Israel's withdrawal from the Occupied Territories.

In any negotiations that take place, knotty geopolitical issues will have to be faced. First is Gaza's viability, which will require land concessions by both Israel and Egypt from the northwest Negev and North Sinai to help alleviate Gaza's population pressures.[7] Second, negotiations must address the sharing of the Temple Mount, for which one option is to create a horizontal international boundary that awards the top of the Mount to the Arabs and its base to Israel. Third, the contradiction between the pressures for separate Israeli and Arab sovereignties and the advantages of functional unity in Jerusalem must be addressed. East Jerusalem has 200,000 Palestinian Arab residents. Its 235,000 Jewish residents would be linked to the 265,000 already living in West Jerusalem. One possible approach might be a federation of the two municipalities for infrastructure operations and a metropolitan government that combines city-region functions through special authorities. Fourth is the development of joint Israeli-Palestinian mechanisms to ensure the equitable sharing of the water resources of the mountain and coastal plain aquifers that underlie the West Bank, Israel, and Gaza. Fifth, a mechanism for arbitrating the right of return for Arab refugees displaced in Israel's War of Independence must be developed. And sixth, Israel must withdraw from the handful of settlements it has built in Gaza, as well as most of those within the West Bank.

In addition, any permanent solution will require the territorial contiguity of the Palestinian West Bank. Creating land hinges between the northern, central, and southern West Bank sectors will necessitate the uprooting of nearly all the Israeli settlements along the north-south axis. Another territorial challenge will be linking Gaza to the rest of Palestine. The shortest distance between northeastern Gaza and the southwestern West Bank is approximately twenty-five miles. If neither a tunnel road nor an elevated highway is feasible, an alternative may be a land corridor under joint Israeli-Palestinian control, which would permit free north-south movement within Israel, as well as east-west movement within a Palestinian state.

In the face of current political tensions, the Israeli invasion of the West Bank in spring 2002, and widespread bloodshed on both sides, hope for a final resolution of the conflict, which will require flexibility by both negotiating parties, will probably hinge on the level of war weariness of each, as well as the weight of outside pressures.

Shifting Alliances among Arab States

Shifting alliances among the Arab states of the Middle East are an ongoing aspect of the geopolitical scene. Ideology, economics, personalities, successful coups, and big-power interests and support all play a part in the shifts between friendship and hostility among Middle Eastern states.

Egypt, the cornerstone of the Arab world, has vacillated in its orientation, leaning toward Britain, then the Soviet Union, and now the United States. This has complicated its relations with Sudan, Yemen, Libya, and Saudi Arabia.

Warm ties between Egypt and Sudan, which cooperated in the development of the Aswan High Dam (completed in 1971), soured with the presidency of Muhammed al-Nimeiry, who turned to the USSR as Egypt was turning to the West. They swung back after a coup attempt against Nimeiry allegedly backed by Libya and local Communists. Libya became more influential in Sudanese affairs when a military coup replaced the Nimeiry government in 1985.

The Gulf War saw sometime allies, as well as frequent enemies, on opposite sides. Sudan, Libya, and Yemen supported Iraq, while former enemies Egypt and Saudi Arabia joined the Allies, as did Syria. Yemen, in particular, suffered as a result of having backed the losing side during the war. The Saudis, who had been so supportive of North Yemen in the 1970s and '80s, expelled 8.5 million Yemeni workers, adding to Sana's economic woes. This was followed by a civil war in 1994, when the South failed once more in its attempt to become independent of the North. The area around Aden was devastated in this fighting.

Radical Islamic groups in Yemen continue to carry out sporadic terror bombings, while kidnapping of foreigners is not only a customary event, but also provides a substantial source of income to dissident groups. The bombing of the U.S.S. *Cole* in the port of Aden in 2000 raised suspicions about the Yemeni government's commitment, or even desire, to contain anti-American terrorism.

Geopolitical tides have continued to shift since the Gulf War. For much of the 1990s serious tensions continued to mar the relations among the various Arab states. Ties between Cairo and Khartoum became especially strained in 1991, when the Sudanese regime halted its cooperation with Cairo in the use of Nile water. Four years later, Egypt broke diplomatic relations with Sudan, accusing its regime of supporting an Islamic fundamentalist attempt to assassinate President Mubarak. The sheltering of terrorists by Khartoum drew UN condemnation and, in 1998, the United States destroyed a suspected chemical weapons plant in Khartoum.

Relations between Egypt and Libya were equally strained during much of the decade, with military clashes taking place along their border. In addition, the terrorist activities of the Qadaffi regime against the United States and Europe led to UN imposition of sanctions in 1992. Tensions within the region also remained high between Chad and Libya, which had intervened militarily in a civil war in Chad and seized much of the northern part of that country. These tensions eased only in 1994, when in response to an International Court of Justice arbitration award Libya withdrew its troops from the Aouzou Strip, over which it had maintained control since the war.

Without their former Soviet patron, Libya, Sudan, and Yemen have become increasingly hard-pressed to sustain their hostility against Egypt (and, in the case of Yemen, against Saudi Arabia). Yemen was the first to seek rapprochement with the Saudis, as both countries agreed in 1995 to negotiate a long-standing dispute over their fifteen-hundred-mile boundary, which lies astraddle the Rub al Khali, in areas of oil and gas potential. The accord, which calls for an outside body to conduct the boundary demarcation, was finally signed in 2000.

In 1999 diplomatic ties between Egypt and Yemen were restored, as the two countries signed bilateral trade and joint manufacturing agreements and pursued a cooperative effort to help resolve the Somalia conflict, in furtherance of their mutual Red Sea security interests. Sana has also cooperated with European energy companies in developing the country's oil and gas resources and created closer relations with the EU.

Toward the end of the decade, Egyptian-Sudanese relations warmed anew. The two countries agreed to cooperate in Nile River navigation between Aswan and Halfa, and trade and diplomatic relations were reactivated. In the year 2000 a joint defense agreement was signed, while Egypt has also sought to mediate the Sudanese civil war, in which hundreds of thousands of southerners have been killed in fighting or have died from rampant disease and starvation.

Cairo's stake in resolving this war is nearly as great as that of the Khartoum government. Both Egypt and northern Sudan are almost totally dependent upon Nile waters. The White Nile, which contributes about 40 percent of the total flow, is especially important because its headwaters are in Lake Victoria, in a region of year-round rainfall, while the Blue Nile provides its floodwaters only in the summer. Because the White Nile and smaller tributaries course through areas controlled by the southern rebels, its flow is vulnerable to various diversionary actions. This is the case especially for the Junglei Canal, a project designed to save water that is usually lost through evaporation. Because of the civil war, only three-quarters of the length of the proposed canal has been completed.

At the same time, Sudan has continued to maintain close links to Libya and has facilitated a rapprochement between that country and Egypt. Libya and Egypt reestablished full diplomatic ties in 2000, following the restoration of commercial relations the previous year. This action was a direct consequence of the efforts of Qadaffi to break the wall of isolation between Libya and the West. The Libyan ruler handed over two Libyan suspects in the Lockerbie bombing trial, paid compensation for London policewomen shot to death from the Libyan embassy in 1984, and renounced terrorism. These moves have resulted in the lifting of UN sanctions and restoration of diplomatic ties with Britain, Italy, and other European states, a process spearheaded by Italy. For Cairo, the links to Libya represent an opportunity to enhance economic and trade ties and to engage Libya in broader regional issues.

Egypt had been suspended from the Arab League in 1979 and, while it was welcomed back in 1989, it had not been able to exert its full leadership potential as long as it remained at odds with its nearest Arab neighbors. Its reentry freed it to take major regional initiatives, including efforts to mediate the Arab-Israeli conflict.

As long as the Arab states remain under authoritarian regimes, changes in their foreign policies will be dependent on the whims of one or a handful of individuals. The introduction of democratic, parliamentary governance within the Arab world might not bring about a change in the pattern of shifting alliances. However, open debates about policy would at least give fuller consideration to the rationale for such shifts.

Oil, Pipeline Routes, and Politics

Nothing better reflects the instability and unpredictability of the Middle East than its system of oil and gas pipelines and the impact of politics and wars upon their use. Iraq's first major pipeline to the Mediterranean extended from Kirkuk in the northern part of the country to Haifa in Israel. Built in 1934, it was closed during Israel's War of Independence, never to open again. A branch line was then constructed from Haditha in Iraq to Tripoli in Lebanon, via Syria. A much larger pipeline was built from Kirkuk to the Syrian port of Baniyas, only to be closed by Damascus, owing to tensions between Iraq and Syria over the latter's backing of Iran during the Iran-Iraq war. The line was reopened in 2001 with the permission of the United Nations, which oversees the "food-for-fuel" program for Iraq. The Iraqis have expressed an interest in building a new and larger line.

Other examples of the influence of war and politics on pipelines within the Middle East abound. The two Kirkuk-Dortyol-Ceyhan lines from Iraq to Turkey skirt Syria. They were closed during the Gulf War and not opened again until six years later. The Iraq-Saudi pipeline from the Rumaila fields in southern Iraq, the country's largest producers, to Yanbu on the Red Sea has remained closed since the war. Iraq is now permitted to export this petroleum by tanker from a new terminal at Mina al-Bakir at the head of the Persian Gulf. The huge Trans-Arabian pipeline—Tapline, completed in 1950—extends for 1,040 miles from Al-Dammam through Jordan and Syria to Sidon (Saida) in Lebanon. It was closed during the Arab-Israeli war of 1967, when Syria lost the Golan Heights to Israel, and has remained mothballed ever since. To replace Tapline, an even larger line with three times the throughput capacity was built by Saudi Arabia. Called "Petroline," it extends from Saudi Arabia's Gulf coastal fields to the country's western provinces and the Red Sea oil terminus and refining center of Yanbu.

The American stake in Saudi Arabia's oil quickly led to a major military and economic alliance between the two countries. For the United States, this was a commitment of strategic necessity. By the middle of World War II, the center of gravity of world oil reserves had shifted from the U.S. Gulf of Mexico/Caribbean region to the Middle East. Middle Eastern reserves, which were then estimated at nearly half of the world's total, have now climbed to over two-thirds.[8] Saudi Arabia alone has 25 percent of the total world reserves. Iran, Iraq, and Kuwait have another 28 percent. While the United States remains one of the world's major oil producers (ranking behind Saudi Arabia and Russia and on a par with the North Sea producers), its domestic output is far outstripped by demand. In fact, in the year 2000 imports represented 60 percent of total U.S. consumption. As a measure of the relative decline of the United States as an oil producer, U.S. output was 34 percent of the world total in 1960, 21 percent in 1970, and under 12 percent in 2000.[9]

Although a minor oil exporter, Sudan has also been caught up in oil pipeline politics. Oil fields have been developed in the Muglad Basin of the south's Kordofan province, just north of the province of Bahr el-Ghazal and the Upper Nile provinces. A 930-mile pipeline from Muglad to Port Sudan on the Red Sea has been completed. This route is the scene of heavy rebel activities because it lies along the dividing line between north and south Sudan. Highly vulnerable to attack, the line has been continuously cut by rebel forces since oil began to flow in 1998. Should Khartoum and the southerners ultimately agree to peace negotiations, the question of sovereignty over the oil-bearing areas and the division of royalties will most assuredly be a major issue.

The Turkish Straits continue to present international political problems, although they no longer are the focus of the historic struggle for strategic control that had embroiled them in wars and international controversies. Instead, it is Ankara's fear of oil spills that now pervades the politics of the straits. The completion of the new pipeline from the Tenghiz oil fields in Kazakhstan to Russia's Novorossiisk on the Black Sea has aggravated Turkey's fears of oil leaks and spills from large tankers traversing the Bosporus. However, the Montreux Convention limits Turkey's ability to restrict the movement of civilian shipping or to require the use of local ship pilots in navigating the narrow waters. It is the environmental concern that so strongly motivates Turkey to support the proposed 1,080-mile pipeline from Baku through Georgia and Turkey to its Mediterranean port of Ceyhan, whose construction was scheduled to begin in 2002.

Closure of the Suez Canal between 1967 and 1975 was a blow to the export of oil from the Middle East. This closure and cutoffs of some of the overland pipeline routes made it imperative to develop a new system for moving the Gulf's oil. One solution was the building of supertankers. These vessels, which are too big to transit the Suez Canal, proved themselves capable of transporting petroleum around South Africa's Cape of Good Hope more efficiently and cheaply than it could be transported via Suez, even after the reopened canal was deepened in 1980. Supertankers continue to play an important role, although they no longer carry the majority share of oil exports to Europe and the United States.

Another shift in the Gulf transportation scene related to the remarkable growth of the Japanese economy, followed by that of the Asia-Pacific Rim as a whole. Direct shipments to that region from the Gulf via the Indian Ocean had no need for Suez and Mediterranean pipeline systems. The growth of Asia-Pacifica has continued, and now accounts for 60 percent of all Saudi petroleum shipments, while the EU has dropped to second-largest market and the United States to third.

Conclusion

The Middle East is by no means the only geopolitical region to have experienced violent turbulence and sweeping changes during the past half century. However, it is unique in the rapidity with which the power balance and geopolitical orientations of the region have see-sawed. This instability is due to the deep fissures both within and among the twenty-four states of the region and to their heavy dependence on support from the Great Powers. Alterations in the fortunes of those powers have a profound impact on the economics and politics of their clients within the region.

The major external forces that have influenced regional change are a succession of events: the crumbling of the European colonial system; the deep penetration of U.S. and Soviet power; the collapse of the Soviet empire and attendant increase in the influence of the American superpower; the current diplomatic controversies over the sanctions imposed upon Iraq pursuant to the 1991 Gulf War; the sharp growth in world demand for oil and natural gas; the impact of globalism on the culture, economy, and politics of most Middle Eastern states; and, most recently, the pressures placed upon Arab states to cooperate with the United States and its allies in the War against Terrorism. These have affected such intraregional forces as the ascendance of military elites that led the overthrow of monarchies; Marxism and various forms of national socialist ideologies that centralized governments and economies; conflicts between states and separatist movements within and across them; the struggle between secularism and the rising tide of Islamic fundamentalism; and the Arab-Israeli conflict.

The diversity of the Middle East as a geopolitical arena and its polynodal regional power structure inhibit the establishment of stable regional or subregional geopolitical units. Their absence limits the more effective use of human and material resources through sharing and transfer mechanisms. Rather than presenting a regional mosaic whose diverse parts complement one another, the Middle East is an assortment of competing states and interest groups. In this competition, Turkey, Egypt, Iran, Iraq, Saudi Arabia, and Israel are all important power centers.

Intraregional trade remains relatively limited, inasmuch as the chief trading partners of the Middle Eastern states with the largest economies lie outside the region. There are a few exceptions. Saudi Arabia serves as an important market for products from smaller, economically weak states, such as those that lie across its Red Sea waters, and some of its Arabian Peninsula neighbors. Lebanon also, because of its Gateway or exchange functions, transships some of its imports to other Middle Eastern states and provides them with financial services and food and textile products. Bahrain serves as a banking and financial service center for the Arabian Peninsula countries.

Aside from the close links among the states of the Gulf Co-operation Council, which have recently expanded their functions to include a free trade agreement among the members, political ties among the region's states are fragile. As discussed previously, various attempts to achieve full-scale political mergers ended in failure, save for the United Arab Emirates and Yemen, although the latter remains deeply divided along its former north-south lines.

More promising than attempts at full-blown mergers of countries are functional ties that have limited objectives. Egypt, Jordan, and Syria have completed an electricity line that links their electric grids. Other examples are the freshwater transfer agreement between Turkey and Israel; the proposed underwater natural gas pipeline from Egypt to Israel, with a planned extension to Turkey; and the agreements between Egypt and Sudan on defense and Nile navigation.

Water remains a major cause for tension and dispute, since as much as 90 percent of the region's major streams and many of its aquifers cut across international boundaries.

Thus not only is Turkey's diversion of the Tigris-Euphrates headwaters opposed by Syria and Iraq, but also control of the Southeast Anatolian Water Project could become a major issue in the negotiations between Ankara and the Turkish Kurds in their demands for independence.

Agreement between Syria and Israel over the Golan Heights is hampered by Syrian insistence that peace depends on Israel's withdrawal not only from the Golan Heights, but also from a ten-meter strip along the northeastern shore of the Sea of Galilee, Israel's main reservoir, which lay within the bounds of the former Palestine Mandate. Israel and the Palestinian Authority are at odds over Israeli control of the mountain aquifer under the West Bank, which is rapidly being depleted.

In the Persian/Arab Gulf, the Shatt al Arab and maritime boundaries remain sources of contention. Conservation practices, recycling, desalinization, the sale of freshwater, and establishing water pricing policies are measures that need to be taken to address the region's water problems, but political fragmentation is a major obstacle to their implementation.

While the region has abundant petroleum and natural gas, many of the disputes over these energy resources occur in connection with land or maritime boundaries that are in areas populated by minorities who seek independence or autonomy. This is the case with Iraq's petroleum fields located in the Kurdish north and the Shia south, which stiffens Baghdad's opposition to those separatist movements. Iran's major oil lies within its heavily Arabic province of Khuzestan, while in the north of the country Iranian Azerbaijan has important potential reserves of both oil and gas. This complicates the search for solutions to that country's irredentist conflicts. Oil has also become an important factor in the Sudanese civil war.

Other obstacles to regional stability are the massive numbers of foreign workers in Saudi Arabia and the Gulf States; use by terrorist groups operating in one country of bases in neighboring countries for training and supply purposes; Iraq's possible development of weapons of mass destruction; transborder nomadic migrations; and the presence of refugees from war and civil strife. Sudan, Eritrea, Somalia, Turkey, Iraq, Kuwait, Iran, and Afghanistan have large numbers of refugees. Of the over three million Palestinian refugees, one-third have languished in camps in Lebanon, Jordan, Syria, Gaza, and the West Bank for over half a century, enduring hardship and creating instability in those lands.

All of these obstacles, plus disparities of wealth, land degradation and other environmental problems, and agricultural production deficits present formidable challenges that are more difficult to tackle owing to the political fragmentation of the Shatterbelt.

The magnet of the circumterral seas of the Middle East continues to attract major external powers, even as their comparative influence has changed. Russia retains some influence over the course of events in the Persian Gulf, through its contacts with Iran and Iraq, and in the eastern Mediterranean, where it continues to back Syria. While the United States remains the prime military force in the Gulf and maintains strategic supremacy there, it is reliant on Britain's political and air support to enforce the no-fly zone policies in Iraq. It also is encountering mounting criticism from European and Arab states for its failure to develop an alternative to sanctions as a way of breaking the political stalemate over Iraq. France, which has been particularly active in seeking oil arrangements with Baghdad, as well as with Tehran, has been among the leading critics of Washington's policies toward Iraq and of its efforts to isolate Iran.

For Washington, the Persian/Arab Gulf remains as strategically important as ever. The security of the Gulf has required the placing of American military and surveillance facilities in Saudi Arabia in the interests of protecting the access of much of the Maritime Realm to Middle Eastern oil supplies. Arms sales to Riyadh, the largest customer for U.S. military hardware, are another measure of the importance of the relations between the two countries. The economic ties between the two have broadened as Saudi Arabia has become the fifth-largest trading partner of the United States and the recipient of the largest share of U.S. investments in the Middle East.

In a region as unstable as the Middle East, geopolitical forecasts are risky. With this caveat, it can be noted that present trends suggest that the current geopolitical atomization may be decreased as new subregional blocs emerge. However, there are significant "ifs"—if the Arab-Israeli dispute is finally resolved and if Turkey is admitted to the EU, the western half of the Middle East might become part of a Euro-Mediterranean expansion of Maritime Europe and the Maghreb. Egypt is already strongly oriented, militarily and economically, to Europe and the United States, as is Israel. A Libya without the mercurial Qadaffi would probably gravitate more strongly into the Egyptian orbit in a strategic sense, and it is already tied economically to Europe. Israel, Lebanon, Syria, and Jordan in a Levant at peace would be logically drawn into an expanded Euro-Mediterranea by economic and cultural ties, as well as common strategic interests.

Israel recently joined the "Western Europe and Others" regional grouping in the United Nations because it has been banned by Arab states from the Asian regional group. This may be a forerunner of the geopolitical linking of the Levant and northeast Africa to the western Mediterranean basin and Atlantic Europe. Also, as a leading high-technology economy and society, an Israel at peace with its neighbors could provide a bridge to high-tech Maritime Europe.

On the eastern border of the Middle East, Iran is gradually emerging from the international isolation that it has imposed on itself and has been reinforced by Western sanctions in reaction to Tehran's sponsorship of international terrorism, including support of the Hizbollah in southern Lebanon. With the rise of reformist elements within the fundamentalist regime that began with the election of President Mohammed Khatami and a reformist parliament in 1997, formal diplomatic and trade relations have begun to be reestablished with European and moderate Arab states.

At the same time, Tehran has sought to offset U.S. pressures and Washington's strategic primacy within the Middle East by developing closer ties to China and Russia. Iran has been aided by Moscow in developing medium-range strategic missiles aimed at putting it on a par with Pakistan, Iraq, and Israel, and has negotiated agreements to become a major supplier of natural gas to India. In the late '90s, Russia also completed the nuclear energy plants for Iran at Bushehr on the Persian Gulf that been started with the help of West Germany in the 1970s. These steps suggest that Tehran will seek to play an independent geopolitical role and link itself to the world's diverse geostrategic regions, without joining any of them.

Iran could become the core of a powerful, independent geopolitical subregion with considerable influence over its neighbors. For example, parts of Central Asia, which historically have been exposed to Persian culture, might gravitate toward Tehran, if its regime were to move toward a balanced relationship between religion and politics, while abandoning its support of international terrorism. However, Iran's Shia religion continues to be an obstacle to closer ties with some Sunni neighbors in both the Arab world and Muslim lands to the east of Iran.

Were the western part of the Middle East to become absorbed within the Maritime European orbit and Iran to maintain its separate geopolitical stance, the remainder of the region—Iraq, Saudi Arabia, the Gulf States, Afghanistan, and Sudan—would continue to constitute a Shatterbelt, albeit considerably smaller than the present one. Polarization within such a reduced Shatterbelt region might be intensified if the United States continues to maintain a strong military and economic presence in Saudi Arabia and Russia succeeds in rebuilding close ties with an Iraq freed of international sanctions but still ruled by Saddam Hussein. The influence of Iran within the Gulf is also likely to grow. Afghanistan might well break up under pressures from Pakistan and Iran, while Pakistan itself might crumble, with one or more of its parts becoming oriented to the Middle East.

What can be predicted with some certainty about the Middle East Shatterbelt is that it will continue to be a region of conflict and shifting alliances. What cannot be predicted with any measure of confidence is how these alliances may shift and what the region's borders may be.

Notes

1. Reader Bullard, *Britain and the Middle East* (London: Hutchinson's University Library, 1951), 28–47.

2. Bullard, *Britain and the Middle East*, 48–65.

3. Richard C. Duncan and Walter Youngquist, "The World Petroleum Life-Cycle" (paper presented at Petroleum Technology Transfer Council Workshop at the University of Southern California, Los Angeles, October 22, 1998).

4. Central Intelligence Agency, "Major Land Disputes around the World: Selected Disputes, July 18, 2000," pamphlet, 7 pp.; Central Intelligence Agency, "Disputes International," *The World Factbook 2000* (Washington, D.C.: Gov/CIA, 2000).

5. Alan J. Day, *Border and Territorial Disputes* (Harlow, England: Longman, 1982), 214–19.

6. Day, *Border and Territorial Disputes*, 222–25.

7. Saul B. Cohen, "Gaza Now! Prospects for a Gaza Microstate," *Mediterranean Quarterly* (Spring 1992), 60–80.

8. U.S. Department of Energy, Energy Information Administration, "Annual Energy Review," in *World Almanac and Book of Facts 2000* (Mahwah, N.J.: Primedia Reference, 1999), 163–64.

9. Andrew Boyd, *An Atlas of World Affairs*, 10th ed. (London: Routledge, 1998), 19–21.

CHAPTER 12

The Southern Continents: The Quarter-Sphere of Marginality

Geopolitically the "Southern Continents" consist of Sub-Saharan Africa and South America from the Amazon basin and Columbia's Cordillera ranges southward. Africa and South America face each other across the South Atlantic, while their opposite coasts border the Indian and Pacific Oceans, respectively. These landmasses and their adjoining ocean areas cover a quarter of the globe and hold 15 percent of the world's population.

In a geostrategic sense, the two continents constitute a "Quarter-Sphere of Marginality."[1] They play a minimal role in the strategic relationships among the world's three geostrategic realms. While these Southern Continents have been dominated by the U.S. and EU power centers since the end of the Cold War, the strategic impact upon the Maritime Realm of events that take place in them is slight.

Radical changes in military technology and the global economy are responsible for this marginalization. Mobile ocean-based naval and air strike forces, long-range aircraft and missiles, and global-spanning surveillance satellites have deprived the land and naval bases of the Quarter-Sphere of meaningful roles in world geostrategic competition.

Changing international trade patterns and major improvements in the canals that bisect the Old and New World hemispheres have also contributed to this marginalization. An increasing share of Persian/Arab Gulf oil now goes to the Asia-Pacific Rim via the Indian Ocean. In addition, oil pipeline capacity overland from the Gulf to the eastern Mediterranean has been expanded, while the Suez Canal has been deepened and its docking facilities expanded since its reopening in 1975. All of this has reduced the importance of the trans-African route around the Cape of Good Hope to Western Europe. The Panama Canal, now under full Panamanian sovereignty, has also been modernized. It handles most of America's east coast trade destined for the U.S. west coast and the Pacific Rim, as well as South America's west coast trade with the eastern United States.

Economically, the postindustrial regions of the world are no longer as dependent upon the Southern Continents for their storehouses of raw materials as they once were. The Quarter-Sphere now suffers from overproduction of minerals and certain commercial crops, as well as competition from other parts of the world, substitutes for their commodities, and changing consumer tastes. Wars, civil strife, authoritarian regimes, and political instability, especially in Africa, but also in some parts of South America, have further discouraged investors. As a result, Sub-Saharan Africa and South America have failed to attract the capital flows, technology transfer, and specialization of industry that has revolutionized so many of the formerly underdeveloped economies of Asia. In addition, much of the potential trade with the developing world, especially food, is stifled by tariff, quota, or domestic subsidy policies of the highly developed countries. Exceptions to this decline in investment interest are pockets of modernity in South Africa, Brazil, Argentina (at least until its financial collapse in 2002), and Chile.

Most of the world's least-developed countries are located within the Quarter-Sphere, which has a minimal share of world trade in goods and services—approximately 4 percent. Its relationships with the industrialized world are based more on humanitarian grounds than on mutual self-interest. In Sub-Saharan Africa, poverty, disease (especially the AIDS pandemic), lack of education, starvation, high death rates, and warfare within and among states evoke the attention and intermittent compassion of the wealthy nations and the international community, but their considerations are neither strategic nor economic.

Colonial/Imperial Background

This view of the marginality of the Quarter-Sphere is a major departure from past geopolitical perspectives relative to the Southern Continents. Panregionalism, the widely held theory of north-south relations, persisted long after it had become outdated. It had been rooted in the proposition that the Southern Continents were the "exploitable world" and vital to the progress of northern, industrialized societies. This had been a cornerstone of German *geopolitik* doctrine and was, in effect, a rationale for U.S. and European imperialism.[2] The race for the anticipated riches of Sub-Saharan Africa resulted in the fierce European colonial struggles of the late nineteenth and early twentieth centuries. Similarly, U.S. policy toward Latin America was motivated by the desire to gain monopoly control over the resources and markets of the continent to its south, to the exclusion of European interference.

European penetration of Africa dates back to the discovery period of the fifteenth century. However, it began in earnest with the explorations and footholds that were established in the late eighteenth and nineteenth centuries. This is conveyed in the names accorded to the West African coast—"Grain and Pepper Coast," "Slave Coast," "Gold Coast," "Ivory Coast." The "Copperbelt" of Northern Rhodesia/Zambia and southeastern Congo (Katanga) is another example.

A rationale offered for European intervention in Africa during the nineteenth century was assumption of the "white man's burden" as the duty of Christian powers to stop the slave trade and "civilize the natives." However, the main motive was economic exploitation. The rapid industrialization of Europe between 1870 and 1890 stimulated the search for new markets, not only within Europe and North America, but also in Africa and Asia. In addition, it produced the capital surpluses that were required to exploit the mineral riches and agricultural potential of these tropical regions. Population growth in Europe resulted in massive overseas emigration after 1880, not just to the United States, but also to the African colonies, where white immigrants could help their mother countries retain political control.[3] Congo is a most egregious example of the ruthlessness with which native Africans were exploited in the search for riches. Britain's colonial interest was not sparked by Henry Stanley's three explorations of the great river during 1871–84, following those of David Livingstone. However, these explorations did prod Belgian king Leopold to establish the Independent State of the Congo as his private preserve. His pursuit of the "wonderful natural wealth" that Stanley ascribed to the Congo led to the exploitation first of rubber and ivory, and then of the copper resources of the river's upper basin.

All of the concessions that were awarded by Leopold utilized forced labor. The brutality of this system sparked widespread outrage. In response, the government of Belgium eventually annexed the territory from Leopold in 1908, establishing the Belgian Congo and ameliorating the conditions somewhat.

While the African rubber trade declined steeply with the shift of the industry to the plantations of Southeast Asia, copper remained a significant export, although today it is exceeded in importance by diamonds. Other minerals (such as cobalt, zinc, tin, and uranium), petroleum (from offshore deposits at the mouth of the Congo), tropical hardwoods, and plantation crops remain the backbone of the modern Congo (Zaire) economy. In addition, some of the substantial hydroelectric potential of the great river has been harnessed, although most of it remains untapped. However, the Congo basin never proved to be as rich as the early explorers and exploiters assumed. Poverty of soils, climatic rigor, disease, labor force instability, and competition from crops and minerals of other parts of the world prevented the region from attaining its perceived potential.

Economics also played a central role in fostering of the pan-Americanism that was first enunciated by the United States in the Monroe doctrine—the concept of an isolated hemisphere to be shielded from the conflicts of the rest of the world. The interventionist policies of Theodore Roosevelt, the control of the Panama Canal, "dollar diplomacy," and Franklin D. Roosevelt's Good Neighbor Policy were manifestations of the same objective—to keep Latin America as a strategic reserve for the United States. During the 1930s and early '40s, the idea of a unified hemisphere capable of achieving self-sufficiency was seized upon by American isolationists as a rationale for not intervening in the struggle between Europe's democracies and its Nazi and Fascist regimes.

The U.S. view of South America's economic importance was strongly influenced by the perceived potential of the Amazon basin (also referred to as "Amazonia" or "Amazonas"). It had long been held to be one of the richest regions of the world, with vast, unexploited mineral, forest, and agricultural resources and access to ocean shipping. This perception was fed by Brazil's rubber boom, which followed Charles Goodyear's invention of vulcanization in 1839. Most of the rubber came from the wild Para rubber tree in the upper Amazon, which gave Brazil a monopoly on the rubber trade. The boom lasted until the early twentieth century and attracted settlers from the country's northeast, many of whom were put to work under conditions of virtual slavery.

With the shift to plantation rubber in Malaya and Sumatra toward the end of the nineteenth century, the Amazonian boom collapsed, as did the African rubber boom. While the Ford Motor Company reintroduced rubber plantations in 1927 and established the Town of Fordlandia in the Amazon, it abandoned the scheme after World War II, owing to the scarcity of workers.

The idea that the western hemisphere could be self-sufficient was as much a fantasy as the concept of a self-sufficient Eur-Africa. Rather than sustained development, South America's economy has been marked by booms and busts. This was the fate of the mining centers of Peru and, in Brazil, of the brazilwood industry, the sugar plantations of the northeast, the gold of Minas Gerais, the coffee of the Paraiba Valley in eastern São Paulo state, and now the hardwoods of Amazonas. Similar experiences have taken place with the nitrates of northern Chile and the sheep ranches of Patagonia. The economic history of the continent has been one of rapid exploitation and then depletion. Yet the search for quick fortunes continues today with the processing of the coca leaves of Colombia into cocaine and the growing of both sun and shade varieties of Colombian coffee.

The concept of a north-south strategic alignment is not only flawed economically, but it is also misleading spatially. Much of South America is closer to Africa and as near to Maritime Europe as it is to the eastern United States. Moreover, East and southern Africa are closer to Arabia and the Indian subcontinent than to Europe, and the latter have had significant historic ties with these Indian Ocean and Arabian Sea lands.

In many ways, the Cold War struggles between the Maritime and Communist powers that took place within the Southern Continents represented extensions of the panregional concepts. Ironically, much of the struggle took place after it had become generally apparent that these were not the global resource storehouses that they had once been thought to be. Africa became a Shatterbelt, as Marxist regimes were established in Mozambique, Angola, Guinea, Benin, Ethiopia, and the People's Republic of the Congo (Brazzaville), while the West mounted major efforts with the help of its base in white-ruled South Africa to unseat the Mozambique and Angola regimes. China, too, penetrated the region, acquiring influence in socialist Tanzania as it helped with arms and the building of the Tazara (Tan-Zam) railway.

Despite Soviet efforts to foment Marxist rebellions in various South American countries, it was not able to establish solid footholds within the region, thus sparing the continent from becoming Shatterbelt. Uruguay, Peru, and Colombia were torn by Marxist terrorist activities, but did not fall under Moscow's sway.

In Chile the Communist Party joined forces with the socialists to enable Salvador Allende Gossens to become the first popularly elected Marxist president in Latin America. However, after three years in office, Allende was overthrown by a military coup, covertly supported by the United States. Argentina also experienced considerable unrest, first when it was caught between Peronista and Communist forces during the period that followed the first ouster of Juan Perón in the late 1950s and again after he, and then his widow, regained power from 1973 to 1976. However, the military junta that then took power conducted its "dirty war" against both the Marxists and the Peronistas, thereby keeping the country within the Western orbit. That South America did not become a Shatterbelt despite all of this turbulence was because the Soviet Union was too far removed from the region to offset U.S. power.

Just as panregionalism was a flawed theory geopolitically, so were theories that promoted the concept of a unified Southern Continent region centering around the South Atlantic basin. An example was Mackinder's 1943 view of the world in which South America and Africa were treated as one of the world's five geopolitical divisions: "If these [tropical rainforests] were subdued to agriculture and inhabited with the present density of tropical Java, they might sustain a thousand million people, always provided that medicine had rendered the tropics as productive of human energy as the temperate zone."[4]

This concept of a unified South Atlantic geostrategic realm is as removed from reality today as it was when presented over a half century ago. The two Southern Continents had as little in common then as now. Today, they conduct only minor trade with one another and they have no military alliances and little cultural contact. Each has strong links to Europe and the United States. The Pacific Ocean is of increasing importance to western South America, as the Indian Ocean is to eastern Africa.

Part I: South America

THE GEOGRAPHICAL SETTING

Cultural geographers find it convenient to divide the western hemisphere along the cultural divide of the Rio Grande and to separate Anglo-America from Latin America. This does not apply geopolitically. The strength of the ties between the United States and Middle America, especially Mexico, have overridden the barrier functions of the river as an economic and cultural divide.

Another western hemispheric divide is framed by the physical environment—the line of the northern Andes–Columbian Cordilleras and the southern Venezuelan-Guiana Highlands that border the Amazon and separate Middle from South America. This is the divide along which this author has drawn the geopolitical boundary. South America is a triangle fronting on two oceans, the Atlantic and Pacific. Two physical features of great magnitude profoundly influence the political map—the Andes mountains and the Amazon Basin. The Andes, with their adjoining forests and deserts, separate western from eastern South America. The Panama Canal has strengthened this condition of separation, making it easier for northwestern South America to communicate with the Caribbean and the North Atlantic than to communicate overland with the rest of South America.

The rain forests, climate, and sparse settlements of Amazonas reinforce the barriers between South and Middle America, as well as between the western and eastern parts of South America. Use of the river as a unifying transportation artery between the west coast countries and Brazil has limited value, not only because of the Andean barrier, but also because of slow and uncertain shipping schedules.

Additional forces, other than the Andes and Amazonia, also tend to fragment South America geopolitically. These include the linguistic, cultural, and racial differences that can be traced to many factors, such as sailing directions, local resources, and intra-European rivalry, as was behind the Partition of Tordesillas, which divided the region between Spain and Portugal in 1493. In the sector controlled by Spain, a system of administrative organizations known as "viceroyalties" formed powerful, quasi-independent political units. These included Peru, New Granada (Colombia, Venezuela, and Panama), and Charcas (whose core was Bolivia). The separate river communication systems that these units developed led to the open sea and thence to differing overseas contact points, reinforcing the isolation of the viceroyalties from one another. Finally, several countries are dependent on similar commodities, which limits the possibilities for intraregional trade while spurring national competition for foreign markets.

It is noteworthy that, save between Argentina and Chile, the crests of the Andes do not serve as national boundaries. In the south, where the Andes form a single range, they are sufficiently high, narrow, and unpopulated to warrant a barrier boundary function. To the north, where three distinct ranges are separated by high valleys, and in the center, where there are two ranges and one high valley, they form a wide but habitable zone. There the basins within the Andes serve as zones of unity, not of separatism. The rain-forested areas on the eastern slopes of the mountains serve as the barriers.

An important facet of the geopolitical structure of South America is its population distribution. On the western side of the continent, the populace has historically been highland oriented. The Spanish settled in the mountains for the minerals. They found the

Indians already there, and this coincidence of minerals and labor supply kept the European population in the highlands.

Some attempts were made to bring Indians down to the Pacific coast to help develop ports. Most of these efforts ended in disaster. The indigenous peoples were unadapted to rainy lowland conditions, succumbed to tropical diseases, and sought to escape the repressive labor conditions imposed upon them. In the drier parts of the west coast, such as the semitropical savannahs and, to the south, the deserts of Peru, the Incas had developed an irrigation culture. But their numbers were small. When the Europeans later sought to develop plantation agriculture along the tropical forested coasts of the northern Andean countries (and also in coastal Brazil), they imported slaves from Africa or indentured laborers from the East Indies.

Thus the centers of western South American population—the capital cities and business nodes—are in the highlands, in the Bogotá Basin, the Basin of Quito, the Peruvian Highlands, and the Bolivian Plateau. Only in central Chile is the population concentrated in the lowland, which here is a broad, moist, and temperate valley bordered by the narrow, high Andes to the east and the low, coastal ranges along the Pacific.

The concentration of populations in the highlands of South America is carried over through much of Central America and Mexico, reinforcing the principle that higher altitudes in tropical and subtropical regions cancel out the negative impacts of low latitudes. The process of vertical zonation of climate brings decreasing temperatures with increasing elevation, while changing conditions from hot, tropical climates at the lowest elevations to moderate to cool temperatures at the higher ones.

Proximity of the Andean highlands to the coast and improvement of transportation and communications offer considerable potential to those highlands for a seaward orientation, and thus for increased urbanization. In modern times, with improved health and medical facilities and air-conditioned buildings, the potential exists for a partial shift of the population to the seacoasts. However, this is only likely to occur after the highland centers become so overcrowded that the states involved have little alternative but to engage in massive coastal developments.

In contrast to the population of the western side of the continent, the population of eastern South America is located in Atlantic coastal regions. These include the fertile, drought-prone to well-watered coastal plains that stretch from northeastern Brazil to Bahia Blanca in Argentina. They are backed by the low East Brazilian Highlands, behind which are level, grassland plateaus. In the south, the major population penetration into the interior, along the Paraná estuary, is a strong reflection of the economic orientation of that area to ocean ports and international trade, as well as of its moderate, midlatitude climate.

While most of South America's population lives in western, coastal-rimming mountains or on the eastern coastal plain and accessible plateaus, the Interior is a hollow core because of rain forest, dry grassland, and Patagonian desert. The weight of the continent's population and resources is on the eastern side. Brazil, Uruguay, Paraguay, and Argentina have over 215 million people, while the western side—Colombia, Ecuador, Peru, Bolivia, and Chile—has only 100 million.

GEOPOLITICAL FEATURES

The geopolitical features of South America have remained remarkably immature for a continent that has enjoyed national independence for so long a period. For example, it lacks either historic or contemporary national capitals with sufficient regional reach to unify the eastern or western sections, let alone the entire continent.

Ecumene

In western South America, the national ecumenes of Colombia, Ecuador, Peru, and Chile are all confined to mountain basins hundreds of miles from each other. Indeed, Peru's ecumene, which is centered at Lima and extends to Callao on the coast, is fifteen hundred miles from Chile's core area, which runs from Santiago southward to Concepción.

On the Atlantic side, the different national ecumenes are closer to one another, but those of Brazil and Paraguay are still substantially removed from the geographically connected ecumenes of Argentina and Uruguay. Brazil's Historic Core and first ecumene was its northeast. Early settlement had been attracted to the northeast coast because of its suitability for growing sugar. The focus for the development was the zone extending from Salvador (the country's first capital, in the state of Bahia), to Recife in Pernambuco. The sugar plantation culture flourished, based on the large-scale importation of slaves from Africa. When the industry collapsed in the nineteenth century due to soil exhaustion, overseas competition, and the abolition of slavery, the region's economy declined, as Brazil's settlement and economic activities shifted southward to where the present ecumene is located. The northeast is now an impoverished, drought-prone region—a far cry from its era of prosperity.

This ecumene extends along the coast from Rio de Janeiro to São Paulo and thence to the coastal Santa Catarina and Rio Grande do Sul provinces of the south. The hydropower and minerals (gold, diamonds, and rich iron reserves) of Minas Gerais provided the capital and material basis for the late nineteenth- and early twentieth-century industrialization of Rio de Janeiro, where the new ecumene had begun to emerge. Reinforcing Rio's economic growth, Volta Redonda, located within the interior fifty miles from Rio, was developed after World War II into one of the world's largest integrated steel complexes, and it now supplies half of the country's iron and steel.

From Rio, the ecumene then spread southward, as the coffee plantations of São Paulo's hinterland led to the next Brazilian economic boom. Over the years, the plantations, always in need of fresh soils, moved from northeastern São Paulo state to its northern and western sections, as well as southward into the state of Paraná. It was coffee that provided the capital for São Paulo's industrial growth.

By the 1960s São Paulo had become the focus of the Brazilian ecumene, and it remains so to this day. It is the main financial center of South America and the continent's largest, richest, and most urbanized area, with a city population of ten million and a population in the suburbs of eight million. Its broad industrial base includes electronics, telecommunications equipment, pharmaceuticals, chemicals, food, and textiles.

If the Brazilian ecumene eventually merges with that of Argentina-Uruguay, which focuses on the Río de la Plata estuary, it will be owing to São Paulo's economic power. However, this expansion is only a long-range prospect, because the distance between Porto Alegre in Brazil and Montevideo-Buenos Aires is 450 miles.

Effective National Territory

The Effective National Territory of Brazil's interior savannah (the Cerrado) and its far south grasslands may someday connect with the Uruguayan and Argentine Pampas—all

Figure 12.1   South America: Major Geopolitical Features

areas capable of attracting population and economic development—but this, too, is a long-term prospect. The same holds true for vast tracts of fertile, uncultivated lands in eastern Paraguay and eastern Bolivia, whose development would be hastened by improved rail, highway, and air services to the Brazilian coast. Serving as major barriers to the merger of the Brazilian, Bolivian, and Paraguayan ENTs are not only the limited capacity of their ranching-grazing economies to support larger populations, but also the location of the Pantanal region between them. The Pantanal, which is a vast wetland that extends across the Paraguay River and is subject to seasonal flooding, is virtually unusable during that period.

Boundary and Territorial Disputes

A number of boundary or territorial issues also inhibit regional cooperation.[5] Chile has territorial claims in Antarctica that partly overlap Argentine and British claims. Bolivia lost the Atacama Desert to Chile through wars in 1883 and 1929. As a result, Bolivia no longer has a sovereign corridor to the sea and it continues to harbor the desire for territorial restitution. The two countries also have a dispute over Río Lauca water rights.

Two sections of the boundary between Brazil and Uruguay are in dispute. One is in the area of Río Quarai (Río Cuareim). The other involves the islands at the confluence of the Río Quarai and the Uruguay River.

Colombia has a maritime boundary dispute with Venezuela in the Gulf of Venezuela. In addition, Nicaragua challenges Colombia's possession of the Archipelago of San Andrés y Providencia, which lies off the Mosquito Coast of Nicaragua and is a center for tourism and transshipment of cocaine from Colombia to the United States.

Ecuador and Peru have had a long-standing, bitter conflict over their boundary in the Amazon region. After sporadic fighting in the 1980s, the early 1990s, and again in 1995, they finally concluded an agreement in 1999, arbitrated by Argentina, Brazil, Chile, and the United States. This confirmed Peru's claim to the border as running along the high peaks of the Condor Range and provided Ecuador with a patch of Peruvian land in Amazonas (one square mile) to honor its military dead. The accord provides for integrating the economies of the two countries, especially in the border region, and for linking their electric grid systems. It also gives Ecuador navigation and trading rights on the Amazon River and its tributaries within Peru.

The Falkland Islands (Islas Malvinas) are United Kingdom–administered, but claimed by Argentina, which launched an ill-fated military invasion of the islands in 1982. While Buenos Aires has not renounced its claim, the dispute has been dormant since that war. Argentina also lays claim to the United Kingdom–administered South Georgia and South Sandwich Islands, two thousand miles east of Tierra del Fuego in the South Atlantic. During the Falklands conflict, Argentine troops invaded South Georgia, but were driven off by the British. Another dispute between the two countries is over territorial sovereignty in Antarctica, where they have overlapping claims.

GEOPOLITICAL FORCES OF SEPARATION AND ATTRACTION

Forces of Separation

A variety of centrifugal forces—physical, economic, social, and political—divide South America and contribute to its geopolitical fragmentation.[6] These include separate historical orientations and cultures, disputes over territorial expansions and frontiers, and the absence of significant trade links among the countries. (The trade links have increased substantially with the establishment of Mercosur, the east coast free trade bloc.) The inability of Brazil to exercise a dominating regional role up to now, despite having 58 percent of the population of the region, is a significant deterrent to regional cohesiveness.

The continent's fragmentation has been exacerbated by the separation of various racial and ethnic groupings on both national and regional levels. Examples are the Afro-Brazilian enclaves of northeastern Brazil; the black populations of Colombia's Pacific and Caribbean coasts; and the Indians of the Andes, the Eastern Andes Piedmont, Amazonas, and the upper Orinoco. Laws perpetuating or protecting the large farm estates known as *latifundia* have helped to keep these populations *in situ*.

The areas of South America that are favorably endowed physically represent oases of prosperity in otherwise impoverished tropical and semitropical areas that suffer from poor soil, droughts or flooding, distance from the sea, and mountain barriers to efficient land communication. The population that did move onto the fertile highland basins developed surpluses that encouraged the development of commerce and industry. As these prosperous population nodes industrialized, they attracted the rural impoverished. The result was the development of the dominant city, which attracts hundreds of thousands of landless people who cannot be housed or employed within the city because population has outstripped the economic base. Provincial centers, overshadowed by the major urban centers and generally bypassed by highly centralized national governmental structures, tend to wither. The South American experience bears out the comment of Montesquieu that concentration leads to depopulation by depriving local centers of the vigor of being themselves capitals.[7]

Also contributing to geopolitical immaturity has been stop-and-go national economic development and international political attention. Sporadic South American development efforts all too often have been related to crisis politics, such as was brought on by droughts in Brazil or elections in Argentina, and then have been put aside as the emergencies have subsided. The situation has been aggravated by the failure of the United States to apply an even, steady flow of political attention, economic aid, and capital investment to the region. Instead, it has usually reacted to crises with programs that rarely outlast the presidential administration that launched them. In recent decades, the influx of immigrants to the United States from such countries as Colombia and Ecuador, as well as the flow of drugs from Colombia and, earlier, Peru, has commanded much attention from Washington. Inasmuch as these occurrences have long-term impacts, they may stimulate the United States to take a long-range approach to its Colombian development aid, along with its drug interdiction programs.

Forces of Attraction

Despite the forces of fragmentation that separate the western and eastern portions of the continent, there are major attractions that connect the two. Most importantly, there is the common Latin culture that binds all of South America, a bond that transcends the differences between Brazil, with its Portuguese history and language, and the rest of the countries of the continent. In addition, the very dominance of eastern South America is a magnet for the western half.

There is some complementarity of economies between the east and west coast countries. Western South America has a relatively stronger mineral base than the east and this can become a basis for broadening exchange. Air routes currently offer alternatives to the barrier effects of mountains and tropical rain forests. Also, upstream waterways connect Manaus in Brazilian Amazonas to Iquitos to the west, in Peru, and to central Ecuador and that country's road system. Southward from Manaus up the Rio Madeiro, the water route runs to Porto Velho in Brazil. From there a road extends westward into Peru. However, these overland connections are still under development. The feeders of one branch of the Trans-Amazon Highway have been completed to connect with the Bolivian and Peruvian system, although the main highway stops far short of the Colombian border. Similarly, a northern perimeter Amazonian highway does link up with the Venezuelan and Guyanan road systems, but does not extend beyond Brazil's Roraima state in the direction of Colombia. In addition, a gas pipeline has been completed from Bolivia's gas fields to São Paulo, while another has been completed from interior southern Argentina through Uruguay to Brazil's southern coast at Porto Alegre. Dam building across the Paraná River has proven to be another force of attraction and unified action. The Yacyreta Dam, built across the Paraná River border between Paraguay and Argentina, began to generate electricity in 1994. Another dam is being planned upstream by the two countries at Corpus. Still farther upstream, Brazil and Paraguay collaborated in building the giant Itaipu dam across their common river border, just above the Iguaçú Falls.

Regional Economic Organizations

One manifestation of the forces of attraction is regional organization. South America's two major forces of attraction are Mercosur (Mercado Común del Sur, the Southern Cone Common Market) and the Andean Group. The members of Mercosur, the regional free trade association established in the 1991 Treaty of Asunción, are Brazil, Argentina, Uruguay, and Paraguay. Chile and Bolivia are associate members, having concluded free trade agreements with Mercosur. The organization's full member states, with their 215 million population, have combined gross domestic products of approximately $1.5 trillion and represent the world's third-largest trading bloc and market. Trade within the four states of the bloc has tripled in the decade since its founding. This can be attributed not only to free trade among its members, but also to reduced common tariffs on imports from outside the bloc. In addition, foreign investments have soared, attracted by the size of the Mercosur market, especially that of Brazil, which receives ten times as much foreign capital now as it did a decade ago.

Mercosur's economic strength has enabled it to be used as a vehicle for the development of regional infrastructures. In addition, its political leverage upon member states is substantial. For example, the requirement of democratic government as a condition for entry into the bloc represents a radical break in political history for a continent that has been plagued by dictatorships and corruption for most of the past two centuries. This policy has helped to forestall attempted coups in Paraguay.

For a while Chile made a strong effort to join Mercosur as a full member. As the year 2000 ended, however, it pulled back from this request, seeking as an alternative a free trade agreement with the United States, a proposition in which Washington appeared interested. Chile's ambivalence may have weakened Mercosur's own interest in pursuing the Free Trade Area of Americas that was proposed by President Clinton in 1994 and is being strongly promoted by President George W. Bush.

Brazil views itself as the key to any western hemispheric economic bloc that would embrace all of South America and is suspicious of any move by Washington that would adopt a "Chile-first" strategy. Indeed, Brazil may resist the Washington-sponsored Free Trade Area of Americas because of its fear that the proposal represents the designs of the United States for economic dominance of the hemisphere. As South America's largest market by far, with an economy twice as large as that of Russia and India together, Brazil and its leaders expect to be treated as equals by the United States. This applies not only to economic negotiations, but also to Washington's crafting of political decisions that affect the region, such as its policy toward Colombia.

The Andean group, which was created in 1969, includes Bolivia, Chile, Colombia, Ecuador, Peru, and Venezuela (the latter geopolitically in Middle America). Because it represents economically struggling and unstable countries, it is far less important than Mercosur. The exception is Chile, which has the highest per capita income in South America. The function of the group has been largely confined to developing common regulations to control foreign investment.

While there has been some discussion about expanding Mercosur's free trade arrangements to all of South America by including the Andean group, such agreements between the eastern and western South American lands are apt to have little economic impact until a solid transportation and communications infrastructure is in place. Even if an accord were to be signed by the two trading blocs, it is not likely that the Andean states would be drawn into Brazil's economic and geopolitical orbit, nor be able to develop meaningful contacts with Argentina and Uruguay. The U.S. market is far more important to the Andean community than is Brazil or other Mercosur states, and the Ibero-Indian culture of the Andes is far removed from that of Portuguese-rooted Brazil or the European-Spanish countries to its south.

PROSPECTS FOR CONTINENTAL UNITY

Brazil is the key to continental unity. It is clearly the dominant political and economic power within South America and one of the major regional powers of the world. It dwarfs its neighbors in population (173 million out of a total of 315 million, or 55 percent), in area (3.3 million square miles out of a total of 6.4 million square miles, or 52 percent), and in GDP ($1.05 trillion, or 70 percent).[8] Possessing common borders with every other South American state with the exceptions of Chile and Ecuador, the South American regional giant is geographically positioned to influence and pressure the other states, especially as various transcontinental transportation and energy projects are brought to completion.

Factors that favor the economic development prospects of Brazil are the attractiveness of its vast market to investment capital, and its rich natural resources of bauxite, gold, iron, manganese, nickel, phosphates, uranium, timber, and hydropower. It has made rapid strides in petroleum development and now produces three-fourths of its total needs. Agriculture is also a strength, with farm exports representing over one-third of total exports. The Cerrado has become the site of rapidly growing commercial agrobusinesses. With a more reliable climate than the coastal states, these interior savannahs have become the major center for soybean, high-quality cotton, and beef production.

Thus the state of Mato Grosso has become the country's leading producer of soybeans, its second-largest rice grower, and its fourth-largest raiser of cattle. Soybeans are now transported by barge down the Madeira River to the Amazon River port of Itacoatiara and then transshipped to ocean-going vessels. Additional links to open the region to further development are a proposed twelve-hundred-mile, all-weather highway north to the port of Santarem on the eastern end of the Amazon and a rail link from southern Mato Grosso to the Ferronorte rail line to São Paulo and the port of Santos. With cheaper shipping and low-cost production on newly cleared land within its ENT, Brazil has increased its world share of the export trade in soybeans from 11 to 26 percent from 1995 to 2000 (the U.S. share during this period dropped from 73 to 53 percent). Prospects are good that the Brazilian world market share will continue to increase.[9]

Meanwhile, São Paulo state remains the world's largest coffee producer. When these crops are added to sugarcane, oranges and other fruits, wheat, rice, chicken, and tobacco, Brazil's agricultural future is bright. Farm products play an especially important role in balancing trade with Brazil's major commercial partners—the United States, Germany, the Netherlands, and Argentina.

The breadth of the country's industrial economy also contributes to its economic strength. Output includes iron and steel products, cement, papers, textiles, fertilizers, electronics, telecommunications equipment, motor-vehicle assembly, and civilian aircraft. Brazil competes with Canada as the world's third-largest producer of such airplanes.

However, while Brazil is clearly the only country capable of spearheading South American geopolitical unity, it is also limited by its domestic problems in how rapidly it can promote such unity. Widespread poverty, inflation, and the racial divide between the black (6 percent) and "brown" (or mixed, 38 percent) populations and the white population plagues the country. While the racial divide is not overt in interpersonal terms, it is reflected economically, with nonwhites suffering from much higher rates of unemployment and poorer education. The fact that so many of these problems are concentrated in the northeast is evidence of the divide.

Expansion of its overseas links with Maritime Europe and the United States would provide Brazil with additional economic and political power and enable it to take a lead role in forging an integrated eastern South American geopolitical region. Such a region would include Brazil, Argentina, Uruguay, Paraguay, probably Chile, and possibly Bolivia.

A recent measure of Brazil's increased importance to the United States as well as its own aspirations for world power is the April 2000 agreement between Washington and Brasília. The agreement enables the United States to use the Brazilian air force base at Alcantara, which is located to the east of the Amazon delta, on the Atlantic, and is an ideal location for the launching of spacecraft and communications satellites by the United States. In return, Brazil will receive funds to acquire or develop and produce its own rockets and unmanned space vehicles.

While the potential of geopolitical unity for eastern South America is promising, for the western, Andean portion prospects for integration are much weaker. The central and northern Andean countries are torn by internal violence and crossborder conflicts. Moreover, unlike the east, which has recently made strides in solidifying democratic governments, these states remain largely in the grip of authoritarian regimes.

The endemic turmoil in western South America is fueled by drug trade revenues that support both Marxist rebels and right-wing militias. The situation is most acute in Colombia, where large-scale coca production has replaced most of the acreage that has been eradicated in Peru, Ecuador, and Bolivia during the last decade. The bulk of the Colombian production is in the south and southeast, where the largest Marxist guerrilla movement, the Revolutionary Armed Forces of Colombia (FARC), exercises control over most of the region, gaining strength from the taxes that it levies on the growers of coca and poppies and on the drug producers.

This income has enabled the rebel movement to maintain a strong force of seventeen thousand fighters that has fought the Colombian army to a standstill. A smaller rebel movement—the People's Liberation Army—operates in the northeast, where it supports itself through extorting money from oil producers. These guerrillas target oil fields and pipelines. In 2001 they cut the country's main oil pipeline, from Cano Limón to Covenas, for 266 days. Arrayed against both rebel movements are right-wing militias that have waged terror campaigns against the leftists. None of these groups can be controlled by the weak central government.

The alliance between the rebels and the drug cartels will have to be broken if peace is to come to Colombia. The areas controlled by right-wing militias, as well as the Marxist guerrillas, are all involved in the growing, production, and trade. The country now supplies 80 percent of the world's cocaine, as well as two-thirds of the heroin that is consumed in the United States. The United States has become increasingly involved in the effort to rout out the drug producers, committing hundreds of millions of dollars to programs designed to entice farmers to shift from coca production to other crops and joining with Colombian military forces to search out and destroy cocaine production sites and trade links. There is no guarantee that the campaign will succeed. If it does, there is always the possibility that coca growing might shift back to neighboring Andean countries, where it had been largely eradicated with U.S. help. Also, other parts of the world might take up the slack, such as the Golden Crescent of Afghanistan (although the Taliban recently eradicated the opium poppy crop there), Pakistan, and Iran or the Golden Triangle of Myanmar, Thailand, and Laos, which are major producers of opium poppies and heroin.

In November 1998, Colombia's President Andres Pastrana made a bold attempt to end the war between the government and the FARC. To facilitate peace talks, he set aside a vast area of twenty-five thousand square miles as a demilitarized zone (DMZ) in which the FARC were given control—in effect a state within a state. However, the negotiations that ensued produced few tangible results. The DMZ became the FARC safe haven and base from which it strengthened itself militarily. At the beginning of 2002 FARC initiated a wave of kidnappings and murders aimed at Colombian political leaders. In reaction, President Pastrana ended the abortive negotiations on February 20, 2002, and ordered government forces to retake the demilitarized zone. Hard-liner Alvarado Uribe, committed to crushing FARC, was elected president in May 2002.

With the resumption of the Colombian civil war, the government has turned to the United States for assistance. While Washington has responded with military aid in addition to what it has dedicated to the antidrug campaign, it has not provided troops for the battle against the FARC.

The outlook is dim for the people of Colombia caught up in the renewal of this long and bloody conflict. It is unlikely that government troops will be able to defeat the FARC, and the involvement of right-wing paramilitary groups adds to the exposure of civilians to indiscriminate attacks. These events increase the possibility of Colombia's implosion, which would also have a fragmenting effect on the rest of the northern Andes countries.

The Colombian civil war has involved Ecuador, which provides a rear base for smuggling arms and exporting drugs; the Peruvian Amazon, through which the FARC receives smuggled weapons; and Venezuela, whose porous western border is a conduit for Colombian drug smugglers.

All of this tends to destabilize already unstable regimes. Peru, having put down the Shining Path maoist revolt at the beginning of the 1990s and enjoyed a brief period of democracy, has been caught up recently in a political crisis. Its president, Alberto Fujimori, admitted to electoral fraud and was then deposed, putting into question Peru's capacity to maintain a stable government.

Ecuador is even more unstable, having been shaken by the collapse of five different governments since 1996. One bright note is its recently signed agreement to end its territorial dispute with Peru, which may ease the economic pressure placed on it by its heavy military expenditures. However, in January 2000, a military junta seized control of the country.

In Bolivia, a former dictator General Hugo Banzer, was voted into power in 1997. This augured poorly for the prospect of democracy and stability in the country. (He became ill in 2001 and was replaced by Vice President Jorge Quiroga.) Such Andean instability gives Brazil little incentive to reach beyond its dominance over eastern South America to bring about the political unity of the continent as a whole.

From a developmental perspective, the South American continent is still in a stage of differentiation. Drives for national self-sufficiency by South America's various countries have promoted this differentiation. The first indications of progress toward specialized integration are the growth of trade and communications links among Brazil, Argentina, and Uruguay. Now that Brazil has turned away from economic isolation as a development strategy, movement toward the higher level of specialized integration is likely to be hastened.

Argentina cannot be written off as a major contributor to the region's prospects for unity. Its economy remains South America's second largest, despite its huge international debt of over $130 billion, hyperinflation, and fiscal collapse. Half a century ago Argentina was a wealthy country with substantial resources, a strong industrial and agricultural base, and a large, well-educated middle class. Dogged by years of military rule and corruption, misguided populist nationalism, economic protectionism, and fiscal and political mismanagement, it has sunk to its current low point.

During the 1990s the government abolished trade barriers, sought international capital, and privatized most of its holdings. In the process it accumulated a huge foreign debt that it spent without restraint on domestic programs and held to a fixed exchange rate too long. The problem was not economic globalization per se, but the rush to embrace it. Fiscal instability has rekindled strong nationalistic and antiglobalism sentiments. However, an inward-facing, self-sufficient economy is not a long-range recipe for restoration to economic health. Ultimately the benefits to be gained from an open economy linked to that of Brazil should overcome the isolating effects of the current nationalistic sentiments. The breadth and depth of Argentina's economic and human resources should speed the country's recovery and restore it to political and economic stability. At such time, it will play an important role in the geopolitical development of the region.

Part II: Sub-Saharan Africa

Since the collapse of the European colonial system, Sub-Saharan Africa has sunk into a state of de-development. The world's poorest region, it is geopolitically atomized, torn by recurrent conflicts among and within its forty-two national states. These states essentially follow the territorial frameworks that were established during the colonial period. There is growing consensus that these national frameworks are flawed because they have failed to account for many of the drives for territorial sovereignty of ethnic, tribal, and religious groups that are subsumed within them.

One recipe for reducing conflict is a larger number of smaller, more homogeneous states. Another school of thought takes the opposite view, holding that substantially larger states are the answer to the African crisis. For example, A. S. Gakwandi proposed a new political map of Africa with only seven states, as a way to resolve the current problems of border disputes, refugees who have been separated from their homelands, and the liabilities of landlocked states. The rationale is that a balance among a handful of states that are ethnically and religiously diverse, but economically viable, would promote political stability.[10] The position of the Organization of African Unity (OAU), however, is that all member states should respect the borders existing at the time of their independence, and that to attempt to redraw them would be an invitation to the spread of conflict in a region already torn by widespread violence.

POST-COLONIAL POLITICAL FRAMEWORKS

Postcolonial Africa has experienced many efforts to break up existing states and to forge unions among them. Separation has often led to bitter warfare, heavy loss of life, devastation of the countryside and cities, and massive flows of refugees. The most prominent have been secession attempts in Nigeria and the recurrent attempts in Congo/Zaire. The Ibo of oil-rich southeast Nigeria established the independent state of Biafra in 1967, seven years after the country gained its freedom from Great Britain. In a war that lasted three years before the defeat of Biafra, more than one million Biafrans are said to have died of starvation.

Shortly after Zaire (now the Democratic Republic of Congo, DRC) became independent in 1960, Katanga (Shaba), the mineral-rich province in the southeastern plateau portion of the country, seceded. The Katangese waged a civil war for three years before the rebellion was put down by UN and Belgian troops, whose aim was to save Zaire from anarchy and maintain the stability of the copper industry. Patrice Lumumba, the leftist prime minister, failed to secure UN intervention when the rebellion broke out and turned for help to the Soviet Union. He was dismissed by President Joseph Kasavubu and was subsequently murdered by the troops of Colonel Joseph Mobutu, head of the army. Mobutu eventually succeeded in crushing the rebellion and seized power in 1966 with the help of Belgian troops and the U.S. Central Intelligence Agency, initiating a dictatorial and exploitative regime.

Five years after Uganda was established as an independent republic in 1962, its southern province of Buganda sought to secede. Buganda had had a long history as an independent kingdom before becoming a British protectorate. It rebelled against the abolition by the central government of the high degree of autonomy that had been guaranteed to it when Uganda became independent. However, the rebellion was quashed.

Shortly after Angola won its independence from Portugal in 1975, the Kongo people in the oil-rich Cabinda exclave, the main source of the country's petroleum, were unsuccessful in their struggle to establish a separate state. However, a major rebellion broke out in Angola that year between the Marxist government and the UNITA rebels. The conflict raged continuously until Jonas Savimbi, UNITA's founder and leader, died in battle in 2002, resulting in peace. The rebel's diamond-rich highland base, plus U.S. and South African military support, had enabled them to maintain a "state within a state" throughout the fight that displaced one-quarter of the country's inhabitants. Political and economic absorption of refugees and the rebels will be a formidable challenge.

One example of a successful separatist struggle has been the experience of Southwest Africa (Namibia), which rebelled against South African rule and gained its independence in 1989. The territory had had a history separate from that of South Africa. A German protectorate in the late nineteenth century, it was occupied in World War I by South Africa, which administered it under a League of Nations mandate. The South Africans refused to surrender this mandate to the UN trusteeship system in 1945. In the 1970s a nationalist guerrilla movement, the South West Africa People's Organization (SWAPO), based largely in Angola, organized a guerrilla war against Pretoria's rule that culminated eventually in the establishment of the separate state of Namibia.

A second secession occurred in the Horn of Africa. The Arabic-speaking Eritreans are oriented toward trade and fishing, unlike the highland Ethiopian farmers. The coastal territory, which had first been occupied by Italy in the 1880s, was administered as a separate colony until merged with Ethiopia when the Italians conquered that country in 1935–36. From the 1960s onward, the Eritreans fought for their freedom. In the late 1970s they forged an alliance with the Tigrinya-speaking Ethiopian rebels in a struggle to overthrow Ethiopia's Amharic-controlled Marxist regime. After three decades, and at the cost of 100,000 to 150,000 fatalities, the regime was overthrown, and shortly thereafter Eritrea was able to become an independent, secular republic. While Eritrea separated from Ethiopia peacefully in 1993, the two countries waged war from 1998 to 2000 over a border dispute.

On the Somali coast, Britain, France, and Italy had all established colonies during the previous century, each centering around a strategic port. Britain created a protectorate around the port of Berbera on the Gulf of Aden. London's objective was to have a presence on the Somali coast to counter French-controlled Djibouti, which had been developed in 1862 as a commercial and strategic rival to Aden. In addition, Britain was interested in securing a food supply, especially mutton for Aden, from the Somali herdsmen. Italy followed suit in 1889 by establishing a protectorate along the central coast, focusing on the port of Mogadishu, which overlooked both the Gulf of Aden and the Indian Ocean. Italy expanded the territory southward in the years that followed.

The British and Italian colonies merged to become the independent Republic of Somalia in 1960. (French Somaliland did not join, and gained its own independence, as Djibouti, in 1977.) Torn by clan fighting, Somalia splintered into a number of unstable parts in the civil war of 1991. The conflict that broke out after the separation of Eritrea from Ethiopia and the dismemberment of Somalia will be discussed in the section on Compression Zones.

Attempts to create larger African states through federations or mergers have, for the most part, been unsuccessful. In 1959, Mali and Senegal formed the Mali federation, only to have it dissolved the next year. Guinea and Ghana, which had joined in a symbolic union in 1958, expanded that union to include Mali in 1961. This merger had no practical effect and ended in 1966, when Ghana's Kwame Nkrumah was deposed.

The East African experience with regional unions was similarly disappointing. While Uganda, Kenya, and Tanganyika were still under British rule, the idea of an East African federation was promoted. A Royal Commission (1953–55) proposed that the three territories establish a federated framework with functions that would include transportation, communications, and taxation. The proposal was not implemented at that time because it called for eventual control by native Africans, and it was therefore strongly opposed by the white settlers. An East African Community (EAC) was formed by the three countries after independence (1967), but it made little headway because of conflict between Uganda and Tanzania over Tanzanian control of the Kagera region in northwest Tanzania, on the southwestern shore of Lake Victoria. The EAC was formally dissolved in 1977, but it was revived in February 2001 as an economic bloc.

In Southern Africa, Southern Rhodesia became a member of the Federation of Rhodesia and Nyasaland. The federation was broken up in 1963. A year later, Northern Rhodesia (Zambia) and Nyasaland (Malawi) became independent. In 1965 the white minority government of Southern Rhodesia (Zimbabwe) declared itself independent of Britain—it later renamed itself the Republic of Rhodesia—and instituted complete separation of the voting franchise along racial lines. UN economic sanctions and African nationalist guerrilla warfare ultimately led, in 1980, to legal independence under black majority rule. An attempt to unite the Portuguese colonies of Cape Verde and Guinea-Bissau failed in 1980 and a confederal arrangement between Senegal and the Gambia (called "Senegambia") was dismantled the following year.

There were a few limited successes in merging former colonies. The Gold Coast and British Togoland were united in 1957, when the two colonies gained their independence, to form Ghana. In 1961 the southern part of the British Cameroons joined the French Cameroons to form Cameroon, while the northern British Cameroons passed to Nigeria. Three years later the island of Zanzibar merged with Tanganyika to form Tanzania. This union provided Zanzibar with considerable autonomy in internal affairs. However, religious and economic differences between the two territories introduced friction early on. Zanzibar is almost completely Muslim and the large majority of Tanganyikans are Christian or of traditional faiths. In addition, the impoverishment of the island of Zanzibar, as a result of the collapse of the world clove market, and the erosion of its autonomy in recent decades has given rise to a strong Zanzibari secessionist movement. Cloves had been the mainstay of Zanzibar and the nearby island of Pemba. With the steep drop in prices and demand, these offshore islands have sought to shift to a tourist economy, but this industry's development has not yet had the desired impact.

The durability of the union of Zanzibar and Tanganyika is increasingly in doubt. Should Zanzibar become independent, it could benefit from its location to become a Gateway state linking East Africa to South Asia and Middle Eastern areas oriented to the Indian Ocean. This would mark a return to its traditional role, which goes back to the eleventh and twelfth centuries, when traders from the Persian Gulf settled in Zanzibar to develop commerce with the East African coast. In the nineteenth century, the island served as the center for the ivory and slave trades from East Africa to the Middle East and lands beyond.

Continental and regional African economic frameworks have also had limited impacts.[11] In its 1980 Lagos Plan of Action, the OAU, which had been established in 1963, set forth the goal of creating a single Pan-African Common Market by the year 2000—a goal that remains elusive. Also in 1963, at the Yaounde Convention, eighteen French-speaking African states and Madagascar formed the Economic Community of West and Central Africa, to whose exports the Common Market accorded tariff-free access. The organization made little coordinated progress, save for sharing a common currency tied to the French franc. A European development fund was also established in connection with the agreement, which did prove a valuable source of aid.

The successor to the Yaounde Convention was the Lome Agreement of 1975, which called for free movement of goods and people among and between the African signatories and the European Community (EC).[12] This objective has yet to be fully realized. The sixteen original African members formed a new geographical regional community—the Economic Community of West African States (ECOWAS), which included both French-speaking nations and Nigeria and other former British colonies.

The Lomé Agreement was initially sponsored by both France and Britain, reflecting a European decision not to disengage from Africa despite widespread tensions over decolonization. By 1999 the Lomé Agreement had been expanded to include a total of seventy-one states, including fifteen from the Caribbean, eight from the Pacific, and forty-eight from Africa. The fifteen EU members are committed to providing all seventy-one states (also known as the ACP, or Africa, Caribbean, and Pacific, states) with aid and access to the EU market. However, Europe's Common Agricultural Policy, which protects European farming, limits the promised access to its markets.

Expanding its function, ECOWAS has become a political cover for the troops of Nigeria and other West African states to send peacekeeping forces to Liberia and Sierra Leone, countries torn by civil wars. Liberia's war started in 1989 and Sierra Leone's in 1992. Despite a 1997 peace declared in Liberia, the rebellion resumed in 2000. The war in Sierra Leone continued to rage, despite the presence of Nigerian and other peacekeeping troops. Rebel forces there control the southeastern part of the country, the heart of the diamond-mining and diamond-trading industry. With this resource and Liberia's help, the rebels were able to purchase arms with which to continue the war. The war ended officially in January 2002 when UN troops were withdrawn and the former rebels participated in May national elections. Whether the peace will be honored by both sides remains to be seen.

Similarly, another regional economic grouping, the Southern African Development Community (SADC), which intervened in the Democratic Republic of Congo, has sought to turn itself into a regional security force. In effect, the civil war there was expanded into a regional conflict. Angola, Zimbabwe, and Namibia, acting on behalf of SADC, sent peacekeeping troops into Congo to save the Laurent Kabila regime from being toppled by rebels. The rebels were supported by forces from Rwanda, Uganda, and Burundi. Thus, three Southern African states became arrayed against three East African Nilotic countries.

The foreign forces remained in the country after the assassination of Kabila, ostensibly to support the new regime and bring peace to the country. A stronger motive for their remaining appears to have been to continue to loot the country of its diamond wealth in the areas that they occupy. Recent agreements were made to withdraw the various outside armies. It is uncertain whether they will be upheld. South Africa, by far the largest and most economically powerful of SADC members, has opposed this intervention. Without South African support, SADC has little political or economic power.

ECOWAS and SADC are the most important of the present regional groups. There are others, such as the Common Market for Eastern and Southern Africa and the Economic Community of Central African States. All of these organizations, however, have made little progress in furthering regional economic integration, in part because of the protectionist policies of the various states.

GEOGRAPHICAL BACKGROUND

Africa south of the Sahara is quite different from South America geographically, and thus it is different geopolitically. The African population is more widely scattered for several reasons.

One is the broad spread of arable lands throughout the higher areas of the tropical and sub-tropical parts of the continent. Another is the limited extent of the various coastlines. A third is the multiplicity of widely separated river systems, each of which tends to attract denser settlements to the lower and middle courses.

No single coastal area in Sub-Saharan Africa possesses the population and economic concentrations that are found in Brazil and in the La Plata estuary. Moreover, no single country is as dominant over its region as is Brazil in South America. For example, Sub-Saharan Africa's largest country, Nigeria, has 125 million people, or one-fifth of the population of the African subcontinent, in contrast to Brazil, where over half of South Americans live. Also unlike Brazil, Nigeria is torn by regional and religious factionalism.

Another distinction between the two Southern Continents is racial and ethnic distribution. Africa is predominantly black racially, with Europeans, Indians, and Arabs combined representing under 5 percent of the total. However, Africa is subdivided into over one thousand ethnolinguistic groups. South America is essentially white or mixed race, with pockets of black populations along the coasts and a scattering of Indian groupings, and has only two major linguistic groupings—Spanish and Portuguese.

Much of Sub-Saharan Africa's 7,800,000 square miles is unsuited to absorbing the rapidly increasing population. Tropical rain forests, poor and dry savannah soils, and deserts are all impediments to agriculture and settlement. Most of the subcontinent consists of high plateau that has experienced successive geologic uplifts, and much of it is inaccessible to the coast. The smooth, emerged coastal plains are narrow, covering a much smaller proportion of the land area than do coastal plains in other continents, and they afford few good, natural harbors. Where these plains do occur, they frequently are too dry and therefore are lightly populated or quite narrow and blocked off from the interior by highlands. Some coastal areas were also depopulated by slaving activities.

Development of modern urban economies has been inhibited by lack of such large, coastal populations in much of the region. There are important exceptions, however. These include the mouths of the Niger and the coastal lands along the Gulf of Guinea to the west and east, the lower Congo, the southwestern and eastern coasts of South Africa, coastal Tanzania, and eastern Madagascar. The rich oil and gas reserves of the Niger Delta and the Gulf of Guinea waters have played the key role in the developments of their coastal lands, although much of the revenues that have been generated by the energy resources have been squandered by corrupt regimes, rather than applied to basic development purposes.

Transportation

The railroad has not played the pioneering nation-building and economic development role in Sub-Saharan Africa that it has played elsewhere in the world, especially in the United States, Western Europe, the Eurasian Heartland, in southern Brazil, and the Pampas of Argentina. In those cases, railways served to attract large-scale settlement, first agricultural and then urban, and became the backbones of national ecumenes. On the African subcontinent, the role of railroads has been limited to transporting minerals and commercial crops to the sea for export, rather than serving as frameworks for dense population and economic activities.

Indeed, instead of becoming nation-building agents, most of the railroads have been centrifugal forces. The Katanga (Shaba) railway in southeastern Congo runs to Benguela on the Atlantic coast of Angola, rather than to the political capital of the DRC in Kinshasa, which is located on the lower course of the River Congo. Another rail line from Shaba connects with the Zambian and Zimbabwean systems to the port of Maputo on Mozambique's Indian Ocean coast. While the Katanga secession movement of the early 1960s was ultimately quashed, the separatist tendencies of the Katangese have been reinforced by geographical isolation, and have resurfaced during the most recent Congo rebellion. This is despite the fact that Shaba's land connections to the rest of Congo have been improved in recent years.

Another important railway that has failed to attract broad economic development is the Tazara (Tan-Zam) Railway. It was built in the 1970s by China (fifteen thousand Chinese workers were involved in the construction) in its efforts to gain influence in East Africa. The line extends for eleven hundred miles and connects landlocked Zambia to the sea via Tanzania's port of Dar es Salaam. The railway's geopolitical significance is that it has freed Zambia from having to export its major copper resources through the Zimbabwean rail system to either the Mozambique ports of Beira and Maputo or the ports of South Africa. In recent years the railroad has been paralleled by a highway and an oil pipeline. While the Tazara line has been economically important to Zambia, it has not appreciably helped to broaden the country's economy, nor has it served as the spine of a corridor of major settlement and economic activity for either Zambia or Tanzania.

In general, transportation remains the Achilles' heel of Africa's economic development efforts. Rail freight rates are much higher than in other parts of the developing world—50 percent higher than in Latin America and twice as high as in Asia. Road systems are even more problematic, as they suffer from continuing deterioration due to inadequate maintenance that is exacerbated by unfavorable conditions relating to climate, vegetation, and terrain.

Economy

The per capita income of many countries in Sub-Saharan Africa is less than one dollar a day. The pervasive poverty is aggravated by an international debt to foreign governments and international lenders that is four times the subcontinent's annual exports. At the end of the year 2000, the industrial nations of the world agreed to provide debt relief to the twenty-two poorest countries—eighteen of these were located within Sub-Saharan Africa (the other four were in Latin America). In addition, the region is plagued by inadequate capital investment (less than 2 percent of world capital flows), HIV-AIDS and other diseases, civil strife, and war. As a result, the southern continent has moved backward economically, and now has an aggregate annual output that barely surpasses that of Belgium.[13] This poverty has placed the region in a continuing condition of political as well as economic dependence on the outside world.

While minerals, including petroleum, and commercial crops and fibers are important generators of export currency, their revenues cannot support the continent's vast subsistence agricultural and urban population. Swings in international mineral prices and high foreign tariffs on agricultural products contribute to economic instability. In addition, corruption syphons off much of the export income into the pockets of the political and economic elite. Periodic crop failure brought on by drought and plant disease devastate the rural countryside, forcing waves of hunger-stricken subsistence farmers to abandon their homes for crime-ridden urban slums in the major cities that cannot support existing populations, let alone absorb these newcomers. The refugees from famine, as well as those fleeing war-torn areas, gain some measure of security and access to food from international relief agencies, but remain rootless in their cities of refuge. The flight from countryside to city is also accelerated by the land consolidation that goes hand in hand with agricultural development efforts to increase farm productivity.

The tragic consequences of this massive flight is reflected painfully in the urban anarchy that prevails in Lagos. This Nigerian megacity has grown from a peaceful center of 200,000 half a century ago to a city of thirteen million. It lacks any semblance of an urban infrastructure, as the continuing streams of newcomers take shelter in shanty towns and in the devastated areas, amid open sewers and with limited access to potable water. Disease is rife, children are unschooled, and crime is endemic. Yet Nigerian migrants keep fleeing the drought-stricken Sahel to the cities, and UN estimates are that Lagos could grow to a population of twenty-three million in a decade and a half. Unless a major international effort is made to stabilize Lagos and the other megacities of the Third World, there is little prospect that the urban tragedy can be ameliorated.

A major challenge for Sub-Saharan Africa, as in so many parts of the developing world, is to find ways of increasing farm output and incomes of small farmers. In many African countries, 60 to 80 percent of the population consists of an impoverished rural peasantry. The figures for oil-rich Nigeria and Angola, for example, are 60 and 70 percent respectively. Even in South Africa, which has the most advanced economy of the region, the rural populace is 50 percent.

The role of manufacturing in the region's economy remains very limited, except in South Africa. An indicator of Africa's lag in this sector is its minimal participation in world merchandise trade. While developing nations as a whole now account for more than one-third of the world's total merchandise exports, Sub-Saharan Africa's share of world trade is only 2 percent. Of its total foreign trade, less than 10 percent is intraregional. Of the rest, more than half goes to Europe and a substantial portion goes to the United States. This lack of exchange contributes to the atmosphere of isolation and atomization and feeds long-held antagonisms and hostilities among the member states of the region.

Under these woeful human and economic conditions, it is clear that Sub-Saharan Africa lacks the capacity to advance without massive economic and technical aid and capital investment from the developed world. Ameliorating the plight of the rural poor, by improving rural health, fighting disease, providing safe water and sanitation, and reducing illiteracy, will require far greater investment than has heretofore been provided. The aid that the region has been receiving in the form of grants and loans has amounted to billions of dollars over the decades, and it annually accounts for 10 percent of the economic activity of the subcontinent. However, it has proven to be insufficient and has not been used effectively.

Even if aid were to be increased, together with the major loan forgiveness package that has been initiated, much greater attention would have to be given to the elimination of corruption and the encouragement of interstate cooperative projects. However, such steps will have limited impact unless the conflicts that sap the human and economic development capacities of Sub-Saharan Africa can be radically reduced. Regrettably, regional geopolitical structural trends provide little evidence that the atomization that is both cause and effect of Africa's current economic and political plight will soon run its course.

GEOPOLITICAL FEATURES

In its geopolitical features and patterns, Sub-Saharan Africa is the least mature region of the world's geopolitical system, and there is little likelihood that it will soon evolve coherent geopolitical structures that could overcome the current regional atomization.

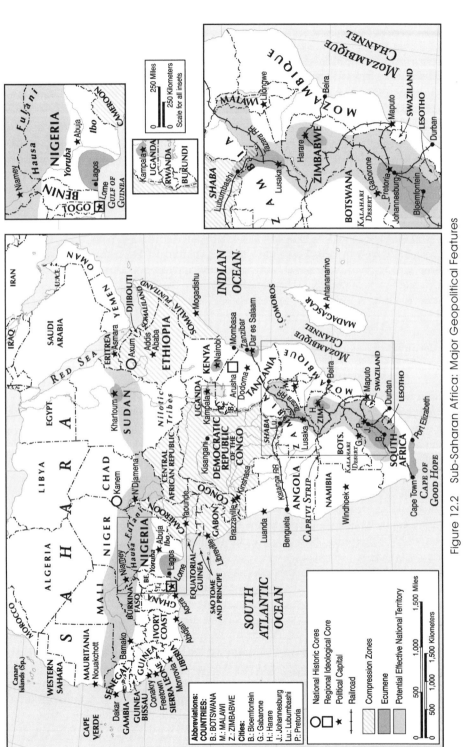

Figure 12.2 Sub-Saharan Africa: Major Geopolitical Features

Historic Regional Core

No single place can lay claim to have planted the seed of Sub-Saharan African unity and thus fulfill the role of historic political core. The leading early proponent of Pan-Africanism, Kwame Nkrumah, led Ghana to independence from his base in Accra. Although Ghana received considerable economic and technical aid from both the United States and the Soviet Union, falling world cocoa prices and ill-conceived, large-scale development projects led to economic chaos and the overthrow of Nkrumah in 1966. Since then, Ghana has lost its role as a Third World ideological leader, and the country is just beginning to pull itself out of the poverty, political instability, and military rule that depressed it for approximately a quarter of a century. The country's prosperity had once been dependent upon cocoa for 75 percent of its foreign exchange; it now receives only 15 percent of its foreign earnings from this source and depends upon its forest and such minerals as gold, bauxite, diamonds, and manganese to fill the gap left by plummeting cocoa prices.

Lomé, the capital of Togo and the founding site for ECOWAS, has also failed to become a rallying point for regional unity. The same applies to Arusha in Tanzania, which was the site for President Julius Nyerere's 1967 Arusha Declaration, in which he called for African socialism, egalitarianism, hard work, and self-reliance. The declaration had a powerful influence within Africa during this period, and the city became the headquarters of the East African Community. However, the EAC was later disbanded because of intraregional conflict. Thus, Arusha did not sustain the spirit of Pan-Africanism in changing political and economic times and it became merely an interesting historical footnote. The fifty-three-nation OAU is not even headquartered in Sub-Saharan Africa. Instead, it is located in Addis Ababa, Ethiopia, where it has had no opportunity to serve as an ideological rallying point for the Sub-Saharan continent. The OAU is scheduled to be replaced in 2002 by a new organization—the African Union. Modeled after the European Union, this new organization would have much broader powers than the present one and would have the aim of achieving political and economic integration among the present members. Thus, a common parliament, central bank, and court of justice and a single currency are envisaged.[14] It is much too early to speculate on the possibilities of the emergence of a powerful new African Union. The fact that its staunchest backer is Muammar al-Qadaffi of Libya—a country not even geopolitically part of Sub-Saharan Africa—is reason alone to suggest that the prospects of the proposed OAU substitute are dim.

Political Capitals

Similarly, no current political center holds the potential for becoming a contemporary regional political core. Nigeria's federal capital, Abuja, which replaced Lagos as the seat of government in 1991, is the center of government for West Africa's largest and most powerful country. However, Nigeria's cohesiveness is undermined by political strife and violence. Lagos, the largest urban center, has been the scene of unrestrained ethnic strife between the Yoruba and Hausa and has become a geographical symbol of national disunity.

South Africa's Pretoria might have been a candidate to become Southern Africa's political capital, but it is more representative of the colonial past than it is of future African unity. Built by the white colonizers, the city has little in the way of a symbolic built landscape that can evoke black African political aspirations. Moreover, the leaders of South

Africa have only recently evinced interest in seeking regional influence. For most of the period following Nelson Mandela's ascension to the presidency in 1994, the new black regime has been absorbed in national, not regional, affairs.

Ecumene

Since national ecumenes are so weakly developed, it is little wonder that there are few traces of a regional ecumene in Sub-Saharan Africa. The subcontinent's only well-developed national ecumene is in South Africa. This economic and population core area extends across the Transvaal from its hub in greater Johannesburg, northward toward the border of Zambia and southeastward across the Drakensburg Mountains to the coast from Durban southward to Port Elizabeth. However, the main South African ecumene has no physical connection with the economic core area of adjoining Zimbabwe.

One development that may some day lead to a Southern Africa regional core is the potential extension of South Africa's ecumene into Mozambique via the Maputo Development Corridor. This is an improved rail and toll highway corridor that runs northeastward from Johannesburg through Swaziland to the Mozambique coast at Maputo. A natural gas pipeline from fields in the Transvaal also extends through the Corridor. Maputo's economy has been strengthened by steel and aluminum plants anchoring the eastern end of the corridor, while a ribbon of dense population is beginning to form along the transit way. However, intensive industrial development in Swaziland and the interior sections of Mozambique are still in the distant future. A smaller transnational ecumene—the Copperbelt—extends from northeastern Zambia into Congo's southeastern Shaba.

Effective Regional Territory

Two vast grassland areas—the Southern African savannah, which extends from the Transvaal through Zimbabwe and Zambia, and the West African Sahel have the potential for becoming Effective Regional Territories. However, the obstacles to the mergers of the ENTs in these areas are formidable. Scarcity of rainfall, disease (both cattle and human), and distance from open seas thwart the potential for oceanic trade. The Sahel, which extends from Senegal through Mauritania, Mali, Burkina Faso, Niger, and northern Nigeria and thence into Sudan and Ethiopia, suffered disastrous droughts and famines in the 1970s and 1990s. This brought devastation to the region and resulted in the depopulation of vast areas, rather than to absorption of the additional populations that Effective National and Regional Territories must be able to attract.

Boundaries

Another major geopolitical feature—boundaries—also reflects the geopolitical immaturity of the region. Some of Sub-Saharan Africa's borders have never been clearly demarcated and remain in dispute. Others, while demarcated, separate territories that are claimed by two or more states and are the sources of often bitter conflict. These boundaries cut across ethnotribal, linguistic, or religious groupings, leaving substantial minorities on one side of the border who seek to reunite with transborder kinfolk (see table 12.1).[15] Tables 12.1 and 12.2 present current and latent boundary and territorial disputes and note their status.[16]

Table 12.1   Sub-Saharan Africa: Current Boundary and Territorial Disputes

Countries	Disputed Boundary	Disputed Territory
Cameroon	International boundary—delimitation in Lake Chad (involves Chad, Niger, Nigeria)	
Comoros		Claim Mayotte Ile from France; Iles of Mwali and Nzwani secessionists seek return to France
Congo/DRC-Congo/Brazzaville	Most of Congo R. boundary indefinite except in Stanley Pool area	
Ethiopia-Eritrea	Land boundary	Badme Triangle Boundary demarcated 2002
Ethiopia-Somalia		Somalia claims southern half of Ethiopia's Ogaden Desert region
Gabon-Equatorial Guinea	Maritime boundary—oil-rich waters of Gulf of Corisco Bay	Sovereignty over islands
Gabon-Nigeria	Maritime boundary—oil-rich waters of Gulf of Guinea	
Gambia-Senegal	Short section of boundary indefinite	
Madagascar		Glorioso Iles and Juan de Nova II., from France
Niger		12,000 square miles of northern Niger claimed by Libya
Somalia		Divisions between Somaliland, "Puntland," and rest of Somalia
Swaziland		Claims territory held by South Africa

Many of the boundary conflicts cannot be separated from broader disputes over control of natural resources, access to the sea, and reunification of peoples. Nor can they be disentangled from civil strife and governmental instability in a particular country, which may lead to the porousness of its borders—a major contributor to conflict in Sub-Saharan Africa. Uncontrolled borders permit guerrilla groups to operate from bases outside a country and to make transborder strikes, drawing adjoining states into the conflict. Congo/DRC and Zambia were used as bases for Angolan rebels in their battle for independence against the Portuguese. Later Angola served as the organizing center for Namibian rebels in their campaign to gain freedom from South Africa. Zambia was accused by the Angolan government of permitting the UNITA rebel movement to maintain itself by selling diamonds across the porous Zambian border and bringing back military supplies. As another example, Mozambique provided a secure headquarters for the leadership of the Zimbabwean rebel guerrillas in their fight for independence.

Table 12.2   Sub-Saharan Africa: Latent Boundary and Territorial Disputes

Countries	Disputes
Cameroon-Niger	Bakassi Pen. and nearby Is. divided between the two countries. Military clashes in 1990s. Rich offshore oil deposits.
Chad-Libya	43,000 sq. mi. Aozou Strip in northern Chad claimed by Libya. War in 1980s. Awarded to Chad by ICJ in 1993. Rich in uranium.
Ghana-Togo	Pan-Ewe secessionist movement in southern Togo. Quiescent since 1980s.
Kenya-Somalia	Dormant dispute in Kenya's northeastern province over rights of Somalian majority to join Somalia.
Lesotho-South Africa	South Africa sovereignty over Transkei, which received independence in 1976 and was absorbed by South Africa in 1994.
Namibia-Botswana	Sovereignty over Kasikili Is. in Linyanti R. resolved in favor of Botswana by ICJ in 1999.
Senegal-Mauritania	Dispute over grazing rights in southern Mauritania. Clashes in 1989.
Tanzania-Malawi	Dispute in Lake Malawi.

Note: ICJ – International Court of Justice.

Guinean rebels operating from Sierra Leone and Liberia have launched transborder attacks against Guinea's army, devastating parts of the country's southwestern and southeastern border regions. Botswana shelters Lozi tribesmen from Namibia, who use bases there to attempt to create a separate Lozi state in Namibia's Caprivi Strip and parts of southwest Zambia. The narrow Caprivi Strip, fifty miles wide and three hundred miles in length, juts into Botswana and Zambia, several hundreds of miles from Namibia's major centers, and is highly vulnerable to border incursions by the Lozi rebels.

The most volatile of such current situations is the border between Congo/DRC and Rwanda. Rwandan Hutu guerrillas who had fled into eastern Congo have used bases there to launch transborder raids against the Tutsi-controlled government in Rwanda. Burundi rebels, also operating from Congo territory, have mounted raids against Burundi's Tutsi regime. It was because of the inability, or lack of desire, of Congo's president, the late Laurent Kabila, to put an end to the Rwandan Hutu raids that the Rwandan government, joined by Uganda, sided with the Congolese rebels seeking to overthrow Kabila. Ironically, the Tutsi president of Rwanda, Paul Kagame, had initially sided with the Kabila insurgency, which overthrew the Congolese dictator, Mobutu Sese Seko, because Mobutu had permitted the Rwandan Hutus to take refuge in eastern Congo.

In the Horn of Africa, the long-running rebellion of the Eritreans against Amharic Ethiopian rule spanned the regimes of both Emperor Haile Selassie and Haile Maryam Mengistu, who overthrew Selassie in 1974. In the 1980s the Eritreans joined forces with Ethiopian rebels from the province of Tigre and together they eventually overthrew the Soviet-supported Marxist government of Mengistu, spelling the end of centuries of Amharic domination. In 1993 the new Ethiopian government, now controlled by the leader of the former rebels, Meles Zenawi, agreed to the independence of Eritrea. Inasmuch as the separation left Ethiopia landlocked, the Eritreans granted it a free port at Aseb, which is connected to Ethiopia by highway. It appeared that peace had finally come.

However, the former allies soon stumbled into war with one another over parts of the 625-mile boundary that had never been delineated. The focus of the fighting was possession of the Badme (Yirga) Triangle. With large numbers of battle-hardened troops on both sides, what started as minor skirmishes in 1998 developed into full-scale war. A cease-fire brokered by the OAU in the summer of 1999 was broken a year later, when the Ethiopians pushed into Eritrea, displacing upwards of a million Eritreans. A second cease-fire was signed in September 2000, with both sides agreeing to return to the line that existed before the initial Eritrean invasion.

A small UN peacekeeping force was deployed within a sixteen-mile buffer zone along this line, and both countries have agreed to the demarcation of the border by the United Nations. An Independent Boundary Commission completed the demarcation in April 2002. The cost of the conflict between these former allies has been one hundred thousand soldiers killed, widespread devastation of the landscape, and massive displacement of Eritrean refugees. The economic development of two of the world's poorest countries has been pushed backward even further.

As a result of the conflict, and despite the peace accord, landlocked Ethiopia has shifted from using the Eritrean port of Aseb as its main outlet for trade to using Djibouti and Berbera. A large share of the country's imports and exports now move via the 487-mile railroad from Djibouti to Addis Ababa. This slow and antiquated line, completed in 1929, must climb a tortuous mountain route to reach the capital on the Ethiopian plateau, eight thousand feet above sea level. The smaller port of Berbera, in the breakaway state of Somaliland, has become increasingly important as an entrepôt for Ethiopia. The former British Somaliland has become politically stable through the establishment of a representative, clan-based government. While Berbera has no railway, its highway connection to Addis Ababa via the Ethiopian commercial center of Harar is the easiest and fastest of the transit ways. Large food shipments for famine relief entered through Berbera in 2000 and the Ethiopian government is cautiously developing other economic relationships with Somaliland.[17]

Most of the Sub-Saharan Africa's border disputes are the legacy of colonial boundary making, just as so much of the civil strife within the region's various states is a product of dividing up territories to suit European colonial aims or to accommodate competing aims. As noted earlier, there is a difference of opinion about whether to tamper with these borders to make states more ethnically cohesive or to enlarge them to create more economically feasible states.

Landlocked Areas

The especially large number of landlocked countries, fifteen in all, is a unique geopolitical feature of Sub-Saharan Africa. These countries are Mali, Burkina Faso, Niger, Chad, the Central African Republic, Uganda, Rwanda, Burundi, Zambia, Malawi, Zimbabwe, Botswana, Swaziland, Lesotho, and Ethiopia. The only other region that begins to approximate such a density of landlocked states is Central Asia, Afghanistan, and the Caucasus, which in combination have eight such national units.

Sub-Saharan Africa's landlocked states are among the poorest in the world, possessing lower per capita incomes than even their own coastal neighbors, most of whom rank among the world's least-developed countries. These landlocked countries are dependent upon costly, slow, and often unreliable land and river corridors to the open seas. Rising oil costs and plunging prices of commodities play havoc with already fragile economies, while transit fees levied by coastal states add to the costs of imports and exports. Lack of direct access to the oceans also inhibits economic specialization and thus adds to the economic weakness of these states.

In the center of the region, Lake Chad has shrunk to 5 percent of its 1963 size because of the construction of large-scale irrigation projects that have diverted the waters from the feeder streams. The problem has been compounded by less-than-normal monsoon rains during this period. The ecological damage that has been done to the lake's fisheries and the impact of shoreline retreat are causes of considerable political tension among the four states that border the water body—Nigeria, Niger, Cameroon, and Chad.[18]

Without secure access to the sea, the sovereignty of landlocked states is often compromised and they are subject to military, as well as economic, pressures from their neighbors. A driving force behind the various attempts to establish federations in both East and West Africa has been the incentive for their landlocked countries to link up with coastal states to gain such access. This was also a major factor in the establishment of the Southern African Development Community (SADC), for it offers the landlocked states of Zambia, Zimbabwe, Malawi, Botswana, Swaziland, and Lesotho not only the promise of lower common tariffs, but also cheaper and more efficient transportation to the sea.

Even the coastal states have landlocked interior sections, and these are the least-developed parts within those countries. The southern coastal parts of the West African countries that adjoin the Atlantic Ocean were developed by the European colonial powers for their agricultural, forest, and mineral resources. In the process, these sea-oriented regions were also Christianized. However, the Europeans had little interest in developing the northern grassland portions of their colonies and allowed them to languish economically. The fact that the populations of these interior regions were Muslim added a religious dimension to the schism. The current bitter struggles between northern and southern Nigeria are a reflection of this economic/religious rift.

Ironically, the northern belt was once the locus of great medieval Muslim Kingdoms (the Mali, Sungali, and Kitari) founded by Arab traders who had drawn their wealth from the trans-Saharan trade in gold, salt, and slaves. However, the mobility of the desert- and grassland-based camel men and horsemen lost its effectiveness when they tried to penetrate the coastal equatorial rain forests. This left these areas open to sea power and allowed the Portuguese at the end of the fifteenth century, and the other European powers who followed, to establish coastal bases. From there, European imperialism eventually took control of the interior. The Europeans created the trade that led to the control of mineral and slave wealth, and to the establishment of cities and commercial agriculture. This shifted the economic balance from the interior to the coast, a condition that continues to this day. With the discovery of coastal and offshore oil and gas deposits in recent decades, the gap between coast and interior has widened.

PROSPECTS FOR REGIONAL POWER CENTERS

No single state within Sub-Saharan Africa has the potential to become a major, or first-order, power that can gain ascendancy over the subcontinent. At best, the prospects are for regional, or second-order, powers to emerge that will be able to dominate the subregions within which they are located.

While Sub-Saharan Africa is divided into five subregions—East, West, Central, Southern, and the Horn of Africa—only two of them, West and Southern Africa, have the potential to become cohesive geopolitical units led by a regional power.

Central Africa is the most geopolitically problematic of the subregions, now that Congo has imploded as an organized state. This subregion has become a Compression Zone, as has the Horn of Africa on the eastern side of the continent. Several factors prevent East Africa from developing a cohesive core. One is the fairly even balance in population and resources among its three large states—Kenya, Uganda, and Tanzania. Another is the civil strife between the Hutu and Tutsi populations that has torn Rwanda and Burundi apart. Historically cool relations between Uganda and Tanzania have also played a role. In 1978 Uganda invaded Kagera, the tin-mining and coffee-producing region of northwest Tanzania, seeking to annex it. The Tanzanians counterattacked the following year, liberating Kagera and then capturing Kampala, Uganda's capital. They drove Idi Amin from office and kept their occupation forces in Uganda until 1981.

It is in the remaining two regions—Southern Africa and West Africa—that prospects for regional cohesion are greatest, because each has a large and relatively powerful leading state, with Nigeria in West Africa and South Africa in Southern Africa. However, even though these countries are much stronger than their neighbors militarily and economically, each has internal weaknesses that will have to be overcome before it can play a successful regional power role.

Southern Africa

South Africa is, by far, the most powerful state economically, not only in southern Africa, but within the subcontinent as a whole. It has an economy that is three times as large as the combined economies of the thirteen other members of the SADC and accounts for 40 percent of the GNP of all of Sub-Saharan Africa. Nevertheless, the South African government was initially unwilling or unable to influence SADC with respect to the war in Congo. It has opposed sending troops there to help the Kabila regime and has failed in its aim of having SADC act by consensus on security matters or in developing common tariff and banking arrangements. In only one instance has South Africa turned from diplomacy and economics to influence affairs within SADC countries. This was in 1998, when it sent troops into Lesotho to reinstate the elected government of Ntsu Mohele, which had been toppled in a coup. The reason for intervention in this case was strategic, because Lesotho is totally enclosed within South African territory. Recently, South Africa has modified its position with respect to involvement in regional conflicts. While it remains reluctant to impose its will upon warring states and peoples, it has adopted a proactive role as mediator and peacekeeper. Thus it is seeking to mediate the Congo civil war and has dispatched peacekeeping troops to Burundi, Congo, Ethiopia, Eritrea, and the Comoros.

At first glance, South Africa would appear far closer to becoming a regional power than would Nigeria. Economically, its per capita income is five times that of Nigeria and its manufacturing sector seven times as large. Unique among African states, it ranks as a middle-income, developed country, blessed with abundant natural resources, such as gold, diamonds, chromium, platinum, coal, iron, uranium, and copper. South African corporations have invested heavily in southern Africa. In addition, it has a broad agricultural base that includes maize, wheat, sugarcane, fruit, vegetables, beef, poultry, dairy, and fish products.

South Africa has not only by far the strongest industrial manufacturing and service base of any African country, but it is also a major manufacturer of military arms and possesses excellent transportation and financial service networks. Moreover, the vicious apartheid system was dismantled through peaceful means when Nelson Mandela was elected president, replacing white with black rule and sparing South Africa the violence that has torn apart so many other African nations in their quests for independence. And stability was maintained as Thabo Mbeki succeeded Mandela to the presidency in 1999.

Despite the breadth of its human and material assets, South Africa contends with major problems. The diversified economy continues to be controlled by whites, who constitute only 15 percent of the country's population of forty-five million people. There is an enormous income gap between blacks (who are 75 percent of the population) and others ("coloureds" and Asians, as well as whites), as 10 percent of the population owns half the wealth. Other serious problems are unemployment (30 percent of the workforce), poverty, crime, and HIV-AIDS. (This disease has spread so widely that the country's population has the highest infection rate in the world.) Because manufacturing is so advanced and employs only 15 percent of the workforce, opportunities for the black majority are limited. Another problem is that 90 percent of the arable land requires irrigation, while periodic droughts reduce employment opportunities in commercial agriculture. This marginalizes the many subsistence farmers who still make up a sizable portion of the rural populace, which is half of the country's total.

With so much of the South African economy being white controlled, the potential for interracial strife remains. In their relations with their former masters, the black majority has thus far adhered to the nonviolent philosophies of such leaders as Nelson Mandela, Bishop Desmond Tutu, and Thabo Mbeki. However, a more radicalized generation of younger black South African leaders could try to redress current economic disparities by seeking to gain partial control of large industries or by seeking large-scale land expropriations, as has been occurring in Zimbabwe under the authoritarian regime of Robert Mugabe. There, the large landholders, who are mostly whites, own 75 percent of the Zimbabwean farmland, although they number only 4.5 percent of the farmers. Mugabe has encouraged black squatters to seize white-owned properties, adding to the turmoil in a country whose economy is in a state of near collapse. Without an improvement in the economic status of the black population of South Africa, political and economic turmoil is always a possibility.

In the regional arena, the very fact that the economy of South Africa is so much more highly developed than that of the rest of Southern Africa, and indeed the entire subcontinent, means that South Africa has little reason to pursue intraregional trade. Nearly all of the country's foreign trade is with Maritime Europe, the United States, and Japan. The EU is its largest trading partner, drawing 37 percent of total South African trade. The fear of neighboring states is that South African manufactures would overwhelm their incipient industries were SADC to become a vehicle for reducing tariffs. They also perceive the strength and sophistication of South Africa's armed forces as a source of possible political and economic pressure against them. These considerations, in addition to South Africa's domestic racial and economic disparities and its reluctance to become overly involved in SADC security affairs, suggest that it will be many years before South Africa is able to exercise fully its capacities as a regional power.

Next to South Africa, the two largest countries in Southern Africa are Angola and Mozambique. Both have been torn by major civil wars and both are deeply impoverished. Of the two, Angola has the better prospects for strengthening its economy and becoming a strong force within the region. It has rich natural resources, including its leading exports of petroleum and natural gas, as well as diamonds, timber, and foodstuffs. In fact, it is Sub-Saharan Africa's second-largest oil producer.

What has undermined both its economy and society is the bitter civil war that has raged since its independence from Portugal in 1975. The Marxist government that then gained control with the help of the Soviet Union and its Cuban surrogate has maintained its position against the rebels, even though its patrons withdrew at the end of 1991. At the same time, South Africa and the United States ceased their support of the UNITA rebels, who are essentially drawn from the Ovimbindu, Angola's largest ethnic group, with 40 percent of the total population. Nevertheless, peace remained elusive, as a UN-sponsored peace initiative broke down in 1999. The struggle continued between the government based in Luanda and UNITA, with the latter financed by its illegal sale of diamonds from the areas under its control. The economic development of the country remains stalled; the United Nations peacekeepers left; the rebels controlled the countryside; the government controlled the cities; and the stalemate continued. Savimbi's death in battle in February 2002 brought dramatic change. The stalemate was broken and peace was achieved.

Despite the civil war and the devastation of the country, Angola plays a role as a regional intervener. Not only has it participated in the SADC-Congo/DRC military venture, but also, in 1997, it dispatched troops to the Republic of Congo (Congo-Brazzaville) to intervene in a civil war there. Its interest in the Congo was twofold: (1) during the Cold War, the "People's" Republic of the Congo was ruled by a Marxist party that had signed a treaty of friendship with the Soviet Union and looked to Angola as a model and (2) the Republic of the Congo adjoins the northern border of Angola's Cabinda exclave (Congo/DRC surrounds it from the south). Securing Cabinda from internal separatist movements, as well as threats from both Congo/DRC and the Congo-Brazzaville, is of the highest priority for Angola. The exclave accounts for two-thirds of Angola's petroleum, while its rich, offshore fields have considerable development potential.

Mozambique, which had also gained independence from Portugal in 1975 under the leadership of a marxist party, the Frelimo, was torn apart by civil war as well. The new Marxist regime was backed by the Soviet Union and Cuba, while the main supporter of the rebel Renamo movement was South Africa. A lengthy campaign of guerrilla warfare devastated the country and the struggle continued throughout the decade. This was despite a nonaggression pact signed in 1984 that was to have put an end to South African support of Renamo in return for Mozambique withdrawing its assistance to the African National Congress in its struggle against apartheid. The civil war finally ended in 1992, but the country continues to struggle, with the return of more than one million war refugees and the ravages of the worst drought of the century. With a resource base far more limited than that of Angola, prospects are that Mozambique will continue to be mired in poverty and torn by civil strife.

West Africa

Nigeria, by far the most populous of African states (125 million) and possessing vast oil resources, has aggressively intervened in the affairs of other West African states. As the region's military giant, it has organized and led military interventions in Liberia and Sierra Leone, operating within the framework of ECOWAS. In other displays of regional power, it maintains military advisers in Gambia and Chad and has used trade as a weapon to secure the compliance of the regimes of Benin and Niger.

Nigeria's entry into the Liberian conflict started with the rebellion by Charles Taylor in 1989. Nigerian jets and gunboats sought to stop Taylor's invasion and keep President Samuel Doe in office. The conflict raged until 1997, when Nigeria shifted its support to Taylor, enabling him to get the upper hand, impose a cease-fire, and gain the presidency through an election. While the cost of the Nigerian involvement was estimated at $2 billion, the Nigerian military has profited richly from control of Liberia's diamond and hardwood trade.

Sierra Leone, long torn by unrest, became a battleground when a military coup overthrew President Joseph Momoh in 1992. The Nigerian intervention was mounted that year, when the Sierra Leone government requested help in defending itself against rebels based in Liberia and aided by arms that funnel through that country. In the ensuing year, the Nigerians succeeded in preventing the rebels from gaining control of Sierra Leone's various governments. However, they could not quell the rebel campaign of terror, maimings, and kidnappings that devastated the country.

Wearying of the continuous support of the conflict, Nigeria brought the two sides together in 1999 and forced the government to share power with the rebels. The truce was soon broken, as the rebels took five hundred UN peacekeepers hostage and attacked Freetown. The Nigerians, the core of the UN's single-largest peacekeeping force, withdrew their troops in June 2000 in response to the disenchantment of the Nigerian populace with the costly and unproductive nine-year intervention. However, the war weariness of the Sierra Leoneans brought about peace in 2002, and national elections followed.

Despite these displays of regional power, the Nigerian domestic scene has been in turmoil because of corruption, mismanagement, and ethnic and religious strife. While a civilian government has recently been established after years of military rule, the regime remains unstable. The Muslim Hausa and Fulani of the North, who make up nearly 30 percent of the population, are perennially at odds with the Christian Yoruba of the southwest and the Ibo of the southeast, each of which makes up approximately 20 percent of the populace. The massacres of the Ibo that touched off the Biafra civil war continue to haunt the country, and the recent efforts of some of the northern Muslim states to introduce Sharia (Islamic law) have sharpened the divide between north and south. This divide could eventually lead to the breakaway of the south, which remains impoverished despite its vast oil resources, to form a separate state.

The north-south division is compounded by the volatility of the "Middle Belt"—the "bread basket" of central Nigeria, which lies between the middle courses of the Niger and Benue Rivers. There the region is torn apart by ethnic, religious, and intercommunal fighting aggravated by drought, starvation, and poverty. While the Niger dams projects that were begun in the 1960s have helped to develop farming in the Middle Belt, the friction among the different tribes and clans, many of which have migrated from the north, keeps the region in continuing turmoil at a local communal level and is the source of increasing numbers of refugee camps within the belt.

Revenues from vast petroleum resources in the Niger Delta in southeastern Nigeria and in the Gulf of Guinea (the Bights of Guinea and Biafra) have done little to allay the poverty that grips approximately one-third of the region's population, or to reduce the nearly 30 percent unemployment rate. Much of these revenues have been looted or squandered by military rulers. Moreover, prolonged droughts in the Sahel of northern Nigeria, as well as the collapse of fishing in Lake Chad, which has shrunk as a result of the droughts, have pushed hundreds of thousands of migrants to the cities of the south. They cannot be readily absorbed there, and their presence further exacerbates the civil strife.

With the decline of agriculture, especially at the subsistence level, Nigeria, once a food exporter, must now import food. While the regime in the federal capital of Abuja—the first democratically elected government in sixteen years—may be able to take the lead in mounting major peacekeeping efforts among its strife-torn neighbors, as it did in Liberia and Sierra Leone, its political and economic staying power as a regional influence remains tenuous. Olusegon Obasanjo's election to the presidency in 1999, after a succession of military regimes, raised hopes among Nigerians that internal conflict would come to an end. However, the violence has continued. Until Nigeria coalesces around widely accepted national goals, stabilizes its government, and learns to use its oil revenues wisely, its role as a regional power is likely to be limited and its regional policies unpredictable.

Elsewhere in West Africa, much of the region continues to be caught up in civil strife and border wars. However, three countries stand out as having gained stability from their early years of turmoil and strife—Ghana, Benin, and Gabon.

Ghana has been led by Jerry Rawling, who first seized power in a military coup and then assumed the presidency in 1982. The country has overcome its period of disunity and economic distress to stabilize its economy and expand it through free market innovations. Agriculture remains Ghana's economic base, but its mineral and forest products industries have been expanded with the help of outside investment. Its ties to the West appear firm.

Benin abandoned its Marxist system in favor of private enterprise a decade ago. Since that time it has moved to popular elections and a multiparty system that has made it a model of an open society in West Africa. While Benin is dependent on subsistence agriculture and cotton, its prospects for economic development have improved with the discovery of oil off its shores. Tiny Gabon, with by far the highest GDP in the region, enjoys relative stability thanks to an economy supported by oil exports. Important oil reserves have also been found in tiny Equatorial Guinea and Chad. The former, with a population of under half a million, has doubled its per capita income in the past decade. Landlocked Chad, with a population of over eight million, is one of the world's poorest countries, but it has vast reserves in its south. A large pipeline is under construction that will enable the beginning of pumping from the fields near Kome to Douala on the Cameroon coast. It remains to be seen whether anticipated revenues will be equitably distributed among the population or monopolized by the political, military, and business elite, as has been the case in much of Africa and the Middle East.

COMPRESSION ZONES

During the past decade, two Compression Zones have developed in Sub-Saharan Africa— Central Africa and the Horn of Africa. Until a decade ago, Central Africa was the scene of intense competition for influence between the Soviet Union and the United States allied with France and other European countries. The rich mineral base of Congo/Zaire and the centrality of its location was perceived as being so vital to American geostrategic interests that Washington turned a blind eye to the rampant corruption and human rights abuses of its Congolese client, Mobutu Sese Seko, and to the venal behavior of Western mining corporations. France became heavily involved in the Central African Republic and the Republic of Cameroon in order to secure its supply of uranium and oil. Benin and Guinea had Marxist regimes, while the former in particular looked to Moscow and other Eastern European countries for assistance. While access to minerals was of some interest to the Soviets also, their prime motivation in these countries, as well as in Congo, was in supporting Marxist governments and expelling the Western countries from much of the region.

While the Great Powers are no longer involved in Central Africa, it continues to be torn apart. Not only has Congo imploded, but Congo-Brazzaville remains caught up in civil war. Upheavals in the Central African Republic have required the intervention of UN peacekeeping forces. Cameroon is ruled by an authoritarian government, as is Equatorial Guinea.

The bellwether of Central Africa is Congo/DRC—the largest country of the region. Its population of fifty million is 70 percent of Central Africa's total and its land area of 900,000 square miles represents 60 percent of the total. The intervention of countries from Southern and East Africa has converted West Africa from its Shatterbelt status during the Cold War to a Compression Zone. Although Congo's neighbors claim that their interests lie in bringing peace to the country, their main motives seem to be gaining access to its rich resources and cutting off the bases of rebels who operate against their own countries from different parts of Congo.

The conflict in Congo/DRC began in 1998, the year after Laurent Kabila toppled the dictatorial regime of President Mobutu Sese Seko, with the strong support of Rwandan Tutsi government troops, as well as forces from Burundi and Angola. Domestic dissatisfaction with the Kabila regime soon led to the outbreak of civil war in the eastern part of the country. Many of the rebels were Banyamulenge Tutsi, born in Congo but denied citizenship by both Mobutu and Kabila. Kabila's army was then backed by Hutu refugees who had been driven out of Rwanda in 1994 and had been using Congo as a base for crossborder incursions aimed at destabilizing Rwanda's Tutsi government.

Aided by mass defections from the Congolese army, the rebels swept across eastern Congo to the gates of Kinshasa and also seized the port of Matadi, the capital's lifeline for food, arms, and electric power. Kabila was saved by the military forces from Zimbabwe, Angola, and Namibia, acting in the name of the twelve-country SADC, which were then joined by troops from Chad and Sudan. The rebels were pushed back to their eastern bases. Fighting continued until September 1999, when a tentative peace accord, brokered by Zambia, was reached, but the accord was soon breached and fighting resumed.

Centrality of location often offers strategic advantages to a country, but for Congo it is a serious handicap. Its government has been unable to form a cohesive unit because its threefold physical divisions—east, west, and south—are separated by an impassable interior. This leaves Congo prey to outside pressures, especially from well-armed states to the east and south lured by Congo's rich resource base.

The Horn of Africa also has shifted from a Shatterbelt drawn into the Great Power struggle within the Middle East to a Compression Zone. Somalia and Ethiopia have fought over the Ogaden, Ethiopia and Eritrea plunged into a bloody war, and Somalia has broken apart. In Somalia, the United States and the United Nations failed in their efforts during the early 1990s to quell the interclan and intertribal fighting. Since then no central government has existed and Somalia has frequently been cited as a failed state.

Rebels in northern Somalia (the former British Somaliland) seceded in 1991 and established the independent state of Somaliland. This country fronts on the gulf of Aden and contains Berbera, the former Soviet naval and missile base that is one of the few pieces of real estate in Sub-Saharan Africa with geostrategic importance. Together with Djibouti and Aden (on the opposite shore), it commands the southern gateway to the Red Sea.

Along the northeastern coast of the Horn, another rebel group broke away to create "Puntland," taking its name from the Red Sea coastland called "Punt" by the ancient

Egyptians. The new territory centers around the port and commercial center of Bossasso, where the Gulf of Aden enters the Indian Ocean and trades in food and frankincense. The separatist leaders have not dismissed the possibility of rejoining a reconstituted Somalian Federation. Meanwhile they have brought stability to Puntland, as have the Somaliland rulers to their land, where they have been able to create a modicum of harmony among the clans and bring basic services to their people. What is left of Somalia continues to be strife torn. Ultimately, its hope for recovery from anarchy may rest upon a confederation of three or four quasi-independent "statelets."

Conclusion

The two Southern Continents seem destined to remain the "Quarter-Sphere of Geostrategic Marginality" for the foreseeable future. Washington's rationale for involvement in Colombia is not dictated by long-range strategic or humanitarian considerations, but by an attempt to find a quick fix to a domestic drug addiction problem through interdiction of the production and trafficking in cocaine and heroin from there.

While the United States has strategic interest in western South America that are based on the drug trade, its strategic interests in Angola and Nigeria are based on their petroleum resources. However, in the case of neither drugs nor oil do these interests rise to the level of possibly requiring military intervention.

To put matters in strategic perspective, would the United States and the West go to war to secure their access to West Africa's oil resources as they did in Kuwait? The answer, in all likelihood, is "no." Kuwait was strategically important, not only because of its own oil reserves, but also because it was the gateway to the bulk of the Middle East's Gulf deposits. Both currently and potentially, the strategic stake of the Maritime Realm in the oil resources of the Middle East is incomparably greater than its stake in those of West Africa.

Geopolitical structures are not immutable. Those structures that emerged from World War II have changed radically with the collapse of the former Soviet Union and the ascendance of China as a world-class power. Looking into the distant future, we can anticipate geopolitical changes coming to Sub-Saharan Africa partially as a result of geopolitical developments in neighboring regions.

The coastal countries and offshore islands of eastern Africa, especially Tanzania, Zanzibar, Madagascar, the Seychelles, Comoros, Maldives, and Mauritius, might be drawn into a new Indian Ocean geostrategic realm. Such a realm would be dominated by India, as discussed in the chapter on South Asia. The Horn of Africa is likely to remain under the shadow of events in the Middle East.

The western half of Sub-Saharan Africa might also, in the long run, emerge from its current state of geostrategic marginality to become a new geopolitical region linked to the Maritime Realm. This would depend upon the abilities of Nigeria and South Africa to achieve strong national cohesiveness and take the lead in making ECOWAS and SADC tightly knit economic and political subunits that could then be linked within a broader geopolitical region. Such a region might also be strengthened by the addition of new states in the lower Congo and Shaba, in the eventuality that Congo/DRC divides into three states. These would consist of one centering around Kinshasa and western Congo, a second centering around Lubumbashi and Shaba in the southeast (Katanga), and a third in eastern Congo or the upper Congo basin that would probably be oriented to East Africa and the Indian Ocean Realm. South Africa signed a free trade pact with Mercosur in December 2000, with the express goal of decreasing its trade dependence on Europe and the United States. However, it is highly unlikely that this accord could lead to a set of strong economic and geopolitical links between the two Southern Continents.

South America's prospects for developing into a geopolitical region that is well integrated into the Maritime Realm depends upon the destiny of Brazil, the continent's only regional power. Its central position within South America enables it to influence events in much of the continent's "Southern Cone"—the geographical triangle that extends from the southern headwaters of the Amazon and the southern Peruvian Andes to Patagonia.

The prospects for the creation of such a region have been improved by the recent turn in relations between Brazil and Argentina. Historically, Brazil's major geopolitical focus has been its rivalry with Argentina for leadership of the La Plata estuary and dominance over the three states that act as buffers between the two countries—Uruguay, Paraguay, and Bolivia. Brazil and Argentina have now achieved a rapprochement that enhances the ability of Brazil to lead the region toward integration and to guarantee peace and stability. The rapid restoration of Argentina to economic recovery is also important to the region's unity prospects.

Extending such a region to include the Andean countries of Colombia, Ecuador, and Peru is unlikely because of the barrier effects of the Amazon region and the Andes. These three states are likely to remain isolated and marginal to the mainstream of Maritime Realm action. Centripetal forces within the states might lead to their implosion.

However, the larger part of South America, led by Brazil, could forge a regional identity that would derive strength from balanced ties with North America, Maritime Europe, and the Pacific Rim, rather than remain dominated by the United States, as it currently is. Under such circumstances, much of South America could overcome its current geopolitical marginalization and take its place as an important component within the global geopolitical system.

The description of the Southern Continents as a "Quarter-Sphere of Marginality" is not to suggest that, because their instability does not undermine the structural balance of the international system, they should be ignored in the grand scheme of world geopolitics. The great powers cannot be indifferent to the fate of these conflict-ridden and economically depressed parts of the world. In addition to humanitarian considerations, it is important to note that local conflicts can get out of hand and destabilize other states, that they can create large numbers of refugees who stream toward the developed world, and that they can become breeding grounds for international terrorism. Peace and economic development within these regions would add to the geopolitical stability of the world system.

Notes

1. Saul B. Cohen, "Global Change in the Post-Cold War Era," *Annals of the Association of American Geographers* 81, no. 4 (1991): 551–80.

2. John O'Loughlin and Herman Van der Wusten, "Political Geography of Panregions," *Geographical Review* 80 (1990): 1–20.

3. Norman Harris, *Intervention and Colonization in Africa, 1884–1914* (Boston: Houghton, Mifflin, 1914), 3–19.

4. Halford Mackinder, "The Round World and the Winning of the Peace," *Foreign Affairs* 21, no. 4 (1943): 204–5.

5. Central Intelligence Agency, "Disputes International," *World Factbook 2000* (Washington, D.C.: Gov/CIA, 2000).

6. Philip Kelley, *Checkerboards and Shatterbelts: The Geopolitics of South America* (Austin: University of Texas Press, 1987), 48–83.

7. Charles Louis de Montesquieu, *The Spirit of Laws,* Book XIV, trans. Thomas Nugent, Library of the Classics (1906, reprint; New York: Hafner, 1949), 221–34.

8. Central Intelligence Agency, *World Factbook 2000* (Washington, D.C.: Gov/CIA Publications, 2000), 2, 3, 5.

9. Jennifer L. Rich, "Brazilians Are Coming on Fast in Soybean Wars," *New York Times,* 10 July 2001, C1–2.

10. A. S. Gakwandi, "Towards a New Political Map of Africa," in *Politics, Economy and Social Change in the Twenty-First Century,* ed. A. I. Asiwaju (London: Hurst, 1996), 252–59.

11. Peter J. Taylor, ed., *World Government* (New York: Oxford University Press, 1990), 188–201.

12. Morag Bell, *Contemporary Africa: Development, Culture and the State* (London: Longman, 1986), 98–11.

13. Joseph Kahn, "World Bank Cites Itself in Study of Africa's Bleak Performance," *New York Times,* 1 June 2000, 6.

14. Norimitsu Onishi, "African Bloc Hoping to Do Better as the 'African Union,'" *New York Times,* 12 July 2001, A3.

15. J. V. R. Prescott, "Africa's Boundary Problems," *Optima* 28 (1980), 3–21.

16. Central Intelligence Agency, "Disputes International," *World Factbook 2000;* Alan J. Day, ed. *Border and Territorial Disputes* (Longman, 1982), 95–178.

17. "Somaliland, the Nation Nobody Knows," *Economist,* 14 April 2001, 42.

18. Andrew C. Revkin, "Lake's Rapid Retreat Heightens Troubles in North Africa," *New York Times,* 27 May 2001, F4.

CHAPTER 13

Epilogue

During the Cold War, global equilibrium was sustained by balanced competition between the U.S. and Soviet superpowers. Following the collapse of the Soviet empire, U.S. policy makers and those of many other nations assumed that the overwhelming economic and military might of the United States would impose a new state of equilibrium upon the world. Such might was applied in the Gulf War, Somalia, Bosnia, and Kosovo without bringing regional or global stability. The war in Afghanistan and against global terrorism demonstrates definitively that winning wars and maintaining global stability requires a multilateral effort involving all of the world's power centers and many other national states.

The conflict in Afghanistan has been widely characterized as signaling a new era in both war and global affairs. However, it is not the actual combat that is unique. Many arenas of battle have required major adjustments to terrain, climate, guerrilla forces, and the geopolitical interests of surrounding countries. What is unique about the this war is that its geographical limits are indeterminate. Terrorist cells extend well beyond the boundaries of Afghanistan and actions against other states that sponsor or harbor terrorists are required. Afghanistan is but the first step in the broader war against global terrorism.

September 11 also marked a new kind of war on the home front for Americans, most of whom had not experienced the ravages of domestic and international terrorism that have taken such a fearsome toll in other lands. The psychological, personal, and economic impact stemming from the devastation of the World Trade Center and the Pentagon will persist long after the conflict in Afghanistan is ended and lower Manhattan is rebuilt.

Will the war against international terrorism fundamentally change the world geopolitical scene? The basic global geopolitical structure remains intact, as Washington discovered in its efforts to knit together a coalition. What may change is the nature of the relationships among the various parts of the structure.

To conduct the war, the United States had to turn, not only to its allies in NATO and other parts of the Maritime Realm, but also to other major power cores—Russia, China, and India—as well as to Pakistan and other countries. Essential to the crafting of the war strategy was the sharing of military and financial intelligence, permission to overfly airspace, and use of land, air, and sea bases in Middle Eastern, Central Asian, and South Asian lands that surround Afghanistan. The common fear of terrorism that motivated many coalition members had the effect of beginning to erode the divisions in the world geopolitical system that were so sharp during most of the last half of the twentieth century. While sophisticated

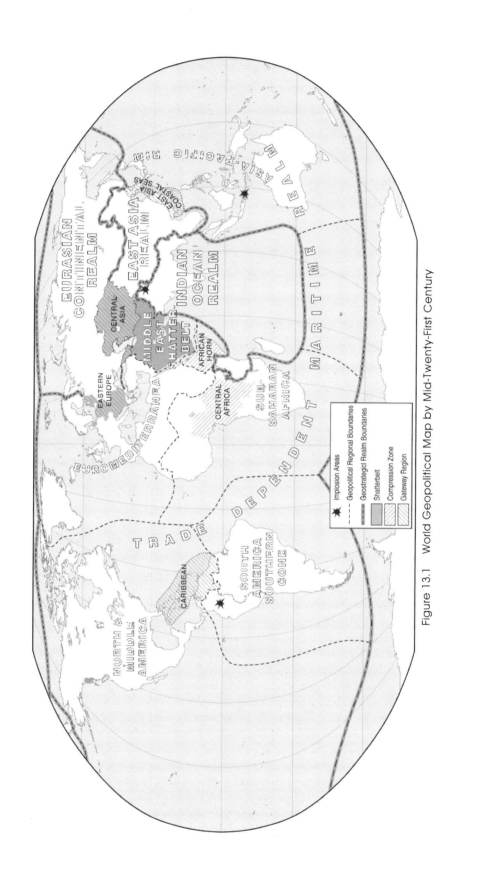

Figure 13.1   World Geopolitical Map by Mid-Twenty-First Century

communications, financial instruments, and weaponry had increased the danger from terrorism, national leaders recognized that, when acting in concert, they had access to far greater resources to overcome the challenge.

Negotiations over establishment of the coalition had consequences reaching far beyond the mission to fight terrorism. They opened opportunities for some countries to pursue other goals. Russia's drive to become accepted as part of the Westernized world has been accelerated and its application to join the World Trade Organization may be speeded up. China's admission to the WTO, an important step in expanding its world markets, is likely to lead more quickly to stronger Asia-Pacific Rim and Trans-Pacific capital and trade links.

The threat of Islamic fundamentalist movements to Uzbekistan and Tajikistan from Afghan bases was an incentive for those countries to give the U.S. air and land forces access to their bases. For Iran, which had long supported the Afghan Northern Alliance, the war represented an opportunity to eliminate the Taliban, which it considered a dangerous enemy. For Pakistan, cooperation with the United States on the use of its military bases meant renewal of large-scale economic aid and the possibility of eventual lifting of the freeze on deliveries of American-built fighter planes that had been purchased a decade ago, which had been held up because of Islamabad's nuclear testing.

Strategic imperatives also presented complications. The need for the United States to reassure India that revival of military and economic agreements with Pakistan would not come at New Delhi's expense resulted in an American commitment to oppose Pakistani-sponsored terrorism in Kashmir. In addition, new economic aid and military sales to India became the subject of U.S.-India deliberations.

The variety in breadth and intensity of responsiveness to the U.S. call for a global War against Terrorism reflects the differing national interests and geopolitical settings of the members of the international community. The geographical patterns of these responses correspond closely to the current world geopolitical map.

The Maritime Realm states were the most committed to supporting the United States in the conduct of the war. Troops, aircraft, naval vessels, and intelligence assistance were offered by Canada and by the Maritime European countries of Britain, France, Germany, Italy, and Spain, with London taking a lead role politically as well as militarily. Turkey, too, strongly supported the campaign. In the Asia-Pacific Rim, Australia offered troops and Japan dispatched three naval vessels—an unprecedented step for Tokyo, which had heretofore been bound by the policy of maintaining military forces for home defense only.

Outside the Maritime Realm, participation was narrower. In the Heartlandic Realm, Russia provided airspace overflight and intelligence assistance and consented to the use of former Soviet bases in Uzbekistan, Tajikistan, and Kyrgyzstan. Also, the flow of Russian arms to the Northern Alliance increased. Iran assisted with weapons to the Northern Alliance and permitted airspace overflight. China expressed unequivocal support of the war, but did not become directly involved in its conduct.

Within the independent geopolitical region of South Asia, both the Indian and Pakistani governments announced strong support. There was considerable risk to Pakistan's Musharaff government in joining the coalition and providing key military bases, in view of the violent opposition of Pakistan's Islamic fundamentalist movements and the large numbers of pro-Taliban refugees and al Qaeda escapees and sympathizers within the country. Former close ties between Pakistani military intelligence and the Taliban make their proffered intelligence assistance a contribution to be treated with caution.

The most ambiguous contributions to the war were those of Arab Middle Eastern Shatterbelt states, where opposition to the American bombing was widespread and often violent, causing regimes that had joined the coalition to participate half-heartedly. Saudi Arabia placed limitations on the use of American air bases on its territory. In Egypt, the influence of Islamic fundamentalism caused the Mubarak regime to condemn a lengthy bombing campaign. Lebanon refused to freeze the assets of the Lebanon-based Hizbollah, which Washington had listed as a terrorist group. Syria continued to sponsor Palestinian terrorist groups aimed at Israel and, together with Iran, to support the Hizbollah. Yasser Arafat, who also "joined the coalition," failed to move against the terrorism of the Intifada in Israel. Kuwait, Bahrain, Qatar, and Oman allowed unhampered use of U.S. bases and other facilities located within their countries. Only Jordan offered to send troops to aid in the fighting. Israel was kept under wraps. Such a mixed response was to be expected of a region that is so fragmented by internal divisions, especially by the struggles between Islamic fundamentalist forces and the regimes of many of these countries.

The global war against terrorism is being conducted against the background of the present, dynamic world geopolitical structure. There will be structural changes, some unexpected, and others that can be anticipated. Figure 13.1 represents the likely world geopolitical map by the mid-twenty-first century. While this map is speculative, these are the directional changes that I expect in the geopolitical patterns and features during the next half century.

A new Indian Ocean Realm is likely to emerge, as India's economic and military dominance is felt throughout the basin and New Delhi joins the ranks of world powers. The relative weakening of Pakistan will strengthen India. This realm would embrace the coastlands of East Africa on the western side of the Indian Ocean Basin and Myanmar on the Basin's Bay of Bengal–Andaman Sea eastern side. It could act as a counterbalance to Chinese pressures against the Asia-Pacific Rim and have a strong influence upon the Rim and East and South Africa.

Eastern Europe, the Trans-Caucasus, and Central Asia could emerge either as Gateway or Shatterbelt regions. The geostrategic importance to Moscow of these regions, located along Russia's western and southwestern borders, cannot be overstated. Russia's vital interests are based on its strategic vulnerability to a potentially hostile presence, such as NATO would represent if expanded into the eastern Baltic and Black Seas; the stationing of U.S. troops in the Caucasus or Central Asia; the presence in neighboring countries of ethnic Russian and Slavic Russophile groups who look to Moscow for physical security and cultural support; and the spread of Islamic fundamentalism from seven republics in southern Russia (such as Chechnya) should they fall into the hands of radical Islamic regimes. Russian interests also include the maintenance of access for Russian investment to the rich oil and gas reserves of Central Asia and the Trans-Caucasus and, above all, strategic control over the regions mentioned above for directing transit of their new energy pipeline infrastructures across Russian territory.

Reassurance over these concerns could encourage Moscow to work together with the West in converting the Eastern European Trans-Caucasus and Central Asian regions into a broad Gateway zone. Otherwise, they would become Shatterbelts. In the latter case, geographical proximity and other features would give Russia a strategic advantage in countering Western penetration efforts.

September 11 appears to have significantly altered U.S.-Russian relations, portending an era of friendship and accomodation. If the agreement on nuclear missiles reduction could be followed by accords on the Anti-Ballistic Missile Treaty, and on the issue of NATO expansion, combined with Russia's desire to be accepted as a Westernizing nation, this would be the prelude to the emergence of Eastern Europe as a Gateway region. Central Asia and the Trans-Caucasus could also develop as Gateways if the partnership between the United States and Russia, whereby Moscow consents to U.S. use of land and air bases in Uzbekistan, Tajikistan, and Kyrgyzstan, is followed by the joint exploitation of the region's oil and gas resources.

The NATO-Russia Partnership grants Moscow an equal voice on such issues as military cooperation and nonproliferation, although NATO retains control over core military decisions. A reasonable alternative to NATO expansion is to include the East European countries as partners. They would benefit and derive security from military cooperation with NATO. However, they would not be entitled to Alliance weaponry, nor would Russia face the strategic threat of having NATO bases on its doorstep.

No geopolitical discussion of any part of the Russian periphery can take place without reference to oil and natural gas. The future development of these resources in both the Trans-Caucasus and Central Asia is of great interest to the West. To Russia, this zone is important in terms of both its energy resources and its strategic military value.

The extensive Russian military involvement in the affairs of Georgia and Armenia during the past decade reflects the depth of Moscow's strategic interest in the Trans-Caucasus. For its part, Washington has made considerable efforts to expand its influence within Georgia through foreign aid support of Western oil interests seeking to build a pipeline from Baku in Azerbaijan across Georgia to the Black Sea and providing military trainers.

Within the Maritime Realm, the present region of Maritime Europe and the Maghreb would expand into a new region, Euromediterranea, which would encompass Turkey, the Levant, and northeastern Africa.

The creation of such a region would hold profound geopolitical implications for the United States. The major burden for Maritime Realm strategic and economic responsibilities in these lands would shift from the United States to Maritime Europe. Emergence of the new region hinges upon a number of eventualities. One is Turkey's admission to the EU and its continuing market-oriented economic reforms, which would link it more closely to the global economy.

Resolution of the Arab-Israeli conflict through establishment of a Palestinian state in nearly all of the West Bank and in Gaza is also a key requirement. Prospects presently appear quite dim for resolution of that conflict. However, a convergence of elements might ultimately bring the warring sides to the negotiating table. These include the escalation of bloodletting, the suffering and economic privation of the Palestinian Arabs, and the tensions and remorseless pressures building up in Israel as a result of Palestinian Arab terrorism. Additional strains will be generated because of the West's concerns that continuation of the conflict will increasingly undermine its relationship with Arab oil states and the Muslim world as a whole. Washington's effort to mobilize support from key Arab states to help meet the U.S. objective of overthrowing Saddam Hussein has galvanized the Bush administration to take a more active role in trying to mediate the conflict.

Resolution of the Cyprus dispute is another prerequisite. If the island is to be reunified, a Greco-Turkish condominium over a confederated Cyprus/North Cyprus state may have to be established as the first step.

A further requirement is modernization of the Egyptian economy and democratization of its governance structure to address Europe's concerns. This would strengthen Cairo's leadership role within the Arab lands of the Levant and northeast Africa.

The rationale for the emergence of Euromediterranea is geopolitically compelling. If it gains the military capacity to match its economic power, Maritime Europe will be well positioned to replace American leadership within the western rim of the present Middle East or at least share equally in the diplomatic and economic burdens.

For Washington, a Euromediterranea could mean substantial reduction of its current military and economic aid programs to Israel, Egypt, and Jordan. At the same time, the United States would be relieved of a good many political entanglements that would be assumed by Europe.

Should the western rim of the Middle East become geopolitically reoriented to Europe, the Middle East Shatterbelt would be reconstituted. It would then consist of the Arabian Peninsula, the Persian/Arab Gulf, Iraq, Iran, and Afghanistan. In addition, the region's eastern border might be extended to include Pakistan's Pashtun areas, because neither Afghanistan nor Pakistan are cohesive national units. There is a strong likelihood that, despite the extraordinary efforts by the Allied powers to rebuild Afghanistan as a unified state, it will not be possible to overcome the ethnic, tribal, and spatial divisions that have torn the country apart.

Pakistan, too, may implode as a result of the pressures of Islamic extremism, as well as Pashtun separatism, and the inability of its military regime to contain these forces. The outcome could be the emergence of a "Pakhtoonistan" that straddles a mountainous eight-hundred-mile borderland between Pakistan and Afghanistan. This state would include the Pashtun tribal areas of eastern and southern Afghanistan with those of western Pakistan from just north of Quetta, in northern Baluchistan, through the federally administered Tribal Areas and the North-West Frontier Province.

The Caribbean is likely to emerge as a Gateway region. It could become a bridge connecting the countries of a new South American Southern Cone region (see cone shape, fig. 13.1), North and Middle America, and Euromediterranea. In the post-Castro era, Cuba, along with Venezuela, could play a key role in creating this Gateway.

The emergence of the Southern Cone region would be based upon the development of Brazil into one of the world's important powers. Its sheer size, resource base, and military power relative to its neighbors should enable it to dominate all of the Amazon basin, as well as a weaker Argentina that could no longer rival its northern neighbor economically, militarily, and in size of population. The Southern Cone would also include Uruguay, Paraguay, Chile, Bolivia, and the Amazonian sectors that now belong to Colombia, Ecuador, and Peru—states threatened by implosion.

Perhaps the most far-reaching potential geopolitical change is the prospective East Asia Coastal Seas Gateway region that would link much of the present East Asia Realm to the Asia-Pacific Rim. It would also link the Asia-Pacific Rim to the Russian Far East.

The new Gateway would be composed of China's "Golden Coast," Taiwan, and a unified Korea. In all likelihood, the Golden Coast would not break away from North and Interior Continental China as an independent state, but would be a quasi-independent one in confederation with China. Confederation could also be the path taken by Taiwan. In both cases, a "Hong Kong Plus" model might be the vehicle whereby they could enjoy economic and a modicum of political independence, such as UN membership and worldwide diplomatic representation. At the same time, as demilitarized states, they would come under China's protection and be junior partners in the political confederation.

The Asia-Pacific Rim would contract geographically as a result of the change in political status of Korea, the implosion of Indonesia, and the expansion of the Indian Ocean

Realm. Nevertheless, under the leadership of Japan, it would remain a cornerstone of the Maritime Realm and derive strength from the East Asia Coastal Seas Gateway.

The world envisaged on the map in figure 13.1 is one of an interdependent geopolitical structure with the promise of greater equilibrium than exists at the turn of the twenty-first century. The continuing evolution of such a world system will put great pressure on the United Nations to effect major institutional changes that would reflect the system's increased hierarchical specialization and complexity. Within the Security Council, the current group of five permanent members is likely to be expanded to include Japan, Germany, India, and Brazil—all existing or potential major powers. As the number of national states continues to increase, membership in the General Assembly could well increase within the next quarter century from the current 200 to between 250 and 275 states.

State proliferation is taking place at the same time that globalization is making it more of a challenge for states to control their national economies and preserve certain valued aspects of their national cultures. At the same time, irredentist movements take advantage of global telecommunications, travel, currency, and eased restrictions on trade to secure weaponry and manpower in support of their struggles for national freedom. Global institutional religious ties are also increasingly important, as they reinforce faiths that have become the driving forces of nationalism in so many parts of the world.

Readjustments within the UN structure might give greater voice to the rising number of regional powers and limited voting weight to those in the quasi-state category. Regional bodies, such as the EU, NAFTA, Mercosur, and ASEAN, will develop into major political-economic forces within the world system, thus some means of formal accommodation for them should be worked out. While a radical reorganization of the UN would no doubt meet considerable opposition from those states that benefit from the status quo, without institutional innovations that reflect the sweeping global geopolitical changes ahead, the world body will run the risk of becoming ineffective and irrelevant.

The increase in the numbers of major and regional powers, and the strengthening of regional organizations, will not eliminate disturbances in the system. These will persist as new states join the international community and unresolvedconflicts between existing states continue to rage. However, such disturbances will be more easily contained by an international system that has more nodes at different geospatial levels and more links between and among those nodes. This will build a more diverse and dense global network that is more capable of withstanding the shocks to the system from various disturbances.

In an increasingly complex geopolitical world, pervaded by the influence of globalism, power will be even more widely dispersed and hierarchy weaker, so that no single state or realm can expect to be dominant. The twenty-first century will become the "Global Century," not the "American" or the "Pacific" one. The very complexity of the system will require the leadership of all of the major and regional powers to keep the world in balance in the face of dynamic changes. As the "first among equals" of the great states, the United States will have ample opportunity to apply its power in international affairs with wisdom, determination, and consistency, while remaining mindful of the limitations, as well as the responsibilities, inherent in the exercise of this power.

Bibliography

Agnew, John. *Geopolitics: Re-visioning World Politics*. London: Routledge, 1998.

——. *Mastering Space: Hegemony, Territory and the International Economy*. London: Routledge, 1995.

——. *Place and Politics*. London: Allen and Unwin, 1987.

——. *Western Geopolitical Thought in the Twentieth Century*. New York: St. Martin's, 1985.

Ardrey, Robert. *The Territorial Imperative*. New York: Atheneum, 1966.

Baransky, N. M. *Economic Geography of the U.S.S.R.* Preface and translation by S. Belsky. Moscow: Foreign Languages, 1956.

Bell, Morag. *Contemporary Africa: Development, Culture and the State*. London: Longman, 1986.

Bertalanffy, Ludwig von. *General System Theory*. New York: George Braziller, 1968.

Blouet, Brian. *Halford Mackinder: A Biography*. College Station: Texas A&M University Press, 1987.

Bowman, Isaiah. *The New World*. Yonkers-on-Hudson, N.Y.: World Book, 1922.

Boyd, Andrew. *An Atlas of World Affairs*, 10th ed. London: Routledge, 1998.

Bracken, Paul. *Fire in the East*. New York: HarperCollins, 1999.

Brandt, Willy. *North-South: A Programme for Survival*. London: Pan, 1980.

Braudel, Ferdinand. *The Mediterranean and the Mediterranean World in the Age of Philip II*. 2 vols. 'Translated by Sian Reynolds. New York: Harper & Row, 1973.

Brecher, Michael. *The New States of Asia*. New York: Oxford University Press, 1966.

Brigham, Albert Perry. *Geographic Influences in American History*. New York: Chautauqua, 1903.

Brown, Seyom. "Inherited Geopolitics and Emergent Global Realities." In *America's Global Interests,* edited by Edward K. Hamilton, 166–97. New York: Norton, 1989.

Brunn, Stanley D., Jeffrey A. Jones, and Shannon O'Lear. "Geopolitical Information and Communications in the Twenty-First Century." In *Reordering the World,* edited by George J. Demko and William B. Wood. Boulder, Colo.: Westview, 1999.

Brzezinski, Zbigniew. *Game Plan*. New York: Atlantic Monthly Press, 1986.

——. *The Grand Chessboard*. New York: Basic, 1997.

——. *Out of Control: Global Turmoil on the Eve of the Twenty-First Century*. New York: Scribner's, Macmillan, 1993.

Bullard, Reader. *Britain and the Middle East*. London: Hutchinson's University Library, 1951.

Bush, George H. W. "Toward a New World Order." 11 September 1990, *Public Papers of the Presidents of the United States, George H. W. Bush, 1990*. Washington, D.C.: Government Printing Office, 1991. Reprinted in O'Tuathail, Gearold. *Critical Geopolitics: The Politics of Writing Global Space,* 131–34. Minneapolis: University of Minnesota Press, 1996.

"Central America's Border Order." *Economist,* 13 March 2000, 42.

Central Intelligence Agency. "Major Land Disputes around the World, Selected Disputes, July 18, 2000." Pamphlet, 7 pages.

———. *The World Factbook 2000.* Washington, D.C.: Gov/CIA, 2000.

Chanda, Nayan. "Cam Ranh Bay Manoeuvres." *FEER* (28 December 2000, 4 January 2000).

"China Survey." *Economist,* 8 April 2000, 13.

Chou, Oliver. "Navy Boss Outlines Force of the Future." *South China Morning Post,* 22 April 1999.

Chrone, G. R. *Background to Political Geography.* London: Pittman, 1969.

Churchill, Winston. "Iron Curtain" speech. Graduation address, Westminster College, Fulton, Mo., March 5, 1946. Excerpted in *Internet Modern History Sourcebook,* August 1977.

Cohen, Saul B. "Asymmetrical States and Geopolitical Equilibrium." *SAIS Review* 4, no. 2 (Summer/Fall 1984): 193–212.

———. "Gaza Now! Prospects for a Gaza Microstate." *Mediterranean Quarterly* (Spring 1992): 60–80.

———. *Geography and Politics in a World Divided.* New York: Random House, 1963. 2d ed. New York: Oxford University Press, 1973.

———. "Global Change in the Post-Cold War Era." *Annals of the Association of American Geographers* 81, no. 4 (1991): 551–80.

———. "A New Map of Geopolitical Equilibrium: A Developmental Approach." *Political Geography Quarterly* 1, no. 3 (1982): 223–42.

Cohen, Saul B., and Lewis D. Rosenthal. "A Geographical Model for Political Systems Analysis." *Geographical Review* 61, no. 1 (1971): 5–31.

Collingwood, Robin George. *The Idea of Nature.* Reprint, Oxford: Oxford University Press, 1993.

Cressey, George. *The Basis of Soviet Strength.* New York: McGraw-Hill, 1945.

Crosette, Barbara. "Europe Stares at a Future Built by Immigrants." *New York Times Week in Review,* 2 January 2000, 1, 4.

Davis, Anthony. "Blue Water Ambitions." *Asia Week* 26, no. 11 (24 March 2000): 1.

Day, Alan J. ed. *Border and Territorial Disputes.* Harlow, England: Longman, 1982.

"Denmark and Greenland, Ultima Motives." *Economist,* 17 February 2001, 55.

Diehl, Paul F., ed. *A Road Map to War.* Nashville: Vanderbilt University Press, 1999.

Dorpalen, A. *The World of General Haushofer: Geopolitics in Action.* New York: Farrar and Rinehart, 1948.

Drozdiak, William. "Old World Reinvents Itself as Model for New Economy." *International Herald Tribune,* 19 February 2001, 1, 11.

Drucker, Peter. *The New Realities.* New York: Harper & Row, 1989.

———. *Post Capitalist Society.* New York: Harper Business, 1983.

Duncan, Richard C., and Walter Youngquist. "The World Petroleum Life-Cycle." Paper presented at Petroleum Technology Transfer Council Workshop, University of Southern Californie, Los Angeles, October 22, 1998.

Ekholm, Erik. "After Fifty Years, China Youth Remain Mao's Pioneers." *New York Times,* 26 September, 1999, A12.

Elau, Heinz. "H. D. Lasswell's Developmental Hypothesis." *Western Political Quarterly* 21 (June 1958): 229–42.

Fairgrieve, James. *Geography and World Power.* London: University of London Press, 1915.

Fitzgerald, C. P. *The Chinese View of Their Place in the World.* London: Oxford University Press, 1964.

"France and Germany: Scenes from a Marriage." *Economist,* 24 March 2001, 27–30.

French, Howard W. "Still Wary of Outsiders, Japan Expects Immigration Boom." *New York Times,* 14 March 2000, A1, A14.

Friedman, Thomas. *The Lexus and the Olive Tree.* New York: Farrar, Straus & Giroux, 1999.

———. "The Mean Season." *New York Times,* 9 September 1999, A23.

Fukuyama, Francis. "The End of History?" *National Interest* 16 (Summer 1989): 3–18.

———. *The End of History and the Last Man.* New York: Free Press, 1992.

———. *The Great Disruption: Human Nature and the Reconstitution of Social Order.* New York: Free Press, 1999.

Gakwandi, A. S. "Towards a New Political Map of Africa." In *Politics, Economy and Social Change in the Twenty-First Century,* edited by A. I. Asiwaju. London: Hurst, 1996.

Gambetta, Léon. Quoted in Norman Harris, ed., *Intervention and Colonization in Africa*. Boston: Houghton, Mifflin, 1914.

Giblin, B. "Élisée Reclus, 1830–1905." In *Geographers Bibliographical Studies,* edited by T. W. Freeman. London: Mansell, 1979.

Ginsburg, Norton. "On the Chinese Perception of World Order." In *China's Policies in Asia and America's Alternatives,* edited by Tang Tsou. Chicago: University of Chicago Press, 1968.

"Go West Young Han." *Economist,* 23 December 2000, 45–46.

Gyorgy, Andrew. *Geopolitics*. Berkeley: University of California Press, 1944.

Harris, Norman. *Intervention and Colonization in Africa,* 1884–1914. Boston: Houghton, Mifflin, 1914.

Hart, B. Liddell. "The Russo-German Campaign." In *The Red Army,* edited by B. Liddell Hart, 100–126. New York: Harcourt, Brace, 1956.

Hartshorne, Richard. *The Nature of Geography*. Lancaster, Pa.: Association of American Geographers, 1939.

———. "The United States and the 'Shatter Zone' in Europe." In *Compass of the World,* edited by H. Weigert and V. Stefannson. New York: Macmillan, 1944.

Hennig, Richard. *Geopolitik, die Lehre vom Staat als Lebewesen*. Leipzig: Hirzel, 1931.

Henrikson, Alan K. "Diplomacy for the 21st Century: 'Re-crafting the Old Guild.'" Paper presented at the 503d Wilton Park Conference, "Diplomacy: Profession in Peril?" Published in *Current Issues in International Diplomacy and Foreign Policy.* Wilton Park Papers, Vol. 1. London: H. M. Stationery Office, 1998.

Hepple, Leslie. "Geopolitics, Generals and the State in Brazil." *Political Geography Quarterly* 5 (Supplement 1986): S79–S90.

Hooson, David, ed. *Geography and National Identity*. Oxford: Blackwell, 1994.

Huntington, Samuel P. "The Clash of Civilizations?" *Foreign Affairs* 72 (1993): 22–49.

———. *The Clash of Civilizations? The Debate*. New York: Council on Foreign Relations, Simon and Schuster, 1996.

———. *Political Order in Changing Societies*. New Haven, Conn.: Yale University Press, 1968.

Jefferson, Mark. "The Civilizing Rails." *Economic Geography* 4 (1928): 217–31.

Jones, Stephen B. "Global Strategic Views." *Geographical Review* 45, no. 4 (1955): 492–508.

———. "The Power Inventory and National Strategy." *World Politics* 1, no. 4 (July 1954): 421–52.

———. "A Unified Field Theory of Political Geography." *Annals of the Association of American Geographers* 44, no. 2: 111–23.

———. "Views of the Political World." *Geographical Review* 45, no. 3 (1955): 492–508.

Kahn, Joseph. "World Bank Cites Itself in Study of Africa's Bleak Performance." *New York Times,* 1 June 2000, 6.

Kaplan, Robert D. "The Coming Anarchy." *Atlantic Monthly* 273, no. 2 (1994): 44–46.

———. *The Coming Anarchy: Shattering the Dreams of the Cold War*. New York: Random House, 2000.

Kelley, Philip. *Checkerboards and Shatterbelts: The Geopolitics of South America*. Austin: University of Texas Press, 1987.

———. "Escalation of Regional Conflict: Testing the Shatterbelt Concept." *Political Geography Quarterly* 5, no. 2 (1986): 161–86.

Kennan, George. "The Sources of Soviet Conduct." *Foreign Affairs* 25 (1947): 566–82.

Kennedy, Paul. *Preparing for the Twenty-First Century*. New York: Random House, 1993.

———. *The Rise and Fall of the Great Powers*. New York: Random House, 1987.

Kissinger, Henry A. *The White House Years*. Boston: Little, Brown, 1979.

———. *Does America Need a Foreign Policy? Towards a Diplomacy for the 21st Century*. New York: Simon & Schuster, 2001.

Kjellén, Rudolph. *Staten som Lifsform*. 1916. Published in German as *Der Staat also Lebenform*. Leipzig: Hirzel, 1917.

Kliot, Nurit, and Stanley Waterman, eds. *The Political Geography of Conflict and Peace*. London: Belhaven, 1991.

Kolossov, Vladimir, and John O'Loughlin. "Pseudo-States as the Harbingers of a New Geopolitics: The Example of the Trans-Dniester Moldovan Republic." *Geopolitics* 3, no. 1 (Summer 1998): 151–76.

Korn, Daniel A. *Ethiopia, the United States and the Soviet Union, 1974–1985*. London: Croom Helm, 1986.

Krotkin, Joel. *The New Geography: How the Digital Revolution Is Reshaping the American Landscape*. New York: Random House, 2000.

Kuzio, Taras. "Borders, Symbolism and Nation-State Building." *Geopolitics and International Boundaries* 2, no. 2 (Autumn 1997): 36–56.

Lacoste, Yves. "Editorial: Les Géographes, l'Action et la Politique. *Herodite* 33 (1984): 3–32.

———. *La Géographie Ça sert, d'Abord, à Faire le Guerre*. Paris: Maspero, 1976.

Lintner, Bertil. *Cross-Border Trade in the Golden Triangle*. Durham, England: Boundaries Research Press–University of Durham, 1991.

Lonsdale, Richard, and J. Clark Archer. "Empty Areas in the United States, 1990–1995." *Journal of Geography* 96, no. 2 (March/April 1997): 108–22.

Lukacs, John. *The End of the Twentieth Century and the End of the Modern Age*. New York: Ticknor and Fields, 1993.

Mackinder, Halford. *Democratic Ideals and Reality*. London: Constable, 1919. Reprint, New York: Norton, 1962.

———. "The Geographical Pivot of History." *Geographical Journal* 23, no. 4 (1904), 421–44. Reprinted in Mackinder, *Democratic Ideals and Reality*, 265–78. New York: Norton, 1962.

———. "The Round World and the Winning of the Peace." *Foreign Affairs* 21, no. 4 (1943).

MacLachlan, Ian, and Adrian Guillermo Aguilar. "Maquiladora Myths: Locational and Structural Change in Mexico's Export Manufacturing Industry." *Professional Geographer* 50, no. 3 (1998): 315–31.

Madriaga, Javier Solana. "Growing the Alliance." *Economist*, 13 March 1999, 23–28.

Mahan, Alfred T. *The Influence of Sea Power on History: 1660–1783*. Boston: Little, Brown, 1890.

———. *The Problem of Asia and Its Effect upon International Policy*. Boston: Little, Brown, 1900.

Malin, James. "Space and History, Part 2." *Agricultural History* 18 (July 1944): 65–126.

March, Andrew L. *The Idea of China*. New York: Praeger, 1974.

Merk, Frederick. *The Monroe Doctrine and American Expansion*. New York: Knopf, 1967.

Modelski, George. *Long Cycles of World Politics*. Seattle: University of Washington Press, 1987.

———. "The Study of Long Cycles." In *Exploring Long Cycles*, edited by George Modelski. Boulder, Colo.: Lynne Riener, 1987.

Montesquieu, Charles-Louis de. *The Spirit of Laws*. Book XIV. Translated by Thomas Nugent. 1906. Reprint, Library of the Classics, New York: Hafner, 1949.

Meyer, Karl E., and Shareen Blair Brysac. *Tournament of Shadows: The Great Game and Race for Empire in Central Asia*. Washington, D.C.: Corneial and Michael Bessie/Counterpoint, 1999.

Murphy, Alexander B. "International Law and the Sovereign State System." In *Reordering the World*, edited by George J. Demko and William B. Wood. Boulder, Colo.: Westview, 1999.

"Myanmar's Where the Indian and Chinese Navies Meet." *Stratfor Commentary*, 27 January 2000.

Mydans, Seth. "East Timor's Dream of Oil. " *New York Times*, 20 October 2000, A13.

"Nations of the World." *World Almanac and Book of Facts 2000*. Mahwah, N.J.: Primedia Reference, 1999.

Newbigin, Marion. *The Mediterranean Lands*. New York: Knopf, 1924.

Nijman, Jan. *The Geopolitics of Power and Conflict: Superpowers in the International System, 1945–1992*. London: Belhaven, 1993.

Nitze, Paul H., Leonard Sullivan Jr., and the Atlantic Council Working Group on Securing the Seas. *Securing the Seas*. Boulder, Colo.: Westview, 1979.

O'Brien, R. *Global Financial Integration: The End of Geography*. New York: Council on Foreign Relations Press, 1992.

O'Loughlin, John, and Herman Van der Wusten. *The New Political Geography of Eastern Europe.* New York: Belhaven, 1993.

———. "Political Geography of Panregions." *Geographical Review* 80 (1990): 1–20.

O'Neill, Robert. "Australia and the Indian Ocean." In *The Southern Ocean and the Security of the Free World,* edited by Patrick Wall. London: Stacey International, 1977.

O'Sullivan, Patrick. "Antidomino." *Political Geography Quarterly* 1 (1982): 57–64.

O'Tuathail, Gearold. *Critical Geopolitics: The Politics of Writing Global Space.* Minneapolis: University of Minnesota Press, 1996.

O'Tuathail, Gearold, Simon Dalby, and Paul Routledge, eds. *The Geopolitics Reader.* London: Routledge, 1998.

Painter, Joe. *Politics, Geography and "Political Geography."* London: Arnold, 1995.

Paret, Peter, ed. *Makers of Modern Strategy.* Princeton: Princeton University Press, 1986.

Parker, Geoffrey. *Geopolitics: Past, Present and Future.* London: Pinter, 1998.

———. *The Geopolitics of Domination.* London: Routledge, 1988.

———. *A Political Geography of Community Europe.* London: Butterworth, 1983.

Perlez, Jane. "Blunt Reason for Enlarging NATO: Curbs on Germany." *New York Times,* 7 December 1997, A17.

Pierre, Andrew J. *The Global Politics of Arms Sales.* Princeton: Princeton University Press, 1982.

Prescott, J. V. R. "Africa's Boundary Problems." *Optima* 28 (1980): 3–21.

Rand McNally. *World Facts and Maps.* 2000 Ed. Skokie, Ill.: Rand McNally, 2000.

Ratzel, Friedrich. *Politische Geographie.* 3d edition. Munich: R. Oldenbourg, 1923.

———. *Politische Geographie der Vereinigtnen Staaten.* Leipzig: R. Oldenburg, 1897.

———. "Die Gesetze des Raumlichen Wachstums der Staaten." *Petermanns Mitteilungen* 42 (1896): 97–107. Reprinted as "The Laws of the Spatial Growth of States." Translated by Ronald Bolin. In *The Structure of Political Geography,* edited by Roger Kasperson and Julian Minghi. Chicago: Aldine, 1969.

Renner, George T. *Human Geography in the Air Age.* New York: Macmillan, 1942.

Revkin, Andrew C. "Lake's Rapid Retreat Heightens Troubles in North Africa." *New York Times,* 27 May 2001, F4.

Rosecrance, Richard. *The Rise of the Trading State.* New York: Basic Books, 1986.

"Russia's World," *Economist,* 9 May 1998, 21.

Ryan, Bruce. "Australia's Place in the World." In *The Australian Experience,* edited by R. L. Heathcote. Melbourne: Longman's, 1988.

Said, Edward. *Culture and Imperialism.* New York: Vintage, 1994.

"St. Kitts Ponders Request for Bombing Range." *New York Times,* 22 March 2001, A5.

Sciolino, Elaine. "It's a Sea! It's a Lake! No. It's a Pool of Oil." *New York Times* 21 June 1998, 16.

Segal, Gerald. "Does China Matter?" *Foreign Affairs* 78, no. 5 (June 1999): 24–36.

Semple, Ellen Churchill. *American History and Its Geographic Conditions.* Boston: Houghton Mifflin, 1903.

———. *The Geography of the Mediterranean World.* 1915. Reprint, New York: Henry Holt, 1931.

Seversky, Alexander de. *Air Power: Key to Survival.* New York: Simon & Schuster, 1950.

Shelley, Fred., J. Clark Archer, Fiona M. Davidson, and Stanley D. Brunn. *Political Geography of the United States.* New York: Guilford, 1996.

Schwartz, Benjamin I. "The Maoist Image of World Order." In *Image and Reality in World Politics,* edited by John C. Farrell and Asa P. Smith. New York: Columbia University Press, 1968.

Siegfried, Andre. *The Mediterranean.* Translated by H. H. Hemming and Doris Hemming. London: Jonathan Cape, 1948.

Singh, Govand. *A Political Geography of India.* Allahabad, India: Central Book Deposit, 1969.

Slessor, John. *The Great Deterrent.* New York: Praeger, 1957.

Smith, Dan. *The State of War and Peace Atlas.* London: Penguin, 1997.

"Somaliland, the Nation Nobody Knows." *Economist,* 14 April 2001, 42.

Spear, Percival. *Modern India.* Ann Arbor: University of Michigan Press, 1961.

Spencer, Herbert. "The Social Organism.." Reprinted in *The Man versus the State,* edited by Donald Macrae. Baltimore: Penguin, 1969.

Spykman, Nicholas. *America's Strategy in World Politics.* New York: Harcourt, Brace, 1942.

———. *The Geography of Peace.* New York: Harcourt, Brace, 1944.

Sulzberger, C. L. *The Coldest War.* New York: Harcourt, Brace, Jovanovich, 1974.

"Survey Taiwan." *Economist,* 7 November 1998, 14.

Taylor, Peter. *Political Geography.* 2d ed. Harlow, England: Longman Scientific and Technical, New York: Wiley, 1989.

Taylor, Peter J. ed. *World Government.* New York: Oxford University Press, 1990.

Trubowitz, Peter. *Defining the National Interest.* Chicago: University of Chicago Press, 1998.

Tung, William L. *China and the Foreign Powers.* Dobbs Ferry, N.Y.: Oceana, 1970.

Turner, Frederick Jackson. "The Significance of the Frontier in American History." Paper presented at the American Historical Association Meeting, Chicago, 1893. Reprinted in Turner, *The Frontier in American History.* New York: Henry Holt, 1920.

Tyler, Patrick E. "The China Threat, Some Experts Insist, Is Overrated." *International Herald Tribune,* 16 February 1999, 2.

U.S. Department of Energy, Energy Information Administration. "Annual Energy Review." In *World Almanac and Book of Facts 2000.* Mahwah, N.J.: Primedia Reference, 1999.

Wallerstein, Immanuel. *The Capitalist World-Economy.* Cambridge: Cambridge University Press, 1979.

———. "European Unity and Its Implications for the Interstate System." In *Europe: Dimensions of Peace,* edited by B. Hettne. London: Zed, 1988.

———. *Geopolitics and Geoculture: Essays on the Changing World-System.* Cambridge: Cambridge University Press, 1991.

———. *Historical Capitalism.* London: Verso, 1983.

———. "The World-System after the Cold War." *Journal of Peace Research,* 30 no. 1 (1993): 1–6.

Walsh, Edmund. "Geopolitics and International Morals." In *Compass of the World,* edited by H. W. Weigert and V. Stefansson. New York: Macmillan, 1944.

Weigert, Hans. *Generals and Geographers.* New York: Oxford University Press, 1942.

Werner, Heinz. *Comparative Psychology of Mental Development.* Rev. ed. New York: International University Press, 1948.

Werner, Heinz, and Bernard Kaplan. "The Developmental Approach to Cognition." *American Anthropologist* (1956): 866–80.

Whittlesey, Derwent. *The Earth and the State.* New York: Henry Holt, 1939.

———. "The Horizon of Geography." *Annals of the Association of American Geographers* 35, no. 1 (March 1945): 1–36.

———. "The Impress of Effective Central Authority on the Landscape." *Annals of the Association of American Geographers* 25, no. 2 (June 1935): 85–98.

———. "The Regional Concept and the Regional Method." In *American Geography: Inventory & Prospect,* edited by Preston E. James and Clarence F. Jones. Syracuse: Association of American Geographers and Syracuse University Press, 1954.

———. "Sequent Occupance." *Annals of the Association of American Geographers* 19, no. 3 (September 1929): 162–65.

Wook-ik Yu. "Seoul: The City of Vitality." *IGU Bulletin* 50, no. 1 (2000): 5–19.

World Bank Atlas: 1999. Washington: World Bank, 1999.

Index

411

About the Author

Saul B. Cohen is a teacher, author, and lecturer in the field of political geography. Among the leaders in the revival of political geography as a discipline following World War II, he has consulted to U.S. and foreign government agencies. His first volume, *Geography and Politics in a World Divided* (1963, revised 1973) and other works and numerous articles have focused on geopolitical theory and issues inherent in world order. He has also written extensively on the Arab-Israeli conflict and Middle East geopolitics.

Professor Cohen's works in geography and educational policy include thirteen volumes and over one hundred articles focusing on such additional themes as environment, resource networks, and location analysis. He is editor-in-chief of the *Columbia Gazetteer of the World* and the *Oxford World Atlas*.

In his university career he has been professor of geography at Boston University, visiting professor at the U.S. Naval War College, professor and director of Clark University's School of Geography, president of Queens College, CUNY, and is university professor emeritus at Hunter College, CUNY.

A Boston native and World War II veteran, he received his A.M., M.A., and Ph.D. degrees from Harvard College and Harvard University. A life-long commitment to education improvement has led to service on numerous national governmental research and policy committees. Elected to the New York State Board of Regents in 1993, he currently chairs the Regents Committee on Higher Education. He lives in New Rochelle, New York, with his wife, Miriam. They have two daughters and seven grandchildren.